Behavioural Economics and Experiments

Behavioural Economics and Experiments addresses key topics within behavioural economics, exploring vital questions around decision-making and human nature. Assuming no prior knowledge of economics, the book features wide-ranging examples from literature, film, sport, neuroscience and beyond.

Ananish Chaudhuri explores the complex relationships between human behaviour, society and decision-making, introducing readers to the latest work on heuristics, framing and anchoring, as well as ideas around fairness, trust and social norms. The book offers a fresh perspective on issues such as:

- Decision-making under uncertainty
- Firms' pricing decisions
- Employment contracts
- Coordination failures in organizations
- Preventing bubbles in financial markets

This is an ideal introduction for students of behavioural economics, experimental economics and economic decision-making on economics, public policy, psychology and business-related programmes, and will also be accessible to policymakers and curious laymen.

Ananish Chaudhuri is Professor of Experimental Economics at the University of Auckland. He has taught at Harvard Kennedy School, Wellesley College, Rutgers University and Washington State University.

Behavioural Economics and Experiments

Ananish Chaudhuri

LONDON AND NEW YORK

First published 2021
by Routledge
2 Park Square, Milton Park, Abingdon, Oxon OX14 4RN

and by Routledge
605 Third Avenue, New York, NY 10158

Routledge is an imprint of the Taylor & Francis Group, an informa business

© 2021 Ananish Chaudhuri

The right of Ananish Chaudhuri to be identified as author of this work has been asserted by him in accordance with sections 77 and 78 of the Copyright, Designs and Patents Act 1988.

All rights reserved. No part of this book may be reprinted or reproduced or utilised in any form or by any electronic, mechanical, or other means, now known or hereafter invented, including photocopying and recording, or in any information storage or retrieval system, without permission in writing from the publishers.

Trademark notice: Product or corporate names may be trademarks or registered trademarks, and are used only for identification and explanation without intent to infringe.

British Library Cataloguing-in-Publication Data
A catalogue record for this book is available from the British Library

Library of Congress Cataloging-in-Publication Data
A catalog record has been requested for this book

ISBN: 978-0-367-46394-6 (hbk)
ISBN: 978-0-367-46393-9 (pbk)
ISBN: 978-1-003-02853-6 (ebk)

Typeset in Garamond
by Deanta Global Publishing Services, Chennai, India

Access the Support Material: www.routledge.com/9780367463939

For Ananrita, who missed out last time and should hopefully be ready to read this soon.
For Ishannita, who asks a lot of questions and keeps me on my feet.
For Indira, who makes me "want to be a better man".
And for Utpal, who would have enjoyed seeing this book out in print.

Contents

List of figures xiv
List of tables xviii
Acknowledgements xix
Preface xxi

1 How we decide 1

2 Experiments in behavioural economics 30

3 Gut feelings and effortful thinking 50

4 Expected utility theory and prospect theory 89

5 Probabilistic thinking 117

6 Thinking strategically 145

7 The ultimatum game 172

8 Market implications of the ultimatum game 203

9 Trust and trustworthiness in everyday life 217

10 Trust and trustworthiness in markets 241

11 Cooperation in social dilemmas 264

12 The carrot or the stick: Sustaining cooperation in social dilemmas 287

13 I will if you will: Resolving coordination failures in organizations 309

| 14 | Behavioural analyses of markets | 342 |
| 15 | Asset bubbles in markets | 373 |

References 403
Index 419

Descriptive contents

List of figures	xiv
List of tables	xviii
Acknowledgements	xix
Preface	xxi

1 How we decide   1

Introduction	2
Descartes's error?	5
How do economists and psychologists approach decision making?	6
Infusing psychology into economics: the guessing game	8
Types of decision making	12
Ana's problem of choice	13
Ana cannot buy everything she wants; her choices are constrained	13
Ana knows what she can afford, but how does she choose among these?	16
Ana knows what she can afford and how she should choose. What *should* she buy?	21
Two examples of how to use this tool	22
How realistic is this "normative" model? Let's look inside the brain	23
Concluding remarks	26
Notes	27

2 Experiments in behavioural economics   30

Introduction	30
The rise of experimental economics	32
Elements of experimental design	35
A brief history of experimental economics	36
Experiments in economics and psychology: similarities and differences	40
Criticisms of experimental economics	41
In lieu of a conclusion: experimental economics: the path forward	47
Notes	48

3 Gut feelings and effortful thinking   50

Introduction	50
The power of gut feelings, or System 1 thinking	53

■ Descriptive contents

	Limits to System 1 thinking and the need to engage System 2	57
	Why do we need to worry about Systems 1 and 2?	62
	Choice over time: smaller–sooner versus larger–later rewards	76
	Concluding remarks	85
	Notes	87
4	**Expected utility theory and prospect theory**	**89**
	Introduction	89
	Risk neutrality and risk aversion	91
	The Allais Paradox	101
	Prospect theory	106
	Explaining the paradoxical behaviour in Allais and elsewhere	110
	Loss aversion, mental accounting and the endowment effect	111
	Loss aversion and overconfidence	112
	Concluding remarks	114
	Notes	115
5	**Probabilistic thinking**	**117**
	Introduction	117
	Probabilities are dicey and often hard to get our heads around	121
	One further detour on the way to the jury decision-making problem	123
	Back to the jury decision-making problem	126
	Michael Bloomberg's stop-and-frisk policy	128
	Indira, the mature mother	129
	Dependent or independent? Connected or unconnected? Conjunctive and disjunctive fallacies	131
	Regression to the mean	137
	Concluding remarks	142
	Notes	143
6	**Thinking strategically**	**145**
	Introduction	145
	The prisoner's dilemma	149
	Yossarian and Nately's choices revisited	152
	Prisoner's dilemma in the animal world	155
	Tit-for-tat strategies in prisoner's dilemma games	156
	Let us talk of Yossarian and Nately one last time	158
	Men are from Mars, women are from Venus: battle of the sexes	160
	Battle of the sexes: the game played by Della and Jim	161
	Hunt a stag or a rabbit? The stag hunt game and pay-off-ranked equilibria	162
	Please, why don't you go first? Games where players move in sequence	165
	Concluding remarks	170
	Notes	171

7	**The ultimatum game**	172
	Introduction	172
	The ultimatum game	173
	Intentions, as well as outcomes, matter	179
	Criticisms of the findings of Güth and his colleagues	182
	Behaviour in the ultimatum game: fairness or altruism?	183
	Raising the monetary stakes in the ultimatum game	184
	Fear of punishment or fear of embarrassment?	188
	Do norms of fairness differ across cultures?	195
	An even more ambitious cross-cultural study	198
	Concluding remarks	201
	Notes	201
8	**Market implications of the ultimatum game**	203
	Introduction	203
	Fairness as a constraint on profit-making	204
	Economic consequences of norms of fairness	207
	Fairness and inequality	209
	Concluding remarks	215
	Note	216
9	**Trust and trustworthiness in everyday life**	217
	Trusting strangers	217
	Is trust nothing but altruism? How about reciprocity?	223
	The role of expectations in the decision to trust	225
	Is a trusting decision analogous to a risky one?	228
	Do trust and trustworthiness go together?	231
	Does trust pay?	233
	Concluding remarks	239
	Notes	240
10	**Trust and trustworthiness in markets**	241
	Introduction	241
	Trust and trustworthiness in agency relationships	242
	Further economic implications of fairness and trust	252
	The Grameen Bank experience	253
	Extrinsic incentives can crowd out intrinsic motivations	254
	Intrinsic motivations, sustainability and climate change	256
	Extrinsic incentives and crowding out of intrinsic motivations	258
	Trust and growth	260
	Concluding remarks	262
	Notes	263

11 Cooperation in social dilemmas — 264

- An example of a social dilemma — 264
- Are smaller groups better at addressing collective action problems? — 268
- Are contributions caused by confusion on the part of the participants? — 270
- Looking for alternative explanations — 273
- Do participants display a herd mentality? — 277
- Turning the prisoner's dilemma into a stag hunt game — 278
- Concluding remarks — 282
- Notes — 285

12 The carrot or the stick: Sustaining cooperation in social dilemmas — 287

- Introduction — 287
- Sustaining social norms by punishing free-riders — 287
- On the cost effectiveness of costly punishments — 290
- The possibility of "perverse" punishments — 293
- Are punishments more effective in the long run? — 295
- The "verdict" on costly punishments — 296
- Sustaining cooperation via means other than punishments — 297
- Sustaining cooperation in non-sorted groups — 298
- Cooperation in sorted groups — 302
- An intergenerational approach to cooperation — 305
- Concluding remarks — 306
- Notes — 307

13 I will if you will: Resolving coordination failures in organizations — 309

- Coordination failures in real life — 309
- Experimental evidence on coordination failures — 313
- The minimum effort coordination game — 316
- Talk is cheap; or is it? Using communication to resolve coordination failures — 321
- Money talks: the role of incentives — 325
- When in Rome ... creating culture in the laboratory — 330
- From the laboratory to the real world: do these interventions work? The story of Continental Airlines — 335
- From the real world, back to the laboratory: are you partners or strangers? — 337
- Concluding remarks — 340
- Notes — 341

14 Behavioural analyses of markets — 342

- Introduction — 342
- Demand — 343
- Supply — 345
- The theory of competitive equilibrium — 347
- Consumer and producer surplus — 350
- But ... does it work in real life? — 352

	Robustness of the market equilibration process	357
	Posted offer markets	360
	Posted offer markets and market power	362
	Fairness in posted offer markets revisited	363
	Policy interventions in markets	365
	Concluding remarks	368
	Notes	370
15	**Asset bubbles in markets**	**373**
	Introduction	373
	Studying asset bubbles in the lab	376
	I don't understand why the fundamental value is declining!	380
	Rational speculation and the role of expectations	383
	Unleashing (and leashing) our animal spirits	387
	Passions within reason: the role of experience in curbing bubbles	393
	Concluding remarks	398
	Notes	400

References   403
Index   419

Figures

P.1	Differences in deceased organ donations across 36 Western countries	xxiii
1.1	Toy *Tyrannosaurus Rex*: an example of a model	6
1.2	Chosen numbers in the guessing game with target = 1/2	9
1.3	Chosen numbers in the guessing game with target = 2/3	10
1.4	Interim interval bounds on choices in the guessing game	10
1.5	Choices in the guessing game by different subject pools	11
1.6	Ana's budget constraint	14
1.7	Slope of Ana's budget constraint	14
1.8	Example of consumption bundles worth more than, less than or exactly $100	15
1.9	The effect of a change in Ana's income on her budget constraint	15
1.10	The effect of a change in the price of Good X on Ana's budget constraint	16
1.11	The effect of a change in the price of Good Y on Ana's budget constraint	16
1.12	Ana's consumption space	17
1.13	The basis of choice: indifference curves	18
1.14	Indifference curves cannot intersect	18
1.15	Various other (possibly problematic) shapes of indifference curves	19
1.16	Slope of Ana's indifference curve(s)	19
1.17	Finding Ana's most preferred consumption bundle out of those that are affordable	21
1.18	A closer look at Ana's best possible consumption bundle	22
1.19	Graphical analysis of the overall effect of a fall in the price of Good X from $20 to $10	23
1.20	Graphical analysis of the overall effect of a rise in the price of Good Y from $10 to $25	23
3.1	Bored man	51
3.2	People with forced smiles	52
3.3	People with Duchenne smiles	52
3.4	Simple heuristics for detecting heart attacks	55
3.5	The Müller-Lyer Illusion: which line is longer	60
3.6	The Stroop Task: upper case or lower case	60
3.7	The Müller–Lyer Illusion explained	61
3.8	Experimental design in Fathi, Bateson and Nettle (2014)	64
3.9	Experimental results in Fathi, Bateson and Nettle (2014)	64

3.10	Minimal cue from Rigdon et al. (2009)	65
3.11	Cards with different length lines from Asch (1956)	66
3.12	Four cards	72
3.13	Time inconsistency	82
4.1	Emma's risk neutral straight-line expected utility function U(W) = 3W	93
4.2	Jessie's concave utility function	94
4.3	Another example with a concave utility function	96
4.4	Logan's concave utility function	98
4.5	Jim's convex utility function	100
4.6	Potential probability weighting function	107
4.7	Value function	109
5.1	Age at first marriage in New Zealand	119
5.2	Red ball–blue ball example	123
5.3	Average time taken by two groups of athletes to run 100 metres	138
6.1	Pay-off matrix for the prisoner's dilemma game with Bonnie and Clyde	150
6.2	The prisoner's dilemma game from Bonnie's perspective	150
6.3	The prisoner's dilemma game from Clyde's perspective	151
6.4	Nash equilibrium of the prisoner's dilemma game	151
6.5	Pay-off matrix for the game between Yossarian and Nately	153
6.6	Nash equilibrium in the game between Yossarian and Nately	154
6.7	Pay-off matrix for Yossarian–Nately game where Nately has no dominant strategy	159
6.8	Nash equilibrium in the Yossarian–Nately game where Nately has no dominant strategy	159
6.9	Pay-off matrix for the battle of the sexes game with Della and Jim	161
6.10	Equilibria in the game played by Della and Jim	162
6.11	Pay-off matrix for the stag hunt game	163
6.12	Equilibria in the stag hunt game	164
6.13	Game tree of the sequential game between Della and Jim	166
6.14	Della's pay-offs in the sequential game	167
6.15	Nash equilibrium in the sequential game between Della and Jim	167
6.16	The sequential game between Caroline's and Spicer's, with Caroline's as the first mover	168
6.17	The sequential game between Caroline's and Spicer's, with Spicer's as the first mover	169
7.1	Structure of the ultimatum game	174
7.2	Distribution of offers in the Güth et al. ultimatum game	176
7.3	Distribution of offers in the second repetition of the Güth et al. ultimatum game	177
7.4	Structure of the Falk et al. ultimatum games	180
7.5	Comparison of offers in the ultimatum game and the dictator game	183
7.6	Breakdown of offers, acceptances and rejections in Cameron's high stakes ultimatum game	187
7.7	Structure of the Bolton and Zwick cardinal ultimatum game	190

■ Figures

7.8	Evolution of play in the various games	192
7.9	Distribution of offers in the ultimatum game in four different locations	196
8.1	Inequality and life expectancy in countries	210
8.2	Inequality and index of social and health problems in countries	211
8.3	Inequality and rate of teenage pregnancy in countries	211
8.4	Inequality in the US	212
9.1	Structure of the trust game	219
9.2	Amounts sent by various senders in the Berg et al. (1995) trust game	221
9.3	Responder behaviour in the Berg et al. (1995) trust game	222
9.4	Average amount sent across the five different treatments in Chaudhuri et al. (2016)	235
9.5	Average proportion returned across the five treatments in Chaudhuri et al. (2016)	236
9.6	Perceived unfairness and desire to punish across the four treatments in de Quervain et al. (2004)	238
10.1	Average rent offered in trust and penalty treatments	248
10.2	Effort demanded and actual effort provided in the trust and penalty treatments	249
10.3	Effort demanded and actual effort provided in SRT and WRT	250
10.4	Impact of fines in the day-care centres	259
11.1	Structure of the public goods game	266
11.2	Pattern of decaying contributions in public goods games	268
11.3	Results from the public goods game with different group sizes and MPCRs	270
11.4	Pattern of contributions in the public goods game with partners and strangers and a surprise restart	273
11.5	Contribution patterns of different types of participants from Fischbacher et al. (2001)	275
11.6	Pay-off matrix of the generic prisoner's dilemma game and of a modified version of the game in Rabin (1993)	280
11.7	Contributions in the public goods game broken down by optimists, realists and pessimists	281
12.1	Average contributions in the partners and strangers treatments with and without punishments	289
12.2	Contributions in and subjects' choices of sanctioning and sanction-free institutions	290
12.3	Role of punishment effectiveness on efficiency	292
12.4	Pro-social and antisocial punishments across different societies	295
12.5	Effectiveness of punishments over the long horizon	296
12.6	Effects of communication in the public goods game	299
13.1	Pay-off matrices for the battle of the sexes game and the stag hunt game	312
13.2	Announcements and bonuses with fixed and randomly re-matched groups in the minimum effort game	340
14.1	Step-like demand function	343
14.2	Shifts in demand	345

14.3	Step-like supply function	346
14.4	Shifts in supply	347
14.5	The process of achieving market equilibrium	348
14.6	Shifts in demand and supply in the petrol market	350
14.7	Consumer and producer surplus	351
14.8	Step-like demand and supply functions with buyers and sellers (Smith 1962)	354
14.9	Results from a continuous double auction market	357
14.10	Results from a continuous double auction market with relatively flat demand and supply curves	358
14.11	Results from a continuous double auction market with producer surplus larger than consumer surplus	359
14.12	Results from a continuous double auction market with a horizontal supply curve and a shift in demand	360
14.13	Posted offer market with lots of buyers and three sellers	362
14.14	Price ceiling and price floor	366
14.15	Impact of a price ceiling	367
15.1	US housing market bubble	374
15.2	South Sea Company bubble	376
15.3	Results from an asset market experiment	379
15.4	Results from asset markets with flat fundamental value	381
15.5	Results from no speculation asset markets	386
15.6	Results from asset markets with depleted self-control traders, non-depleted self-control traders, and a mix of both types of traders	390
15.7	Results from asset markets with high and low overconfidence traders	392
15.8	Peak price periods in asset markets	395

Tables

3.1	List of matches: round 16 of the 2019 US Open Men's Tennis Tournament	55
3.2	Where are the rich customers around the world?	58
4.1	Presentation of lotteries in gain or loss frame	105
4.2	Presentation of lotteries with the same expected value in gain or loss frame	106
5.1	Breakdown of test results	130
5.2	Probability of hits following hits and/or misses	140
6.1	Isha playing the prisoner's dilemma game repeatedly against an opponent using the grim trigger strategy	157
7.1	Offers made in high stakes ultimatum games	186
7.2	Percentage of inequitable offers rejected by the responder	192
7.3	Rates of acceptance of offers from human and computer proposers	194
7.4	Offers across the diverse small-scale societies	199
9.1	Cox's (1994) modified dictator game	224
9.2	Average amount sent across various treatments in Ortmann et al. (2000)	227
9.3	Modal transfers, earnings and returns across different treatments in Chaudhuri et al (2017)	236
11.1	Interaction of group size and MPCR in Isaac and Walker (1988b)	269
13.1	Two stag hunt games, each with a dominated strategy, leading to different results	315
13.2	Pay-off matrix: Van Huyck et al. (1990) minimum effort coordination game	317
13.3	Typical pattern of effort choices by individuals within groups in Van Huyck et al. (1990) minimum effort coordination game	318
13.4	Typical pattern of minimum effort choices across all groups in Van Huyck et al. (1990) minimum effort coordination game	319

Acknowledgements

One does not manage to write a book like this without the assistance of many. I am grateful to the Department of Economics and the University of Auckland for providing me with the research and study leave during which I worked on this manuscript. The break from teaching and administrative responsibilities allowed me to read, think and write uninterruptedly. Much of my research in this area has been made possible by funding from the Royal Society of New Zealand Marsden Fund as well as the University of Auckland via the Faculty Research Development Fund and the Vice-Chancellor's Strategic Development Fund. I appreciate this support.

Two groups of people deserve special thanks for having served as guinea pigs as I tried out ideas and arguments. These include my students from Econ 271: Special Topics in Economics (Behavioural Economics) at the University of Auckland during the latter half of 2019 as well as my students from MLD 302: Behavioural Decision Making at Harvard Kennedy School during Spring 2020. I am grateful to a number of these students for taking the time to provide extensive feedback on what worked and what did not. These include Grace Brebner, Karishma Singh, Logan Templer and Jessie Zhang at Auckland. Emilio Angulo, Nathan Hodson and Rebecca Yao at the Kennedy School were kind enough to let me use ideas and figures from their written assignments. Nathan, in particular, helped carry out the survey on conjunction fallacy and write a case study for Chapter 5.

Iris Bohnet, Academic Dean at Harvard Kennedy School, made it possible for me to visit and teach there during the early part of 2020. This was huge opportunity and I am deeply thankful for her graciousness. It goes without saying that the Kennedy School provided an incredibly stimulating environment, one which broadened my horizons and also helped immensely in thinking through some of the topics discussed. This includes the students in my class, who frequently forced me to think deeper about the topics and their potential policy applications, particularly Todd Link, Lennart Kuntze and David Stansbury. I am also very grateful to Suzanne Cooper and Laura Medeiros for facilitating my visit.

My intrepid research assistant Jessie Zhang did an absolutely fantastic job of proof-reading the manuscript, finding references and generally correcting my mistakes. Eva Gottschalk at the Kennedy School and Yaxiong (Sherry) Li at Auckland helped in many ways, particularly in creating the diagrams in the book. I am very grateful for their assistance.

Over the years, a large group of people have kindly taken the time to discuss ideas with me and also often provided extensive feedback on various parts of this book. They include Quentin Atkinson, Nandita Basu, Gary Bolton, Geoffrey Brooke, Scott Claessens,

Acknowledgements

David Cooper, David Dickinson, Tony Endres, Ernst Fehr, Kyle Fischer, Simon Gächter, Ryan Greenaway-McGrevy, Tim Hazledine, Martin Kocher, Dmitriy Kvasov, Jim Murphy, Charles Noussair, John Panzar, Abhijit Ramalingam, Bradley Ruffle, Antonio Rangel, Al Roth, Andrew Schotter, Alexander Smith, Barry Sopher, Asha Sundaram and James Tremewan. I am deeply indebted to them for taking the time out of their busy schedules to help me. I do apologize to anyone I may have left out of the list.

Three anonymous reviewers provided extremely valuable feedback which has led to significant improvements in the book's exposition. I thank them sincerely. Andy Humphries, my editor at Routledge persevered with me for a long time, while I served a seven-year prison sentence; sorry, I meant to say a seven-year term as Department Chair! I doubt I would have completed this project were it not for Andy's persistence. I am also grateful to Natalie Tomlinson, who took over from Andy. I thank Chloe James, Emma Morley and Cathy Hurren for shepherding this project through and Yvonne Doney for her expert copy-editing.

I am indebted to my wonderful wife Dr Indira Basu for her constant support. She has made tremendous sacrifices on my behalf and marrying her was by far the smartest thing that I have ever done. Of course, life is made constantly interesting, enchanting and challenging by our beautiful daughters, Ishannita and Ananrita, who are growing up to be charming and empathetic young women. The three of them have often been forced to act as a captive audience while I tried out new ideas and arguments. Isha and Ana have also often willingly and cheerfully lent a hand in making up tables and figures, usually without any financial remuneration. My father, Utpal, passed away as I was getting started on the book. He would have been happy and proud to see this in print. And just in case you are wondering, I did not forget my mother. I have dedicated a whole new forthcoming book to her!

Of course, at the end of it all, as we say in all our academic papers, I alone am responsible for any errors that may appear in the following pages. Feel free to write and tell me if you do not agree with something I have said and you have counter-examples. Also feel free to let me know if you are aware of other applications or anecdotes that might be relevant. I hope I have managed to convey some of the passion and excitement that characterizes research in these topics and I hope you enjoy reading the book. You can find out more about my research and other activities on my website: https://ananishchaudhuri.com.

Finally, in case you could not quite place the "want to be a better man" allusion, Jack Nicholson says this to Helen Hunt in the James Brooks film, *As Good as It Gets*.

Ananish Chaudhuri
Cambridge, MA and Auckland, NZ

Preface

At any point in time, a large number of people around the world are waiting for an organ transplant. There are also a lot of people who could choose to donate their organs, especially in the event of their death. It is not the case that every deceased person's organs can be used. It depends on a number of factors, such as age, lifestyle, manner of death, etc. For instance, I am a healthy male in my early fifties. I don't smoke and drink only moderately. I am in reasonably good shape physically. If I died from an accident tomorrow, doctors could potentially use my organs to save multiple lives. But this has to happen quickly, soon after my death. However, in order for this to happen, I (and my family members) have to agree beforehand that doctors can harvest my organs upon my death.

The problem is "easier" in the case of some organs, such as kidneys, than others like heart, liver or lungs. We need only one kidney to lead a healthy life. This creates the potential for "live" donations. So, if my partner needed a kidney, I could (and would happily) donate one of my two fully functional kidneys to her. But this may not work, since my kidneys need to be a match for hers. This means that not only does she need a kidney, she needs it from a matched partner. In the US, the average waiting time for a kidney transplant is three to five years.

In 2012, the Nobel Prize in Economics went to Al Roth of Harvard Business School. Al Roth has long been known for his contributions to both economic theory and experimental economics. But, to a large extent, Roth's Nobel Prize was awarded in recognition of his contributions toward facilitating kidney exchanges. What is it that Roth, along with his collaborators, Tayfun Sonmez and Utku Unver of Boston College, accomplished?

Consider two couples: Al and Barbara, and Charlotte and David. Al needs a kidney and so does Charlotte. Barbara and David are perfectly happy to donate a kidney to her/his partner but neither is a match for the respective partner. However, David's kidney is a match for Al, while Barbara's is a match for Charlotte. This sounds promising; but suppose Al and Barbara live in Boston, while Charlotte and David live in San Francisco. How do the couples go about finding one another? Social media? Maybe. Let us say they do. Now consider the medical and logistical challenges. Al and Barbara will have to show up to a hospital at the same time as Charlotte and David. Doctors need to remove the kidneys from Barbara and David to start with. Barbara's kidney now needs to be flown to San Francisco, while David's needs to be transported to Boston. Typically, either planes or helicopters are standing by to fly the kidneys to their designated destination. Once the kidneys arrive at their respective places, the team of surgeons, nurses, anaesthetists and others who helped remove

Barbara's kidney now need to transplant David's kidney in Al, while Barbara's kidney goes to Charlotte, where the same procedure has to be carried out. Just imagine, the time, effort and personnel needed to pull off this one exchange.

But wait! Parties to the transaction may have second thoughts at the last moment. What if one of the couples pulls out? Also, how do you know that this is the best possible matched pair, since there could be many such pairs in the US, and possibly around the world? Who decides which are the best matches? Who puts them in touch with one another? How do you make sure that this complex daisy-chain of paired kidney swaps will be pulled off correctly? This is where Al Roth stepped in. Having done extensive work matching students to high schools in New York and matching medical residents to medical schools in Boston, Roth and his collaborators were extremely well placed to figure out the answers to these questions. In recent times, Roth and his team have undertaken exchanges involving 13 pairs of donors and recipients, including ones located outside the US. In 2019, I heard Roth deliver a keynote speech on his kidney-exchange work at a conference in Dijon, France. It was probably the most fascinating talk I have ever heard; mostly because it sounded nothing like an academic talk, but, rather, like the plot from an episode of *ER* or *Grey's Anatomy*.[1]

While Roth's work with kidneys have literally been a lifesaver for many, the fact is that for many other transplants, like a heart or liver or lungs, there is no possibility of "live" donations. We need a pool of healthy deceased donors who are willing to donate their organs. Now, take a look at Figure P.1. It is clear that rates of deceased organ donation are quite different across countries. The countries included are mostly Western, developed, industrialized, rich and market-based democracies, which share many cultural and economic norms. But even if you look at countries located literally next door to each other, such as the Netherlands and Belgium, you will see big differences. Belgium is doing better than the Netherlands and has access to many more organ donors.

As you look at this picture, you could start to formulate arguments as to what could cause these differences. You may be tempted to frame these differences in terms of these countries' culture, history and demographics. But it turns out that there is a very simple reason why these differences come about. Believe it or not, these differences are caused by a single question on driver's licence forms. Some countries in the world ask applicants: "Would you like to be an organ donor? If so, check the box below." Other countries state: "We will assume that, in the event of your death, you will be willing to donate your organs. If you are not willing to do so, then check the box below."

The countries that implement the "opt-out" option are referred to as countries with "presumed consent"; that is, we assume that you have given consent to donating your organs unless you specifically tell us otherwise. On the other hand, the countries that rely on the "opt-in" option are called "informed consent" countries; the assumption being that you have not consented to donating your organs unless you explicitly indicate this on your driver's licence.

It may be surprising, but the fact is that, in the first case, people do not check the box, and, therefore, do not become organ donors. In the second case, people also do not check the box, and, therefore, become organ donors by default! Now go back and look at the figure again. Guess what is common to all the countries that have higher rates of organ donation? *They all provide the second "opt-out" option: Check the box if you do not want to donate your organs.*

Figure P.1
Differences in deceased organ donations across 36 Western countries. Re-created on the basis of data in Abadie and Gay (2006).

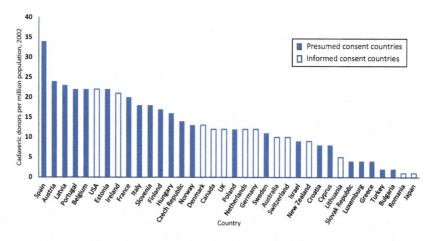

You are in (i.e., you are an organ donor) unless you explicitly opt out by checking the box. The countries that do not do so well on the organ donation scale are the ones that provide the "opt-in" option: *Do you wish to donate?* You are out (i.e., not a presumed organ donor) unless you wish to opt in by checking the box. All of this over a simple decision (or the lack of one) to check a box!

Behavioural economists refer to this as the *framing effect*, or, at times, *changing the default*. You can achieve enormous shifts in behaviour simply by changing the way a particular question or problem is framed. Think about this. If you or someone close to you is waiting to receive a liver or kidney, it may make a huge difference as to whether you are in Spain or New Zealand all because someone at the Department of Motor Vehicles decided how the organ donation question should be framed.

Organ donation, of course, is not an issue that faces many of us. I actually do not know anyone who has had an organ transplant. But this kind of behaviour is not restricted to organ donations. In their book *Nudge*, Richard Thaler of Chicago's Booth School and Cass Sunstein of Harvard Law point out that similar issues of choice arise when people plan for their retirement. Most organizations around the world have a system for matching employee contributions to a pension fund. At the University of Auckland, where I work, I contribute 6.5% of my salary towards retirement saving (called "superannuation" over here downunder; in the US, the common term is a 401(K)) and the university matches this. So, anyone who manages to put away (say) $6,500 in a year, gets another $6,500 in employer contributions for a total of $13,000. One catch: typically, you cannot touch this money until you are 65, which is the usual retirement age in many countries, at least in New Zealand. But, given compound interest, amounts saved grow quickly. For most of us – indeed I will go out on a limb and say for all of us – it makes perfect sense to sign up to such plans. Unless someone is a financial wizard and knows of a secret recipe which can double one's investment year on year, it is a safe bet to assume that we should sign on for such plans where employee contributions are matched by the employer. This is, as they say, a "no-brainer". But by now, you know where I am headed. A lot of people do not sign up!

Is it because the ones not signing up are financial wizards who have better ideas on how to invest their money? No! It is simply because, around the world, some employers choose the "opt-in" option: they ask the employee to check a box if they wish to join. Many employees do not check this box and do not join. Other employers rely on the "opt-out" option. They enrol employees automatically. Employees can check a box if they do not wish to join. Most employees do not check this box and, therefore, remain enrolled.

As Thaler and Sunstein point out: in one firm with a default contribution rate of 3% of salary, more than one-quarter of workers contributed exactly that amount to the plan, even though the employer matched contributions dollar for dollar up to 6% of salary. Once the firm switched to a 6% default, workers started contributing the same proportion. A 2013 report in the *Guardian* found that approximately one year after the UK introduced automatic enrolment with an opt-out feature, there were 1.6 million more savers in workplace pensions. Only 9% chose to opt out.

This is a serious issue because, around the world, many people do not manage to save enough for retirement, hence poverty rates among the elderly are quite high and the aged are often overly reliant on the social safety net, such as Medicare in the US. This led Richard Thaler and his collaborator Shlomo Benartzi to propose the Save More Tomorrow (SMT) plan. Under this plan, people commit in advance to allocate a portion of their future salary increases towards retirement savings. I discuss later why it is easier to get people to give up a larger proportion of their *future* salary rather than their *current* salary. Seventy-eight per cent of the people offered the SMT plan elected to use it; 80% remained enrolled through the next three pay raises. The average saving rates for SMT plan participants increased from 3.5% to 11.6% over the course of 28 months.

Do you want other examples of such seemingly irrational behaviour? All around the world, offices have a coffee corner. They work on an honour system. You can help yourself to a cuppa but, in return, you are expected to leave some money in the box. Not surprisingly, some people leave money, others don't. But if you want more people to leave money, then you can resort to a simple trick. Put a pair of eyes on top of the donation box. Or even better, add a message underneath the pair of eyes: *Put 50 cents in the box; we are watching you.* No one is really watching! It is just a pair of eyes drawn on a piece of paper. But with the watching eyes, more people will put money in.

It was 2001 and I was working at Washington State University. My wife was offered a post-doctorate at Tufts Medical School (in downtown Boston) and I managed to get a job at Wellesley College, a highly selective all-women's college just outside of Boston. My wife and I decided to drive across the country. Over a week, we drove around 3000 miles across the US; along the way, we stopped at places like Butte, Montana; Rapid City, South Dakota; Wisconsin Dells, Chicago, Youngstown, Ohio and so on. At each of these places we ate lunch and dinner and sundry other meals. At the end of each meal, we left a tip even though we knew full well that we would not go back to any those places, and, even if we did, we would certainly not go back to the same restaurant. So, even if the waiting staff at any of these establishments thought poorly of us for not leaving a tip, it should not have mattered much to us. We would never see them again! Why was I leaving money? Was I afraid that the waiter/waitress would call me names? So what? I was not going to be around to hear that. As they say, "Sticks and stones …". Why do I care if someone, whom I will never see again, calls me a name?

How irrational is this? As Dan Ariely of Duke points out, humans are "predictably irrational". People make apparently irrational choices but there is some method to the madness.

It is not simply that people are irrational, but there is a degree of predictability, or, in other words, pattern, to their irrationality. This, in turn, suggests that if we understand the underlying patterns and commonalities, we can use those insights to design better policy. This is going to be one of my principal goals here: to discuss how to understand such irrationality and how to make use of that insight in the design of public policy.

But there are nuances here. There is, at least, one particularly distinctive aspect to the different types of behavioural irrationalities mentioned. This distinction applies to how people respond if and when you draw their attention to this issue. For instance, if I highlight the apparent irrationality involved in the case of checking (or not checking) boxes in the case of organ donation or contributing to retirement funds, you will most likely take this information on board and will (ideally) change your decision. But in the case of the watching eyes or leaving tips in restaurants that you will never go back to, you will most likely not change your behaviour even if I pointed out the "error" of your ways. The well-known Cornell economist and author, Robert Frank, suggests that there are some "mistakes" we might rectify when pointed out (such as the organ donation or retirement savings example), but there are other "mistakes" we will not correct even when brought to our attention; such as tipping in restaurants that one will never go back to. Why?

These are the kinds of questions that I will address in this book. I intend to provide a broad overview of research in human decision making: the things we get right and the ones we get wrong, an accounting of our biases, and, more importantly, how to understand these so that we can design better policies. In recent years, behavioural economics has emerged as an exciting new area of research, since these are the kinds of questions on which it is shedding light. Part of the appeal of behavioural economics comes from the fact that it enriches the traditional approach in economics by infusing it with key insights from human psychology. This, in turn, holds the promise of making a serious difference in terms of public policy. This contribution of behavioural economics to public policy and the recognition of the difference it can make to people's lives is also why a number of Nobel Prizes in Economics in recent times have been awarded to people working in what is perceived as behavioural economics research (though I am not entirely sure if the recipients themselves would necessarily attach this label to their work). But maybe this is beside the point; behavioural economics is clearly a broad church and happy to include people from disparate backgrounds.

A non-exhaustive list of Nobel Prize winners for work in behavioural economics includes Daniel Kahneman and Vernon Smith in 2002, Elinor Ostrom in 2009, Al Roth in 2012, Robert Schiller in 2013, Richard Thaler in 2017 and, most recently (at the time of writing in early 2020), Abhijit Banerjee, Esther Duflo and Michael Kremer in 2019. In retrospect, other recipients such as Thomas Schelling (2005), George Akerlof (2001), Reinhard Selten (1994), Maurice Allais (1988) and Herbert Simon (1978) would certainly qualify for the "behavioural economist" sobriquet and the reason that they are not usually thought of as being in that mould is that they predated the prevalence of the term. I also include Muhammad Yunus, the founder of Grameen Bank in Bangladesh, and the winner of the 2006 Nobel Peace Prize, among this group.[2] Work done by some of the above and many others have led to startling and significant new discoveries that have contributed to our understanding of human decisions and human foibles.

■ Preface

The book is designed to be an introduction to this area. It is meant for people who are curious to know what behavioural economics is all about. In doing so, I am providing an overview of a host of issues, rather than engaging in deep dives in any one. Many of the topics discussed can form the basis of entire courses and often do. For instance, I spend two chapters on the heuristics and biases literature, but these and their applications to policy design and choice architecture can be an entire stand-alone course. Those who are interested in deep dives can and should follow up with other more advanced texts and/or courses dedicated to specialized topics and sub-fields. My point is to draw the horse near the water and get it thirsty; how much it drinks is the horse's call. I do not assume much in the way of technical expertise other than exposure to basic numeracy and concepts in probability. I do understand that many of the terms in this paragraph are relative; some topics will feel like a deeper dive than others and some will find the material more quantitatively challenging than others. Some of this reflects my own preferences and expertise. I know more about some topics and their applications than others, since I have done more work in those areas. Some basic numeracy skills are unavoidable, such as in the material on decision making under uncertainty. But at all points, I will try my best to explain the material so that it is accessible to a general audience.

So, all I am really asking for is a healthy dose of curiosity about the world around us and why we (individuals/groups/societies/governments) make the decisions that we do. And, as I tell my students, the reason for asking them to do some numerical calculations is not because I want to torment them, but because it forms an integral part of logical thinking. This is not that different from learning how to code, study logic, or, for that matter, learn Latin. Of course, no one speaks Latin but studying it helps us understand the structure of most Western languages, such as English, French, Italian or German. Studying these topics with the aid of some basic maths helps develop a formal way of thinking that is often essential in complex decision-making tasks.

Providing an overview of human decision making is not a particularly easy undertaking since "behavioural economics" actually means different things to different people, and, depending on who is teaching the course, the course content may be very different. Earlier, I stated that behavioural economics is a discipline that infuses economic thinking with insights from psychology. But this presupposes that there is a well-defined domain of economic thinking and an equally well-defined set of psychological principles that can be applied to the former in order to generate more realistic predictions of human behaviour. This is not necessarily true, because economists often disagree with one another about central assumptions in the field, as do psychologists. Given that, at the end of the day, both disciplines are really off-shoots of philosophy and are primarily interested in understanding human decision making, there are clear overlaps in research questions. But there is not necessarily agreement about first principles. For instance, social psychologists are often at loggerheads with evolutionary psychologists over things such as the role and impact of nature versus nurture. Economists also disagree about crucial matters such as the impact of inflation and the role of governments in regulating industry. Matters have been made complicated, or possibly more exciting, by the entry of neuroscientists who are now routinely trying to peek inside the black box of the brain via techniques such as functional magnetic resonance imaging (fMRI) to try to understand the nuances of decision making. I will touch upon some of these neuro-economic findings at various points in the text.

As noted, my aim is to reach out to the novice who wants an introduction to the area, who is looking to dip his or her toe in the water. The topics covered reflect my views on what such a person should know and needs to know. Reasonable people will differ on the selection of those topics as well as the depth and breadth. But I am reasonably confident that the coverage will serve a wide range of people and most readers will emerge on the other side with some new-found insights and a new perspective on thinking about social problems.

The book can be used by different types of readers. It is primarily designed to serve as a textbook for a one-semester course in decision making. The topics covered should provide ample material for 12–14-week long semesters of approximately 75–90 minutes of contact time per week. Such courses will most likely be undergraduate courses. Second- or third-year courses could probably rely on this material alone. Fourth-year seminar type courses or graduate level courses would probably find it useful to get students to read some of the actual articles discussed in the book. I teach this material, or variants thereof, at undergraduate level at the University of Auckland. I have also used this for my graduate course in Experimental Economics, where I supplement this with other material and journal articles. I am aware of colleagues who use the book for other applied Master's level courses, as well as people who use it for first year interdisciplinary honours-type seminars.

Second, the book can be used by a lay reader looking to get a handle on the topic. This current book is, in many ways, an extension of my earlier book *Experiments in Economics: Playing Fair with Money*. That book was meant for a general audience with no background in Economics nor anything related to it. David Cooper of Florida State University wrote a very positive review of that book in the *Journal of Economic Literature*. Among other things, he said the following:

> … What this book is perfect for is giving interested readers who are not professional economists a flavour of what experimental economics does and why it is important. It is the book I gave my mother when she wanted to understand what I was always babbling about (she loved it!) …

So, to all those of you who work in this area and struggle to explain what you do to your parents, here is the book you want to buy as the next Mother's Day/Father's Day gift. Lay readers could easily skip some of the more technical parts and I indicate the parts that such readers should feel free to ignore without hampering their understanding of other parts of the book.

But, less facetiously, practitioners from a wide range of fields and those working in public policy should be able to get value out of this book. During Spring 2020, I used this material to teach "MLD 302: Behavioural Decision Making" to students at Harvard Kennedy School.[3] Most of these students were pursuing Master's degrees in public policy or public administration. Some came from Tufts University's Fletcher School of Government, while others from the Chan School of Public Health. I think I had one or more students from Harvard's Graduate School of Design. I also had a number of members from the American Leadership Initiative at the Kennedy School. These are typically people who have already had a distinguished career and are looking for a new challenge or a shift in vocation/avocation toward pursuing a new goal. Some of them are lawyers or entrepreneurs. Both formal and informal feedback suggested that all of these people found parts of the material interesting, thought-provoking and applicable to things that they were working on or were interested in. So, if you are a public policy practitioner, then there should be something in this book for you. If nothing else, you can use this as a substitute for doing MLD 302 at Harvard Kennedy School.

Third, the book can be a useful supplementary or recommended text for undergraduate or graduate courses in experimental economics that devote a substantial amount of time to issues such as ultimatum, trust, social dilemma and coordination games. The same is true for a variety of upper-level courses in microeconomics or game theory, where the instructor might wish to discuss experimental findings and behavioural implications of the theoretical models of behaviour.

Fourth, findings in this area have broad overlaps with social psychology, organizational behaviour, management and other business-related disciplines, and, as such, the book should appeal to researchers and students in those areas as well. Parts of the material, especially ones related to heuristics and biases, rightfully belong to the psychology literature. This material may be well known to students with a background in psychology. However, chances are that these students will get value from the discussion of strategic thinking and the variety of experimental games.

The material on trust, gift-exchange and how to resolve problems of coordination failure in organizations should be of particular interest to human resource managers and might provide insights into ways of motivating their workforce. Parts of the book dealing with strategic thinking, Bayesian updating, and the concepts of fairness and trust and their economic implications should be of interest to social and evolutionary psychologists. I spend quite a bit of time on problems of collective action; this, again, should find wide applicability to a range of issues across disciplines.

I can think of no better way to end this preface than to quote from John Maynard Keynes' preface to the *General Theory of Employment, Interest and Money*, which eloquently sums up what I would like to say to the prospective reader.

> The composition of this book has been for the author a long struggle of escape, and so must the reading of it be for most readers if the author's assault upon them is to be successful – a struggle of escape from habitual modes of thought and expression. The ideas which are here expressed so laboriously are extremely simple and should be obvious. The difficulty lies, not in the new ideas, but in escaping from the old ones, which ramify, for those brought up as most of us have been, into every corner of our minds.

NOTES

1 Much of this work is complex and technical in nature. I have certainly not done justice to the breadth and scope of this work here. If you find this interesting, you should certainly read Al Roth's eminently readable book: *Who Gets What – and Why: The New Economics of Matchmaking and Market Design*.
2 These were the early days in the rise of behavioural economics, but Yunus was very clearly relying on behavioural insights from economics and psychology in his work to combat poverty in

Bangladesh. But possibly because it was early days and because behavioural economics, particularly behavioural development economics, was still considered far outside the mainstream of Economics, Yunus had to settle for the Peace Prize rather than the Prize in Economics. Knowing Yunus, I doubt the distinction mattered to him. In case you are not aware, the Peace Prize is handed out in Oslo, Norway, while all the other prizes are awarded in Stockholm, Sweden. It is also the case that the Nobel Prize in Economics is very much a late-comer and was not part of Alfred Nobel's original endowment. The Economics prize was instituted in 1969 by the Swedish Reserve Bank and is actually referred to as the Sveriges Riksbank Prize in Economic Sciences in Memory of Alfred Nobel. This is why the other "real" Nobel Prize winners like the ones in literature, physics or chemistry do not consider the Economics Nobel Prize as a real Nobel Prize!

3 At the Kennedy School, courses are allocated to different teaching areas. Mine belonged to MLD: Management, Leadership and Decision Making.

1 How we decide

In this chapter, I talk about

- The assumption of "rationality" in the social sciences;
- The concept of "bounded rationality";
- The role of social norms and conventions in guiding rational behaviour;
- How economists and psychologists differ in their approach to the study of decision making and how behavioural economics combines insights from both;
- The "guessing game" as an example of this merger of economic and psychological input;
- The canonical problem of choice facing an economic consumer as a demonstration of the "normative" approach in economics.

VIGNETTE 1:

3 February 1953: "The day the music died." Buddy Holly's death in a plane crash in Iowa on this day has been immortalized in many ways including in Don McLean's classic "American Pie".[1] But the story goes that Holly, Richie Valens and others were supposed to take a bus but had chartered the plane at the last minute. They had been on the road for a while and Holly wanted to arrive early so that everyone could do their laundry.

VIGNETTE 2:

In 2019, James Holzhauer, a professional sports-bettor from Las Vegas, set the world of *Jeopardy!* on fire and became one of the highest earning players of all time. In his fourth game on April 9, he won $110,914 in a single day, which broke the previous single-game *Jeopardy!* winnings record of $77,000 set by Roger Craig in 2010. Holzhauer became particularly well known for selecting big value clues at the outset in an attempt to uncover the Daily Doubles and when he found them, he bet it all every single time thereby ending up with huge cash earnings.[2]

VIGNETTE 3:

In 1994, the players of Major League baseball in the United States of America went on strike. This led to the cancellation of 938 games overall, including the entire post-season and the World Series. Team owners were demanding a salary cap and came up with a new revenue-sharing plan, which required the players' approval. The players' union rejected the offer, which they thought was unfair to the players and merely a way to address problems of disparity among the owners. After prolonged negotiations failed to break the impasse, the acting commissioner, Bud Selig, called off the rest of the season on September 14. The move to cancel the rest of the season meant the loss of $580 million in ownership revenue and $230 million in player salaries. Thus, the players essentially walked away from $230 million collectively because of what they considered was an unfair offer. The average salary of players at this time was about $1.2 million per year. This in turn resulted in a loss of more than twice that amount for the owners.

VIGNETTE 4:

One part of the British daytime show *Golden Balls* works like this: two contestants face each other and decide on a pool of cash that varies from one pair to the next. The pool is typically in the thousands of pounds if not hundreds of thousands. Each contestant is given a set of two balls; one can be opened to reveal the message "Split" written inside, while the other, when opened, says "Steal". Each contestant knows the content of the message inside each ball; that is, whether the message inside says "Split" or "Steal". The contestants are given some time to discuss their options and indicate what decision they will take. If both choose "Split", they each receive half the jackpot. If one chooses "Steal", while the other chooses "Split", then the contestant choosing "Steal" will win the entire pool of money and the one choosing "Split" gets nothing. If both contestants choose "Steal", then neither contestant wins anything. Different pairs arrive at different outcomes. In some, both members choose "Split" and share the pot. But there are plenty of instances, where one member in the pair chooses "Split", while the other chooses "Steal" even after promising repeatedly that (s)he will choose "Split". In such cases, the one choosing "Split", the "nice" option, is left with nothing.

One episode (back in February 2008), saw Sarah from Manchester and Stephen from Hartlepool facing each other. The pot was £100,150! Stephen and Sarah discussed the situation at length, with each promising solemnly and repeatedly that each was going to choose "Split", thereby walking away with about £50,000 each. Then came the time to reveal their respective choices. Stephen chose "Split" as promised, but Sarah, who had at times tearfully promised to choose "Split", actually chose "Steal", walking away with the entire jackpot, leaving Stephen with nothing.

INTRODUCTION

We make hundreds, if not thousands of decisions over the course of a day; big and small. Some of these are inconsequential, while others are much less so (though this is probably relative to the individual and not everyone is as equally vested in all decisions).[3] Some of these may not have financial or economic implications but many do; in fact, in a sense it may not be inaccurate to say that most do. For instance, your decision to take this course or buy this book or even read this book required a number of trade-offs; another course you could have taken, another book you could have read or another activity you could have pursued. This is the "opportunity cost" of doing what you are doing; the value of the best alternative activity foregone. The opportunity cost of holding loads of cash in your wallet is the interest income you are foregoing by not putting your money in the bank. The opportunity cost of our fantastic family trip to Europe was the part of the mortgage that could have been paid off had we not taken the trip. In some cases, assigning a dollar cost to the foregone alternative activity is easier. But, if you think hard about it, you could also possibly assign a dollar value to other things; activities that you gave up in order to pursue this current activity. Economists call this "imputed value"; the idea that you could and should assign a value to activities.[4] When you decide to undertake a particular activity, you have implicitly decided not to undertake another activity.

So, how do we make up our minds when confronted with decisions involving multiple choices? This is no easy matter as Theodore Geisel (popularly known as Dr Seuss) points out in his book *Oh, The Places You'll Go!* (1990), a book supposedly written for young children but one which contains profound insights for adults too. Geisel writes that at times the reader may find himself/herself in a place where the streets are not marked, where some windows are lit but others are dark; a place where he/she could fall down and sprain a body part. Does the reader dare to go in, or should he/she stay out? Geisel ends this part by stating that often the reader will find that it is not at all a simple matter "for a mind-maker-upper to make up his mind".

Some of these decisions are purely individual ones such as: should I get the extended warranty on my big screen television. How about on my iPhone? Should I buy a lottery ticket? But others go beyond just individual decisions, to decisions made by groups, such as the bargaining between players and owners in Major League baseball. Or a company trying to decide whether to cut prices or not to match a competitor; United and Continental trying to decide whether to merge or not ... and the response of competitors to a merger; Novartis deciding how much to invest in R&D on a new cancer drug and when to stop.

Other examples include: people trying to decide whether to contribute money towards building a local park or another similar charity; a Persian-rug seller haggling over the price and deciding how quickly to lower the price; a Hadza man in Tanzania deciding whether to join another hunter in order to jointly hunt a large prey for the day, or just try to catch a smaller animal on his own; an employee deciding how hard to work when the employer is away.

But I digress. To get back to the point: we are constantly making decisions and many of these have financial implications. So, it would be good if we knew more about how we make these decisions. While human decision making is of interest to a wide cross-section of researchers, it is probably safe to say that economics and psychology are the two disciplines that spend the most time worrying about this.

Economists start by assuming a certain amount of rationality on the part of humans. It is actually possible to argue over what "rationality" means, and scholars in different disciplines often do. My working definition, or, better yet, my understanding of what economists understand by "rationality", is that when faced with choices, humans engage in a clear-headed calculation of the benefits and costs; we possess foresight and are able to undertake complex calculations, and finally, that we are interested in maximizing what economists refer to as *utility*.[5] Furthermore, we do not have the luxury of choosing anything we want.

Our choices are *constrained*, in the sense that they depend not only on what we want, but also on what we can afford. Left to myself, I always prefer to fly business-class, but my professorial salary prevents me from doing this much of the time.

These are reasonable assumptions and even if one does not necessarily agree with this definition of rationality (say the one about self-interest), one could think of these assumptions as being normative (what should happen); that is, prescribing a course of action rather than being descriptive. After all, it makes sense that individuals should look to maximize happiness; firms should maximize profit. A firm that does not maximize profit will be driven out of the market. So, in a sense, when economists think of humans, they have in mind Mr Spock or Sheldon Cooper.

Psychologists, on the other hand, typically start by assuming humans are "boundedly rational";[6] again, one could argue about what exactly this means, but my definition of "bounded rationality" is that we have limits on our cognitive abilities; we face constraints of time, computing ability and foresight; we often fall prey to biases and errors of judgement. Some problems are hard, some others we experience only infrequently. This implies that we have more experience and expertise with some problems than with others. Buying groceries does not pose much of a challenge; we do it all the time. But buying a computer requires more research; buying a car even more so. Buying a house is a decision we make infrequently.

Anyone who has bought a house knows how stressful this is. Which is the right house? Will it still be "right" when the kids are older? What neighbourhood? Which school zone? Close to the ocean? Better lifestyle but a longer commute. Or close to the highway, reducing commuting time but being in a less nice area. Which bank to approach for a loan? Which has the better rates? This bank is giving away a flat-screen TV while the other will pay the lawyer's fee. A third is offering a low "teaser" rate. Which one works out better over the course of the loan lasting 25 years? Often, we look at a house which just "feels right" and so we ignore other factors that go against our judgement. The Duke psychologist Dan Ariely, supposedly an expert on human decision making, talks about how he found himself driving home in a brand-new, small, bright-red Audi convertible before he realized that, as the father of two young children, the car was far from what he and his family really needed. Even the most sophisticated and computationally savvy person struggles with these choices. This means that the possibility of making mistakes are higher, the less facility we have with the task at hand.

But is this all primarily about self-interest? What is best for me? What makes me and my close ones better off? We want to achieve the optimal outcome. We want to buy the right house in the right school zone, sign up for the right retirement plan, get the best possible health insurance and choose the best possible combined mobile phone and broadband package. But we often fail to do so just because some of these decisions are really complex. We get confused or run out of patience or are just too tired at the weekends to deal with this.

But is there nothing beyond self-interest? What about emotions? Empathy? Altruism? Good-will? Morality? Should we primarily rely on reasoning without passion or should we let our passions guide us, but within reason? Uniquely among primates, humans exhibit an ability to engage in large group social living and frequent cooperation with non-related kin. There must be institutions in place that allow for such cooperation to emerge and to become established, often based on social norms and conventions. This, then, is yet another way in which the assumption of self-interest becomes suspect.

It is not too far from the truth to suggest that much economic thinking is underpinned by the principle of Utilitarianism espoused by Jeremy Bentham (1748–1832). Bentham said that our primary goal should be to engage in dispassionate reasoning, and that we should choose the course of action that achieves the greatest happiness for the largest number. A contrarian view was put forth by David Hume (1711–1776), who said: "Reason is, and ought to be the slave of passions; and can never pretend to any other office than to serve and obey them." This, then, is yet another way the psychological view of human decision making differs from the economic view: by explicitly allowing for the role of what may be broadly called "emotions", where I am using this term loosely to include all such things as intuition, empathy, feelings and passions.

DESCARTES'S ERROR?

The French philosopher, mathematician and scientist, Rene Descartes, is supposed to have said: *Cogito ergo sum. I think, therefore I am.* But what Descartes was really implying harked back to the days of Aristotle and is referred to as the mind–body dualism. Without going into the details, the crux of the matter is that there is a clear distinction between reason, which is seen as being superior to, and more useful than, emotions. Descartes was effectively arguing that it is our reasoning ability that makes us human; rational processes must be unencumbered by emotions. In his book *Descartes' Error*, the UCLA neuroscientist, Antonio Damasio, challenges this duality and suggests that rationality requires emotional input; in the absence of emotions (or "passion"), most of us would be incapable of carrying out normal day-to-day activities. Damasio's first example involved Phineas Gage.

On September 13, 1848, Gage was heading up a work gang blasting rock for the Rutland & Burlington Railroad, near the village of Cavendish, Vermont. The work involved boring a hole in the rock, adding blasting powder and a fuse, and using a 3.5 feet long tamping iron to pack in sand, clay, or other inert material into the hole above the powder in order to contain the blast's energy and direct it into surrounding rock. On this day, a charge went off prematurely. The tamping iron that Gage was holding went in through his left cheek, pierced the frontal lobe of his brain and stuck out from the right side of his skull. While Gage lost consciousness temporarily, he was soon sitting up and managed to make the 30-minute cart-ride to the physician's surgery. Gage survived and went on to live for another 12 years, at times earning a living as a "freak" in circus shows. But in the days that followed the accident, Gage was no longer the same person. He was impulsive and foul-mouthed. He drank and got into fights. Physicians now believe that this dramatic difference in Gage's behaviour was caused by significant damage to the frontal lobe of his brain.

Damasio then goes on to discuss a patient of his – Elliott. Elliott had a good job and was doing well until it was discovered that he had a tumour in his frontal lobe. The tumour was removed with significant damage to the brain. Elliott's life soon fell apart. Elliott had not lost his reasoning ability. Damasio soon learned Elliot's cognitive faculties were unharmed. He performed well on IQ tests and other measures of intelligence. His memory, both short- and long-term, functioned well, and his language skills, perception, and ability with maths were all still present. But he just could not complete the tasks he was assigned at work, where he might spend an entire afternoon trying to figure out how to categorize his documents.

■ How we decide

Soon, Damasio realized that he had been preoccupied with Elliot's intelligence. But what was missing was not intellect. Damasio writes: "He was always controlled, always describing scenes as a dispassionate, uninvolved spectator. Nowhere was there a sense of his own suffering, even though he was the protagonist." Damasio asked Elliot to look at lots of emotionally charged images, like pictures of burning buildings, gruesome accidents, and people about to drown. Elliot remained curiously dispassionate about the images. Now Damasio had a better picture of Elliot's interior life:

> Try to imagine not feeling pleasure when you contemplate a painting you love or hear a favourite piece of music. Try to imagine yourself forever robbed of that possibility and yet aware of the intellectual contents of the visual or musical stimulus, and also aware that once it did give you pleasure. We might summarize Elliot's predicament as to know but not to feel.

What is my point? My point is that the matter of thinking is not as straightforward as it sounds, and it seems that, at times, reason needs explicit emotional input in order to complete tasks. So, for psychologists, humans look not like Sheldon, but more like Leonard Hofstadter or Penny.[7]

HOW DO ECONOMISTS AND PSYCHOLOGISTS APPROACH DECISION MAKING?

Look at Figure 1.1. Suppose I asked you, "What is this?" Your immediate answer would be that it is a dinosaur. The more discerning of you (or fans of the "Jurassic Park" films) may even say that it is a *Tyrannosaurus Rex*. This is how my students typically respond. But it is

Figure 1.1
Toy *Tyrannosaurus Rex*: an example of a model

not really a *Tyrannosaurus Rex*, right? It is a long-discarded toy dinosaur that I dug up from my daughters' playthings. In fact, it is a "model" of a *Tyrannosaurus Rex*. The model is based on what we know from the available fossil record. In fact, I remember visiting the Museum of Natural History in New York and having an interesting and informative discussion of everything that Spielberg got wrong about the Velociraptor in his films. The model may not be exact and may well get some aspects wrong, but it serves a useful purpose. It tells us how this particular animal most likely looked or behaved.

This is the economics approach to understanding human behaviour: Start with a "model", essentially a theory, based on some assumptions about behaviour. See what predictions this model makes about behaviour in different circumstances and then see if actual behaviour corresponds to this "model". If not, then possibly tinker with the model to make it more realistic. The arguments that apply to the case of dinosaurs, also apply to the case of thinking about human behaviour: All models are wrong, but some models are useful. Of course, the predictions of the model depend on the assumptions underlying the model, and so, if the assumptions are questionable, then the model's predictions may go awry. But, nonetheless, starting with a model and making adjustments along the way is a good way to approach many scientific questions. In the next chapter, I address in more detail some of the issues regarding these assumptions and what it means to actually test the assumptions underlying such a model. But rather than getting side-tracked into this debate right now, let me continue.

Psychologists, on the other hand, typically start by focusing on the "target" behaviour; typically, an interesting and frequently observed pattern of behaviour or phenomenon. Instead of trying to write down an assumption-based model of such behaviour, psychologists prefer to collect data on such behaviour. Once a particular phenomenon has been documented many times, psychologists then call it a "theory", which is really a different name for a model, because once a theory is formulated, it can then be used to make predictions about future behaviour under similar circumstances. The psychology approach then, is descriptive.

Consider the example of "ego depletion theory" proposed by Roy Baumeister. Baumeister had two groups of participants placed in two separate rooms around a table. In one room, the table had a bowl of freshly cut cauliflowers. The table in the other room had a bowl of freshly baked cookies, whose aroma filled the room. Participants were forbidden from consuming any of the contents of the bowls in either room. Afterwards, both sets of participants were given challenging mathematical problems to solve. It turned out that the group that had been in the room with the cookies gave up much more quickly on trying to solve the problems, as opposed to the people in the room with the cauliflowers.

His findings led Baumeister to the following conclusion. Many tasks in day-to-day life require us to exert self-control. But there is a limit to how long and how much self-control we can exert. The people who had to refrain from eating the cookies had to exercise much greater self-control than those asked to stay away from the cauliflowers. As a consequence, the people in the room with the cookies had used up most of their quota of self-control, and hence had a harder time concentrating on the mathematical problems that followed. The people facing cauliflowers had a larger reserve of self-control left over and hence persisted at the problem-solving task much longer.

Baumeister went on to call this "Ego depletion theory"; the idea that over the course of time, our ability to exert self-control diminishes. This is why most of us find it much easier to resist dessert (or chocolates) earlier in the day when our stock of self-control is high, but find resistance more difficult at night, when our stock of self-control is running low. This is also why most supermarkets are laid out the way they are. All supermarkets pretty much have their fruit and vegetable aisles in the front as you walk in; the ice creams and other desserts are stocked on the shelves towards the back, as you are nearing the completion of your shopping. The argument is that we find it much easier to pick up the large tub of ice cream once we have loaded our trolley with fruits and vegetables. If a supermarket put the ice cream isle at the front, they would find fewer buyers for it.[8]

This is an example of the descriptive psychological approach: going from a regularly observed phenomenon to building a theory about a potential explanation of those observations. One drawback to this descriptive approach, however, is that there are instances when a particular phenomenon may be explained by more than one theory. In such cases, it becomes difficult to know whether something is caused by one reason or another. This also, at times, makes it difficult to predict future behaviour and has occasionally created problems with the replicability of experimental results. There is nothing inherently superior about one approach or the other. They are different ways to figure out the foibles of human behaviour and each has its advantages and disadvantages. This is partly why behavioural economists have come to rely on elements of both approaches and have done so with great benefit, as I hope to convince you in the pages that follow.

INFUSING PSYCHOLOGY INTO ECONOMICS: THE GUESSING GAME

In order to get a better handle on what I am talking about and how psychological insights can enrich economic reasoning, let us play the "guessing game". Here is how the game is played. I carry out the following exercise in many of my classes and lectures. I hand out small slips of paper and ask each member of the group to choose a number between 0 and 100. *The winner is the person who comes as close as possible to one half of the average number chosen in the group.* The actual fraction used (often called the "target") does not have to be one half. It could be another fraction, such as two-thirds. I then collect all the sheets, enter all the numbers into an Excel spreadsheet, calculate the average and then take half of that average. I find the person whose choice is closest to this and give him/her a small monetary reward.[9]

You will get a lot more out of the next few paragraphs if you try playing the game. Put the book down, think about it for a bit and then write down a number.

So, what number did you choose? If you are like Sheldon Cooper, then you probably chose zero! In fact, this is what dispassionate reasoning in line with traditional economic thinking will suggest. Why? Suppose everyone chooses 100. Then the average for the group is 100. One half of the average is 50. In that case, you should choose 50 to come as close as possible to one half of the average. But suppose everyone thought that! In that case, everyone chooses 50, so the average is 50 and one half of the average is 25. So, should you choose 25? No, because if everyone figured this out and chose 25, the average would be 25 and you should choose 12.5 to come as close as possible to one half of the average. If you continue this process (or "iterative" thinking to throw in some economic jargon) then the only number that survives is zero. Everyone should choose that. Again, using jargon, this is the equilibrium outcome. Over time, everyone should converge to zero; over time, those who choose other things should learn the folly of their ways. Of course, that does not quite help if you only get one shot at playing this game.

But I am sure it will not come as a surprise to you to learn that this is not what happens. In fact, you will seldom "win" if you chose zero. If the target is one half then you are more likely to win if you chose something in the ballpark of 13, that is, applied two levels of reasoning from 50 to 25 to 12.5. Rosemarie Nagel, of the University of Pompeu-Fabra, has done extensive work on this problem and how people think through it. Figure 1.2 shows the typical pattern of choices.

What do you notice? There is a big spike at 50. These are people who stopped at the first step. Then there is a spike at 30 with smaller spike at around 25. These are people who went to the second step of homing in on 25. Then there is a large cluster between 10 and 17. These are people who went to the third step of 12.5 and then made some upward or downward adjustments. In fact, there are few choices at zero or close to it. The average choice for this group is 27 while the median is 17. This means around 50% of the choices lie below 17, which is reasonably close to the third step of 12.5.

What if the target was two-thirds? Figure 1.3 shows this. Once again, iterated thinking suggests that people should choose zero using an analogous argument. Suppose everyone chooses 100. Then the average for the group is 100. Two-thirds of the average is 67. But if everyone chose 67, then the average is 67 and two-thirds gets you to 45. Repeating this process again gets you to 30, and so on. Once again, Nagel found that very few people actually chose zero. There is a spike at around 67, then a bunch of choices between 40 and 50, with small spikes at 40, 45 and 50, a big spike at 35 and a bigger one at 25. So, while the spikes are not exactly at 67, 45, 30 and so on, they are in the ballpark with some deviations, since every individual is adding small upward or downward adjustments.

What is even more interesting is when Nagel looked at what she called "interim intervals". Clearly, people are not going to pick the exact targets. So, Nagel looked at reasonable intervals around the target; so, in the case of the one-half target, not exactly 50 but numbers

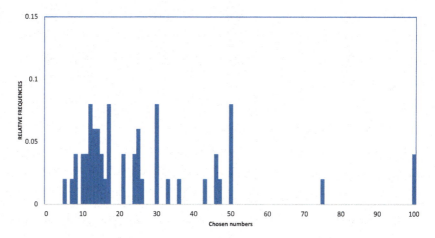

Figure 1.2
Chosen numbers in the guessing game with target = 1/2. Re-created on the basis of data in Nagel (1995)

■ How we decide

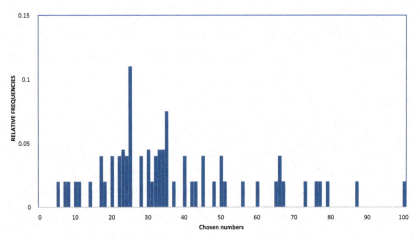

Figure 1.3
Chosen numbers in the guessing game with target = 2/3. Re-created on the basis of data in Nagel (1995)

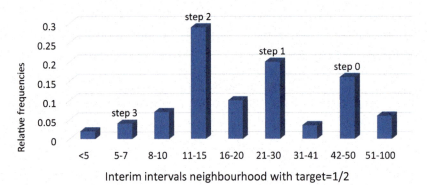

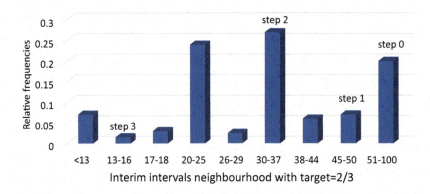

Figure 1.4
Interim interval bounds on choices in the guessing game. Re-created on the basis of data in Nagel (1995)

a little bit higher or lower than 50. Figure 1.4 shows these interim intervals. A few things stand out. First, there are very few zero choices. Second, a lot of the choices do fall in the interim intervals that we expected. For instance, if you look at the top panel of Figure 1.4, then you notice that in the one-half target game, a lot of the choices cluster around 50, 25 and 12.5. If you look at the bottom panel for the game with the two-thirds target, a similar pattern emerges. Finally, the bulk of the choices are contained within the first three intervals. For the one-half target game, the bulk of the choices lie within the three clusters, around 50, around 25 and around 12.5. For the bottom panel, the convergence is less pronounced. Theory predicts choices of 67, 45, 30 and so on. There are a lot of choices between 51 and 100 but few choices around 45, but then there is big spike around 30.

So, simply homing in on zero is not going to do the trick. You need to actively anticipate what others in the group are doing. Now, at this point, many people say: but these are students, playing for small stakes of money. How seriously do they take the game? Do they even understand what the "correct" answer is? Colin Camerer, of Caltech, got tired of people asking him this question. So, he had a bunch of people play this game, including CEOs of leading companies at a retreat, portfolio managers from investment banks and Economics PhD students. Figure 1.5 shows what happened. If most people chose zero, then we expect the bars to all cluster around zero. The more spread out the bars are, the more scattered the choices are, with more choices further away from zero. It is clear that the CEOs and portfolio managers did not choose zero. In fact, the proportion choosing zero is much higher among the Caltech students. When I carried out this experiment at Harvard Kennedy School, I also had a lot of students who chose zero. I do not believe it is the case that these people are necessarily smarter than others. They may be, but it is also possible that, in looking around the room, they are forming judgements about their peers: what they know, how many levels of thinking they will apply.[10]

Economists sometimes call these models of "cognitive hierarchy" or "Level-k thinking". There may be some naïve types who stop at the first step, say, by choosing 50 in the one-half target game. Let us call this "Level Zero" thinking: everyone will choose 100, so the average is 100 and, therefore, one half of the average is 50.[11] Then there is a second type that applies Level One thinking, which takes them to 25; then there is a Level 2 type that goes to 12.5. Actually, it is a little bit more complicated than that. Excluding the naïve Level Zero types, each type might actually be considering how many players of which type there are in the group and conditioning their responses based on that. This is why you get quite a bit of dispersion in the stated responses rather than the choices homing in exactly on 50, 25, 12.5 and so on.

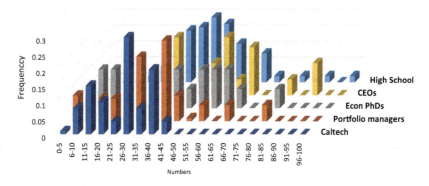

Figure 1.5
Choices in the guessing game by different subject pools. Re-created on the basis of data in Camerer (2003)

But you feel like asking: What does this have to do with real-life? My daughters love watching a show titled *Family Feud* and sometimes they cajole me into watching with them. Two teams compete to win points. Here is a part of one episode that I watched. One team was given the following category: "Things people lose while on vacation." The team is given a number of options, such as wallet, passport, money, etc. In the meantime, the show's organizers have polled a random group of 100 people and asked each of them the same question. The challenge for the team is to pick the most popular choice among those external respondents. So, for instance, if the most frequent choice among those other 100 people is "wallet", then the team will earn the most points if they also pick "wallet"; the team gets fewer points if they pick the second most popular choice, even less if they choose the third most popular choice and so on. So, all of a sudden, it does not matter what you think you would lose while on vacation, but you need to anticipate what a random group of 100 people outside the studio thinks you would lose while on vacation. If you think that this is a trivial example, then bear in mind that a majority of people pick stocks on the basis of their familiarity with the name. They think that other people will also be familiar with the name and will pick that stock as well, implying that this stock is likely to perform better than others. In all these cases, you need to anticipate what others in your peer group will do.

John Maynard Keynes, the father of modern macroeconomics, wrote:

> professional investment may be likened to those newspaper competitions in which the competitors have to pick out the six prettiest faces from a hundred photographs, ... so that each competitor has to pick not those faces which he himself finds prettiest, but those which he thinks likeliest to catch the fancy of the other competitors, [who are] ... looking at the problem from the same point of view. ... We have reached the third degree where we devote our intelligences to anticipating what average opinion expects the average opinion to be.

In many of these instances then, if you applied nothing but equilibrium reasoning, you would most likely not "win". Your better option would be to look around, get a sense of the room, think of how many levels of reasoning your peers might apply. In short, pure reasoning is not enough. Of course, you need to engage in some amount of reasoning, since stopping at the first step is also not the recipe for success. But this needs to be complemented by some amount of emotional input and psychological intuition about those you are interacting with; in short, reason leavened with passion: this is the very essence of behavioural economics.

TYPES OF DECISION MAKING

Broadly speaking, we can think of three types of decisions we are frequently called upon to make. First, decisions that involve one person and probably does not impact others. For example, buying a lottery ticket; deciding whether to buy the new iPhone or put the money in a savings account; taking out a mortgage. Second, decisions that involve small groups or one-on-one bargaining situations. For example, bargaining for a good price; whether to take part in collective action such as marching for climate change or protesting a regime's rule. Here, what we do often depends on what others are doing and our beliefs about them. Many such decisions involve strategic thinking, in the sense that they often require us to anticipate how the other party may respond to choices we make. At times, we need the tools of game theory to think through these situations. But, equally, many such decisions are influenced by notions of social norms; what is fair; what is appropriate; what is expected. Third, there are decisions that we make in markets with many buyers and sellers. Often, an individual will have limited power over the prices that prevail in these markets, given that (s)he is one of many in the market. So, at times, these decisions may be similar to individual choice problems – how much do you want to buy at a given price in the supermarket – but not always.

I end this chapter by discussing the canonical economic approach to a consumer's choice problem. Those of you who have done Economics before this will be familiar with much of this material. Even if you have not done Economics before, this is not essential for our purposes. Feel free to skip to the section headed "How realistic is this 'normative' model? Let's look inside the brain", where I present the results of some fMRI (functional magnetic resonance imaging) studies to understand what happens inside the brain when we make choices among various options. This will not hamper your ability to follow the rest of the material from the next chapter onward. But those of you from other disciplines may find this interesting and useful. It will give you a flavour of what I mean by the "normative" approach in economics.

ANA'S PROBLEM OF CHOICE

Ana's dad gave her $100 for her birthday and told her that she can choose how to spend this money. Suppose that Ana can spend it on two goods. In a feat of imagination, let us call them Goods X and Y. Certainly, Ana can save some money for later, but let us assume (without loss of generality, to throw in some jargon) that she does not need to worry about saving. (Or, her father gave her more than $100 and she has put some of this away under her mattress to hide it from her big sister Isha, who is in the habit of claiming money she finds lying around the house under the principle of "finders keepers", or, as she has recently learned, "possession is nine-tenths of the law".) So, for now, Ana intends to spend $100 that she has at her disposal.

ANA CANNOT BUY EVERYTHING SHE WANTS; HER CHOICES ARE CONSTRAINED

So how should Ana spend her money? Well, it depends, first of all, on what X and Y cost. This will dictate what she can afford. Suppose X costs $20 per unit ($P_X$ = $20) while Y costs $10 per unit ($P_Y$ = $10). (So maybe X is a film ticket and Y is a large tub of popcorn.) How many of each can she afford? What if she spent her entire $100 on X? Since X costs $20 each, she can buy 5 of these. How about Y? She can buy 10 of these since they cost $10 each. This allows us to draw Ana's *budget constraint*. She can buy either 5 units of X or 10 units of Y, or any combination of the two that add up to $100. Figure 1.6 shows this budget constraint. At one extreme, Ana buys 5 of X and zero of Y; at the other extreme, she buys 10 of Y and zero of X. If we join these two extreme points (or the two intercepts) with a straight line, then this is Ana's budget constraint. She can choose either of the two extremes, or, more likely, another intermediate point on the line such that the total is $100. For instance, she can buy 4 units of X, costing $80, and 2 units of Y, costing $20, for a total of $100. Or 3 of X costing $60

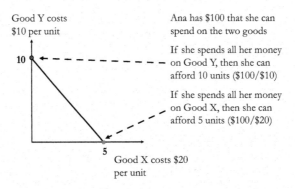

Figure 1.6
Ana's budget constraint

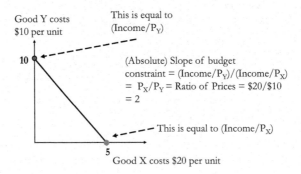

Figure 1.7
Slope of Ana's budget constraint

and 4 of Y costing $40, etc. The line is negatively sloped because, in order to buy more of one good, Ana needs to give up some of the other. We will refer to a possible pair of choices of X and Y as a *"consumption bundle"*.

Figure 1.7 shows that the absolute slope of the budget constraint is given by the ratio of the two prices (P_X/P_Y). This is because the slope of a line is given by the rise over the run. In this case, the rise is (Income/P_Y) while the run is (Income/P_X). Simple algebraic manipulation shows that this is the same as (P_X/P_Y). Of course, this is the absolute slope (or the magnitude of the slope) since the actual slope is negative. Given the supposed values of P_X and P_Y, this value is equal to ($20/$10) which is 2. This simply implies that you can buy 2 units of Y for each unit of X; that is., if you buy one more of X, then you will need to buy two fewer of Y.

Figure 1.8 shows the nature of Ana's choices. She can afford any consumption bundle that lies on the budget constraint but nothing that lies beyond (to the north and east) of that line. Of course, she can consume inside the shaded triangle, but, as I argued above, she wants to spend the entire $100 and, therefore, will operate on the line itself, rather than under the line.

What happens if Ana's mum (who is more fiscally responsible and conscious about not spoiling the children) adds $20? In that case, Ana will have $120. If Ana has $120, then, at the two extremes, she can either buy 6 units of X ($120/$20) and zero of Y, or she can buy 12 units of Y ($120/$10) and zero of X. In this case, her budget constraint shifts out and to the right, parallel to its former self. Or, suppose Ana, out of a sense of charity, decides to give

Figure 1.8
Example of consumption bundles worth more than, less than or exactly $100

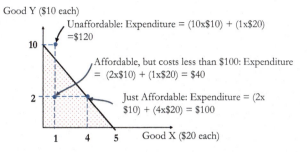

Figure 1.9
The effect of a change in Ana's income on her budget constraint

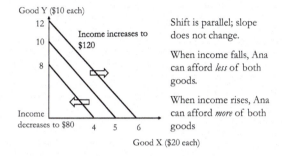

$40 of her $120 to Isha. (Ostensibly, Isha is only "borrowing" this money, but Ana knows that she is never seeing that $40 again!) Then Ana will be left with $80. If Ana has only $80, then she can buy 4 of X ($80/$20) and zero of Y, or she can buy 8 of Y ($80/$10) and zero of X. If that happens, then her budget constraint shifts inward to the left, but once again in a parallel manner. Figure 1.9 shows what happens in each case.

Let us go back to the case where Ana has $100. What happens if the price of either X or Y goes up or down? Suppose the price of X changes. Since the price of Y has not changed, the intercept of the budget constraint on the Y-axis remains unchanged. Ana can still buy 10 of Y and zero of X if she wishes. But now she can buy more or less of X depending on whether X has become less or more expensive. If X has become cheaper than $20 per unit and Ana spends her entire $100 on X, then she can buy more than 5 units. In this case, the budget line swivels outward around the Y intercept. However, if X has become more expensive than $20 per unit and Ana spends her entire $100 on X, then she can buy fewer than 5 units. In this case, the budget line swivels inward around the Y intercept. Figure 1.10 shows the respective situations.

On the other hand, if the price of X does not change but Y becomes more or less expensive, then the intercept of the budget constraint on the X-axis remains unchanged. Ana can still buy 5 of X and zero of Y if she wishes. But now, she can buy more or less of Y depending on whether Y has become less or more expensive. If Y has become cheaper than $10 per unit and Ana spends her entire $100 on Y, then she can buy more than 10 units. In this case, the budget line swivels outward around the X intercept, whereas if Y has become more expensive than $10 per unit and Ana spends her entire $100 on Y, then she can buy fewer than 10 units. In this case, the budget line swivels inward around the X intercept. Figure 1.11 shows the respective situations.

■ How we decide

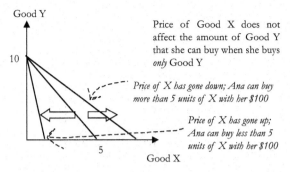

Figure 1.10
The effect of a change in the price of Good X on Ana's budget constraint

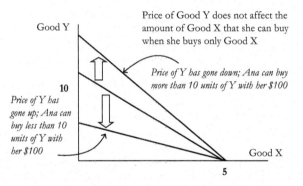

Figure 1.11
The effect of a change in the price of Good Y on Ana's budget constraint

ANA KNOWS WHAT SHE CAN AFFORD, BUT HOW DOES SHE CHOOSE AMONG THESE?

Ana now has a clear idea of what she can afford. But there is a second part to the problem. How does Ana choose a particular combination of X and Y? Economists assume that consumption of goods yields *utility*, which is economese for happiness or satisfaction. Consumption bundles that offer more utility are preferred to those that provide less utility. Utility is measured on an "ordinal" scale. An ordinal measure is one where we assign a higher number to things that are more preferred, but the numbers are not meaningful *per se*. Examples of ordinal measures are things like academic degrees, academic ranks or military ranks. If you want to indicate that a professor (or a lieutenant) is ranked higher than a lecturer (or a captain), then an ordinal measure will assign a higher score to the former than the latter, but the score itself is meaningless. You can assign the former a 5 (or 100) and the latter a 2 (or 10) if you wish. The number itself is irrelevant as long as the preferred option is awarded a higher number. (On the other hand, a "cardinal" measure is one where the numbers have a particular meaning, such as when measuring height, weight, age or distance.)

Let me digress briefly to highlight the distinction between "total utility" and "marginal utility". Clearly, the value we ascribe to goods (or bundles) and, therefore, the price we are willing to pay, depends on the utility we get from them. But then why are diamonds so much more expensive than water? Doesn't water provide more utility? This is the so-called "Diamond–Water Paradox" or "Paradox of value" posited by Adam Smith. In his treatise, "An Inquiry into the Nature and Causes of the Wealth of Nations", Smith wrote in 1776:

The word VALUE, it is to be observed, has two different meanings, and sometimes expresses the utility of some particular object, and sometimes the power of purchasing other goods which the possession of that object conveys. The one may be called "value in use;" the other, "value in exchange." The things which have the greatest value in use have frequently little or no value in exchange; on the contrary, those which have the greatest value in exchange have frequently little or no value in use. Nothing is more useful than water: but it will purchase scarcely anything; scarcely anything can be had in exchange for it. A diamond, on the contrary, has scarcely any use-value; but a very great quantity of other goods may frequently be had in exchange for it. Water may be more essential, but the higher price of diamonds is dictated by its scarcity.

The fact that an additional unit of water is worth much less than an extra carat of diamond is not because of total utility calculation but because an additional unit of diamond is worth a lot more than the additional unit of water. In other words, the *marginal utility*, the extra utility we get from consuming one more unit of the same good, is higher for diamonds than for water. The price of a good, then, is often determined by how abundant or scarce the it is.

So, the first thing we need is for Ana to be able to rank her bundles; the ones she prefers should get labelled with higher scores while the ones that are inferior should be given lower scores. Figure 1.12 depicts the situation. Suppose Ana has been given the bundle, E. I have created four quadrants around E, for reasons that will become clear momentarily. What can we say about bundles like G, that lie to the north and east of E, that is, bundles in the first quadrant? All bundles such as G, which contain either more of X or more of Y or more of both, must be better than E. So, Ana should score these bundles higher. How about a bundle like F? F has less X and less Y than E, so E must be preferred to F. This implies that consumption bundles like F, that lie in the third quadrant, will be inferior to E and be awarded lower scores. Given all such possible consumption bundles, we want Ana to be able to say that either she likes one better than the other, or that she is indifferent between the two since they both yield the same utility. Finally, we need Ana's preferences to be "transitive". If given

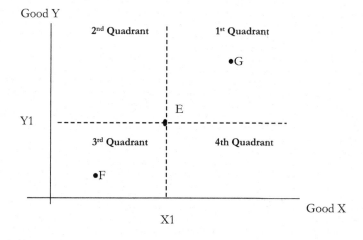

Figure 1.12
Ana's consumption space

■ How we decide

two choices, E and G, Ana says that she prefers G over E, and given two choices E and F, she says that she prefers E to F, then if asked to choose between G and F, Ana should prefer G to F. This is a basic assumption regarding consistency of choices. This assumption is often violated in real life with consequences for many things, such as voting patterns, but this is far beyond our scope for now.[12]

What we need next is to create a set of "indifference curves" for Ana. An indifference curve shows a combination of consumption bundles that give Ana the same utility. This, in turn, implies that if we want to look for consumption bundles that give Ana the same utility as E, then these bundles must lie either in the second or the fourth quadrant; that is, they must contain either more Y and less X compared to E (those in the second quadrant), or they must contain more X and less Y compared to E (in the fourth quadrant). So, just like the budget constraint, the indifference curve must also have a negative slope: if you want more X (Y) then you have to give up some Y (X). I claim that Ana's indifference curves look like the ones in Figure 1.13. Indifference curves that lie to the North and East yield higher utility.

In Figure 1.13, I have drawn all the indifference curves as being parallel to one another. This is because indifference curves for the same person cannot intersect. Or maybe they can, but we do not want them to. Why? Take a look at Figure 1.14. In that figure, bundles E and A lie on the same indifference curve; so, they must both yield the same utility to Ana. This means Ana would be indifferent between E and A. But bundles E and B both lie on the same indifference curve, so they must also yield the same utility to Ana. Hence,

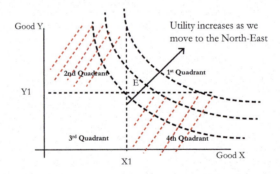

Figure 1.13
The basis of choice: indifference curves

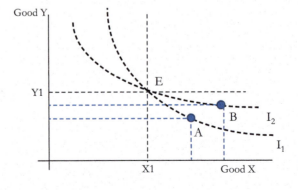

Figure 1.14
Indifference curves cannot intersect

Ana should be indifferent between E and B. But then, using the transitivity assumption, given a choice between A and B, Ana must be indifferent between the two. But this cannot be right. B contains more of X and more of Y than A, so Ana should strictly prefer B to A. So, a *reductio ad absurdum* situation. If indifference curves intersect, then we end up with bundles that are simultaneously preferred and not preferred. This could happen, but would be pretty absurd.

Why must the indifference curves look like the ones in Figure 1.13, bowed inward toward the origin? Look at Figure 1.15, where I have drawn three other possible indifference curves to illustrate my point. All three are negatively sloped, and contain more X if it contains less Y, or vice versa. What is the problem if Ana's indifference curves look like one of these? It is possible but, for the time being, I am going to rule out that possibility. I will come back to this question shortly to explain what the problem would be in such a case. So, it is not so much because this is what indifference curves look like, but because other shapes create difficulties and lead to some strange predictions. So, think of this as the outcome of a *reductio ad absurdum* process, which brings us to this shape by ruling out all other shapes.

Earlier, I mentioned that the slope of the budget constraint is given by the ratio of the prices, that is, (P_X/P_Y). What about the slope of the indifference curve? Figure 1.16 illustrates this. Suppose Ana moved from consuming at Point A on this indifference curve to Point B; that is, she reduced her consumption of Y and increased her consumption of X. But, in going

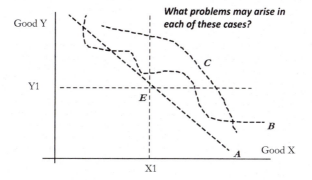

Figure 1.15
Various other (possibly problematic) shapes of indifference curves

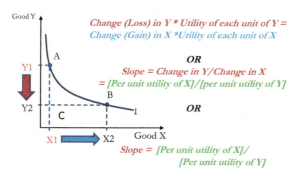

Figure 1.16
Slope of Ana's indifference curve(s)

from A to B, she is still on the same indifference curve. Therefore, her total utility must be unchanged. This implies that any loss in utility from the reduced consumption of Y must be made up by the gain in utility from the increased consumption of X. We can write this as:

$$\text{Change}(\text{Loss}) \text{ in Y}^* \text{ Utility per unit of Y}$$
$$= \text{Change}(\text{Gain}) \text{ in X}^* \text{ Utility per unit of X.}$$

We know that the slope can be defined as the rise over the run (or, as in this case, Change in Y/Change in X). This implies that the slope of the indifference curve is given by:

$$\text{Slope of indifference curve} = \text{Change in Y/Change in X}$$
$$= \text{Utility per unit of X/Utility per unit of Y.}$$

Another term for utility per unit is marginal utility; since marginal utility is really the increase or decrease in utility from consuming one more or less unit of a good. So, we can rewrite the above:

$$\text{Slope} = \text{Utility per unit of X/Utility per unit of Y}$$
$$= \text{Marginal Utility of X/Marginal Utility of Y.}$$

Essentially, in moving from one point to another point on her indifference curve, Ana is calculating how much utility per dollar of X or Y she needs to give up. If X gives Ana more utility per dollar than Y, then she should buy X, or vice versa. Keep making this adjustment until, dollar for dollar, X and Y yield just about the same utility. Stop there.

There is one other point I need to note. Notice how I have argued that the indifference curves are bowed inward? This is based on one other assumption, which typically goes by the fancy name of "diminishing rate of marginal substitution" and is, in turn, based on the *principle of diminishing utility*. If you ignore the jargon, it is what it says and happens to be rather intuitive: it simply says that as we consume more of the same good, the extra utility (marginal utility) we get from each additional unit goes down. So, suppose Ana's dad takes her to Mission Bay in Auckland and lets Ana choose to eat as much ice cream as she wants. The first one tastes great; gives her lots of utility; the second still good; the third one not so much ... by the fourth or fifth, her tummy starts to ache. This, in turn, has an implication for the slope of the indifference curve. Notice that as Ana moves from a point like A to a point like B (and you should draw this out), she will need to be given larger and larger quantities of X for every unit of Y she gives up. This is due to diminishing marginal utility; as she consumes more and more X, she gets less and less utility from each additional unit of X, and in order to keep utility constant, she needs lots more X to make up for the loss in utility from consuming less Y. Or, as she consumes more and more X, the extra utility she gets from each additional unit is smaller; while as she consumes less and less Y, Y becomes more valuable to her; so, as she gets closer and closer to the X-axis, for any given increment in X, she is willing to give up less and less Y.

The point here, is that Ana is willing to give up some Y for X and vice versa. But, the inward bowed shape of the indifference curve suggests that this is not 1:1; in fact, the rate at which she is willing to trade off Y for X is not constant. It changes as she moves down the indifference curve from A to B. At A, or around it, she is consuming lots of Y and little X; so, she is willing to give up a rather large amount of Y to get a little more X. But at B, or around it, she is consuming lots of X and little Y; so, she is no longer willing to sacrifice much Y. If you still take away more Y from her, you will need to give her lots more X to compensate her.

ANA KNOWS WHAT SHE CAN AFFORD AND HOW SHE SHOULD CHOOSE. WHAT *SHOULD* SHE BUY?

Now, what should Ana consume? Of course, she wants to consume as much of X and Y as she can, but she is not really free to choose anything she wants. Her choices are constrained by what she can afford. This is the essence of the economic concept of *constrained maximization*; that is, Ana must choose that consumption bundle which gives her maximum happiness, subject to the fact that this is something that she can actually afford, which in turn is decided by her budget constraint. Figure 1.17 illustrates Ana's choice problem.

Left to herself, Ana wants to pick a consumption bundle on the highest possible indifference curve; so, anything on I_2 is better than anything on I_1, which, in turn, is better than I_0. But Ana is not free to choose anything she wants; she can only choose the best bundle she can afford. This means that she must choose a consumption bundle that lies on *both* the budget constraint and the highest possible indifference curve. By this reckoning, she cannot choose any bundle on I_2 even though she would like to, since these bundles lie beyond her budget constraint and are, therefore, unaffordable. She can choose bundles on I_0, but she can do better. The best possible bundle that she can choose is the one that lies exactly at the point where the indifference curve I_1 touches the budget constraint. This is affordable since it lies on the budget constraint, and is also the bundle that gives her the maximum utility; anything more becomes unaffordable.

To use jargon, the best possible consumption bundle, that yields the highest utility and is also affordable, is the one that lies exactly at the point where the indifference curve I_1 is tangent to the budget constraint. Figure 1.18 makes this clear.

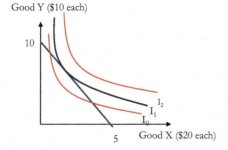

Figure 1.17
Finding Ana's most preferred consumption bundle out of those that are affordable

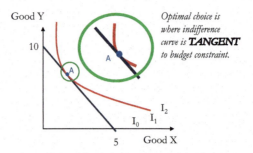

Figure 1.18
A closer look at Ana's best possible consumption bundle

We are close to the finish line. But, before we end, let us go back to the strange looking indifference curves in Figure 1.15. Why did I rule them out? Suppose the indifference curve looks like A, that is, a straight line. If you now look at the budget constraint in Figure 1.6, then you will realize a problem. If the indifference curve is indeed a straight line as in A, then one of three things will happen. One possibility is that the indifference curve has a larger slope, that is, it is steeper, than the budget constraint. If that happens, then, in order to maximize her utility, Ana will consume only X and zero Y. If, on the other hand, the indifference curve is flatter than the budget constraint, then Ana will consume only Y and zero X. Finally, if the indifference curve has the *same slope* as the budget constraint, then Ana will be maximizing her utility when the indifference curve lies on top of the budget constraint. Here, Ana could consume only Y and zero X, or only X and zero Y, or any combination of X and Y that lie on the budget constraint. This is fine, but it will make it difficult to pinpoint Ana's choice and, therefore, make it difficult to predict how Ana might respond if her income or prices change. This is not to say that this cannot happen, but that it results in some strange choices. For the time being, I am ruling out these strange choices. If you look at indifference curves B and C, you will realize that they also pose similar problems. B, for instance, has undulating up and down segments, such that some bundles on the same indifference curve contain more of both goods. This cannot be correct, since that would violate the transitivity principle for the same reason that indifference curves cannot intersect in Figure 1.14.

TWO EXAMPLES OF HOW TO USE THIS TOOL

Before concluding, I want to show two examples of how to use this tool. I do this in Figures 1.19 and 1.20. Figure 1.19 depicts a situation where the price of Good X has fallen from $20 per unit to $10 per unit. Initially, Ana is consuming at the point M on indifference curve I_1. Given that the price of Y has not changed, when the price of X falls, the budget constraint swivels out to the right. Now, Ana finds a new point of tangency and moves to point N on indifference curve I_2. At N, she is consuming a little bit less of Y, whose price has not changed, and more of X, which has become cheaper.

Figure 1.20 shows a situation where the price of Y has gone up from $10 per unit to $25 per unit. Here, the budget constraint swivels inward around the X intercept since the price of X has not changed. Ana moves from point M to point N, where she is buying more X, whose price has not changed, because she is now buying less of Y, which has become more expensive.

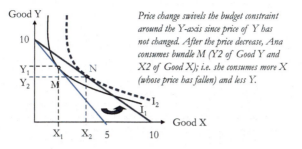

Figure 1.19
Graphical analysis of the overall effect of a fall in the price of Good X from $20 to $10

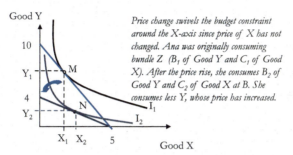

Figure 1.20
Graphical analysis of the overall effect of a rise in the price of Good Y from $10 to $25

I will leave you with a brief discussion of something economists talk about a lot: income and substitution effects. You see, when a particular good, Y, becomes more expensive, and especially if that good constitutes a substantial part of our budget, we feel the pinch in two ways. One, because Y is more expensive, we try to look for a suitable alternative. This is the *substitution effect*. To what extent we can substitute another good for Y depends on whether there are close substitutes or not. So, typically, when Y becomes more expensive, we tend to buy less of Y and more of X. But equally, when Y becomes more expensive, given our income has not changed, it is as if we have less money at our disposal and our purchasing power has gone down. This is the *income effect*. In Figure 1.20 the combined effect is that when Y becomes more expensive, we reduce Y and substitute more X for Y given the substitution effect, but the increase in the consumption of X is not as much as it would otherwise be, because of the income effect; it feels as if we have less money. So, the net effect is a large reduction in the consumption of Y and a small increase in the consumption of X.

HOW REALISTIC IS THIS "NORMATIVE" MODEL? LET'S LOOK INSIDE THE BRAIN

Do people really behave like this? Do they actually go through all these complex calculations of budget constraints and indifference curves, and look for points of tangency? Of course not! But they behave as if they are doing this. Just as the lack of knowledge of its grammar does not prevent us from speaking a language, similarly, just because we do not actually carry out all these computations, it does not mean that we are not engaging in essentially this type of thinking.

Every time you go shopping and you compare prices, this is effectively what you are doing, you are looking at the price and your mind is going through a quick calculation of the utility per dollar. There is a sale on Ben and Jerry's this week; so maybe get that instead of the Häagen Daz. Ana sees a cute top in the store window but then when she looks at the price, she decides that it is not worth it. What does that mean? It means that the utility calculus in her mind has told her that the happiness from the top is not enough to cover the cost.

Let me give you another example, taken from Robert Frank's book *The Economic Naturalist* (2007). You have all seen drinks vending machines. You put in your money, press the desired button and a can of the chosen beverage drops down. Most of you are probably too young to have seen these, but, once upon a time, there used to be these things called newspaper vending machines. These were much simpler contraptions: you put in the money, pressed a lever and the entire lid of the machine opened to reveal all the newspapers inside. Why the difference? Why does the lid of the drinks vending machine not open to reveal all the drinks inside? Alternatively, why does the newspaper vending machine not dispense one newspaper at a time? This is because of marginal utility calculation. It is fine for the newspaper vending machine to allow you access to all the newspapers and assume you will take only one, since the marginal utility of a second newspaper is very small. But, if the drinks vending machine lid opened up, then it is highly likely you will grab a couple more.

So, the normative model seems like a reasonable approximation of behaviour: that consumers are looking to maximize utility per dollar by comparing utility per dollar of X with utility per dollar of Y; if the former is larger, then buy more X, and vice versa. Stop when the two are approximately equal. This led the noted economist Paul Samuelson to formulate his "Revealed Preference Theory". He argued that because we cannot look inside people's brains, we cannot know for sure what their preferences are and how much utility they are getting from their consumption. But we can certainly see their purchasing habits. How much of X and Y they buy at various prices and how they adjust their purchases when income or prices change tells us enough about whether and how they are maximizing their utility and this, in turn, tells us about their preferences. So, in reality, the sequence in our minds is: preferences leading to utility leading to choices. Samuelson said that because we can only observe choices, we can follow the reverse sequence: Start with choices and work our way backwards to understand utility, and then, preferences.

But what if we could look inside people's brains? In the 1990s, a budding group of neuroscientists, led, to an extent, by Paul Glimcher of New York University, started to become interested in how people make choices about what to buy and at what price. Over time, this group has earned itself the sobriquet of "neuroeconomists". They realized that we could take a peek inside the brain by having people make decisions while inside an fMRI machine. Functional magnetic resonance imaging measures brain activity by looking at changes in blood flow to different parts of the brain on the basis of the idea that such blood flow in the brain and neuronal activity are correlated. When an area of the brain is in use, blood flow to that region also increases, and so this particular area will "light up".

Above, I have argued that the crux of the problem boils down to comparing choices. When we decide to buy (and consume) a good, it gives us happiness (utility). But, when we have to pay for it, this is a cost and causes a sensation of pain. The act of choice involves equating marginal utilities, or essentially trading off the happiness of consumption with the pain of payment. So, by looking at what parts of the brain are implicated in the acts of making these choices, we can draw inferences about how we are making these choices.

Brian Knutson of Stanford, along with collaborators at MIT and Pittsburgh, gave people a series of straightforward purchasing choices. Twenty-six subjects were given an endowment of $20.00 to start with and could use some of this money to purchase one or more goods. They are shown a good, say a box of Godiva chocolates, asked what they might be willing to pay for it, and then shown the price. The actual price of the goods varied from $8.00 to $80.00 but were heavily discounted. At the end of the session, one of their choices was randomly selected. If, for that specific choice, a participant had offered to pay a price that was higher than the stipulated price of that good, they were deemed to have purchased the product. In such cases the price was deducted from a subject's endowment and the good was shipped to them.

Knutson and colleagues found that preference is correlated with higher activation in the nucleus accumbens (NAcc), in the sense that there is greater activity in the NAcc when subjects are shown a good that they prefer more than others. The NAcc is a part of what is known as the basal forebrain and is generally recognized for its role in the "reward circuit" of the brain. When we do something rewarding, dopamine neurons (along with other types of neurons) in an area of the brain called the ventral tegmental area (VTA) are activated. These neurons project to the NAcc, resulting in an increase in dopamine levels in the NAcc. Furthermore, Knutson and his colleagues also found that when there was a difference between the price subjects were willing to pay (WTP) and the price they were shown, that is, the price they have to pay, there is greater activation in the medial prefrontal cortex (mPFC). This is as expected, since the prefrontal cortex is well known for its role in executive decision making, resolving conflicting signals and engaging emotional responses. Finally, Knutson and his colleagues found that there is activation in the insula when shown the price of a good. We know that, among other things, the insula "lights up" in brain scans when subjects feel or anticipate pain. So, the act of paying, or at least the thought of having to pay, actually causes "pain" in our brain.[13]

Hilke Plassmann, John O'Doherty and Antonio Rangel at Caltech provide corroborating evidence via fMRI scans. Their design is slightly different from that of Knutson. They had 19 subjects taking part, who were all given a show-up fee. To make the choice problem even more salient, these subjects were asked not to eat anything for at least four hours prior to the experiment. Then they are shown a series of sugary and salty "junk" foods (such as bags of lollies) and asked how much they are willing to pay for each. These are cheaper items than the ones in the Knutson study and so the amounts they can bid are limited to lie between $0 and $3. Following this, the computer randomly generates a price for each of the goods. If the price the subject was willing to pay (say $3) is greater than the random price generated by the computer, then the subject gets to buy that particular good; if not, then no purchase takes place. This meant that whether the subjects got to eat a snack at the end of the session (almost five hours since their last meal) depended on what they bid on various goods and whether they managed to purchase any or not. So, the stakes were high indeed.

At the end of the session, subjects have to pay for the goods they have bought, out of the initial endowment they were given at the beginning. Plassmann et al.'s results are similar to those of Knutson's, if not quite the same. They found that as subjects make this decision, there is much greater activation in the medial orbitofrontal cortex (mOFC) of the brain. Functions of the mOFC include encoding actual or inferred value. It also plays a role in inhibiting responses and emotional appraisal. What Plassmann and colleagues did not find is activation in the nucleus accumbens, the brain's reward centre. But this may not be surprising and may be due to the way the information is presented. In Knutson, the good (such as a box of chocolates) is shown first and participants have some time to just look at the goods. This is followed by questions about price or willingness to pay. This allows for the brain's reward centres to become activated via a dopamine surge before the cold price calculations come into play: How much is this worth? How much should I pay? How much am I being asked to pay?

In contrast, Plassmann and her colleagues were presenting all the relevant information up-front; asking questions about the willingness to pay along with showing the good to the participants. This means that the calculating parts of the brain are activated earlier in Plassmann's subjects compared to Knutson's subjects. And not surprisingly, both Knutson and Plassmann found that, when confronted with a choice, the prefrontal cortex, tasked with making executive decisions, appraising emotional responses and resolving conflict, became activated.

Remember Phineas Gage and Damasio's patient Elliott? Both suffered damage to the frontal lobe, and both became incapable of emotional regulation and also incapable of making "proper" decisions when confronted with a multiplicity of choices. So, contra Samuelson: we do not necessarily need to infer utility and preferences by looking at choices. We can take a peek into our brains, and activation in different areas can tell us what we prefer and, therefore, how we make choices and, more importantly, what we will choose in a particular situation given a choice of goods and prices. So yes, our brains are actually trying to equate utility per dollar for different goods; we are just not necessarily aware of the machinery grinding away in the background. So, the next time you are at the shopping centre trying to decide whether to buy the cashmere sweater or the expensive perfume, or a make-up set or a shaving kit, or a fancy jacket for your partner as an anniversary gift and you feel a headache coming on, don't fret. This is simply your prefrontal cortex trying to figure out the point of tangency between your indifference curve and your budget constraint. At times, and increasingly, this leads to "choice overload", where confronted with too many choices, we give up. So, go ahead and get him/her a gift-card. Let your partner deal with the choice problem and the accompanying headache.[14]

CONCLUDING REMARKS

This chapter is designed to set the tone and provide context for the rest of the discussion in this book. I started by providing a definition of rationality, primarily involving maximizing our own happiness. Then, I discussed how actual behaviour deviates from the type of maximization suggested by this view of rationality. I argued that such deviations stem from two sources: first, the fact that some problems are complex or experienced infrequently. Therefore, we often struggle to figure out what the best possible course of action is in such situations. Second, we tend to abide by social norms and conventions even if they militate against maximizing personal happiness. This is often governed by the role of emotions, as suggested by David Hume. Along the way, I touched upon how damage to the frontal lobe of the brain can adversely impact one's ability to regulate one's emotions. This may have devastating consequences for rational decision making, even though much of the other brain functions are intact.

I provided an overview of how economists and psychologists approach the study of human decision making: what are the differences and what are the areas of overlap. I talked about the Guessing Game as an example of how infusing psychological insights can lead to better decisions in this game, rather than just following the logic of rational maximization.

I then presented material that is somewhat more technical in terms of the choice problem facing Ana. I discussed the constraints on Ana's choices: in the form of the budget constraint. I presented the tool of indifference curves to categorize Ana's choices and used the two together to identify the consumption bundle that Ana will choose. I provided a couple of extension examples to highlight how economists use this tool to study behaviour.

Finally, I turned to the newly emerging and exciting field of neuroeconomics to take a peek into people's brains. I presented the results of some fMRI studies that explore what happens when we are confronted with choices. I showed that these brain scans provide corroboration to the normative model of economics. There is, indeed, lots of activity in the brain's reward centres and areas dealing with conflict and executive decisions, mostly in keeping with how the normative model thinks of how these choices are made.

NOTES

1. If, as is likely, you were born in the 21st century, then it is likely that you have headphones stuck in your ears pretty much 24/7 and that you have no idea who Buddy Holly or Don McLean are. Please take my advice: go to YouTube or Spotify or wherever it is you get your music from and listen to the song. And while you are at it, check out Buddy Holly's "Peggy Sue" and McLean's haunting "Vincent (Starry Starry Night)" about Vincent Van Gogh.
2. However, the record for most wins in *Jeopardy!* is still held by Ken Jennings, who won 75 games! In early 2020, Holzhauer faced off against Jennings and another past champion, Brad Rutter, for what was billed as the Tournament of All Time Greats. Jennings won that tournament fairly easily, though Holzhauer was the runner-up, winning $250,000.
3. For instance, Sheldon Cooper from *The Big Bang Theory* insists on a thermostat setting of 68° Fahrenheit; most of us are probably not too fussed with one or two degrees higher or lower. Many economists will argue that *all* our decisions have economic implications. For example, the thermostat setting will almost certainly have an impact on the heating bill. I am not going that far. I will primarily focus on issues that are overtly financial/economic in this volume.
4. For instance, this is a conversation that I often have with my wife, when she insists on looking (these days increasingly on the internet) for a bargain. I often forego searching for bargains, especially on items that are not hugely expensive, such as small appliances. I figure that I might have to spend an extra couple of hours in order to save $50. But this is not really a saving, since to me those extra hours are valuable. I could have spent those hours reading, writing, watching films or listening to music. In fact, if someone asked me: how much are you willing to forego in order *not* to spend extra time looking for a bargain, I might say that I am willing to pay as much as $50. So, even if I save $50 in the end, effectively this additional saving is cancelled out by the imputed value of my extra time, which is also $50. So, in order for the bargain to make sense, it must save me more than the imputed value of my time. Of course, my wife, and increasingly my daughters, respond by saying that I put a disproportionately large value on the opportunity cost of time. It is also true that the advent of online shopping has dramatically reduced the opportunity cost of looking for bargains, implying that unless one's opportunity cost is extremely high, it makes sense to look for savings on all reasonably expensive items. Of course, some derive happiness from the act of shopping itself.

5. I will have more to say about the economic concept of utility shortly. For now, let us think of utility as happiness or satisfaction. For a business, this may be akin to profit. At one extreme, one can think of a pure *homo economicus*, as a straw-man. This is someone whose utility depends solely on his/her monetary pay-offs. But, as I will discuss at length in this book, maximizing utility is not the same as always acting in one's self-interest. People may well get utility from being generous, kind, and helpful to others even at the cost of one's self-interest.

6. The phrase "bounded rationality" is attributed to the polymath Herbert Simon. Simon's view counters the traditional "rationality" assumption of economics; that we humans face a variety of constraints on our choices, but we seek to maximize happiness (or utility) subject to those constraints, referred to as "constrained optimization". Simon's view is that we face limits on our cognitive abilities, and, therefore, we do not necessarily behave as the maximizers that economic theory would posit. This may not be a comprehensive definition of bounded rationality but it is close enough and should suffice to highlight the distinction between the different approaches adopted by economists and psychologists.

7. Avid fans of the show will know that throughout the 12 seasons of the show, we never actually get to learn what Penny's maiden last name is; or even if she has a more formal name like Penelope. However, for part of the show, she is married to Zack Johnson, though there is no indication that she ever called herself Penny Johnson, primarily because she was oblivious to the fact that she was actually married. She does take on Leonard's last name after she marries him.

8. In recent years, this theory has been subject to controversy since a number of other researchers have failed to replicate some of these findings. I am going to ignore this debate for now. This is not because the debate is not important, rather, it is beyond our scope. Here, I am less interested in debating the replicability of research findings than I am in providing a good example of the psychological approach of moving from observation to theory for a novice reader. I believe that this example serves the purpose.

9. I do this a lot; in fact, every time I teach. So, over time, I have shelled out quite a bit of money from my own pocket.

10. This kind of iterated thinking, where you try to anticipate what others are thinking, or what others are thinking that you are thinking and so on is often refereed to as *theory of the mind*. This is different from thinking through the various steps of the guessing game to get to zero and must necessarily require one to be able to empathize with others or be able to create a mental model of others' thinking. One can use the term "empathy" for this. My point is this: in all such situations of iterative thinking it is often necessary to infuse "pure reasoning" with something else; call it empathy, feelings, intuition or something else. I have chosen in this book to refer to such things as emotional input but others may prefer a different word than "emotion".

11. Some researchers use the convention of calling this Level 1 thinking, where Level Zero thinking may imply choosing a number at random from between zero and 100. I will stick with the convention of calling this Level Zero where this implies choosing 100 (or the highest possible number in the range of numbers). This does not do any harm to the intuition or the arguments presented here.

12. I wrote much of this book during the early part of Spring 2020 when I was in Cambridge, MA, and Democratic primaries were in full swing. A person would violate transitivity if they said that they preferred Sanders over Buttigieg and Buttigieg over Biden, but then professes to prefer Biden over Sanders. This happens quite a lot. For the time being, all we need is for Ana to not do that.

13. Incidentally, it is well documented that the more "ephemeral" or less salient the act of paying, the less painful it seems to us. This often makes us buy more than we otherwise would. So, paying with a credit card is less painful than paying with cash. Things like digital wallets, digital currency or frequent flyer miles make the act of payment even less salient. It makes it feel as if we are not really paying anything, even though these are still real money.

14. Some of you may well be aware of the futility of buying gifts. It is well known that, when asked, most gift recipients value the gift they have received less than what the gift-giver paid. This means that when asked how much they are willing to pay for a particular gift, recipients indicate a dollar-value that is less than the price actually paid by the one giving the gift! So, to the recipient,

the gift is worth much less than to the giver. This suggests that the easiest thing to do would be to just give cash (or yes, a gift card) and let the recipient deal with all the hassles of making a choice. But, as my older daughter continually admonishes me: gift cards indicate a complete lack of thoughtfulness! Hence, your choice: being perceived as being thoughtless or being cheap! As fans of *The Big Bang Theory* will appreciate, gift-giving is a serious and complicated business. Sheldon Cooper, whose emotional appraisal mechanisms are somewhat compromised, suffers tremendous stress at the thought of gift exchanges during the festive season. This is because Sheldon knows that Penny will insist on giving him a gift for Christmas, and he wants to make sure that he gives her a gift in return that matches the exact value of the gift that Penny has given him. So, he goes out and buys a large number of gift baskets, each of different value. The plan is that, once Penny gives him a gift, Sheldon will pretend to go to the bathroom on the ruse that he is suffering from intestinal discomfiture. He will quickly run to his bedroom, look up the value of Penny's gift online, and then give her a return gift of appropriate value from the large set of gift baskets he has at his disposal. Then, Penny hands him a used napkin. She explains that Sheldon's hero, Leonard Nimoy, came to the Cheesecake Factory where Penny works, and he actually used this napkin to wipe his mouth. Sheldon is beside himself at the thought that he is holding in his hand a napkin that actually contains Leonard Nimoy's DNA. He runs to his bedroom, gets *all* of the gift baskets he has bought, gives them to Penny and says that it is nowhere near enough to compensate Penny for what she has given him!

2 Experiments in behavioural economics

In this chapter, I talk about:

- *The rise of experimental economics; how it came to become part of mainstream research in economics;*
- *The similarities and differences between the approaches adopted by economists and psychologists;*
- *The history of experimentation in economics;*
- *Issues regarding experimental design;*
- *Criticisms of the experimental method, including issues of external validity;*
- *Experimenter demand effects;*
- *The prospects of experimental economics in the coming years.*

INTRODUCTION

So, you want to figure out why someone did what they did or what someone might do when confronted with a particular circumstance or choice? What do you do? Traditionally, researchers have followed two different paths. The first of these is to rely on surveys. This is essentially the same as asking people. Surveys are straightforward and usually yield valuable insights. But at the same time, there are drawbacks to this approach as well. The problem is that sometimes people's response to what they would do in a particular situation does not predict accurately what they would really do when actually placed in that situation; that is, there is a disconnect between attitudes (stated preferences) and behaviour (actions). This implies that, at times, people's attitudes do not correlate well with their behaviour. It is also the case that we are not always good at articulating our reasons.

This essentially means the following: suppose I asked you whether you were willing to contribute $50 for a good cause and you said yes. But when eventually the envelope gets passed around and you have to actually part with the money, you may renege on that promise completely or put in less than $50. I am not saying that you will do it, but it has been known to happen. Moreover, responses in these questionnaires may differ substantially from behaviour, not because the respondent is trying to mislead the researcher, but because the respondent may possess an incorrect perception of his/her own and of others' views or reactions. That is, the respondent might honestly think that he/she will behave in a certain way in a particular situation, but when that specific situation comes to pass, he/she actually behaves differently.

Here is an example of such dichotomy between attitudes and behaviour, taken from the literature in social psychology. In the early 1930s, Richard LaPiere wanted to discover if people who had various prejudices or negative attitudes towards members of other ethnic groups would actually demonstrate these behaviours in an overt manner. For approximately two years, LaPiere travelled around the USA with a young Chinese couple. They stopped at 184 restaurants and 66 hotels. They were refused service only once, and, on the whole, received a better than average standard of service from the establishments visited. After returning from two years of travelling around, LaPiere wrote to all the businesses where he and the Chinese couple had dined or stayed. In a letter, which gave no indication of his previous visit, he enquired whether they would offer service to Chinese customers. While virtually none of the establishments had actually refused service, in the survey, the majority expressed the opinion that they would not serve the Chinese visitors. There are many other examples of such dissonance between attitudes and behaviour.

The second avenue of exploration, as opposed to relying on survey questionnaires, has been to look at naturally occurring field data generated by a real-life economic phenomenon. That is, if you wanted to understand whether and why people contribute to charity, then you might dig up data on charitable contributions and analyse those data. This has been the more traditional and usual approach in economics. In order to understand behaviour, one needs to look at data that pertain to a particular phenomenon. For instance, suppose we want to know the impact on unemployment of an increase in the minimum wage or large-scale migration into a particular region.[1] In such cases, the recourse is to compare two otherwise similar regions, one of which has recently experienced an increase in the minimum wage (via new legislation) or a sudden influx of new immigrants as opposed to a second region that has not experienced anything similar.

In fact, the famous American economist and the recipient of the Nobel Prize in 1970, Paul Samuelson, wrote in his undergraduate textbook (which, until recently, was the most popular text in universities, not only in the US but across the world):

> (e)conomists cannot perform the controlled experiments of chemists or biologists because (they) cannot easily control other important factors. Like astronomers or meteorologists, (economists) generally must be content largely to observe.

Richard Lipsey, prominent economist from the London School of Economics, makes the impossibility of experimentation in Economics even more explicit:

> Experimental sciences, such as chemistry and some branches of psychology, have an advantage because it is possible to produce relevant evidence through controlled laboratory experiments. Other sciences, such as astronomy and economics cannot do this.

Given this non-experimental view, economists have traditionally adopted a more theoretical approach that relied on building mathematical models of behaviour in order to explain, understand or predict behaviour in a variety of economic transactions. These models start from a series of *ex ante* assumptions that are typically based on the researcher's intuition about the state of affairs. Then they go on to make predictions about changes in behaviour that would result from those underlying assumptions. The success of such models is measured by their internal coherence. In fact, the 1986 Nobel Laureate, Milton Friedman, suggests that the assumptions made by economists in building theoretical models do not propose to represent how the world works exactly. They merely proceed on the assumption that these are "as if" propositions, distilling regularities in behaviour that happen to be useful in deriving predictions. Therefore, even though a lot of theorising in economics depends crucially on the assumptions we make about individual preferences and behaviour, these assumptions should not be treated as empirical hypotheses to which the theory is committed.

This is also because any attempt to test theoretical models is subject to the Duhem–Quine problem. Since theories must be applied in a specific context in order to test them, it is virtually impossible to test a single theoretical hypothesis in isolation. Researchers need to make a series of supplementary assumptions in order to apply the theory to the context within which it is being tested. Consequently, if the theoretical postulates are not borne out by the data, it is often difficult to disentangle whether the hypothesis itself is incorrect or whether the problem lies with one or more of the supplementary assumptions.

This prompted Vernon Smith to argue:

> Consequently, we come to believe that economic problems can be understood fully just by thinking about them. After the thinking has produced sufficient technical rigor, internal coherence and interpersonal agreement, economists can then apply the results to the world of data.

As a result, often economists were not overly concerned with empirical validation of the assumptions or predictions of theoretical models. Even when empirical validation was sought, it was usually via finding a natural experiment that might generate data suitable for testing a particular theory.[2] However, one problem with field, that is, naturally occurring, data is that such data may not always be available, or may not be available in the exact form that is needed to answer a particular question. Moreover, since the data are generated by a one-time economic phenomenon, they may not necessarily be in the form that allows us to make causal inferences; that is, whether a particular phenomenon, X, caused another phenomenon, Y. A natural experiment is also impossible to replicate.

THE RISE OF EXPERIMENTAL ECONOMICS

So, the question is, given this traditional view of economics as an essentially non-experimental science, how did experimental economics come to occupy an entrenched position in the mainstream of economics? The idea that data capable of helping us to understand important economic phenomena could be generated via controlled laboratory experiments is of recent vintage and did not take hold until the last two decades of the 20th century. In many ways, the rise of experimental economics coincided with the widespread application of game theory in economics to study strategic decision making. Even though the rise of game theory can be traced back to the work of John von Neumann and Oskar Morgenstern, it was only in the 1970s that economic theory models came to rely on and apply concepts derived from game theory. Given that game-theoretic assumptions rely on innate beliefs and preferences, finding natural datasets to test the validity of these models is practically impossible. Experiments, however, provided a tractable way of addressing research questions of this nature.

Charles Plott of Caltech, who, along with Vernon Smith, is a pioneer of the field, writes that part of the increased acceptance of experiments was also caused by a shift in the way that economists thought about the role of economics in general and economic theory in particular. In the middle decades of the 20th century, the prevailing view was that because economic phenomena were extremely complex, the only way to study them was to study economies "in the wild", and to either build theories to explain economic phenomenon or to understand the statistical properties of ongoing processes. But gradually, the emphasis began to shift from studying particular economies as they are found in the wild to studying general theories, models and principles that govern the behaviour of economic phenomena. Part of this was certainly due to the increasing influence of game-theoretic concepts. The argument became that general theories must apply to special cases. It is possible to generate simple yet real economies in the laboratory to which the general theory should be applicable. Laboratory experiments can then be used to test and evaluate the predictive capacities of general theories, as well as set up contests between which, of many theories, are better able to explain and predict complex economic phenomena.

Vernon Smith makes the point that the study of decision making by suitably motivated individuals in the laboratory has important and significant applications to the development and verification of theories. Results of laboratory tests can serve as rigorous empirical pre-tests of economic theory, prior to the use of field data tests.[3] Results obtained via experiments can be directly relevant, not only to evaluating theories, but also to inform further theory development.

As a result, in recent times, social scientists have turned to incentivized decision-making experiments in order to understand human behaviour in economic transactions. The field of "Experimental Economics" is essentially an empirical approach to understanding such behaviour. Here, researchers analyse decisions made by participants in a variety of economic "games" (or "experiments") that have been specifically designed to simulate a particular economic transaction that the researcher wished to study. Participants in such experiments are remunerated and the amount they receive depends on the decisions they make during the experiment.

So, a crucial difference between experiments and surveys is that the decisions that participants make in these experimental games are not hypothetical. In these experiments, participants are paid money based on their performance in the task. The rewards are designed to be large enough and salient enough in order to compensate participants for the opportunity cost of their time (i.e., whatever they might have earned in an alternative job for the duration of the experiment). These payments render the decisions made in the experiment real, since there is now a substantial amount of money riding on those decisions. Furthermore, this compels the participants to pay attention to the task at hand rather than cavalierly checking off boxes on a questionnaire. Thus, while answers on survey questionnaires can often be no better than self-serving "cheap talk", by paying people money on the basis of their decisions and thereby inducing participants to pay close attention to what they (and others in their group are doing), decisions made in economic experiments are better able to elicit true preferences and beliefs. Essentially, experimental economists ask participants to put their money where their mouth is.

The above is not meant to suggest by any means that either surveys or work done using naturally occurring data are not valuable. They can be valuable complements to data collected via experiments. But there are situations where they suffer from limitations. This is particularly true in situations involving strategic decision making, where people's actions are influenced by their beliefs about the actions of others. However, such beliefs are not observable and getting natural data on them is nearly impossible. But if one designs a suitable experiment where people's decisions determine how much they get paid, then their actions may allow us to draw conclusions about their beliefs. Experiments, then, are particularly useful for studying situations that require strategic decision making. This is one reason why the rise of research in experimental economics has coincided with the prominence of game theory in economic analysis.

In the early years of experimental economics, researchers tended to rely on experiments run using pen and paper and a convenient sample of university students. But, increasingly, researchers are relying on more elaborate computerized experiments carried out in computer laboratories with purpose designed software. This has been made possible by rapid advances in computing facilities, which, in turn, has allowed researchers to generate voluminous amounts of data suitable for sophisticated econometric analysis. Researchers are also increasingly moving away from exclusive reliance on student subjects. They are carrying out field experiments with adult members of society or members of specialized groups who may be more representative of the population or of the subject pool whose behaviour is of primary interest.

Participants typically arrive at a classroom or computer laboratory. They are given instructions for the experiment. Usually, such instructions are given using abstract, context-free language. The idea is that the use of neutral language prevents the participants from being influenced to behave in a particular manner by what they believe the researcher is trying to study; a phenomenon that usually falls under the rubric of "experimenter demand effects". However, in recent years, as experiments have become more elaborate, researchers are increasingly relying on instructions that use emotive terms and provide an explicit context to the experiment. This is because if the context itself is relevant to the performance of subjects and helps subjects make sense of the task they are being asked to perform, then it is not necessarily the case that abstract, context-free experiments provide more general findings. This is especially true for tasks that are complex and place significant demands on the participants' cognitive skills. I am going to leave a more detailed discussion of this issue to more advanced courses and/or textbooks.

With very few exceptions, interactions are anonymous. This means that while participants may know other people who show up for a particular session, nevertheless, when they are put together into separate pairs or groups while undertaking a joint decision or transaction, they are not privy to the identity of the other pair or group members. At the end of the session, participants are paid their earnings from the experiment privately. The payment that participants get depends on the decision(s) that they make during the course of the experiment. Again, with very few exceptions, payment is performance dependent and it is unusual for the participants not to be paid or to be paid a fixed amount (independent of performance) in an economics experiment.

This is one of the ways in which experiments in economics differ from those in psychology, where remuneration for participants is not always performance dependent. Sometimes, participants in psychology experiments are paid a flat fee, sometimes they receive course credit, and, at times, some of the participants are paid at random. The important distinction here is that compared to economists, psychologists put less emphasis on pay-off dominance or reward salience.

ELEMENTS OF EXPERIMENTAL DESIGN

I am going to touch upon a few other related issues very quickly. In running an experiment, one has to make a number of decisions. First, should it be one-shot or repeated? The advantage of a one-shot experiment is that it is clean and easy to understand. They are often better approximations of theoretical models, and, therefore, serve as better tests of the underlying theory. But all experiments put their subjects in an unfamiliar circumstance and this problem is exacerbated by the use of neutral, context-free instructions. What if subjects do not get it right in the first attempt? What if they take time to learn? In that case, the experimenter may be better off with having subjects make decisions repeatedly. But if the same players interact with each other over and over again, this allows them to build reputations and signal future moves. If one wants to avoid that and preserve the one-shot nature of interactions, then one option is to have random re-matching of subjects from one round to the next. Such random re-matching can take two different forms: one where there is some probability, albeit small, that the same two players can meet more than once and a second, where this possibility is excluded, so that it is guaranteed that one player will not meet another more than once. Clearly, given the nature of the task and the size of the group, the latter usually requires more subjects than the former.

Experiments can utilize *between-subjects* and *within-subject* designs. The first means that each subject takes part in only one treatment. Some are assigned to a control treatment, while others to various other experimental treatments. The experimenter then compares the outcomes of the treatment condition(s) to the control condition. On the other hand, one can use within-subject treatments, where each subject takes part in both the control condition as well as the treatment condition(s). Here, the comparison is between the subject's behaviour (and change thereof) between the control and treatment conditions. It is essential to make sure that there are appropriate control treatments. Doug Davis (of Virginia Commonwealth) and Charlie Holt (of University of Virginia), two pioneers of experimental economics, emphasize that it is extremely important not to vary too many parameters simultaneously but instead to introduce careful incremental changes to the experimental design. Varying too many things at once might introduce confounds and make it difficult to study the real impact of the treatment variable.

Experiments can be *single-blind*, meaning that while a particular subject is not aware of the decisions made by other subjects, the experimenter can see all such decisions. Or, they can be *double-blind*, meaning even the experimenter cannot see who made what decisions.[4]

Finally, a topic that has become controversial in recent times: how do you pay subjects, especially when they have interacted for more than one game or for more than one round, as is almost always the case with most studies? The traditional approach is to pay for all rounds. But some argue that this may create a *wealth effect*, implying that as the experiment progresses, the subject is earning more and more money, which may alter decisions. Given that the payments in typical experiments are rather small, in my opinion, potential wealth effects are not a large concern. One way of avoiding this is to avoid telling subjects how much they are making over time. This is, obviously, easier if they are taking part in a series of distinct tasks as opposed to repeating the same task many times. One alternative proposed by those who are suspicious of the "pay for all rounds" approach, especially where subjects are repeatedly undertaking the same task numerous times, is to select one round at random at the end of the session and pay for only that round. But that does not necessarily solve the problem. Suppose, in an experiment, a subject makes 50 (100) decisions but is paid for only one of those. The subject then knows that each decision has only 1/50th (1/100th) chance of being relevant. This leads to a loss of reward salience since each decision now has a small probability of paying off; this is not all that different from survey responses. Finally, it has been argued, by some, that if the task is complex and there is significant learning involved, then it may make sense to pay for the very last round, which best reflects the subject's facility at the task.

Another pioneer of experimental economics, Andrew Schotter of NYU, along with long-time collaborator Antonio Merlo of the University of Pennsylvania, explore this payment question in a series of experiments. In these studies, subjects are asked to find the correct answer in a complex mathematical task. Getting the answer correct is difficult, and somewhat beside the point. The idea is to see how close subjects come to the correct answer (much like throwing darts and trying to hit the bullseye) and whether they get better at it (come closer to the correct answer) over time. Subjects in their experiments take part in two different treatments: learn-while-you-earn and learn-before-you-earn. As would be obvious from the names of the treatments, in the first one, the subjects earn a small amount of money in each round, as is the traditional practice. In the second treatment, however, subjects first get to play a number of rounds without earnings, then earn a much larger amount (a large multiple of the per-round earning in the learn-while-you-earn treatment) in the last round. Merlo and Schotter find that subjects who take part in the learn-before-you-earn treatment do much better at coming closer to the correct answer. This is, at least partly, because the subjects who get paid every round adopt a more myopic approach, where they focus on whether they "won" or "lost" in each round. The subjects in the other treatment, who did not have to worry about getting paid each round, engaged in much greater experimentation, and in doing so, ended up learning about the underlying problem much better over time.

For all of these design questions, there is no single correct answer. The ideal experiment design will depend on the nature of the task and the research question(s) involved. However, it is highly likely that any of you who are confronted with these questions at some point would have, by that time, undergone significantly more training and exposure to proper research techniques and would be well placed to make these calls.

A BRIEF HISTORY OF EXPERIMENTAL ECONOMICS

(This section relies heavily on two sources: (i) Roth A., 1995; (ii) Friedman, D. and Sunder, S., 1994.)

It is difficult to pin down exactly which was the first economic experiment, though Al Roth suggests that Daniel Bernoulli, in trying to understand people's responses to the St

Petersburg Paradox, was the first person to carry out what would be considered an economic experiment. The St Petersburg Paradox involves playing the following game. Suppose one has to pay a fee to enter a lottery which has the following pay-off structure. A fair coin is tossed and the game ends once tails comes up. If the first toss throws up tails, then the game ends and the player wins $1. If the first toss is heads and the second toss is tails, then the player wins $2. If the first two tosses are heads and the third is tails, then the player wins $4. If the first three tosses are heads and the fourth results in tails, then the player wins $8, and so on. So, with probability 1/2, the player gets $1; with probability 1/4 he/she gets $2; with probability 1/8 he/she gets $4; etc. The expected value of this lottery is infinite and hence a risk neutral player should be willing to pay an infinite amount to play this lottery. However, in practice, people would be willing to pay a finite, and most likely small, amount to play this lottery. I will discuss this paradox, its resolution and other associated issues at length in Chapter 4.

However, in modern times, one of the first experiments was carried out by L. L. Thurstone, who was interested in experimentally determining the shape of an individual's indifference curves as part of choosing the optimal consumption bundle. I discussed this choice problem in the previous chapter. He carried out an experiment where each subject was asked to make a large number of hypothetical choices between commodity bundles consisting of hats and coats, hats and shoes, or shoes and coats. Based on detailed data for one particular subject, Thurstone went on to conclude that one could define indifference curves that accurately described the choice data, and it was feasible and practical to estimate indifference curves in this way. Thurstone's experiments, of course, were subject to the criticism that economists often raise against the experiments carried out by psychologists; that Thurstone was asking his subjects for hypothetical responses and it is not always clear as to how reliable such hypothetical responses are.

In 1944, John von Neumann and Oskar Morgenstern published their book: *Theory of Games and Economic Behavior*. This book brought attention to a powerful theory of individual choice and a new theory of interactive strategic behaviour, and had a profound influence on subsequent experimental work. It also exposed economists to the idea of decision making under uncertainty and the concept of expected utility. This, in turn, and in many ways building upon the early experiments on individual choice by Thurstone, led a number of economists to try to experimentally test various aspects of Expected Utility Theory. I will discuss this in more detail in Chapter 4, when I talk about Expected Utility Theory and Prospect Theory.

Understanding behaviour in markets is a major preoccupation of economists and the beginning of experimentation into the process of price formation in markets can be traced back to the work of Edward Chamberlin at Harvard in the 1940s. Chamberlin wanted to study how markets worked and how prices were formed. In order to do, so he had his students participate as buyers and sellers in simulated markets. Buyers were assigned values for a fictitious good being sold by the sellers who, in turn, were assigned costs of production. The underlying theoretical assumption is that both parties are interested in making the maximum profit. For buyers, the profit is obtained as the difference between the buyer's valuation and the price paid. For sellers, this is calculated as the price received minus the cost of production. Chamberlin allowed buyers and sellers to walk around the room and engage in decentralized bilateral negotiations, and did not use any monetary rewards. His aim was to understand how a process of bargaining between these hypothetical buyers and sellers led to the determination of prices in these markets.

Vernon Smith, considered one of the founders of modern experimental economics, was a student of Edward Chamberlin and took part in the experiments carried out by the latter. Later, as an assistant professor at Purdue University, Smith realized that one could analyse theoretical propositions in economics using the experimental approach as adopted by Chamberlin. In the 1960s, Smith started using experiments to study price formation in markets. In many ways, these experiments laid the foundation for what we refer to as the field of experimental economics today.

Smith created a laboratory market where buyers and sellers could trade one (or more) units of a good. Buyers are assigned valuations that reflect their maximal willingness to pay for a single unit of the good, while sellers are assigned costs, which is the minimum amount they are willing to accept. For buyers, this surplus is the difference between their willingness to pay and the price they actually paid, while, for sellers, it is the difference between the price received and the minimum acceptable amount (which is designed to reflect their cost of production). Smith demonstrated that while the microeconomic system he had created in the laboratory in the form of a simple market deviated significantly from the assumptions made in the classical theory (for instance, the assumption that one needed a large number of buyers and sellers in order to get price-taking behaviour), by and large, these markets showed reliable patterns of convergence to the predicted equilibrium. I will discuss this in much greater detail in Chapter 14.

Contemporaneously, following the publication of von Neumann and Morgenstern's work, strategic decision making in the context of bargaining games came to occupy a central position in the minds of both economists and game theorists, and such strategic considerations came to influence how economists looked at different market structures, such as oligopolies. Merrill Flood reports results from experiments studying behaviour in prisoner's dilemma games conducted in the 1950s by Flood in collaboration with his colleague Melvin Drescher. Much of this work was based on the pioneering work in game theory undertaken by John Nash, which led to the discovery and the widespread use of the Nash equilibrium concept in strategic decision making. It also won Nash a Nobel Prize in Economics in 1994 and made him the protagonist of the hit film *A Beautiful Mind*, directed by Ron Howard and starring Russell Crowe as Nash. Flood found behaviour in this game to be much more cooperative than theory predicted, which led to an attempt to better understand and explain how people approached these situations in real life.

Also in the middle decades of the century, a group of talented mathematicians at Princeton, including John Nash, Lloyd Shapley and John Milnor, began an empirical tradition they called "gaming", which consisted of analysing economic transactions that require strategic thinking, particularly in the form of anticipating an opponent's moves. At the same time, an overlapping group of mathematicians and psychologists at RAND Corporation in Santa Monica and other groups around the country began to conduct experiments informed by the emerging literature in game theory. (I will have much more to say about such situations involving strategic thinking in Chapter 6.) In 1952, an interdisciplinary conference was organized at the RAND Corporation where a large part of the discussion and a number of papers presented dealt with reporting and interpreting the results of experiments. At least three of the participants at that conference were to have a major subsequent impact on the development of experimental economics – Jacob Marschak, Roy Radner and Herbert Simon.

Thomas Schelling reported on a series of experiments designed to understand how people go about making decisions in circumstances where successful outcomes relied on coordinated actions. He argued that, in these circumstances, it is often the case that people might be able to coordinate their actions better by relying on "focal" actions. For instance, Schelling asked a group of students the following question:

> You are to meet somebody in New York City. You have not been instructed where to meet; you have no prior understanding with the person on where to meet; and you cannot communicate with each other. You are simply told that you will have to guess where to meet and that he is being told the same thing and that you will just have to try to make your guesses coincide.

Schelling found that a majority of respondents agreed to meet at noon and at the information booth of Grand Central Station. There is nothing that makes Grand Central Station a location with a higher payoff but its tradition as a meeting place makes it prominent and therefore a focal point. Schelling went on to expand on this line of thinking and how people's abilities – or lack thereof – to coordinate their actions may have an impact on economy-wide phenomena such as bank-runs or expanding business investments during a recession. (I will discuss such coordination problems in Chapter 13.) Among other things, Schelling devoted considerable time and effort to thinking about nuclear disarmament in the 1960s. His work led to a Nobel Prize in Economics in 2005 and rumour has it that he may have served as the basis of the character of Dr Strangelove, played so memorably by Peter Sellers in Stanley Kubrick's acclaimed film, *Dr. Strangelove or: How I Learned to Stop Worrying and Love the Bomb*.

It is important to note that, parallel to developments in the US, there arose a robust experimental research agenda in Europe by the end of the 1950s and the early years of the 1960s. There, the focus was on understanding boundedly rational behaviour, particularly in the context of studying prices and quantities in different market structures. A leader of this line of research was Reinhard Selten, who would go on to receive the Nobel Prize in Economics (along with John Nash and John Harsanyi) in 1994.

Significant early contributions also came from Charles Plott, who undertook path-breaking work studying issues relating to markets and industrial organization. Some of this early work was in collaboration with Vernon Smith. While Smith's earlier work had focused on the process of price formation in competitive markets, their work extended this to "posted offer" markets; where sellers announce a price and buyers can either buy at that price or not; an institution that more closely resembles the day-to-day markets we encounter in life. A key question was whether such posted offer markets allowed sellers to collude with one another and whether, as a result, prices would tend to be higher in such markets compared to competitive markets. But in addition to this, Plott was also a pioneer in extending experiments to other areas, such as political science, that are typically not considered to be experimental disciplines. In Fiorina and Plott (1978), for instance, Plott and his collaborator use experiments to study decision making in committees. Needless to mention, these experiments would turn out to be harbingers of significant later experimental work in those areas.

By the 1980s and 1990s, game-theoretic models had become solidly entrenched in economic analysis. These models, which placed demands on human cognition and brought issues of beliefs, learning and bounded rationality to the fore, lent themselves readily to experimental validation. Experimental economics gradually began to find greater acceptance and experimental economics became a part of the mainstream. Besides the extensive experimental work being carried out at Arizona (under the leadership of Vernon Smith), at Bonn (under Selten) and at Caltech (under Plott), there were a number of other researchers and laboratories. While an exhaustive list is beyond the scope of this book, a partial list of other active experimental laboratories in the 1980s and 1990s would include Iowa, New York University, Pittsburgh and Texas A&M.

EXPERIMENTS IN ECONOMICS AND PSYCHOLOGY: SIMILARITIES AND DIFFERENCES

(This discussion borrows heavily from Friedman and Sunder, 1994.)

I have already discussed parts of this in Chapter 1, so I will try not to repeat myself too much here. While experimentation in economics is a relatively recent phenomenon, researchers in psychology have been carrying out experiments for much of its modern existence, in order to understand human behaviour. In fact, psychology has always seen itself as an experimental science, as opposed to economics, which has embraced experimentation relatively recently. A partial list of ways in which experiments in economics and psychology differ appears below.

First, as noted already, most economics experiments emanate from a theoretical basis, often as an attempt to test said theories. In psychology, however, there is much less emphasis on writing down *a priori* formal models of human behaviour and the data often take precedence. At times, the development of theory in psychology follows the accumulation of considerable empirical regularities and a new theory or concept finds acceptance if it is better able to explain a body of empirical findings.

Second, economists typically focus on behaviour in specific institutions, such as markets, and much of their experimentation is driven by changes in the rules governing such market structures, while psychologists often prefer to study behaviour in the absence of such institutional constraints. Many of their experiments also deal with non-economic behaviour.

Third, experimental economists typically emphasize a clear incentive structure in the laboratory where the payments to participants are directly related to the decisions that they make. Psychologists often do not rely on monetary incentives, particularly performance dependent payments; at times, they pay a fixed fee or pay some participants at random. Instead, psychologists tend to emphasize the role of intrinsic motivation. In fact, some psychologists, as well as other social scientists, argue against providing salient monetary rewards which are task dependent. They argue that such extrinsically provided motivation in the form of monetary rewards to participants might in fact crowd out intrinsic motivations, which is their primary focus. However, more and more psychologists are resorting to rewarding salience in their experiments.

Finally, economists typically shy away from using deception in their experiments; while psychologists consider this to be less of a problem. Psychologists suggest, with justification, that in some experiments, it is virtually impossible to address the research question adequately in the absence of such deception. This is true, for instance, in the case of Solomon Asch's classic study on conformism and Stanley Milgram's work on obedience to authority. There is also controversy surrounding exactly what constitutes deception; is omitting a piece of information the same as providing incorrect information? This is an involved debate at this point and is well beyond our scope.

CRITICISMS OF EXPERIMENTAL ECONOMICS

In spite of the impressive growth that experimental economics has enjoyed in recent decades, the approach has its detractors who remain unconvinced that decision-making experiments can generate useful data. Here is a list of typical criticisms made against the experimental approach.

First, even now it is the case that the bulk of experimental studies are carried out with convenient samples of college/university students. They are typically young and have little or no experience with the marketplace and, in any case, possess less wisdom and experience than their older, more mature counterparts. This, then, raises the question of whether the data generated via decisions made by students can be representative of other parts of the population. More importantly, can this data provide us with valid clues as to how experienced players may approach the same problem? Do the decisions made by undergraduate students in laboratory experiments provide clues regarding the thinking of CEOs of multi-national corporations or stockbrokers, or even the average person on the street? Do the results obtained from these experiments allow us to make inferences about the behaviour of others outside the laboratory? That is to say, do these experimental results have external validity?

Second, while subjects in these decision-making experiments do get paid for their participation and often at rates that compare well with the opportunity cost of their time, the fact remains that the amounts involved are small. Therefore, one oft-expressed concern is whether the decisions made on the basis of these small amounts allow us to generalize about decisions involving much larger sums of money, that may characterize many real-life transactions.

Third, another concern that arises in the use of experiments is the so-called "experimenter demand effect". Here, the idea is that the very design of the experiment and/or the language of the instructions might provide clues to the subjects about the experimenter's research question. Closely connected to, and indeed following from this concern, is the worry that the instructions may lead subjects to believe that the experimenter wishes them to behave in a particular manner. As a result, participants may end up acting in the way they think they are expected to, rather than in the way they would actually like to behave.

The fourth question relates to whether experiments allow us to make causal inferences. That is, if outcome Y is associated with institution X, then can we say that Y is caused by X?

Last, but by no means least, is the concern regarding external validity of laboratory experiments. This concern is actually not separate from the ones listed above. In fact, the broad question about external validity encompasses many of the criticisms listed above. The question is: *do the decisions made by participants in experiments tell us anything meaningful about how people – and, more importantly, professionals with specific training in certain areas – behave in real life?*

For instance, laboratory experiments routinely demonstrate the emergence of bubbles in markets trading finitely lived assets. But does the fact that undergraduate student subjects in the laboratory routinely create asset bubbles tell us anything about bubbles in real-life asset markets or, indeed, whether such markets will be characterized by bubbles as well? Steven Levitt and John List of the University of Chicago raise this issue of external validity most forcefully:

> Yet unless considerable changes are made in the manner in which we conduct lab experiments, our model highlights that the relevant factors will rarely converge across the lab and many field settings.

The implication here is that it is the results in field settings that matter, and unless laboratory experiments can tell us something about behaviour in the field, then these experiments are meaningless. In many ways, this criticism echoes the same idea that the only meaningful way to learn anything important about economic phenomena is to study economies in the wild, or at least create field experiments that are close approximations of the natural economy.

I will discuss these criticisms in turn, while reserving the most attention to the critical issue of external validity. Some of these criticisms raise questions worth pondering. But the first important point to note is that not all of these are criticisms of the experimental method *per se*. Some of these are essentially arguments in support of carrying out more elaborate experiments.

With regards to the criticism that data generated on the basis of decisions made by student subjects are not reliable predictors of behaviour in the real world, this criticism is increasingly losing its force. If the main desire is to predict behaviour among other parts of the population or for special sub-groups, then one can easily run experiments with subjects recruited from those groups. More and more experimental economists are carrying out elaborate field experiments with specialized subject pools. In Chapters 7 and 8, where I talk about the economics of fairness, I will discuss a large set of field experiments, done under the leadership of Joseph Henrich of Harvard, studying pro-social behaviour among a large number of small-scale tribal societies scattered all over the world. Ernst Fehr of Zurich and John List of Chicago have compared the behaviour of CEOs and students in a trust game, designed to measure levels of trust and reciprocity among the subjects. I will discuss issues of trust and trustworthiness in greater detail in Chapters 9 and 10. They find that, contrary to conjectures that CEOs may be more attuned to the strategic imperatives of the game, they actually display greater levels of trust and trustworthiness than their student counterparts. In Chapter 1, I discussed how different groups of people approach the Guessing Game and showed that some students actually do better in the game than CEOs. Contrary to popular presupposition, it is worth bearing in mind that often there are no significant differences between the behaviour of student subjects and their more sophisticated counterparts. And, in many instances, these differences do not go in the direction that non-experimental researchers expect them to.

Experience can, at times, be counter-productive also. People with experience in a particular area might wrongly apply those lessons and their wisdom to a problem that appears similar but is actually quite different. This is particularly true if experimental instructions provide context. When such context is provided, people often bring their experience in that context into the experiment. A problem arises when their real-life experience in that context is with a situation that differs somewhat from the situation the experimenter is trying to implement through the experimental design. If the subject thinks as if he/she is dealing with the real-world situation that he/she has previously experienced, this may dominate the experimental situation and pay-offs. This may result in a loss of experimental control.

The argument that experimental results are suspect because of the small stakes involved has also been found to be wanting. Experimental economists now routinely carry out experiments with substantial stakes. One common way of doing this is to carry out experiments in less developed countries, where what would be considered relatively small amounts in the developed world represent much larger amounts and, in turn, imply much larger purchasing power. The main finding is that stakes do not matter nearly as much as critics seem to think they would, if at all. In Chapter 7, I will discuss the findings reported by Lisa Cameron of Monash University. She carried out ultimatum game experiments in Indonesia and found that raising monetary stakes does not change behaviour all that much, and, in fact, often led to behaviour that was fairer and more equitable, contrary to the predictions based on individual self-interest.

One common concern with experiments, particularly in the social sciences, is experimenter demand effects. This can mean a number of different things. It is possible that the experimenter, either consciously or even unconsciously, communicates his/her expectations about appropriate behaviour to the participants. This may cause participants to alter their behaviour to conform to those expectations. Or, even if the experimenter does not provide any subtle cues, the subjects may try to infer what it is that the experimenter is trying to figure out and change their responses to correspond to what they think the experimenter wants to hear. This concern applies to survey questions as well.

In the first decade of the 20th century, Wilhelm von Osten, a German mathematics teacher and horse-trainer, claimed that his horse, Clever Hans, could undertake simple mathematical calculations by tapping out the correct answer. Indeed, in numerous demonstrations, it turned out that Clever Hans could actually correctly answer such questions. However, Oscar Pfungst, who was appointed to evaluate Clever Hans' abilities, quickly discovered that the horse could get the correct answer even if von Osten himself did not ask the questions. So, it was clearly not the case that von Osten was providing subtle clues to help Clever Hans solve the problems. But Pfungst discovered that the horse gave the right answer only when the questioner knew what the answer was, and the horse could see the questioner. Pfungst then started to look at the behaviour of the questioner and found that as the horse's taps approached the right answer, the questioner tensed up and his/her posture and facial expression changed to reflect this increased tension, which was released when the horse made the final, correct tap. So, when the experimenter knew the answer, the experimenter's posture and/or facial expressions were providing cues to the horse on when it should stop tapping.[5]

Daniel Zizzo, formerly of East Anglia and now at Queensland, identifies two types of demand effects: (a) cognitive and (b) social. Cognitive demand effects can arise in deciphering the task being undertaken if and when participants make inferences or errors regarding appropriate behaviour in said task.[6] In addition, social demand effects may arise if participants perceive social pressure, either explicitly or implicitly, through the instructions or cues provided by the experimenter, who often occupies a position of authority.

Zizzo relies on the following anecdote to provide an example distinguishing social and cognitive experimenter demand effects (EDE).

> As an illustration of the sense in which social EDE and purely cognitive EDE differ, consider a Western person who has grown up eating with forks and knives and who enters a traditional Chinese restaurant for the first time. She sees both racks with forks and knives and racks with chopsticks—i.e., she knows that both options are available. She and her date (also someone as inexperienced as her) do not see other diners in the restaurant, and they do not receive any explicit or implicit pressure from staff to use chopsticks. She may still choose to ask for chopsticks because, given the menu of available options and the schema she recalls on how one can have a true 'Chinese restaurant' experience—schema which is especially useful due to her unfamiliarity with the decision problem—, she feels it is the better option of the two to maximize her utility from the restaurant meal. This would be the equivalent scenario to that of a purely cognitive EDE. Alternatively, as she enters the restaurant with her date, she may observe a number of other diners, and they are all using chopsticks; or her date, who frequently comes to this restaurant, may raise an eyebrow when she says she is considering asking for fork and knife; or the waiter may make a polite but not so subtle comment that it would be a good idea to consider trying out chopsticks. In all of these alternative cases, in addition to the above purely cognitive effect of task construal, she will feel the social pressure to conform to what peers (the first case) imply is the socially acceptable norm or, more directly, to what experts (the second and third case) require her to do. This would be the equivalent scenario to that of a social EDE.

Zizzo suggests that demand effects that are uncorrelated with the objectives of the experiment are harmless. But demand effects that are either negatively or positively correlated with the true objectives are potentially problematic. Positive correlation, in particular, makes interpretation of results difficult since any result in favour of the experiment's hypotheses may be confounded by such demand effects.

Zizzo offers some strategies to deal with demand effects. These include not using classroom "pseudo-volunteers", minimizing the social interaction between the experimenter (particularly if that person occupies a position of authority, such as a lecturer) and participants, and avoiding loaded language that provides context. He also suggests using "non-deceptive obfuscation" where practicable, so as not to provide clues about the true experimental objective to the participants.

As mentioned above, the use of abstract and context-free language is a way of safeguarding against such experimenter induced demand effects. However, it is also the case that, increasingly, many experimental economists are using emotive language. In doing so, it is important to bear in mind the trade-offs between creating a more realistic experiment and any possible demand effects.

Do experiments allow causal inferences? This criticism is not confined to experiments but applies with equal force to any empirical study. In fact, it may be argued that this criticism applies more to empirical studies based on unique natural experiments which cannot be replicated. One big advantage of experiments with well-defined instructions, rules and parameters is replicability. If a critic does not believe the answers thrown up by a particular study, then it is perfectly feasible to replicate the results under similar conditions. Therefore, if a number of similar experiments with either identical or closely related designs show that, under a given set of circumstances, robust and replicable regularities emerge, it is not unreasonable to conclude that if that same set of circumstances prevail, then the same regularities will also occur. This is the essence of inductive reasoning, the act of going from the specific to the general.

This brings me to what is considered to be the most pertinent and forceful criticism of economic experiments, as levelled by Steve Levitt and John List. Once again, a full discussion of this issue is beyond our scope. It is worth iterating that the question of external validity contains within itself many of the other criticisms that I have listed above. As such, my responses to those other criticisms above also apply to the charge of experiments lacking external validity.

The criticism about external validity contains a fundamental misunderstanding of what role experiments are designed to play. The suggestion that lab experiments lack external validity assumes that the only role for experiments is to tell us something about the real world. There are at least two problems with this criticism. First, while it is true that we would like our experiments to tell us something about the real world, this is not the only goal of experiments. Second, the issue of external validity looms larger for a certain set of studies than for others.

As I have pointed out above, experiments in economics play multiple roles. One of these roles is to test the empirical validity of economic theories (bearing in mind the caveat that any such attempts do run into the Duhem–Quine problem, as noted above). But, as Vernon Smith argues, to the extent that laboratory experiments do create a small-scale microeconomic society, the theoretical predictions that are supposed to hold true for complex real-life phenomena should still be valid within the controlled conditions of the laboratory. It seems to defy reason that theoretical predictions which are wildly off the mark within the laboratory would still perform well in conditions with more confounds and more uncontrolled variables.

As I have also argued above, another major role of experiments is to demonstrate empirical regularities in searching for facts and/or meaning. In doing so, economic experiments essentially play the role of economic models that can lead to further theory building. Moreover, to the extent that many experiments are often comparing the impact on behaviour from changing various institutional parameters, it is not a big concern whether the experiments are carried out with the traditional participant pool of students or other non-traditional participants. In many cases, the different pools will produce changes in behaviour in the same direction, though perhaps of differing magnitude, in response to different treatments. This may be of little concern if it is the direction of change rather than its magnitude that is of primary interest.

Thus, when it comes to the role of experiments in testing theory or searching for facts, external validity does not emerge as a major concern. The area where the issue of external validity does loom large is when experiments are utilized to design policy. Here, there are two responses. First, if the data generated using student participants is considered unreliable, then an obvious response would be to run the experiments with more sophisticated participants. Here, the student experiments can be thought of as pilot studies guiding the design of further experiments with non-student subjects. Second, in many cases – as with the design of auctions for selling broadcasting rights over the electromagnetic spectrum – the questions are difficult, especially because often there is no adequate theory to generate testable predictions. In such cases, carrying out lab experiments prior to field implementation makes perfectly good sense.

One area where the critics have been particularly vocal is in terms of experimental research showing the existence of other-regarding preferences and their applicability to different situations, such as other-regarding preferences in markets for labour. Levitt and List have argued that these results pertaining to other-regarding preferences have little or no external validity and that the only way to address the existence or lack thereof of social preferences is to design field experiments involving subjects who have particular expertise with the task at hand. To illustrate his point, List went to look at behaviour in a market for trading sports cards. List found that when it comes to the behaviour of professional sports cards dealers, social preferences such as generosity do not play a role. But this finding has been challenged by Colin Camerer of Caltech, another stalwart of experimental economics, on the basis of a re-analysis of List's data.

But, and more importantly, as Camerer points out, while it is true that experimental results may not always translate directly to a particular context, it is also true that there might be problems with transfer from one field study to another. Given that a lot of parameters are specific to a particular field context, it is not clear that results of these field studies are more generalizable to other contexts than the results of lab experiments. Camerer writes:

> The guiding idea here is ... "parallelism" ... (the assumption) that the same general laws apply in all settings. ... For example, parallelism does not require that students in a lab setting designed to resemble foreign exchange traders behave in the same way as professional foreign exchange traders behave on trading floors. ... The maintained assumption of parallelism simply asserts that if those differences could be held constant (or controlled for econometrically), behaviour in the lab and the trading floor would be the same. Put differently, if many experimental and field data sets were combined, with sufficient variation among variables like stakes, experience, and subject characteristics, a "Lab" dummy variable would not be significant (assuming it did not plausibly correlate with omitted variables).

Camerer then goes on to conclude by suggesting that:

> generalizability of lab results is an exaggerated concern among non-experimenters ... (T)he scientific perspective that (governs) experimental economics ... is that all empirical methods are trying to accumulate regularity about how behaviour is generally influenced by individual characteristics, incentives, endowments, rules, norms, and other factors. A typical experiment therefore has no specific target for "external validity"; the "target" is the general theory linking economic factors to behaviour. ... Second, when experiments are criticized for limited generalizability that criticism depends on contrasting stereotypes of a

canonical low-stakes, artificial experiment with students and a canonical field setting with self-selected skilled agents and high stakes. Criticisms that depend on these contrasted stereotypes ignore the crucial fact that experiments can be very different and that more experiments can always be conducted.

Charles Plott, echoing Camerer's arguments, suggests that the emphasis on realism is misguided. Experiments are often designed to expose things that are hidden by nature. Therefore, designing experiments to replicate natural settings is not necessarily illuminating. Often, the very simplicity of experiments is what makes them useful. According to Plott, economics is the study of principles that govern the behaviour of mankind in the ordinary business of life. Therefore, simple experiments are often sufficient in uncovering the principles that govern such behaviour. This is particularly because these principles can be better understood not by studying behaviour in equilibrium, but by understanding the structure and institutions that guide behaviour toward that particular equilibrium. Therefore, often it is the simplicity of experiments that is of fundamental importance in order to understand the nature and functioning of specific institutional structures.

IN LIEU OF A CONCLUSION: EXPERIMENTAL ECONOMICS: THE PATH FORWARD

As I write this at the end of the second decade of the 21st century, it is safe to say that experimental economics is now firmly entrenched in the mainstream of economics. So much so that, in a recent paper, Andrew Oswald, a leading scholar of economics at the University of Warwick, comments:

> experimental papers are becoming common in the highest impact-factor journals ... Some economists think that experimental-method papers may even take over as the dominant style of work. I am not sure; it is easy to get carried away with the latest fashions. ... But true-experiment papers will surely make up a much bigger slice of the future of economics than has been common up to this point.

At the beginning of this chapter, I suggested that at its heart, experimental economics is merely an alternative empirical approach to studying economic phenomena. At times, experiments may suffice on their own; at times, it might be useful to supplement them with natural data and/or survey evidence. In some cases, experiments can serve as an important robustness check on findings obtained on the basis of natural data and/or surveys. In other cases, experiments can also serve the role of economic model building by throwing up empirical regularities that, in turn, can lead to the development of new models of economic behaviour.[7]

Experimental economics is currently in the process of making the transition from being a sub-field of economics to the status of another empirical tool for studying economic phenomena. Economists are now routinely turning to experiments in an attempt to validate theory. However, it is still too premature to call economics an experimental science. Among large sections of economists there is still a significant amount of resistance to the reliance on experiments, particularly laboratory experiments. This is due, partly, to lingering questions about the external validity of experiments. I have already addressed this issue in the previous section. But it is also clear, as illustrated by the quote from Oswald above, and the recent track record of Nobel Prize winners, that experiments, whether in the lab or the field, will increasingly play a major role in economic research.

NOTES

1 Here is an example of a natural experiment that allowed a specific theoretical conjecture to be tested. In this case, the conjecture is that large-scale immigration into an area will place downward pressure on wages (particularly blue-collar wages) in that region. The Mariel boatlift was a mass movement of Cubans who departed from Cuba's Mariel harbour for the United States between April 15 and October 31, 1980. The boatlift was precipitated by a sharp downturn in the Cuban economy, leading to simmering internal tensions on the island and a bid by up to 10,000 Cubans to gain asylum in the Peruvian embassy. The Cuban government subsequently announced that anyone who wanted to leave could do so, and an impromptu exodus organized by Cuban Americans with the agreement of Cuban President Fidel Castro was under way. The exodus was ended by mutual agreement between the two governments in October 1980. By that time, up to 125,000 Cubans had made the journey to Florida, most of whom were placed in refugee camps. The Mariel boatlift features prominently in *Scarface*, a 1983 film directed by Brian De Palma, and starring Al Pacino as Antonio "Tony" Montana, a fictional Cuban refugee who comes to Florida in 1980 as a result of the Mariel Boatlift. It turns out that in spite of this massive influx of immigrants, wages did not go down. The reasons as to why those wages did not decline are complex and far beyond the scope of this book.
2 An example of such a "natural experiment" is found in David Card and Alan Krueger's study of what happens to unemployment with an increase in the minimum wage. Theory suggests that a minimum wage should lead to an increase in unemployment. (Most readers will probably understand this but I will address the mechanism behind this in detail in Chapter 14.) On April 1, 1992, New Jersey's minimum wage rose from $4.25 to $5.05 per hour. To evaluate the impact of this rise in minimum wages on local levels of employment, Card and Krueger surveyed 410 fast-food restaurants in New Jersey and contiguous eastern Pennsylvania (where the minimum wage was constant) before and after the rise. Contrary to theory, Card and Krueger did not find evidence that the hike in minimum wage reduced employment.
3 This is particularly because undertaking large-scale studies using field data is resource intensive. They are also hard to replicate. Often, it makes sense to undertake a smaller scale lab study beforehand to understand which aspects are more important than others and therefore demand greater focus, what are the key questions and what type of data needs to be collected.
4 It is worth pointing out that a double-blind protocol in the social sciences is actually less stringent than in the medical sciences. In social sciences, typically, even if the researcher cannot see any decision, the researcher knows who was assigned to which condition. In medical sciences, the researcher is typically unaware of even that: who is in the treatment condition and who is in the placebo condition.
5 It still seems like a major feat to me if Clever Hans could actually make out human expressions and posture. So, while maybe not as interesting as being able to solve mathematical problems, this still seems like a major achievement on the part of Clever Hans. The issue of animal intelligence is, of course, way beyond the scope of this book. But for those interested, I recommend checking out work done with New Caledonian crows by Gavin Hunt and my colleague, Russell Gray, and their many collaborators at the University of Auckland. Their work found remarkable tool manufacturing skills on the part of New Caledonian crows. These skills were the results of a lengthy learning period and are underpinned by brains with large associative regions and the ability to make causal inferences. Russell's website is here: https://unidirectory.auckland.ac.nz/profile/rd-gray.

6 A cognitive demand effect may arise if the experiment or instructions are difficult resulting in a lack of comprehension on the part of the participants. Here, the participants essentially fail to understand or misunderstand the nature of the tasks that they are expected to carry out.
7 Those of you who are curious to know more about where experimental economics may be headed, particularly as an empirical tool, should consider taking a look at a volume that I edited, titled *Research Agenda in Experimental Economics*. A key aim of the volume is to speak to people outside of mainstream economics. One intended group of readers include people working in areas that may not automatically turn towards using experiments in studying their own research questions. Here, the aim is twofold: (1) to reach out to these potential readers and inform them of ways in which experiments are being used by pioneers in those fields and (2) to point out useful avenues of further research. To that end, the chapters in the volume, written by leading scholars in the field, are not intended to summarize work in those fields, but, rather, provide a selection of how experiments are being utilized to address interesting research questions in those areas and what the potential future extensions are. But, equally, the volume also reaches out to experienced experimentalists to illustrate how they can use the items in their tool-kit to address other interesting research questions that are amenable to experimental study.

3 Gut feelings and effortful thinking

In this chapter I talk about:

- Two types of thinking: System 1, which is automatic or instinctive, and System 2, which is deliberative or effortful;
- Situations where System 1 works well;
- Situations where System 1 may be of limited use and System 2 needs to be engaged;
- Some limitations of instinctive thinking or reliance on heuristics;
- Frequently observed decision biases including priming, framing, anchoring, confirmation and hindsight biases;
- Problems of time-consistency in choices as an example of conflict between System 1 and System 2.

INTRODUCTION

It was 2006 and Stephen Colbert was the featured speaker at the White House Correspondents' dinner, an annual event that brings together the movers and shakers of Washington DC: politicians and journalists with a liberal sprinkling of Hollywood glitterati. This was back when Stephen Colbert was still doing "The Colbert Report" on Comedy Central; before he hit mainstream American consciousness by taking over the *The Late Show* from David Letterman on CBS. Depending on who you ask, Colbert was either a massive hit or a big flop. (I belong to the former group, but I digress.) Colbert made headlines for ripping into the then President George W. Bush. Bush had long claimed that he was not a "Brainiac" and that he was the type of guy who relied on his "gut". This led to Colbert's famous riff:

> We are not that different, he and I. We both get it. Guys like us, we are not some brainiac on nerd patrol. We are not members of the "fact"-onista. We go straight from the gut. That is where the truth lies. Right down here in the gut. Do you know that there are more nerve endings in your gut than in your head? You can look it up. Now, I know some of you will say that "I did look it up and that is not true." That's because you looked it up in a book. Next time, look it up in your gut. I did. My gut tells me that's how our nervous system works.

While taking nothing away from Colbert's bravura performance, Bush may have had a point, even though Bush was most likely unaware of this. There is actually serious academic debate as to whether you should or should not follow your gut. Look at Figure 3.1. At one glance,

Gut feelings and effortful thinking

Figure 3.1
Bored man

you can deduce a number of things. This person is bored, frustrated and clearly not enjoying the job at hand. This assessment took nanoseconds. It comes naturally to us and we are continually engaged in such assessment of cues all around us. In fact, facial expressions are quite common across cultures and parts of the world. People around the world look the same when they are happy or sad, bored or angry.

Let me now ask you a slightly more complex question. Look at Figures 3.2 and 3.3. Each figure has a smiling woman and smiling man. Suppose I asked you to compare across the figures: Are you more likely to trust the woman (man) in Figure 3.2 or 3.3? What do I mean? Suppose you were playing the "Split or Steal" game with one of these people and were trying to decide whether to choose "Split" or "Steal". The other person is saying that he/she will choose "Split" for sure. Are you more likely to trust the two people in Figure 3.2 or would you feel more comfortable with the two people in Figure 3.3?

Or, better yet, suppose I asked you to take part in an experiment where you have to play the "trust game" with one of these people? You are going to play each of the four people in the two figures in turn. Each time, you have $10 at your disposal and the other person has no money. You can take the $10, put it in your pocket and walk away. Or you can choose to share some or all of this $10 with one of the four people in the photo. Here is the catch: if you offer any money to the other person, then the experimenter will triple this amount! If you offer $5 to the other person, then the experimenter will actually give $15 to that person. The second person will then have a choice to make. Does he or she want to send any money back to you? The game ends after this second decision and any money sent back by the other person is not tripled. I will discuss this game and research findings about it at length in a later chapter.

■ Gut feelings and effortful thinking

Figure 3.2
People with forced smiles

 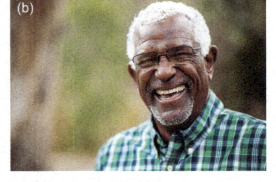

Figure 3.3
People with Duchenne smiles

For now, let me simply say why this game involves you trusting the other person. Suppose you sent $5 to this person, then you have $5 left and the other person receives $15, since the $5 you sent is tripled by the experimenter. None of you knows the other and chances are that you are located in different rooms and not sitting face-to-face. All you can see is a photo of the other person exactly as in the two figures. There is not a whole lot of reason for this person to send any money back to you, which, in turn, means that there is not much justification in you sending anything in the first place. By sending money, chances are, you will not get anything back, so you will be left with less than $10. But, suppose you chose to trust the other person and sent $5. The other person gets $15. He/she sends $7 back to you. You now have $12: the $5 you kept plus the $7 you get back. The other person has $8: the $15 he/she received minus the $7 he/she sent back. Both of you are better off than where you started, where you had $10 and the other person had zero. You have both gained (sure, at the expense of the experimenter, but then you don't really care about the experimenter, do you?). This is, as management people love to say, a "Win–Win"!

In fact, if you sent all $10 to the second person, he/she will have $30. Maybe he/she will send back $15 or even $20. Both of you walk away with a chunk of money. But this does require you to "trust" the other person and the other person to reciprocate your trust; otherwise, it will not work, and you will end up with less than $10. So, let me ask you again: if you were playing against each of the four people in the two figures, who would you trust? Would you send money? How much? Would you send more (or less) to one of the four?

A group of researchers led by Paul Seabright at the Toulouse School of Economics provide an answer. You will most likely trust and send money (or more money) to the two people in Figure 3.3 compared to the two people in Figure 3.2. This is because the two people in Figure 3.3 are demonstrating a genuine or "Duchenne" smile. Look a little more closely. Notice how the muscles around the eyes (the "*orbicularis oculis*") of the two people in Figure 3.3 are crinkled? It turns out that you cannot fake this. If you are genuinely smiling, then these muscles will automatically crinkle. Now, look at the two people in Figure 3.2. They are smiling but this is not a genuine smile since the muscles around their eyes are not crinkled. These people are not considered as trustworthy as people who are expressing a genuine smile.[1] This is not foolproof, but in general people are much more apt to trust those expressing a genuine smile (or another hard-to-mimic signal).

How do Seabright and his collaborators know this? Because they had subjects play the "trust game" against other subjects who were either smiling genuinely (a Duchenne smile) or not. The recipients who were considered to be smiling genuinely, were trusted more. Senders sent them more money than those whose smiles were considered non-genuine.

THE POWER OF GUT FEELINGS, OR SYSTEM 1 THINKING

Surprised? You should not be, according to Gerd Gigerenzer of the Max Planck Institute of Human Development in Berlin. According to Gigerenzer, millions of years of evolution have endowed us with this ability to make quick judgements. In the African Savannah, this may have meant life or death. If there is a slithering noise in the bush behind you, you might be better off jumping, assuming a snake rather than investigating the source of the sound. According to Gigerenzer, evolution has moulded our minds into an adaptive toolbox, so that we can, often, rely on such instincts to good effect. We can rely on our intuition to come up with ecologically rational solutions to complex problems. What does "ecologically rational" mean? Again, as in the case of rationality, views differ. One way to think of ecological rationality is that the rationality of a decision, that is, the usefulness of the decision or the benefit from that decision depends on the circumstances in which it takes place, so as to achieve one's goals (or maximize one's utility) in that particular context. This may be different from pure rationality, in the sense that this may involve taking some short-cuts or intuitive/automatic decisions rather than an elaborate maximization of utility subject to constraints. Gigerenzer calls such shortcuts "heuristics" or "rules of thumb". Or simply "*gut feelings*".

Here are some names for you: Mickey Mantle, Willie Mays, Ty Cobb and Joe DiMaggio. They are considered some of the greatest centre-fielders in baseball history. As Gigerenzer points out, when Mantle or Mays went out to track down a fly-ball, he was usually not computing the parabolic path of the ball and estimating where exactly the ball would come down. He was simply relying on a rule of thumb: fix your gaze on the ball; start running; adjust your running speed so that the angle of gaze remains constant.

It is true that we often feel something is off before we consciously know why we feel this way. We often explain this by referring to a sinking feeling in the gut, or clammy hands or goosebumps, or a rapidly beating heart. Many of these sensations arise in the limbic system of the brain, the part lying at the border of the brain hemispheres and the brain stem. This is the oldest part of the brain, which is also found in lower mammals such as lizards and, therefore, often referred to as the "lizard brain" in popular culture. This is the part that regulates the "fight or flight" response. Faced with situations where we need to act fast, our brains, moulded by millions of years of evolution, are quick to perceive the appropriate response: fight or run; trust or not; elation or disgust. This may happen long before we can consciously analyse or put into words, what it is that we are feeling.

Gerd Gigerenzer's book *Gut Feelings* and Malcolm Gladwell's *Blink* (based in part on Gigerenzer's research) provide intriguing examples and anecdotes of how such instinctive feelings work. Such instinctive thinking is often called System 1 thinking; instinctive responses to an external stimulus; as opposed to System 2 thinking, which is more deliberative and effortful. I will have a lot more to say on the distinction between System 1 and System 2 thinking in what follows.

But this is not the entirety of Gigerenzer's thesis: that our brains are designed to come up with such instinctive responses which serve us well. Gigerenzer's point is more nuanced. Gigerenzer not only suggests that instinctive thinking is beneficial in many circumstances, he also suggests that it is not necessarily the case that complex problems require complex solutions. At times, simple solutions, heuristics or simple rules of thumb can provide solutions that are equally, if not more, effective; their simplicity is often their greatest asset and contributes to their greater efficiency.

Let me provide a trivial example before talking about more elaborate ones. The University of Auckland Business School, where I work, is located in the Sir Owen G Glenn Building. This is a soaring glass and steel structure providing expansive views of the Pacific Ocean and the Auckland Domain (our Central Park), and it has won many architectural awards. It is a delightful place to go to for work every day. The building provides five levels of parking in the basement. The earlier you come, the higher up you can park. But, regardless of when I get to work, and I usually get there reasonably early in the day (usually by 8:30 a.m.), I don't look at any of the empty parking spots but head directly to Level 3 and park at a particular spot just by the elevator or within a few spaces of it. But on days when I go in late and if it is after 9:00 a.m., then I don't bother with Level 3. I proceed directly to Level 4 and park at the corresponding spot on that level. Why? Because this way, at the end of a long day, I don't have to try to recall where I parked or walk around the car park looking for my car, as I see happening to other people. All I need to remember is whether I came in early or late. The rule is simple: early, go to Level 3; late, go to Level 4. And I already know exactly where to look as I get out of the elevator.

In Accident and Emergency departments around the world, triaging in the case of patients arriving with chest pains is critical. Is it a myocardial infarction? Or is it something else? Timely intervention is critical if it is indeed a heart attack in progress. Faced with this, hospitals around the world have devised extensive checklists to accurately identify heart attack victims. These lists call for a number of tests, which require time, the one item in extreme short supply in such cases. In the book *Fast and Frugal Heuristics*, Gigerenzer and collaborators point out that a much simpler set of rules can do at least as well, if not better. Figure 3.4 illustrates this simpler approach.

Sure, you are thinking, this simple rule of thumb gets a lot of cases wrong. Yes, it does, but the point is that far more complex rules get lots of cases wrong, too. As economists like to say, there is a trade-off here: complex rules may be more accurate, but they also take much longer to implement and produce results, time that is often not available. Simple rules have the advantage of saving precious time, and, on average, may work out better than complex rules.

Next, look at the information in Table 3.1. This shows the opponents from the Round of 16 of the 2019 US Open Men's Tennis Tournament. Can you figure out the name of who won each match? Give it a shot before you read on.

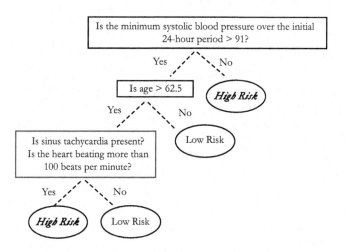

Figure 3.4
Simple heuristics for detecting heart attacks. Re-created on the basis of Gigerenzer et al. (1999), which in turn used data from Breiman et al. (1996)

Table 3.1 List of matches: round 16 of the 2019 US Open Men's Tennis Tournament

Djokovic vs. Kudla	Majcharzak vs. Dimitrov
Wawrinka vs. Lorenzi	De Minaur vs. Nishikori
Koepfer vs. Basilashvili	Rublev vs. Kyrgios
Medvedev vs. Lopez	Berrettini vs. Popyrin
Federer vs. Evans	Shopalov vs. Monfils
Goffin vs. Carreno Busta	Bublik vs. Andujar
Schwarzman vs. Sandgren	Bedene vs. Zverev
Nadal vs. Chung	Isner vs. Cilic

The answer is (and I deliberately arranged it in this manner): the winner was the first named player in the first column and the second named player in the second column. How did you do? Chances are you did pretty well even if you are not a regular follower of tennis. How? Most likely, because you adopted a simple rule of thumb: in each pair, you picked the player who was better known, or at least the player you had heard of before. If you did this, you would have done pretty well. I am not that keen a fan of tennis but know a little bit. Except for a few cases like Goffin vs. Carreno-Busta, Berrettini vs. Popyrin, Koepfer vs. Basilashvili or Schwarzman vs. Sandgren, where I had not heard of the players before, I did pretty well on the others, simply by relying on what Gigerenzer calls the "recognition heuristic". If it was a name I had heard before, this probably meant that they were the better player, so I picked that player.

Harry Markowitz won the Nobel Prize in Economics in 1990 as the pioneer of "Modern portfolio theory", which provides rules for investing money. For example, maximize expected return for any given level of risk, as measured by the variance or standard deviation of the returns; if two assets have the same standard deviation in returns, then pick the one with the higher expected return. Sounds good in theory; in practice, as Gigerenzer and his collaborators found out, many investment bankers do not understand the intricacies of the theory and often fail to convey its essence to investors. Some bankers apply the rule incorrectly. What should a savvy investor do? You can do just as well by simply diversifying your portfolio such that if you have access to three funds, you allocate one-third of your money to each of the three. This simple strategy will often outdo more complicated ones.

Tom Brady, the long-time quarterback for the New England Patriots, is legendary for his ability to make fast decisions in the pocket. He may well be the best quarterback of all times. Brady has won six Super Bowls and was elected to be the Most Valuable Player (MVP) in four of them. He has been the National Football League MVP three times. What makes Brady so good? It turns out that Brady is particularly good at split-second decision making on where to throw the ball in the face of onrushing tacklers. For someone in Brady's position, there is really no time to pause and ponder the alternatives; one needs to decide very quickly and the only way to do that is to rely on one's System 1 – instinctive thoughts translated into reflexive actions.

On January 15, 2009, Chesley Sullenberger was the captain of US Airways Flight 1549. This was an intercontinental flight departing from LaGuardia Airport in New York City and headed for Seattle, with a stop en route in Charlotte, North Carolina. Shortly after take-off, a flock of Canadian geese flew into the plane, resulting in the plane losing power in both engines. Sullenberger quickly realized that there was no way the plane could get back to LaGuardia or any other airport in the locality. Using deft instincts (heuristic: if the horizon is rising, raise the nose; if the horizon is falling, lower it), he guided the plane to a water landing on the Hudson River. All 155 people on board survived. Sullenberger was the last to leave the plane after making sure that everyone else was safely out. Among other accolades, the newly elected President, Barack Obama, invited Sullenberger and his crew to join the Presidential Inauguration ceremony on January 20th. In 2016 Clint Eastwood directed the film *Sully*, with Tom Hanks playing the role of Chesley Sullenberger.

Gigerenzer suggests that "an intuition is neither caprice nor a sixth sense but a form of unconscious intelligence". Talking about the experience later, Sullenberger referred to it as the "the worst sickening, pit-of-your-stomach, falling-through-the-floor feeling". But he also said something else that puts the benefits of relying on gut feelings in context. He said that for 42 years, he had been making small, regular deposits in his bank of experience, education and training. And on that fateful day, this experience paid off. His balance in the experience account was sufficient that he could make a large withdrawal. The above suggests that across a wide spectrum of situations, we can do well by going with our instincts. There are many instances when they can serve us well. But, in order to reap the greatest benefits from our gut feelings, we may need to have substantial expertise in the task at hand. Most of us are not Tom Brady or Chesley Sullenberger. So, it is possible that our gut feelings may not necessarily always serve us well, especially when it comes to problems that are complex, decisions that we encounter infrequently and situations in which we have little experience. So, ultimately, whether you rely on your gut feelings or not may come down to how much familiarity you have with the task in question.

LIMITS TO SYSTEM 1 THINKING AND THE NEED TO ENGAGE SYSTEM 2

Consider the following problems.[2] Try answering them before you read on. You will get more out of them if you do.

Problem 1: A bat and a ball together cost $1.10. The bat costs $1 more than the ball. How much does the ball cost?

Problem 2: If it takes 5 machines 5 minutes to make 5 widgets, how long would it take 100 machines to make 100 widgets?

Problem 3: In a lake, there is a patch of lily pads. Every day, the patch doubles in size. If it takes 48 days to cover the entire lake, how long does it take for the patch to cover half of the lake?

The most common answer to Problem 1 is that the ball costs 10 cents. But this is clearly incorrect; since in that case, that bat must cost $1.10 since the bat costs $1 more than the ball. But, if that were true, then the two together cost $1.20, not $1.10. The correct answer is that the ball costs $0.05 and the bat costs $1.05. But our instincts or System 1 does not come up with this answer since $0.05 is not intuitive. For Problem 2, the answer is 5 minutes, even though our instincts cannot help but say 100 minutes, as most people who were asked this question would say. This is because one machine takes 5 minutes to make one widget. So, 5 machines make 5 widgets in 5 minutes. By that reckoning, 10 machines will make 10 widgets also in 5 minutes. So, 100 machines will need 5 minutes to make 100 widgets. Finally, for Problem 3, the answer is not 24 days as most people respond. The correct answer is 47 days. Since the lily pads double every day, if the pond is half-full after 47 days, then it doubles and gets filled the very next day, the 48th. In all these cases, the answers to these problems seem obvious to our System 1 but the correct answer is not the most obvious one. This led the psychologist Daniel Kahneman to coin the acronym WYSIATI. *What you see is all there is!* But often there is much more than meets the eye.

■ Gut feelings and effortful thinking

So, let us say, that you are not convinced of the limitation of System 1 with these trivial riddles. Here is a weightier question. At the University of Auckland, there is a strong emphasis on inculcating an entrepreneurial spirit in our students. So, I ask my students at various levels, suppose you have managed to set up your business and are looking to expand. Where should you head? Where are the rich customers who can afford the luxuries of life located? When I ask this question of my students, the responses are quick and instinctive: USA, Australia, Singapore, Western Europe.

Are they correct? Well, sort of. In what follows, I have used public data provided by a think-tank based in Washington, DC.[3] The numbers are designed to be illustrative, rather than exact. I have rounded numbers up or down as needed to keep things simple. This data assumed (and this is not controversial) that anyone earning between $20 and $50 per day belongs to the upper-middle class, while those earning more than $50 per day can be thought of as high earners. A simple way to think about this is that these are people who can afford to buy things that are not basic necessities; they have the purchasing power to look at various luxury items. Take a look at Table 3.2. In this table, I have provided information about a selection of countries around the world and how many upper-middle class or high earners they have. My students are correct. The USA has a lot of these people; as many as 292 million of them. Germany has 76 million, while the UK has 59 million and so on. But now look at the lowest four rows of the table. These are not the names that pop into our minds instinctively when we think of "rich" countries.

Notice that China has 154 million of such people. In fact, the number of rich people in China exceeds that in France, Italy and Spain combined. India has more rich people than Australia while Brazil has marginally fewer rich than the UK. Malaysia has twice as many rich as Switzerland. The point is that while the proportion of rich in countries such as China or Brazil are much smaller than the proportion in the USA or Western Europe, China or Brazil have a lot more people! The fact that these countries have a lot more people, and, therefore, even if the proportion of rich is smaller, that still works out to a very large absolute number, is not immediately obvious to System 1.

As I will also hope to convince you, it is not the case that we immediately update our beliefs in light of new information and rectify our mistakes. Businesses, like individuals

Table 3.2 Where are the rich customers around the world?

Country	Population (million)	Earning $20–$50/day	How many (million)	Earning more than $50/day	How many (million)	Earning more than $20/day	How many (million)
USA	324	53%	172	37%	120	90%	292
Germany	81	50%	41	43%	35	83%	76
UK	66	54%	37	34%	22	88%	59
France	65	52%	34	40%	26	92%	60
Italy	59	53%	31	26%	15	79%	46
Spain	46	52%	24	21%	10	73%	34
Australia	25	50%	13	42%	11	92%	24
Switzerland	9	58%	5	38%	3	96%	8
China	1400	10%	140	1%	14	11%	154
India	1300	1%	13	1%	13	2%	26
Brazil	212	20%	42	7%	15	27%	57
Malaysia	33	40%	13	12%	4	52%	17

(after all, business decisions are made by individuals such as the CEO), can also fall prey to such mistakes if the person in charge already has a perspective that is different and does not pause to check whether the initial conjecture is correct or not. Often, once we make up our mind about something, we proceed to act on this, without checking to make sure that we have the facts correct, and if it later transpires that we may not have had the right facts, we do not necessarily change course.

Let us look at the following example.[4] A study of the incidence of kidney cancer in the 3,141 counties of the USA revealed a remarkable pattern. Counties with the *lowest* incidence of kidney cancer are mostly rural, sparsely populated and located in traditionally Republican states in the Midwest, the South and the West. So, does that mean being Republican somehow makes you immune to kidney cancer? Faced with information like this, our instincts immediately try to come up with a narrative to fit the facts. In this case, that narrative goes like this: it has nothing to do with Republicans (or Democrats). The low rates of cancer are due to the clean living of the rural lifestyle: no air pollution, no water pollution, access to fresh food without additives.

But the same study of the incidence of kidney cancer in the USA revealed that the counties with the *highest* incidence of kidney cancer are mostly rural, sparsely populated and located in traditionally Republican states in the Midwest, the South and the West. What is the story that fits this pattern? The narrative could be that rural counties are likely to be poor, with little access to good medical care, consumption of a high fat diet and too much red-meat, and possibly too much tobacco and alcohol. This makes sense.

But wait a second! How can both of these be true? How can rural counties report both very high and very low rates of kidney cancer? It is not the case that the same county has both high and low rates of cancer incidence; some have high and some have low. The key factor is that rural counties have small populations and extreme outcomes are much more likely with small numbers. So, the fact that both the highest and the lowest incidence of cancer are reported by rural counties is due to the fact that they are sparsely populated. Small numbers are much more likely to throw up extreme examples. But the fact "sparsely populated" (and, therefore, small numbers) does not immediately stand out to System 1. This is exactly why we fail to consider that while China's proportion of rich people may be small, its population is huge. Therefore, even a small proportion of a very large number works out to a fairly large number.

System 1, as embodied in automatic/intuitive thinking, operates automatically and quickly, with little or no effort and no sense of voluntary control. System 2, on the other hand, is deliberative and effortful. It allocates attention to effortful mental activities that demand it, including complex computations, but it takes conscious effort to engage System 2. System 1 quickly gets into action as soon as we receive a signal or a threat or a stimulus. One good analogy is to think of System 1 as an elephant that lurches into action quickly, while System 2 is the rider trying to guide the elephant; this can be done but is not easy and requires practice.

Kahneman provides a handy guide to thinking of the types of activities System 1 and System 2 deal with. System 1 helps us: detect that one object is more distant than another; orient to the source of a sudden sound; complete the phrase "bread and …"; Answer 2 + 2; read words on billboards or street signs; drive on empty motorways (on autopilot); detect

■ Gut feelings and effortful thinking

expressions on a face. System 2, on the other hand, enables us to: focus on the voice of a particular person in a crowded room; park in a narrow space; compare two items for their overall value; monitor the appropriateness of one's behaviour in a social situation; tell someone else one's phone number; check the validity of a complex logical argument.

A couple more examples before I move on. Take a look at Figure 3.5, which shows what is known as the Müller-Lyer Illusion. Müller-Lyer's original work was published 1889 and was written in German. An English translation of his work is provided by Ross Day and Hannelore Knuth. Again, you will appreciate the point more if you first try the test yourself. Looking between the arrows, which line segment do you think is longer? Seems obvious, does it not? A is clearly longer than B. Now turn the page and look for Figure 3.7. Still convinced A is longer? The lines are of equal length! But now go back and look at Figure 3.5 again. Line A does seem longer again! Once you have seen Line A as being longer, it seems difficult to "unsee" it. This is System 1 at work. It is hard to overcome your instincts even after the correct answer has been revealed.

Now look at Figure 3.6. This is a version of what psychologists call the *Stroop Task*. The task is simple. Start with the left-hand panel and simply say if the word (Left or Right) is written in upper case or lower case. Now move to the right-hand panel and repeat the exercise. Is the word Upper or Lower written in upper case or lower case? Did you struggle a bit this time? Why? Because, as soon as you see the word, your System 1 got into action and was intent upon reading the word. You had to actually step back, keep your System 1 in check, and engage your System 2 to see if the word was written in upper case or lower case rather than simply reading the word itself. You can do the exercise in reverse. Start with the right-hand panel and state whether the word is located on the left or the right. Then, do the same with the left-hand panel. State whether the word is to the left or the right. Once again, you will find yourself slowing down. This is because your instincts are homing on what the word says. It takes active engagement from System 2 to figure out the location: Is it located to the left or the right?

The Mueller-Lyer Illusion: which line is longer?

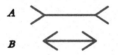

Figure 3.5
The Müller-Lyer Illusion: which line is longer

The Stroop Task
(upper case or lower case)

- LEFT
  - left
  - right
- RIGHT
  - RIGHT
  - left
- LEFT
  - right

- upper
  - lower
  - LOWER
- upper
  - UPPER
  - lower
  - LOWER
  - upper

Figure 3.6
The Stroop Task: upper case or lower case

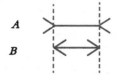

Figure 3.7
The Müller–Lyer
Illusion explained

CASE STUDY 3.1 IDENTIFIED VERSUS STATISTICAL LIVES

I was working on this book in the early part of 2020, while the world was dealing with the COVID-19 pandemic. As the disease spread rapidly across the world, epidemiologists argued for stricter and stricter social distancing measures. Many countries, including my home country of New Zealand, imposed a complete lockdown, with people asked to stay home except for those who were engaged in what were deemed to be "essential services". Many epidemiologists suggested such strict social distancing measures for as long as 18 months.

In his book *Risk Savvy*, Gerg Gigerenzer notes that, in the immediate aftermath of September 11, 2001, many Americans decided that flying was too risky. Instead, they chose to drive. In the 12 months following the attacks, an additional 1,500 people lost their lives on the roads while trying to avoid the risk of flying. This is more than the total number of passengers on the planes used in the 9/11 attack. In deciding to drive instead of flying, people were essentially focusing on *identified* lives, the loss of lives that happened right in front of us on 9/11. Gigerenzer calls this "dread risk", the fear of losing lots of lives in a short span of time. But, in doing so, they were ignoring the additional loss of lives that happened from road accidents, since these happened in a scattered manner and, therefore, did not garner as much attention. This secondary loss of lives, which result from diverting much of our resources to save the lives right in front of us, is referred to as *statistical* lives.

A very similar phenomenon played out during the COVID-19 pandemic. Most medical professionals were keenly focused on saving identified lives. Every day, newspapers reported how many people died of COVID-19 around the world. This is not surprising, since this is exactly what our instincts tell us to do: take all possible safety measures to avoid the pathogen. But we forget that many of those people would have died in the normal course of events, from a variety of reasons, such as heart attacks or flu. After all, approximately 50 million people die every year from a variety of causes, including old age. So, the issue was not so much how many people died from COVID-19, but how many more? In focusing on identified lives, we ignore the loss of statistical lives. It is likely that the total impact of the loss in statistical lives will be greater than any loss of lives due to COVID-19. But those deaths will register less on our collective psyche since they will be diffuse, scattered all over the world and will not be reported on in the same manner.

But what was not adequately recognized or discussed was that, beyond a certain point, it would just not be worth it to keep the economy shut down in order to save more people. As economic activity came to a standstill, businesses went bankrupt. By late March of 2020, more than 6 million people had filed for bankruptcy in the US. The corresponding number at the start of the global financial crisis in 2008–2009, was less than a million. In New Zealand, as international flights essentially stopped, Air NZ's revenue fell from roughly NZ $6 billion per year to only about NZ $500 million.[5] Globally, the massive economic shock of strict physical distancing measures resulted in poverty, hunger and death, particularly in developing countries. It is estimated that a ten-percentage-point increase in unemployment results in a decrease in life expectancy of approximately one to one and one-half year. The diversion of resources, including health facilities around the world, to reducing deaths from COVID-19 meant that other tests, screenings and surgeries were postponed, leading to a sharp spike in death from other causes. Around the world, roughly 80 million children were not vaccinated, leading to a sharp increase in measles, diphtheria and cholera.

My argument here is not that social distancing was not required. Strong interventions were certainly required. But different countries possibly needed different degrees of intervention. More importantly, what was needed was a discussion of the trade-offs. How many lives do we save if we lock down the country for four weeks? What is the economic implication of that? How much will the economy shrink? How many jobs will be lost? How many businesses will go bankrupt? How many people, including children, will start to suffer from mental disorders from this prolonged confinement? My point is simply this: there were hard trade-offs involved. It was not the case of saving lives from COVID-19 versus no impact anywhere else. Like Ana in Chapter 1, even governments and countries face budget constraints. The decision to devote tremendous resources to COVID-19 meant that these resources had to be reallocated from some other activity. It was not clear from the public commentary if the policy makers were always aware of these trade-offs; that diverting resources to saving the identified lives lost due to COVID-19 necessarily implied the loss of lives elsewhere.

What was also not recognized in the panic over the pandemic is that all of this was really based on probabilistic models. A lockdown of 18 months will work better than a lockdown of six months, which is better than four weeks, each imposing a different magnitude of social and economic costs. Much of this depended on the contagion rate: how many additional people did each infected individual pass the disease on to? How many lives will be taken by COVID-19 (identified lives) and how many lives will be lost due to our attempts to prevent the loss of lives from COVID-19 (statistical lives)? The issue of statistical lives does not loom large to System 1.

WHY DO WE NEED TO WORRY ABOUT SYSTEMS 1 AND 2?

The evidence above suggests that, at times, our instincts can prove useful, but equally, at times, they can lead us astray. Often, the particular context or presentation or certain external cues make a big difference. This, in turn, has implications. For instance, consider the following examples taken from Kahneman.

Example 1: Complete the following sentence: Ann approached the bank …

A frequent answer is along the lines: *She needed to withdraw some money from her account.* Here, most respondents are thinking of a financial institution when they hear the word "bank". But an equally feasible response may be: *After paddling hard for an hour, Ann decided to call it a day. Ann approached the bank where her friend was waiting.* Once again, System 1 rushes in to create a narrative and the resulting story can make a big difference to the outcome.

Example 2: You are considering two job candidates for one opening, Alan and Ben. A psychometric test was administered to each candidate as part of the interview process. You have the report from the tests. The test says that Alan is: Intelligent and Industrious but can, at times, be Impulsive, Critical, Stubborn and Envious. Ben, on the other hand, is Envious, Stubborn, Critical and Impulsive but can, at times, be Industrious and Intelligent. Which candidate did you hire? Is it Alan?

Priming

The fact that System 1 responds rapidly can often be used to design choices to achieve better outcomes. The popular name for this is "choice architecture". I will provide some examples in the following pages. Those looking for a more in-depth treatment would be well advised to read Thaler and Sunstein's book, *Nudge*. Let us look at some examples of where one can utilize instinctive feelings into policy choices. Many associations, such as Red Cross or UNICEF, try to attract donations from people and often hire professional fundraisers for this purpose. Now, when it comes to fundraising, what kinds of strategies work better than others? James Andreoni and Ragan Petrie of the University of Wisconsin carried out an experiment with paid participants. They looked at two strategies that are often used by fundraisers. First, what happens when participants can choose to contribute to one of two charities – one where their contributions are anonymous and another where their contributions are made public? Second, what happens when there is "category reporting", that is, rather than providing information about actual contributions, contributions are reported in categories such as up to $100, $101 to $500, $501 to $1,000, etc.

For the first question, Andreoni and Petrie find that participants contribute very little when their contributions are anonymous, while they contribute a lot more when their contributions are made public. Also, when contributions are reported in categories, many more participants increase their contributions to enter the lower end of a higher category. This suggests that, along with the warm glow of donating to charity, there is a bit of vanity involved as well. This is an example of priming, where one's behaviour is conditioned on an external cue provided by the person who is designing the choice mechanism. This is more elaborate than, but quite similar to, the idea of putting a pair of eyes on the "honesty jar" beside the coffee machine that I talked about in the Preface.

In fact, I did not make up the "watching eyes" idea. Moe Fathi, Melissa Bateson and Daniel Nettle of the University of Newcastle in the UK did. Of course, others have undertaken other variations of this experiment. Fathi and colleagues were also interested in raising money for charity and finding mechanisms that make a difference. They implement a 2 × 2 design, as shown in Figure 3.8. Let me explain. Subjects are assigned to one of the four different treatments. The first group sees a donation jar that is filled with loose change, mostly 10p, 20p, etc. coins. A second group sees a similar jar with loose change except there are a pair of watching eyes on a poster right above the jar. The eyes are part of a poster on

■ Gut feelings and effortful thinking

	Jar filled with loose change	Jar filled with large coins
	Jar filled with loose change PLUS watching eyes	Jar filled with large coins PLUS watching eyes

Figure 3.8
Experimental design in Fathi, Bateson and Nettle (2014)

	Jar filled with loose change *Median contribution = 20p* *Large contributions (£1 or £2) = 30%*	Jar filled with large coins *Median contribution = 0p* *Large contributions (£1 or £2) = 23%*
	Jar filled with loose change PLUS watching eyes *Median contribution = 72.5p* *Large contributions (£1 or £2) = 50%*	Jar filled with large coins PLUS watching eyes *Median contribution = 50p* *Large contributions (£1 or £2) = 42%*

Figure 3.9
Experimental results in Fathi, Bateson and Nettle (2014)

the wall that prohibits eating and drinking in the lab. So, it is not the case that the eyes are accompanied with a message asking people to donate. The message accompanying the eyes is irrelevant to the task at hand. A third group sees a jar, except now it is filled with £1 and £2 coins. Finally, the fourth group sees a jar with £1 and £2 coins as well as the poster with the pair of watching eyes immediately on top of the jar. This study allows us to look at two different ways of priming people. Does it matter if the jar contains loose change or large coins? Does it matter if there are watching eyes or not?

Participants in the study are handed a plain brown envelope that contains £5 (made up of 1 × £2, 2 × £1, 1 × 50p, 2 × 20p, 1 × 10p). They are made aware that they can keep the entire amount, or if they wish, they can contribute some or all of this to a deserving charity by putting this money in the jar in front of them. The authors report two key findings: first, the switch from loose change to large coins does not make much difference; in fact, it seems to have little or no effect. But, adding the pairs of eyes makes a big difference in each case. In Figure 3.9, I show what happens.

Let us first compare across rows. When the jar is filled with loose change, the median contribution is 20p and about 30% of the contributions are "large", implying contributions of £1 or £2. Adding a pair of eyes increases the median contribution more than threefold to 72.5p. When the jar is filled with large coins, the median contribution is zero and 23% of contributions are large. Adding a pair of eyes increases the median contribution to 50p and large contributions almost double to 43%. But, looking across columns, if we compare loose change without eyes versus large coins without eyes, or loose change with eyes versus large coins with eyes, we find little or no difference; in fact, contributions go down slightly when the jar is filled with large coins. So, the watching eyes make a big difference, but the more subtle prod of showing people loose change versus large coins (changing the subliminal social norm of what is appropriate: contribute loose change or large coins) did not succeed as well.

What is even more surprising is that it is not just human eyes that increase people's degree of pro-sociality. Mary Rigdon at Rutgers and her collaborators show that a similar effect can be obtained even with a "minimal" cue such as things that look like eyes but are not. I show what I mean in Figure 3.10. The left-hand panel of this figure shows three dots

Figure 3.10
Minimal cue from
Rigdon et al. (2009)

that are simulated to look like a human face (two eyes and a mouth), while the right panel is designed as a neutral control. Rigdon and her collaborators find that even this "minimal cue", three dots arranged to look like a face, leads to greater generosity on the part of participants in a laboratory charity-giving game.[6]

CASE STUDY 3.2 THE "DARK SIDE" OF PRIMING

It is clear that priming techniques can be used in beneficial ways, as discussed above. Police forces all over the world could probably make substantial savings if they replaced police officers using speed-guns by the side of road with large billboards that have a pair of eyes and the message "Drive safely. Don't Speed. We are watching you!". Better yet, put the face of some police officers in a watchful mode. This will, most likely, have a similar effect. Of course, this will mean a loss of revenue from all those speeding tickets, but the cost savings may make up for that. If any of you readers happen to be a police officer or know of a police department that may be interested in trying out a controlled experiment, I am available to work on this.

But priming can also have detrimental effects. Priming can lead to unwanted peer effects and social pressure resulting in conformist behaviour. One of the most well-known examples of the desire for such conformity in groups comes from the experiments carried out by Solomon Asch. Asch carried out his work in the 1950s as the world was trying to recover from the horrors of the Second World War. Asch was interested in exploring how so many ordinary Germans willingly conformed to Nazi propaganda. Asch asked participants to take a "vision test". Participants are shown two cards. The card on the left has the reference line and the one on the right has the three comparison lines. Figure 3.11 shows the relevant information. In reality, all but one of the participants in any group were research confederates of the experimenter. The participants – the real one and the confederates – were all seated in a classroom and each, in turn, was asked which line on the right-hand card was longer than, shorter than, or of equal length to the reference line on the left-hand card. The confederates had been instructed to provide incorrect answers. While a number of the real participants answered correctly, a high proportion (32%) conformed to the majority view of the others even when this view was clearly erroneous, in which the majority said that two lines were of the same length even though they differed by several inches.[7]

We do not necessarily need to look towards mass hysteria to see the detrimental effects of priming. A lot of this happens in everyday life, where we carry around lots of stereotypes in our heads. I once watched a YouTube clip of a young Asian man

 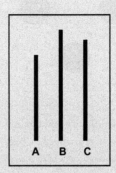

Figure 3.11 Cards with different length lines from Asch (1956)

talking about how hard it was to get into Harvard and how hard it was, even afterward; since he was used to being one of the smarter ones in his high school but, all of a sudden, everyone around him was extremely smart and capable. Below the clip was a comment by someone to the effect that if it was so hard for an "Asian dude", what chance did the correspondent have? This is a stereotype: that Asian students are smart. Here are some others: women are not good drivers; women are not funny and hence do not make very good stand-up comedians; African Americans are not academically oriented and are intellectually inferior; women are better at Arts and not good at STEM subjects.[8]

There are multiple problems with this. For one thing, stereotypes are often wrong. But, more importantly, a group that is subject to such stereotyping may come to believe that the stereotype is accurate and internalize it, to the extent that priming that stereotype (often referred to as "stereotype threat") leads to altered performance on the part of that group. If African Americans believe that they are intellectually less capable than European Americans, then if and when the stereotype is primed, they may actually perform worse. Similarly, if women believe they are not good at maths, then priming their gender identity may actually lead to worse performance in mathematical tasks by women.

Indeed, much evidence suggests that this is true. The psychologists Claude Steele at Stanford and Joshua Aronson of the University of Texas Austin decided to explore this with undergraduate African American students at Stanford. Let me repeat that: these are students at Stanford. In one study, a group of African Americans and European American students were given difficult verbal problems taken from the Graduate Record Examination (GRE). The problems were designed to be challenging on purpose. In one condition, students were told that this was a test of the students' intellectual abilities, and, at the end of the test, students will receive feedback on their ability levels. This was the *diagnostic* condition. In another treatment, the participants were told that this was a test trying to understand how the participants went about solving verbal problems and had nothing to do with intellectual ability. This was the *non-diagnostic* condition. Finally, there was a third *non-diagnostic challenge* condition where the participants were told that this was about ways of problem solving that had nothing to do with intellectual ability. In addition, participants were told that the problems were designed to be challenging. Steele and Aronson's conjecture was that the first diagnostic condition would pose a stereotype threat to the African American students, who may have internalized the idea that African Americans are intellectually inferior. In keeping with this hypothesis, Steele and Aronson find that, after controlling for the students' SAT scores, on average, African American students performed worse than European Americans in the diagnostic condition that primed the stereotype. Performance of the two groups was not different in the other two treatments.

To rule out other potential explanations, in another study, Steele and Aronson had students take part in similar verbal problem solving tasks, except here, the researchers primed ethnic identity directly by asking the participants about their race prior to starting. Once again, in the treatment where participants were asked specifically to note their race, African American students performed worse than European Americans. In another treatment, which was identical in all other respects, except there was no question on race, performance of the two groups did not differ.

Jennifer Steele of York and Nalini Ambady of Tufts undertook a similar study, except this time the target group were women and the choice was about arts or mathematics. Participants in studies by Steele and Ambady were asked to rate how enjoyable (or not) they found a series of activities. The Arts survey items included: writing an essay; listening to music for a class assignment; taking a literature exam; analysing a poem and finally, completing an art assignment for a visual arts course. The Maths survey items included: doing an algebra problem set; computing compound interest; solving an equation; taking a calculus exam and finally, completing a geometry problem set.

In one study, Steele and Ambady primed gender identity by having participants look at a computer screen where a series of words flashed by quickly. The female prime words were ones such as: doll, dress, earring, flower, girl, jewellery, lady, pink, lipstick, etc., while the male primes were words like uncle, tough, man, father, football, blue, boy, beer, etc. Another group of subjects were also shown a series of priming words, but these had nothing to do with gender. Following this, participants were asked to rate the Arts and Maths activities on a zero to nine scale with zero being "not enjoyable at all" and nine being "highly enjoyable". In a follow-up study, Steele and Ambady, like Steele and Aronson, primed gender by specifically eliciting such information prior to the rating of the survey items.

In both studies by Steele and Ambady, the findings were the same. The participants who had been exposed to the female prime words rated the Arts survey items much more highly compared to the Maths survey items. Participants who were shown non-gender specific words did not exhibit any such preference for the Arts survey items. The same was true for the participants who had not been asked about their gender as opposed to those who were asked about gender.

Framing

Framing refers to situations where different ways of asking the same question lead to very different outcomes. I have already talked about this at length in the Preface, where I discussed the problems of organ donations and retirement savings; how a simple change from "opt-in" to "opt-out" makes a big difference. Behavioural scientists typically refer to this as *changing the default option*. As I noted before, changing the default option from opt-in (as done in countries with "informed consent") to opt-out (i.e., "presumed consent"), can make a significant difference in terms of increasing organ donations. The same is true for boosting retirement savings. I alluded to work done by Richard Thaler and Cass Sunstein showing that when a firm offered a default contribution rate of 3% of salary, more than one-quarter of workers contributed exactly that amount to the plan, even though the employer matched contributions dollar for dollar up to 6% of salary. Once the firm switched to a 6% default, workers started contributing that proportion. A 2013 report in the *Guardian* found that approximately one year after the UK introduced automatic enrolment with an opt-out feature, there were 1.6 million more savers in workplace pensions. Only 9% chose to opt out.

Here is another example provided by Daniel Kahneman. Participants in this study are asked to express their preference between two treatments, A and B, affecting 600 people. Except one half of the group gets one message while the other half gets a different message. Half of the group gets the following positively framed information, which is put in terms of lives saved:

Treatment A is predicted to save 200 lives.
With Treatment B, there is a 1/3 chance of saving everyone but there is 2/3 chance of saving no one.

The other half of the group sees the information below, which is more negatively framed in terms of lives lost:

Treatment A is predicted to result in 400 deaths.
With Treatment B, there is a 1/3 chance that no one would die but there is 2/3 chance that everyone will die.

A large majority of respondents chose Treatment A when the message was framed positively in terms of lives saved, while a majority chose Treatment B when the message had a negative framing in terms of lives lost. This is surprising, since the informational content of the two messages are identical. If Treatment A saves 200 lives, then it leads to the loss of 400 lives. If Treatment B has a 1/3 chance of saving everyone, then it has a 2/3 chance of killing everyone. But, simply presenting this information in the form of lives saved versus lives lost makes a huge difference. The policy implication of this is massive because this is not a mistake committed by uninformed lay people. It happens to experts, professionals and policy makers. Simply changing the default may result in differences in which life-saving drugs we fund and which we do not.

A study undertaken by Benjamin Toll and collaborators (made up mostly of a group of psychiatrists and psychologists at Yale) examine the framing effect in smoking cessation measures. These participants received positively framed messages such as, "If you hold on to your reasons for quitting, you will have a better chance of success", "When you quit smoking, you take control of your health. You save your money. You look healthy. You feel healthy", and "If no one smoked, 430,000 lives would be saved in the United States each year." These messages were in contrast to the negatively framed ones: "If you do not hold on to your reasons for quitting, you will have a greater chance of failure", "If you continue smoking, you are not taking control of your health. You waste your money. You look unhealthy. You feel unhealthy", "Because people smoke, 430,000 lives are lost in the United States each year." These researchers found that participants in the positive-frame condition were significantly more likely to report continuous abstinence from smoking.[9]

One final example before I move on. In the early part of 2020 during the COVID-19 pandemic, the New Zealand government decided to award a lump-sum amount to retirees and other beneficiary recipients to help with heating bills in winter. (Remember that in the Southern Hemisphere, March–April–May is autumn and June–July–August is winter.) However, those who were well-off had the option of opting out and not taking this benefit. A colleague of mine at Auckland, Susan St John, argued persuasively that the government could have saved a significant amount of money if, instead, they had asked people to opt in, in the sense that the ones who really needed the help could ask for it, but the ones who did not could do nothing and would have automatically not received the payment.

CASE STUDY 3.3 FRAMING AND MARKETING

I end this section with two light-hearted examples. The first one is taken from Tim Harford's excellent book, *The Undercover Economist*. The information is dated but still makes the point. Harford presents the following menu from the Starbucks on The Strand in London.

Cappuccino	*£1.85*
Hot Chocolate	*£1.89*
Caffe Mocha	*£2.05*
White Chocolate Mocha	*£2.49*
Venti White Chocolate Mocha	*£3.09*

On the face of it, this looks great; lots of interesting choices. Then Harford presents what he calls the "English translation" of the same menu.

Cappuccino (no frills)	*£1.85*
Hot Chocolate (no frills)	*£1.89*
Mix them together (I feel special)	*£2.05*
Use different powder (I feel very special)	*£2.49*
Make it huge (I feel greedy)	*£3.09*

The point is that every single item on the menu costs about the same to produce. After all, it does not cost a whole lot more to make a larger cup of coffee, squirt flavoured syrup, sprinkle chocolate powder or add whipped cream. Yet, the above menu can be very useful in separating the price sensitive customers (the ones buying regular coffee) from the ones who are not so sensitive to the price (the ones ordering the Venti White Chocolate Mocha).[10]

The other similar example comes from Dan Ariely's book *Predictably Irrational*. He highlights the subscription options for *The Economist*.

Internet only: *$59 per year*
Print only: *$125 per year*
Print plus internet: *$125 per year*

Guess what most people do with a pricing scheme such as this. Most people go for the third "Print-plus-internet" option. Why not; you are getting the print version for the same price and on top of that, you are getting the online option for free! Except, the vast bulk of these people will end up reading the magazine online and will never flip through the pages of the printed version. They would be far better off paying $59 per year for the internet only option.

Anchoring

It is often the case in life that we do not evaluate events or outcomes *de novo*, but, rather, start from a reference point, which is usually some sort of status quo. This typically leads to anchoring effects. Some examples will make this easier to understand. Researchers and lecturers around the world carry out the following exercise with a group of people, usually their students. The students are asked to pick small identical slips of paper from a box. The students do not know this but the slips have only one of two numbers written on them: either 10 or 65. So, half of the students get a slip of paper with 10 on it, while the other half gets a slip with 65. Then they are asked to answer the following question: "How many countries are there in the continent of Africa?". The correct answer is 54. But, on average, members of the group who were given 10 will always chose a lower number than those who received 65. It is a trivial thing that has no connection with the Africa question but the act of picking a smaller number establishes a lower anchor (reference point) for one group, while the act of picking a larger number establishes a higher anchor for the other group.

Here is another example. A group of people were split into two. Both were asked about the height of Redwood trees. Except, one group was asked: "Is the height of the tallest Redwood tree more or less than 1,200 feet? What is your best guess?" The other group was asked: "Is the height of the tallest Redwood more or less than 180 feet? What is your best guess?" The average answer for the first group was 844 feet and that for the latter was 282 feet! So, one way to think of anchoring is: *Anchoring = priming plus reference point*. There is a priming element to this via the suggestion of higher or lower numbers. This prime helps to establish the reference point: Are there ten countries in Africa, or 65? Is the tallest Redwood 1,200 feet or 180 feet? But once the reference point has been established, further calculations are done as deviations from that reference point. The "10" group moves up since they know that ten is too few. The "65" group moves down since they feel that 65 is too many. The 180 feet primed group moves up since they are sure that Redwoods are taller than that, while the 1,200 feet primed group moves down since they know that is too much (roughly a 120 storey building), but they cannot escape the inevitable lure of the reference point and adjust up or down rather than starting from scratch and asking: "How tall do I think Redwood trees are?"

We can calculate an *anchoring index* for these problems. In the Redwood trees example, the high anchor is 1,200 feet while the low anchor is 180 feet. This is a difference of 1,020 feet. The average guess by the high anchor group is 844 feet while the average guess by the low anchor group is 282 feet. The anchoring index is defined as

Anchoring index

$$= \frac{\text{Average guess by high prime group} - \text{Average guess by low prime group}}{\text{Value of high prime} - \text{Value of low prime}}.$$

In this case, the numerator is 844 − 282 = 562 feet, while the denominator is 1,020 feet. So, the anchoring index is (562/1020) = 0.55. If the primes are not influential at all and the guesses made by the two differently primed groups are exactly equal, then the anchoring index is zero. On the other hand, if the primes are completely successful and the everyone in the high anchor group chooses exactly the high anchor value as his/her guess while all members of the low anchor group choose exactly the low anchor value, then the index will equal 1.

This matters in different ways. And, as always, this is not just regular people. Professionals fall prey to this as much as the rest of us. In one study by Gregory Northcraft and Margaret Neale, a group of seasoned real estate professionals were shown a house and an asking price. As always, one half of the group saw a high asking price while the second group saw a low asking price. Then, the two groups were asked for their best guess. Not surprisingly, the guesses were far apart, with an anchoring index of 0.41. This implies that if, for example, the high anchor is $100,000 more than the low anchor, then the average guess of the high anchor group was approx. $41,000 more than that of the low anchor group. Furthermore, the real estate agents were absolutely confident in their ability to come up with a reasonably accurate price for the house and were certain that the asking price shown to them at the beginning of the exercise had absolutely no influence on their price predictions.

But, such anchoring also works in other insidious ways. Iris Bohnet is the Academic Dean of Harvard Kennedy School and does a lot of work looking at ways to improve gender equality. She is the author of a critically acclaimed book: *What Works: Gender Equality by Design*. Bohnet talks about how worker evaluations are undertaken at most companies, including educational institutions. Typically, the worker is asked to undertake a self-evaluation, which is then forwarded to the line manager, who usually has a performance appraisal meeting with the worker prior to making a final performance evaluation. Such evaluations are crucial in terms of promotions, merit increases in pay and performance bonuses. This sounds like a robust consultative process; what can go wrong? It turns out that women routinely underestimate their own performance and provide lower ratings for their own performance than men do for their own performance. Guess what? Managers realize this and they do make some adjustments; upwards for women and downwards for men. But, just like everyone else, managers also become anchored by the initial evaluations. So, even after the adjustments are made, women typically end up with lower ratings than men since their evaluations started from a lower anchor.

Confirmation bias

By the time this book is published, we will know the result, but as I write this in the early part of 2020, New Zealand is poised to have a general election in October 2020.[11] The general election will also include a referendum on legalizing marijuana in New Zealand. It is highly likely that as the election and the referendum roll around, there will be lots of discussion around the issue of marijuana, all the pros and cons of legalizing it. Except, chances are, that those who are opposed to it now will still be opposed, while those who are supportive will remain supportive in spite of the chatter on talk-radio, television, in print media and on social media. This is because of something called *confirmation bias*; by and large, we pay attention to information that bolsters our already preconceived notions about things. System 1 does not do very well in terms of looking for disconfirming evidence. This is primarily because looking for disconfirming evidence is effortful rather than intuitive and does not come easily to us.

For instance, suppose you believe that marijuana use is associated with increased juvenile delinquency. Is this right or not? In order to think through this problem, you really need to consider four different groups of people: (1) *Marijuana users who are delinquent*; (2) *Marijuana users who are not delinquent*; (3) *Delinquents who do not use marijuana*; (4) *Non-delinquents who do not use marijuana*. But if you are already convinced that marijuana use causes delinquency, then you will primarily be looking for support for the first of the outcomes above whereas, if you are in favour of legalizing marijuana, then you will keep thinking of all the people you know who smoke pot and never committed any crimes, or all the criminals you know who committed crimes while high on something other than marijuana. But often in order to arrive at the correct answer, we need to look for disconfirming evidence rather than asking questions that bolster our prior position.

Consider Figure 3.12, which shows four cards. Suppose I tell you that these four cards obey the following rule: *If a card has an odd number on one side then it has a vowel on the other side.* Which two cards do you need to turn over in order to prove or disprove this rule? The vast majority of people say: The "3" card and the "A" card. This is incorrect. You certainly need to turn over the "3" card to see if there is a vowel on the other side. But, turning over the "A" card is not useful. The rule did not say anything about a card with a vowel on one side. It is asking about cards that have an odd number on one side. How do you disprove this rule? You do this by turning over the "non-vowel" "C" card. If the "C" card has an odd number on the opposite side, then you have disproved the rule.[12]

It turns out that people are terrible at this. Go ahead, try it out. Take the above problem and test a bunch of your friends who have not taken this course or read this book. See if they pick the "3" card and "C" card; chances are, virtually all of them pick the "3" card correctly but then choose the "A" card, which is incorrect.

There is a silver lining though. While it turns out that most people are not good at this task when placed in an abstract context of numbers, vowels and consonants; they do get better at it if you provide an explicit context. Here is a problem I pose to my students.

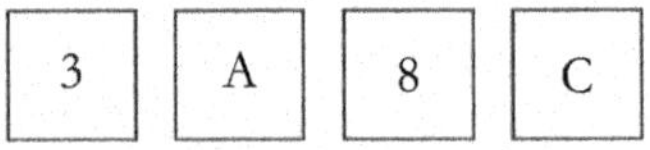

| 3 | A | 8 | C |

Figure 3.12
Four cards

Suppose you are in charge of enforcing safe drinking rules in a restaurant, which caters to young and old. Obviously, the restaurant must abide by the law, which says: *If you are drinking alcohol, then you must be 21 or above.* Obviously, you cannot go around and check every single patron, so you are constrained to a few random checks. Whom should you check?

Once again, our intuition tells us that we need to check people who are drinking, which is correct, and then people who are 21 or older. The latter is, of course, incorrect. This is because there is no compulsion that everyone who is 21 or older needs to be drinking. So, checking the above-21 group does nothing to prove or disprove this rule. What do you need to check in order to make sure that the rule is being followed? You need to check those (or at least some of those) who look younger than 21 and make sure that they are not drinking. So, to establish that the rule is being followed, you will need to check a few people who are drinking to confirm that they are 21 or above (*this is the* modus ponens *part "if P then Q"; if drinking then must be 21 or older*), and then check a few of those who look younger than 21 to confirm that they are not drinking (*this is the* modus tollens *part, which says that you must show "if not Q then not P", or, in other words, if younger than 21 then must not be drinking*).

But, while people do manage to do better on the second type of problem than the first, in the sense that more people get the answer correct for the latter problem than the former, you should not assume that people are generally good at this. There are plenty of examples of people acting on the basis of confirmation bias. I conclude this section by providing one, which goes a long way in explaining some of the political polarization we see around us in recent times.

Charles Lord, Lee Ross and Mark Lepper, of Stanford, had 48 undergraduates, who either supported or opposed capital punishment, look at two purported studies, one seemingly confirming and one seemingly disconfirming their existing beliefs about the deterrent effects of the death penalty. As the authors conjectured, both proponents and opponents of capital punishment rated the study results that confirmed their own beliefs to be the more convincing, resulting in corresponding shifts in their beliefs. The net effect was an increase in attitude polarization. Lord and his colleagues comment:

> People who hold strong opinions on complex social issues are likely to examine relevant empirical evidence in a biased manner. They are apt to accept "confirming" evidence at face value while subjecting "disconfirming" evidence to critical evaluation, and, as a result, draw undue support for their initial positions from mixed or random empirical findings. Thus, the result of exposing contending factions in a social dispute to an identical body of relevant empirical evidence may be not a narrowing of disagreement but rather an increase in polarization.

Hindsight bias

You are on a road-trip with your spouse driving. You approach a fork in the road and your spouse turns right. An hour later, it is clear you are completely lost. You say: "I knew we should have turned left". You have just finished presenting the results of a months-long study on consumer preferences for your company's products. A Senior Executive speaks up and says: "I don't know why we spent so much time and money on this. I could have told you what the results were going to be".

This type of behaviour often goes by the name of *hindsight bias*. And, as they say, hindsight is 20/20! In retrospect, we all know better; we all knew what the right course of action was all along. Baruch Fischhoff of Carnegie Mellon has done extensive work in this area. One study Fischhoff carried out goes like this. Immediately prior to Richard Nixon's historic trip to China, Fischhoff and his collaborators asked a group of respondents to rate the likelihood of certain events, such as: Nixon will meet with Chairman Mao, Nixon will declare the event a success, etc. Following the trip, those same respondents were brought back. Of course, now everyone was aware exactly which of those events had transpired. The respondents were now asked: how did they think they had rated the likelihood of each of those events before they had taken place? Needless to mention, for all the events that had actually happened, respondents thought that they had assigned a much higher likelihood to those events in the ratings they gave prior to those events actually happening. Given that Fischhoff and his collaborators had data on those predictions prior to the events, they could easily compare the two sets of predictions: (i) predictions before the event and (ii) predictions after the event of how they had predicted those events before the events happened. It is hardly necessary to say that they did not match up. Knowing what had actually transpired made people believe that they had known all along as to what would transpire. They were much more likely to say that they had actually predicted the events that happened (or assigned high probability to events that ended up happening). Fischhoff summarized it in one of his articles succinctly: "Hindsight is not equal to foresight". Knowledge of an outcome increases our beliefs about the degree to which we could have predicted that outcome *ex ante* (beforehand). A key problem with hindsight bias is that it prevents us from learning from our mistakes and taking lessons that can prevent the same mistake in the future. A possible remedy is to invest in acquiring hindsight; think of what could go wrong. This is a problem for lots of areas of public policy as well as medical decision making. If the patient has died and the surgeon is now sure that he knew all along what the problem was, then why did he not end up with a better outcome?

The $20 auction and the sunk cost fallacy

I often carry out this exercise in my classes. Plenty of others (such as Max Bazerman at Harvard Business School) do too, with similar results. I start my lecture by taking a $20 note out of my wallet and tell my students that I was going to sell it to the highest bidder. I then invite students to bid on it with one small caveat. This is an "all pay" auction. That means that everyone who bids an amount must pay the highest amount that they bid, *even if they are eventually outbid by someone else*, with only the highest bidder winning the money. But the losers must also pay whatever they bid. This is not as unusual as you think and there are plenty of real-life examples. Think about running for public office in the US. Every candidate spends substantial amounts of money, but there can only be one winner, with the expenses incurred by everyone else providing no benefit. Similarly, as I write this in the middle of the COVID-19 pandemic, companies around the world are in a mad race to develop a vaccine. They will spend billions of dollars in doing so, and finally, only one (or a handful) of them will be successful; the one or ones whose vaccine eventually goes to the market.

As my $20 auction starts, there is a general sense of amusement: a titter here, a nervous chuckle there. But eventually, someone or the other takes the plunge and bids $1. If the bidding stops there, then this person would have won $20 for $1 and will be better off by $19.

But soon, others join the fray and the bid amounts start to increase. Pretty soon, bids start to approach $20, and in most cases, they go over; people actually start to bid more than $20 for $20! Why? Suppose you have bid $20 while someone outbids you by going up to $21. If this person wins the $20, then this person has lost $1, while by being outbid you are now looking at losing the entire $20 you bid. (Bear in mind that if there are two people, one of whom has bid $20 and the second $21, then I, as the auctioneer, am looking at making $41 for a $20 note.) So, even though people have to bid above $20, they do it, because now it is a question of minimizing losses. I usually stop once the bids go above $20 and do not take money from the students. But, if I did, I could make a hefty amount if I wanted.

This behaviour lies at the crux of the sunk cost fallacy; the idea that people often pursue goals even when the benefits fall short of the costs. People do not want to stop because they have already invested time, money, etc., and if they stop, they lose what they have already invested. This is a clear violation of the principles of utility maximization we discussed in a previous chapter; one where we are expected to carefully consider the marginal benefits and marginal costs. But we get trapped in this behaviour often. Countries keep on fighting ruinous wars even when it is clear that nothing remotely resembling victory is possible. Candidates keep campaigning even when it is clear that the additional costs of doing so will outweigh any potential benefits, given the virtually zero chance of victory.[13] Actually, the fact that they have incurred substantial costs is the reason for doubling down and getting in deeper. This is analogous to the situation where we buy tickets to watch a film but, halfway through viewing it, we realize that it is terrible. Any additional benefit of continuing to watch the film is simply not worth our time. But we still watch it till the end because we have spent money on the ticket. But the money for the ticket is a sunk cost in any case; we will not get this back regardless of whether we finish watching the film or not. But the fact that we have incurred a cost, even if sunk, often makes us stick it out, see things through to the end, even if any potential benefit falls far short of the cost. And no, policy makers are not immune to the sunk cost fallacy. If anything, they may be even more prone to this type of thinking.

CASE STUDY 3.4 THE STORY OF AUCKLAND'S CITY RAIL LINK

A few years ago, the city of Auckland embarked on an ambitious infrastructure project of building an inner-city rail tunnel in order to provide commuters to Auckland's Central Business District a quicker commute. In the aftermath of the COVID-19 pandemic, my Auckland colleague, Tim Hazledine, wrote an article calling for the entire project to be scrapped.[14] He argued that this was a classic example of the sunk cost fallacy. According to Tim, when the City Rail Link was first proposed, those faster commutes were estimated to be worth (on a net present value basis) about $2 billion, and the construction cost was originally estimated to be about $2 billion also. Then, in April 2019, with $700 million already spent, the costs were revised upward to $4.4 billion with no change in the estimated benefits and no guaranteed finish date.

> In April 2020, the City Rail Link management announced that, because of COVID-19, costs would rise further and the impending May budget should make allowances for this. No mention was made of the possibility that COVID-19 may actually reduce the benefits of the rail link, through more people continuing to work at home rather than commute. Tim added:
>
> Adding in some substantial costs missing from the official calculations, the costs of disruption to business and citizens during the build, and the cost of the huge subsidy on the price of rail tickets, it seems sadly reasonable to predict that we now have a $5 billion+ monster on our hands. Even with more sunk costs incurred since last year, we are looking, in the best scenario, at having to fork out another $4 billion to finish a possibly $2 billion value project.

CHOICE OVER TIME: SMALLER–SOONER VERSUS LARGER–LATER REWARDS

One particular situation where the conflict between System 1 and System 2, between acting instinctively versus engaging in effortful deliberation, becomes especially salient is when it comes to making choices over time. Psychologists often refer to this as choosing between *smaller-sooner* versus *larger-later* rewards. Usually, when confronted with a reward, our instinctive impulse is to grab it; without realizing that if we could restrain ourselves and exercise some self-control, then we may well end up with a larger reward, albeit at a later date.

Walter Mischel (1930–2018) was a psychologist at Columbia University. He is credited with having devised the *marshmallow test* paradigm in the 1990s.[15] Here is what Mischel did. He brought a large number of young children into a room, one at a time. Each child was presented with a marshmallow on a plate and given the following choice. They could eat the marshmallow if they wished. But if they waited for a span of time, say 10–15 minutes, then they could have two marshmallows. With that, the experimenter walked off, leaving the child in the room alone with the marshmallow. So, the choice for the child is simple: enjoy one marshmallow now, or wait 15 minutes and double your marshmallow endowment; a stark choice between a smaller-sooner or larger-later reward. As you can guess, some children went ahead and ate the marshmallow in front of them, while others exercised self-control and held out for the second marshmallow. Mischel and his collaborators then tracked these children over a number of years and made a startling discovery. The children who were able to exercise self-control and delay gratification by holding out until they received a second marshmallow ended up with more successful outcomes in life, in terms of things like school performance. This line of work has shown that the ability to delay gratification early in life can be a good predictor of success later in life.

What does children choosing to eat one marshmallow now or two marshmallows later have to do with the rest of us? This entire parable is not about marshmallows; it is about the ability to delay gratification or hold out for a larger-later reward as opposed to grabbing the smaller-sooner one. These kinds of choices arise for us adults all the time; for instance, when we make choices over time such as whether and how much to save. Earlier in this chapter, I discussed issues of framing choices. I suggested that changing the default rule can result in more people signing up for retirement savings schemes. In doing so, these people are typically much better off post-retirement, in the sense of having higher savings than those who chose not to join a similar scheme. This decision is also a choice between smaller-sooner versus larger-later rewards. Should I take what is left of my salary after paying for essentials like rent and groceries and spend it on current consumption, for example, electronics, holidays, etc.? Or should I defer some of this, save this money, earn interest on it, so that I have a larger amount later on? This is not to suggest that one should not enjoy the pleasures of life, but the issue is one of balance: doing too much consumption may mean not having enough left over for retirement. Of course, you also do not need to overdo the savings bit, since all work and no play is no fun. Once again, this gets down to the question of trade-offs and opportunity costs.

The choice between whether to consume now or save up money for retirement is similar to investment decisions, where the returns of the investment will occur at a later point in time. Say Jessica has saved up NZ $1,000 from her babysitting jobs. Should she buy the new iPhone 11 or save this money? Buying the new iPhone will certainly make her quite happy. The alternative for Jessica would be to put this money into an interest-bearing account, such as a term deposit. Given that Jessica's dad does some day-trading, she could also ask him to invest this money for her into buying a financial asset. This would imply that Jessica will have more than $1,000 in the future so she can buy the iPhone plus something else, say Beats Solo 3 wireless headphones. The question is: would the second alternative offer greater happiness than buying the iPhone now? If it does, then Jessica would be well advised to save the $1,000 and invest it in an interest-bearing financial asset. This then, is the version of the marshmallow test that Jessica is facing. Buy the iPhone now, or wait and buy the iPhone plus the headphones in, say, one year from now.

The basic question here is: when someone like Jessica is considering an investment where the returns are available at a later date, how does she equate returns at different points in time? Or in other words: what is a particular sum now worth in the future? Another way of asking the same question is: what is something available in the future worth now?

While this can refer to any choices such as marshmallows or iPhones, it is easier to calculate the trade-offs if we convert it into monetary amounts. So, the question is: does Jessica buy something with her $1,000 today or wait? To keep things simple, let us assume that if Jessica chooses to invest her money, then it will be locked in for one year and she will only be able to get the (hopefully) higher amount in one year's time. So, how much is today's $1,000 worth in one year's time? Of course, this depends on the interest rate. (Since this is not a course in macroeconomics, we will ignore inflation so that the purchasing power of $1 today is the same as that of $1 in one year's time. This does not do any harm to our arguments; so, as economists like to say: we can do this without any loss of generality.)

Suppose the interest rate is 10%. How much will today's $1,000 be worth in one year's time? It will be worth $1,100, since Jessica will earn $100 worth of interest on her $1,000 investment. The interest earned is the opportunity cost of spending the $1,000 right now instead of waiting and earning $1,100 in one year's time. Of course, the opportunity cost should also factor in the length of the delay: is it one year or two years or three years or more? For the time being, and to keep things simple, I will assume that the choice is between now and one year's time.

Now let me ask you a different question; actually, two questions.

Question 1: Would you take $1,000 today or $1,100 in one month from today?

Question 2: Would you take $1,000 in one year from today or $1,100 in one year and one month from today?

You have to make a commitment today by choosing one option for Question 1 and one option for Question 2. Essentially, Question 1 is asking you to choose between $1,000 today and $1,100 in one month. Question 2 is taking the exact same choice and shifting it out one year in the future. So, effectively, you will have the same choice in one year's time: $1,000 today or $1,100 in one month. The choices are the same. Except, you are being asked what *you will choose today* and *what you think you will choose in exactly one year's time*.

If you are consistent, then you should do one of the following. Either, for the first question, you choose $1,000 today, and for the second question, you pick $1,000 in one-year from today. This means that your utility calculation is such that, in both cases, you prefer the smaller-sooner reward of $1,000 rather than waiting for the larger-later reward of $1,100. Or, you choose $1,100 in one month from today for Question 1, and $1,100 in one year and one month from today for Question 2. Here, you are happy to delay gratification and hold out for the larger-later reward in both cases.

But, confronted with these choices, a significant proportion of respondents choose $1,000 today over $1,100 in one month for Question 1, but they then go on to say that they prefer $1,100 in one year and one month over $1,000 in one year for Question 2. So, they are not willing to wait one month to get an extra $100 now, but they are sure that in exactly one year's time, when confronted the exact same choice, they will be willing to wait for the larger reward! We are *patient in the future*. Individuals with such preferences are described as *present-biased*. This is why we say things like the following: Next month, I'll quit smoking. Next week, I'll catch up on the required reading. Tomorrow morning, I'll wake up early and exercise. After Christmas, I'll start eating better. Next month, I'll start saving for retirement.

We are not willing to give up the smaller-sooner reward now, but we are sure that we will be able to do so tomorrow or in one week or in one year. Of course, when that time comes, whether it is tomorrow or next week or next year, we are faced with the same choices and take the smaller-sooner reward while hoping to do better in the future's tomorrow, or the future's next week, and so on. This is also why most of us are doomed to fail in following through with our New Year's resolutions, no matter how much we promise to hold ourselves to them. As Richard Thaler points out: the bias is systematically (if not universally) in favour of the present. For instance, you seldom (never?) hear statements like the following: I plan to watch more TV next year. I plan to eat more cookies next year. I plan to smoke more cigarettes next year. I plan to borrow more on my credit card next year. I plan to exercise less next year.

What does "present bias" mean?
The material in this section is somewhat technical and many readers may wish to skip this. For those interested, I am going to try and explain some of the intuition here. In doing so, I will be making some simplifications. The papers and models that deal with present bias can be complex. I am certainly not going to do justice to the complexities here. But I feel that it might be useful for some to get a flavour of these ideas and those who find this of interest can pursue this later.

The issue of present bias is tied closely to the concept of discounting future pay-offs, though they are not the same. In one sense, we can think of present bias as discounting the future "too much", that is, putting much less weight on future pay-offs than we should. It is also possible to think of "present bias" as a situation where how much we discount future pay-offs changes over time. It is important to understand that, depending on how one views the future (or one's probability of reaching that future), present bias may be perfectly reasonable. I am going to try to provide a broad overview of why people seem to make inconsistent choices in the examples given above.

I need to emphasize that there are actually two related, yet distinct, questions here. The first of these is the choice between smaller-sooner and larger-later rewards. This has to with self-control and the ability to delay gratification. A number of behavioural problems, such as addiction, can be explained by appealing to an inability to delay gratification. The other issue here is that we are often unable to resist the smaller-sooner reward in the present, but believe that we will be able to do so in the future.

Why do we choose $1,000 today instead of $1,100 in one month? And if so, why are we so convinced that we would choose differently in one year's time? Why do we choose the chocolate cake over celery sticks for an afternoon snack today but believe firmly that we will choose the celery sticks if given the exact same choice tomorrow (or next week)? When given a choice between a high-brow film or a low-brow one this weekend, why do we choose the low-brow film but are certain that we will choose the high-brow one if given the same choice in a week's time?

We cannot resist the impulse now but believe that we will be able to resist the impulse in the future. But this belief in the degree of patience of our future selves makes it even more difficult for our current selves to exert self-control. We think: it does not matter if I give in to my impulses now because I will do much better (start exercising, smoke less, drink less, eat less fatty food and so on) tomorrow or in one week or one month or one year.

But, before I can explain this, I need to revisit Jessica and her choices. Should Jessica take the $1,000 today or hold out for a larger sum tomorrow? What is this larger sum? If the interest rate is 10%, then in one year this sum will be $1,100. Does Jessica want something more than $1,100? Maybe Jessica is extremely impatient and finds waiting painful. (As a child she always preferred one marshmallow now over two in 15 minutes.) Or not. Maybe, Jessica realizes the value of waiting to get an extra $100 in interest. In order to understand Jessica's choice, we need two separate concepts. The first is the prevailing interest rate in the market, which is the same for everyone, and the second is more personal and relates to Jessica's own degree of patience. Obviously, this second factor relating to the degree of patience will be likely to vary from one person to the next.

In order to better grasp this issue, we need to use the concept of *net present value*. Given a choice between $1,000 today and $X in one year, which would you choose? How large does $X need to be? The economist's answer is: this depends on the prevailing interest rate. Sometimes, the *interest rate* is also referred to as the *discount rate*. (Going forward, please bear in mind that the interest rate and the discount rate mean the same thing and can be used interchangeably.) Let us continue with the assumption that the interest rate (discount rate) is 10%. So, $1,000 today is worth [$1000+[(0.10)*$1000]] = [(1+0.10)*$1000] = [(1.10)*$1000] = $100 in one year. This implies that if Jessica's choices are governed by only the prevailing

■ Gut feelings and effortful thinking

market interest rate, then she should be indifferent between $1,000 today and $1,100 in one year. So, if Jessica is perfectly consistent, then only the current interest rate should matter for her as she calculates the trade-off between spending $,1000 now or waiting for $1,100 in one year. This, in turn, allows us to calculate Jessica's discount factor.

In order to define the discount factor, we need to turn this question on its head by asking: What is $1,100 in one year's time worth today? The answer is $1,000. How do we know this? We, of course, know this already because we have calculated this above. But, notice that if $1,000*(1.10) = $1,100, then that also implies that $1,000 = \dfrac{\$1100}{1.10}$. Now, how did we get to 1.10? We got there by adding {1 plus 0.10}, or in other words, {1 plus the interest rate of 10% (0.10)}. Let us use δ to denote the discount factor. In this instance, we will define the discount factor as $\delta = \dfrac{1}{1.10}$ or $\delta = 0.909$. But, more generally, the discount factor is defined as $\delta = \dfrac{1}{1+\text{interest rate}} = \dfrac{1}{1+\text{discount rate}}$. If the interest rate (discount rate) is 10%, then the discount factor is 0.909. If the interest rate is 5%, then the discount factor is given by $\delta = \dfrac{1}{1+\text{interest rate}} = \dfrac{1}{1+0.05} = \dfrac{1}{1.05} = 0.952$. If the interest rate is 20%, then the discount factor is 0.83. The higher the interest rate, the smaller the value of the discount factor. This is simply because when the interest rate is higher, the opportunity cost of spending $1,000 now is also higher. It is more costly to not save $1,000 if the interest rate is 20% as opposed to if it is 5%. With 20% interest, Jessica is giving up $200 in interest, while with 5%, she is foregoing $50.

But, as I note above, Jessica's discount factor may or may not be the same as the one dictated by the market interest rate. She may have a more or less patient disposition. This implies that in order to not spend the $1,000 and save it, she requires an interest rate that is higher than the current market interest rate. So, people are willing to wait one year for a return that is equal to the market interest rate or higher. Unless you are a stoic or a masochist, it is highly unlikely that anyone will choose to wait for one year to get *less than* the market interest rate. So, it seems reasonable to assume that most of us are happy to settle for the current market interest rate or something more than that.

So, what rate Jessica is willing to settle for may well depend on her psychological disposition and how patient she is. At one extreme, she can be fully rational and use the market interest rate as her reference point. Or she may be looking to get a higher return than that. Let us think of this rate as Jessica's *implicit discount rate (implicit interest rate)*, the interest rate that she wants, in order to forego spending the $1,000 today. Suppose her implicit discount rate is 20%, while the actual market interest rate is 10%. This means Jessica is willing to take $1,000 today but she is willing to wait if she can get [$1000*(1+0.20)] = [$1000*(1.20)] = $1200 in one year's time. Another way of saying this is: Jessica is indifferent between $1,000 today and $1,200 in one year.

This, in turn, implies that the higher someone's implicit interest rate, the more that person will prefer smaller–sooner over larger–later rewards. Someone who is guided by the market interest rate is not impatient at all. But, as someone's implicit interest rate rises, the person needs a larger and larger sum of money in the future to make them willing to save $1,000 today. If Isha's implicit interest rate is 5%, then she is indifferent between $1,000 today and $1,050 in one year. If Ana's implicit interest rate is 10%, then Ana is willing to trade $1,000 today for $1,100 in one year. Jessica, with her 20% implicit interest rate is indifferent between $1,000 today and $1,200 in one year. If Avala's implicit interest rate is 25%, then Avala wants $1,250 in one year in return for $1,000 today. If Tingmeng wants $1,500 in one year in order to forego $1,000 today, then Tingmeng's implicit interest rate is 50%. This, in turn, also implies that out of all these people, Tingmeng is the most impatient. She needs the largest amount ($1,500) in one year's time, in order to save $1,000 today. Avala is less impatient than Tingmeng. Jessica even less than Avala, Ana even more so, and finally, Isha is the least impatient (most patient) of the lot since she is asking for the lowest implicit interest rate out of the five.

But here is an alternative way of thinking about this problem. Suppose Logan is looking at getting a series of $1,000 payments. To keep things simple, let us stick to two periods. So, Logan will get $1,000 today and $1000 in one year. $1,000 today is worth $1,000 today, but how much is $1,000 in one year's time worth today? Once again, we can apply the net present value formula. Suppose the prevailing discount rate (interest rate) is 10%, then $X today will be worth [$X*(1+0.1)] in one year. So, effectively the question we are asking is: what amount ($X) does Logan need to invest at 10% today to get a return of $1,000 in one year?

So, it must be the case that [$X*(1+interest rate)] = [$X*(1+0.10)] = [$X*(1.10)] = $1000. We have done this exercise above. We can write this as $X = [($1000)/(1.10)] = [(1/1.1)]*$1000 = $909. So, if the prevailing discount rate is 10%, then $909 today will be worth $1,000 in one year. Or, in other words, Logan should be indifferent between $909 today and $1,000 in one year. So, as we saw above, Logan's discount factor (δ) = (1/1.1) = 0.91 (approx.). Or, to repeat, the discount factor $\delta = \dfrac{1}{1+(\text{discount rate})}$, where the discount rate is the same as the prevailing market interest rate. This also implies that the following statements mean the same things. (a) Given the interest rate (discount rate) of 10%, Logan is indifferent between $909 today and $1,000 in one year. (b) Given the interest rate (discount rate) of 10%, Logan is indifferent between $1,000 today and $1,100 in one year.

If all that matters for Jessica or Logan is the discount factor (δ), then Jessica or Logan are behaving rationally. But, as we also noted above, for most people it is not the actual discount rate that matters, but the implicit discount rate, since different people differ in their degree of patience; their ability to delay gratification. People differ in how much you need to give them in the future, for them to forego a particular sum of money today.

Usually, for most people, behaviour is guided by the *beta-delta* ($\beta*\delta$) *model*. This is referred to as *quasi-hyperbolic discounting*. If $\beta = 1$; then $\beta*\delta = \delta$. Someone like this is perfectly happy to forego $1,000 today for $1,100 in one year with 10% interest rate. But this is not true for many who are less patient and for these people $\beta < 1$ or $\beta*\delta < \delta$. What are the implications of having a β of less than 1?

Suppose the prevailing interest rate (discount rate) is 5%. If Isha's discount factor (δ) is determined by exactly that discount rate, and Isha is fully rational, then for Isha, $\beta = 1$ and $\beta*\delta = \delta = [1/1.05] = 0.952$. For any investor whose decisions are guided by the prevailing market interest rate, $\beta*\delta = \delta = \dfrac{1}{1+\text{discount rate}(\text{interest rate})}$. Let us assume that *all* investors take the market interest rate as given, so that their discount factor (δ) is determined by the market interest rate. In other words, $\delta = \dfrac{1}{1+\text{discount rate}}$. If the discount rate is 5%, then δ is 0.952; if discount rate is 10%, then δ is 0.909; if discount rate is 20%, then δ = 0.83, and so on.[16]

■ Gut feelings and effortful thinking

But as we have seen, this is one extreme, and, for most people, their implicit interest rate is different from (higher than) the market discount rate. What I am saying is that we will assume that these individual differences are driven primarily by differences in β. If the prevailing interest rate is 5%, then Ana's δ is 0.952. But suppose, for Ana, β = 0.9. This means that Ana's β*δ = 0.857, which means that, for Ana, $1,000 in one year is worth approx. $857 today. But this also implies that Ana is effectively asking for an implicit discount rate of approx. 17%. This is because she will need to invest $857 at 17% in order to get $1,000 in one year. Taking another example, suppose Jessica's β = 0.8. Then Jessica's β*δ = 0.762 (assuming the prevailing interest rate is 5%, so δ = 0.952). This means that for Jessica, $1,000 in one year is worth approx. $762 today. In turn, this also means that Jessica is asking for an implicit interest rate of approx. 31%, since this is the interest rate that one needs in order to turn an investment of $762 today into $1,000 in one year.

To fix ideas, let us look at two extreme cases. If Jaclyn is completely present biased then her implicit interest rate is infinite, so that any future pay-off is worth zero! (1/infinity=zero!) Completely present biased means that no matter what the future pay-off is, Jaclyn will always take the amount available today. She has no patience at all and no matter how large the amount available in the future (how large the larger-later reward is), she will always choose the smaller-sooner reward. This in turn implies that for Jaclyn, β = 0 so that β*δ = 0. On the other hand, given a market interest (discount) rate of 5%, if Isha is indifferent between $1,000 today and $1,050 in one year, her behaviour is governed exactly by the prevailing discount (interest) rate. She is not present biased at all, so that for Isha, β = 1 and β*δ = δ. Her implicit interest (discount) rate is the same as the market interest (discount) rate.

The above then explains why some people are better at holding out for the larger-later reward than others. For the former group β is larger than the latter group. Now, let us turn to the other related question: why people prefer $1,000 today over $1,100 in one month while remaining convinced that they will take $1,100 in one year and one month instead of $1,000 in one year's time? They are unable to wait for the larger–later reward now but are sure they will be able to do so tomorrow/next week/next year.

Much of this has to do with the fact that we underestimate the power of β. Figure 3.13 highlights this point. Right now, we prefer to take the $1,000 rather than wait one month for

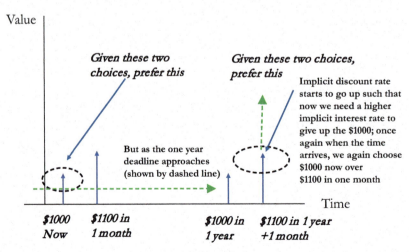

Figure 3.13
Time inconsistency

$1,100. But we are certain that we will be able to hold out in the future. And so, we indicate a preference for $1,100 in one year and one month. One year goes by and we are now faced with the *same choice* as right now. $1,000 today or $1,100 in one month! All of a sudden, waiting for the $1,100 in one month starts to look more challenging and we flip again, because in our minds we now need a higher than 10% interest rate to make the wait worth its while. It is as if, during the intervening period, our implicit discount rate has started to increase so that when the one year is over, we need much more than 10% to give up the smaller-sooner $1,000 in order to wait for the larger-later $1,100. We end up choosing the $1,000 again.

CASE STUDY 3.5 TYING ODYSSEUS TO THE MAST: HOW TO MAKE COMMITMENTS AND STICK TO THEM

So, are we doomed then? Are we always going to fall prey to choosing the smaller-sooner reward over the larger-later reward, hoping that it will not matter now since our future self will surely be patient enough to choose the larger-later reward? Not really. For one thing, just as Walter Mischel found with the children, there are individual differences; some of us have better self-control than others. So, not everyone is liable to fall into the trap. But, what if you do not have the requisite self-control? There are still things you can do to commit to the larger-later reward, but the first step is to understand that if your current self is not able to resist the temptation, then your future self will not be either. This is crucial. Better yet, assume that your future self will not be able to exercise self-control. The good news is that there are ways of doing this, and in order to do so, a good place to start is with the story of Odysseus, who is also known as Ulysses, as told in Homer's *Odyssey*.

The Trojan War is over and Odysseus is making his way back to his home in Ithaca. Odysseus is told by the Goddess Circe that his route back home will take him past the Island of the Sirens. The Sirens are mythological creatures who look like beautiful women and sing wondrous melodies to passing sailors. But, if and when sailors try to approach the island to listen to the songs from closer quarters, they end up wrecking their ships on the rocky shores and suffering a painful death. Odysseus knows that he needs to navigate his ship around this island. He also realizes that no matter what he thinks now, when they approach the island, he will give in to the temptation of listening to the songs from closer quarters, and he will most likely instruct his sailors to guide the ship closer to shore, thereby wrecking it. Odysseus is curious and does want to hear the sirens sing but he also wants to make sure that his future self is not in a position to jeopardize his own life and the lives of his sailors. So, what does he do?

He gets his sailors to tie him to the mast and he gives his sailors pieces of beeswax, which they can use to plug their ears. This way, Odysseus is sure they cannot hear him or the song of the sirens. In turn, they will not be tempted to row closer to shore and they will also ignore any entreaties from Odysseus to do so. Odysseus gets to hear the sirens, and as the ship goes by, he does repeatedly ask his crew to take him closer to the shore, but with their ears plugged, they cannot hear him. This way, Odysseus makes sure that they navigate the island safely. What Odysseus is really doing is making an up-front commitment of getting himself tied to the mast, so that no matter how much his future self wants to go closer to the island to listen to the Sirens' songs, the ship will be safe. So, in effect, Odysseus is forcing his future self to not deviate from the original plan.

It turns out that all of us can engage in similar commitments to make sure that we do not fall to preference reversals. There is considerable evidence out there. I will talk about work undertaken by Nava Ashraf of Harvard, Dean Karlan of Yale and Wesley Yin of Chicago. Ashraf and her colleagues travelled to the Philippines and partnered with the Green Bank of Caraga, a rural bank in Mindanao. First, they got a bunch of the bank's customers to answer questions like the ones we have seen before, to select for people who exhibit the type of preference reversals discussed above via quasi-hyperbolic preferences. Half of these people were offered a new account called SEED (Save, Earn, Enjoy deposits). The other half were either assigned to a control group that received no further contact, or a marketing group that received a special visit to encourage them to save more using the existing savings products available; so, this last group was asked to save more but not offered the opportunity of opening a SEED account.

The SEED account is purely a commitment device that restricts access to the deposits in that account per the client's instructions at the time of opening the account. But, other than that, the account offers no other advantages, and more importantly, does not offer a higher interest rate. There are three distinct features of these accounts. First, the depositors had to agree to restrict access to these funds until they had reached a goal. The goal could be a specific date or a specific amount. Out of 202 people who signed up for a SEED account, 140 chose a date (typically coinciding with a celebration) while 62 opted for an amount. In addition, all of these people were encouraged to set a specific savings goal, which would be written on a "Commitment Savings Certificate". Second, depositors could choose to get a piggy bank for a small fee. The piggy bank came with a lock that can only be opened by the bank and not the account holder. So, the depositor would actually have to go to the bank to take any money out of the piggy bank. But the lock is flimsy and could be broken easily. 167 out of 202 clients signed up for the piggy bank. Finally, clients also had the option of making automated direct deposits into the SEED account from other accounts, but very few opted for this option.

Ashraf and her colleagues found that, after twelve months, the average bank account savings of the SEED group was 411 pesos higher relative to the control group and represented an 81 percentage-point increase from pre-intervention saving levels. Given this, why do we not see more such commitment devices? Ashraf et al. point out that, at times, such commitments work in other ways. Christmas Clubs were popular in the US in the early 20th century; such clubs committed members to a schedule of deposits and restricted withdrawals. David Laibson of Harvard points out that, in recent years, defined contribution retirement plans, housing mortgages and withholding too much tax to be claimed back later serve as similar commitment devices. In

> many developing countries, individuals rely on informal rotating savings and credit organizations (ROSCAs), which are akin to Christmas Clubs. But why do formal banks not offer more of such devices? Ashraf et al. suggest that not enough people are aware of their quasi-hyperbolic preferences, and so the costs of offering such devices for formal banks probably outweigh their revenue earning potential.

CONCLUDING REMARKS

We have now come to the end of one of the longer chapters of this book. In this chapter, I have discussed the distinction between System 1 and System 2 thinking. System 1 is automatic; System 2 is deliberative. System 1 is like an elephant that lurches into action as soon as a stimulus presents itself. System 2 takes time to get engaged, but once it does, it serves as the rider trying to steer the elephant; possible but not necessarily easy. I have highlighted situations where relying on System 1 (or heuristics) can be useful. At times, this may depend on how much expertise or experience we have with the matter at hand. I have also shown that relying on heuristics can drive us astray at times. They can make us fall prey to systematic biases in our judgement such as priming, framing or anchoring. Yes, knowledge of these biases and acknowledgement of their existence allows us to better design choices and can help us nudge people in desirable directions, but, equally, we have seen that many of these biases have a "dark side", leading to unintended consequences such as with ethnic or racial stereotypes. This is not to suggest that heuristics are not useful, but they do require us to be mindful of the situation and ask whether we are utilizing the heuristic properly. Engaging System 2 requires effort but it is almost always useful to engage in effortful thinking; even if it is to simply decide: "No it is okay, we will be on the highway for a while so turning on cruise control is fine. We can reassess when we hit the next construction or traffic jam."

I have also shown that this conflict between System 1 and System 2 looms especially large when it comes to choosing between smaller-sooner and larger-later rewards. I pointed out that there are actually two related, but slightly different, issues here. The first is that we need to exert self-control (engage System 2) in order to delay gratification and hold out for the larger-later reward, rather than grabbing the smaller-sooner reward. The other issue is that we often fall into the trap of thinking that while we may not be able to resist the temptation today, we will be able to do so in the future. We are present biased right now, but patient in the future. This latter belief actually exacerbates the tendency to choose the smaller-sooner reward now. I have also discussed that one way to avoid falling into this trap is to make an active commitment, like Odysseus or the depositors in the Philippines who chose the SEED account, in order to tie your future self to the mast. But, doing so requires that you recognize and concede the fact that your future self will be no more patient than you are currently. If you are not aware of this part of your psyche, then you may not feel the need to adopt such commitment devices. But, on the basis of current evidence, I think it is safe to say that pretty much all of us can use such commitment devices in one activity or another: to tackle problems of smoking, drinking, overeating, under-saving for retirement or restricting screen time. I will end this chapter with one last case study that shows why reliance on heuristics can be bad for labour market outcomes of minorities.

■ Gut feelings and effortful thinking

CASE STUDY 3.6 ARE EMILY AND GREG MORE EMPLOYABLE THAN LAKISHA AND JAMAL?

It is well documented that there is significant racial inequality in the US labour market. Compared to European Americans, African Americans are twice as likely to be unemployed, and earn nearly 25% less when they are employed. In the early 2000s, Marianne Bertrand of Chicago and Sendhil Mullainathan of MIT set out to understand why. Before I get to Bertrand and Mullainathan's contribution, let me talk a little bit about standard theories for such disparate outcomes between the races. Even now, as you read this, your System 1 is thinking: of course, discrimination! Yes, possibly, but let us engage our System 2 for a minute and delve a little deeper.

Typically, economists make a distinction between two types of discrimination, taste based and statistical. Taste-based discrimination is exactly what it sounds like. Here, a White/Christian/Muslim/Jewish/High Caste/Male employer does not wish to offer employment to a Black/Muslim/Jewish/Muslim/Low Caste/Female employee, simply because the former does not wish to work with the latter. This kind of discrimination may actually be quite costly for the employer if he/she is passing up on highly qualified candidates. These employers would eventually start to lose out to other employers who do not engage in this type of discrimination. While taste-based discrimination is certainly around, it is on the wane, at least partially because of laws and regulations prohibiting such explicit discrimination.

An alternative to this type of discrimination is statistical discrimination. Here, employers may use an observable signal such as gender or ethnicity as a proxy for unobservable skills. For instance, when I was younger and single I paid more for car insurance than I do now. The assumption here is that a married, 50-something with children will be a safer driver and less prone to risk taking than an unmarried, single 25-year-old.

A slightly more sophisticated form of statistical discrimination assumes that signals may be more reliable for certain groups than others. So, the same level of education or a degree from the same college may be considered more credible for a white applicant than a black applicant. (Maybe the black applicant is not as good but got admitted due to affirmative action.)

Bertrand and Mullainathan set out to see which of these may explain why African Americans fare worse in the job market, compared to European Americans. First, using Census data, they created a set of popular names for children born to White parents such as Emily and Greg, and a separate list of most popular names preferred by Black parents. Then they undertook an experiment, where they sent out hundreds of resumes in response to help-wanted advertisements in Chicago and Boston newspapers. Typically, two resumes are identical except one has the name Emily Walsh or Greg Baker, while on others, the names are Lakisha Washington or Jamal Jones. Of course, they do more than that; some resumes are better in the sense that they show more qualifications or fewer gaps in employment history. But the point is the same: for each job, the employer will receive at least two identical resumes, one with a "white" sounding name and the second with a "black" sounding name.

In total, the authors responded to more than 1,300 employment ads, sending out nearly 5,000 resumes. The results indicate large racial differences in call-back rates to a phone line with a voice mailbox attached and a message recorded by someone of the appropriate race and gender. Job applicants with white names needed to send about ten resumes to get one call-back; those with African American names needed to send around 15 resumes to get the same result. Then the authors get down to teasing out which form of discrimination may lie at the heart of these disparate outcomes. This is a great paper and easy to read since it does not require a lot of technical knowledge. In the interest of parsimony, I am going to refrain from elaborating further on the details. The authors do not find evidence to support either of the two discrimination theories: taste-based or statistical. Instead, they find something else. I will let the authors tell you what their conclusions are.

> The uniformity of discrimination across occupations is also troubling for a statistical discrimination interpretation. ... These facts suggest that perhaps other models may do a better job at explaining our findings. ... Employers receive so many resumes that they may use quick heuristics in reading these resumes. One such heuristic could be to simply read no further when they see an African American name. Thus, they may never see the skills of African American candidates and this could explain why these skills are not rewarded.

NOTES

1. In biological terms, a Duchenne smile is impossible to fake and therefore provides a "hard to mimic" signal. Since we have no voluntary control over the muscles around our eyes, they will crinkle only when someone is smiling genuinely indicating pleasure or happiness. "Hard to mimic" means that you cannot willingly fake this.
2. These questions are taken from work done by Shane Frederick of the Yale School of Management and are part of what has come be to known as the cognitive reflection test (CRT). Frederick was trying to demonstrate how, in such problems, our instincts immediately come up with an answer, which upon reflection, turns out to be incorrect.
3. Centre for Strategic and International Studies (CSIS); https://csis.org.
4. This is taken from Daniel Kahneman's book *Thinking Fast and Slow*.
5. At the time, the New Zealand dollar was worth around 60 US cents.
6. Rigdon and her colleagues find that this greater increase in generosity is driven to a large extent by men, who become much more generous in the face condition as opposed to the control condition. For women, there is no difference. I am going to refrain from elaborating, since there is voluminous literature on gender differences in economic transactions. I have chosen not to explore this topic here. There are other books and papers which undertake comprehensive reviews of this topic, including my Harvard Kennedy School colleague Iris Bohnet's critically acclaimed book. *What Works: Gender Equality by Design*.
7. The National Geographic Channel has an excellent show called *Brain Games* hosted by Jason Silva. There is an episode on the Asch study using real participants. You can see it here: www.youtube.com/watch?v=BOBhKR4MK3w.
8. STEM stands for Science, Technology, Engineering and Mathematics.

9   I am grateful to Rebecca Yao at Harvard Kennedy School for providing me with this excellent example. I will have a bit more to say on this topic in the next chapter where I talk about prospect theory.
10 *Venti* is Italian for "twenty". The reason it is called "Venti" is that this largest serving from Starbucks is literally 20 oz. of coffee.
11 Update: Subsequent to this, in the October 2020 elections, the left of centre Labour Party led by Jacinda Ardern swept to power, handily defeating the right of centre National Party. The marijuana referendum lost by a razor-thin margin with 51% opposed and 49% voting in favour.
12 This is actually a problem of logic often referred to as *modus ponens* and *modus tollens*. The general proposition says that if you want to test the truth (or lack thereof) of a conditional proposition such as "*If P then Q*": then you must examine two things. First, does P imply Q? This implies that if the antecedent "P" holds, then the consequent "Q" may be inferred. This is the *modus ponens* part. But that is not sufficient. You must also show a second part. And the second part involves showing "not Q" implies "not P"; in other words, it is not enough to show that whenever P is true, Q must be true, but you must also show that whenever the consequent does not hold "not Q", then the negation of the antecedent "not P" may be inferred. This is the *modus tollens* part. In English, this implies that if you hold the view that "all marijuana smokers are delinquents", then you need to demonstrate that whenever you find a marijuana smoker, that person must be a delinquent. But this is not enough. You must also show that every person who is a non-delinquent is also a non-marijuana smoker. Simply showing the first part or showing that some marijuana smokers are also delinquents is not enough. So, if you want to establish or falsify the proposition "If rose then red", you need to show the following. First, all roses are red, and second, all non-red flowers are not roses. If you find a non-red rose then the rule has been falsified. The card choice task was introduced by Peter Cathcart Wason in 1968 as a test of deductive reasoning. This and other variants of this task are usually referred to as Wason Selection Tasks.
13 This lesson was driven home to my students and I by the campaign for the Democratic nomination in 2019–2020. It was a very large field with at least 18 candidates vying for the nomination. They were all spending lots of money on advertisements and maintaining field offices with support staff long after it was clear that many of them had no chance of securing the nomination. While the benefits in this particular instance are rather ambiguous, it is hard to imagine how even a liberal accounting of benefits could outweigh the costs beyond a certain point for some of the marginal candidates.
14 Hazledine, Tim. "Tank the Tunnel". Newsroom, May 11, 2020. www.newsroom.co.nz/ideasroom /2020/05/11/1162413/tank-the-tunnel.
15 You will find this more interesting if you take a look at some of these studies. You can do this by going to YouTube and searching for "marshmallow test" or "Walter Mischel" or both. I can guarantee that you will find the videos hilarious. If you want to waste some more time, then check out Justin Wilman, who has a very popular show called *Magic for Humans*. Search for his take on the marshmallow test. I am certain that you will enjoy it.
16 This is a gross simplification of the beta–delta model. It is also true that even the discount factor, δ, may vary from one person to the next. Here, we are making the simplifying assumption that the discount factor for everyone is based on the prevailing interest rate and that interest rate is also the same for everyone. So, any differences in how we value future pay-offs arises from β, which varies from one person to another.

4 Expected utility theory and prospect theory

In this chapter, I:

- *Extend the heuristics and biases literature presented in the previous chapter;*
- *Provide a quick overview of the canonical expected utility theory of economics;*
- *Discuss the Allais Paradox, that calls into question key assumptions of the expected utility model;*
- *Explore deviations from the canonical expected utility model;*
- *Provide an overview of Kahneman and Tversky's prospect theory, including the concepts of reference points, differential treatment of gains and losses and loss aversion;*
- *Utilize these concepts to discuss the principles of the endowment effect and overconfidence and their applications to economics.*

INTRODUCTION

You have all seen the signs specifying penalties for littering along highways. Have you ever wondered why the fines are so large? For instance, one sign might say that the fine for littering is US $2,000! Why is the fine for flicking a candy wrapper out of your car window so high? The answer is that, while the magnitude of the fine is very large, the *expected* fine is small. What is the expected fine? It is the magnitude of the fine multiplied by the probability of getting caught. You see, if everyone who littered got caught, then we could impose a $50 fine on everyone and this fine would likely be enough to deter litterbugs. But on a highway, what are the chances of actually getting caught? Is it 1 in 100? If so, then the expected fine for littering is (1/100)*$2,000 = $20. This is much smaller than $2,000 but still a substantial amount. Given the low probability of getting caught, in order to deter littering, the amount of the fine needs to be large.

This example demonstrates the concept of expected value. Lots of things in life are probabilistic. When I buy a big 75-inch OLED television, there is a chance that it could topple over and break, which may imply the need to have the super-cover warranty on it. If I go mountain climbing or downhill skiing I could fall and break a leg. This may require having adequate health insurance. Should I get flood insurance on my house? Well, that depends on the location of the house; how flood prone is the area? What is the probability of a flood? What is the expected loss in the event of a flood? How much will it cost me in ongoing insurance premia?

■ Expected utility theory and prospect theory

In New Zealand, as in many other countries around the world, such as Canada, healthcare is provided by a public system. This essentially means that if you have a heart attack or an accident, you can show up at your local hospital emergency room and they will take care of you. New Zealand does provide for private insurance. If you require treatments for non-life-threatening problems such as cataracts, hip replacements, kidney stones or a tonsillectomy, and you go to the public system, you may have to wait for a while until a suitable opening is available. But if you have private insurance, then you can get this addressed faster via the private system. So, should you have private insurance or not? It depends to an extent on your risk tolerance. Are you happy to wait for an opening in the public system or do you want to get this done immediately? As a result, a lot of people I know in New Zealand do not have private insurance. Some of them keep a sum of money aside in case of emergencies since you always have the option of paying out of your pocket in the private system. But it all comes down to expectations. What are your chances of developing kidney stones? What is your pain threshold? Are you willing to wait for the public system? Or do you want to spend the extra money to take out private insurance so that you can be treated immediately? Most of these outcomes pose a degree of uncertainty and what you decide to do is a matter of your perceptions of these risks.[1]

So, suppose you are asked to place a bet that a random card drawn from a deck of 52 cards is an ace. If the card turns out to be an ace then you win $5; otherwise you get nothing. What are the chances that a random card will turn out to be an ace? Four out of 52, or 1/13. So, there is only a 1 in 13 chance of you winning this bet. This means that if the prize is worth $5, then your expected winnings are (1/13)*$5, or just 38 cents. This means that, in expectation, you should expect to win only $0.38. So, if you paid $1 to buy a ticket for this lottery with a winning prize of $5, then you would expect to lose about $0.62. Even if the winning prize was $10 and you paid $1 for a ticket, you should expect to lose around $0.23. This is because with a prize of $10, your expected winnings are (1/13)*$10, which is around $0.77.

This is true of most gambling games. Even if the prize is very large, the probability of winning that prize is very small; meaning the expected value of the win is relatively small, which is why fines for littering need to be large in magnitude. So, suppose someone offers you the following bet. A ten-sided die is tossed. If the number "10" comes up, then you win $25. But if any of the other numbers, such as 1 through 9, come up, then you get nothing. Let's say that you can buy a ticket for $3 in order to accept this bet. Should you accept it? Probably not. Because, the chance of winning the $25 prize is 1/10. This means that your expected winnings is (1/10)*$25 = $2.50. But you are paying $3 to enter the game. Of course, once in a while someone will earn the grand prize of $25, but on average, you would expect to lose 50 cents per game: the expected win of $2.50 minus the ticket price of $3.

The same is true for most lotteries or casino games at a much larger scale. Even if the jackpot is very large, the probability of winning is vanishingly small. For example, suppose the jackpot for a particular lottery is $40 million and the ticket costs $25. Should you buy a ticket? It depends. Suppose, 5 million people buy tickets. Then your expected probability of winning is 1/5,000,000. This means that even if the jackpot is $40 million, the amount you expect to win is: (1/5,000,000)*(40,000,000) or $8. Of course, someone, or more than one, will win, but, on average, most people will lose and their expected loss is ($25-$8) =

90

$17. This implies that the expected value of any win is typically less than the price of the lottery ticket or the price of entering the casino game. This is why the house usually wins. Of course, people do routinely accept these bets and we will see shortly how this decision may be justified.

The expected value of a gamble is the sum of the value of each possible outcome multiplied by the probability of that outcome. For example, if there is a 70% chance of winning $500 and a 30% chance of losing $100, then the expected value of the gamble is (0.70)*(500) + (0.30)*(-100) = $320. The expected value is the amount I would earn per event on average if the event were repeated many times. Let us look at two different lotteries. Which would you prefer? (A) 50% chance of losing $100 and 50% chance of winning $500 or (B) 25% chance of losing $400, 25% chance of winning $100 and 50% chance of winning $600. What is the expected value of lottery A? 0.50*(-100) + 0.50*(500) = $200. The expected value of lottery B is 0.25*(-400) + 0.25*(100) + 0.50*(600) = $225. The expected value of the second lottery (B) is higher than the first (A) and so you should choose the second over the first.

Let us take another example. Which would you prefer? (C) 50% chance of losing $100 and 50% chance of winning $600 or (D) 25% chance of losing $400, 25% chance of winning $100 and 50% chance of winning $600. What is the expected value of lottery C? 0.50*(-100) + 0.50*(600) = $250. The expected value of lottery D is 0.25*(-400) + 0.25*(100) + 0.50*(600) = $225. In this case you should prefer the former (C) over the latter (D). So, in all these cases, the answer is clear. You should pick the lottery with the higher expected value.

One final example. Which would you prefer? (E) 50% chance of losing $100 and 50% chance of winning $500 or (F) 25% chance of losing $500, 25% chance of winning $100 and 50% chance of winning $600. What is the expected value of lottery E? 0.50*(-100) + 0.50*(500) = $200. The expected value of lottery F is 0.25*(-500) + 0.25*(100) + 0.50*(600) = $200. The expected values are equal and so in this final example, you should be indifferent between the two lotteries.

RISK NEUTRALITY AND RISK AVERSION

But, now consider the following lottery, which has come to be known as the St Petersburg Paradox. I explained this game back in Chapter 2 but, in case you do not recall this, let me describe the game once more. You are asked to toss a fair coin. The game ends as soon as tails comes up. If you get tails on the very first toss, then the game ends and you win $1. If tails comes up on the second toss, that is, the first toss is heads, followed by tails then you win $2. If the first two tosses are heads and the third is tails, then you win $4 and so on. So, with probability 1/2, you win $1; with probability 1/4 you win $2; with probability 1/8 you win $4; etc. How much should you be willing to pay for this gamble? The first step, of course, is to calculate the expected value of this lottery. What is the expected value? In order to calculate it, we first need to calculate the probability of getting tails for the first time, in a given round. The probability of getting tails on the very first toss is 1/2. The probability of getting tails for the first time on the second toss is 1/4. If you get a tails on the second toss, then you must have got heads on the first toss. So, the probability of tails on the second toss is Probability(Heads)*Probability(Tails) = (1/2)*(1/2) = 1/4. Following the same logic, the probability of getting tails for the first time on the third toss is Probability(Heads)*Probab ility(Heads)*Probability(Tails) = 1/8 and so on. How much should you expect to win on average? With probability 1/2 you win $1, with probability 1/4 you win $2, with probability 1/8 you win $4, etc. So, the expected value is ($0.50 + $0.50 + $0.50 + ...). The expected value of the game is infinite! Yet, few people would be willing to pay a lot of money to accept this gamble.

The resolution, proposed by Daniel Bernoulli in 1738, was that the "value" of this lottery is not the same as its monetary value.[2] Instead, people attach some subjective value, or "utility", to monetary outcomes. Thus, people do not seek to maximize expected values, but instead seek to maximize expected utility. The argument is that just as we get utility from consuming goods, so do we get utility from money (which can be used to buy goods). So, if Emma is looking at two monetary pay-offs (essentially two different levels of wealth) W_1 and W_2 with corresponding probabilities p_1 and p_2, then the expected value of the lottery to Emma is simply $(p_1)*(W_1) + (p_2)*(W_2)$. However, what Bernoulli is saying is that this may not be what Emma's primary concern is. Emma is looking at the utility she gets from these monetary amounts and is making her decisions on the basis of that utility. So, Emma's utility is some function of her wealth, and this function may well be different from the actual monetary value. We will denote this utility by "U" and write this function as U(W), meaning that utility is a function of wealth. It is entirely possible for U(W) to be equal to W; meaning that for Emma or others like her, it is possible that their utility is the same as their wealth. For example, if I give Emma $100, then she gets 100 units of utility.

But what Bernoulli is suggesting is that this may not necessarily be the case, and for some people, utility is different from wealth. As noted above, this implies that when we calculate the expected value of a lottery, we multiply the different pay-offs with the corresponding probabilities, and sum these up. So, if a lottery has two different prizes, W_1 and W_2, with associated probabilities of p_1 and p_2 respectively, then the expected value of the lottery = $(p_1)*(W_1) + (p_2)*(W_2)$. But, the expected utility from this lottery may or may not be the same as its expected value. In order to calculate the expected utility, we need to look at the utility Emma gets from the two prizes W_1 and W_2. We will refer to the two utility values as $U(W_1)$ and $U(W_2)$ respectively. Then, to calculate Emma's expected utility, we need to multiply these utilities with their corresponding probabilities, and sum them up. So, we will define Emma's expected utility as Expected Utility = $(p_1)*\{U(W_1)\} + (p_2)*\{U(W_2)\}$. Of course, as wealth increases, utility will increase too. If Emma gets a bigger prize, she is happier. But the key question is: does utility increase at the same rate as wealth? The answer is no, not for everyone. Let us now turn to look at some examples to understand what this means.

Suppose Emma's utility function is positively sloped and linear in her wealth. Positively sloped means that when Emma's wealth goes up, her utility goes up too. "Linear" means that if we graph Emma's utility against her wealth, then the resulting relationship will be an upward sloping straight line.[3] This implies that Emma's utility function takes the form: U(W) = kW, where k is some positive constant. Some examples of this are U(W) = W, with k = 1; U(W) = 3W, with k = 3 or U(W) = (1/2)W, with k = 1/2. It turns out that for Emma (and others like her), if the utility function is a straight line, then all they care about is the monetary value. The utility calculation is not that important, since it will yield the same answer as the one with monetary pay-offs. This is because, here, utility is always some positive multiple of money. What this means is that, in deciding whether to accept a gamble or not, all that someone like Emma will look at is simply the expected value. If the expected value is positive, Emma will take the lottery. Given a straight-line utility function, the utility calculation will yield a similar answer, so, it is not essential to calculate the utilities. Let me explain.

Suppose Emma's utility function is given by U(W) = 3W. Let us say that Emma has $10,000 currently. Emma is offered the following lottery. She can toss a coin and if heads comes up, she will lose $1,000, while if tails comes up, she will win $1,000. Should Emma accept this lottery? If she does, then she has a 1/2 chance of ending up with $9,000 and a 1/2 chance of ending up with $11,000. Her expected utility from staying with her endowment of $10,000 is U($10,000) = 3*10,000 = 30,000. Her expected utility from playing the lottery is (1/2)*U(9,000)+(1/2)*U(11,000) = (1/2)*(27,000)+(1/2)*(33,000) = 30,000.

Notice two things. First, the two options have exactly the same expected utility, and thus Emma will be indifferent between the two of them. Second, in order to answer this question, Emma could simply have looked at the lottery: 1/2 chance of winning $1,000 and 1/2 chance of losing $1,000. What is the expected value? Zero. So, she should be indifferent between sticking with her $10,000 and accepting this gamble. People who behave like Emma are called *risk neutral*. For a gamble with an expected value that is identical to that of not gambling, a risk neutral person is indifferent between gambling and not gambling, because their expected utility from gambling is identical to the utility they get from not gambling. In general, a risk neutral person will take whichever option has higher expected value, since maximizing expected value maximizes their expected utility as well. Figure 4.1 illustrates this situation.[4]

Before moving on, let us look at a couple more examples. Suppose Emma is given the following choice: 1/2 chance of losing $1,000 and 1/2 chance of winning $2,000. Would she still prefer to stick with her $10,000 or will she accept the lottery? Here, she has a 1/2 chance of ending up with $9,000 and a 1/2 chance of ending up with $12,000. In this case, Emma will strictly prefer the lottery. Let us see why. Her expected utility from staying with her endowment of $10,000 is U($10,000) = 3*10,000 = 30,000. Her expected utility from playing the lottery is (1/2)*U(9,000)+(1/2)*U(12,000) = (1/2)*(27,000)+(1/2)*(36,000) = 31,500. This is greater than 30,000, and, hence, Emma will opt for the lottery. But Emma could have arrived at the same conclusion simply by looking at the monetary values of $9,000 and

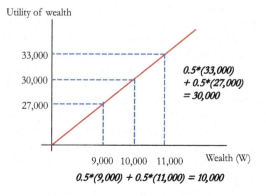

Figure 4.1
Emma's risk neutral straight-line expected utility function U(W) = 3W

■ Expected utility theory and prospect theory

$12,000. If there is a 1/2 chance that she will lose $1,000 and a 1/2 chance that she will win $2,000, then her expected value is (1/2)*(-$1,000) + (1/2)*($2,000) = $500. Note that this is simply 1/3 of the net change in expected utility, or that the net change in expected utility is simply three times the change in expected value. Therefore, looking at only one of these is sufficient and calculating expected value is simpler. Since the expected value is positive, Emma will accept the gamble. In order to arrive at this conclusion, Emma can, of course, calculate the corresponding expected utility values, but she does not need to. If her utility function is a positively sloped straight line, then simply looking at the expected monetary amounts will yield the same insight.

Finally, what if the lottery looks like this: 1/2 chance of losing $2,000 and 1/2 chance of winning $1,000. Would she still prefer to stick with her $10,000 or will she accept the lottery? Here, she has a 1/2 chance of ending up with $8,000 and a 1/2 chance of ending up with $11,000. In this case, Emma will strictly prefer to stick to her original endowment of $10,000. This is because Emma's expected utility from staying with her endowment of $10,000 is U($10,000) = 3*10,000 = 30,000. Her expected utility from playing the lottery is (1/2)*U(8,000)+(1/2)*U(11,000) = (1/2)*(24,000)+(1/2)*(33,000) = 28,500. This is less than 30,000, and hence, Emma will avoid the lottery. But, Emma could have arrived at the same conclusion simply by looking at the monetary values of $8,000 and $11,000. If there is a 1/2 chance that she will lose $2,000 and a 1/2 chance that she will win $1,000, then her expected value is (1/2)*(-$2,000) + (1/2)*($1,000) = -$500. Since the expected value is negative, Emma will not accept this gamble. As before, the net change in expected utility is simply three times the net change in expected value. This is simply because if $U(W) = 3W$, then change in $U(W)$ is three times the chance in wealth (or, a bit more formally, $\Delta U(W) = 3\Delta W$).

However, not everyone is like Emma. Some are like Jessie, whose utility function is not a straight line but a curved one, like the one shown in Figure 4.2. Let us first understand how Jessie's utility of money differs from Emma's. For Emma, as wealth increases, utility always increases at the same rate. It does not matter how much money Emma has to start with. If Emma's wealth increases from $10,000 to $11,000, then her utility increases by 3,000 from 30,000 to 33,000. If Emma's wealth increases from $100,000 to $101,000, her utility increases by the same amount of 3,000: from 300,000 to 303,000. It does not matter whether

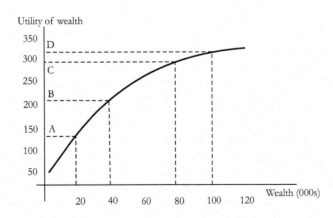

Figure 4.2
Jessie's concave utility function

Emma is poorer (with only $10,000) or richer (with $100,000). An increase of $1,000 gives Emma the same increase in utility at all levels of wealth.

But Jessie views the same outcomes differently, usually because Jessie's preferences are different from Emma's. For Jessie, as wealth increases, utility also increases, but by smaller and smaller amounts. Look at Figure 4.2. Suppose Jessie's wealth goes up by $20,000. The change in her utility will depend on how much money she had when she was given this additional $20,000. If she had $20,000 to start with then her wealth changes from $20,000 to $40,000, her utility goes up by a large amount from point A to point B. But, for the same $20,000 increase in Jessie's wealth from $80,000 to $100,000, her utility increases by a much smaller amount; from point C to point D. So, unlike Emma, the changes in Jessie's utility are not constant. As Jessie's wealth increases, for any given change in Jessie's wealth, Jessie's utility changes by smaller and smaller increments. This is usually referred to as the principle of *diminishing marginal utility*.[5] For every $20,000 increase in Jessie's wealth, she does get more utility, but her utility increases by smaller and smaller amounts, as shown in Figure 4.2. People like Jessie are *risk averse*.

If Jessie's utility function looks like the one in Figure 4.2, typically referred to as a *concave function*, which is increasing but becoming flatter as it increases, what is a good way of representing this utility function? One easy function (and one that I will use here) is $U(W) = \sqrt{W}$ (i.e., utility obtained is the square root of wealth).[6]

Now, let us look at how Jessie will respond, if given the same choice as Emma. Jessie has $10,000 currently. She is offered the following lottery. She can toss a coin and if heads comes up, she will lose $1,000, while if tails comes up, she will win $1,000. Earlier, we saw that if Emma accepts this lottery, then she has a 1/2 chance of ending up with $9,000 and a 1/2 chance of ending up with $11,000. The expected value of this lottery is zero and, therefore, Emma would be indifferent between sticking with her $10,000 and accepting this lottery. It turns out that this no longer holds true for a risk averse person like Jessie.

Now, if Jessie decides to stick with her initial $10,000, then her utility is given by: $U(W) = \sqrt{W} = \sqrt{10000} = 100$. What if she chooses to accept the gamble? In that case, she is looking at the following options: with 1/2 chance, she wins and ends up with $11,000. In this case, her utility is $U = \sqrt{11000} = 104.88$. Or, with 1/2 chance, she loses and ends up with $9,000. Then her utility is given by $U = \sqrt{9000} = 94.87$. What is her *expected utility*? In order to calculate this, we need to multiply these utilities with their corresponding probabilities, and sum them up. So, Jessie's expected utility is: (1/2)*(104.88) + (1/2)*(94.87) = 99.88. This is less than the 100 in expected utility that Jessie gets if she simply hangs on to her $10,000 to start with. Thus, even though gambling and not gambling have the same *expected value*, not gambling has the higher expected utility for someone like Jessie, who is risk averse.[7] In general, a risk averse person will always stick with the "sure thing", rather than accept a lottery of the type described here.

In Figure 4.3, let us look at another example of risk aversion with a different set of numbers. But, as before, I will continue to assume that Jessie's utility function is concave and is defined as $U(W) = \sqrt{W}$, i.e. $U(W) = W^{1/2}$. Suppose Jessie's current wealth is $8,000. Should she accept a gamble where she has a 1/2 chance of losing $4,000 and a 1/2 chance of winning $4,000? By now, we know the answer: if she is risk averse, then she will probably not accept this gamble. But typically, as economists, we need to put down some numbers and calculate things before we can make a definite conclusion.

■ Expected utility theory and prospect theory

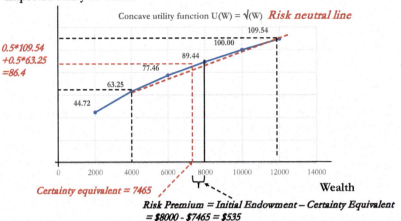

Figure 4.3
Another example with a concave utility function

Notice that if Jessie does choose to play this lottery, then she has a 1/2 chance of ending up with $4,000 and a 1/2 chance of ending up with $12,000. The expected value of the lottery is (1/2)*($4,000) + (1/2)*($12,000) = $8,000, which is the same as Jessie's current wealth. A risk neutral Emma will be indifferent between sticking with $8,000 and playing the lottery. However, we already know that a risk averse Jessie will prefer to stick with $8,000, rather than accept this gamble. Why? This is because, if Jessie simply holds on to her initial wealth of $8,000, then her utility is $U(W) = W^{1/2} = (8,000)^{1/2} = 89.44$. On the other hand, if Jessie does accept the gamble, then with 1/2 chance she gets $4,000, and with 1/2 chance she gets $12,000. The utility she gets from $4,000 is $U(W) = W^{1/2} = (4,000)^{1/2} = 63.25$. The utility she gets from $12,000 is $U(W) = W^{1/2} = (12,000)^{1/2} = 109.54$. What is her expected utility in this case? It is (1/2)*(63.25) + (1/2)*(109.54) = 86.395, which I will round up to 86.4. This is clearly less than 89.44, which is what Jessie gets if she simply hangs on to her $8,000 (Figure 4.3).

In addition to this, Figure 4.3 highlights two other key concepts: *certainty equivalent* and *risk premium*. But before I explain these, let us think a little bit more about the choices facing Jessie. It is clear that, given a choice between a sure $8,000 and a lottery paying $4,000 with 1/2 chance and $12,000 with 1/2 chance, Jessie prefers the sure $8,000 because this yields higher utility for her. In fact, Jessie may well be willing to settle for something slightly less than $8,000, which may still yield her higher utility than the lottery. The certainty equivalent of a lottery/gamble (risky situation) is the amount of money that makes Jessie indifferent between receiving that amount for certain and taking on the gamble. So, Jessie prefers the certain $8,000 above the gamble because the former yields 89.44 in utility while the latter only yields 86.4. This implies that, *given a choice between the lottery (1/2 chance of $4,000 and 1/2 chance of $12,000), Jessie should be willing to settle for something even less than $8,000 as long as that amount yields more than 86.4 of utility.* But how do we find out what this other amount is?

Figure 4.3 also allows us to do this. In order to answer this, we need to turn our previous question on its head. Earlier, we started with a monetary amount and asked what utility was provided by that amount. Now, we need to start with the utility received and work our way to the monetary amount. We know that if Jessie accepts the lottery, then she gets a utility of 86.4. So, what we need to do is to find the monetary amount that yields this amount of utility. How do we do this? If $U(W) = \sqrt{W}$, this implies that $W = (U)^2$. So, if the utility is 86.4, then the corresponding level of wealth must be $(86.4)^2$, which is $7,464.96. Let us round this up to $7,465. (Note: $\sqrt{7,464.96} = 86.4$.) This means that Jessie would be indifferent between receiving $7,465 and accepting the lottery, since they both yield the same expected utility. This is Jessie's certainty equivalent, the amount $7,465. This means that if Jessie is facing a lottery of this type, 1/2 chance of $4,000 and 1/2 chance of $12,000, then Jessie will certainly prefer a sure $8,000 over the lottery. In fact, if push comes to shove, a risk averse Jessie will prefer to take any amount above $7,465 rather than the lottery, since $7,465 provides the exact same expected utility as the lottery and anything above that amount will provide more utility.[8]

In turn, Jessie's risk premium is the difference between the expected value of the gamble and Jessie's certainty equivalent. This is the amount Jessie is willing to forego in order not to take part in the lottery. This means: suppose you ask Jessie what sure amount she will be happy to accept instead of the lottery (1/2 chance of $4,000 and 1/2 chance of $12,000). Jessie will say that she far prefers getting the expected value of the lottery for sure, which is $8,000. In fact, she is willing to go down to a sure payment of $7,465 rather than accept this lottery. The difference between Jessie's initial endowment of $8,000 and the CE of $7,465, which is equal to $535, is her risk premium. This means that if a risk averse person like Jessie finds herself in a situation where she can keep her current wealth or be exposed to (say) an act of nature, where with 1/2 chance she might end up with $4,000 and with 1/2 chance she might get $12,000, then Jessie strictly prefers to stick with her current wealth of $8,000. In fact, Jessie is willing to insure herself against being subjected to the act of nature that may reduce (or increase) her pay-off, because she just does not like the uncertainty. In that case, Jessie will be willing to pay as much as $535 ($8000 - $7565) to avoid subjecting herself to the probabilistic outcome. Most of you will understand that this is the essential principle behind buying insurance. If we are faced with a situation where we could end up worse off, we are willing to pay to avoid that eventuality.

CASE STUDY 4.1 EMILIO AND THE FLAT-SCREEN TV

Emilio has just bought a fancy new 65-inch OLED smart television for $5,000.00. The salesperson tells Emilio that these televisions tend to be quite delicate and so he should take out insurance. Should he, and if so, how much? Suppose there is a 10% chance that the television will topple over from his entertainment unit and get smashed to pieces, and a 90% chance that nothing will happen. In this case, with 10% chance Emilio ends up getting zero, while with 90% chance nothing happens and Emilio's $5,000 television remains intact. So, the potential pay-offs are $0 with 10% chance, and $5,000 with 90% chance. Emilio is risk averse and his utility of wealth is $U(W) = \sqrt{W}$. If the TV breaks (10% chance), then Emilio's wealth is zero and so his utility is zero. If the TV does not break (90% chance), then his utility is $U(5,000) = \sqrt{(5,000)} = 70.71$. What is his expected utility? It is $(0.1)*(0) + (0.9)*(70.71) = 63.64$. What amount of money is equivalent to this level of utility? The answer in this case is the

■ Expected utility theory and prospect theory

square of 63.64, which is approximately $4,050. This is Emilio's certainty equivalent, which, in turn, means that Emilio will be willing to pay as much as $950 in order to avoid the possibility of the TV breaking. So, Emilio's risk premium is $950. He will probably pay less than this for insurance, but this is the maximum he should be willing to pay. For instance, if the probability of the TV breaking is 0.01 rather than 0.1, then Emilio's certainty equivalent is approx. $4,900 and his risk premium would be just about $100. In the latter case, if Emilio forks out more than $100 in super-cover warranty, then he is paying too much.

CASE STUDY 4.2 LOGAN'S JOB OFFERS

Logan is a risk averse individual with utility of wealth function $U(W) = \sqrt{W}$. He has just finished his Bachelor's degree in Economics at the University of Auckland and is considering two job offers. He has the option of taking Job #1, which pays a fixed salary of $54,000 per year. He has a second option, Job #2. This one is with a start-up that is offering to pay a base salary of $4,000 per year; however, there is a 50:50 chance that an app being developed by this company will be highly successful, in which case, Logan will receive a bonus of $100,000 per year on top of the $4,000 base salary. Which job should Logan choose?

The answer to this question appears in Figure 4.4.[9] The intuitive answer is that Logan will choose the job that pays a fixed salary since he is risk averse and likes the

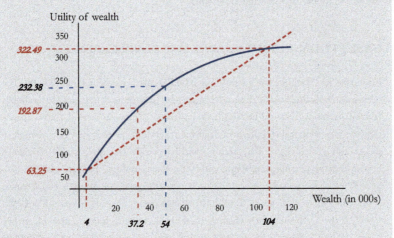

Figure 4.4
Logan's concave utility function

certainty of Job #1. But this is not necessarily correct because we have already seen that all probabilistic choices have a corresponding certainty equivalent. So, whether Logan will accept or forego Job #2, will depend on what the certainty equivalent of Job #2 is and whether Job #1 guarantees Logan more or less than that sum. If Logan takes Job #2, then with 1/2 chance he gets $4,000, and with 1/2 chance he gets $104,000. The utility of $4,000 is $\sqrt{4000} = 63.25$, while the utility of $104,000 is $\sqrt{104000} = 322.49$. Logan's expected utility from taking Job #2 is $(1/2)*(63.25) + (1/2)*(322.49) = 192.87$.

There are two ways to check whether Logan should accept Job #1 or Job #2. We have just found that Job #2 comes with an expected utility of 192.87. What utility is offered by Job #1? The answer is $\sqrt{54000} = 232.38$. This is greater than the expected utility of 192.87 offered by Job #2. So, Logan should prefer Job #1 over Job #2. But there is another way of arriving at the same answer. If Logan takes Job #2, then he gets 192.87 units of utility. What is his certainty equivalent? In other words, what is the equivalent "sure" amount that will provide Logan with the same amount of utility? To answer this, we need to find the square of 192.87, which is $37,198.84. This means that Logan will be willing to forego Job #2 with its probabilistic payment scheme, for any other job that pays at least approx. $37,200 or more. Job #1 pays quite a bit more than that. So, Logan will prefer Job #1; in fact, he would settle for a job with a fixed salary that is smaller than $54,000, as long as that job pays more than his certainty equivalent for Job #2, which is approx. $37,200.

CASE STUDY 4.3 JIM HOLTZHAUER, THE RISK SEEKER

In the Preface I alluded to the recent *Jeopardy!* winner, Jim Holtzhauer, who, every time he hit a "Daily Double", bet it all, and typically won big in all the games that he won. Jim is a risk lover. In any population, the majority of people show some degree of risk aversion with a smaller number of people who are risk neutral. People who are risk loving are usually a small minority. In his day job, Jim Holtzhauer is a sports bettor in Las Vegas. Risk lovers tend to prefer taking a gamble over the sure thing. So, how would someone like Jim respond, if he were faced with the same choices as Logan? In Jim's case, let us change things around a bit and put this more explicitly in the context of placing bets in a high-stakes game of poker.

Jim is currently sitting on $54,000. He is facing a bet where with 1/2 chance, he can lose $50,000, leaving him with $4,000; or with 1/2 chance, he can win $50,000, giving him $104,000. I am sure that you can see that the choices facing Jim are the same as those facing Logan: take the "sure" $54,000 or take the gamble (1/2 chance of $4,000 and 1/2 chance of $104,000). How does Jim choose? In general, risk lovers tend to choose the gamble over the sure thing, since usually they derive more utility from the former than the latter. But we still need to check.

■ Expected utility theory and prospect theory

While people who are risk averse tend to have concave utility functions, for risk lovers, the utility function is convex. This means that as wealth increases, the utility of wealth increases and it increases at an increasing rate; that is, rather than becoming flatter for higher levels of wealth, as in the case of risk aversion, a convex utility of wealth function becomes steeper for higher levels of wealth. One potential example of such a utility function is $U(W) = W^2$, that is, utility obtained is the square of wealth. Figure 4.5 depicts the utility function for a risk lover like Jim.

In this figure, to keep the numbers manageable, I denote wealth in thousands of dollars and utility (which is the square of wealth) in millions of units. Whether Jim sticks with the sure $54,000 or takes the gamble depends on which of these provide him with higher utility. What is Jim's utility if he sticks with the $54,000? The answer is $(54,000)^2$ = 2,916 million. What happens if he accepts the gamble? He will either end up with $4,000 or $104,000. The utility derived from $4,000 is $(4,000)^2$ = 16 million. The utility from $104,000 is 10,816 million. What is Jim's expected utility from the gamble? It is equal to (1/2)*(16 million) + (1/2)*(10,816 million) = 5,416 million. This is much larger than the 2,916 million Jim gets from sticking with the $54,000. Therefore, Jim will prefer to take the gamble rather than staying with the sure thing.

Does this mean that someone like Jim will always take the gamble regardless of what the "sure" amount is? No, even a risk lover like Jim has a certainty equivalent. Except, a risk averse person's certainty equivalent is smaller than the initial endowment, implying that a risk averse person is willing to give up some money to avoid having to face the gamble. For a risk lover, the opposite is true. His/her certainty equivalent is higher than the initial endowment. This means that the risk lover needs

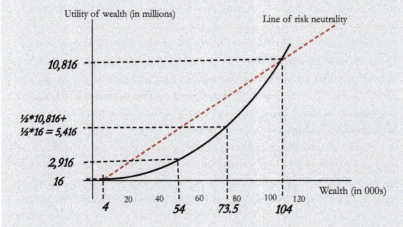

Figure 4.5
Jim's convex utility function

to be paid more in order to take the "sure" thing and forego the gamble. How do we calculate this? The technique is the same as for risk aversion.

What is Jim's expected utility when he takes the gamble? It is equal to 5,416 million. In order to find Jim's certainty equivalent, we need to find the amount of money that yields Jim this same amount of utility. Given that $U = W^2$, this implies that $W = \sqrt{U}$. If U is 5,416 million, then the corresponding level of wealth is $\sqrt{(5,416 \text{ million})}$ = \$73,600. This implies that as long as the "sure" amount is less than \$73,600, Jim will always choose the gamble. However, Jim will be indifferent between accepting the gamble and accepting \$73,600 for sure. If Jim is offered more than \$73,600 for sure, then he will choose that sure amount over the gamble.

THE ALLAIS PARADOX

The expected utility theory is an elegant model that provides a good description of how people should approach probabilistic decisions regarding states of wealth (otherwise known as decision under risk). But, as always, between the conception and the reality falls the shadow. It turns out that, when it comes to probabilistic choices, people's actual behaviour often deviates from the dictates of expected utility theory. This may be caused by many factors, including the fact that people do not have good intuition when it comes to probabilities, people treat gains and losses differently and people seem to treat events with a small chance of happening quite differently from events that have a higher probability. The first demonstration of this apparent irrationality was provided by the French economist Maurice Allais (1911–2010; Nobel Prize in Economics 1988).

Allais asked respondents to choose between the following pairs of lotteries:

Pair #1: What would you choose: Choice A or Choice B?
Choice A: \$5,000,000 with probability 0.10, \$1,000,000 with probability 0.89 and \$0 with probability 0.01.
Choice B: \$1,000,000 with probability 1.
Pair #2: What would you choose: Choice C or Choice D?
Choice C: \$5,000,000 with probability 0.10 and \$0 with probability 0.90.
Choice D: \$1,000,000 with probability 0.11 and \$0 with probability 0.89.

It turns out that a majority of respondents choose B over A for the first pair, but then choose C over D for the second pair. This is a problem, because it is fine to choose B over A, but if so, then that person must prefer D over C. Or, if someone chooses A over B, then he/she must prefer C over D. Choosing B over A for the first pair and C over D for the second is a violation of independence because of what is often referred to as the "common consequence effect". To understand why, see below.

First, I am going to rewrite the choices in each pair. For Pair #1, I am going to leave Choice A alone but rewrite Choice B as Choice B*. For Pair #2, I am going to rewrite Choice C as Choice C* while leaving Choice D alone. Notice that doing this does not change those lotteries at all; they are merely a different way of stating the same choice.

Pair #1:

Choice A: $5,000,000 with probability 0.10, $1,000,000 with probability 0.89 and $0 with probability 0.01.

Choice B: $1,000,000 with probability 1.

Choice B*: $1,000,000 with probability 0.11 and $1,000,000 with probability 0.89. (Note: 0.89 + 0.11 = 1.)

Pair #2:

Choice C: $5,000,000 with probability 0.10 and $0 with probability 0.90.

Choice C*: $5,000,000 with 0.10, $0 with probability 0.89 and $0 with probability 0.01.

(Note: 0.89 + 0.01 = 0.90)

Choice D: $1,000,000 with probability 0.11 and $0 with probability 0.89.

Now that we have lottery B as B* and C as C*, we can delete B and C. This leaves us with the following choices:

Pair #1:

Choice A: $5,000,000 with probability 0.10, $1,000,000 with probability 0.89 and $0 with probability 0.01.

Choice B*: $1,000,000 with probability 0.11 and $1,000,000 with probability 0.89.

Pair #2:

Choice C*: $5,000,000 with probability 0.10, $0 with probability 0.89 and $0 with probability 0.01.

Choice D: $1,000,000 with probability 0.11 and $0 with probability 0.89.

But notice that some elements are common to A and B* ($1,000,000 with probability 0.89) and the same is true for C* and D ($0 with probability 0.89).

Since these elements are common to the two lotteries, we can delete them from each; this is the "common consequence" part I referred to above. What do the lotteries look like now?

Pair #1:

Choice A: $5,000,000 with probability 0.10 and $0 with probability 0.01.

Choice B*: $1,000,000 with probability 0.11.

Pair #2:

Choice C*: $5,000,000 with probability 0.10 and $0 with probability 0.01.

Choice D: $1,000,000 with probability 0.11.

It turns out that lotteries A and C (or C*) and lotteries B (or B*) and D are identical. So, if one chooses A over B, then that person must prefer C over D, or vice versa. But this fact that the lotteries are the same is not obvious to most of us. This then, raises questions about our ability to reduce compound lotteries and think through more complicated probabilistic choices, an essential requirement for expected utility theory.

Inspired by the work done by Allais, starting in the mid-1970s, Daniel Kahneman (at the University of British Columbia) and Amos Tversky (1937–1996, of Stanford) set about documenting more such examples of our lack of facility with probabilistic choices.[10]

Kahneman and Tversky opined that this inability to readily (or intuitively) grasp the intricacies of probabilistic choices pose challenges for the conclusions drawn from expected utility theory. This requires us to view such choices differently. Their work in this area led to them formulating an alternative to expected utility theory. This alternative formulation has now become widely known as "prospect theory". Following on from Allais' description of how we usually fail to see through the "common consequence" effect, Kahneman and Tversky started by looking at the "common ratio" effect.

Kahneman and Tversky asked 95 respondents which of the following options they prefer in each pair.

Pair #1:
Choice A: An 80% chance of $4,000.
Choice B: $3,000 for sure.
Pair #2:
Choice C: A 20% chance of $4,000.
Choice D: A 25% chance of $3,000.

A large majority (80%) of respondents preferred Choice B in Pair #1, while a majority (65%) expressed a preference for Choice C in Pair #2. Here, the fallacy in these choices is more obvious compared to the Allais paradox. This is because in going from A to C (or from B to D), all that has happened is that the probabilities have been multiplied by the same fraction: one-fourth. 80% versus 20% between A and C, and 100% versus 25% in B and D. Once again, this implies that anyone who prefers A over B must prefer C over D, or vice versa, but this is not what happened.

The next pair of lotteries Kahneman and Tversky looked at constitutes another example of the "common consequence" effect and illustrates a clear violation of the postulates of expected utility theory. Seventy-two respondents were given the following pair-wise choices:

Pair #1:
Choice A: $2,500 with p = 0.33; $2,400 with p = 0.66 and $0 with p = 0.01.
Choice B: $2,400 with p = 1.
Pair #2:
Choice C: $2,500 with p = 0.33; $0 with p = 0.67.
Choice D: $2,400 with p = 0.34; $0 with p = 0.66.

Seventy-two per cent of respondents chose B in Pair #1, but 83% chose C in Pair #2. This is hard to explain using expected utility theory. The expected values of the four choices are $2,409 for A, $2,400 for B, $825 for C and $816 for D. So, if someone is risk neutral, then the choice is clear: A over B, and C over D. But maybe people are not risk neutral. Suppose they assess utility according to some other utility function U, which can either be concave or convex. We can show that no matter what form this utility function takes, it is impossible to reconcile the choice of B over A and then C over D using the tenets of expected utility theory. This is because if people choose B over A, then it must be the case that they assess the expected utility of lottery B to be higher. This implies:

$$U(2,400) > (0.33)*U(2,500) + (0.66)*U(2,400).$$

Transposing. sides we can rewrite this as U(2,400) – (0.66)*U(2,400) > (0.33)*U(2,500).
This implies (0.34)*U(2,400) > (0.33)*U(2,500). Call this *Inequality 1*.

But, if people choose C over D, then it must be the case that expected utility from C is greater than that from D. Or, (0.33)*U(2,500) > (0.34)*U(2,400). Call this *Inequality 2*. But these two inequalities are mutually exclusive and cannot hold simultaneously.

In expected utility theory, assessments of outcomes are independent of the status quo, in the sense that it does not matter what the starting point (in terms of an initial endowment) is. In the examples we studied above, for instance, Jim choosing between bets, the calculation of expected utility did not depend on his initial endowment of $54,000. Similarly, the way Logan feels about Job #2 does not change based on the sure payment in Job #1, as long as Job #1 pays more than the certainty equivalent for Job #2. But Kahneman and Tversky discovered that, when asked, people made very different choices based on at least two things: first, the initial starting point (which can be thought of as the reference point or status quo). Second, whether the lottery represents a gain or a loss, particularly with reference to the status quo. They posed the following problem to their respondents.

Situation 1: Suppose you have won $1,000 on a game show. In addition to these winnings, you are now asked to choose between Choice A: 1/2 chance of winning of $1000, or Choice B: Winning $500 for sure.

Situation 2: Suppose you have won $2,000 on a game show. In addition to these winnings, you are now asked to choose between Choice C: 1/2 chance of losing of $1000, or Choice D: Losing $500 for sure.

Notice that the two situations are identical in terms of final wealth states in expectation. In either case, the respondent ends up with $1,500 (either for sure or in expectation), except in one case there is a "gain" in going up from $1,000 to $1,500, while, in the second case, there is a "loss": going down from $2,000 to $1,500. Regardless, expected utility theory tells us that one either prefers the sure amount in both cases or the expected amount in both cases. But it turns out that respondents are much more likely to choose the sure amount of Choice B ($500 for sure) in the first case, while they choose the expected value described in C (1/2 chance of losing $1,000) in the second case. This suggests two things: one, that people are making their decisions over *changes* in wealth, rather than the final wealth levels, and two, they take different views when it comes to losses as opposed to gains. Regarding the second issue, people prefer to lock in a sure gain rather than opt for probabilistic gains, but when it comes to losses, people prefer a probabilistic loss over a sure loss.

A starker demonstration of this differential treatment of gains and losses comes from the following example. Respondents are presented with identical lotteries with the same expected value, except one set is framed as a gain (a "gain frame") while the other is posed as a loss (a "loss frame").

Pair #1 in Gain Frame:
Choice A: 80% chance of winning $4,000.
Choice B: Win $3,000 for sure.
Pair #2 in Gain Frame:
Choice C: 20% chance of winning $4,000.
Choice D: 25% chance of winning $3,000.

Pair #1 in Loss Frame:
Choice A: 80% chance of losing $4,000.
Choice B: Lose $3,000 for sure.
Pair #2 in Loss Frame:
Choice C: 20% of chance of losing $4,000.
Choice D: 25% chance of losing $3,000.

For ease of exposition, I represent the information in tabular form in Table 4.1, along with the expected value in each case and the proportion of respondents who chose each lottery. The key comparison here is between the two Pair #1s in the gain and loss frames, respectively. When it came to a win (Pair #1 in gain frame, Column 1), 80% went for the sure win of $3,000 over the expected win of $3,200. But in the loss domain (Pair #1 in loss frame, Column 3), 92% chose the larger expected loss of $3,200 over the sure loss of $3,000. This is certainly not driven by an inability to understand expected values. If we compare the Pair #2s in each frame, where all pay-offs are probabilistic, in the gain frame (Column 2), a majority (65%) chose the larger expected gain of $800 over a smaller expected gain of $750. In the loss frame (fourth column), most people preferred the smaller expected loss of $750 over the larger expected loss of $800. This suggest that there are at least two things people seem to care about. First, they seem to treat sure gains/losses differently from expected gains/losses. Second, they seem to apply very different calculations when it comes to gains as opposed to when it comes to losses.

Table 4.2 presents another illustration of the same phenomenon, except, rather than asking people to choose between lotteries of different expected value, for the lotteries in Table 4.2, the expected values of the lotteries are held fixed. Once again, we see a similar pattern of choices: if we focus on Pair #1 in each case, that is, if we compare across

Table 4.1 Presentation of lotteries in gain or loss frame

Gain frame		Loss frame	
Pair #1	Pair #2	Pair #1	Pair #2
Choice A: 80% chance of winning $4,000. {Expected gain = $3,200} {Chosen by 20%} Choice B: Win $3,000 for sure. {Sure gain = $3,000} {Chosen by 80%}	Choice C: 20% chance of winning $4,000. {Expected gain = $800} {Chosen by 65%} Choice D: 25% chance of winning $3,000. {Expected gain = $750} {Chosen by 35%}	Choice A: 80% chance of losing $4,000. {Expected loss = $3,200} {Chosen by 92%} Choice B: Lose $3,000 for sure. {Sure loss = $3,000} {Chosen by 8%}	Choice C: 20% chance of losing $4,000. {Expected loss = $800} {Chosen by 42%} Choice D: 25% chance of losing $3,000. {Expected loss = $750} {Chosen by 58%}

Source: Kahneman and Tversky (1979)

■ Expected utility theory and prospect theory

Table 4.2 Presentation of lotteries with the same expected value in gain or loss frame

Gain frame		Loss frame	
Pair #1	Pair #2	Pair #1	Pair #2
Choice A: 90% chance of winning $3,000. {Expected gain = $2,700} {Chosen by 86%} Choice B: 45% chance of winning $6,000. {Expected gain = $2,700} {Chosen by 14%}	Choice C: 0.2% chance of winning $3,000. {Expected gain = $6} {Chosen by 70%} Choice D: 0.1% chance of winning $6,000. {Expected gain = $6} {Chosen by 30%}	Choice A: 90% chance of losing $3,000. {Expected loss = $2,700} {Chosen by 8%} Choice B: 45% chance of losing $6,000. {Expected loss = $2,700} {Chosen by 92%}	Choice C: 0.2% chance of losing $3,000. {Expected loss = $6} {Chosen by 27%} Choice D: 0.1% chance of losing $6,000. {Expected loss = $6} {Chosen by 73%}

Source: Kahneman and Tversky (1979)

Columns 1 and 3, we find that when it came to gains (Column 1), 86% prefer a 90% chance of winning $3,000 over a 45% chance of winning $6,000. But in the loss domain, the opposite happened (Column 3). 92% prefer a 45% chance of losing $6,000 over a 90% chance of losing $3,000. This is despite the fact that the expected win or loss is identical in each case ($2,700). Kahneman and Tversky referred to this pattern of choices as *preference reversals*.

PROSPECT THEORY

Armed with this additional evidence, Kahneman and Tversky were now in a position to put forth their alternative to expected utility theory, which, after some deliberation, they decided to call "prospect theory", since lotteries can also be thought of as "prospects".[11] The first key element within prospect theory is the *probability weighting function*. Under expected utility theory, in order to calculate the expected utility of a lottery, we multiply the utilities of different pay-offs with the corresponding probabilities, and sum these up. Kahneman and Tversky proposed that people do not look at probabilities objectively; rather, they weigh them differently, based on their magnitude. So, if there are two lottery prizes W_1 and W_2, with corresponding probabilities p_1 and p_2, then, under expected utility theory, we calculate expected utility as $U(W) = (p_1)*U(W_1) + (p_2)*U(W_2)$. But under prospect theory, it is not the probabilities themselves that matter, but, instead, people attach a decision weight to those probabilities. Therefore, under prospect theory, the expected utility of the same lottery is given by the following expression: $U(W) = \pi(p_1)*U(W_1) + \pi(p_2)*U(W_2)$, where π is a function that assigns a value to each probability, which is different from the probability itself.

Figure 4.6 depicts some plausible probability weighting functions. The probability weighting function has the following properties. It is discontinuous at the end points; $\pi(0) = 0$ and $\pi(1) = 1$. But other than zero and one, it "overweights" small probabilities and "underweights" large ones. So, for probability values that are less than some cut-off probability (p*), that is, as long as p < p*, the subjective value of that probability appears to be larger than the objective value of the probability, that is, $\pi(p) > p$; the probability appears to be larger than it really is. For probability values higher than this cut-off, that is, p > p*, $\pi(p) < p$, implying that large probabilities are "underweighted", the subjective probability appears to be smaller than the objective probability. How this happens depends on the exact functional form of

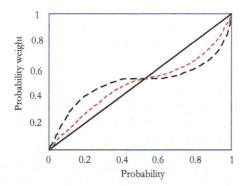

Figure 4.6
Potential probability weighting function

the probability weighting function. For example, it may be the case that for some functional form, π(p) > p for p < 0.30 (overweighting); π(p) = p at around 0.30~0.35 and π(p) < p for p > 0.35 (underweighting). This means that even if some events have a very low probability, in our minds we overweight it and the subjective probability appears to be much larger that is actually (objectively) is. This is why we routinely buy lottery tickets, even though the probability of winning the jackpot is vanishingly small. Similarly, we often underweight large probabilities.[12]

CASE STUDY 4.4 COVID-19 ONCE MORE

In Chapter 3, Case Study 3.1, I discussed the global response to the COVID-19 pandemic. Here is another related perspective on this. Earlier, I showed what the pattern of responses are if you asked people to choose one of the following lotteries. *Choice A: Would you prefer to win $3,000 for sure or would you prefer to win $4,000 with an 80% probability? Choice B: Would you prefer to lose $3,000 for sure or would you prefer to lose $4,000 with 80% chance?* We saw that a vast majority of respondents choose the first option in Choice A but the second in Choice B. This means that people prefer to win $3,000 for sure over winning an expected $3,200 in Choice A. But, when it comes to Choice B, they prefer to lose an expected $3,200 over a sure loss of $3,000. So, people prefer a smaller sure gain over a larger probabilistic gain. But they prefer a larger probabilistic loss over a smaller sure loss. Kahneman and Tversky referred to this phenomenon as *loss aversion*.

Here is how loss aversion played a role in the response to the pandemic. Many epidemiologists in both New Zealand and elsewhere were adamant about strict social distancing measures in an attempt to suppress the disease, no matter what the cost. But in doing this, the epidemiologists are focusing on what is often referred to as identified lives; the loss of lives we can see right in front of our eyes. This is the fear of losing a lot of lives in a short span of time. Therein, lies the connection with the lottery. Faced with the prospect of a large-scale loss of lives, medical professionals are willing to accept much larger probabilistic losses further down the road rather than accept smaller sure losses due to people succumbing to COVID-19. Part of this also

> has to do with the underweighting of large probabilities. We have argued that the "sure" thing looms large in our psyche, so the sure losses are harder to ignore. But the probabilistic losses are less obvious, especially because if the probability of the event is high, as long as it is not equal to 1, we will tend to underestimate that probability.[13]

The second key component of prospect theory is the *value function*, which is defined on changes in wealth or welfare starting from a reference point (usually the status quo), rather than the utility function for final wealth levels, as in expected utility theory. The value function has three key features. First, gains and losses are defined relative to a reference point. Most of the time, the reference point is simply the original status quo; for example, for a gambler who has been losing, getting back to even may be the reference point. It may be against expectations; someone who expected a stock to return 7% but obtained only 2%, he/she may actually view this as a five-point loss, rather than a 2% gain.

A second key feature of the value function (somewhat similar to risk aversion in expected utility theory) is that our perceptions of both gains and losses are characterized by diminishing marginal sensitivity in each direction – successive incremental changes have a smaller and smaller marginal impact. For example, it is easier to distinguish between a four-degree change in temperature when the temperature rises from 2° to 6° than a four-degree change when the temperature increases from 22° to 26°.

A third and final feature is the phenomenon of loss aversion; losses loom larger than gains. The aggravation that one experiences from losing a sum of money is greater than the pleasure associated with gaining the same amount and these changes are felt far more strongly under prospect theory than under expected utility theory. Loss aversion is also reflected in the fact that people are more likely to lock in sure gains rather than opt for potentially larger gains in expectation. But, when it comes to losses, people wish to forego a sure loss and prefer to hold out for a potentially larger loss in expectation. A different way of saying this is: starting from some reference point (quite possibly current wealth or a similar status quo), people are risk averse in gains and risk seeking in losses. *They prefer a smaller sure gain over a larger probabilistic gain, implying that in the gain domain, people behave as if their certainty equivalent is less than their current endowment.* We know from our earlier discussion that this is a feature of risk aversion. On the other hand, *in the loss domain, people opt for the larger probabilistic amount rather than the smaller sure amount; they behave as if their certainty equivalent is larger than their initial endowment, a feature associated with risk seeking.*

Figure 4.7 shows the value function. "O" is the reference point. The shape of the value function highlights the features discussed above. There is a kink at the reference point, indicating that gains and losses are evaluated differently. The increase in value coming from a gain from O to A (measured by O–X) is much less than the loss of value experienced by a loss from O to B (measured by O–Y). Alternatively, we can say that the increase in value coming from a gain from O to A (measured by O–X) is much less than the increase in value coming from avoiding a similar loss from B to O (measured by O–Y). The curve also flattens out in either direction, implying that larger gains and losses have a proportionally smaller impact on the value gained or lost.

Figure 4.7
Value function

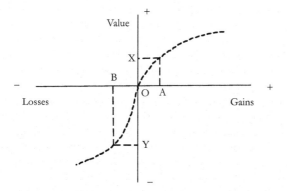

CASE STUDY 4.5 TECHNICAL DIGRESSION

Much of the material in this section is mathematically challenging and so many readers may feel free to skip this next bit without losing much in terms of understanding what the value function implies in terms of decision making.

If we define the magnitude of potential gain (or loss) by x, then one possible functional form of the value function is: $V(x) = |x|^{\alpha}$ for $x \geq 0$ (i.e., for gains); otherwise $V(x) = -\lambda(|x|)^{\alpha}$ for $x < 0$ (i.e., for losses), where $|x|$ stands for the absolute magnitude of the gain or the loss, with $\lambda > 1$, where λ is the coefficient of loss aversion and is typically estimated to be around 2.25 ~ 2.5. That is, losses matter more than twice as much as gains. The fact that the value function exhibits diminishing marginal sensitivity (implying that the curve flattens out more and more for both gains and losses of larger and larger magnitude) has a striking implication. It means that the value function is concave in gains (i.e., people will tend to be risk averse in the gain domain), but it is convex for losses; people will be risk-seeking for gambles involving losses. We have addressed the intricacies of this earlier and I will refrain from elaborating further.

Let us look at a numerical example to fix ideas. Suppose Eva's value function is defined as: $V(x) = |x|^{0.8}$ for $x \geq 0$ (gains) and $V(x) = -2(|x|)^{0.8}$ for $x < 0$ (losses), where $|x|$ is the absolute value of the gain or the loss. How does Eva feel about flipping a fair coin, where, if the coin lands heads, she will win $600, while if it lands tails, she will lose $500? Notice that the expected value of the lottery is positive, since the magnitude of the gain ($600) is greater than the magnitude of the loss ($500) and there is a 1/2 chance of either happening. For the sake of simplicity, let us assume that Eva uses the actual probability of 1/2 in calculating expected utilities, rather than using the probability weighting function. (The conclusions remain unchanged if we use the probability weighting function, except the calculation becomes more complicated.)

What is Eva's utility if she does nothing? In this case, there is no gain or loss and her utility is zero. But what if she agrees to flip the coin? With 1/2 chance she gets $600, in which case her utility is $(600)^{0.8}$, and with 1/2 chance she loses $500, in which case her utility is $(-2)*(500)^{0.8}$. What is her expected utility in this case? $U = (1/2)*(600)^{0.8} + (1/2)*(-2)*(500)^{0.8} = -60.81$. Loss aversion makes this favourable gamble unattractive.

■ Expected utility theory and prospect theory

EXPLAINING THE PARADOXICAL BEHAVIOUR IN ALLAIS AND ELSEWHERE

There are now two components of risk attitudes: the probability weighting function and the value function. These two may be in reinforcing directions, or in opposing directions. Let us now go back and re-visit the Allais Paradox. Recall that Allais posed the following choices to his respondents and the latter typically chose B over A in Pair #1 but C over D in Pair #2. The question was, what explains this pattern of choice? Now we can answer this better.

Pair #1: What would you choose: Choice A or Choice B?
Choice A: $5,000,000 with probability 0.10, $1,000,000 with probability 0.89 and $0 with probability 0.01.
Choice B: $1,000,000 with probability 1.
Pair #2: What would you choose: Choice C or Choice D?
Choice C: $5,000,000 with probability 0.10 and $0 with probability 0.90.
Choice D: $1,000,000 with probability 0.11 and $0 with probability 0.89.

In lottery B, the "sure thing" of getting $1,000,000 million for sure looms large, while the 0.89 probability on $1,000,000 million in lottery A is underweighted, making A relatively less appealing than the certain million in B. However, in C and D, both probabilities of 0.10 and 0.11 are overweighted, making C the relatively more attractive choice.

Next, let us look at the common ratio effect, where going from Pair #1 to Pair #2, all probabilities are multiplied by one-quarter. Once again, we saw that people tend to choose B over A and C over D.

Pair #1:
Choice A: An 80% chance of $4,000.
Choice B: $3,000 for sure.
Pair #2:
Choice C: A 20% chance of $4,000.
Choice D: A 25% chance of $3,000.

This can now be explained by appealing to the fact that Choice B offers a "sure" thing, while the 0.8 probability in Choice A is underweighted. But in Pair #2, both of the small probabilities are overweighted, thereby making Choice C the more attractive option over Choice D.

Finally, in the game show example, we saw that people made dramatically different choices depending on whether they have already won $1,000 and are facing a further gain (either $500 for sure or 1/2 chance of winning $1,000), or they have already won $2,000 but are now facing a loss (either $500 for sure or 1/2 chance of losing $1,000). In the first example, $1,000 serves as the reference point ($1,000 is the new 0); outcomes above this are viewed as gains. In the second example, the reference point is $2,000 and outcomes below this are viewed as losses. This is because people are risk averse in gains and risk seeking in losses. In the gain domain, when the expected values are the same, they prefer the sure thing over the probabilistic outcome and choose the gain in $500 for sure. In the loss domain, when the expected values are the same, people prefer the probabilistic outcome over the sure thing and choose the 1/2 chance of a $1,000 loss.

LOSS AVERSION, MENTAL ACCOUNTING AND THE ENDOWMENT EFFECT

In this section and the next, I will discuss how the ideas contained in prospect theory, particularly the concept of loss aversion, apply to a variety of day-to-day decisions, both big and small. I discuss the endowment effect in this section. In the next section, I will address issues of overconfidence. In both cases, I will show how these interact with ideas of loss aversion and what the implications may be. Consider the following two situations.

Situation A: Sherry has bought two $80 tickets to the theatre for her friend Bella and herself. When she arrives at the theatre, she opens her wallet and discovers that the tickets are missing. $80 tickets are still available at the box office. Should Sherry buy two more tickets to see the play?

Situation B: Sherry has arrived at the theatre intending to buy two tickets that cost $80 each. Bella is supposed to join her there. When Sherry arrives at the theatre box office, she discovers to her dismay that the $160 with which she was going to make the purchase is missing. $80 tickets are still available at the box office. She has a credit card. Should Sherry buy the tickets and just charge them to her credit card?

When queried about the two above-mentioned situations, a majority of respondents say "No" for Situation A and "Yes" for Situation B. Why? The answer has to do with a number of concepts we have explored up until this point and include: framing, mental accounting and sunk costs. The price of the tickets is sunk and should be ignored. But, as Richard Thaler has shown, we assign expenses to different mental accounts. It appears that in our minds, "lost ticket" gets charged to a "recreation" account which is now depleted. Therefore, most respondents say "No" in Situation A. But, "additional cost" comes out of a "wealth" account and so in Situation B, most respondents say "Yes".

Let us now consider a different situation, also highlighted by Richard Thaler, that extends the previous idea.

Scenario A: It is 1998. Michael Jordan and the Chicago Bulls are about to play their final championship game. You would really like to get a ticket to the game. How much are you willing to pay?

Scenario B: It is 1998. Michael Jordan and the Chicago Bulls are about to play their final championship game. You have a ticket to the game. How much are you willing to sell it for?

Thaler reports that, on average, respondents who do not have a ticket say that they are willing to pay $330 to buy a ticket. For those who supposedly have a ticket, when asked how much they are willing to sell it for, the answer, on average, is $1,920!

Kahneman, Jack Knetsch (of Simon Fraser) and Thaler refer to this as the *endowment effect*. The mere act of possessing something renders it much more valuable to us; so much so that we ask for a much higher selling price for a good we possess (say, an expensive bottle of wine) than we are willing to pay to buy the exact same good. It turns out that the endowment effect applies not only to valuable items or things we have had for a long time but even to things that we have possessed for short periods of time. Kahneman and colleagues took a group of students and divided them into three groups: "Buyers", "Sellers" and "Choosers". "Sellers" were given mugs with the university logo on it and asked to name a selling price between $0.25 and $9.25 in $0.25 increments. "Buyers" had no mugs and were asked if they are willing to buy a mug from one of the sellers at those different price points. Finally, "Choosers" are asked, for each of those price points, whether they would rather take the mug or an equivalent amount of money. Essentially, sellers are being asked for their minimum acceptable price (ask) for the mugs, while the buyers (and choosers) are being asked for the maximum price they are willing to pay (or bid) for a mug.

Roles (and mugs) are allocated randomly and, hence, we would expect the bids and asks to be similar. However, on average sellers ask for $7.12, buyers $2.87 and choosers $3.12. So, the price the sellers put on the mugs, which they had been given a few moments ago, is much higher than the price the buyers are willing to pay for those same mugs. A plausible reason behind this behaviour is loss aversion. The fact of possessing the mug changes the reference point for the sellers; for them it becomes a matter of losing something, while for buyers it is a gain. We have already seen that the loss in value from a loss of a particular magnitude is much greater than any potential gain in value from an equal gain. Hence, sellers who have the mug ask for a much higher price to compensate them for the large loss in value they experience from losing the mug.

LOSS AVERSION AND OVERCONFIDENCE

Negotiations, particularly those over legal disputes or management–union bargaining, often fail and end up in binding arbitration. It is usually much better if the parties can achieve a negotiated settlement since arbitration is costly, in terms of both time and money. Arbitration is also highly uncertain, since there is no guarantee which of the two final offers the arbitrator will accept. At least part of the reason why negotiations often end in impasse is that negotiators often suffer from overconfidence. If and when negotiations end in impasse and parties end up in binding arbitration, typically the arbitrator ends up selecting one offer or the other (say, either the management offer or the union offer). This implies that there is a 50% chance of one's offer succeeding. Yet, negotiators on each side believe that there is a 64.5% chance of success, which just cannot be true because the two sides' chances of success cannot add to more than 100%

A key issue behind successful negotiations is whether the issue is framed as a gain or a loss. For example, suppose union and management are bargaining over wages. Management is willing to pay $16/hour and union is asking for $20/hour with both sides agreeing to $18/hour. Is this a loss for management now that they have ended up paying $2/hour more than they were willing to pay? Or is it a gain given that they are paying $2/hour less than what they may have been forced to pay? Framing the negotiation as a gain or a loss may have bearing on ultimate success.

Two key factors affecting negotiations are: one, awareness of overconfidence, and second, perspective taking. What does the other side know in order to believe that they have a reasonable chance of success? This often requires CEOs (or senior leaders) to make sure that they have someone willing to play Devil's advocate rather than being surrounded by "yes men".

Margaret Neale and Max Bazerman have spent considerable time studying negotiations. In one such study, student participants take on the role of management negotiators against experienced confederates playing the role of union negotiators. Confederates are told to use a pre-determined reciprocal rule, based on concessions made by management negotiators. The two sides are negotiating over a number of issues, including wages, medical plan, holiday pay, paid sick days and night-shift differentials. Neale and Bazerman hypothesize that: (1) *Negotiators who frame negotiations in terms of losses will use fewer concessionary processes during the negotiation and have less successful outcomes than will negotiators who frame negotiations in terms of gains.* (2) *Individuals who are overly confident about the accuracy of their judgement of the probability of success in final offer arbitration will use fewer concessionary processes and have less successful outcomes than will those who are realistically confident about the accuracy of their judgements.*

Prior to the actual negotiations starting, participants undergo training. The training is designed to achieve two things. First, to put them in a "gain" or "loss" frame of mind. The second is to create more realistic expectations. Participants in the "loss" frame are told: *Any concessions beyond those granted will represent serious financial losses to the company. Please remember that your primary objective is to minimize such losses to the company. I cannot emphasize the severity of the situation enough.* Participants in the "gain" frame are told: *Any union concession from their current position will result in gains for the company. Please remember that your primary objective is to maximize such gains for the company. I cannot emphasize the importance of these gains to the company enough.*

Separately, participants in *realistic confidence* treatment are briefed that negotiators often tend to be overconfident and believe that their probability of success is higher than it is in actuality. Participants in the *overconfident* treatment are not given any special instructions, with the implicit assumption that the lack of exposure to any de-biasing will ensure that they will tend to be overconfident in their beliefs. This then generates a 2 × 2 experimental design with four different treatments: gain frame and realistic; gain frame and overconfident; loss frame and realistic, and finally, loss frame and overconfident. A key metric measured by Neale and Bazerman is how many negotiations end in successful resolution. Readers will most likely be easily able to anticipate the results at this point. Participants in the loss frame and overconfident treatment fared worst and managed to reach agreement in only 36% of cases. At the other extreme, negotiators in the gain frame and realistic treatment reached resolution in nearly 83% of cases. Those in the loss frame and realistic treatment successfully resolved 62% of cases while those in the gain frame and overconfident treatment did so in 73% of cases.

The perils of overconfidence are pervasive. In order to plan effectively, every organization must make forecasts of uncertain events. Are organizations good at making well-calibrated forecasts? Itzhak Ben-David, John Graham and Campbell Harvey suggest not. They analysed over 10,000 forecasts made by Chief Financial Officers of thousands of firms over many years. Results show that actual market returns fall inside these executives' 80%

confidence intervals only about one-third of the time. Brad Barber and Terrance Odean have studied the impact of overconfidence in investments. For investors with a moderate amount of wealth, the best return is obtained from investing in an index fund or buying a diversified portfolio and holding it for a number of years. In one study, Barber and Odean looked at 66,465 households that held an investment account with a broker between 1991 and 1996. On average, investors sold 75% of their investments in any given year. The average investor earned 16.4%, which was less than 17.9%, the average market return during this period. Twenty per cent, or 12,100 accounts that had the highest turnover earned 11.4%. Barber and Odean also studied 35,000 investment accounts sorted by gender. Women achieved better results than men because they were less subject to overconfidence. Women had turnover rates of 53%, while for men this was 77%. We have already seen that excessive buying and selling does not pay; accounts with high turnover end up doing worse on average. So, not surprisingly, men, who tend to engage in a greater volume of buying and selling, experience lower returns.

Finally, here is yet another example of loss aversion at work. Investors typically tend to sell stocks/mutual funds whose price has gone up and hang on to those whose price has gone down. Why? The discrepancy can be explained by appealing to loss aversion and reference points. We are risk seeking in losses but risk averse in gains. So, we tend to sell "winners" to lock in sure gains rather than waiting for potentially larger probabilistic gains. But, when it comes to "losers", we become risk seeking. We tend to forego the sure loss and opt for "holding", which may result in potentially larger probabilistic losses.

CONCLUDING REMARKS

In this chapter, I have discussed the issues that arise in making decisions when the outcomes are probabilistic. I have focused on decision making under risk, where risk is defined as situations where the probabilities of various outcomes are known. Uncertainty refers to situations where those probabilities are not specified. The early part of the chapter develops the concepts of expected value and the theory of expected utility. We saw, via the St Petersburg Paradox, that in calculating the potential pay-offs from different probabilistic outcomes, people base their decisions primarily on expected utility, rather than expected values. Those who base their decisions on only the expected values are referred to as risk neutral. But the majority of people are risk averse in the sense that their utility functions are concave and flatten out with increasing wealth. This implies that as wealth increases, each additional dollar generates proportionally smaller and smaller amounts of additional utility. I defined the concepts of "certainty equivalent" and "risk premium" and showed that, broadly speaking, risk averse individuals prefer a certain guaranteed payment as long as the certain payment is equal to or above the certainty equivalent of the gamble. I also discussed the relatively rare case of risk loving individuals who tend to prefer probabilistic pay-offs over certain ones and whose certainty equivalent for the exact same gamble will be much higher than that of a risk averse individual.

Following this, I looked at challenges to expected utility theory, first via the work of Allais, and then via Kahneman and Tversky's prospect theory. We introduced the probability weighting function, showing that, in general, people tend to overweight small probabilities and underweight large ones. People also seem to assess outcomes as gains and losses starting from an initial reference point. They then behave differently in the domain of gains and losses. The increase in utility (or value) obtained from a gain of a particular size is much smaller than the reduction in utility (or value) experienced from a loss of an equivalent size. People are risk averse in gains; implying that they prefer sure gains over potentially larger probabilistic gains, but they are risk loving in losses. They prefer to go for larger probabilistic losses over smaller sure losses; a phenomenon that has been referred to as "loss aversion". I then concluded the chapter by discussing how loss aversion may lead to the endowment effect and how it may impact economic transactions such as negotiations or bargaining, especially if coupled with overconfidence.

NOTES

1 I need to point out an important caveat here. I will often use the terms risk and uncertainty synonymously, much as they are used in day-to-day parlance. However, to economists, these are two different and distinct concepts. Both of these are probabilistic events, meaning that they are not certain and occur with some probability. Risk refers to circumstances where these probabilities are known. Uncertainty or ambiguity refers to situations where these probabilities are unknown. Most of the examples I will talk about in this chapter are about risk, since I will typically assume that the probabilities are known. This is not true in many cases where the actual probabilities are unknown. As Donald Rumsfeld, who was George W. Bush's Defense Secretary during the second Iraq War noted: there are often "known unknowns" and "unknown unknowns". Rumsfeld took a lot of ribbing, but the fact is that these are actually legitimate concepts in logic, philosophy and statistics.

2 The paradox takes its name since Daniel Bernoulli was a resident of the city and published his arguments in the Commentaries of the Imperial Academy of Science of Saint Petersburg (Bernoulli, 1738).

3 "Linear" implies a straight line that passes through the origin, while "affine" is also a straight line but one that intersects the Y-axis at a point different from the origin.

4 This and other diagrams in the rest of the chapter are not drawn to scale. But readers should be able to follow the intuition easily.

5 The principle of diminishing marginal utility lies at the heart of progressive income taxation. Typically, as income increases, we pay a higher proportion of our income in taxes. The assumption is that for someone who earns $30,000, an additional $1,000 is worth more in terms of utility than for someone who earns $300,000. So, the second (richer) person should be willing to pay more in taxes out of an extra $1,000 than the former. Alternatively, for someone making $300,000, paying a larger proportion out of a $1,000 increment is less painful than for someone making $30,000. This means that the first $30,000 of one's income is typically taxed at a lower rate than the last $30,000, for someone making $300,000. In New Zealand, for instance, we pay 10.5% out of the first $14,000 of income, then 17.5% between $14,000 and $48,000, 30% between $48,000 and $70,000 and finally, 33% for income above $70,000. Therefore, if someone makes only $14,000, this person is paying a tax of 10.5 cents for each additional dollar. But, beyond $70,000, the income earner is paying 33 cents out of every additional dollar.

6 Other functions will work too, such as $U(W) = (W)^k$ with $0 < k < 1$ (i.e., k is a positive fraction). Or $U(W) = \log W$. But, in order to keep things simple, I will work with $U(W) = \sqrt{W}$. This is the same as saying $U(W) = W^{1/2}$ or $U(W) = W^{0.5}$, such that here, k is 1/2. This is simpler than the other formulations and is a good way of getting a handle on the concept of risk aversion. The concavity of the utility function is a measure of how risk averse an individual is. More concave utility functions imply greater risk aversion. So, someone with a utility function of $U(W) = W^{1/8}$ is more risk averse than someone with $U(W) = W^{1/4}$, who, in turn, is more risk averse than someone with $U(W) = W^{1/2}$.

7   You might be thinking that 99.88 and 100 are very close. Yes, but this is because of the functional form and the lottery pay-offs I have chosen in this instance. If I change the utility function or the size of the pay-offs, then these numbers will be much further apart. We will look at some examples like this shortly.

8   Don't take my word for it; check. Take an amount higher than $7,465 and make sure it yields more than 86.4 units of utility. Take, for example, $7,600. You will find that it yields 87.18 units of utility and so is strictly preferred to the lottery.

9   As before, this diagram is not drawn to scale.

10 I elaborate on some of these issues further in the next chapter. Kahneman would go on to win the Nobel Prize in Economics in 2002, along with Vernon Smith. Amos Tversky would most likely have shared the prize with them, but, unfortunately, Tversky had passed away and the Nobel Prize is not awarded posthumously. Tversky has made tremendous contributions to many areas of cognitive psychology. I say more about some of his work on the "hot hands" fallacy in the next chapter. For those interested in learning more about Kahneman, Tversky and their collaboration, an excellent book to read is *The Undoing Project* by Michael Lewis.

11 The evolution of prospect theory from expected utility theory is a good example of the distinction between the economic and psychological approaches to modelling choice. Expected utility theory is an elegant and coherent model of choice under risk, but one that struggled to explain choices under certain situations. So, when the model was confronted with human behavioural data, the model could not predict certain choices well. Prospect theory, on the other hand, is a completely descriptive theory that starts by looking at a large amount of data regarding choices in different situations. Once Kahneman and Tversky were confident that they had established well-defined patterns in the data, they were ready to propose an alternative theory. In this second case, the development of theory follows from, and is a consequence of, the observed regularities in the data.

12 This part, unfortunately, gets a little technical. But most readers can ignore some of this and go with the intuition of the probability weighting function. A potential form of the probability weighting function shown in Figure 4.6 is $\pi(p) = \dfrac{p^\gamma}{\left\{p^\gamma + (1-p)^\gamma\right\}^\gamma}$. Smaller values of γ imply a more dramatic s-shape. So, in Figure 4.6, the less curved line might be when γ is 0.7, while the more curved line could be for γ equal to 0.55. Of course, if γ is equal to 1, then the function is exactly equal to p for all values of p.

13 In saying this, I am not taking a strong stance on what the appropriate response is, since the responses varied considerably among countries. The stringency of the response was also crucially dependent on the timing of the policy intervention. I am simply highlighting how some of the material we have discussed have obvious and immediate policy applications. My point is that COVID-19 is certainly not the last pandemic we will face; neither is this the last time we will be forced to make decisions under acute duress facing the large-scale loss of lives. Like it or not, we live in a world full of trade-offs. So, when confronted with difficult decisions such as pandemic response, policy makers will be well-served if they bear in mind the issues of identified lives versus statistical lives, the underweighting (overweighting) of large (small) probabilities and the associated phenomenon of loss aversion. This will almost certainly lead to more well-informed debate and (one hopes) better policy.

5 Probabilistic thinking

In this chapter, I talk about:

- *The difference between correlation and causation;*
- *Omitted variable bias;*
- *Prior and posterior probabilities;*
- *Bayesian thinking and Bayes' Rule;*
- *The application of Bayesian thinking to legal and medical decision making;*
- *Conjunctive and disjunctive fallacies;*
- *Regression to the mean.*

INTRODUCTION

In a particular city, there are two cab companies: the Blue Cab Company and the Green Cab Company. This was before the advent of Uber and Lyft and GPS tracking that can pinpoint exactly where a car is at any point in time. The Green Cab Company is much larger and owns 85% of the cabs in the city; Blue cabs account for the remaining 15%. Around dusk one day, a cab was involved in a fatal hit-and-run accident. There is an eyewitness. The witness is certain that it was a Blue Cab. The police tested the witness' accuracy. They asked the witness to correctly identify and distinguish between Blue and Green cabs in identical circumstances; same time of day and similar light. The witness correctly identified Blue Cabs as blue and Green Cabs as green 80% of the time and got it wrong in 20% of cases. The police think 80% accuracy is pretty good. They are convinced that the eyewitness got it right and start focusing on drivers in the Blue Cab company only. Should they be so certain? I will come back to this shortly, but for now, let me digress a bit.

I love the film *12 Angry Men*. I have watched it many times and often, while teaching Behavioural Economics, I use one of my early lectures to show this film to my students. I show the 1957 black and white version starring Henry Fonda, Martin Balsam, George C. Scott and Ed Begley Sr. rather than the later remake with Jack Lemmon, James Gandolfini and Tony Danza.

A juvenile boy stands accused of killing his father. The film starts with the judge handing the case to the jury and the latter moving to the jury room to deliberate. At the first vote, 11 out of 12 jurors are convinced that the boy is guilty; the sole hold-out is Henry Fonda, Juror No. 8. He does not say that he is certain the boy is not guilty; he just wants to talk a

■ Probabilistic thinking

little about the evidence, while the others try to convince him about the boy's guilt. Among other things, the film is a see-saw battle between System 1 and System 2 thinking. Most of the jurors know in their gut that the boy is guilty and find it astounding that Juror No. 8 does not share their certitude. At the beginning, at least, Juror No. 8 is the only person who seems willing to be the rider rather than the elephant; to take a step back and ask questions about what the evidence really shows rather than relying on his gut feelings about what is right. The other aspect of the movie that is worth highlighting is the role of probabilities. Over and over again, when a juror claims that he is certain something did or did not happen, Juror No. 8 asks: "Is it possible?".

At one point in the film, Henry Fonda says that he would like to find out "if an old man who drags one foot when he walks, 'cause he had a stroke last year, could get from his bedroom to his front door in 15 seconds." At this, Juror No. 3 comments: "You're talking about a matter of seconds! Nobody can be that accurate." Fonda responds: "I think testimony that could put a boy into the electric chair should be that accurate."

The reason why I enjoy this film so much is that it encapsulates many of the recurring themes in this book: System 1 versus System 2 thinking; our conscious and unconscious biases; getting our heads around decisions when outcomes are certain versus uncertain (deterministic versus probabilistic) and the role of emotions in such decision making. At a later point in the film, Fonda says:

> It's always difficult to keep personal prejudice out of a thing like this. And wherever you run into it, prejudice always obscures the truth. I don't really know what the truth is. I don't suppose anybody will ever really know. Nine of us now seem to feel that the defendant is innocent, but we're just gambling on probabilities – we may be wrong. We may be trying to let a guilty man go free, I don't know. Nobody really can. But we have a reasonable doubt, and that's something that's very valuable in our system. No jury can declare a man guilty unless it's sure.

The Blue Cab–Green Cab problem did not come up in the film, but a number of other probabilistic events did. Could the old man who limps badly get to the front door in time to see the boy running down the stairs and out of the building? Could he really hear the boy yell "I will kill you" when an L-train was roaring past his window? Could a woman, who was not wearing her glasses, watching out through her window, see the boy stab his father through the windows of that L-train even if the train was completely empty? I am not going to say any more. If you have seen the film, then you will appreciate this chapter even more; if you have not seen this film, then you need to rectify this shortcoming at the earliest available opportunity.[1]

No one knows for sure. There were no eyewitnesses as there often are not. But, as Juror No. 8 keeps iterating, it is all about the probabilities; is it possible? Is it probable? How likely is it? Is it a high probability event or a low probability event? It turns out that we are not naturally good at thinking in terms of chances. When it comes to probabilities, our gut feelings often misguide us. To use Kahneman's WYSIATI paradigm, when it comes to probabilities, the need to look carefully and dig deeper is all the more important because, when it comes to probabilities, there is often much more to what you see.

CASE STUDY 5.1 IF THEY ARE SO POOR, WHY DO THEY HAVE SO MANY BABIES?

I hear this a lot; I hear this from people in developed countries about those in poorer countries; the ones Donald Trump referred to as "s—thole" countries. I hear this from rich folks, about the poor in their own country. I hear it from Hindus about Muslims in India and from rich, affluent Whites about Blacks and Latinos in the US. What does this mean? As far as I can make out, the argument is that "those people" are poor because they have so many babies and need to care for them. So, the reckless act of procreating over and over again is the root cause of poverty. Why can't they be more like us? Why can't they keep their libido in check?

It is certainly true that poorer countries (lower per capita income) have higher birth rates compared to richer countries (higher per capita income) that have fewer children and lower birth rates, where birth rate is defined as simply the number of live births per thousand persons. This is, at least, partly due to the fact that people in richer countries are getting married much later in life. This implies that they start to have babies later in life (because even now, most babies are born to married parents, rather than out of wedlock), and, in turn, end up with fewer babies. Looking at New Zealand, in 1961, the median age at first marriage was 25 for men and 22 for women. This is shown in Figure 5.1. By 2016, the median age for men was 32 and for women 30. Much of the change happened before 2004–2005 and has been steady since then. The pattern would be similar for other developed nations. But even within the same country, birth rates start to drop as income levels rise. And, as Hans and Ola Rösling and Rönnlund point out in their fascinating book *Factfulness*, there are no differences across religious groups. The same pattern holds true for all countries, whether they are majority Christian, Muslim or something else. As incomes rise, birth rates decline. So, no, there is nothing particularly strange or other-worldly

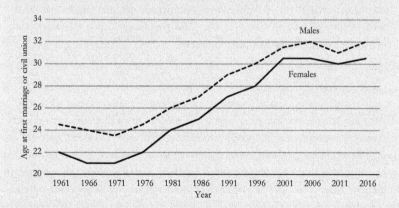

Figure 5.1
Age at first marriage in New Zealand

about (say) Muslims as opposed to Christians. The pattern is the same. As per capita income rises, the birth rate falls in Christian countries as they do in Muslim, Hindu or Buddhist countries.

When I ask my students about why this may be the case, a common answer is contraceptive use or lack thereof. This is incorrect because even in poorer countries there is widespread knowledge of contraceptives. The answer to this riddle is simple: opportunity cost. I defined opportunity cost earlier. At its core, opportunity cost is the cost of an activity/good/service that you give up in order to get something else. So, the cost of taking a vacation may be foregoing interest on savings or reducing your mortgage. With rising incomes, there are more opportunities, particularly for women. Equally, in developed countries around the world, the amount of education needed for a given job has increased. People are studying longer and working harder. Now, the cost of having a baby needs to be considered against the consequent loss of income from a woman's wages, a trade-off that was not required when jobs for women were few and far between. It is also true that, for women, there is a "biological clock", implying that there is a limit to how late in life women can have children. This in turn implies that women who start having children later in life (as in most industrialized nations) will end up having *fewer* children compared to women who may start to have children much earlier in life.

So, two points: first, most people are getting the direction of the causality wrong. It is not that more babies lead to poverty. Rather, poverty results in people having more babies, since the opportunity cost of having a baby is lower. Second, if you want to implement a policy aimed at reducing the birth-rate, then one option is to enact policies that raise income levels. But, more importantly, a critical intervention would be creating opportunities for women, both in education and employment.

Does correctly understanding this causality matter? Yes! Very much so! Misunderstanding this causality (and the real reason for a high birth rate) led to China's misguided one-child policy; India's forced sterilization policy for adult males in the early to mid-1970s during the Prime Ministership of Indira Gandhi and Peru's forced sterilization programme among the tribal population such as the Quechua in 1995 under the Presidency of Alberto Fujimori.

Just as establishing causality is often tricky, people also often mistake correlation for causality. Just because two things go together, it does not mean that one causes the other. Sometimes, these correlations are purely coincidental; economists call these "spurious" correlations. At other times, the correlation between two variables is caused by a third "omitted" variable, that lurks in the background and is not immediately perceived. For example, the consumption of ice cream and swimming pool drownings tend to be positively correlated. Does this mean that a child is more likely to drown in a swimming pool after consuming ice cream? No. The point to note is that both of these things tend to happen in the summer. In the summer, when the weather turns hot, we consume more ice cream and also get in the pool more often.

I love to ask my students about a headline I saw in the *New York Times*: "Happy children do household chores". What does this mean? Does being happy cause children to do chores around the house? Or is it that doing chores makes children happy? The answer is neither. It just happens that there are some families where, possibly due to parenting style, children tend to have a happy disposition and also take part in household chores. The omitted variable here is the attributes of those families or of the parenting style or both.

Let us consider a more elaborate policy-relevant topic. Is unemployment good or bad for health? In general, most economists would argue that unemployment is bad; besides its immediate impact on the ability to earn a living, it has other auxiliary adverse effects such as a loss of self-esteem or loss of feelings of self-worth. In fact, estimates suggest that an increase in the unemployment rate results in lower life expectancy on average. Yet, it is also generally found that when unemployment rates increase, the mortality rate declines. How can both of these be true?

The answer lies in the fact that the second finding above is at the aggregate, economy-wide level. If you look at the economy as a whole, when unemployment rates go up, mortality rates fall. But this is most likely driven by a third omitted factor. One potential answer provided by health economists is the following: during booms when jobs are easy to find, it is difficult to find good care for the elderly. This means that, at times of low unemployment, mortality rates among the elderly rise. But, during recessions, when unemployment is high and jobs harder to find, it is easier to find care persons for the elderly, leading to an improvement in quality of care and therefore a fall in the mortality rate. But the crucial point to recognize here is that we are talking about two different things moving in unison; the unemployment rate among younger adults going up results in the mortality rate of the elderly going down due to better quality care; similarly, more jobs for the younger adults implies a fall in the quality of care for the elderly, leading to a rise in the mortality rate in times of higher unemployment.

PROBABILITIES ARE DICEY AND OFTEN HARD TO GET OUR HEADS AROUND

In Chapter 3, I talked about Kahneman's discussion of the incidence of kidney cancer in the 3,141 counties of the USA. Counties with the lowest incidence of kidney cancer are mostly rural, sparsely populated and located in traditionally Republican states in the Midwest, the South and the West. But, counties with the highest incidence of kidney cancer are mostly rural, sparsely populated and located in traditionally Republican states in the Midwest, the South and the West.

How can both of these statements be true? We found that the answer lay in the small number of observations in each case; rural counties have small populations and small populations are more likely to throw up extreme outcomes. As Kahneman notes:

> The fact that rural counties are "sparsely populated" (and therefore result in a small number of observations) does not immediately stand out to System 1. We must actually exert mental effort to see that the following two statements mean exactly the same thing: (a) Large samples are more precise than small samples. (b) Small samples yield extreme results more often than large samples do.

■ Probabilistic thinking

Let me give you two further examples taken from Kahneman's work (much of this done with his long-time collaborator, Amos Tversky).

Suppose, at the University of Auckland, 40% of students study Arts, 15% study Medicine, 15% study Business and Economics, 15% study Engineering, and 2% study Computer Science. The remaining study other disciplines. Consider Tom, a student at the University of Auckland, whose characteristics are described below.

> Tom is of high intelligence, although lacking in true creativity. He has a need for order and clarity and for neat and tidy systems in which every detail finds its useful place. His writing is dull and mechanical, occasionally enlivened by somewhat corny puns and flashes of imagination of the sci-fi type. He has a strong drive for competence. He seems to have little feel and little sympathy for other people and does not enjoy interacting with others. Self-centred, he nonetheless has a deep moral sense.

The question is: what does Tom study? Once again, you might want to try this thought experiment before you continue. What do you think Tom studies? A vast majority of people, when asked, say that Tom studies Computer Science.

This is most likely not going to be true. Why? Because you have already been told that 40% of students (a plurality) study Arts. So, absent of any further information, you should assume that any particular student picked at random is likely to study Arts, more than any other subject. Now, look at the paragraph that describes Tom. Does it really tell you all that much about Tom? If every 40 out of 100 students study Arts, surely some of them will be dull and mechanical writers and have a strong drive for competence. Kahneman calls this the *representativeness* bias. We read words like "neat and tidy systems", "dull and mechanical writing", "flashes of imagination of the sci-fi type", "strong drive for competence" and our System 1 immediately starts screaming "computer science", ignoring the fact that only two out of 100 students would fit that label. There are very few computer science students.

Let us turn to the next example. Below, I will provide a description of Linda. You will then need to choose the sentence that you think is the most likely description of Linda. Once again, you will find this more fun, if you try it before continuing.

> Linda is thirty-one years old, single, outspoken and very bright. She majored in philosophy. As a student, she was deeply concerned with issues of discrimination and social justice and also participated in antinuclear demonstrations.

Which statement below best describes Linda?

> Linda is a bank clerk.
> Linda is an insurance salesperson.
> Linda is a bank clerk and she is active in the feminist movement.

Most frequent response? Linda is a bank clerk and she is active in the feminist movement. But how can this be right? Among the set of people who are bank clerks, there must be both feminists and non-feminists. The probability that Linda is a bank clerk is the sum of two different probabilities: the probability that Linda is a feminist bank clerk, plus the probability that Linda is a non-feminist bank clerk! This means that the probability that *Linda is a bank clerk* must be greater than or, at best, equal to, the probability that *Linda is a feminist bank clerk*. At best, the two probabilities would be equal if there are no non-feminist bank clerks. But the probability (Linda is a feminist bank clerk) cannot be greater than the probability (Linda is a bank clerk). Kahneman calls this the *conjunction fallacy*; the idea that the probability of a subset of an event cannot be greater than the probability of the event itself. For example, it would be a conjunction fallacy to state that "the set of seven-letter words ending in 'ing'" is larger than "the set of seven-letter words with 'n' as the sixth letter". This is because every seven-letter word ending in "ing" has "n" as the sixth letter![2]

ONE FURTHER DETOUR ON THE WAY TO THE JURY DECISION-MAKING PROBLEM

I have kept you waiting for quite a while. It is time to get back to the Blue Cab–Green Cab problem that I started with. Actually, I need to make another detour. Sorry about that. This is like when you are waiting at the doctor's office and your name is called. You jump up, waiting to be seen, only to realize that it is only the nurse who wants to take your temperature and blood-pressure and you wait again, this time in a smaller room.

But I hope the wait will be worth it. First, one more game. Take a look at Figure 5.2. Isha has two boxes: A and B. Box A has 2 red balls and 1 blue ball. Box B has 1 red ball and 2 blue balls. Isha tosses a fair 6-sided die. If 1, 2 or 3 comes up, she will pick Box A; if 4, 5 or 6 come up, then she will pick Box B. So, each box has a 1/2 chance of being picked. Once she has picked a box, she reaches inside and randomly chooses one of the three balls in the box. She then brings it out and shows the ball to you. You need to guess which box the ball came from.

Suppose the ball Isha has picked up is red. What is the chance that the red ball came from Box A? A surprisingly common answer from my students is 1/3. Why? Well, because the chance that Box A is picked is 1/2 and the chance of getting a red ball from Box A is 2/3. So (1/2)*(2/3) = 1/3. But this cannot be right! Because this would mean that there is

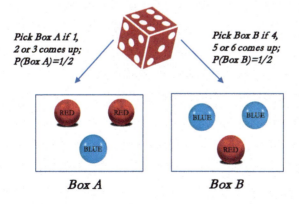

Figure 5.2
Red ball–blue ball example

■ Probabilistic thinking

a 2/3 chance of getting a red ball from Box B. At worst, since there are 6 balls, 3 red and 3 blue, the probability of getting a red ball must be, at least, 1/2. This probability of picking a red ball in the absence of any additional information is called the *prior probability*. Each box has a 1/2 chance of being picked. So, at the very beginning, before anything has happened, the chances of getting a red ball is the same as that of a blue ball; 1/2. However, the fact that a ball has been picked and shown to you and the fact that this ball is red conveys additional information to you. Most of us tend to ignore this additional piece of information.

This is what the contestants on the famous game show *Let's Make a Deal* with Monty Hall did. Monty would show contestants three doors. Behind one door was a grand prize, while behind the other two were zonks, things of no value. The contestant had to pick a door. Once the contestant had picked a door (say Door 1), Monty would open one of the other two doors to reveal a zonk. Suppose Monty opened Door 2. Then he would ask the contestant if he/she wanted to stay with Door 1 or switch to Door 3. The vast majority of contestants decide to stick with their original choice, ignoring the fact that Monty's choice of opening one of the doors carries meaningful information.

At the beginning, the chances of the grand prize being behind one of the three doors is 1/3 each. So, if a contestant picks Door 1, then he/she has picked the grand prize with 1/3 probability. This implies that there is a 2/3 probability that the grand prize is behind Doors 2 or 3. When Monty reveals that there is a zonk behind Door 2, this must imply that the probability of the grand prize being behind Door 3 has increased from 1/3 to 2/3. This, in turn, implies that the contestant will be better off, *on average*, by always switching. Not convinced? Suppose there are 100 doors. You have chosen Door 1. Monty now opens, one by one, 98 other doors from 2 through 36 and 38 to 100. Only Door 1 and Door 37 remain unopened. Will you still stick with Door 1 or will you switch to Door 37? The important point here is that Monty gets to decide which doors to open. The fact that Monty did not open Door 37 conveys meaningful information. You should promptly switch to Door 37. It may not necessarily work for you, but over many trials, those who switch will always do better than those who do not.

So, what about that red ball? In order to understand the answer to this question, we need to think of something called *conditional probabilities*: the fact that the probability of something happening given that something else has already happened. In this case, we need the probability that it is Box A, given that a red ball has been picked. Essentially, two things must happen. *First, Box A needs to be picked. Next, given that Box A has been picked, Isha needs to pick a red ball out of Box A.* This means that we need to find the probability that it is a red ball from Box A, or, putting it differently, that it is a red ball *and* it is from Box A *given* that a red ball has been picked. Here, the word *given* really means *divided by*.

So, we need Pr(From Box A given that it is a red ball), which is often written as Pr(Box A|Red Ball). More formally, Pr(Box A|Red Ball) = Pr(Box A & Red Ball)/Pr(Red Ball). Transposing sides, this also means that Pr(Box A & Red Ball) = Pr(Box A|Red Ball)*Pr(Red Ball). But, Pr(Box A & Red Ball) must be the same as Pr(Red Ball & Box A). And, in that case, using a similar argument as above, it must be true that Pr(Red Ball & Box A) = Pr(Red Ball|Box A)*Pr(Box A). This, in turn, also implies that Pr(Box A|Red Ball)*Pr(Red Ball) = Pr(Red Ball|Box A)*Pr(Box A) = Pr(Box A & Red Ball) = Pr(Red Ball & Box A).[3]

So, we need the probability of the event that it is a red ball from Box A, that is, Pr(Box A & Red Ball). Then we need to divide this by Pr(Red Ball), that is, the probability of picking a red ball to start with. We have just shown that Pr(Box A & Red Ball) = Pr(Red Ball|Box A)*Pr(Box A). The chance of getting a red ball after Box A has been chosen is 2/3, since Box A contains 2 red and 1 blue ball. The chance of Isha picking Box A is 1/2. This means that the probability of the event that it is Box A and it is a red ball, that is, Pr(Box A & Red Ball) is (2/3)*(1/2) = (2/6) = (1/3).

But we are not done. Remember, we need Pr(Box A|Red Ball). We said that this is equal to Pr(Box A & Red Ball)/Pr(Red Ball). We have just found the value of the numerator. Pr(Box A & Red Ball) = (2/3)*(1/2) = (2/6) = (1/3). We now need the denominator. What is the chance of getting a red ball? If you think about it, there are two ways that Isha can get a red ball. She could have picked Box A and the red ball came from that box. We have already found this probability. It is 1/3. But there is a second way in which Isha could have picked a red ball. She could have picked Box B and then picked a red ball out of that. This is the probability that it is Box B and it is a red ball, or Pr(Box B & Red Ball). This probability must be equal to Pr(Red Ball|Box B)*Pr(Box B). The probability of picking a red ball out of Box B is 1/3 since Box B contains 1 red and 2 blue balls. The probability of picking Box B is 1/2. This means that Pr(Red Ball|Box B)*Pr(Box B) = (1/3)*(1/2) = 1/6.

Now, we can say the following:

$$\Pr(\text{Box A} \mid \text{Red Ball}) = \frac{\Pr(\text{Box A \& Red Ball})}{\Pr(\text{Red Ball})}$$

$$\Pr(\text{Box A} \mid \text{Red Ball}) = \frac{\Pr(\text{Red Ball}|\text{Box A}) * \Pr(\text{Box A})}{\Pr(\text{Red Ball}|\text{Box A}) * \Pr(\text{Box A}) + \Pr(\text{Red Ball} \mid \text{Box B}) * \Pr(\text{Box B})}$$

$$\Pr(\text{Box A}|\text{Red Ball}) = \frac{\left(\frac{2}{3}\right)*\left(\frac{1}{2}\right)}{\left(\frac{2}{3}\right)*\left(\frac{1}{2}\right)+\left(\frac{1}{3}\right)*\left(\frac{1}{2}\right)} = \frac{\frac{2}{6}}{\frac{2}{6}+\frac{1}{6}} = \frac{2}{3}$$

So, our prior probability (before we had any additional information) that the red ball came out of Box A was ½, given that there are 6 balls of which 3 are red. But, now that Isha has shown us a red ball, we need to update our prior probability and come up with a *posterior* probability, which is now higher and equal to 2/3. The formula above owes its origin to Thomas Bayes and is popularly known as Bayes' Rule.[4]

Here is one other example to help you fix this idea in your mind. Trust me, the pain will be worth it, when you see the applications and understand their implications. Suppose we are interested in probability of an outcome D, and D can be generated in two ways: either through A or B. Then, we can write, Pr(D) = Pr(A&D) + Pr(B&D) = Pr(D|A)*Pr(A) + Pr(D|B)*Pr(B). Suppose you have a factory which produces Kookaburra balls and there are two machines which produce them: one new (A), and another old (B).[5] A produces 80 and

■ Probabilistic thinking

B produces 20 balls per day. One per cent of A's production is defective and 2% of B's production is defective. What is the probability that a randomly selected kookaburra ball is defective?

Since machine A produces 80% (0.8) of the balls and the probability of a ball from machine A being defective is 0.01, the probability that a ball is defective and from machine A is 0.008. Since machine B produces 20% (0.2) of the balls and the probability of a ball from machine B being defective is 0.02, the probability that a ball is defective and from machine B is 0.004. So, the total probability of getting a defective ball is 0.008 + 0.004 = 0.012. So, if we know that a ball is defective, what is the chance of that ball being from machine A? This is (0.008)/(0.012) = 2/3. And if we know that a ball is defective, the chance of that ball being from machine B is (0.004)/(0.012) = 1/3.

We can argue this in a different way that allows us to exploit the theorem provided by Reverend Bayes. The probability of a ball from machine A being defective is 1% or $Pr(D|A) = 0.01$. The probability of a ball from machine B being defective is 2% or $Pr(D|B) = 0.02$. The probability that a ball is produced by machine A is $Pr(A) = 0.8$, and for machine B this is $Pr(B) = 0.2$. Plugging these numbers into the equation we wrote earlier:

$$Pr(D) = Pr(\text{Defective Ball} | \text{Machine A}) * Pr(\text{Machine A})$$
$$+ Pr(\text{Defective Ball} | \text{Machine B}) * Pr(\text{Machine B})$$
$$= 0.01 * 0.8 + 0.02 * 0.2 = 0.008 + 0.004 = 0.012$$

Suppose a ball is picked at random and it turns out to be defective. What is the chance that this ball came from machine B; that is, Pr(Machine B|Defective Ball)? What do we need to find? For the numerator, we need to find Pr(Machine B & Defective Ball). For the denominator, we need to find the ways in which we can get a defective ball.

$$Pr(\text{Machine B} | \text{Defective Ball}) = \frac{Pr(\text{Machine B \& Defective Ball})}{Pr(\text{Defective Ball})}$$

$$= \frac{Pr(\text{Defective Ball}|\text{Machine B}) * Pr(\text{Machine B})}{\{Pr(\text{Def Ball} | \text{Machine A}) * Pr(\text{Machine A}) + Pr(\text{Def Ball} | \text{Machine B}) * Pr(\text{Machine B})\}}$$

$$= \frac{0.02 * 0.2}{0.01 * 0.8 + 0.02 * 0.2} = \frac{0.004}{0.012} = \frac{1}{3}$$

So, we get the same answer as we did before.

BACK TO THE JURY DECISION-MAKING PROBLEM

Now, finally, let us get back to the jury room. You have heard the evidence and everyone around is convinced that the eyewitness and the police are correct. Surely, they say, you cannot believe otherwise. The eyewitness is right in 80% of cases! That is a very high probability and makes the others convinced that there is no reason to doubt the accuracy of the eyewitness. But you have now taken a course in behavioural decision making and you know all about WYSIATI and base-rates. You know that it is not necessarily the case that "what you see is all there is"; sometimes, there is more. You may remember the China example from Chapter 3; there may be fewer rich people as a proportion but there are so many more people that even this small proportion works out to a large number. Similarly, you are thinking, I know what the eyewitness says: she thinks she saw a Blue Cab, but there are so many Green Cabs in this city. It was dusk; the light was not great, and it seems that it is easy to confuse the two colours.

So, you ask for some paper and a pen and you start writing this down. You need to make sure that you have this right before you can try convincing the others, who are absolutely certain that there is no doubt. Eighty-five per cent of the cabs in the city are green; 15% are blue. This means that Pr(Cab is Green) = 0.85; Pr(Cab is Blue) = 0.15. The eyewitness correctly identified the cab's colour under identical circumstances in 80% of cases. So, Pr(Cab is identified as Blue when it is really Blue) = 0.8. However, the eyewitness was not right 100% of the time. She got it wrong in 20% of cases. This means that Pr(Cab is identified as Blue when it is really Green) = 0.2.

So, what is the true probability that the Cab is really Blue when it has been identified as Blue? As before, we need two things. We need the probability that the cab is really Blue and is identified as Blue in the numerator. In the denominator, we need all the ways that the cab can be identified as being Blue. Here, the cab can be identified as Blue in two ways: correctly; that is, it is identified as Blue when it is really Blue, or incorrectly: it is identified as Blue when it is really Green. The latter situation is called a *false positive*. So, we need:

$$\Pr\big(\text{Cab really Blue}|\text{Cab is identified as Blue}\big)$$

$$= \frac{\Pr\big(\text{Cab is really blue and is identified as blue}\big)}{\Pr\big(\text{Cab is identified as Blue}\big)}$$

$$= \frac{\Pr(\text{Cab identified Blue}\,|\,\text{Cab really Blue}) * \Pr(\text{Cab really Blue})}{\big\{\{\Pr(\text{Cab identified Blue}\,|\,\text{Cab really Blue}) * \Pr(\text{Cab really Blue})\} + \{\Pr(\text{Cab identified Blue}\,|\,\text{Cab really Green}) * \Pr(\text{Cab really Green})\}\big\}}$$

$$= \frac{0.8 * 0.15}{0.8 * 0.15 + 0.2 * 0.85} = \frac{0.12}{0.12 + 0.17} = \frac{0.12}{0.29} = 0.414$$

This means the actual probability that the cab is really Blue when it has been identified as Blue is just about 41.4%; not only is it much less than 80%, it is less than one-half! There is a less than 1/2 chance that the cab is actually Blue.

Now, you have the more difficult job of explaining all of this to other members of the jury, who are certainly in no mood to hear about your probability mumbo-jumbo and do not care what your behavioural economics teacher taught you. If you really want to know how to get your point across, then watch the film. It provides great lessons in how to negotiate;

how to convince others who are dead set against you and know for sure that they are right and you are wrong.

Chances are, you are not going to be able to explain Bayes' Rule to your colleagues. And if you tried, you will find eyes glazing over and people giving you dirty looks. So, here is an easier way of explaining this. Now you are thinking: if there is an easy way of explaining this, then why did he subject us to all this mathematical torture? The answer is that the easy way is only easy as long as you understand the hard way. What you need to say to other members of the jury is this:

> Look, suppose there are 1,000 cabs in this city. 850 of them are Green, while 150 are Blue. If the eyewitness is right 80% of the time, that means the eyewitness will correctly identify 120 of the 150 Blue Cabs. *But*, given a 20% chance of making a mistake, the eyewitness will identify 20% of Green Cabs as Blue Cabs. This means that there will be 170 Green Cabs that will be *incorrectly identified* as Blue Cabs. This means that there are more cabs that are *incorrectly identified* as Blue than are *correctly identified* as Blue. Is it possible that the eyewitness is mistaken?

Notice that if you work out the chances here, you still get the same result. There are 120 cabs that are identified as Blue when they are really Blue. But there are another 170 cabs that are identified as Blue when they are really Green. This means that there are 290 (120+170) cabs in total that are identified as Blue. So, what is the chance that the eyewitness is correct? It is 120/290 = 41% (approx.). Chances are that if you keep your cool, like Henry Fonda in *12 Angry Men*, and simply say: "Is it possible?", one or more other members of the jury will come around to see your point of view eventually.

MICHAEL BLOOMBERG'S STOP-AND-FRISK POLICY

In the lead-up to the US Presidential Election in 2020, the former Mayor of New York City, Michael Bloomberg, was vying to be the Democratic nominee. He endured significant criticism for vastly expanding the "stop-and-frisk" policies in the city.[6] This is where police are deployed primarily in African American neighbourhoods and accost young African Americans in search of drugs and weapons. The idea was that doing this would lead to a reduction in crime since Bloomberg believed, and was on record for stating in a speech at the Aspen Institute in 2015:

> 95% of your murders and murderers and murder victims fit one M.O. You can just take the description and Xerox it and pass it out to all the cops. They are male minorities 15 to 25.

But this does not make a lot of sense, and the clue to why it does not is hidden in Bloomberg's quote itself. The people who were being pulled over were in the *minority*. So, unless you are prepared to argue that every single African American is prone to criminality and none of the European Americans are, then the policy does not make sense. Even if the degree of criminality is higher among African Americans and lower among European Americans, the fact is that there are far fewer of the former and far greater numbers of the latter. So, even if the probability of criminality among the European Americans is lower, the fact that there are so many more of them implies that if your aim is to get those drugs and weapons off the streets, you might as well pull-over as many European Americans as African Americans, or even more of the former, since there are so many more of them. Remember China: there may be a lower proportion of rich people but the total population is very large.

During the primary season in late 2019 and early 2020, Bloomberg went on to repudiate his previous remarks and apologized. Patrick Lynch, the then President of the Patrolman's Benevolent Association of New York City released a statement where he said that the apology was too little and too late. Lynch suggested that Bloomberg could have saved himself the trouble if he had listened to the police officers on the street.[7]

INDIRA, THE MATURE MOTHER

Indira is a smart and accomplished professional with advanced degrees. But, along the way, she did not really have time to have children. Remember, I said at the beginning of this chapter that, in the Western world, we are studying longer and getting married late. This means that we are also having children later in life. Indira is now 35 and expecting her first child. She is worried that her baby may have Down's Syndrome, which is more common in babies born to older mothers.[8] This does not mean that younger mothers cannot have babies with the syndrome; it simply means that as a woman gets older, her chances of having a baby with Down's Syndrome increases rapidly. For instance, the chances that a 25-year-old mother will have a baby with the syndrome is 1 in 1,300. This probability increases to 1 in 1,000 for a 30-year-old mother, 1 in 365 at 35, and 1 in 90 at 40.

Typically, the first step in screening for Down's is to undertake a nuchal translucency. This is an ultrasound technique usually carried out at around ten weeks of pregnancy. It is designed to measure the thickness of fluid build-up at the back of the baby's neck. Higher than normal thickness can be an early indication of Down's. A more reliable screening test is the maternal blood serum test, which can be carried out at around the same time (approx. 11–13 weeks into pregnancy). One can undergo an amniocentesis, which can tell you for certain whether chromosomal abnormalities are present or not. But this is an invasive procedure that requires inserting a needle into the uterus to pull out amniotic fluid for testing. There is a small chance of miscarriage when undertaking an amniocentesis. A lot of mothers stop with the maternal blood serum test. They look at what the probabilities are and the decide whether to continue with the pregnancy or terminate it at that point.

Indira has just received a phone-call from her obstetrician telling her that she has tested positive on the maternal blood serum test. This means that her unborn child may have Down's Syndrome. Naturally, she is concerned. She asks the doctor how accurate the test is, and the doctor tells her that the test is accurate 90% of the time. This means that if 100 mothers whose babies have Down's Syndrome took this test, then the test will correctly predict that the baby has Down's in 90 cases (which is usually referred to as a true positive) and in the remaining ten cases, the test will fail to predict the existence of the syndrome (a false negative; the baby has the syndrome but the test fails to pick that up). Indira is well informed and knows that most tests are not infallible. There is a chance of a "false positive". This means that the test will say that the baby has Down's even though the baby does not. Indira finds out that there is a 5% chance of a false positive. This means that five out of every 100 mothers will be told that their babies have Down's even though they do not.

■ Probabilistic thinking

The question for us is to figure out exactly how big is the probability that Indira's baby has Down's. Remember that, as with most things in life, there is seldom certainty about events; all we have to rely on are probabilities. How high is the case fatality for a certain disease? Is it 0.1% or is it 1%? These have radically different implications for formulating policy.

Before we get to the mathematics, let us just write down some numbers. The *prior probability* that a 35-year-old mother will have a baby with Down's is 1 in 365, or 0.00274. Because this is not an easy number to deal with, I am going to pretend that the prior probability is 1 in 100, or 0.01. This will make the calculation a little easier. The maternal blood serum test is accurate in 90% of cases. This means that the test correctly predicts the existence of the syndrome in 90 out of 100 cases (true positives) but fails to indicate the existence of the syndrome in 10 out of 100 cases (false negative). The test also results in a false positive in 5% of cases. This means that out of 100 mothers who take this test, for five mothers the test suggests the presence of Down's Syndrome incorrectly (a false positive). This means that in 95 out of 100 cases the test also accurately predicts the absence of the condition when the baby does not have Down's (true negative). This implies that if we start with 1,000 35-year-old mothers who take the maternal blood serum test, 1% of them will have babies with Down's. This amounts to ten mothers. This, in turn, also implies that 990 mothers will not have Down's babies. Of the ten mothers who have babies with Down's, nine will be identified correctly. Of course, there is one mother who will get a "false negative"; she will get a negative test even though her baby most likely has Down's. This is a problem too. But, given a 5% "false positive" rate, out of the 990 mothers whose babies do not have Down's, 5% of them, or approx. 50 (the actual number is 49.5) will get a positive test result. The other 940 will get a "true negative". Table 5.1 illustrates this breakdown.

Fortunately, Indira is well aware of Bayes' Rule. She now knows that there are 59 mothers who have received positive tests. But out of them, only nine actually have babies with Down's Syndrome. So, the chances that Indira's baby has Down's Syndrome is 9/59 = 0.15, or just about 15%. This is much higher than the prior, which was 1 in 100, or 1%. So, the chances of Indira having a baby with Down's Syndrome has gone up dramatically, by 15 times, but it is certainly not 90%. Remember, this simple numerical example is worked out with a prior of 1 in 100, which is just about one-third of the true prior of 1 in 365. This will make a big difference in the actual calculations. As I noted before, that actual prior is about 1 in 365. If we use the actual prior of 1 in 365, which is about 1/4 of our make-believe prior of 1 in 100, then the posterior probability will also go down by about 1/4.

So, why don't we now go back and work with the actual numbers? We want the probability that Indira's baby has Down's Syndrome (DS) given that she has tested positive. This is given by:

Table 5.1 Breakdown of test results

	Baby has Down's Syndrome	*Baby does not have Down's Syndrome*	*Total*
Positive test	9 [True positive]	50 [False positive]	59
Negative test	1 [False negative]	940 [True negative]	941
Total	10	990	1000

$$\Pr(\text{Baby has DS}|\text{Positive Test}) = \frac{\Pr(\text{Baby has DS and Test is Positive})}{\Pr(\text{Getting a Positive Test})}$$

What else do we know? We know that the prior probability of having a baby with Down's Syndrome is 1 in 365. So Pr(Baby has DS) = 1/365 = 0.00274. This in turn implies that the prior probability of the baby not having the syndrome is 0.9973. Let us call this Pr(No DS) = 0.9973. We also know that the probability of getting a positive test if and when the baby has DS is 90%. So Pr(Getting Positive Test given that the baby has DS) = 0.9, or Pr(Positive Test|Baby has DS) = 0.9. Finally, Pr(Getting Positive Test given that the baby *does not* have DS) = 0.05, or Pr(Positive Test|No DS) = 0.05.

For the numerator, we know that:

$\Pr(\text{Baby has DS and Test is Positive})$

$= \Pr(\text{Positive Test}|\text{Baby has DS}) * \Pr(\text{Baby has DS})$

$= 0.00274 * 0.9 = 0.002466.$

Remember that a positive test can come about in two ways: correctly and incorrectly. So, for the denominator of the equation above, we can write:

$\Pr(\text{Getting Positive Test})$

$= \Pr(\text{Getting Positive Test}|\text{Baby has DS}) * \Pr(\text{DS})$

$+ \Pr(\text{Getting Positive Test} | \textit{No DS}) * \Pr(\text{No DS})$

$= (0.9 * 0.00274) + (0.05 * 0.9973) = 0.002466 + 0.04987 = 0.0523.$

What is the probability that the baby has DS given that Indira has received a positive test? This is:

$$\Pr(\text{Baby has DS}|\text{Positive Test}) = \frac{\Pr(\text{Baby has DS and Test is Positive})}{\Pr(\text{Getting a Positive Test})}$$

$$= \frac{0.002466}{0.0523} = 0.047 = 4.7\%.$$

Again, this probability of 4.7% is magnitudes larger than the prior, which was 0.00274 or 0.2%, but nevertheless, it is still a reasonably low number, and again, nowhere close to 90%.

DEPENDENT OR INDEPENDENT? CONNECTED OR UNCONNECTED? CONJUNCTIVE AND DISJUNCTIVE FALLACIES

It is often the case that a particular outcome depends on one thing going right or wrong, or a bunch of things going right or wrong. For instance, a space shuttle may crash if even

■ Probabilistic thinking

one out of multiple systems malfunction. Similarly, a number of different events all have to happen together in order for you to hit a "Trifecta" in horse-racing. The distinction between "conjunctive" and "disjunctive" fallacies refers to the distinction between dependent and independent events; the difference between an outcome that comes about when a number of things all happen together, or an outcome that will come about even if only one out of multiple things happen. The word "conjunctive" means relating to or forming a connection or combination between things. "Disjunctive" refers to a lack of connection.[9] So, an easy way of thinking about this is to think of "connected (conjunctive) events" and "unconnected (disjunctive) events". It is also important to understand that the two go together, in the sense that it is not quite possible to define these as separate events. There are not two questions here, in the sense of whether something is a conjunctive fallacy or whether it is a disjunctive fallacy. There is really one question: are these events conjunctive/connected (dependent) or disjunctive/disconnected (independent)?

Providing some examples will make this easier to understand, rather than getting bogged down in the semantics. Here is one posed by Max Bazerman at Harvard Business School to his MBA students and discussed in his book, *Judgment in Managerial Decision Making*. Suppose I asked:

Which of the following events is the most likely, second most likely and least likely? Event A: Drawing a red marble from a bag containing 50% red and 50% blue marbles. Event B: Drawing a red marble 7 times in succession with replacement from a bag containing 90% red and 10% blue marbles. Event C: Drawing at least 1 red marble in 7 tries with replacement from a bag containing 10% red and 90% blue marbles.

Bazerman points out that when respondents are presented with these three events, the typical pattern of response is that P(B) > P(A) > P(C). So, people seem to believe that the event with the highest probability is drawing a red marble 7 times in succession with replacement out of a bag containing 90% red and 10% blue marbles. They believe that the second most likely event is drawing a red marble out of a bag containing 50% red and 50% blue marbles. The third event, drawing at least 1 red marble in 7 tries with replacement from a bag containing 10% red and 90% blue marbles is assigned the lowest probability. This would be an example of the conjunctive fallacy, where people fail to understand that the outcome of drawing a red marble 7 times in succession is actually quite unlikely, since 7 things would have to go right for this to happen.

Let us go ahead and calculate the probabilities. The probability of Event A, the chance of getting a red marble out of a bag that contains 50% each of red and blue marbles, is easy. It is exactly 50% (0.5). How about the probability of Event B, the chance of drawing 7 red marbles in succession with replacement out of a bag with 90% red and 10% blue marbles? Here, it is likely that the base rate, that there is a 90% chance of getting a red marble, is driving people astray. They are not adequately accounting for the fact that even though the chance of picking one red marble is very high, the chances of picking a red marble seven times in a row may not be high. The probability of picking a red marble out of the bag with replacement is an independent event, and here, seven of these events have to occur in unison. So, what is the actual probability that this outcome of seven red marbles in succession will happen? The probability of getting the first red marble is 90% or 0.9. The probability that the second marble is also red is 0.9*0.9 = $(0.9)^2$ = 0.81. The probability that the first three are red is 0.9*0.9*0.9 = $(0.9)^3$ = 0.729. So, the probability that the first seven marbles are all red is $(0.9)^7$ = 0.478 (approx.). Hence, the probability of this event happening is less than one-half, meaning that Event B is certainly less likely than Event A.

How about the third event: the probability of getting at least one red marble out of seven tries with replacement out of a bag with 90% blue and 10% red marbles? Notice that this is really the same question as Event B, but rephrased in the following way: *What is the probability of getting seven blue marbles in succession and with replacement out of a bag containing 90% blue and 10% red marbles?* This is because, if you do not get at least one red marble in seven tries with replacement, then it must be the case that in each of those seven tries, you have picked a blue marble. But we already know the answer to this question. What is the probability of getting seven blue marbles in succession and with replacement from a bag containing 90% blue and 10% red marbles? The answer is $(0.9)^7$ or 0.478. This, in turn, implies that the probability of this event *not* happening, or, in other words, the probability that you will get at least one red marble in one of those seven tries, is 1 − 0.478 = 0.522. Where does this leave us? We have just found that the probability of Event A is 0.5, that of Event B is 0.478 and that of Event C is 0.522. This means that Event C is more likely than Event A and Event B is the least likely, or P(C) > P(A) > P(B).

The following example discussed by Bazerman makes the conjunctive/disjunctive distinction clearer.

> It is evening now and you have to catch a flight in a hurry for an urgent business meeting tomorrow in _____. There are 5 airlines that have morning flights that will get you to _____ in time. The probability of a seat opening up in any one of those flights is 30%, 25%, 20%, 15% and 25%. What are the chances that you will make the flight?

On the face of it, the situation seems bleak because it appears that there is at most a 1 in 3 (30%) chance of you getting a flight on the first airline; the probabilities are even lower on the other airlines. But the key question here is: are these events connected or not? If they are all connected in the sense that if a seat does not open up on the first airline then it is unlikely to open up on any other airlines, then you would be correct: you have a 30% chance of getting on a plane. For instance, suppose the city you are flying to is playing host to a giant convention. Then all the airlines will face similar pressures, the events will be connected (i.e., they are not independent) and if your chances of getting on to one airline goes down, then this will affect all the other airlines too. But, on the other hand, if these are not connected (i.e., they are independent) and depend on idiosyncratic factors such as each airline's booking practices, flight routes, or tomorrow's weather on those routes resulting in flight delays or not, then of course, your chances of getting a flight are much higher than 30%.

Why? Because if the events are independent, then you will have to miss out on getting a seat on five different flights independently of each other; that is, five bad things (you not getting a seat of any of the five flights) will have to happen in unison. And we have seen that the probability of five independent "good" or "bad" things happening in unison are typically low. In this particular case, for you to be *not* able to get on any flight, means that you do not get a seat on any of the five airlines. What is the probability of that? The probability that you will not get a seat on the first airline is 70% (since there is a 30% chance of getting a seat); the probability that you will not get a seat on the second or the third or the fourth or the fifth airline is 75%, 80%, 85% and 75%, respectively. For you not to get a seat, *all* of these events must happen. So, what is the probability that you will not get a seat on any of the flights? This probability is equal to $(0.7)*(0.75)*(0.8)*(0.85)*(0.75) = 0.2678$ or approx. 27%. So, if there is an approx. 27% chance that you will not be able to get on any one of those five flights, then there is a 73% chance of you getting on at least one of those five flights. One is all you need, and in this case, your chances are pretty high; almost 3 out of 4.

CASE STUDY 5.2 THE CONJUNCTION FALLACY REVISITED

Earlier in this chapter, I discussed Kahneman's "Linda problem" as an example of the conjunction fallacy.

> Linda is 31 years old, single, outspoken and very bright. She majored in philosophy. As a student, she was deeply concerned with issues of discrimination and social justice and also participated in antinuclear demonstrations.

Typically, people are asked variants of the question: what best describes Linda? A much larger proportion of people say that Linda is a feminist bank clerk as opposed to the proportion of people who say that Linda is a bank clerk. This is interpreted as a conjunction fallacy because the probability that Linda is a feminist bank clerk cannot be higher than the probability of Linda being a bank clerk, since feminist bank clerks must be a subset of the set of bank clerks.

Gerd Gigerenzer argues that this mistake makes perfect sense. According to him, when people are asked about the best description of Linda, they are not thinking of sets, subsets or probabilities; rather, they are thinking in much more qualitative terms, and, to them, it seems intuitive that Linda is a feminist. Lots of people make this mistake, including those who are well versed in such matters. Gigerenzer suggests that this is not surprising at all. In fact, Gigerenzer says that if people are asked the question in a different way, the responses are different. For instance, if people are asked: Out of (say) 100 people, how many are likely to be bank clerks and how many are likely to be female bank clerks, then they get this right, since they now realize that they are being asked about the count of feminist bank clerks rather than their description.

But, Gigerenzer's approach seems a little forced to me. If Kahneman's question is too subtle and leaves enough scope for misinterpretation, then Gigerenzer seems to be hammering in the intent of the question by asking people to specifically focus on the fact that feminist bank clerks must be a subset of all bank clerks. But most questions in real life are not as clear-cut as that, and people do need to have an intuitive appreciation of likelihood. My student at Harvard Kennedy School, Nathan Hodson, told me a funny anecdote. He told me about a survey of US Congressional staffers, many of whom work long hours for not much pay. When asked, a majority of respondents said that there was a 20% chance that he or she would quit his/her current job, but then went on to say that there was a 50% chance that he/she would quit Congress altogether. But this cannot be right! If the chance of quitting Congress is 50% then the chance of quitting a job inside Congress must be at least 50%, if not more; it cannot be less.[10]

Nathan and I came up with three questions that were designed to look at the conjunction fallacy, along with the fallacies of events that are conjunctive/connected and disjunctive/disconnected. We took as our inspiration the tragedy of the Space Shuttle, *Challenger*. On Tuesday, January 28, 1986, the shuttle broke apart 73 seconds into its flight, killing all seven crew members aboard. It is believed that the failure was caused by the failure of O-ring seals used in the solid rocket booster joints that were not designed to handle the unusually cold conditions that existed at this launch. The O-ring seals were a mundane and inexpensive item but caused the space shuttle to disintegrate.

This led us to think of problems where the functioning of machines depends on any one component out of many working fine, or all components performing properly. For instance, the space shuttle blew up because one rather insignificant component failed to work properly. On the other hand, aeroplanes are typically built with a number of fail-safe devices so that even if one component does not work, the plane will still avoid a crash as long as other components hold up. Here are the questions we made up:

Question 1: The functioning of a particular machine is dependent on two safety valves: A and B. The machine will operate fine as long as one of the safety valves is functioning properly. Valve A has a 10% chance of failure while Valve B has a 5% chance of failure. Suppose you are in charge of maintaining this machine. How certain can you be that the machine will not break down?

Question 2: The functioning of a particular machine is dependent on two safety valves: A and B. In order for the machine to operate perfectly, *both* valves must function well. Valve A has a 10% chance of failure while Valve B has a 5% chance of failure. Suppose you are in charge of maintaining this machine. How certain can you be that the machine will not break down?

Question 3: The functioning of a particular machine is dependent on two safety valves: A and B. In order for the machine to operate perfectly, *both* valves must function well. The valves have been known to fail when subjected to extremely stressful conditions such as extreme heat or cold. Valve A fails in the most extreme 10% of conditions while Valve B fails in the most extreme 5% of conditions. Suppose you are in charge of maintaining this machine. How certain can you be that the machine will not break down?

The first question requires people to understand that the machine will work well as long as one of the valves are working. So, the way to approach this problem is to ask: What are the chances that both valves will fail at the same time? Valve A fails

10% of the time; so, the probability that Valve A fails is 0.1. Valve B fails 5% of the time; so, the probability that Valve B fails is 0.05. For the machine to fail, *both* valves must fail at the same time. This is similar to the catching a plane problem above, that in order for you not to get a seat at all, you must fail to get a seat on any of the five airlines. If the functioning of the two valves is independent of each other, then what is the probability that both valves will fail at the same time? The answer is (0.1)*(0.05) = 0.005. So, what is the chance that the machine will fail? 0.005 or 0.5%. This means that you can be 99.5% (1 − 0.05 or 100% − 0.5%) certain that the machine will function properly.

The second problem requires people to understand that as long as the valves can fail independently of each other, the probability of failure is higher. In this case, the way to approach the problem is to ask: What is the chance that the machine will not fail? Given that Valve A fails with 10% chance, that is, with 0.1 probability, and Valve B fails with 5% chance or 0.05 probability, the probability that Valve A works is 90% (0.9) and that of Valve B working is 95% (0.95). The machine will work as long as both Valve A and Valve B are working. This happens with a probability of (0.9)*(0.95) = 0.855, or 85.5%. This, in turn, implies that the machine can fail with a probability of 0.145, or 14.5%. (100% - 85.5%).

Finally, the third problem was designed as a test of the conjunction fallacy. Here, the probability of Valve B failing is clearly a subset of the probability of Valve A failing. This is because the question says that when it gets extremely hot or cold, under the most extreme 10% of cases Valve A will fail, and under the most extreme 5% of cases Valve B will fail. This implies that all we need to worry about is the failure of Valve A, since any time Valve A fails, Valve B must also fail and so any time Valve A fails the machine will fail. Valve A fails 10% of the time. So, you can be certain that the machine will work 90% of the time.

Another way to think about Question 3 is: The machine will fail if Valve A fails or Valve B fails or both fail. We already know from Question 1 above that the probability of both failing is 0.5%. So, in that case, the machine will work well in 99.5% cases. If Valve B fails 5% of the time, the machine will work 95% of the time. Finally, A fails 10% of the time, implying that here, the machine will fail 10% of the time but work 90% of the time. We only need to worry about the largest chance of failure here, which is 10%, because the risk of Valve B failing (at 5%) is nested within the risk of Valve A failing (at 10%). The key thing to recognize here, is that the failure of Valves A and B are not independent; they are connected. Every time it gets too hot or too cold, the valves may fail. So, what I need to worry about is which of the two valves fail more often. It does not matter if Valve B is working (happens 95% of the time) or not working (happens 5% of the time), because if Valve A fails (happens 10% of the time) then the machine stops working.

Do people understand this? Nathan and I posed this question on Prolific, an online platform based in the UK.[11] We also had an additional nine responses from students in a course in Behavioural Economics. We really did not expect most people to get the answers right. What we were really keen to understand is whether they understood the conjunction fallacy inherent in the last problem. The key comparison was between Questions 2 and 3. Did they understand that there was a 14.5% chance of the machine failing in Question 2 but only a 10% chance of the machine failing in Question 3?

We found that slightly more people got Question 3 correct than Question 2 (40.5% compared to 38.1%). This shows that Question 3 was not impossibly difficult compared to Question 2. But we also found that many more people displayed the cognitive error in Question 3: 48.8% went for 15%, by simply adding probabilities rather than accounting for their nesting, with very few people choosing the other wrong answers. By comparison, in Question 2, which is purely mathematical, no single wrong answer was chosen by so many people. This suggests that when people were faced with a question of nested probabilities, there was a tendency towards answering an easier question than the one being asked.

This might explain why the conjunction fallacy arises. Rather than answering a question about multiple different probabilities, many people answer an easier question. Perhaps in the Linda and Tom examples, the easier question is "what ties together the information I have given you?" When it comes to the congressional staffers who claim to be more likely to leave Congress than to leave their team, perhaps they are answering a question about how close they feel to their colleagues. It is not that they are more likely to leave their team than to leave Congress altogether, it is that they feel more attached to their team than to Congress as a whole. That answer makes a lot more emotional sense, fits the data, and shows the dangers of overlooking the conjunction fallacy.[12]

REGRESSION TO THE MEAN

Like most Israeli adults, Daniel Kahneman also served in the Israeli Defence Forces and spent part of his time with the Air Force. There, he noticed a pattern among pilots flying sorties. At the end of each session, the pilots who had done well were praised by the instructors while those who had made mistakes received a scolding. Invariably, the ones who had been praised went on perform worse the next time, while those who had been scolded improved. This led the instructors to believe that scolding rather than praising was the way to go, since praising led to reduced performance while scolding improved it.

Let us take a look at Figure 5.3 to get a visual overview. Here, we have a group of athletes who are running 100 metres. The group on the left had run 100 metres in 19.05 seconds on average on the first day and were chastised. The next day, they ran the 100 metres in about 18.35 seconds on average, shaving almost 0.7 seconds off their time, on average. The other group on the right had run the same 100 metres in 18.35 seconds on average on the first day and were praised for their efforts. The next day, their average speed decreased to about 19.15 seconds on average. This is an illustration of the same phenomenon; the chastised ones got better; the praised ones deteriorated.

■ Probabilistic thinking

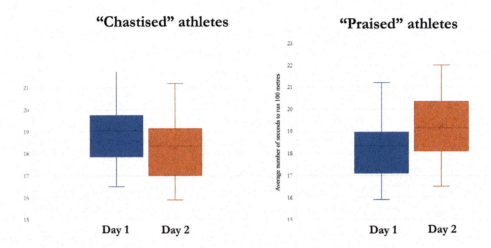

Figure 5.3
Average time taken by two groups of athletes to run 100 metres

In reality, this is explained by a concept called *regression to the mean*. This simply implies that all of us, pilots, athletes, runners and basketball players, have a benchmark level of performance. On any given day, we may perform slightly better or worse than the benchmark. If we do better one day, then chances are we will do worse the next day and "regress" towards the benchmark; if we do worse on one day, then chances are we will "progress" towards the benchmark by performing better the next day. What this suggests is that if you look at a particular snapshot of performance, then you may find behaviour to be above or below average. But if you took observations over a much longer period, then you will find behaviour conforming to the mean. This is another manifestation of the fact that it is hard to extrapolate from small samples, which are more prone to throw up extreme outcomes.

Picking stocks is a highly imprecise science where random factors play a large role, even if investment bankers would have you believe otherwise. Suppose you took a group of investment bankers, with similar skills, background and experience and looked at their performance in a given year. Some would do better than others. If you go back and compare the performance of those below and above the average in any year, it is highly likely that you will find that those who performed above the average the previous year have performed worse the following year. And, if you do this for a number of years in a row, then chances are that that the average performance of an investment banker will be similar to the overall average for all investment bankers. Baseball players who hit well above their batting average in their rookie season are likely to do worse their second; this is the so-called "Sophomore slump". Some call this the *"Sports Illustrated* cover jinx", exceptional performances which result in a player being featured on the cover, are likely to be followed by periods where performance dips, that is, regresses to the mean.

The concept of regression comes from genetics and was popularized by Sir Francis Galton, a cousin of Charles Darwin. Galton observed that extreme characteristics such as height in parents are not passed on completely to their offspring. Rather, the characteristics in the offspring regress toward the mean. By measuring the heights of hundreds of people, he was able to quantify regression to the mean, and estimate the size of the effect. Galton suggested that the difference between a child and his/her parents for some characteristic is proportional to the parents' deviation from typical people in the population. If the parents are each two inches taller than the averages for men and women, then on average, the offspring will tend to be shorter than the parents by some fraction of two inches. For height, Galton estimated this coefficient to be about two-thirds. So, if a male parent is two inches taller than the average male, then the male offspring will be shorter than the parent but taller than the average male by about one and one third inches.[13]

CASE STUDY 5.3 THE "HOT HANDS" FALLACY

Anyone who has been to a basketball game would have heard statements along the lines of: *"Steph Curry is a streak shooter"*. Or, *"Get the ball to Klay Thomson; he has 'hot hands' today"*. This belief in streak shooting or "hot hands" is prevalent not only among fans but also among the players. These phrases express a belief that a player's performance during a particular period is significantly better than what his or her overall record would suggest. This is not confined to basketball. Baseball fans talk of hitting streaks while gamblers believe that they are on a winning streak. This belief appears to originate from the fact that people often fail to realize that small observations are more likely to throw up more extreme outcomes, as in the incidence of kidney cancer in rural counties discussed earlier. People seem to think that if they toss an unbiased coin, then, even in short sequences, the coin should exhibit approximately 50% heads and 50% tails. In cricket, for instance, winning the toss at the start is often crucial because the winning captain gets to decide whether to bat or bowl first, which, depending on the weather, the quality of the pitch, etc., can make a big difference in the outcome of the game. It is not unusual for commentators to refer to certain captains as being "lucky" or "having a streak" in the sense that they make the right call more often than not. In reality, the probability of winning or losing the toss is always 50:50. But it is not just fans who believe in "streaks" and "hot hands"; players do too.

Thomas Gilovich of Cornell, along with Robert Vallone and Amos Tversky (of Stanford), decided to look into this in a more scientific manner. The first step, of course, was to get an accurate understanding of what it is that players and fans mean when they talk about a streak or having hot hands. A survey of basketball fans yielded the following insights. Ninety-one per cent of fans believe that a player has a better chance of making the next shot after having made the last two or three shots than he does after having missed his last two or three shots. Sixty-eight per cent believed something similar about free-throws; that a player has a higher chance of making the shot following a successful first shot (a hit), rather than following a miss. Eighty-four per cent of fans thought that it was important to pass the ball to someone who has just made several (two, three or four) shots in a row, since this player now had "hot hands".

In order to study this, Gilovich and his colleagues first approached the Philadelphia 76ers. This was back in 1985, so most of the names may be unfamiliar to today's readers, but perhaps not all. First, they looked at the probability of a player making a shot (getting a hit) following recent histories of hits and misses. Table 5.2

■ Probabilistic thinking

Table 5.2 Probability of hits following hits and/or misses

Player	I Prob(hit following miss)	II Prob(hit following hit)	III Prob(hit following 2 misses)	IV Prob(hit following 2 hits)
Clint Richardson	0.56	0.49	0.47	*0.50*
Julius Erving	0.51	*0.53*	0.51	*0.52*
Lionel Hollins	*0.46*	*0.46*	0.49	*0.46*
Maurice Cheeks	*0.60*	0.55	*0.60*	0.54
Caldwell Jones	*0.47*	0.45	*0.48*	0.43
Andrew Toney	*0.51*	0.43	*0.53*	0.40
Bobby Jones	*0.58*	0.53	*0.58*	0.47
Steve Mix	*0.52*	0.51	*0.56*	0.48
Darryl Dawkins	0.71	0.57	*0.73*	*0.58*

presents some results. In the first column, I show the probability of getting a hit following a miss, while the second column shows the probability of getting a hit following another hit. The third and fourth columns show the probability of a hit following two misses and the probability of a hit following two hits respectively. The point to remember is that if the "hot hands" fallacy is correct, then the probability of a hit following a hit should be higher than the probability of a hit following a miss. Similarly, the probability of a hit following two hits should be higher than that following two misses. Now let us compare Columns I and II (hit following miss versus hit following hit), or Columns III and IV (hit following two misses versus hit following two hits). For each comparison, I have highlighted in italics the larger of the two numbers. Two things clearly stand out. First, the numbers are not all that different. Indeed, the authors find that except for Darryl Dawkins, there is no correlation between the probability of a hit following a hit and the probability of a hit following a miss. Second, for most players, the probability of making a shot following a miss is actually higher than that following a hit.[14]

But maybe, this is not what fans (or players) mean when they talk about a "streak". Maybe what they have in mind are frequent and prolonged periods during which a player's hit rate is higher than his overall average. (This is actually not possible, since if a player has frequent periods of hitting above his average, then this would also lift his average.) The basic idea is *stationarity*; that a player's performance cannot be better than his overall average for prolonged sequences. Gilovich and colleagues look at this in two ways. First, they partition the record of each player into non-overlapping sets of four shots, and then they break these into three sequences: high (three or four hits out of four), moderate (two hits out of four) and low (zero or one hit out of four). If a player exhibits "hot hands", then his record must include more high-performance sets than expected by chance. Unfortunately, there is no evidence in favour of this.

Alternately, maybe players have "hot" or "cold" nights rather than hot or cold streaks. Since the authors have the distribution of shots made for each player over many games, it is easy to calculate the overall mean and the variance for each player. If a player tends to have hot or cold nights, then those nights would tend to show higher variance than would be predicted by the overall average and variance. But once again, the authors fail to find evidence that the variance calculated on a game-by-game basis is different from the overall variance.

Of course, looking at shots taken during a game may be misleading. If a player is indeed in the midst of a streak, then the opposing team may put more effort into guarding him; this may mean that the player has to take more difficult shots. One way of holding other things constant is to look at free-throw performance. Is a player more likely to hit following a hit than following a miss? Most fans believe that if a player has a lifetime average of making 70% of his free throws, then on average, there is a 74% chance that he will have a hit following a hit, while the chances of having a hit following a miss is 66%. For this, the authors look at data from the Boston Celtics for the 1981–82 season. Once again, the data, based on free throws taken by the Boston Celtics, does not bear this out. Five of the nine players, including Larry Bird and Chris Ford, tended to be more accurate following a miss rather than a hit, while the remaining four including, Robert Parish and Kevin McHale, were more accurate following a hit than a miss.

Finally, maybe having faith in "hot hands" is not so bad, especially for the players. Maybe players have an intuitive feel for when they are hot or not and so they are better able to predict when they are likely to make the next shot even if the pattern of hits and misses is not different from the player's lifetime average. In order to test this, Gilovich and his colleagues approached the men's and women's basketball team in Cornell University. Players were paired up, alternating between the role of "shooter" and "observer". Before each shot, both the player and the observer were asked to predict independently whether the player will make the next shot or not. Everyone was paid a fixed sum for participation. In addition, they were told that they could bet "high" (win 5 cents for a hit; lose 4 cents for a miss) or "low" (win 2 cents for a hit; lose 1 cent for a miss) on every shot. Players were encouraged to bet "high" if they were feeling hot.

If players can predict their hits and misses, then their bets should correlate with their performance. Neither the shooters nor the observers were good at predicting outcomes, with virtually zero correlation between their predictions and the actual outcome. Possibly not so surprisingly, there was strong correlation between the prediction and the performance on the previous shot; when the shooter hit, both the shooter and the observer predicted a hit on the next attempt; same with misses. The authors conclude by saying that this is yet another example of a "cognitive illusion", where we identify patterns even though none exists. This is yet another example of our common failing to understand random processes and to extrapolate from small observations. But this has consequences. In the context of basketball, this means players will be passing to someone who is "hot" even though this player may also be more heavily guarded, while not passing to another less guarded player. In the world of investment, this may mean handing over our money to someone who has just outperformed the

> market, in the belief that this broker is hot. Chances are, he will regress to the mean
> and his performance will go down and we would have been better off going with the
> broker who has underperformed and who will move up toward the average (assuming
> of course, that the two have the same lifetime average).[15]

CONCLUDING REMARKS

In this chapter, I have highlighted the fact that humans are not very good with dealing with probabilistic events. Among other things, here are a few key take-aways from this chapter.

First, just because two things go together (are correlated), does not mean that one causes the other. Furthermore, establishing causality is not straightforward, as we saw in the example of the poor having more babies. It is not that having more babies causes poverty, but that those living in poverty will inevitably end up having more babies since the opportunity cost of having a baby is low for poor women.

The next big take-away was the idea of base rates. It is commonly observed that most accidents happen in close proximity to our homes. This is because we do most of our driving from and to home. So, the base rate of having an accident closer to home is higher. It is also the case that a small fraction of a very large number can be a large number, as we saw in the case of China. A small proportion (10%) of rich people in a population of 1.4 billion still works out to 140 million rich; a fairly large number.

The third and possibly most important take-away is the distinction between prior and posterior probabilities as calculated via Bayes' Rule; the idea that available information can and should be used to update prior beliefs. This is also probably one of the more complex ideas in this chapter (and indeed in this book), and something that is not intuitive at all to most people. Consequently, it is easy to get this wrong. But, as I discussed in the context of stop-and-frisk in New York City, the consequences of getting this wrong can be devastating.

Fourth is the idea that we need to understand which events are independent (disjunctive) and which are not independent (conjunctive). This has significant implications for our ability to understand how or what may go right or wrong, and may make a difference between Chesley Sullenberger landing his plane safely without any functioning engines or the space shuttle *Challenger* blowing up because an O-ring failed.

I concluded this chapter by highlighting the important concept of regression to the mean. For most of us in most walks of life, the best predictor of future performance is past performance. We will most likely do as well as our lifetime averages. This is the idea of stationarity, that performance will oscillate around the average and will not stay above or below the average for very long. So, if someone does significantly better than the average in one period, chances are that they will do worse in the next period. The same is true for someone who is having a slump. Of course, this does not rule out someone getting better or worse over time. This is where we have an upward or downward trend rather than oscillations around the average. But, in that case, this will become obvious fairly quickly. For people with established records, chances are they will perform around their lifetime averages.

NOTES

1. *12 Angry Men* (1957); screenplay by Reginald Rose; directed by Sydney Lumet; producers: Henry Fonda and Reginal Rose; Orion–Nova Productions.
2. For example, "forcing" and "porcine" are both seven-letter words and both have N as the sixth letter but "porcine" does not end in "ing".
3. In general, if A and B are two outcomes, then $Pr(A|B) = Pr(A\&B)/Pr(B)$. This means (via transposing sides) that $Pr(A\&B) = Pr(A|B)*Pr(B)$. But $Pr(A\&B)$ is the exact same thing as $Pr(B\&A)$. We can write $Pr(B\&A)$ as $Pr(B|A)*Pr(A)$. This, in turn, implies that $Pr(A\&B) = Pr(B\&A) = Pr(B|A)*Pr(A) = Pr(A|B)*Pr(B)$.
4. Thomas Bayes (1701–1761) was an English statistician, philosopher and Presbyterian minister. Bayes never published this rule or theorem, which was published after his death by Richard Price (1723–1791), a British moral philosopher and mathematician. Price spent most of his adult life as minister of Newington Green Unitarian Church and was a Fellow of the Royal Society.
5. Kookaburra is an Australian bird, whose call sounds literally like someone is laughing. More immediately, as every cricket fan knows, Kookaburra is a company that produces cricket balls. They also produce field-hockey (or, to everyone outside the US, hockey) balls.
6. NPR.org; February 11, 2020; www.npr.org/2020/02/11/804795405/throw-them-against-the-wall-and-frisk-them-bloomberg-s-2015-race-talk-stirs-deba
7. "'Too little, too late': Police union president slams Bloomberg 'stop and frisk' apology". WPIX 11 New York. 2019-11-17.
8. Down's Syndrome is also known as Down Syndrome, or Trisomy. This is a genetic condition caused by the presence of all or part of a third copy of chromosome 21. Down's Syndrome is usually associated with physical growth delays, mild to moderate intellectual disability, and characteristic facial features. Those afflicted with Down's typically have a much lower IQ compared to their peers and usually have a lower life expectancy. There is no cure for this. Babies born to older mothers are particularly susceptible to suffering from Down's.
9. A conjunctive fallacy is not the same as a conjunction fallacy, though the two are related. A conjunction fallacy is one where someone assigns a higher probability to a subset of an event than to the event itself. For instance, stating that "Linda is a bank clerk and she is a feminist" is more likely than "Linda is a bank clerk" is an example of the conjunction fallacy. This is because if Linda is a feminist bank clerk, then she must, first of all, be a bank clerk. This means that feminist bank clerks are a subset of the set of bank clerks. So, the probability of the former cannot be higher than the latter. Conjunctive (connected) fallacies may refer to things that are a subset of a larger set, but they do not have to, in the sense that conjunctive fallacies may refer to any events that occur together without necessarily being subsets of one.
10. www.congressfoundation.org/storage/documents/CMF_Pubs/life_in_congress_aligning_work_life.pdf.
11. Prolific, based in the UK (www.prolific.co) and Amazon's Mechanical Turk based in the US (www.mturk.com) are online platforms that have thousands of registered participants. Researchers can pose their study questions and registered participants can take part in these studies if they wish. Participants are paid to reimburse them for their time. The payment also serves as a means of making sure that the participants take the task seriously.
12. I am very grateful to Nathan Hodson of Harvard Kennedy School for his insights on this topic. Nathan had significant input into the writing of Case Study 5.2. Along with the above three questions, we also asked our respondents to answer the "Tom" question and "Linda" question, except we made Linda an elementary school teacher, rather than a bank clerk. Forty-two per cent of our respondents said that Tom studies computer science, even though the base rate information suggests that he studies Arts, since the statement of the problem says that 40% of students study Arts while only 2% study computer science. When it came to Linda, approx. 57% of respondents stated that Linda is an elementary school teacher who is active in the Feminist movement, while approx. 9% said that Linda is an elementary school teacher.

■ Probabilistic thinking

13 Galton was a polymath known for his contributions to multiple areas of study. But, later, he fell into disrepute for his steadfast support for eugenic policies. His arguments in favour of eugenics were picked up, among others, by Hitler and his followers, resulting in devastating consequences.

14 In the case of Dawkins, the correlation is in the opposite direction than that suggested by the "hot hands" theory. Dawkins was more likely to have a hit following a miss than a hit following a hit. The correlation between the two probabilities for Dawkins is negative.

15 Gilovich and his colleagues conclude by making an interesting observation. In basketball, the belief about streak players seems to apply more to people who play Guard. These players are used to taking long-range three-pointers from the edge of the court. If and when they make a number of these long-range three-pointers, these become memorable events and become imprinted in the minds of the fans. Misses do not register as much. So, the belief in the "streak" may also be thought of as a type of availability bias.

6 Thinking strategically

In this chapter, I:

- *Introduce the concept of games, which are situations involving strategic decision making requiring anticipation of others' actions in that situation;*
- *Discuss games where players move simultaneously and games where players move sequentially;*
- *Define the concepts of dominant strategy, backward induction and Nash equilibrium;*
- *Talk about games with unique equilibrium outcomes as in the prisoner's dilemma game, and games with multiple equilibria as in the stag hunt game;*
- *Address some applications of these games to economic transactions as well as extensions to the natural world.*

INTRODUCTION

A large number of decisions in our day-to-day lives require us to engage in "strategic decision making". What does this mean? It means that what I decide to do in a particular situation will affect the well-being of another person (or group of people) – and, in turn, what someone else does will crucially impact upon my own well-being. Here are some examples of such situations:

- participants choosing between "Split" and "Steal" in the *Golden Balls* TV game;
- people trying to decide whether to join a march for climate change or regime change;
- deciding whether to contribute to a charity or not;
- the local bakery offering a discounted price on pastries just before it closes;
- employees deciding how hard to work when the boss is away;
- Persian rug seller deciding how quickly to lower the price when haggling with a tourist;
- airline companies trying to decide whether to cut prices or not;
- Qantas and Air New Zealand trying to decide whether to merge or not;
- the response of competitors to such a merger;
- Lamelara men in Indonesia deciding whether to join in on the day's whale hunt or not and how to divide the whale if they catch one.

Economists (and increasingly those in many other disciplines) routinely rely on a set of tools called "game theory" to understand how people make decisions in such situations.

Game theory is essentially a language for describing strategic interactions when what happens to one person is affected by another person. Thus, a number of situations that confront us in our day-to-day lives – such as the ones listed above and many others – can be thought of as "games" with us as "players", and they can be analysed using the tools of game theory. While it is always hard to pinpoint when exactly a particular set of ideas arose, most scholars would agree that the origins of game theory can be traced back to the publication of the book *The Theory of Games and Economic Behavior*, written by John von Neumann and Oskar Morgenstern in 1944.

Let me highlight why many of these situations involve strategic decision making by looking at the first example listed above. In the Remuera neighbourhood of Auckland, where I used to live, there is a playground for small children called "Little Rangitoto Reserve". I used to go there often, when my daughters were little. Surprisingly, the equipment in this playground – the slides, the swings, the jungle gym and the monkey-bars – were not provided by the Auckland City Council, but, rather, were bought by local residents on the basis of voluntary contributions. On the face of it, this is probably not surprising to any of you, since you may have experience with similar such ventures or others which rely on voluntary charitable contributions for a good cause. It happens all the time, and, as a result, we tend to forget that this is actually quite an accomplishment.

Let me explain why. Suppose you want to build a similar public park in your neighbourhood, and you decide to approach local households for a certain contribution. Not everyone in the neighbourhood has to contribute for the park to get built. As long as some of the families contribute, you will have enough money for the park. What are the chances that you will be able to raise enough money? The chances are actually good, but there is an inherent social dilemma here. For the time being, suppose (as economists often tend to do) that, by and large, people are self-interested and care (mostly) about their own welfare. It is obvious that if everyone does chip in with a contribution, then the park will get built, and everyone in the neighbourhood can take their children there. Collectively, then, we will all be better off if everyone cooperated.

But consider a purely self-interested individual trying to decide whether to contribute or not. Suppose he/she does not contribute any money to the pot and the park does not get built. Then he/she is not better off, but he/she is not worse off either, since there was no park there before and there will not be one in the future. Suppose this person contributes and the park does not get built but the money is not returned; then he/she is strictly worse off. But suppose he/she does not contribute, but enough money is raised to build the park. Now a park is quite different from (say) a health club, because, once the park is built, it is extremely difficult to keep anyone out, regardless of whether he/she has paid or not. Typically, you cannot really have a membership for a public park. So, even if someone has not paid, this person cannot be prevented from going to the park once it is built. Thus, he/she has not contributed anything but still gets to enjoy a walk in the park with his/her child or his/her dog. This person is then better off, since he/she has not paid anything out of his/her own pocket, but still gets to enjoy the open air of the park and the verdant surroundings. So, then it appears that whether the park gets built or not – for an individual who cares primarily about his/her own self-interest – the practical course of action is not to contribute any money.

Economists refer to this type of behaviour as "free-riding" – taking advantage of other people's contributions. But if everyone reasoned along the same lines, then no one will contribute, and the park will never get built. Joseph Heller summed up this phenomenon eloquently in *Catch-22* while discussing his protagonist Yossarian's reluctance to help build the military officers' club on the island of Pianosa:

> Sharing a tent with a man who was crazy wasn't easy but Nately didn't care. He was crazy, too, and had gone every free day to work on the officers' club that Yossarian had not helped build.
>
> Actually, there were many officers' clubs that Yossarian had not helped build, but he was the proudest of the one on Pianosa. It was a sturdy and complex monument to his powers of determination. Yossarian never went there to help until it was finished; then he went there often, so pleased was he with the large, fine, rambling shingled building. It was truly a splendid structure, and Yossarian throbbed with a mighty sense of accomplishment each time he gazed at it and reflected that none of the work that had gone into it was his.

In the economist's parlance, Yossarian is free riding on the effort put in by the other officers, an occurrence not altogether uncommon in many economic settings which require a group of people to collaborate. Many of you who are used to working with groups of people and are aware of the problems that arise will recognize Yossarian's behaviour. Economists typically argue that, when faced with a group enterprise, such as building the officers' club or a local park, or contributing to charitable causes in general, self-interested humans will inevitably behave like Yossarian, and, therefore, such enterprises are doomed to failure. Economists go on to suggest that in equilibrium – the usual term used is a "Nash equilibrium" after John Nash who first proposed the idea – all self-interested actors will free-ride and no one will contribute towards building the park. Here, the phrase "equilibrium" suggests a lack of any tendency or desire to change. If no one contributes and the park does not get built, then collectively, everyone is worse off and everyone realizes that everyone is worse off. But no individual wishes to change their behaviour. A single individual contributing will not change the outcome (the park will most likely still not get built), while this individual will be out of some cash from their own pocket at no additional benefit to him or her. Everyone realizes that it is better if everyone contributes, but once they are caught in the free-riding trap – the equilibrium – it is extremely difficult to get out of it. The only way to get out of the trap will be for everyone to change their minds simultaneously, which again creates a similar collective decision-making problem which led to us falling into the trap in the first place.

Once again, our intrepid hero Yossarian of *Catch-22* sums up the nature of this equilibrium succinctly in the following conversation with Major Major Major Major (a man whose first name is Major, last name is Major, middle name is Major and one who holds the rank of Major):

> "Suppose we let you pick your missions and fly milk runs," Major Major said. "That way you can fly the four missions and not run any risks."
>
> "I don't want to fly milk runs. I don't want to be in the war any more."
>
> "Would you like to see our country lose?" Major Major asked.

"We won't lose. We've got more men, more money and more material. There are ten million people in uniform who can replace me. Some people are getting killed and a lot more are making money and having fun. Let somebody else get killed."

"But suppose everybody on our side felt that way."

"Then I'd certainly be a damned fool to feel any other way. Wouldn't I?"

Everybody refusing to fly missions is the least desirable outcome in this case – at least from Major Major's and the country's perspective - but if one person does not fly missions while others do, then the person not flying is better off, and eventually, the others will stop flying as well – a Nash equilibrium.

At this point, you might be thinking that not everyone is like Yossarian, or, for that matter, not like an economist! ("No wonder people call it the 'dismal science'," you might be muttering under your breath.) If you do not agree with this assumption, that is fine, because, as I will show you shortly, this assumption is mostly wrong. Yes, people do, in fact, donate large amounts to charity. And they do donate blood and organs to others. Across a vast majority of transactions, humans routinely cooperate with non-related strangers. Maybe because they believe that this is the behaviour expected of them and not to comply with that expectation imposes psychological costs. But I do need to point out that if you are someone who perceives human beings as being essentially kind and cooperative – altruistic – across the board, then, as I will show you (and as many of you probably know from experience), that view would be incorrect as well. People are neither purely self-interested nor purely altruistic, but, rather, they are conditional co-operators whose behaviour is determined to a large extent by what they think their peers will do. I will talk about this at length later. But we need to start somewhere if we wanted to build a model of human behaviour that generates accurate predictions, and economists feel that the assumption of rational self-interest is a good place to start. So, let us start there and see where and how far that gets us. I will get back to Yossarian and Nately shortly, but, before then, let us talk about films. First, Rob Reiner's *The Princess Bride*, and then *Bonnie and Clyde*, starring Warren Beatty and Faye Dunaway.

CASE STUDY 6.1 *THE PRINCESS BRIDE*

An excellent example of trying to anticipate the actions of others in order to figure out how best to respond comes from Rob Reiner's film *The Princess Bride*, starring Cary Elwes. The film buffs among the readers will probably recall the scene where Cary Elwes (the "man in black") is locked in a battle of intellect with Vizzini, the Sicilian played by Wallace Shawn. The battle of wits begins with Cary Elwes putting Iocane powder (a poison) into one of two glasses of wine without Vizzini's knowledge. Vizzini has to figure out which glass has the poison. Of course, getting it wrong means death. In one memorable passage, Vizzini says:

> But it's so simple. All I have to do is divine from what I know of you: are you the sort of man who would put the poison into his own goblet or his enemy's? Now, a clever man would put the poison into his own goblet, because he would know that only a

great fool would reach for what he was given. I am not a great fool, so I can clearly not choose the wine in front of you. But you must have known I was not a great fool, you would have counted on it, so I can clearly not choose the wine in front of me. ... You've beaten my giant, which means you're exceptionally strong, so you could've put the poison in your own goblet, trusting on your strength to save you, so I can clearly not choose the wine in front of you. But, you've also bested my Spaniard, which means you must have studied, and in studying you must have learned that man is mortal, so you would have put the poison as far from yourself as possible, so I can clearly not choose the wine in front of me.

Vizzini's intellect does not help much as finally he picks a glass, drinks the contents and drops down dead. Of course, the dénouement of this scene is that Cary Elwes put poison in both glasses, but the poison does not affect him since he has built up immunity to it.

THE PRISONER'S DILEMMA

The type of game played between Yossarian and Nately is called a *prisoner's dilemma*. When the game was first introduced into popular folklore, most likely by the Princeton mathematician Albert Tucker, it was placed in the context of the following story. A crime has been committed. The police arrest a couple of likely suspects. Let us call them Bonnie and Clyde. The police bring Bonnie and Clyde over to the station and put them in different cells where they can neither see nor talk to one another. One police officer says to Bonnie: "Look, we know you guys did it. But we are pretty sure that Clyde was the primary instigator; you just went along for the ride and then things got out of control. It is not too late to save yourself. All you need to do is to rat on your mate and finger him for the crime; then we can convict him, and he will get ten years in prison, while we will let you go free. But you need to make up your mind quickly, because all we need is one confession. So, if Clyde rats on you first, then he gets the deal and you go away for ten years." At the same time, another officer makes the exact same offer to Clyde. "But what if I keep mum and so does my mate?" asks Bonnie (or Clyde). "Then you can't convict, can you?" "That's true," admits the police officer. "But even then, we will still have enough to convict you of a lesser crime and put each of you in jail for a year." "And if we both rat on each other?" asks Bonnie (or Clyde). "Then we can put both of you away for five years," says the officer.

The resulting interaction between Bonnie and Clyde can be depicted as in Figure 6.1. This is typically called a *pay-off matrix* and is often referred to as the *normal-form* of a game. A crucial point to bear in mind here is that this is a game of simultaneous moves; meaning that both Bonnie and Clyde have to pick their strategy without knowing what the other person has chosen. They cannot communicate, and even if they did, who knows what the other person's word is worth? It is nothing but "cheap-talk". Bonnie (or Clyde) can promise Clyde (or Bonnie) that he or she will remain silent, but does the other person trust that? What if the other person is a back stabber? How much honour can there be among thieves?

■ Thinking strategically

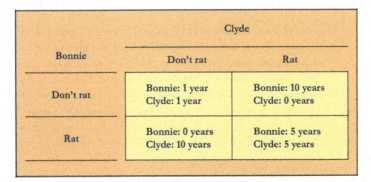

Figure 6.1
Pay-off matrix for the prisoner's dilemma game with Bonnie and Clyde

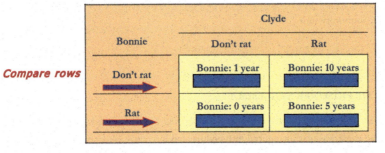

Figure 6.2
The prisoner's dilemma game from Bonnie's perspective

Before continuing, let us make sure we understand how this pay-off matrix works. If both Bonnie and Clyde choose "Don't Rat", then they each get one year in prison. If Bonnie chooses "Don't Rat", while Clyde chooses "Rat" then Bonnie gets 10 years in prison while Clyde gets off scot-free (zero years in prison). However, if Bonnie rats out Clyde while Clyde holds his silence, then Bonnie goes free while Clyde ends up in prison for 10 years. Finally, if they both "Rat" on each other, then they both end up in the slammer for 5 years each.

We will assume that Bonnie will act in her own self-interest (and the arguments that apply to Bonnie apply with equal force to Clyde). In order to compare her choices, we need to compare across the two rows: Don't Rat and Rat; that is, look at the pay-offs that result from Bonnie choosing either "Don't Rat" or "Rat". I have covered up Clyde's pay-offs to allow us to focus on Bonnie's pay-offs (Figure 6.2). What happens if Bonnie chooses "Don't Rat"? She gets 1 year in prison if Clyde also chooses "Don't Rat" or 10 years in prison if Clyde chooses "Rat". But if Bonnie chooses "Rat", then she goes free if Clyde stays silent or she gets 5 years in jail if Clyde also chooses to "Rat". It becomes clear from this exercise that Bonnie is strictly better off by choosing "Rat". This is because Bonnie is not certain what Clyde will choose. But, if Clyde chooses "Don't Rat" then Bonnie gets 1 year from choosing "Don't Rat" and goes free (better outcome than 1 year in jail) if she chooses "Rat". So, the strategy "Rat" is strictly better for Bonnie if Clyde chooses "Don't Rat". What if Clyde chooses "Rat"? Now Bonnie gets 10 years if she stays silent and she gets 5 years in jail (much better than 10 years in jail) if she also chooses "Rat". So, the strategy "Rat" is also strictly better for Bonnie if Clyde chooses "Rat".

150

Regardless, of what Clyde chooses, Bonnie gets a better outcome by choosing "Rat". Game theorists call this a *dominant strategy*, a strategy that does better, that is, yields a higher pay-off, against each and every one of the opponent's strategies. The strategy "Rat" is then a dominant strategy for Bonnie, since regardless of whether Clyde chooses "Don't Rat" or "Rat", Bonnie is better off by choosing "Rat".

But an exact same argument applies to Clyde. This is shown in Figure 6.3, where I have covered up Bonnie's pay-offs to better highlight the choices facing Clyde. For Clyde, we need to compare across the two columns "Don't Rat" and "Rat". If Bonnie chooses "Don't Rat", then Clyde gets 1 year from choosing the same, or freedom if he chooses to "Rat". If Bonnie chooses "Rat", then Clyde gets 10 years from staying silent or 5 years for also choosing "Rat".

Now, consider the pay-offs that result from Clyde choosing "Don't Rat" or "Rat". "Don't Rat" means either 1 year in prison if Bonnie also chooses "Don't Rat" or 10 years in prison if Bonnie chooses "Rat". On the other hand, if Clyde chooses "Rat" then he goes free (much better than 1 year in jail) if Bonnie chooses "Don't Rat" or he gets 5 years in jail (much better than 10 years in jail) if Bonnie chooses "Rat" also. The strategy "Rat" then becomes dominant strategy for Clyde as well; since regardless of whether Bonnie chooses "Don't Rat" or "Rat", Clyde is better off by choosing "Rat".

But if they both rat on each other, then they will both go to prison for five years. Except if only both could have kept their mouths shut, they would have both been better off and spent only one year in jail each! This particular scenario is, in fact, a regular feature of cop shows or films such as *NYPD Blue* or *LA Confidential*. So, in the Nash equilibrium of this game, we would expect both Bonnie and Clyde to rat on each other. Once they arrive at this

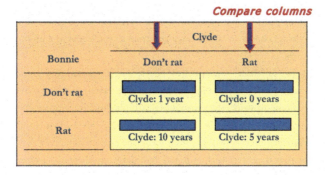

Figure 6.3
The prisoner's dilemma game from Clyde's perspective

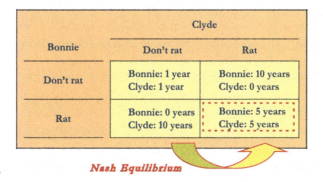

Figure 6.4
Nash equilibrium of the prisoner's dilemma game

■ Thinking strategically

outcome, they both realize that they have missed a trick and collectively would have been better off if they had both chosen "Don't Rat", but once they have arrived at the {Rat, Rat} outcome, both are stuck there, since neither player wishes to deviate unilaterally, since that makes him/her even worse off. This {Rat, Rat} outcome in this game is called the Nash equilibrium, after the Princeton economist/mathematician John Nash (Figure 6.4).[1]

YOSSARIAN AND NATELY'S CHOICES REVISITED

Let us now think about the game between Nately and Yossarian. The difference here is that it is no longer about jail sentences, as with Bonnie and Clyde, who were primarily interested in minimizing time served in jail. We will cast Yossarian and Nately's problem in the form of monetary pay-offs with the implication that both are interested in maximizing those. Just to make sure that we understand this, I will go through the argument once more, since, for the Bonnie and Clyde example, we were talking about jail terms and both Bonnie and Clyde prefer a shorter jail term than a longer one. But, for this next example (and most of the ones following) we will be thinking in terms of money and so, more money is better. Participants now seek to maximize their pay-off in terms of monetary earnings.

Each of Yossarian and Nately can choose one of two strategies: (1) work on building the officers' club; I will call this strategy "work"; (2) not work on building the officers' club, that is, shirk and free-ride on the effort put in by others. I will call this strategy "shirk". The second strategy is analogous to not contributing towards the public park and free riding on the contributions made by others, hoping that the park will get built anyway. I will also assume that the officers' club will get built as long as one person works on the project, except if both of them work, then the club gets built faster. (If you think it is unrealistic for a club to be built by one man, then think of Nately as the leader of a group of co-operators who always choose to "work" and Yossarian as the leader of a group of free-riders who always "shirk".)

For each strategy – "work" or "shirk" – adopted by Nately and Yossarian, they get a pay-off. Suppose we could assign a monetary amount to these. If both Nately and Yossarian (or their respective groups) choose to work, then the club gets built quickly. Suppose the pay-off to each (or each group) from having a club like this built is $12. (Maybe this is the monetary equivalent of the satisfaction they will get from using the club on any given day; or maybe this is the amount that they were willing to pay in order to go there and have a drink at the end of the day.) But now suppose only Nately works and Yossarian does not. Remember, the club will still get built in that case, but now, Yossarian is better off because he can now go there for a drink but has expended no effort in building the club and thus has not incurred any physical or psychological costs. Say this increases his pay-off to $16 at the expense of Nately, who has expended effort. Because effort is costly (in terms of time and physical exhaustion) and Nately has had no help from Yossarian, Nately now gets only $2. The situation is similar if, by some strange quirk of fate, only Yossarian worked and Nately shirked. Then Nately gets $16 while Yossarian gets $2. Finally, if they both shirk, then the club does not get built, and they are neither better off nor are they worse off. Suppose the pay-off in this case of both shirking is $6 each.[2] We can represent this game as in Figure 6.5.

152

Figure 6.5
Pay-off matrix for the game between Yossarian and Nately

	Nately's strategy	
Yossarian's strategy	Work	Shirk
Work	Y's profit = $12 N's profit = $12	Y's profit = $2 N's profit = $16
Shirk	Y's profit = $16 N's profit = $2	Y's profit = $6 N's profit = $6

As with Bonnie and Clyde, in this pay-off matrix, Yossarian chooses one of the two row strategies – work or shirk – while Nately chooses one of the columns – work or shirk. Each of them makes a choice at the same time and before knowing what the other person has decided. Once they have each chosen a strategy, they get a particular monetary pay-off created by the intersection of those two strategies. It is clear that, collectively, Yossarian and Nately (or their respective groups) are better off if they both choose to work. They each get $12.

But is that what individual rationality (as embodied in the decision to maximize monetary pay-off of oneself) suggests? It turns out that the answer is no. Here is why. Let us look at this game from Yossarian's perspective. (Since the situation is symmetric, all the arguments that apply to Yossarian apply with equal force to Nately.) Suppose Yossarian is convinced that Nately will work. What we need to figure out is this: what is Yossarian's best response to the strategy that Nately has chosen? In this case, Nately has chosen "work". Should Yossarian work too? The answer is no. Yossarian is actually better off – gets a better pay-off – by shirking. To understand this, look at the pay-off matrix again, but this time, cover up Nately's pay-offs, just as we did in the case of Bonnie, where we covered up Clyde's pay-offs.

Suppose Nately chooses to work; then Yossarian gets $12 from also working, but gets more – $16 – from shirking. This implies that if Yossarian is only interested in maximizing his own pay-off, then he should shirk. So Yossarian's best response to Nately's decision to work is to shirk. Suppose Nately chooses to shirk; then Yossarian gets $2 from working, but gets more – $6 – from also shirking. This implies that if Yossarian is only interested in maximizing his own pay-off, then he should also shirk. So Yossarian's best response to Nately's decision to shirk is to also shirk.

This then implies that, regardless of what Nately does, Yossarian is better off shirking. Shirk, then, is a dominant strategy for Yossarian. If Yossarian is only concerned with making the most money for himself, then he should choose to shirk no matter what Nately chooses. The presence of this dominant strategy actually makes Yossarian's decision-making problem easier, because now, he really doesn't need to worry about what Nately is doing. Yossarian should always choose to shirk. If Nately works: then Yossarian gets $16 from shirking and only $12 from working. So, if Nately works then Yossarian should shirk. But if Nately shirks: Yossarian gets $2 from working (a very bad outcome for Yossarian) and gets $6 from also shirking. Yossarian, therefore, has a clear, indeed a dominant, strategy: shirk.

But just as we saw in the case of Bonnie and Clyde, since the situation is symmetric and the same argument applies equally well to Nately, he should always shirk too. To see this, look at the pay-off matrix again and focus only on Nately's pay-offs from the different strategies. Nately's perspective is the same as Clyde's, since he also has to choose between one of two columns. As before, cover up Yossarian's pay-offs, just as we covered up Bonnie's pay-offs when we looked at Clyde's choices. It is clear that if Nately always chooses to shirk, then he makes either $16 (if Yossarian chooses to work) or $6 (if Yossarian chooses to shirk); whereas, if Nately chooses to work, then he can make either $12 (if Yossarian chooses to work) or $2 (if Yossarian chooses to shirk). Therefore, the pay-off to Nately from shirking is always greater compared to that from working, regardless of what Yossarian does. Nately is always better off choosing to shirk, just like Yossarian.

This, in turn, implies that neither will work on building the club and the club will never get built; just as I argued above, if everyone is only interested in their own pay-off, then no one would contribute to the public park and the park will never get built. Moreover, once both of them have decided to shirk, they both end up with $6, which is worse than the $12 that they could have each obtained by working together. But unilaterally, neither wishes to change his mind. This is because if one player continues to shirk, then the other player gets even less – $2 – by changing his mind and choosing to work. And so even though they both realize that, collectively, they are worse off by choosing to shirk, no one wishes to change his strategy. Once again, we have the Nash equilibrium outcome (Figure 6.6).

In this game, then, the Nash equilibrium comes about when each player chooses to shirk as their best response to what they think the other player will do. More generally, then, we get a Nash equilibrium when players choose that strategy which they think is their best response – will do the best or yield the highest pay-off – against what their opponent will choose. These games, whether they are played between prisoners or regular people, are generically referred to as "prisoner's dilemma" games; the crux of the problem is that both players can be better off if they cooperate, but individual rationality and the desire to maximize one's own pay-off dictates free-riding on the cooperation of others, which is the dominant strategy. When they both rely on their dominant strategies, they are collectively worse off. There is, thus, a tension between cooperating and maximizing the joint benefit, or free-riding and trying to maximize one's own pay-off at the expense of others.

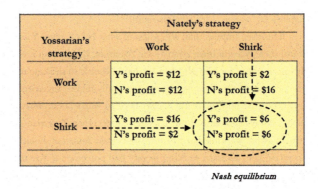

Figure 6.6
Nash equilibrium in the game between Yossarian and Nately

There are many situations in life where we confront a prisoner's dilemma like this. As I mentioned above, the decision of whether to contribute to a public park or not is one such situation. Everyone is better off if everyone contributes, but, individually, I can do better if I free-ride. But if everyone thinks like that, then no one contributes. All countries are better off if every country chooses to reduce their greenhouse gas emissions. But reducing emissions is costly and requires sacrifices. If one country does not reduce its emissions while others do, then this country is better off at the expense of others. But when every country thinks along the same lines, no one reduces their emissions and we get massive global warming. If all fishermen abide by their assigned quotas and one fisherman "cheats" and exceeds his quota, then he is better off – he catches more fish – at the expense of those who are abiding by the quota. But if everyone chooses to do so – since it is a dominant strategy to over-fish if everyone else is abiding by the quota – then we get massive over-fishing and depleting stocks of fish (or other resources). If all of us throw our garbage in designated garbage bins – which might involve some work – then we are all better off. But if one person throws his garbage out on the street, then that person is better off, since he has saved himself the extra effort. But if everyone does the same thing, then we get utter chaos and really dirty streets.

In all these cases, collectively, we are better off if we cooperate, but the cooperative outcome is often hard to sustain, since, if everyone is cooperating, then one person can be better off by reneging and free-riding. But if it makes sense for one person to free-ride, then it does so for others as well, so, the equilibrium is that we all free-ride and we end up with global warming, fast depleting oceans and forests, and dirty streets. And once we arrive at that bad outcome, we might regret it, but we are often unable or unwilling to change the situation, because we would need everyone to change at the same time. One person choosing to cooperate while everyone else free-rides does not change things and makes the one co-operator worse off. But getting everyone to change their minds at the same time poses similar problems of collective action which led to the Nash equilibrium in the first place.

PRISONER'S DILEMMA IN THE ANIMAL WORLD

Bull elephant seals can exceed 20 feet in length and weigh 6,000 pounds, while female elephant seals weigh only 800–1,200 pounds. Why are bull elephant seals so much bigger? The evolutionary explanation is that elephant seals are polygamous, so males must compete for females. Bull elephant seals pummel one another on the beach for hours until one finally retreats, battered and bloody. The winners of these battles command nearly exclusive sexual access to harems of as many as one hundred females and explains why males are so much bigger.

A male with a mutant gene for larger size would be more likely to prevail in fights with other males and this gene would proliferate in the population. In short, the males are big because small males seldom gain access to females. But while the large size is individually beneficial, size becomes a disadvantage as a group, because their size makes it more difficult to escape from the great white shark, their principal predator. If all bulls could cut their weight by half, each would be better off. The outcome of each fight would be the same as before, yet all would be better able to escape from predators.

A similar argument applies to the peacock's tail and the stag's antlers. A larger tail for a peacock signifies better genetic quality and is useful for attracting mates. So, a peacock with a larger tail will do better in the mating market than a peacock with smaller tail. This means that there will be an incentive for peacocks to look for larger and larger tails, or a peacock with a mutation for a larger tail will attract more mates and have more progeny. But larger tails make it more difficult to run away from predators, implying that peacocks with larger tails will be more vulnerable. So, collectively, all peacocks are better off if they could halve the size of their tails without loss of any benefit, but it is in each peacock's individual self-interest to seek a larger tail. A similar argument applies to the stag's antlers. In nature, of course, this balance is mediated by what is known as fitness trade-offs; some peacocks with larger tails attract more mates and leave behind more progeny, but some peacocks with larger tails are more vulnerable to predators and, therefore, leave behind fewer progeny. It is only in the case of humans (super predators) that there is no natural balance, requiring rules, norms and conventions to rein in individual self-interest to promote the social good. I will have much more to say on this when we get to the material on collective action problems and public goods games.

TIT-FOR-TAT STRATEGIES IN PRISONER'S DILEMMA GAMES

Before moving on, I need to point out that prisoner's dilemma-like situations often arise when the interactions are one-off and players have no, or limited, ability to make binding commitments, meaning that they can say that they will do one thing, but when the time comes to take action, they are free to renege and cannot be held to their promises. This – especially the absence of binding commitments – is often the case in real life. If players know that they will interact over and over again, or that they can make binding commitments that can be enforced by a third party, then the outcome might be different.

In games that are played over and again without a known end point, one potential solution to solving such cooperation problems is to engage in *tit-for-tat* strategies.[3] This is where you adopt the following strategy: cooperate to start with, but, from the next period onwards, mimic what your opponent did in the previous period. If your opponent cooperated, then cooperate, but if your opponent defected, then defect. In one sense, tit-for-tat is a forgiving strategy; it punishes the opponent once for defecting, but if the opponent resumes cooperation, the tit-for-tat strategy resumes cooperation as well. In the 1990s, Robert Axelrod, a political scientist from the University of Michigan, asked researchers from all over the world to submit algorithms for playing the prisoner's dilemma game. The idea was that the different strategies will go head to head in a simulated tournament; strategies will be pitted against each other in different rounds and the one that collected more points will move on in the tournament. Anatol Rapaport of the University of Toronto submitted tit-for-tat, which emerged victorious. The important thing to understand is that tit-for-tat will always, on average, do no worse than any other strategy, since it allows itself to be exploited only once.

CASE STUDY 6.2 HOW PATIENT DOES ISHA NEED TO BE (FOR ADVANCED STUDENTS)

The following material can be skipped for many; particularly those who have not covered the material on time consistency in Chapter 3. But for those who have done so and are ready for some challenging material, then the following may be of interest. If you understand the concept of discounting future pay-offs then many of you will also probably realize that in games played repeatedly, the extent we discount the future (how present or future biased we are) can also have a critical impact on our decision to cooperate. The more present biased we are, the more likely we are to go for the higher pay-off from shirking; this is the same as opting for the smaller-sooner reward. But if we are more patient, then we are more likely to hold out for the larger-later reward.

Isha is playing an infinitely repeated version of the prisoner's dilemma game. In each period, Isha has a choice between "Cooperate" and "Defect", and her opponent has those same choices. The game is similar to that played by Yossarian and Nately, except with different pay-offs. You can think of "cooperate" as Yossarian's decision to "work", while "defect" is akin to his decision to "shirk". If Isha and her opponent both cooperate, then they both get $4. If both choose to defect, then they each get $1. If one cooperates while the other defects, then the cooperating player gets $0 while the defecting player gets $8. So, in this pay-off matrix, the first number in each cell refers to Isha's pay-off while the second number is the pay-off to her opponent. But, one twist is that Isha's opponent is known to rely on a *grim trigger strategy* (GTS). This means that if Isha cooperates, then GTS will cooperate. But if Isha *ever* chooses to defect, then GTS *will forever defect from the next period on*.

Clearly, whether Isha chooses to start out by cooperating or not depends on how present biased she is and how much she values future pay-offs.

If Isha and GTS keep cooperating, then Isha keeps getting $4 each period. If Isha defects, then she gets $8 in that period, but because GTS will defect from the next period onward, the best Isha can hope to get is $1 from the next period onward.

Remember, from Chapter 3, that future pay-offs are discounted by βδ (beta*delta), where $\delta = \dfrac{1}{1+r}$. In this context, we will think of "r" as the interest rate that Isha uses

Table 6.1 Isha playing the prisoner's dilemma game repeatedly against an opponent using the grim trigger strategy

		Grim trigger strategy (GTS)	
		Cooperate	Defect
Isha	Cooperate	Isha: $4 GTS: $4	Isha: $0 GTS: $8
	Defect	Isha: $8 GTS: $0	Isha: $1 GTS: $1

■ Thinking strategically

to trade-off between current and future pay-offs. For the sake of simplicity, we will assume that there is no inflation and that Isha's beta is equal to 1.

This implies the following sequence of payments for Isha.[4]

From cooperation: $4 + 4\delta + 4\delta^2 + 4\delta^3 + \ldots$

From defection: $8 + 1\delta + 1\delta^2 + 1\delta^3 + \ldots$

If you think about this for a bit, you will realize that Isha will be more inclined to cooperate for higher values of δ. Why? Suppose δ is 1, this means that by the end of the third period, Isha would have earned $12 from cooperating as opposed to $10 from defecting. But to make things a little bit more realistic, suppose δ is 0.8. Notice that in this case, Isha's pay-offs look the following:

From cooperation: $4 + 4(0.8) + 4(0.8)^2 + 4(0.8)^3 + \ldots$

From defection: $8 + 1(0.8) + 1(0.8)^2 + 1(0.8)^3 + \ldots$

Even with this value of δ, by the end of the fourth period (say), the pay-off from cooperation (4 + 3.2 + 2.56 + 2.048 = 11.808) becomes higher than that from defection (8 + 0.8 + 0.64 + 0.512 = 9.952). In fact, even after period 3, the pay-off to cooperation (9.76) narrowly exceeds that from defection (9.44). What does that imply for Isha's implicit interest rate? Since $\delta = \dfrac{1}{1+r}$, then given a value of 0.8 for δ, we can solve for r, and r comes to 0.25 or 25%. This implies that as long as Isha uses an implicit interest rate of less than 25% (meaning she is willing to forego $100 today for something less than $125 in one year), Isha will be willing to cooperate. Remember, the more present biased a person is, the higher the implicit interest rate he/she needs, in order to give up the smaller-sooner reward. So, someone with an implicit interest rate of 25% is more present biased than someone with an implicit interest rate of 20%. In this case, any person who is willing to live with an implicit interest rate of less than 25% will be willing to cooperate. This, of course, depends on the pay-off numbers in the game and will change if we change the numbers in each cell.[5]

LET US TALK OF YOSSARIAN AND NATELY ONE LAST TIME

We have spent some time talking about prisoners' dilemma games where each player has a dominant strategy. When each utilizes his/her dominant strategy, each ends up with a worse outcome than if they had not mutually relied on those strategies. However, I do not wish people to be left with the impression that all games have dominant strategies for both players. We may well have games where one player has a dominant strategy while the other does not. Consider a modified version of the Yossarian–Nately game as shown in Figure 6.7.

Yossarian's pay-offs are unchanged from the previous game, but Nately's pay-offs are different. Specifically, Nately now gets $10 instead of $16 if Yossarian works and Nately

Figure 6.7
Pay-off matrix for Yossarian–Nately game where Nately has no dominant strategy

Yossarian's strategy	Nately's strategy	
	Work	Shirk
Work	Y's profit = $12 N's profit = $12	Y's profit = $2 N's profit = $10
Shirk	Y's profit = $16 N's profit = $2	Y's profit = $6 N's profit = $6

Figure 6.8
Nash equilibrium in the Yossarian–Nately game where Nately has no dominant strategy

Yossarian's strategy	Nately's strategy	
	Work	Shirk
Work	Y's profit = $12 N's profit = $12	Y's profit = $2 N's profit = $10
Shirk	Y's profit = $16 N's profit = $2	Y's profit = $6 N's profit = $6 *(Nash equilibrium)*

shirks. Think of this as follows. Nately is an honourable man and if Yossarian works but Nately does not, then the latter feels guilty. This implies that he gets only $10 and not the $16 that he would have before. But Yossarian still has a dominant strategy, which is to shirk. This is because if Nately works, then Yossarian gets $16 from shirking as opposed to $12 from working. So, if Nately works, then Yossarian is better off shirking. On the other hand, if Nately shirks, then Yossarian is better off shirking too. If Nately shirks, then Yossarian gets $2 from working and $6 from shirking. So even here, it is a safe assumption that Yossarian will shirk.

What does Nately do? We will assume that Nately is smart enough to figure out that Yossarian still has a dominant strategy, which is to shirk. If Nately anticipates that Yossarian is still going to shirk, even in this game, then what should Nately do? If Yossarian shirks, then Nately gets $2 from working and $6 from shirking. So, if Nately figures out that Yossarian will still shirk, then Nately will shirk too. This means that once again, they will end up at the {Shirk, Shirk} Nash equilibrium; except, this time, only Yossarian has a dominant strategy, and Nately does not. But Nately correctly anticipates the fact that Yossarian will choose to shirk and ends up shirking himself too. This, then, is a game with a dominant strategy for only one player rather than both. Figure 6.8 highlights this.

The above games are all ones that lead to a single Nash equilibrium; in some cases, this is arrived at because both players have a dominant strategy. In other cases, this results from the fact that only one player has a dominant strategy, but the other player correctly surmises that. But it is not the case that all games have to have a single Nash equilibrium. Games can have multiple equilibria. I will talk now of such games.

MEN ARE FROM MARS, WOMEN ARE FROM VENUS: BATTLE OF THE SEXES

Pat and Chris are wondering what to get each other on their anniversary. Both Pat and Chris love the 1980s game show *Perfect Match* (a show where couples had to answer questions about each other separately to see how well they knew their partners). Pat and Chris decide to put their knowledge of each other to the test. They decide that for their anniversary evening, each of them is going to buy *one* ticket to an event and see if their choices match! Pat loves the opera and would like to go see Puccini's *La Bohème* at the New York Metropolitan Opera. Chris, on the other hand, would rather watch the New York Yankees take on the Boston Red Sox at Yankee stadium.

Here is the point. Pat and Chris would like to coordinate their actions and would ideally like to buy tickets to the same event. If they end up at the opera, then Pat would be the happier of the two, while Chris would enjoy it more if he was sitting behind the home plate at Yankee stadium. But they most certainly want to be together at the same event even if it is the preferred event of the other person. What they do *not* want, under any circumstances, is to mismatch or fail to coordinate; that is, they do not want to end up with each holding a ticket to a different event and spending their anniversary evening separately. There are two feasible outcomes (or equilibria) in this game. One, where they both buy tickets to the opera, where Pat is happier and gets greater satisfaction (or pay-off) compared to Chris, and the other, where they both go to the Yankees game, which makes Chris the happier of the two. But if they fail to coordinate and buy tickets to different events, then they both feel wretched and get pay-offs of zero each. Thus, a failure to coordinate in this situation results in a bad outcome for both. Game theorists and economists, who are not usually renowned for their sense of humour, often refer to this as the *battle of the sexes* game.

In case you are thinking that this is a somewhat contrived example, let me assure you that the noted short story writer, O. Henry, certainly did not think so. O. Henry's short story "The gift of the Magi" provides an excellent example of coordination failure. It is the day before Christmas, and a young couple – James and Della Dillingham – who love each other very much, are in despair. Each wants to buy the other a thoughtful gift, but neither has much money. There are two possessions in which the couple take great pride. One is Jim's gold watch, which is a family heirloom; the other is Della's shining lustrous hair. Suddenly, Della has an epiphany; she cuts off and sells her hair for $20 and uses that money to buy a handsome platinum fob chain for Jim's gold watch. Later, Jim comes back home with Della's gift, a set of beautiful combs, pure tortoiseshell with jewelled rims; just the shade to wear in Della's lustrous (and now vanished) hair. And then Della presents Jim with his gift, the watch chain. At this Jim smiles and says "Let's put our Christmas presents away and keep 'em a while. They're too nice to use just at present. I sold the watch to get the money to buy your combs."

What we have here is a situation where Jim and Della have failed to coordinate their actions. They would be better off if they had managed to coordinate to one of the two outcomes: (1) Della does not cut her hair and does not buy the chain while Jim sells his watch and buys the combs; here, Della would be better off; (2) Della cuts off her hair and buys the chain while Jim hangs on to his watch; here, Jim is better off. But what they have managed to do is to arrive at an outcome where they are both worse off; a failure to coordinate their actions. Let us take a look at how a game theoretic formulation of this game between Della and Jim might be like.[6]

BATTLE OF THE SEXES: THE GAME PLAYED BY DELLA AND JIM

We can depict the game played by Jim and Della using the pay-off matrix shown in Figure 6.9. Once again, we are going to go ahead and assign some arbitrary monetary values to the participants' happiness or satisfaction (which may well be ordinal rather than cardinal). Della has two strategies – (1) *sell hair* (and buy a chain) and (2) *don't sell hair*, while Jim also has two strategies – (1) *sell watch* (and buy combs) and (2) *don't sell watch*. If Della sells her hair and buys the chain while Jim hangs on to his watch (the intersection of the strategies *sell hair* for Della and *don't sell watch* for Jim); then Jim now has a watch *and* the chain and is happy. Della is happy too at Jim's happiness but a trifle wistful about her lost hair. So, her pay-off is slightly lower than Jim's.

On the other hand, if Della keeps her hair while Jim sells his watch to buy the combs (the intersection of the strategies *don't sell hair* for Della and *sell watch* for Jim), then Della now has her hair *and* the combs she so desired. Jim is happy at Della's happiness but a little sad about losing the family heirloom (the watch). So, his pay-off is slightly lower than Della's. But if Della does not sell her hair and Jim does not sell his watch, then they are neither better off nor worse off and they both get zero. Finally, if Della sells her hair and gets the chain, while Jim sells the watch and gets the combs, then neither of them can use his or her gift and they each get zero again.

In this game, neither player has a dominant strategy and we need to look for an equilibrium in *best responses*. This implies that each player wants to choose a strategy that provides the maximum pay-off against what the other player has chosen. If Della chooses *sell hair*, then Jim's best response is to choose *don't sell watch*; this is because Jim gets a higher pay-off of $5 from not selling his watch, compared to $0 from selling his watch. Conversely, if Jim chooses *don't sell watch*, then Della's best response is to *sell hair*. Della gets $3 from selling hair as opposed to $0 from not selling hair. So *sell hair* for Della, *don't sell watch* for Jim constitutes a pair of best responses and leads to one equilibrium outcome shown by the dashed circle in Figure 6.10. Alternatively, if Della chooses *don't sell hair*, then Jim's best response is to choose *sell watch*; he gets $3 from selling his watch, compared to $0 from not selling it. Conversely, if Jim chooses *sell watch*, then Della's best response is to choose *don't sell hair*. Della gets $5

	Jim's strategy	
Della's strategy	Sell watch	Don't sell watch
Sell hair	Della's profit = $0 Jim's profit = $0	Della's profit = $3 Jim's profit = $5
Don't sell hair	Della's profit = $5 Jim's profit = $3	Della's profit = $0 Jim's profit = $0

Figure 6.9
Pay-off matrix for the battle of the sexes game with Della and Jim

■ Thinking strategically

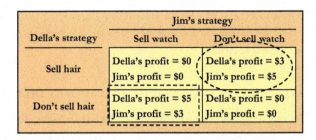

Figure 6.10
Equilibria in the game played by Della and Jim

from not selling her hair as opposed to $0 from selling her hair. So *don't sell hair* for Della, *sell watch* for Jim constitutes yet another pair of best responses and leads to a second equilibrium outcome shown by the dashed rectangle in Figure 6.10. Both of these are perfectly feasible outcomes in this game. However, they both wish to avoid the outcomes where (1) Della sells her hair and Jim sells his watch (as happens in the story) or (2) where neither of them sells anything. In both of these two cases, they get a zero pay-off.

The type of situation encountered by Della and Jim is usually referred to as a *coordination problem*. As noted, Della and Jim would much prefer to arrive at one of the equilibria: either {Sell Hair for Della, Don't Sell Watch for Jim} or {Don't Sell Hair for Della, Sell Watch for Jim}, rather than ending up at the other two outcomes where they both get nothing. There are a number of real-life situations where this kind of coordination problem arises. Driving on different sides of the road is an example. There are many other examples of adopting the same or different standards: these include adopting 110 as opposed to 220 volt electrical appliances; Windows versus UNIX operating systems; VHS versus Betamax video recording and playing standards; PAL or SECAM or NTSC colour encoding systems in television broadcasts and so on. I will discuss this in greater detail in Chapter 13.

HUNT A STAG OR A RABBIT? THE STAG HUNT GAME AND PAY-OFF-RANKED EQUILIBRIA

There is, however, a different type of coordination problem, one that is probably more relevant in everyday life and certainly more relevant in economic organizations. In the "battle of the sexes" game, the trick is to coordinate to one of the two desirable outcomes, rather than fail to coordinate and end up with zero. However, in many economic transactions, the people involved (1) not only need to coordinate to one of the outcomes but (2) at the same time some of these outcomes are more desirable (yield higher pay-offs) than the others. Take the example of a plane taking off on time. In this case, there are at least two feasible outcomes: (1) where everyone works at speed to ensure that the plane takes off on time, an outcome that is desirable from the point of view of the airline company, the passengers and, in most cases, the workers as well; (2) where everyone works at a leisurely pace which often implies delays and problems for the company and consequently for the workers too.

Back in the 1750s, the French philosopher Jean-Jacques Rousseau, in his *A Discourse on Economic Inequality*, alluded to this problem when he talked about two hunters trying to decide whether to hunt a stag or a rabbit. Hunting stag requires coordinated action by both hunters, and it is only when they both work together that they can hunt the stag. The pay-off to hunting a stag is large, with both hunters getting a large amount of meat. However, each hunter has the option of hunting a rabbit. Hunting a rabbit does not require any coordination between the hunters and each can hunt (and catch) a rabbit on his/her own. But if one hunter is trying to catch a stag (and relying on the other's cooperation in this enterprise) while the other hunter sees a rabbit scurrying by and, abandoning the stag hunt sets off in hot pursuit of the rabbit, then the second hunter gets the rabbit for sure while the first hunter gets nothing. In that case, the first hunter would have been better off hunting a rabbit as well, where at least he/she would have guaranteed oneself some meat at the end of the day.

The point is that, even if they have discussed this beforehand and both have promised to hunt the stag, still, there is no way to force one or the other to keep his/her word. So, if a hunter sees a rabbit scurrying past, he/she is perfectly free to break his/her word and go running off after the rabbit, while the other is blissfully unaware of this defection and keeps looking for the stag. Therefore, the two hunters are *both* better off if they work together and hunt the stag; they both get large quantities of meat. Alternatively, they can each hunt a rabbit, in which case they both get some meat, but strictly less than what they could have obtained if they had managed to snare a stag. But if one of them hunts the stag while the other hunts a rabbit, then the first one ends up going home empty-handed while the second one gets the rabbit. So, if there is *any* doubt in the mind of one hunter that the other hunter might not cooperate and might go off on his/her own to hunt a rabbit, then the secure option might be to hunt the rabbit in the first place.

Once again, let us ascribe some monetary pay-offs to the various outcomes, while preserving the basic incentives of the game. Suppose each hunter hunts the stag, in which case they get it and they both earn $8. If one hunter concentrates on hunting the stag while the other one goes off after the rabbit, then the one trying to hunt the stag gets zero while the one going for the rabbit gets $5. Finally, if they both hunt rabbits, then they both get $5. I depict the pay-off matrix for this game in Figure 6.11.

Now, as before, let us look at best responses. Suppose hunter 1 chooses to hunt a stag. What is hunter 2's best response? Hunter 2 gets $8 if he/she also hunts the stag but only $5 if he/she hunts a rabbit. Thus, hunter 2's best response in this case is to hunt the stag. But by the same argument, if hunter 2 is hunting the stag, then hunter 1 is better off hunting the stag as well; getting $8, as opposed to the $5 from hunting a rabbit. Therefore, both hunters choosing to hunt the stag is a feasible outcome or equilibrium of this game. This outcome is depicted by the dashed rectangle in Figure 6.12. But suppose hunter 1 decides to hunt the rabbit. In that case, hunter 2 has no incentive to hunt a stag since he/she will certainly not

Figure 6.11
Pay-off matrix for the stag hunt game

Hunter 1	Hunter 2	
	Hunt stag	Hunt rabbit
Hunt stag	1's profit = $8 2's profit = $8	1's profit = $0 2's profit = $5
Hunt rabbit	1's profit = $5 2's profit = $0	1's profit = $5 2's profit = $5

■ Thinking strategically

get the stag and end up with zero. In this case, where hunter 1 is hunting a rabbit, hunter 2 is better off hunting a rabbit as well, with both getting $5. But by the same argument, if hunter 2 is hunting a rabbit, then hunter 1 is better off doing the same. Therefore, both hunters choosing to hunt rabbits is a feasible outcome or equilibrium of this game also. This is shown by the dashed circle in Figure 6.12.

Figure 6.12 demonstrates the two feasible outcomes. Except that both hunters are *strictly better off*, that is, they both get a higher pay-off, when they work together to hunt the stag, as opposed to when they both go in different directions looking for rabbits. Economists usually refer to the outcome where both hunters hunt the stag as the *pay-off-dominant* outcome, simply because this outcome yields a higher pay-off ($8 each) to both players, compared to the "hunt rabbit" outcome where each only gets $5. The outcome where both hunters hunt rabbit is often called the *secure* outcome, since by doing so, they are both guaranteed $5 each.

In the context of these games, the question often arises as to how to get the two hunters (or a group of participants) to coordinate their actions to hunt the stag, that is, to achieve the outcome that yields the maximum pay-off for everyone involved. Because if there is any doubt in the mind of either of the players, that the other might renege on the promise to hunt the stag, then that person will most likely go off to hunt a rabbit. Thus, both players must be fully convinced and trust that the other player will indeed take part in the stag hunt.

These types of games that allow for two equilibria, one of which yields a higher pay-off than the other, are generically referred to as *stag hunt games*, or at times, *assurance games*. I should point out that Rousseau's description of the stag hunt game is not a stylized example designed to make a point but is a fact of life in many hunter-gatherer societies. The anthropologist Frank Marlowe of Harvard has undertaken extensive field work among the Hadza, a group of nomadic hunter-gatherers who live near Lake Eyasi in northern Tanzania. Here is Marlowe's description of the hunting practices of Hadza men.

> Men do not do as much cooperative foraging as women. ... during the late-dry season, however men will go hunting at night waiting at the few permanent waterholes to ambush game that come to drink. Because other predators like lions and leopards use the same strategy, night hunting is very dangerous and they always do this *in pairs*. Men also help each other track game once it has been hit ... [my emphasis]

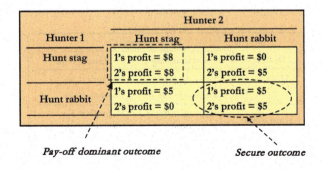

Figure 6.12
Equilibria in the stag hunt game

164

The difference between the stag hunt game and the battle of the sexes game is that, in the latter game, one person is happier in one outcome while the other is happier in the other outcome and both get zero if they fail to coordinate. In the stag hunt game, both players not only need to coordinate to an outcome but, more importantly, they want to coordinate to the outcome that yields a higher pay-off to both. They are both better off in one outcome (where they both hunt the stag) compared to the other outcome (where they both hunt rabbits). It may be worth reminding readers that the outcome where both hunters hunt the stag is the pay-off dominant outcome, since here, both hunters each get a strictly higher pay-off compared to the case where they both hunt rabbits. But the strategy of hunting a stag is risky, because if the other hunter goes off to hunt a rabbit, then the one hunting the stag will return empty-handed. The outcome where they both hunt rabbits, thereby guaranteeing each a positive, albeit smaller, pay-off, is the secure outcome.

This kind of coordination problem is actually endemic to many organizations. It arises in any organization engaged in team production, such as in automobile manufacturing factories or steel mills; generally, anywhere a group of people have to coordinate their actions to achieve the most desirable outcome. Another example occurs in mountain climbing, where the climbers are joined to one another and the progress of the group as a whole is determined by the slowest climber. As a result, these types of problems are also sometimes called a *weak-link* or a *collaboration* game.

Stag hunt-type problems are not confined to human societies and show up among other species as well. The hunting practices of orca are also an example of a stag hunt. Typically, orcas cooperatively corral large schools of fish to the surface of the water and then use their tails to hit the fish and stun them. Since this requires that the fish are not able to escape, it requires the cooperation of many orcas. But each orca is free to wander off on its own and catch its own fish.

PLEASE, WHY DON'T YOU GO FIRST? GAMES WHERE PLAYERS MOVE IN SEQUENCE

Up to this point, I have talked about games where players moved simultaneously; that is, they had to commit to an action without knowing what the other players had decided. But this is not true of all games. There are situations where one player moves first, and the other player gets to see what the first player chose before making their own decision. The Penny–Sheldon gift exchange situation I discussed in Chapter 1 fits this scenario. Sheldon has decided that he is going to wait and see what Penny gets him for Christmas before reciprocating with his own gift.

These situations where players move in sequence rather than simultaneously are referred to as *sequential games*. These games are depicted via the use of *game trees*, rather than the pay-off matrices we used for simultaneous move games. In order to discuss how to think about such sequential games, why don't we go back to Della and Jim Dillingham to see what might change if one moved first and the other moved second? Or, one of them could surreptitiously follow the other and see what the other was up to? Let us say, for the argument, that Della moved first (or that Jim figured out what she was up to). Once again, a key operative assumption is that both wish to maximize their own monetary pay-offs. Figure 6.13 depicts the game tree of the resulting game.

■ Thinking strategically

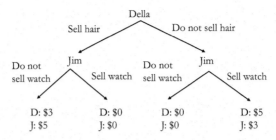

Figure 6.13
Game tree of the sequential game between Della and Jim

Suppose Della moves first and decides whether to sell her hair or not. If Della decides to sell her hair, then Jim knows that he is located on the left-hand branch of the tree. He has two choices: to sell his watch or not. If he decides not to sell his watch, then Della gets $3 and Jim gets $5. If Jim decides to sell his watch, then they both get $0. On the other hand, if Della chose not to sell her hair at the outset, then Jim will be in the right-hand branch of the tree. Once again, he has the same two choices: to sell his watch or not. If he chooses to sell his watch, then Della gets $5 and Jim gets $3. If Jim chooses not to sell his watch, then they each get $0. For each pair of numbers corresponding to the pay-offs, the top number in the pair is Della's pay-off; the bottom number is Jim's.

The way to think through these games is to engage in *backward induction*. This implies that you need to start at the end of the game, or bottom of the tree, with Jim's decision, and then work your way up the tree. This is a simple game with two players, each with two moves, but the same argument will apply to games with many players moving in sequence. What does backward induction mean? The term sounds fancy, but the intuition is very simple. If you have ever tried to solve one of those maze-puzzles that appear in newspapers and magazines, then you will know what I am talking about. If and when you tried, it is highly likely that once in a while you have "cheated" and started from the end, that is, you looked at where you had to go and then figured out how to get there by starting from the end and working your way backwards through the maze to the starting point. That's backward induction! The basic idea is this: the second mover knows what the first mover has chosen. So, the decision should be simple for the second mover. Choose the action that maximizes pay-off based on what the first mover has chosen. But, the first mover should also be able to think through the various options available to the second mover, and, in doing so, he/she should be able to anticipate exactly how the second mover would decide and thereby figure out what move he/she will choose in the very first instance.[7]

So, let us start with Jim's decision if he is in the left-hand branch of the tree following Della's decision to sell her hair. Jim will look at his own pay-off and choose the one which is larger. Jim gets $5 from not selling his watch, while he gets $0 from selling his watch. So here, Jim will choose not to sell his watch. Thus, if Della chooses to start the game by selling her hair, then Jim will choose not to sell his watch. They will end up at the outcome {Sell hair for Della, Don't sell watch for Jim}. What happens if Della chose not to sell her hair at the outset? In this case, Jim is in the right-hand branch of the tree. Here, Jim gets $3 from selling his watch and $0 from not selling his watch. Clearly, then, Jim will choose to sell his watch. The two of them will end up with the outcome {Don't sell hair for Della, Sell watch for Jim}.

166

But, as I said before, Della should be able to anticipate Jim's responses. Della now knows that if she sells her hair, then Jim is in the left-hand branch of the tree and will respond by not selling his watch. Della will get $3 and Jim will get $5. If Della starts by not selling her hair, then Jim is in the right-hand branch and will choose to sell his watch. In this case, Della gets $5 and Jim gets $3. This means that Della can expect to get $3 if she cuts her hair off and $5 if she does not. Clearly, Della should choose not to cut her hair off to start with. Figure 6.14 illustrates this. In this figure, I have retained only the relevant moves for Jim, removed the irrelevant ones, and highlighted the pay-offs for Della. This is because Della can anticipate how Jim will respond to each of her two strategies: sell hair or don't sell hair. It is clear that Della gets a higher pay-off from choosing "don't sell hair" at the outset. If and when she does this, Jim will respond with "sell watch"; Della will get $5 and Jim will get $3. This is also a Nash equilibrium, except in this case, we have arrived at the equilibrium not via looking at best responses as in the game with simultaneous moves, but by relying on the principle of backward induction.

So, in this game where Della moves first and Jim follows, the Nash equilibrium (via backward induction) involves Della choosing not to sell her hair and Jim responding with selling his watch. I have depicted this with the dashed lines and a dashed circle in Figure 6.15. I am sure you will have figured out that this is the Nash equilibrium if Della moves first. The equilibrium will be different if Jim moved first and chose whether to sell his watch or not. If that happened: Jim moved first and chose whether to sell his watch or not and then Della responded by deciding whether to sell her hair or not, then the Nash equilibrium in this game, via backward induction, would be for Jim to not sell his watch and Della to sell her hair, that is, {Don't sell watch for Jim; Sell hair for Della}. In this outcome, Jim gets $5,

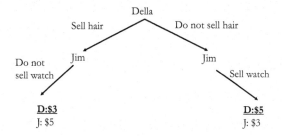

Figure 6.14
Della's pay-offs in the sequential game

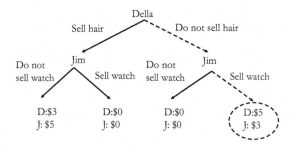

Figure 6.15
Nash equilibrium in the sequential game between Della and Jim

while Della gets $3. I will leave this to you to work out. Recreate Figure 6.13 by allowing Jim to go first. You need to make sure that you put Jim's pay-offs on top this time.

CASE STUDY 6.3 TO ENTER OR NOT TO ENTER; THAT IS THE QUESTION

Consider a hypothetical situation where two coffee-shop chains, Caroline's Coffee and Spicer's Coffee, are competing for market share. Spicer's is the incumbent firm while Caroline's is hoping to enter the market. The game tree for this game between the two is shown in Figure 6.16. Here, the idea is that Caroline's can choose to enter the market or not. If Caroline's does not enter, then Caroline's gets $0 while Spicer's enjoys the monopoly profit of $15 (these could be in millions or billions). On the other hand, if Caroline's does enter the market, then Spicer's can respond with either "peace" or "war". Peace implies Spicer's accommodates Caroline's entry and is prepared to sacrifice some profit as a result. Here, Caroline's gets $5 and Spicer's gets $10. But Spicer's can choose to go to "war", say, via engaging in ruinous price cutting or heavy advertising or both. It could also be that currently Spicer's has only a few stores around town and it lets Caroline's open up in the neighbourhoods that do not have a Spicer's coffee shop without putting up a fight; or Spicer's could choose to fight Caroline's by trying to build a lot more stores. If Spicer's chooses "war", then the outcome is dire for Caroline's, who loses $1, while Spicer's also ends up with a lower profit of $5.

The main question is: if Caroline's can choose to commit first and enters the market, then does Spicer's threat of going to war subsequently make sense? Can Spicer's threaten to go to war if Caroline's enters, and if it does so, will this threat be credible to Caroline's? The answer is no. I explain in Figure 6.16. If Caroline's chooses to enter, a self-interested Spicer's is better off choosing "peace" rather than "war", since "peace" yields $10 for Spicer's as opposed to $5 from "war". Caroline's can then anticipate, that if they choose to enter, then Spicer's will choose to accommodate this entry. This yields a profit of $5 for Caroline's. If Caroline's chooses not to enter, then Caroline's gets nothing. Faced with these choices, Caroline's will choose to enter, and Spicer's will choose to accommodate this entry.

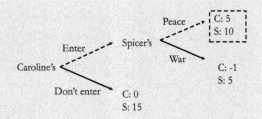

Figure 6.16
The sequential game between Caroline's and Spicer's, with Caroline's as the first mover

The only way Spicer's may be able to stop Caroline's entry would be to change the game completely and seize the first mover advantage. One way of doing so is to make a costly and credible commitment. Having learned about an insurgent company's plans to enter its market, Spicer's seizes the initiative and chooses to move first by deciding to pre-empt entry via building more stores. Spicer's has two choices: build a store at every corner or at every other corner. Caroline's gets to see Spicer's move and can then decide whether to enter or not. I depict this game in Figure 6.17.

Suppose Spicer's opens a store at every other corner. In this case, Caroline's is at the top branch of the tree. Here, Caroline's gets $5 from entering and $0 from not entering; of course, if Caroline's does not enter then they get no profits. Faced with those choices, Caroline's will choose to enter. This means that over on this branch of the tree, the game will have the outcome of Spicer's choosing to open a store at every other corner and Caroline's entering the market in response. In this outcome, Spicer's earns $10 and Caroline's earns $5. Alternatively, suppose Spicer's chooses to open a store in every corner. This puts Caroline's in the lower branch of the tree. If that happened, then Caroline's makes a loss of $2 from entering, and, as before, they get $0 from not entering. This implies that in the lower branch of the tree, Caroline's will choose not to enter, since by entering, they incur heavy losses.

Given Caroline's responses ("enter" following Spicer's choosing to open a store at every other corner or "don't enter" following Spicer's decision to open a store at every corner), Spicer's can now anticipate how Caroline's will respond following each of the two choices. If Spicer's opens a store at every other corner, then the pay-off waiting for them is $10, since Caroline's will respond by entering. On the other hand, if Spicer's chooses to open a store at every corner, then Caroline's responds by not entering (since Caroline's will suffer losses if they do). In this case, Spicer's makes $12. The choice for Spicer's is clear: they get $10 from opening a store at every other corner but $12 from opening a store at every corner. So, Spicer's should go ahead and open a store at every corner, and Caroline's will respond by not entering the market. This is the Nash equilibrium of this second game, arrived at via backward induction. In Figure 6.17, I have depicted the equilibrium with dashed lines.

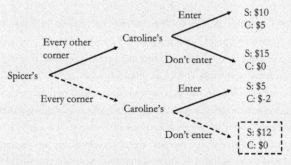

Figure 6.17
The sequential game between Caroline's and Spicer's, with Spicer's as the first mover

CONCLUDING REMARKS

In this chapter, I have shown that decision situations which involve two players (or a few players) often require strategic considerations, including anticipating the actions of others. Such scenarios are often referred to as a "game", with the participants as "players". Such games can involve simultaneous moves (players move at the same time) or sequential moves (players move one after the other). Some games have dominant strategies, resulting in one unique equilibrium like the prisoner's dilemma game. Some games may have a dominant strategy for one player but not the other; except the other player may be able to anticipate and respond to this fact. Other games, often called coordination problems, allow for more than one equilibrium outcome.

Coordination games come in two flavours. Some games, like the battle of the sexes game, allow for two equilibria; one yields a higher pay-off to one of the two players, while the other equilibrium yields a higher pay-off to the other player. But some other coordination problems, like the stag hunt game, have two equilibria: one where both players are better off in terms of pay-off, but a second, secure outcome, guaranteeing a minimum pay-off that players may be tempted to get at if they are risk averse.

The prisoner's dilemma game is often referred to as a "social dilemma" that poses a conflict between cooperation for the common good and free-riding, which is in one's own self-interest and maximizes one's own personal pay-off. We discussed how this game applies to a variety of issues such as global warming or depletion of common resources. It can even be extended to the animal kingdom. Sustaining the cooperative outcome in one-shot interactions may be difficult. But if interactions are repeated, then cooperation is possible. Tit-for-tat strategies, where each player starts by cooperating and then mimics the other player from the next period onwards (cooperate if opponent cooperates; defect if opponent defects) can be key to resolving such problems. One's degree of present biasedness (or lack thereof) matters too. Whether one cooperates to start with or not depends on how one views the trade-off between smaller-sooner and larger-later rewards and the extent to which one values the future.

Turning to games with sequential moves, we defined the principle of backward induction to find the Nash equilibrium. Here, the player who moves second knows what the first player chose, but the first player can also anticipate the second player's choice and can choose his/her own strategy optimally at the outset. The outcome of such games then depends on which player gets to move first.

Earlier in the chapter, I said that it is difficult to sustain cooperation in a prisoner's dilemma game with a known end point (sometimes called a *finitely repeated* prisoner's dilemma). Now that we understand the logic of backward induction, it is easier to understand why this is so; why one needs something akin to an infinite horizon in order to sustain cooperation, as in the game between Isha and an opponent playing a grim-trigger strategy. Suppose Isha and Ana are going to play the prisoner's dilemma game for ten rounds and they both know this. Then, if they are purely self-interested, they will certainly choose to defect in the tenth and last round, knowing that the game ends after that. But, if they are going to defect in the last round and both know that this is what will happen, then, anticipating their tenth-round moves, they should both also defect in the ninth round. By backward induction, they will then defect in the eighth round and the seventh round and so on till the very first round. So, if they know that game has a certain end point, they should start by defecting and keep defecting in each and every round after that until the tenth and last round. This is why, in order to sustain cooperation in this game, one needs to play a game without a known end point; at the very least, in each round, there must be some non-zero probability that the game will continue beyond that round.

NOTES

1 In 2002, John Nash received the Nobel Prize in Economics for his work along with Reinhard Selten and John Harsanyi. He struggled with mental health issues for a large part of his life. Nash's life and contributions are depicted in Sylvia Nasser's book, *A Beautiful Mind*, which was later turned into an Oscar-winning film of the same name, directed by Ron Howard and starring Russell Crowe as Nash.
2 These are meant to be illustrative examples and the pay-offs are not designed to have explicit meaning. One way to think of these pay-offs is that they are ordinal rather than cardinal, but, for those wondering about this, think of it as the following: if the club does not get built then they will have to go a club much further away. This is costly in terms of time and travel and reduces their pay-offs from $12 each (if the local club gets built) to $6 each (if they have to travel to a club much further away).
3 It is difficult to sustain cooperation in games with known end points. I will explain why that is the case later in this chapter.
4 These sequences are known as geometric progressions. The sum of the first series is $\frac{4}{1-\delta}$. The sum of the second series is $8 + \frac{\delta}{1-\delta}$. In order for Isha to cooperate, it must be the case that the pay-off from cooperation is greater than that from defection of $\frac{4}{1-\delta} > 8 + \frac{\delta}{1-\delta}$ or $\delta > \frac{4}{7}(0.57)$.
5 In fact, at the limit, if δ is exactly 0.57, then r is 0.75. This implies that anyone with an implicit discount (interest) rate of less than 75% will find it profitable to cooperate in this game.
6 Of course, one can argue, as O. Henry does, that it is the *failure* to coordinate their actions that provides the greatest proof of their love for one another. At the end of the story, the author comments: "But in a last word to the wise of these days let it be said that of all who give gifts these two were the wisest."
7 Those of you who have played a game called Nim will be aware of the logic of backward induction. This is also true for games like Go or chess, except in those latter two games, the set of strategies is so complex that it is impossible for humans to engage in backward induction effectively; but that is what computer programs designed to play these games do; for every starting move of their opponent, they calculate the strategy commensurate with the backward induction equilibrium.

7 The ultimatum game

In this chapter, I:

- *Talk about the ultimatum game, as a way of exploring preferences for fairness;*
- *Show that humans (and even non-humans) have inherent notions of fairness and that behaviour in this game reflects those predispositions;*
- *Demonstrate that generous offers in this game are not the result of altruism, low stakes or experimenter demand effects; rather, they are the result of the fact that proposers in this game correctly anticipate that small offers may be construed by responders as being unfair and therefore rejected by the latter;*
- *Explore to what extent these results translate to different cultures and societies.*

INTRODUCTION

In 2011, just prior to the Rugby World Cup, Adidas New Zealand got into controversy for the price of the All Blacks jerseys, which cost more than twice as much in New Zealand compared to overseas.[1] According to Adidas New Zealand, the price they set in New Zealand was "relative to the local market". When Kiwi supporters tried to order cheaper overseas jerseys online, Adidas moved aggressively to block such attempts. Public indignation rose so high that some local retailers started selling the jerseys at a loss; even the then Prime Minister John Key weighed in on the debate. What went wrong with Adidas' strategy? Adidas New Zealand was engaging in nothing other than good old-fashioned price discrimination. This is Economics 101, where sellers charge a much higher price to those buyers who are willing to pay up, mostly because they are less flexible in terms of their purchasing decisions.

This is why the person sitting in the seat next to yours on the aeroplane may have paid hundreds of dollars more than you did because they bought their ticket at the last minute while you bought yours two months back. So, what Adidas New Zealand implicitly assumed was that once the World Cup got going – and New Zealand started to win – the fans would catch the fever and, in the heat of the moment, willingly snap up the high-priced jerseys in spite of the much higher prices. But the strategy backfired. Adidas' move was widely condemned as being grossly unfair and one that actually ended up tarnishing the brand.

In February 2007, shareholders of the Tokyo Kohtetsu Company blocked a takeover by a rival steel producer, the Osaka Steel Company, the first time in Japan that shareholders have vetoed a merger approved by the companies' boards. An investment fund, Ichigo Asset

Management, started a rare proxy fight against what it saw as an unfair offer from Osaka. Ichigo, which owned 12.6 percent of Tokyo Kohtetsu, had not been against the takeover *per se*, only against the fairness of the offer. Yoshihisa Okamoto, senior vice president at Fuji Investment Management, said the vote "sends the message that such unfair offers are unacceptable."[2]

Colin Camerer, a leading experimental economist at Caltech, tells the following story:

> I once took a cruise with some friends and a photographer took our picture, unsolicited, as we boarded the boat. When we disembarked hours later, the photographer tried to sell us the picture for $5 and refused to negotiate. (His refusal was credible because several other groups stood around deciding whether to buy their pictures, also for $5. If he caved in and cut the price, it would be evident to all others and he would lose a lot more than the discount to us since he would have to offer the discount to everyone.) Being good game theorists, we balked at the price and pointed out that the picture was worthless to him. (As I recall, one cheapskate (either Dick Thaler or myself) offered $1.) He rejected our insulting offer and refused to back down.

The picture is essentially valueless to the photographer (worth less than $1) and of significant value to Camerer (certainly more than $5). Therefore, there are many ways to divide the gains from exchange which would leave both parties with a profit. Yet the photographer was unwilling to accept any price less than $5 and walked away from a profitable deal. In all of these examples, people are willing to forego money because they consider a particular offer to be unfair. This raises the questions: (1) are humans fair by nature? (2) Does this sense of fairness have economic implications? These are things that I talk about in this chapter.

THE ULTIMATUM GAME

Bargaining (haggling, negotiating) is a frequent part of many economic transactions including bargaining for a higher salary in job contracts or haggling over the price of a carpet or a used car or negotiations between owners and striking workers of a company. Often, as a part of the bargaining process, especially in cases where agreement is proving to be elusive, one party makes an ultimatum offer, a situation where that party says: "This is my best offer, take it or leave it …". This happens, for instance, in the case of binding arbitration where two sides are deadlocked and have failed to arrive at a compromise despite repeated attempts. If that ultimatum offer is accepted then it leads to a resolution, but if not, then it sometimes means substantial financial losses for both parties involved.

In many such situations where the two sides in a dispute – players and owners, management and union – have reached an impasse, one side that may have greater bargaining power or less to lose, might make a *take-it-or-leave-it* offer to the other side – an *ultimatum*. For instance, team owners may join together to lay down an ultimatum to the players' union and threaten the entire season if the players do not agree to the owners' ultimatum. If, however, the recipients of the ultimatum do decide to leave it – possibly because they are unhappy with the offer and the way the available amount on the table is being split, then it usually implies that both sides end up losing money. Rejecting an offer in these circumstances means

■ The ultimatum game

that the aggrieved person is willing to forego a substantial amount of money in order to make sure that the other side loses as well. This is akin to cutting off one's nose to spite one's face.

In the early 1980s, Werner Güth, Rolf Schmittberger and Bernd Schwarze, three economists at the University of Cologne, were studying bargaining behaviour. More specifically, Güth and his colleagues looked at what happens when one party makes such a "take-it-or-leave-it" ultimatum offer to the other. What Güth and his colleagues were interested in understanding was: how do people – especially the recipients of such an ultimatum – respond to it? And do the people who make an ultimatum offer anticipate that response?

In order to study this problem, Güth and his colleagues recruited a group of graduate students at their university and had them take part in a simple game which has subsequently become well known as the *ultimatum game*. Forty-two participants were paired into groups of two to form 21 pairs. One player in each pair is called the *proposer* while the other is called the *responder*.[3]

Each proposer was given a sum of money which ranged from 4 marks to 10 marks. (This was in the days before Germany adopted the Euro as its currency. To keep things simple, in what follows I also often resort to saying "dollars" rather than use different currencies.) Three proposers received 4 marks, three received 5 marks, three received 6 marks, three received 7 marks, three received 8 marks, three received 9 marks and finally three proposers received 10 marks. Each member of the pair knew *exactly* how much money the proposer of the pair was given. Their task was simple. Each proposer was asked to suggest a split of this initial endowment between him and the responder he was paired with. But there was a catch: the responder had to agree for either to receive any money.

That is, suppose a proposer who received 10 marks said: "I want to keep 8 marks and give 2 marks to the responder", then that offer would be communicated to the paired responder and the responder would have to decide whether to accept this offer. If the responder accepted, then the proposer got to keep the 8 marks while the responder received 2 marks. But if the responder did not accept the proposer's offer, then they both got nothing. Figure 7.1 illustrates the situation.

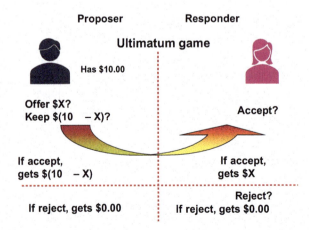

Figure 7.1 Structure of the ultimatum game

174

The proposers and the responders were seated at opposite ends of a large room and, while they were placed in identifiable groups, no proposer ever learned which responder he was paired with. So, what happened? Before you proceed, you might want to put the book down for a couple of minutes and think of the following: suppose you were a proposer and had 10 marks (or 10 dollars), what would you do? How much would you keep? How much would you offer to the responder – someone who is most likely a complete stranger to you and someone you will possibly not meet or interact with in the future? Next, put on your responder hat. You know how much money the proposer you are paired with was given. What is the minimum amount you are willing to accept? 1 cent? 5 cents? 1 dollar? Remember that if you reject the proposer's offer, then you both get zero.

Now, what should we expect to happen? Since the two players move in sequence, we can rely on the principle of backward induction, which says: start with the decision to be made by the last person and work your way backwards. In this case then, let us start with the second decision maker – the responder. When the responder is offered an amount of money, what should she do? Well, if she is someone who believes that some money is better than no money, then she should accept any offer that gives her some money (even if she is offered a relatively small sum), because the consequence of turning down the offer means that she will get nothing. So, the responder should be willing to accept most offers – even meagre ones! (Of course, if the offer is really small – say 10 cents – the responder might be indifferent between making 10 cents and making nothing, in which case the responder might turn the offer down. But we would expect the responder to accept most non-trivial amounts.) Therefore, if the proposer *anticipates* the responder's reaction – that the responder will be willing to accept most non-trivial amounts, even small ones – then the proposer should offer exactly that, a small amount, because the less the proposer offers to the responder, the better off the proposer is (since he gets to keep more of the money), as long as the responder agrees to that division. Suppose we constrain the proposers to making offers in 50 cent increments. Then we really expect those proposers to offer relatively small amounts to the responder – maybe 50 cents, maybe a dollar. Thus, in a Nash equilibrium of this game, we expect that proposers will offer a very small amount to the responder and the responder will accept whatever amount is offered.

In Figure 7.2, I show the various percentages, such as 10%, 20%, 30%, etc. (out of the initial amount) that the 21 proposers offered to their paired responders. Since different proposers received different starting amounts, I need to put all these numbers in percentage terms rather than absolute numbers. The lighter shaded bars show the number of proposers (out of 21) who offered a particular percentage amount, such as the number of proposers who offered 10%, number of proposers who offered 20%, etc. The darker shaded bars show the number of rejections, that is, the number of times a particular offer was turned down. The graph is quite striking. One-third of the proposers (seven out of 21) offered exactly half (50%) of the initial amount to the responder. Seventeen out of 21 proposers (slightly more than 80%) offered the responder *at least 20% or more* of the total amount available. This was surprising to say the least, since the proposers seemed to be offering way more than they had to. The one other puzzling bit here was the rejections. Two of the 21 offers were rejected. As you can see from Figure 7.2, at the extreme left, there are two proposers who wanted to keep the entire amount (100%) and offered the responder nothing (0%). One of these zero

■ The ultimatum game

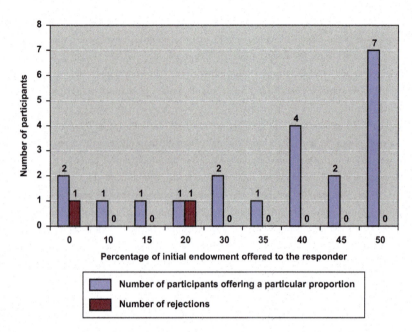

Figure 7.2
Distribution of offers in the Güth et al. ultimatum game. Re-created on the basis of data in Güth et al. (1982)

offers is turned down by the responder. This is hardly surprising since the responder would have obtained nothing in either case, whether he/she accepted or rejected the offer. But the surprise is that in one case, a proposer wanted to keep 80% of the available amount and offered the responder 20% but the responder turned this offer down! The proposer in this case had been given 6 marks to start with, and wanted to keep 4.80 marks and offer 1.20 to the responder. But the responder turned down the 1.20 marks in order to make sure that the proposer did not get the 4.80 marks.

Surprised and intrigued, Güth and his colleagues decided to carry out the exercise again. They brought back the same 42 participants – 21 proposers and 21 responders – a week later and asked them to play the exact same game as before with the same instructions. The only difference was that this time, the proposers most likely received a different amount at the start compared to what they received a week earlier (say 8 marks rather than 5) and they were very likely paired with a different responder this time around. The results – presented in Figure 7.3 – were possibly even more striking. Figure 7.3 is very similar to Figure 7.2. As before, the lighter shaded bars show the number of proposers (out of 21) who offered a particular percentage amount, such as the number of proposers who offered 15%, number of proposers who offered 20%, etc. Again, as before, the darker shaded bars show the number of rejections, that is, the number of times a particular offer was turned down.

A number of things stand out in this figure. First, there were fewer 50–50 splits offered by the proposers (three out of 21 or 14%, as opposed to seven out of 21 or 33% a week before). But the offers were still very generous. Eighteen out of 21 proposers (close to 86% and almost the same number as a week before) offered at least 20% of the available amount to the responder. Even more striking were the rejections. Six of the 21 offers are rejected. In

Figure 7.3
Distribution of offers in the second repetition of the Güth et al. ultimatum game. Re-created on the basis of data in Güth et al. (1982)

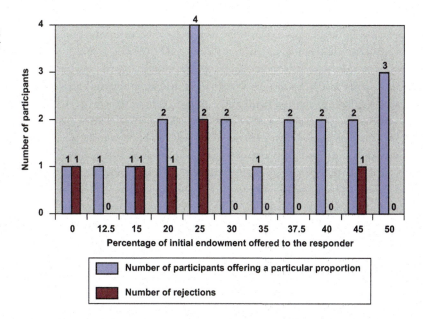

a number of cases, where the proposer wished to keep 80% or more of the available amount and offered the responder 20% or less, the responders turned down the offer.

But two responders said "no" when the proposer offered them 25% of the pie. In absolute amounts, in both cases the proposer had 4 marks to start with and had offered the responder 1 of those 4 marks and the responder turned them down. And, in one case, a proposer, who had received 7 marks to start with, wanted to keep 4 marks (57%) and offered the responder 3 marks (43%) but was turned down, giving both zero!

In order to make sure that these results were not being caused by the inability of the participants to understand the instructions, Güth and his colleagues had them participate in a more difficult decision-making problem to test their analytical skills. Their performance in this more difficult task convinced the researchers that lack of understanding was not driving these results. In reporting these results, Güth and his colleagues comment:

> subjects did not deviate from the optimal outcome because of their difficulties in solving the game. The main reason seems to be that the rational solution is not considered as socially acceptable or fair.

They went on to add that the typical consideration of the responder in this game seems to be as follows: if the proposer left me a fair amount then I will accept; if not and the amount to be sacrificed is not large then I will reject the proposer's offer. Correspondingly, a proposer possibly reasoned like this: even if I offer the responder a small amount, I need to give him/her a sufficient amount so that he/she is better off accepting this amount rather than turning me down and forcing us both to get nothing.

In order to get a better handle on the psychology of the participants, Güth and his colleagues then carried out a further study. Here, they had 37 participants who were asked to allocate 7 marks, but each person was asked to make two decisions – (1) how much would someone in the role of a proposer offer to the responder and (2) what was the minimum amount each person was willing to accept as the responder. The idea is this: if someone says that I want to keep 5 marks out of 7 and give the responder 2 marks (and expects the responder to accept that offer), then we would expect that when this same person was a responder and was offered 2 marks, he/she would gladly accept that amount.

It turns out that the majority of people were remarkably consistent. Fifteen participants out of 37 – as the proposer – offered the exact same amount to the paired responder that they were willing to accept if they were the responder themselves. That is, if they offered 2 marks out of 7 to the responder, then in their role as responder, they were willing to accept 2 marks as well. In many of these cases, the actual splits proposed were 50–50. Seventeen participants showed an explicit recognition of the fact that, in this game, the proposer essentially has the upper hand and thus can be excused for wishing to retain a larger proportion of the available amount. These participants were willing to accept a smaller amount in their role as the responder than they offered to the responder in their role as proposer. That is, suppose as proposers, they offered 3 marks out of 7 to the responder, then as responders, they were willing to accept 3 marks *or less* in a clear recognition of the power asymmetry between the two. But while these participants were perfectly willing to make allowances for this asymmetry as the responder, they were often more reluctant to exploit this power as the proposer. (I will have more to say later about this reluctance to fully exploit one's market power to garner more money for one's own self.) There were only five participants out of 37 who offered the responders less money than the minimum amount they were willing to accept as the responder.

These results clearly demonstrated that people's decisions were not being caused by an inability to understand the game or mistakes, but, rather, that participants obviously had clearly defined notions of what constituted a fair or unfair offer. Proposers were reluctant to make offers that would be construed as being unfair and responders had no hesitation about turning down unfair offers, when made, even if that meant sacrificing substantial amounts, as long as that sacrifice also caused the person making that unfair offer to suffer.

These results caused a stir. To a large extent, this was because neither unfairness nor a concern for relative pay-offs was part of the economist's lexicon at that point. Economists typically tend to rely on the assumption of a rational *homo economicus*, who is primarily interested in maximizing his/her monetary returns in a particular situation, or, more generally, his/her utility (with monetary pay-offs featuring as the prominent component of utility). These results suggested that people seemed to care a lot about normative outcomes such as whether an allocation was fair or not, and, more importantly, they seemed to be quite obsessed about relative pay-offs – that is, how much do I get as the responder *vis-à-vis* the proposer – and were willing to give up non-trivial amounts of money to avoid inequitable outcomes. So, for instance, responders seemed to be happy to give up 2 dollars to spite the proposer out of 8 dollars. This leads to the conclusion that people care considerably about the fairness of outcomes. Responders are willing to turn down money if they believe that a particular allocation is unfair. In making allocations, proposers make allowances for the fact that an offer may get turned down if it appears unfair to the responder, even if it gives the responder a relatively large pay-off in absolute terms.

INTENTIONS, AS WELL AS OUTCOMES, MATTER

One potential confound here is this: when responders turn down inequitable offers – that is, offers which give the proposer a much larger share of the pie compared to the share of the responder – what is it that they are protesting about? Is it the unfairness of the offer – that the proposer is trying to take more of the money to make him/herself better off at the expense of the responder? That is, are they acting in accordance to some implicit social norm that prescribes what behaviour is acceptable in a given situation and what is not? Or are the responders dissatisfied with the outcome of the bargaining process and the fact they are relatively worse off compared to the proposers and it is this relative standing that bothers them? It is conceivable that preferences and reactions to allocations are affected not only by the final outcome of the process but also by how the current decision context transpired. People may be far more willing to put up with unfair outcomes if they are the result of environmental or chance factors, rather than the result of a deliberate act by another person. For instance, people are more willing to exact retribution when a plane crashes because a faulty part was not replaced, rather than when the crash was caused by a storm.

Sally Blount at the University of Chicago's Graduate School of Business decided to examine this phenomenon of aversion to unfair acts as opposed to protesting unfair outcomes. She had MBA students take part in an ultimatum game under different conditions. The first condition was the usual ultimatum game, where participants were randomly assigned to the role of proposers and responders. Proposers had $10 and would offer a split of the initial pie, and responders had the right to accept or reject. In the event of a rejection, neither the proposer nor the responder got any money. In a second treatment – called the *third party* treatment – participants were divided into proposers and responders but the actual allocation of the initial amount ($10) was decided not by the proposer, but by another disinterested participant who stood to gain nothing from the allocation. The responders had the option of rejecting the allocation decided by the disinterested third party and, in the event of rejection, neither the proposer nor the responder got any money. Finally, there was a third – *chance* – treatment, where once again, participants were divided into proposers and responders. There was $10 to be divided, as before, but rather than the proposer or a third party making the decision, the allocation of the money in this treatment was decided by the spin of a roulette wheel which put an equal chance on each outcome (for instance, $10 for the proposer and $0 for the responder, $9 for the proposer and $1 for the responder and so on).

Before playing the actual game, Blount also asked each participant to state the minimum amount he/she was willing to accept if assigned to the role of the responder in the game to be played immediately thereafter. If all that the responders cared about was their *relative standing* in relation to the proposers, that is, they did not want to be too worse off in monetary terms compared to the proposer, then the minimum acceptable amounts stated by participants in these three treatments should not be different. However, if it is the *intentionality* of the act that matters and people care more about intentional acts of unfairness rather than how much money they get relative to another, then we would expect people to be more willing to accept inequitable allocations when the allocation is made by chance (by spinning a roulette wheel) than when the allocation is made by a proposer who stands to gain from the inequity of the offer.

■ The ultimatum game

The results clearly demonstrated that it is the *unfairness* of offers, rather than relative pay-offs, that people care about. In the first treatment, where the offers were decided by the proposer, who got to keep more money by offering the responder less, on average, the minimum amount responders were willing to accept was $2.91 (out of $10). In the case where the allocations were determined by a disinterested third party, the average minimum acceptable amount was $2.08. But in the case where the offer was decided by chance, the minimum acceptable amount on average was $1.20. Thus, people were far less concerned by the unfairness of the outcome and the inequity of final pay-offs when the division was decided by chance than when it was decided by another human, especially a human who stood to gain by making an inequitable offer. Furthermore, in the first treatment, where the proposer would allocate the money, nine out of 17 proposers offered a 50–50 split to the responder, four offered between $4 and $4.50, two offered between $2.50 and $3 and two offered the responder only $0.50. It became clear that responders were much less willing to accept large disparities in the pay-offs with a human proposer as opposed to when the allocation was decided by chance.

Further evidence that intentions matter came from Armin Falk, Ernst Fehr and Urs Fischbacher of the University of Zürich. They had 90 participants take part in four separate, slightly modified ultimatum games. In each game, the proposer was asked to suggest a split of 10 points. (Total points accumulated by the proposers and the responders were later redeemable for cash payments.) But rather than choosing any possible split of the 10 points, Falk and his colleagues restricted their proposers to making *only one of two choices*. I will call these choices A and B. Furthermore, choice A was *always the same in all four games*. Choice A gave 8 points out of 10 to the proposer and 2 points to the responder. Choice B, however, varied from one game to the next. See Figure 7.4 for details on the structure of the game. In one game, choice B gave 5 points to the proposer and 5 points to the responder, that is, in this game, the proposer had a choice between keeping 8 for him/herself and giving 2 to the responder (choice A), or making an equal split giving 5 to each (choice B). Let us call this the "5/5 game". In a second game, choice B gave 2 points to the proposer and 8 points to the responder, that is, in this game, the proposer could choose to retain the lion's share of the pie (8 for him/her and 2 for the responder), or give away 8 to the responder, keeping only 2. Let us call this the "2/8 game". These pay-offs are denoted in parentheses in Figure 7.4. Finally, in another game, choice B gave 10 points to the proposer and nothing to the responder. This game then offered two inequitable choices to the proposer – one inequitable choice where he/she kept 8 and offered the responder 2, and one even more inequitable choice where he/she

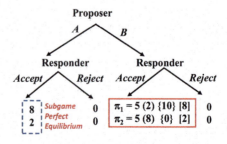

Figure 7.4
Structure of the Falk et al. ultimatum games

kept all 10 and gave the responder nothing. I will call this the "10/0 game". These pay-offs appear within braces in Figure 7.4. They also ran a game which provided the proposer with a trivial choice where both choice A and choice B gave 8 points to the proposer and 2 points to the responder. Here, the proposer had no choice but to keep 8 and offer 2. Regardless of whether the proposer chose A or B, as long as the responder responded by accepting the offer the outcome was the same, 8 for the proposer and 2 for the responder regardless of which branch of the tree was being utilized. These pay-offs are shown within square brackets in Figure 7.4. I am not going to discuss this last game with trivial choices since a discussion of the other three games will suffice to make my point.

In each and every game, the responder could reject the proposer's offer, in which case, they both end up with nothing. Before I tell you the results, and it is quite likely that you have an intuitive feeling for what to expect, let us think of what we expect to happen in this game in terms of acceptance or rejection by the responders. Once again, if responders are only concerned with their monetary pay-offs, then we expect that the 8/2 offer (8 points for the proposer and 2 for the responder) will never be rejected. Intuitively, we would expect that in the 5/5 game, a proposal of 8/2 is clearly perceived as unfair because the proposer could have proposed the egalitarian offer of 5 points for the proposer and 5 for the responder. In the 2/8 game, offering 8/2 may still be perceived as unfair but probably less so than in the 5/5 game, because the only alternative available to 8/2 gives the proposer only 2 points as opposed to the 8 points given to the responder. Thus, we would expect the rejection rate of the 8/2 offer in the 5/5 game to be higher than that in the 2/8 game. Finally, offering 8/2 in the 10/0 game may even be perceived as a fair (or less unfair) action, so the rejection rate of 8/2 is likely to be lowest in this game.

The results were exactly as expected. The rejection rate of the inequitable 8/2 offer was the highest in the first 5/5 game (44.4%). The 8/2 offers were rejected 27% of the time in the 2/8 game and only 9% of the time in the 10/0 game. The variations in these rejection rates suggest that *intentions* behind the original offers is a major factor behind whether the offer is accepted or not. The rejection rates of the alternative offers (5/5), (2/8) and (10/0) are as follows: nobody rejected the 5/5 offer and only one subject rejected the 2/8 offer. Almost 90% rejected the 10/0 offer when made.

The Emory University primatologist, Frans de Waal, and his colleague Sarah Brosnan believe that such notions of fairness are not confined to humans. They carried out an experiment exploring inequity aversion among capuchin monkeys. Two capuchin monkeys are put in transparent cells next to each other. Each monkey has a collection of pebbles in the cell. The experimenter approaches each monkey in turn. The monkey has to hand a rock to the experimenter; in return, the monkey gets a treat. The treat is either a slice of cucumber or a piece of grape, with the latter being the more coveted treat since the monkeys like grapes more than cucumbers. Initially, each monkey gets a piece of cucumber in return for handing a pebble to the experimenter. But, after a few trials, one monkey continues to get cucumber while the other is given a piece of grape. At first, the monkey who gets the cucumber watches the other monkey get the grape, but after a couple of times of this happening, the monkey getting cucumbers gets highly agitated and throws the cucumber away rather than eat it and starts banging against the cell and effectively, starts to protest this unequal treatment for the same work.[4]

But it also appears that chimpanzees (*Pan troglodytes*) may not share this human penchant for fairness. In 2007, Keith Jensen, Josep Call and Michael Tomasello at the Max Planck Institute for Evolutionary Anthropology had 11 chimpanzees participate in an ultimatum game with the exact same format as the Falk, Fehr and Fischbacher study described here, except the chimpanzees were dividing 10 raisins rather than money. But, just as in the human study, the proposer chimpanzees had to choose between two offers A and B. Offer A always gave 8 raisins to the proposer and 2 to the responder, while offer B varied from one game to the next. In one game, offer B gave 5 raisins to each (5/5 game), in a second, offer B gave 2 raisins to the proposer and 8 to the responder (2/8 game), and in a third, it gave 10 raisins to the proposer and none to the responder (10/0 game). Unlike their human counterparts who routinely turn down 8/2 offers when the alternative is 5/5, chimpanzee responders "did not reject unfair offers when the proposer had the option of making a fair offer; they accepted all non-zero offers; and they reliably rejected only offers of zero". It seems that the question of whether notions of unfairness extend to the animal kingdom is not settled and needs further research.

CRITICISMS OF THE FINDINGS OF GÜTH AND HIS COLLEAGUES

There were a number of criticisms aimed at the validity and interpretation of these results. Broadly speaking, these questions could be classified into the following categories. First, the critics suggested that we are conditioned from childhood onward to be sociable and cooperative. Thus, when confronted with a relatively novel situation of the ultimatum game, proposers do not quite catch on that they have the upper hand in the transaction and that they can, therefore, earmark a larger portion of the available amount, giving the responders a smaller share. That is, proposers make generous offers because they are being altruistic, and this does not really have anything to do with the fairness or unfairness of offers. This, of course, does not quite explain why the responders turn money down.

The second criticism was somewhat related to the first and grew out of it. Suppose you brought a group of people into a room and made half of them proposers and half responders. You gave the proposers $10 to divide between the two. This was like manna from heaven. Clearly the proposer is in a position of strength vis-à-vis the responder. But what entitles the proposer to be a proposer and therefore gain this position? The assignment to roles is purely a matter of chance. In this rather ambiguous situation, the proposers might feel less entitled to the money and more inclined to share it fairly with the responders – after all, the proposer could easily have been a responder. Elizabeth Hoffman, Kevin McCabe and Vernon Smith, who have done extensive work in the area, put it in the following way. "It is as if you and I are walking along the street, and we see an envelope on the sidewalk. I pick it up. It contains ten $1 bills. I hand five to you and keep five."

The third criticism was aimed at the relatively small stakes involved. These critics argued that 10 marks (or 10 dollars) was not a large amount and, therefore, the participants may not even have taken the game seriously. Behaviour would be different and more "rational" if the amounts involved were larger, that is, proposers will keep a larger fraction and responders will not be so quick to turn offers down if larger amounts were involved. Turning down a dollar or two is one thing but who would turn down $10 or $20?

The fourth criticism involved a more subtle issue and had to do with what is often called *experimenter demand effects*. This suggests that even if a proposer is interested in pocketing most of the amount given to him/her, he/she may not do so because he/she knows that the experimenter can see his/her decisions and does not want the experimenter to think of him/her as greedy. Thus, it is embarrassment that is preventing the proposers from pocketing most of the money. And similarly, being observed by the experimenter may compel the responder to reject small amounts because he/she does not want to appear desperate or look like a pushover.

BEHAVIOUR IN THE ULTIMATUM GAME: FAIRNESS OR ALTRUISM?

Let us take these criticisms in turn and see if they hold water. First, are proposers motivated by a desire to share? Robert Forsythe, Joel Horowitz, N. E. Savin and Martin Sefton of the University of Iowa answered this question by looking at the differences in behaviour in the ultimatum game and an even simpler game called the *dictator game*. The dictator game is similar to the ultimatum game in that participants are paired into proposers and responders. The proposers are then given an amount of money, such as $10. They are then told to decide on an allocation of this money between the two. But now, the responder does not have a say at all! Thus, any amount the proposer gives to the responder, the latter would have to accept without any option of rejecting that offer.

Here, the prediction based on self-interest is clear. The proposer should simply take all the money and give nothing to the responder. But, comparing the behaviour of the proposers in the ultimatum and dictator games can tell us about the motivations of the proposers. Suppose proposers in the ultimatum game were merely motivated by altruism – a desire to share – rather than fear of rejection. If that is the case, then the offers by the proposers in the two games – the ultimatum game and the dictator game (the latter being purely a decision to share the money) – should be similar. But if proposers in the ultimatum game are motivated by the fear of being punished in the event of unfair offers, then we would expect much more generous offers in the ultimatum game than in the dictator game.

In Figure 7.5, I show the behaviour of the participants from one set of experiments carried out by Forsythe and his colleagues. They report results from two separate sets of experiments, one done in April and the second in September. The left panel shows the distribution of offers in the dictator game while the right panel shows the same for the ultimatum game. I have used slightly different shading for the offers made in April (lighter shading) and

Figure 7.5
Comparison of offers in the ultimatum game and the dictator game. Re-created on the basis of data in Forsythe et al. (1994)

September (darker shading), respectively. In both games, the proposers were given $5 and were asked to suggest an allocation out of this. The x-axis shows the amounts offered and the y-axis the respective proportions of offers, with 2 implying 20%, 4 implying 40% and so on. It is quite clear from comparing the two panels that the proposers in the ultimatum game offer the responders a lot more money than the proposers in the dictator game. It is clear that the modal offer – that is, the offer made by the majority of participants – in the ultimatum game is 50% of the initial amount available. Fifty-five per cent of the proposers offered the responder $2.50 out of the $5.00 given to the proposers at the start of the game. Another 20%–25% offered 40%, that is, $2.00 out of $5.00. Thus three-quarters of proposers in the ultimatum game offered between $2.00 and $2.50 out of $5.00 (i.e., between 40% and 50%) to the responders. In contrast, the modal offer in the dictator game is zero. About 40% of the proposers in the dictator game offered nothing to the responder. Another 30% offered 20% of the available amount, that is, $1.00. So, while 75% of proposers in the ultimatum game offered $2.00 or more (40% or more) out of $5.00, just about 70% of the proposers in the dictator game offered a dollar or less (20% or less).

This was powerful evidence against an explanation based on proposer altruism and lent further credence to the argument that both proposers and responders were reacting in accordance with implicit social norms that dictate fairness in allocations. The conclusion was unequivocal. In the dictator game, where there is no threat of being punished, proposers are rather parsimonious. But in the ultimatum game, the proposers clearly anticipate the fact that if they make unfair offers to responders, then many responders will react adversely to that unfairness by turning down the offer, even if the responder has to forego a substantial amount by doing so. Both proposers and responders exhibit that they have a very clear notion of what constitutes fair or unfair in a particular situation and respond accordingly.

RAISING THE MONETARY STAKES IN THE ULTIMATUM GAME

Would behaviour in the ultimatum game be different with higher stakes? Here, one unresolved issue, of course, is how large is large enough? In 1996, Elizabeth Hoffman, Kevin McCabe and Vernon Smith decided to try the same game with $10 and $100. $100 was certainly a non-trivial amount then, as it is now, especially if you are a student whose opportunity cost of time is certainly less than $100 – especially given that the experiment took around 20 minutes to run. Hoffman, McCabe and Smith decided to examine the question of entitlement as well. So, besides carrying out one treatment where participants were assigned to a role as proposer or responder randomly, exactly as in prior studies, they looked at another treatment where these roles were decided on the basis of performance in a trivia quiz. Those who scored high in the quiz got to be proposers, while the rest got to be responders. The proposers in this ultimatum game were told that they have "won" the right to divide this money with the idea that having won this right would imply a greater sense of entitlement among the proposers and might lead to more parsimonious offers.[5]

What Hoffman, McCabe and Smith found was startling. In those experiments where participants were randomly assigned to the role of proposers and responders, as in the original study by Güth and his colleagues, the offers made by proposers to responders in the game played with $100 were *remarkably similar* to the offers made in the $10 game. There were 24 proposers in the $10 game and 27 in the $100 game. In both cases, the modal offer (i.e., the offer made by a majority of proposers) was 50% – either $5 out of $10 or $50 out of $100. And in both games, pretty much all the offers ranged between 30% and 50%, that is, between $3 and $5 in the $10 game, and between $30 and $50 in the $100 game. Except, in the $100 game, there was one person who wished to keep the entire $100 (which was acceptable to the responder), while no proposer wanted to keep it all in the $10 game. And in the $100 game, there were two subjects who offered $60 (60%) to the paired responder – that is, these two were willing to give up $60 and keep $40! Little wonder that these offers were accepted.

When it came to the games where people have "earned" the right to be proposers by doing well on the trivia quiz, offers were more parsimonious. There were 24 proposers who played the $10 game and 23 who played the $100 game. There were fewer offers that gave the responder 40% or more, and more offers that gave the responder 10%. In this case, a number of proposers appeared to believe that the responders would be willing to accept a smaller portion of the pie, such as 10% (probably because the proposers have "won" the quiz and feel entitled to claim a larger share of the booty). But, quite surprisingly, the responders were clearly not willing to accede to this sense of entitlement on the part of the proposers and were quite willing to turn down inequitable offers, even in the $100 game. This was because the rejection rates (i.e., the rate at which proposed offers were turned down by the responders) were much higher in the $100 game as well. In the $10 game, only three out of 24 offers were rejected, while in the $100 game, five out of 23 offers were rejected. In the $100 game, three out of four offers where the responder was offered $10 were rejected, and out of five cases where the responder was offered $30 with the proposer keeping $70, two were rejected! Thus, a number of participants in the $100 game rejected amounts of money that were greater than or equal to the entire stake in the $10 game. This suggests that the expectations of what constitutes as fair is different between the $10 and $100 games.

The Hoffman, McCabe and Smith study suggests that if the roles of proposer and responder are assigned randomly, then offers tended to cluster around 50% and this was true whether the stakes are $10 or $100. Thus, multiplying the stakes tenfold did not lead to any appreciable changes in proposer behaviour. When the roles were assigned on the basis of performance in a trivia quiz, proposers seem to feel entitled to keep more of the money and make more parsimonious offers, but this legitimacy was not necessarily accepted by the responders and, especially in the $100 game, the parsimony of the proposers led to discord and higher rejection rates.

These results went a long way in answering the proposition that behaviour would be different and more in keeping with the self-interest assumption, if only the stakes were higher. It turns out that this is not true, and, in fact, if roles are assigned randomly, then there is a slight movement towards more equitable offers with increased stakes. But is $100 high enough? Would behaviour be different if the sum of money was even larger?

One problem with using really large sums of money is that these studies are funded by research grants and most researchers do not have unlimited amounts of money at their disposal. But there is a way out of this and that is to run these experiments in a less developed country. Given that there are large differences in purchasing power, even small sums in developed countries amount to much larger sums in less developed ones. Thus, the same amount

■ The ultimatum game

of dollars goes a much longer way in less developed countries and allows the researcher to run experiments with stakes that amount to many times the monthly income of participants.

Lisa Cameron decided that to really answer the question about stakes, we need to look at behaviour with even greater amounts of money. In 1994, she travelled to Gadjah Mada University in Yogyakarta, Indonesia. At that time, the per capita gross domestic product of Indonesia was $670, which was about 3% of the gross domestic product per capita in the US. Cameron had participants play the ultimatum game with Rp 5,000 Rp 40,000 and Rp 200,000 (approximately $2.50, $20 and $100 respectively, with the then exchange rate of $1 = Rp 2,160). The largest of these three stakes was approximately three times the average monthly expenditure of the participants. These were unarguably high stakes.

It is possible that behaviour may be different if we were dealing with millions of dollars, but most of us are not dealing with millions on an everyday basis. Furthermore, it is not clear if that would make a difference either. If Bill Gates was playing an ultimatum game with Warren Buffet – those are the people who can afford to play the ultimatum game with millions of dollars – and Buffet offered Gates $200,000 out of $1 million, then it is quite conceivable that Gates might turn the offer down. $200,000, after all, does not mean as much to Gates as it does to most of us. Table 7.1 shows the offers made by the proposers using the three different stakes: Rp 5000, Rp 40,000 and Rp 200,000. The average amount offered is around 40% in all three cases and the modal amount is 50% in each case.

Figure 7.6 provides a more detailed breakdown of offers, acceptances and rejections. In a small number of cases, the responder filled in an incorrect answer to the question "How much will you receive if you accept?" In these cases, Cameron assumed that the responder did not understand the game fully and so the response is marked as a problem rather than as an acceptance or rejection. In this figure, I have shown data from three games, each played for two rounds. The first round is always identical, with stakes of Rp 5,000. Proposers have to decide how to split this amount between him/her and the responder. In the second round of Game 1, the stake remains unchanged. In Game 2, the stake increases from Rp 5,000 in Round 1 to Rp 40,000 in Round 2. Finally, in Game 3, the stake increases from Rp 5,000 in Round 1 to Rp 200,000 in Round 2. In each panel of Figure 7.6, the x-axis denotes the proportion of the pie that the proposer wished to keep and the y-axis shows the relevant proportion of each such allocation.

Surprisingly, or in the light of what I have said above, not surprisingly, in the game with Rp 200,000, offers of 10% and 20% of the available amount (Rp 20,000 and Rp 40,000, respectively) were rejected by the responders. In the Rp 40,000 game, offers of 25%, 30%

Table 7.1 Offers made in high stakes ultimatum games

	Game 1 (Rp 5,000)	*Game 2 (Rp 40,000)*	*Game 3 (Rp 200,000)*
Average proportion offered	40%	45%	42%
Modal offer (offer made by a majority of participants)	50%	50%	50%
Acceptance rates	69%	91%	90%

Created on the basis of data provided in Cameron (1999)

The ultimatum game

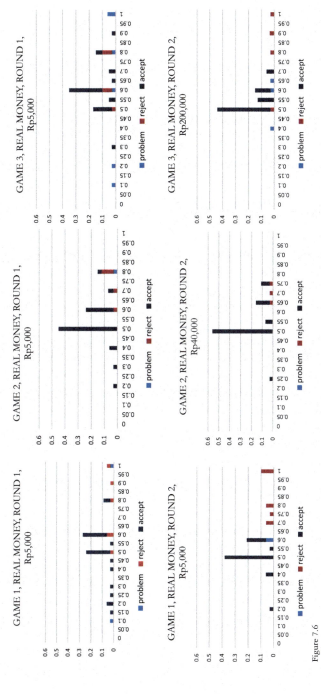

Figure 7.6
Breakdown of offers, acceptances and rejections in Cameron's high stakes ultimatum game. Re-created on the basis of data in Cameron (1999)

and 35% (Rp 10,000, Rp 12,000 and Rp 14,000, respectively) were turned down as well. Cameron's conclusion: *the examination of proposer behaviour in these games does not show any movement toward the Nash equilibrium outcome as the stakes increase.* Remember, Nash equilibrium reasoning suggests very small offers by proposers and acceptance by responders. Cameron goes on to argue that "proposer behaviour is invariant to stake changes", that is, offers do not become more parsimonious even when large sums of money are concerned. Possibly because, as I pointed out above, in the case of inequitable offers of 25% of the available amount or less, responders routinely turn down substantial amounts of money if they feel that the offer is unfair.

Cameron also found that there was an increase in the rates of acceptance of offers as the stakes increase, but she suggests that this may not necessarily reflect a greater willingness on the part of the responders to accept a given amount, but is, rather, due to the fact that as the stake size grows, proposers in general tend to make more generous offers, which makes those offers more likely to be accepted. So, if Warren Buffet did get together with Bill Gates to play the ultimatum game, chances are, Buffet will offer Gates 40%–50% of the pie and Gates will accept.

FEAR OF PUNISHMENT OR FEAR OF EMBARRASSMENT?

What about the criticism that generous offers by proposers are caused by an unwillingness to appear greedy in the eyes of the experimenters, who can observe the decisions made? Elizabeth Hoffman, Kevin McCabe, Keith Shachat and Vernon Smith ran some dictator game experiments using a complicated "double-blind" protocol. Normally in experiments, a participant is not aware of whom he/she is paired with, but the experimenter can see all the decisions. Thus, there is anonymity between the participants but not between the participants and the experimenter. This protocol is called "single-blind". A double-blind protocol refers to a situation where the decisions made by all participants are completely anonymous in that neither the other participants nor the experimenter learns what a particular participant decided.[6] Usually, experimental economists carry out double-blind protocols by assigning letters or numbers to participants and participants then picking a letter or number at random. Participants then make decisions on pieces of paper which are deposited in a locked box so that the experimenter cannot see those decisions. The experimenter then pays the participants on the basis of the numbers or letters assigned and deposits these payments into another locked box. Participants pick up the payment that matches their letter or number from the locked box using keys given to them at the beginning of the session. The experimenter does not know which participant was assigned a particular letter or number and, therefore, has no way of matching the decisions with a particular participant.

Using this complex protocol guarantees that the participants will be convinced that no one – neither the other participants nor the experimenter – will ever learn what each individual participant decided. Hoffman and her colleagues actually ran another even more stringent double-blind protocol where they used one of the experimental participants as the monitor for the entire session. This participant, who was taught what to do at the beginning of the session, was in charge of running the entire session and did not have any prior knowledge about the experimenters' purpose. Furthermore, Hoffman and her colleagues also looked at a treatment where not only did they use a double-blind protocol, but also reinforced the proposer's sense of entitlement to the money by having them participate in a trivia quiz where those in the top half of the group got to be proposers while the rest were responders.

In previous dictator experiments, around 20% of proposers offered nothing to the responder, while another 20% offered half the available amount. When Hoffman and her colleagues looked at dictator games where the right to be a proposer was "earned" on the basis of performance in the trivia quiz, 40% of the proposers offered nothing and another 40% offered only 10% or 20% of the pie to the responder. When they added the double-blind protocol on top of that – that is, proposers earned the right by winning in the trivia quiz and there was anonymity between both participants and between the participant and the experimenter – over two-thirds of proposers offered nothing and 84% offered 10% or less. Hoffman and her colleagues suggested that being observed by the experimenter – and possibly thought greedy – seemed to matter, and that it is conceivable that it is this fear of being thought greedy that leads to generous offers in the ultimatum game, rather than allowances for implicit social norms of fairness or the fear of being punished for unfair offers.

Of course, this elaborate double-blind protocol coupled with a sense of entitlement generated by winning the quiz might have created a different type of experimenter demand effect. It is possible that participants may have construed the elaborate procedures as a signal that they really should keep the money, given that most transactions in real life are often not nearly as anonymous as this.

Gary Bolton at Penn State and Rami Zwick at the University of Auckland provided an eloquent answer to this question and demonstrated beyond doubt that it was the fear of punishment that was driving behaviour in the ultimatum game. Bolton and Zwick compared the behaviour of participants in the ultimatum game with another game that they called the *impunity game*. Let me explain the impunity game first. In this game, players are paired up into proposers and responders exactly as in the ultimatum game. Also, exactly as in the ultimatum game, the proposer is given a certain sum of money and asked to suggest a split of this money between the proposer and the responder. The responder is informed about the split offered by the proposer and asked whether he/she wishes to accept or reject that allocation. If the responder accepts the offer, then the allocation is implemented, with the proposer keeping the amount he/she wanted to and the responder getting the rest. However, if the responder rejects the offer, *then the proposer still gets the amount he/she wanted to keep but the responder gets nothing*. So, the difference from the ultimatum game is that, in the impunity game, a rejection by the responder does not have the power to hurt the proposer by taking money away from him/her. The threat of punishment to the proposer for making an unfair offer is removed in the impunity game.

Bolton and Zwick decided to look at behaviour in the ultimatum game, first with a double-blind protocol, which preserves anonymity between the participants and the experimenter, and then with a single-blind protocol, where the experimenter gets to observe participant decisions. They also decided to compare the behaviour of the proposers in the ultimatum game with that in the impunity game. The reasoning is as follows: suppose proposers make generous offers in the single-blind ultimatum game because they do not want to be perceived as being greedy or unfair by the experimenter. Then we should expect to see less generous offers in the double-blind ultimatum game, where the experimenter

■ The ultimatum game

could not observe individual decisions, as compared to the single-blind protocol, where the experimenter could see all decisions. On the other hand, if generous offers in the ultimatum game are driven by the fear of being punished in the event of making an unfair offer, then we should observe far more parsimonious offers in the impunity game, where there is no threat of punishment (since even if the responder rejects the offer, in this game, the proposer still gets to keep the amount he/she wanted for him/herself), compared to the ultimatum game, where the responder's rejection will cost the proposer his/her share of the pie.

Bolton and Zwick also made a change to the way the games were carried out. In most prior studies, proposers were given an amount (say $10) and asked to suggest a split of this amount between the proposer and the responder. The changes made by Bolton and Zwick included the following. First, each proposer played the game ten times, but, each time, the proposer was paired with a different responder. Second, in each round the proposer had $4 and in each round the proposer could make one of two choices – (1) an *equitable* choice, which gave $2 to both the proposer and the responder or (2) an *inequitable* choice which gave the proposer more money than the responder.

Figure 7.7 highlights the structure of the Bolton and Zwick study, which involves a binary choice for the proposers, either an equitable choice or an inequitable choice. Bolton and Zwick then look at three variants of this game: (1) a single-blind protocol; (2) a double-blind protocol and (3) the impunity game. Let me explain.

The proposer starts the game by either choosing the equitable offer or the inequitable offer (labelled in neutral and non-emotive terms). If the proposer chooses the equitable offer

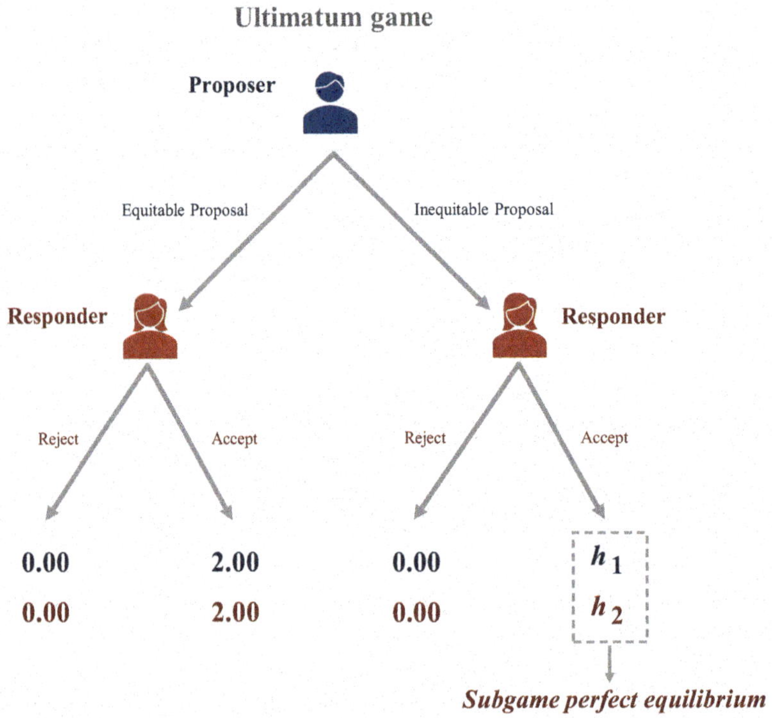

Ultimatum game

Proposer

Equitable Proposal / Inequitable Proposal

Responder   **Responder**

Reject   Accept   Reject   Accept

0.00   2.00   0.00 h_1
0.00   2.00   0.00 h_2

Subgame perfect equilibrium

Figure 7.7
Structure of the Bolton and Zwick cardinal ultimatum game

and the responder accepts (which is highly likely), then each gets $2. If the responder rejects (which seems unlikely), then both get zero. On the other hand, the proposer can choose the inequitable offer to start with. If the responder rejects the offer, then, as usual, both get zero. But if the responder accepts, then the proposer gets h_1 and the responder gets h_2. But the amounts corresponding to these inequitable offers are different in different rounds. Sometimes the inequity in pay-offs was small, while in other cases, the difference was larger. More specifically, the actual choices for the five inequitable offers were {$2.20, $1.80}, {$2.60, $1.40}, {$3.00, $1.00}, {$3.40, $0.60}, {$3.80, $0.20}. Since each proposer played ten games, he/she faced each of these above five choices twice.

Notice that, in each of the five choices, the sum adds up to $4, and that the first of these five offers is more equitable than the last, which gives the responder only $0.20 (i.e., 5% of the pie) and the level of inequity increases between the first and the last choice. Once again, if participants are motivated by purely monetary considerations, then self-interested preferences dictate that the proposer should always offer an inequitable split such as {$3.40, $0.60} or {$3.80, $0.20}, regardless of how inequitable it is, and the responder should accept.

The game protocols are similar. In the single-blind protocol, the responder does not know which proposer he/she is paired with but the experimenter has access to this information. In the double-blind protocol, there is both subject–subject as well as subject–experimenter anonymity. The impunity game is also similar, except, in the impunity game, if the responder rejects, then the proposer still gets h_1 as in the ultimatum game (with potential pay-offs of $2.20, $2.60, $3.00, $3.40 or $3.80) but the responder gets nothing, that is, h_2 is set to zero in the impunity game.

Again, to remind you about the central comparison here, if it is experimenter observation that matters, then we would expect proposers to choose the inequitable offer more frequently in the double-blind ultimatum game compared to the single-blind ultimatum game. On the other hand, if it is the fear of punishment that is the primary motivation behind proposer choices, then we would expect more inequitable choices in the impunity game, where the responder cannot retaliate to the inequity (and reduce the proposer's pay-off) by rejecting the offer, compared to the ultimatum game where rejection is meaningful and deprives the proposer of his/her pay-off.

The results clearly supported the punishment hypothesis. In the single-blind ultimatum game, 56% of all proposer choices were one of the inequitable choices and around 20% of these offers were rejected. The equitable offer of $2 each for the proposer and the responder was never rejected by the responder. Rejection rates were also higher as the offers became more inequitable. The choices in the double-blind ultimatum game were not all that different from those in the single-blind ultimatum game. There was a small increase in the proportion of inequitable offers by the proposers – 63% of the offers were inequitable ones in the double-blind protocol, as opposed to 56% in the single-blind protocol. Once again, there were also substantial rejections by the responders. Bear in mind what we said before. It is possible that responders may reject small offers in the ultimatum game in order not to be seen as desperate or a pushover by the experimenter. Using this logic, we would expect many more responders to accept small offers in the double-blind ultimatum game than in the single-blind ultimatum game. Remember that the responder could be offered $1.80, or $1.40, or $1.00, or $0.60, or $0.20 out of $4. Table 7.2 provides a breakdown of the rejection rates.

■ The ultimatum game

Table 7.2 Percentage of inequitable offers rejected by the responder

Inequitable offers to the responder	$1.80	$1.40	$1.00	$0.60	$0.20
Single-blind ultimatum game	7.7	11.8	57.1	77.8	100.0
Double-blind ultimatum game	13.3	7.1	67.0	70.0	100.0

Created on the basis of data provided in Bolton and Zwick (1995)

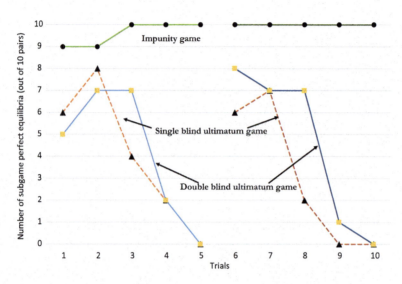

Figure 7.8 Evolution of play in the various games. Re-created on the basis of data in Bolton and Zwick (1995)

A few things stand out from this table. First, offers that were grossly inequitable – offering the responder only 20 cents out of the $4 available – were turned down in every single case regardless of whether the experimenter could observe actions (single-blind protocol) or not (double-blind protocol). Furthermore, more than 50% of offers that gave the responder $1 or less were turned down. Overall, the differences between the two treatments – single-blind versus double-blind – were not very pronounced. To observe really different behaviour, one must look at the impunity game, where the threat of punishment was removed. Here, 98% of the offers made by the proposers were inequitable offers and *none of these – not even when the proposers offered the responder $0.20 out of $4 – were turned down*! The evidence was incontrovertible. When the responders could not retaliate by rejecting unfair offers, the proposers felt no compunction in making inequitable offers; and when the responders knew that their rejection was not going to hurt the proposer, the responders did not bother engaging in such punishment either.

Finally, recall that regardless of any changes in pay-offs, the subgame perfect equilibrium in each game is the same. The proposer should choose the inequitable offer to start with; following that, the responder will accept any offer, no matter how small, assuming even a small amount such as $0.20 is better than nothing. So, over time, we expect to see more and more plays of the game to coincide with this subgame perfect outcome. We expect this to happen in all three forms of the game: single-blind, double-blind and impunity. Of course, by now we know that it is not going to happen, but, nevertheless, the evolution of play in the three different treatments is still instructive. Figure 7.8 shows this information.

There are ten pairs in each of the three conditions: single-blind, double-blind and impunity. In keeping with the way the data are presented in the original study, I break up the data for the first five rounds and the second five rounds. This is done to show whether there is any learning over time and whether the patterns are radically different between the two sets. Three things stand out: first, for each of the three games, the evolution of play is similar between the first five and second five rounds. Second, the evolution of play is remarkably similar for the single-blind and double-blind games, showing that behaviour in these games is not different. Finally, the pattern of play is starkly different for the impunity game. Almost all plays of the game here are in keeping with the subgame perfect equilibrium prediction: the proposer chooses the inequitable choice and no offers are rejected, no matter how small, by responders who realize that their rejection does not have the power to hurt the proposer, and, therefore, do not bother rejecting any offers. Bolton and Zwick's results then provide compelling evidence in favour of the punishment hypothesis. It is the possibility of being rejected for making small offers that prompts proposers into making generous offers, rather than experimenter demand effects (i.e., any concerns of being perceived as being unfair by the experimenter).

CASE STUDY 7.1 LOOKING INSIDE THE BRAIN WHILE PLAYING THE ULTIMATUM GAME

In Chapter 1, I introduced the burgeoning field of neuroeconomics, where researchers ask participants to take part in decision-making games while ensconced inside an fMRI machine. Alan Sanfey at Radboud University in Holland, along with his colleagues, decided to look inside the brain while people take part in an ultimatum game. Nineteen participants play a series of ultimatum games in the role of a responder over 20 rounds lasting 36 seconds each. Each participant plays ten times against a human proposer and another ten times against a computerized proposer. Prior to the experiment, each participant is introduced to ten other participants that he/she will be paired with over the course of the study. In each round, each participant was shown a photo of another person or a photo of a computer along with the offer. However, the actual offers were pre-determined and, even in the human rounds, the offers did not actually come from the human proposer but via the pre-set algorithm, even though the responder may have thought that the offer came from the proposer whose photo was being shown. (This amounts to deception, which may, at times, be necessary, but still should be avoided as far as practicable for reasons alluded to in an earlier chapter.)

The actual game is similar to the set-up in Falk et al. discussed earlier. There are only four offers possible: two fair or relatively fair offers: {$5, $5} and {$7, $3}; and two other "unfair" offers: {$8, $2} and {$9, $1}, where the second number denotes the pay-off to the responder. Of course, {$5, $5} is fair while {$7, $3} less so, but {$7, $3} is certainly more fair than the other two.[7] Each responder sees five {$5, $5} offers, one {$7, $3} offer, two {$8, $2} offers and two {$9, $1} offers, amounting to a total of ten offers when playing another human and another set of ten when playing against a computer, albeit in different sequences. The same set is repeated, albeit in different

Table 7.3 Rates of acceptance of offers from human and computer proposers

	Percentage of offers accepted			
	{$5, $5}	{$7, $3}	{$8, $2}	{$9, $1}
Human proposer	100	95	52	40
Computer proposer	100	95	85	65

Created on the basis of data in Sanfey et al. (2003)

orders for different participants. Each round begins with a 12 second separation interval. Then, for human trials, each responder gets to see a name and a photo of the paired proposer for 6 seconds. Then they get to see the proposed offer, which would be one of the four splits shown above for 6 seconds. Finally, they had to indicate whether they accepted or rejected the offer by pressing one of two buttons on a button box. Table 7.3 shows Sanfey et al.'s findings.

These results are very much in keeping with those reported by Blount, who showed that people apply fairness attributions and expect larger offers from human proposers as opposed to computers. It is clear that the rate of acceptance of "unfair" {$8, $2} or {$9, $1} offers is much higher when such offers come from computers as opposed to other humans. But what is more intriguing is what happens inside the brain when the responders get one of the "unfair" offers such as {$8, $2} or {$9, $1}, as opposed to one of the "fair" offers of {$5, $5} or {$7, $3}. Sanfey et al. find that there is significant activation in the bilateral interior insula upon receiving an unfair offer. The bilateral anterior insula is typically associated with negative emotional states such as pain and distress or hunger and thirst. It is part of the autonomic nervous system that regulates a variety of processes that occur without requiring conscious effort, such as heartbeat, blood flow, breathing, and digestion. This evidence suggests that humans react with almost a visceral sense of disgust when confronted with an unfair offer.

Not surprisingly, the researchers also find activation in the anterior cingulate cortex (ACC), which deals with conflict and impulse control, because, after all, there is a trade-off here between expressing anger via rejecting an offer and turning down money. There is also activation in the pre-frontal cortex (PFC), particularly the dorsolateral pre-frontal cortex (DLPFC), which, as we have discussed earlier, is tasked with receiving stimuli from different parts of the brain and then making decisions about what action to implement. So, the PFC is getting at least two different stimuli: one that says: "This offer is unfair; it is insulting; we should turn this down." Another part of the brain says: "Well yes, but money is money; why leave money on the table? This is a mistake." The PFC then has to make an executive decision about which of these to prioritize. Sanfey et al. further show that, in the case of unfair offers, the amount of activation in the bilateral anterior insula is greater than that in the DLPFC. The "insult effect" of an unfair offer outweighs any regret we may feel about leaving money on the table and we end up turning such offers down.

DO NORMS OF FAIRNESS DIFFER ACROSS CULTURES?

Most of the above studies used university students as participants and were concentrated on participants in the US and, in the case of the original study by Güth and his colleagues, Germany. It should be clear from the discussion above that the prevailing norm as to what constitutes a fair offer influences behaviour in the ultimatum game. But different cultures may have very different ideas of what constitutes "fair". Thus, while the above studies may provide us clues regarding what university students in Western market-based economies conceive as fair, is it possible to generalize those results to other countries and other cultures?

The first attempt to answer this question was undertaken by Alvin Roth and his colleagues, Vesna Prasnikar, Masahiro Okuno-Fujiwara and Shmuel Zamir during 1989–1990. Roth and his colleagues decided on an ambitious project which involved recruiting university students across four different locations – Pittsburgh, Ljubljana (in Slovenia, which used to be part of Yugoslavia; in what follows I will frequently use Yugoslavia to refer to Slovenia), Tokyo (in Japan) and Jerusalem (in Israel). This was one of the first attempts to look at behaviour in the ultimatum game across a number of (very) different cultures. A typical session had 20 participants and they were divided into ten pairs of proposers and responders. Each of the ten proposers interacted with each of the ten responders, so that, by the end of the session, each participant had participated in ten rounds of play. Needless to mention, proposers and responders were anonymous to one another and were identified by numbers only. In the US, in every round, each proposer had $10 to divide. In keeping with purchasing powers prevailing at the time, the amount to be divided was made equal to 400,000 dinars (YUD) in Yugoslavia, 20,000 yen (JPY) in Japan and 20 shekels (ILS) in Israel. However, because these amounts were different, proposers in each country were asked to suggest a division of 1,000 tokens, where the total tokens earned by participants were converted into real money at the end of the session.

An ambitious cross-country project like this poses a number of ancillary problems. Two of these are (1) language effects and (2) experimenter effects. The first one refers to the fact that, since the instructions to participants are written in four different languages (English, Slovenian, Japanese and Hebrew), this might lead to differences in behaviour. For instance, as these authors point out, the words "bargaining", "negotiating" and "haggling" are roughly synonymous but quite possibly convey very different messages depending on which word is being used. Pepsi for instance, much to its chagrin, found out about the pitfalls of translation when Pepsi's tagline "Come alive with the Pepsi generation" was translated into "Pepsi brings your ancestors back from the grave" in Chinese. Along the same lines, Frank Perdue's chicken slogan, "It takes a strong man to make a tender chicken" was translated into Spanish as "It takes an aroused man to make a chicken affectionate." The slogan for Coors beer, "Turn it loose", was translated into Spanish as "Suffer from diarrhoea".[8]

This problem is handled by first writing out the instructions in English and then translating them into the language of the country concerned and then back-translating them into English to make sure that the act of translating the instructions does not distort the meaning of the instructions. The initial translation and back-translations are done by different people.

The second problem arises from the fact that different people are running the experiments in different countries and there is a chance (possibly low) that the participants may

■ The ultimatum game

respond differently to the different demeanours or personalities of the different experimenters. This problem was solved by having each of the experimenters run sessions in Pittsburgh. By keeping the location fixed, any differences in behaviour due to a particular experimenter's personality can be pinpointed. The Slovenian data was gathered by Prasnikar, who also ran the first Pittsburgh sessions, with Roth observing. The remaining Pittsburgh data were gathered by Zamir (who also ran the experiments in Jerusalem) and Okuno-Fujiwara (who ran the sessions in Tokyo as well), with Roth and Prasnikar observing. There were no systematic differences in behaviour based on who was running the session.

Figure 7.9 shows the types of offers made in the four locations. In this figure, I show only what happened in the tenth (and last) round of interactions. It is conceivable that participants, particularly proposers, engage in some amount of experimentation – that is, trying out different things – in the first few rounds. Furthermore, they probably learn valuable information from both acceptances and rejections of offers during those early rounds. Thus, it stands to reason that the offers made in the very last round reflect in-built preferences and norms better than the data from the first few rounds.

The graph looks complicated but really is not. The horizontal axis shows the percentage of the amount available that the proposer offered to the responder. The vertical axis shows the proportion of proposers who offered a particular percentage to the responder. There are four sets of bars. The first set shows the offers that were made in Israel. The second set shows the offers made in Japan. The third shows the offers in Yugoslavia, and the final set of bars (at the very back) shows the offers made in the USA. So, looking at the bars for Israel – the very first set – we find that no one offered 0% to the responder. About 5% of offers gave the responder 10% of the pie while another 5% offered 17.5%. Ten per cent of offers gave the responder 20%, and 32% offered the responder 40%.

A few things stand out from this figure. Not surprisingly, the proposers seldom offered more than 50% of the pie to the responder. (There is one exception. In the United

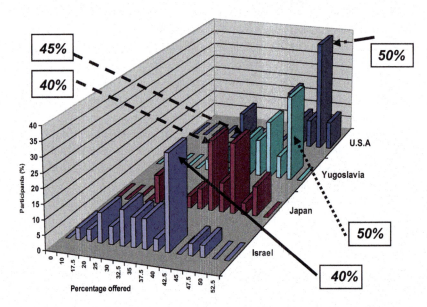

Figure 7.9
Distribution of offers in the ultimatum game in four different locations. Re-created on the basis of data in Roth et al. (1991)

States – look at the very last set of bars – around 10% of all offers in the last round were "hyper-fair", in that these proposers offered 52.5% of the pie to the responder, keeping only 48.5% themselves, a lower share. Of course, these offers were all accepted.) Second, overall the offers look similar in that in no country do we see extremely parsimonious offers as the theory predicts.

But if we look more closely, then there are differences. One thing that you should notice is that in Israel (the very first set of bars), the modal offer (i.e., the offer made by the most subjects) is 40%. Around one-third of all offers gave the responder 40% of the pie. In Japan (the second set of bars) there are two modes – 40% and 45%. Roughly 25% of offers each were of either 40% or 45%. However, in Yugoslavia and the USA, the modal offer is 50%. Thirty per cent of all offers in the last round gave the responder 50% in Yugoslavia and 40% of offers gave 50% to the responder in the US. Statistical tests confirmed the following: offers in the USA and Yugoslavia were equally generous, while the offers in these two countries were more generous than the offers in Japan, which in turn was more generous than the offers in Israel.

If we now look at the rejection rates, then we find that across all rounds, roughly 28% of all offers were rejected in the US, 29% in Yugoslavia, 22% in Japan and 28% in Israel. Thus, while the rejection rates were broadly similar across countries, what was surprising is that, if we look at the tenth and final round only, then we find that the rejection rates in the two low-offer countries – Japan and Israel – were actually lower than the other two. Rejection rates in the tenth and final round were 14% and 13%, respectively, in the two low-offer countries, Japan and Israel, and these rates were lower than the 19% and 23% rejection rates in the USA and Yugoslavia, respectively.

Looking at these patterns of behaviour, one could hypothesize that the difference among subject pools is in something like their "aggressiveness" or "toughness". But if it is indeed the case that there are differences in aggressiveness across the four countries, then we would expect the responders in each country to share that characteristic. This should then lead to high rates of disagreement and rejected offers in the two countries (Japan and Israel) where the offers are low in general. But that is not the case. Instead, the two countries where offers are low (Japan and Israel) do not exhibit any higher rates of disagreement than the high-offer countries (the USA and Yugoslavia).

The authors conclude:

> This suggests that what varies between subject pools is not a property like aggressiveness or toughness, but rather the perception of what constitutes a reasonable offer under the circumstances. That is, suppose that in all subject pools it seems reasonable for the first mover to ask for more than half the profit from the transaction and that what varies between subject pools is how much more seems reasonable. To the extent that offers tend toward what is commonly regarded as reasonable, and assuming that offers regarded as reasonable are accepted, there would be no reason to expect disagreement rates to vary between subject pools, even when offers do. Our data thus lend some support to the hypothesis that the subject-pool differences observed in this experiment are related to different expectations about what constitutes an acceptable offer ... Consequently, we offer the conjecture that the observed subject-pool differences are cultural in character.

■ The ultimatum game

The work done by Roth and his colleagues went a long way towards addressing the issue of cultural differences. Their results showed that there were both similarities and differences across cultures. The similarity was that in no country were the proposers as parsimonious as the theory would suggest and the vast majority of offers gave the responders 20% or more of the pie. But there were differences. The modal offers were lower in Japan and Israel compared to Yugoslavia and the US, and offers in general were less generous in the former two countries compared to the latter two.

AN EVEN MORE AMBITIOUS CROSS-CULTURAL STUDY

However, while it is true that the four above countries do represent very different cultures, are students across these countries all that different? Maybe the students are much more alike than the citizens of these nations at large. If so, then maybe we should look further and deeper to search for cultural differences in behaviour. In the mid-1990s, a far more comprehensive cross-cultural study of behaviour in the ultimatum game than anything attempted before was initiated under the auspices of the MacArthur Foundation Norms and Preferences Network.

Joseph Henrich, an anthropologist at the University of California, Los Angeles (UCLA) was undertaking field work among the Machiguenga, a group of horticulturalists in the tropical forests of south-eastern Peru. Henrich had heard about the ultimatum game results discussed above from his dissertation adviser, Robert Boyd. Henrich decided to have the Machiguenga play the ultimatum game. Henrich's findings were surprising and deviated substantially from the findings of studies prior to this. The Machiguenga behaved very differently from the participants in the studies mentioned above. The most common offer made by Machiguenga proposers was 15% and, despite many low offers, not a single offer was rejected. This was doubly surprising given that Machiguenga live in small villages where people interact with other village members quite regularly and have very limited contact with strangers – an environment that we would expect would make the people more predisposed towards sharing, reciprocal motivations and fairness.

Henrich shared his findings with Robert Boyd, a noted anthropologist at UCLA, and Colin Camerer, a leading experimental economist at Caltech. Both Boyd and Camerer were also members of the Norms and Preferences Network. The obvious question was this: were the Machiguenga results anomalous or were these results indicative of far more substantial cultural variations in behaviour that is not captured by the predominantly student participants in the previous studies? Boyd and Herbert Gintis, who were at this time the directors of the Preferences Network, decided to organize and fund a tremendously ambitious programme of cross-cultural experimental work.

They put together a group of 12 experienced field researchers working in 12 countries over five continents and gathered data for 15 small-scale societies exhibiting a wide variety of economic and cultural conditions. The societies studied included the Orma in Kenya, the Hadza and the Sangu in Tanzania, the Torguud Mongols and the Kazakhs in Mongolia, the Lamalera in Indonesia, the Au and the Gnau in Papua New Guinea, the Achuar in Ecuador, the Machiguenga in Peru, the Tsimane in Bolivia, the Mapuche in Chile and the Ache in Paraguay. Some of these are foraging societies, some practise slash-and-burn horticulture, some are nomadic herding groups and some are sedentary, small-scale agricultural societies.

Needless to mention, given the complexity of the task involved, it was impossible to control for differences in language or experimenters (as Roth and his colleagues did). Thus, the researchers, who were already involved in anthropological field work in these countries, carried out the experiments on their own in these respective societies using the local language or local dialect. The experimenters tried to maintain anonymity by having proposers make offers and responders make acceptance/rejection decisions in seclusion, but still, given the small-scale and tight-knit nature of many of these communities, the level of anonymity is certainly less than in usual laboratory studies of behaviour.

The findings, published in 2004 in the book, *Foundations of Human Sociality* edited by Joseph Henrich, Robert Boyd, Samuel Bowles, Colin Camerer, Ernst Fehr and Herbert Gintis, suggested that (1) there is no society where behaviour is commensurate with the extreme self-interest hypothesis that posits that proposers would keep a lion's share of the pie; (2) there is much more variation between groups than has been previously reported. The norm of what constitutes fair behaviour varies substantially across these societies and, more importantly, this variation coincides with differences in the patterns of interaction in everyday life.

Table 7.4 provides a broad overview of behaviour in the ultimatum game across these diverse societies. I have arranged the societies in increasing order of the average offers made.

Table 7.4 Offers across the diverse small-scale societies

Group	Country	Mean offer	Modes	Rejection rates	Low offer (less than 20%) rejection rates
Machiguenga	Peru	0.26	0.15/0.25	0.05 (1 of 21)	0.10 (1 of 10)
Hadza (Small camp)	Tanzania	0.27	0.20	0.28 (8 of 29)	0.31 (5 of 16)
Quechua	Ecuador	0.27	0.25	0.15 (2 of 13)	0.5 (1 of 2)
Mapuche	Chile	0.34	0.50/0.33	0.07 (2 of 30)	0.2 (2 of 10)
Torguud Mongols	Mongolia	0.35	0.25	0.05 (1 of 20)	0.00 (0 of 1)
Gnau	Papua New Guinea	0.38	0.4	0.4 (10 of 25)	0.50 (3 of 6)
Hadza (Big camp)	Tanzania	0.40	0.50	0.19 (5 of 26)	0.80 (4 of 5)
Au	Papua New Guinea	0.43	0.3	0.27 (8 of 30)	1.00 (1 of 1)
Achuar	Ecuador	0.42	0.50	0.00 (0 of 16)	0.00 (0 of 1)
Orma	Kenya	0.44	0.50	0.04 (2 of 56)	--- (0 of 0)
Ache	Paraguay	0.51	0.50/0.40	0.00 (0 of 51)	0.00 (0 of 8)
Lamalera	Indonesia	0.58	0.50	0.20 (4 of 20)	0.38 (3 of 8)

Created on the basis of data provided by Heinrich et al. (2004)

As you can see, the variations are substantial. At the low end, we have the Machiguenga, Quechua and Hadza (small camp) where the average offers are around 25% of the pie and the modal offer also hovers around the 25% mark. (Remember, in the cross-cultural study in Israel, Japan, Slovenia and USA carried out by Al Roth and his colleagues the lowest mode was in Israel and that mode was 40% of the pie.) At the other end of the spectrum, we have the Achuar, Orma, Ache and Lamalera. Among the Achuar and the Orma, proposers on average offer a little more than 40% of the pie, which is very similar to what we find in the industrialized country studies. The Ache and the Lamalera are even more generous and, on average, make "hyper-fair" offers, where the proposers, on average, offer a larger share of the pie (51% and 58% respectively) to the responders.

Looking at the column for rejection rates, we find that these rates tend to be low. In industrialized nations, on average, five out of ten offers (50%) that give the responder less than 20% are rejected. But, regardless of whether the offers are in general parsimonious, as among the Machiguenga and the Quechua, or very generous, as among the Achuar, Orma, Ache and Lamalera, very few offers are rejected. This suggests broad agreement among the proposers and responders as to what constitutes a fair offer in these societies. Strangely enough, among the Machiguenga and the Quechua, where the average offer is around 25% and the modal offer is also around 25%, these low offers are readily accepted by the responders, as are the much more generous offers made among the Achuar, Orma, Ache and Lamelera, where the average and modal offers hover around half the pie.

The large variations across the different cultural groups suggest that preferences or expectations are affected by group-specific conditions, such as social institutions or cultural fairness norms. While it is difficult to pinpoint the causes of behavioural differences across these extremely diverse societies, to the researchers involved in this work, two reasons stood out. The first of these, that seems to predict whether offers are generous or stingy, is the pay-off to cooperation – that is, how important and how large is a group's pay-off from cooperating in day-to-day economic production. For instance, among the Machiguenga, who are entirely economically independent and rarely engage in productive activities that involve others besides family members, the proposers made very low offers. On the other hand, Lamalera whale hunters, who go to sea in large canoes manned by a dozen or more individuals requiring close cooperation between them, make more generous offers.

The second factor that seemed to have predictive power in explaining offers was the extent of market integration. How much do people rely on market interaction in their daily lives? The researchers found that, by and large, those who engage in greater interaction make more generous offers in the ultimatum game. It seems, then, that the more market orientated a society is, the more equitable are the offers made by the proposers. The researchers tentatively suggest one plausible explanation of this behaviour. When faced with a novel situation (the experiment), the participants looked for analogues in their daily experience, asking: "What familiar situation is this game like?", and then acted in a manner appropriate for that situation.

Once again, the primary lesson arising from this very broad and ambitious cross-cultural study is that a social norm regarding what is a fair allocation – rather than pure self-interest – is the primary driving force behind offers in the ultimatum game, even though that actual norm is substantially different from one society to another. Thus, offers in some societies, such as the Machiguenga and the Quechua, are very low while those among the Ache and Lamalera are more generous, but, in all cases, there is little conflict between proposers and responders, showing that while the idea of what is fair may be different *across* these societies, *within* those societies there is broad agreement regarding this and both proposers and responders behave in accordance with this mutually shared understanding of what constitutes a fair offer.

CONCLUDING REMARKS

In this chapter, I argued that human beings seem to possess inherent norms or predispositions for fairness and are willing to reject unfair deals at substantial personal costs. I used the ultimatum game first introduced by Werner Güth and his colleagues to illustrate this point. I showed that proposers in this game routinely make more generous offers than they need to. Such generous offers are not made out of a sense of altruism or any concerns with being perceived as being unfair by the experimenter. These offers are motivated by the fact that proposers realize that making very small offers may be construed as being unfair by responders, who may choose to reject such offers, in which case the proposer ends up with nothing. I have shown that raising the stakes does not make a difference to this pattern of behaviour; indeed, there is some evidence to suggest that, with higher stakes, the proposers tend to make more equitable offers. We saw that such notions of fairness seem to extend to different cultures and societies; however, there seems to be substantial variation in what is considered to be "fair" across these different groups. There is some, though not a lot of, variation among industrialized nations, but there is much more variation in small-scale hunter-gatherer societies, depending on their degree of market integration.

Finally, I should point out the following. At the very beginning of this book, I said that humans deviate from the assumption of self-interest in two major ways. Sometimes, we deviate because some problems are hard and there are limits to our cognitive and/or computational abilities. The first few chapters of the book up until this point focused on demonstrating examples of decision scenarios where this was true: situations where there are significant cognitive demands resulting in a failure to maximize pay-offs. These are the "mistakes" that we will be likely to correct if and when our attention is drawn to them. But, equally, at times our deviation from self-interested behaviour results from our desire to behave according to ingrained norms, the norm of fairness being one such. In this chapter, I have shown examples of responders leaving money on the table and walking away from substantial pay-offs just because they considered a particular offer to be unfair. I also discussed the 1994 Major League Baseball negotiations, where the players collectively walked away from a large pay-off simply because they believed that the owners were being unfair. These deviations from the assumption of self-interest are "mistakes" that we make with full deliberation and ones we will not correct even if and when they are labelled as such.

NOTES

1 "All Blacks" is the colloquial term for New Zealand's (Rugby Union) national team, since they wear an all-black jersey. Similarly, the South African team is known as "Springboks" and the Australians as "Wallabies".
2 Reuters (2007, February 22). 'A first in Japan: shareholders block a takeover', *New York Times* (World Business).

■ The ultimatum game

3 Actually, Güth and his colleagues called them Player 1 and Player 2, respectively. Different authors use different terms in their papers. Rather than use different terms all the time, I will stick to the convention of calling the first player 'the proposer' and the second player 'the responder' in the rest of this chapter.
4 Interested readers can watch a clip on YouTube here: www.youtube.com/watch?v=meiU6TxysCg.
5 It is, of course, debatable whether a trivia quiz creates a genuine sense of entitlement. Those who end up as the "losers" might feel aggrieved and question whether performance in a trivia quiz is the appropriate or adequate way of creating a legitimate entitlement for those who "won".
6 Double-blind protocol in medical studies refers to an even more stringent condition where even the principal researcher does not know which patient is assigned to which group – for instance, which patient is in the treatment group and which is in the placebo group. This would dictate that all experimental sessions are run with research assistants who have no idea about the researcher's hypotheses or purpose. While this is feasible, it is often not practicable, and, in any case, the evidence, at least in the case of studies in experimental economics, suggests that this does *not* make a big difference.
7 It is also generally true that across a wide range of experiments, responders are typically happy to accept approx. 30% of the pie while they reliably reject offers of 20% of the pie or less.
8 I need to thank Nandita Basu for providing me with these examples.

8 Market implications of the ultimatum game

In this chapter, I:

- *Discuss the implications of the ultimatum game results and notions of fairness for a variety of market transactions, including bargaining over prices or negotiating salaries;*
- *Demonstrate how such fairness concerns may actually lead to customers withholding demand and desisting from buying something even if it is valuable;*
- *Make connections between such notions of fairness and the global debate on inequality.*

INTRODUCTION

As I pointed out at the beginning of the book, the starting point of much economic thinking is the assumption of individual rationality, implying that in most situations involving strategic decision making, the people making those decisions care primarily about their own monetary pay-offs or their utility where that utility is mostly a function of the monetary pay-offs accruing to them or their kin. In most cases, such calculations of self-interest are predicated on beliefs that others are like us and everyone else is also involved in maximizing his or her own self-interest. Typically, such attempts at maximizing utility or profit do not involve overt moral or ethical considerations; neither do they involve notions of what is fair. This idea is not new. Adam Smith wrote about moral sentiments, but, in 1776, he also commented in his book, *An Inquiry into the Nature and Causes of the Wealth of Nations*:

> It is not from the benevolence of the butcher, the brewer, or the baker, that we expect our dinner, but from their regard to their own self-interest. We address ourselves, not to their humanity but to their self-love, and never talk to them of our own necessities but of their advantages.

But, as the voluminous evidence from ultimatum games demonstrate, the assumption of self-interest is incomplete at best. We have seen that notions of fairness play an important role in a variety of situations. A potential critique is that the evidence I have provided in the previous chapter comes from stylized experiments and may be applicable to situations like bilateral bargaining. But do they apply to more diffuse and decentralized market transactions? The answer is in the affirmative and this is what I turn to next.

FAIRNESS AS A CONSTRAINT ON PROFIT-MAKING

One of the early attempts to understand whether norms of fairness may act as an active constraint on profit-seeking or might lead to different outcomes than the ones predicted by the self-interest model was undertaken in the mid-1980s by Daniel Kahneman, a psychologist at Princeton, and two economists, Jack Knetsch of Simon Fraser University and Richard Thaler of Cornell. They used an extensive questionnaire to understand people's predispositions towards a multitude of strategies adopted by businesses. Here is an example:

> A hardware store has been selling snow shovels for $15. The morning after a large snowstorm, the store raises the price to $20.

Respondents were asked to rate this move as (1) completely fair; (2) acceptable; (3) unfair and (4) very unfair. Out of 107 respondents to this question, 82% considered this unfair or very unfair.

Their findings illustrate the role that norms of fairness play in day-to-day pricing decisions and how these norms can serve as a constraint on unfettered profit-making. Kahneman and his colleagues provide a number of examples of this phenomenon. Below, I discuss some of these.

Exploitation of increased market power

The market power of a business reflects the ability of the business to charge its customers a higher price. For instance, in the event of a snowstorm, the seller obviously has increased power to raise the price, because people's need for the shovels has increased. Very often, when faced with an emergency, people wish to stock up on essentials; this creates an opportunity for the seller to jack up the prices of those commodities. By and large, respondents seem to believe that such price-gouging is unfair because such an action would constitute opportunistic behaviour. There are a number of examples of the opposition to exploitation of shortages:

> A severe shortage of Red Delicious apples has developed in a community and none of the grocery stores or produce markets has any of this type of apple on their shelves. Other varieties of apples are plentiful in all of the stores. One grocer receives a single shipment of Red Delicious apples at the regular wholesale cost and raises the retail price of these Red Delicious apples by 25% over the regular price.

Only 37% of 102 respondents considered this price increase acceptable. Similarly, firms with market power often use that power to increase profits by charging different customers different prices depending on their willingness to pay a higher price. Cinemas charge a much higher price for admission on weekday evenings and on weekends than during a weekday. Airline companies charge a much higher price to those customers buying tickets at the last minute compared to those who bought their tickets way in advance for the same class of service. This is referred to as *price discrimination*, where the seller is essentially trying to get from each customer the most that he/she is willing to pay for the good. I discussed aspects of this when I talked about the pricing of All Blacks jerseys by Adidas in the previous chapter.

But the survey results suggest the addition of a further restraint. Many forms of price discrimination were considered outrageous.

> A landlord rents out a small house. When the lease is due for renewal, the landlord learns that the tenant has taken a job very close to the house and is, therefore, unlikely to move. The landlord raises the rent $40 per month more than he was planning to do.

Out of 157 respondents, only 9% thought this was acceptable while a whopping 91% considered this unfair. On a different question, a majority of respondents thought it unfair for a popular restaurant to impose a $5 surcharge for Saturday night reservations. The near unanimity of responses to questions like these indicate that pricing strategies that deliberately exploit the dependence of a particular individual is generally considered offensive by most.

The context for pricing decisions

The next two questions look at what happens when a business increases price in an attempt to protect its profit.

> Suppose that, due to a transportation mix-up, there is a local shortage of lettuce and the wholesale price has increased. A local grocer has bought the usual quantity of lettuce at a price that is 30 cents per head higher than normal. The grocer raises the price of lettuce to customers by 30 cents per head.
>
> A landlord owns and rents out a single small house to a tenant who is living on a fixed income. A higher rent would mean the tenant would have to move. Other small rental houses are available. The landlord's costs have increased substantially over the past year and the landlord raises the rent to cover the cost increases when the tenant's lease is due for renewal.

These increases were considered acceptable by 79% and 75% of the respondents, respectively. This suggests that it is acceptable for firms to protect themselves from losses even if this means raising prices.

But 77% of 195 respondents thought that the following was unacceptable:

> A small company employs several workers and has been paying them average wages. There is severe unemployment in the area and the company could easily replace its current employees with good workers at a lower wage. The company has been making money. The owners reduce the current workers' wages by 5%.

The rule seems to be that the seller can certainly protect themselves against losses. But, in the last instance, the firm is lowering wages not to cover losses, but to exploit the fact that workers are now finding it more difficult to find jobs in the region and that this places those workers at a disadvantage vis-à-vis the firm.

Enforcement

Sixty-eight per cent of respondents in this survey said that they would switch their patronage to a pharmacy five minutes further away if the one closer to them raised its prices when a competitor was temporarily forced to close, and, in a separate sample, 69% indicated that they would switch if the more convenient store discriminated against its older workers. In traditional economic theory, compliance with contracts depends on enforcement. But buyers and sellers may be willing to abide by norms of fairness even in the absence of any explicit enforcement. The following scenarios illustrate:

> If the service is satisfactory, how much of a tip do you think most people leave after ordering a meal costing $10 in a restaurant that they visit frequently?

The average tip (as stated by 122 respondents) was $1.28.

> [how about] ... in a restaurant on a trip to another city that they do not expect to visit again?

Here, there are 124 respondents and the average tip was $1.27. The respondents evidently do not treat the possibility of enforcement as a significant factor in the control of tipping. This is entirely consistent with the widely observed adherence to a 15% tipping rule in the US, even by one-time customers who have little reason to fear embarrassing retaliation by an irate server. In the Preface, I already talked about our cross-country odyssey from Washington to Boston, where we left handsome tips at restaurants in cities that we will almost certainly never return to.

The important question, though, is: do firms, which the theory assumes maximize profits, also fail to exploit some economic opportunities because of unenforceable compliance with rules of fairness? The following questions elicited expectations about the behaviour of a garage mechanic when dealing with a tourist as opposed to a regular customer.

> A man leaves his car with the mechanic at his regular]/[A tourist leaves his car at a] service station with instructions to replace an expensive part. After the [customer/tourist] leaves, the mechanic examines the car and discovers that it is not necessary to replace the part; it can be repaired cheaply. The mechanic would make much more money by replacing the part than by repairing it. Assuming the [customer/tourist] cannot be reached, what do you think the mechanic would do in this situation?

Roughly the same proportion of respondents (60% in the case of the regular customer and 63% in the case of the tourist) thought that the mechanic will choose to replace the part in order to make more money. Here, again, there is no evidence that the public considers enforcement a significant factor. The respondents believe that most mechanics (usually excluding their own) would be less than saintly in this situation. However, they also appear to believe that the mechanics who would treat their customers fairly are not motivated by the anticipation of sanctions, since they think that the mechanic will treat the regular customer and the tourist in the same way even though there is no possibility of repeat business from a tourist.

Fairness in labour markets
Given that norms of fairness seem to apply to a variety of pricing decisions, we would expect that this might extend to labour markets as well. In labour markets, it is often observed that the wages paid to workers do not decline, even in the face of persistent unemployment when firms could easily hire workers more cheaply and, therefore, could choose to offer lower wages

even to the existing workers. But, very often, whether a particular transaction is considered fair or not depends on what the relevant reference point is. Market prices and the history of previous transactions between a seller and a buyer can serve as reference transactions. The role of prior history in wage transactions is illustrated by the following two questions:

> A small photocopying shop has one employee who has worked in the shop for six months and earns $9 per hour. Business continues to be satisfactory, but a factory in the area has closed and unemployment has increased. Other small shops have now hired reliable workers at $7 an hour to perform jobs similar to those done by the photocopy shop employee. The owner of the photocopying shop reduces the employee's wage to $7.

Out of 98 respondents, 17% thought this was acceptable while 83% considered this unfair. I will have more to say on this particular topic of fairness in labour markets shortly.

ECONOMIC CONSEQUENCES OF NORMS OF FAIRNESS

The findings of the study by Kahneman and his colleagues suggest that:

> many actions that are both profitable in the short run and not obviously dishonest are likely to be perceived as unfair exploitations of market power. ... Further, even in the absence of government intervention, the actions of firms that wish to avoid a reputation for unfairness will depart in significant ways from the standard model of economic behaviour.

The above is all fine and good but, after all, the results reported above are based on responses to survey questions and, as I pointed out in the introduction, at times, actual behaviour does deviate from stated attitudes. For instance, a respondent might say that he/she will not patronize a firm that is engaging in price-gouging by jacking up the price of an essential commodity in an emergency, but, when push comes to shove, the buyer might easily give in. Now the problem here is that it is very hard to show that people are *not* buying something in protest, since it is impossible to prove a negative.

Bradley Ruffle, of Ben Gurion University in Israel, decided to set up an experiment to test if buyers do indeed refrain from buying at prices they consider to be unfair. Ruffle focused on situations where the seller puts a price tag on his/her product and the buyer has the option of either buying at that price or not buying at all. In economics, these are referred to as *posted-offer* institutions. Most retail stores operate on this principle, in the sense that when you walk into the store, each item has a price tag and you can either buy at the indicated price or not and there is no scope for haggling over the price. The car company Saturn in the US, for instance, has a no-haggling policy, as opposed to most other car sellers, who allow for negotiations over the price. Honda has a similar no-haggling policy in New Zealand, with a fixed price for their cars. Such a no-haggling policy turns the sale of these cars into a posted-offer institution. Economists have usually tended to focus exclusively on the behaviour of sellers in such a context, without realizing that if buyers are motivated by norms of fairness and care about relative pay-offs, then they might actually refrain from buying the good at times, which, in turn, has implications for these markets.

■ Market implications of the ultimatum game

In a posted-offer market, sellers post prices which buyers can either accept or reject. Acceptance yields the seller a pay-off determined by the difference between the price he/she posts and his/her cost on each unit sold. The buyer earns the difference between his/her valuation for the good and the price that he/she pays. If the buyer rejects the price, then neither party earns any surplus. Thus, a posted-offer institution is a natural multi-player extension of the ultimatum game.

What does valuation of a good mean? The idea behind valuation is this: economists assume that when a person buys a good, that person has a maximum price he/she is willing to pay depending on the satisfaction (happiness/utility) that he/she gets from it. Suppose you are willing to pay $200 to go to see Bruce Springsteen play at Giants stadium. Why are you willing to pay $200? Because you have thought about the satisfaction you will derive from attending this event and you think that, at most, this is worth $200 to you. Now suppose you manage to get a ticket for $150. Then, in the parlance of the economist, you have enjoyed a surplus of $50, which is your *consumer surplus*. So, any time you are willing to pay a certain amount for something and you end up paying less than the maximum you were willing to pay, you enjoy a surplus. The *producer surplus*, on the other hand, is the difference between the price at which a seller sells the good and the cost of producing it. *Producer surplus* is essentially an alternative term for profit. I will discuss these two concepts in greater detail in Chapter 14.

Ruffle recruited 92 participants at the University of Arizona and set up a series of posted-offer markets with buyers and sellers. It is assumed that the sellers are selling a homogeneous good. In each market, buyers and sellers interact for 20 rounds. In each round, the sellers have a number of units of a homogeneous good available for sale. In each round, the buyers are assigned a particular valuation for each unit of the good that he/she buys. Similarly, in each round, the seller is assigned a particular cost for each unit that he/she sells. Ruffle looks at the impact of a number of different conditions.

(1) *Number of buyers and sellers*: in some cases, there are *two* buyers in the market, while, in other cases, there are *four* buyers. The number of sellers is always held constant at *two*.
(2) *Relative profits of the buyers and the sellers*: Compared to the buyer, the seller always enjoys a much larger share of the profit on each unit sold. In some cases, the seller's share is *three* times that of the buyer's. Suppose it costs the seller $12 to produce a T-shirt. The buyer is willing to pay as much as $20 for it. In this case, the total surplus to be split is ($20 − $12) = $8. Suppose the seller puts a price of $18 on the shirt and the buyer agrees to buy it. Then the seller gets a surplus of ($18 − $12) = $6 while the buyer gets a surplus of ($20 − $18) = $2. Thus, the seller's share of the surplus ($6) is three times that of the buyer's ($2). In other cases, the seller's share of the profit is *six* times that of the buyer's. Suppose, as in the previous example, the buyer's valuation is $20 while the seller's cost is $13 rather than $12. In this case, the total surplus is ($20 − $13) = $7. Suppose the seller quotes a price of $19 and the buyer buys at that price. Then the seller's share of the surplus is ($19 − $13) = $6 while the buyer's share is ($20 − $19) = $1; therefore, the seller's share of the surplus is six times that of the buyer's.
(3) *Information available to buyers and sellers*: Finally, in some cases, the buyers know the sellers' costs and the sellers know the valuations of the buyers, while in other cases the

buyers and the sellers not only know the costs and valuations, respectively, but *in addition they are shown the profit that each party will make for various transactions*. The intention here is to make "the earnings inequality salient to the buyers in an attempt to incite them to forego profitable purchases".

What Ruffle finds is that indeed *demand withholding* by buyers – where the buyers essentially refuse to buy at prices that give most of the surplus to the sellers – is a factor in these markets. The effect of such withholding is more pronounced when (1) there are two buyers rather than four; (2) when the surplus accruing to the seller is six times that accruing to the buyer and (3) when the buyers are made aware of this inequitable distribution of the surplus by providing them with information about the profits accruing to each party. In one session of this particular treatment, one buyer boycotted the market *entirely* for six out of 20 periods, thereby foregoing the possibility of earning any money in those periods. Bear in mind that if the buyer participates, then the buyer will make positive profit, but these profits will be small compared to the ones that the seller will make. By not participating at all, the buyer is making sure that neither he nor the seller makes any money at all. This is very similar to turning down small offers in the ultimatum game, except here, such rejection comes in the explicit context of a market transaction.

Such demand withholding does often induce the sellers to lower the price charged in later periods and a lower price, in turn, implies a more equitable sharing of the surplus between the buyer and the seller. The fact that two buyers are often more successful in acting in a coordinated manner and withholding demand, compared to four buyers, can be explained by appealing to the fact that the choice to withhold poses a free-rider problem for the buyers. Buyers benefit from withholding their demand (since that would result in lower prices and a greater share of the surplus for them later on) but each buyer prefers the other buyers to do the withholding. Such coordinated action to withhold demand proves more successful when there are two buyers as opposed to four buyers. Four buyers are often much less successful in upholding the covenant, with sellers resisting buyers' attempts at demand withholding and refusing to lower prices. Eventually, one or more of the buyers gives in. Two buyers, on the other hand, manage to coordinate much better and are successful at driving prices down.

Ruffle concludes:

For a given price, the punishment to sellers of rejecting a profitable purchase is greater the more extreme the earning inequality. The observation that, for a given number of buyers, withholding is more frequent the larger the surplus inequality is therefore consistent with fairness.

FAIRNESS AND INEQUALITY

In their book, *The Spirit Level*, the epidemiologists Kate Pickett and Richard Wilkinson of York University, UK document how societies characterized by high degrees of inequality perform worse on various measures of social and economic well-being. This is an excellent book, well worth reading, with three caveats. First, the data pertain primarily to the

■ Market implications of the ultimatum game

rich industrialized nations but there is plenty of other evidence to suggest that the primary insights will extend to less developed nations as well. Second, the data are very much at an aggregate macroeconomic level of entire countries. Therefore, they do not tell us much about within country differences. There may be significant variations within a country, particularly large ones like the US. However, that is not entirely germane to our discussion. Finally, the results are all in the nature of correlations; we can see which variables tend to move together; it is not really possible to infer a causal story. For instance, if countries high in inequality achieve worse outcomes for its children, we do not necessarily know whether it is the inequality that is driving the outcomes or whether countries that fail to make adequate provisions for its children will tend to become more unequal over time. Nevertheless, Wilkinson and Pickett make a compelling case for the adverse consequences of rising inequality. Below, I present some of the facts and figures from this book.

Figure 8.1 shows that as a country's degree of inequality increases, the life expectancy of its citizens drops. The typical measure of income inequality is the Gini coefficient. The closer the value of the Gini coefficient to zero, the greater the degree of equality. On the other hand, as the Gini coefficient becomes larger and approaches one, the degree of inequality within a country increases.[1] As is clear from Figure 8.1, for a country like Japan, with relatively greater equality, life expectancy at birth is more than 81 years, while at the other extreme, for countries with a relatively high level of inequality, such as the USA or Singapore, life expectancy is lower and is around 76–77 years. Clearly, the relation is not exact. For instance, all the Scandinavian countries are characterized by low inequality, but within them, life expectancy is much lower in Denmark compared to Sweden (and both are lower than Japan). This is because inequality is not the only factor that impacts life expectancy. There are other factors, such as diet or prevalence of smoking, that also contribute. But the overall, picture is unmistakeable. As income inequality rises, life expectancy falls.

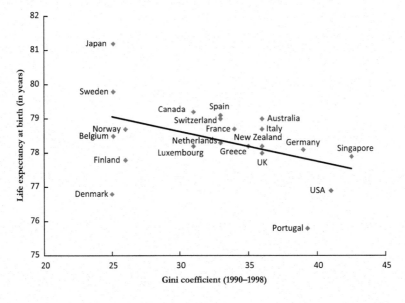

Figure 8.1
Inequality and life expectancy in countries.
Re-created on the basis of data in Wilkinson and Pickett (2009)

210

Figure 8.2 shows what happens to a composite index of social and health outcomes as inequality rises. The horizontal axis here measures the underlying Gini coefficient. But the vertical axis shows the values of a composite index that is created by looking at a variety of social and health problems. The index is computed by looking at a number of factors, including life expectancy, mathematics and literacy scores among high school students, child mortality, imprisonment rates, homicide rates, teenage pregnancies, trust, obesity, mental illnesses (including drug and alcohol addiction) and social mobility. Each of these variables is measured, scaled and signed appropriately, so that the composite index which is created is one such that a higher score on this index indicates worse outcomes for each of the variables (such as lower life expectancy, lower maths and literacy scores, higher rates of child mortality, imprisonment and homicides and so on). It is clear from Figure 8.2 that as inequality increases, these social ills become more pronounced. Once again, at the lower end of inequality we have Japan and the Scandinavian countries that report lower levels of such social problems, while at the higher end we have a country such as the USA, high in inequality and high in social and health problems.

The final piece of evidence is Figure 8.3, which shows rates of teenage pregnancies. It is well documented that such young mothers are ill-equipped to rear children, which in

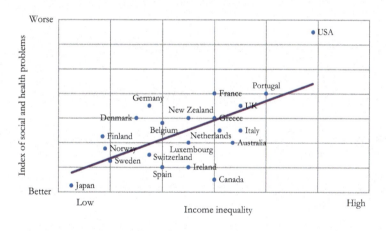

Figure 8.2
Inequality and index of social and health problems in countries. Re-created on the basis of data in Wilkinson and Pickett (2009)

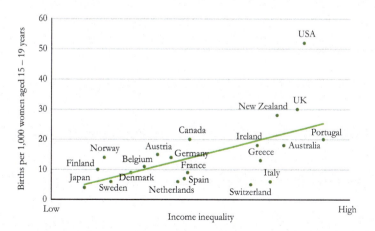

Figure 8.3
Inequality and rate of teenage pregnancy in countries. Re-created on the basis of data in Wilkinson and Pickett (2009)

■ Market implications of the ultimatum game

turn leads to a cascade of social ills. Once again, the same pattern emerges. Countries with low income inequality achieve much better outcomes than countries with higher income inequality.

Findings such as these or those reported in books such as Thomas Piketty's *Capital in the 21st Century* have set off a global debate about the adverse impact of inequality and the need to reduce inequality to achieve better economic outcomes. But, three psychologists from Yale, Christina Starmans, Mark Sheskin and Paul Bloom, argue that we are misinterpreting the data and findings. They argue that it is not inequality *per se* that people object to, but, rather, they care more about equity and fairness. People are willing to live with some amount of inequality if they are convinced that this has risen out of differences in effort rather than lack; people are willing to accept economic inequality as long as there is social mobility and people can change their circumstances via hard work.

Michael Norton of Harvard Business School and Dan Ariely asked a large number of respondents to estimate the degree of income inequality in the US. Not surprisingly, people were not very good at it. Mostly, they do not seem to comprehend how rich the "super rich" are and believe the income distribution to be much more equitable than it actually is. But do they prefer complete equality? No. Absolute equality (implying a Gini coefficient of zero) implies that the bottom 10% of income earners get 10% of total income, the bottom 20% get 20% of income, the bottom 50% get 50% of income and so on. Is this what their respondents preferred? No. The respondents were happy to live with a certain amount of inequality. This level of inequality is a far cry from the actual level of inequality that prevails in the US, but, nevertheless, it was not the case that people preferred complete equality.

Figure 8.4 shows the results from the Norton and Ariely study. The top bar shows that the top 20% of income earners in the USA earn nearly 85% of all income. The second 20% account for around 10% of all income earned. So, taken together, the top 40% earn around 95% of all income! The share of the bottom 40% is so small that these are not visible in this figure. The middle bar is what people suppose the distribution to be. For example, they believe that the top 20% earn almost 60% of income rather than 85%, which is the actual figure. They also believe that the bottom 40% (the parts of the bar shaded with diamonds or with dots) earn about 10%, which is much higher than is the case. The most relevant bar for our purposes is the bottom horizontal bar. Look at the left-most dashed/shaded area representing the top 20%. Respondents are saying that, on average, they are okay with this

Figure 8.4
Inequality in the US.
Re-created on the basis of data in Norton and Ariely (2011)

212

top 20% earning just over 30%, and the bottom 40% earning (the areas to the right shaded with diamonds or with dots) just about 25%.

Starmans and her colleagues suggest that this is not surprising because voluminous evidence suggests that both adults and children choose fairness over equality. For example, in one study, 6–8-year-old children had to award erasers to two boys who had cleaned up their room. If there were an unequal number of erasers to be distributed, the children preferred to throw away an extra eraser rather than create an unequal distribution. But when they are told that one boy did more work than the other, they awarded the extra eraser to the hard worker. In fact, when one recipient has done more work, six-year-olds believe that he or she should receive more resources, even if equal pay is an option. Likewise, although infants prefer equality in a neutral circumstance, they expect an experimenter to distribute rewards preferentially to individuals who have done more work.

This preference for inequality is not restricted to situations where one person has done more work, but also extends to rewarding people who have previously acted helpfully or unhelpfully. When three-year-olds witnessed a puppet help another puppet climb a slide or reach a toy, they later allocated more resources to the helpful puppet than to a puppet that pushed another down the slide, or hit him on the head with the toy.

Consider a situation with two individuals, identical in all relevant regards, where one gets $10 and the other gets nothing. This is plainly unequal, but is it fair? Starmans et al. find that it can be, if the allocation was random. Adults consider it fair to use impartial procedures such as coin flips and lotteries when distributing resources. Research undertaken by Gary Bolton, Jordi Brandts and Axel Ockenfels also suggest that, at times, a fair procedure can be a substitute for a fair outcome. That is, people might be willing to accept an unfair offer if they believe that the offer was the result of implementing a fair policy. In their study, proposers in an ultimatum game have three choices initially – (A): a hyper-fair offer of (200, 1800), that is, 200 experimental dollars for the proposer and 1,800 for the responder; (B): an equitable offer of (1,000, 1,000) and finally (C): an inequitable offer of (1,800, 200). They found that 41% of the inequitable offers (C) were rejected.

In a second study, the offers were generated by throwing dice rather than being generated by an actual human proposer. They looked at an asymmetric lottery which puts a very high, 98%, probability on the inequitable offer C and a symmetric lottery which puts an equal 33% probability on all three choices. They found that the rejection rates of the inequitable offer C were very similar with the asymmetric lottery and with human proposers, but the rejection rates were much lower for the symmetric lottery. The authors conclude that the fairness of the outcomes and the fairness of the procedures both matter, and that a fair procedure may be a substitute for a fair outcome.

This study appears to be quite similar to the one conducted by Sally Blount, yet there is a subtle difference. In Blount's study, people were willing to accept unfair offers when these offers were chosen by a lottery but not when they were made by other participants. In the study by Gary Bolton and his colleagues, people were willing to commit beforehand to accepting the outcome of a lottery knowing full well that the outcome may be bad for them, as long as they were certain that the lottery itself was fair, that is, the lottery placed a roughly equal probability on the fair and unfair outcomes. Children seem to have similar views. In the erasers-for-room-cleaning studies described above, if children are given a fair 'spinner' to randomly choose who gets the extra eraser, they are happy to create inequality.

Inspired by some of these results, Ingvild Almås, Bertil Tungodden and other collaborators at the Norwegian School of Economics decided to embark on an ambitious cross-country study trying to understand people's attitudes towards inequality. Their study includes participants from 60 countries around the world that account for nearly 80% of humanity. These include developed countries such as the USA, UK, Switzerland, Australia and the Netherlands; middle income emerging economies such as China, Brazil, India and South Africa; as well as less developed nations such as Bangladesh, Rwanda, Zambia and Zimbabwe. Tungodden and his colleagues essentially ask their respondents, what hypothetical level of the Gini coefficient they would find acceptable and whether it matters if the corresponding level of inequality is arrived at via "luck" or "merit". Needless to mention, respondents are not actually asked questions about the Gini coefficient, they are essentially asked about their desired level of income inequality (should the bottom 10% of income earners get more or less than 10% of total income? Should the top 10% get more or less than 10% of total?, etc.) that allows the researchers to create the imputed values of the Gini coefficient implied by these underlying preferences for income distribution.

Tungodden and his colleagues report a number of findings. First, there is much less tolerance for income inequality in more developed countries than in less developed countries. So, if we plot the imputed value of the Gini coefficient going from zero to one (computed on the basis of the desired income distribution expressed by citizens of a particular nation) on the X-axis and Gross Domestic Product (GDP) per capita on the Y-axis, then we get a negatively sloped line. This suggests that citizens of more developed countries actually have a lower tolerance for inequitable income distribution than citizens of less developed countries.

But what was more striking was how people responded when asked about the role of luck or merit. Tungodden and colleagues asked their respondents what level of income inequality they are willing to live with (and what this implies for the magnitude of the corresponding Gini coefficient) if and when this income inequality comes about purely as a result of luck. Averaging over all countries, the value of the imputed Gini coefficient is approx. 0.45 (45%). This means that when income inequality is purely the result of luck, on average respondents around the world are willing to live with an intermediate level of inequality. But what if income inequality is the result of merit? What average value of the Gini coefficient are people willing to accept in that case? The average Gini coefficient in this case turns out to be a shade above 0.7 (70%), which is considered a high degree of income inequality. So, if people are convinced (or can be convinced) that the observed income inequality is the result of differences in merit and/or effort, then they seem to be willing to live with a much higher level of income inequality.

The researchers then looked at how people in different countries react to a high degree of inequality brought about by luck or skill. For our purposes, let us say that people are asked whether they are willing to live with a hypothetical Gini coefficient of 0.6 or above, where this is brought about purely as a matter of luck. Respondents from the majority of countries stated that they would not be comfortable with this, with some notable exceptions: China, India, Indonesia, Algeria, and Nigeria. But, when asked if they were willing to live with a Gini of 0.6 or above if the resulting inequality came about due to merit, the vast majority of respondents (including those in both developing and developed countries) stated that this would be acceptable to them.

CONCLUDING REMARKS

In the previous chapter and this one, I have provided evidence that people are willing to turn down a deal offering substantial monetary amounts if they believe that they are being treated unfairly. This unfairness can take two forms. At one level, people care about relative pay-offs in the sense that they might reject offers that give the other party a lot more than them. To paraphrase the economist, Robert Frank, this concern for relative standing can be summed up succinctly by saying that a person would feel quite happy if he/she is driving a BMW while everyone around him/her is driving a Toyota, but the same person would be quite unhappy if the people around him/her were driving Ferraris. (Or, as Frank humorously comments: a person is happy as long as he makes more than his wife's sister's husband.) But, at the same time, I have shown that rejection of offers cannot be attributed to a concern for relative standing only. Intentions matter as well. People are perfectly happy to accept inequitable offers generated by computers (where no attribution of intentions is possible) but are unwilling to accept the same offers if made by another human, especially if that human stands to benefit from the offer being accepted.

Adam Smith is typically associated with his advocacy of the "invisible hand" in the form of market forces to decide who gets what and when. But, in his 1759 book, *The Theory of Moral Sentiments*, Smith wrote:

> How selfish soever man may be supposed, there are evidently some principles in his nature, which interest him in the fortunes of others, and render their happiness necessary to him, though he derives nothing from it, except the pleasure of seeing it. Of this kind is pity or compassion, the emotion we feel for the misery of others, when we either see it, or are made to conceive it in a very lively manner. That we often derive sorrow from the sorrows of others, is a matter of fact too obvious to require any instances to prove it; for this sentiment, like all the other original passions of human nature, is by no means confined to the virtuous or the humane, though they perhaps may feel it with the most exquisite sensibility. The greatest ruffian, the most hardened violator of the laws of society, is not altogether without it.

This preference for egalitarianism and fairness has significant implications for markets and the economy. As I have shown above, people may actively refrain from buying goods if they believe that they are being fleeced. Trying to extract too much profit from the buyers may lead to sellers losing their business, and in some cases, such as the Adidas and All Blacks jersey pricing example, may end up tarnishing the brand.

I then extended the ultimatum game findings to a broader macroeconomic perspective to make connection with the ongoing global debate on inequality. My point here is that the findings of the ultimatum game do not just apply to microeconomic issues such as pricing or bargaining, but have much broader philosophical implications for how we structure our societies. It does appear that, while much of the global debate revolves around how to address inequality, this is not the most pressing problem. People are much more concerned about fairness and equity rather than income inequality. They are willing to live with higher inequality as long as they are convinced that this resulted from merit and hard work rather than sheer luck. And, contrary to popular belief, luck plays a much bigger role behind success. A child born to married and educated middle-class European American parents in Princeton is already off to a much better start than a child born out of wedlock to a teenage mother in Newark. But such inequities can be mitigated as long as there is adequate social mobility and people can improve their lot via effort. So, the bigger problem may not be so much the inequality in income distribution, but, rather, the fact that in some developed countries, particularly the USA, the scope for social mobility has been reduced significantly in recent years via the implementation of policies such as tax cuts or reduction in expenditure in other public goods, which help the less well-off disproportionately more.

A case in point is the 2019 scandal where a number of powerful people, including film stars and hedge fund managers, were found guilty of paying prestigious universities to get their children admitted under false pretences, where the children may not have obtained admission on their own merit. This was a failing not only on the part of the parents, but the institutions involved too. But such practices guarantee that there are fewer opportunities and, consequently, less social mobility. It is possible that people care more about this than income inequality *per se*. This is certainly a topic that is open to further research.

NOTE

1 The value of the Gini coefficient can either be expressed in decimals between 0 and 1 or in percentages between 0% and 100%. In what follows I may use one or the other (e.g., 0.6 or 60%) convention, depending on the source being discussed. This is a trivial issue. In either case, lower values (such as 0.3 or 30%) mean greater equality, higher values (such as 0.7 or 70%) mean greater inequality.

9 Trust and trustworthiness in everyday life

In this chapter, I:

- *Introduce the trust game and discuss how notions of trust and reciprocity play a role in economic transactions;*
- *Show that predispositions to trust are robust to different ways of posing the question;*
- *Demonstrate that trust is different from generosity and is typically based on expectations of reciprocation from the trustee;*
- *Explore how trust is different from decision making under risk and that, while we use the words trust and trustworthiness interchangeably, they are not exactly similar responses; a trusting person is not necessarily trustworthy but a trustworthy person is trusting;*
- *Examine the role of framing and how levels of trust and reciprocity can be enhanced by making sure that each participant in a situation involving trust and reciprocity interpret the situation in the same way as every other participant.*

TRUSTING STRANGERS

In Victor Hugo's *Les Misérables*, Jean Valjean, an ex-convict recently released from prison and overwhelmed by the vicissitudes of life, shows up at the doorstep of Monseigneur Myriel. To Valjean's surprise, the bishop welcomes him warmly, inviting him to share his supper and offering him a bed for the night. Even more remarkable, he treats Valjean with unfailing courtesy and ignores the stigma of his past. But rising stealthily in the middle of the night, Valjean steals the bishop's silver. Later, he gets caught by the police, who bring him back to the bishop. This time his crime will bring him life imprisonment. However, Monseigneur Myriel pretends that the silverware is a legitimate gift and, in a gesture of supreme kindness, he takes his most prized possession, a set of candlesticks, and gives them to Valjean as well. As Valjean is leaving, the bishop says: "Don't forget that you promised me to use this silver to become an honest man". This level of trust reposed in, and kindness shown to, a complete stranger would be beyond most of us.

Yet, many day-to-day transactions in life require us to trust strangers. For instance, every time we buy things on eBay or TradeMe and hand over our credit card details, we are essentially assuming that the seller will honour that trust and not rip us off. Similarly, when we pay our lawyer or accountant or car mechanic on the basis of hours of work, we trust these individuals to correctly represent their total hours. The concept of trust cuts across disciplines. Besides economists, people in many other disciplines, such as politics or sociology or management sciences, talk about the role of trust – trust among nations, among groups, among workers in organizations, between unions and management. In economic transactions, trust is often important in reducing the costs of transacting deals. So much so that economists have now come to believe that such trust among strangers has implications for the economy's performance as a whole. Countries whose citizens are more trusting experience faster economic growth compared to those whose citizens are less trusting. I will discuss the implications of trust among citizens for a country's development in the next chapter.

Such trust is ubiquitous in many situations. In 2002, I was attending the Annual Meeting of the American Economic Association in Atlanta, Georgia. I was interviewing for jobs at the meeting. I took a cab to a hotel where I was supposed to meet the representatives of a particular university, only to realize upon arrival at the hotel that I had neither their room number nor their phone number. In order to get this information, I had to go back to the main conference hotel. I had very little time left before the appointment. I asked the cab driver to take me to the main conference hotel. Once there, I told him to wait while I ran inside to get this information from the bulletin board. Now, this was a bustling hotel with hundreds of conference attendees milling around. Once I went in, I could have easily walked out via another door and stiffed the cab driver out of his fare. He could have never found me once I went into the lobby. There were many other taxis around, and I could have easily jumped into another one. This would have saved me – and cost the driver – around $15. Yet, when I asked him to wait, he did so without protest. I came out with the necessary information shortly and we drove back to the first hotel where my appointment was. We engage in transactions like these all the time. Yet, if you think about it, there was no guarantee for the cab driver that I would come back and pay him. But he trusted my word and waited for me.

In rural areas in many parts of the world, farmers routinely place fresh produce on a table by the side of the road. The table has a box attached to it where people can put money in. The idea is that people driving by can pick up some of the produce and, in turn, leave money in the box. Here, the farmer is essentially trusting people to leave money in return for produce since, with no one watching, someone can just as well pick up the goods and *not* leave any money in the box. Yet, most people do leave money. Charities often rely on a similar practice when they leave candy bars (with a price on them) on the counter in petrol stations and retail stores. You are supposed to pick up a candy bar and leave the asked for amount in a box next to them.

While we may be convinced that trust plays a crucial role in many transactions, the important question is: how should we go about measuring trust? After all, if we want to engage in any sort of quantitative comparisons between organizations, groups or countries to understand if the members of one group are more trusting than those of another, it is useful to have a handy way of measuring trust.

Joyce Berg, John Dickhaut and Kevin McCabe of the University of Minnesota came up with an elegant game to measure trust. In their game – called the *investment game* – participants are paired up. (Subsequently, this game has become more popularly known as the "trust game". In what follows I may use these terms interchangeably, but please note that both "investment game" and "trust game" refer to the same game studied by Berg et al.) One person is called the "sender" and the other person the "receiver".[1] Senders and receivers are placed in different rooms and no one knows whom he or she is paired with. Both the sender and the receiver are given $10. Each sender is then told that she can simply keep all of that money, say "Thank you very much" and leave. The game will end if she does so. In this case, the sender will have $10 and the receiver will have $10. But if the sender wishes, she can send a part of or all of the $10 to the paired receiver. If the sender sends any money at all, then the experimenter will *triple* that amount and give that tripled amount to the receiver. So, for instance if the sender sends $5 to the receiver, then the experimenter will triple that and give $15 to the receiver. Then the receiver is told the following: he can simply keep the entire amount sent to him and leave. The game will end at that point. Or if he wants, he can send some of this amount back to the paired sender in the other room. In any case, the game ends with the receiver's decision – regardless of whether he decides to send back any money or not – and any money sent back by the receiver is *not* tripled. Figure 9.1 illustrates this game.

What do you think happens in this game? First, following the principle of backward induction, let us start with the receiver's decision. The receiver has been sent a sum of money – say $15 – by a sender whom he does not know and will most likely never meet again. The receiver knows that the game will end after his decision. A self-interested receiver has no incentive to send any money back. If the receiver is sent any amount, then the receiver should simply keep all of it and send nothing back. Now let us put ourselves in the shoes of the sender. If the sender correctly anticipates the receiver's reaction, that is, the receiver has no incentive to return any money, then it would be foolish to send any money in the first place. By doing so, the sender makes herself vulnerable to being exploited by the receiver and would probably be worse off.

But there is an alternative way to think about this situation. Suppose the sender decides to *trust* the receiver and sends him all of the $10. The $10 gets tripled to $30. Now the sender has nothing while the receiver has $40 (remember both senders and receivers get $10 to start with). Suppose the receiver, knowing that he can exploit the sender's trust by returning nothing, decides to *reciprocate* the sender's trust by sending back $20. Then the sender ends up with $20 while the receiver ends up with ($40 – $20) = $20 as well. (Or maybe the

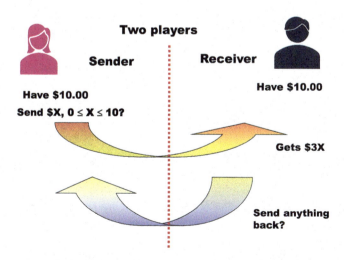

Figure 9.1
Structure of the trust game

receiver sends back $18, in which case the sender ends up with $18 and the receiver ends up with ($40 − $18) = $22.) In both of these cases, both the sender and the receiver are better off than they would have been if no money had changed hands. If no money changes hands, then both the sender and the receiver make only $10. There are numerous other splits possible. But the noteworthy thing about this second scenario is that in all those cases that the sender *trusts* the receiver and the receiver turns out to be *trustworthy* and *reciprocates* the sender's trust, the sender and the receiver end up with more money than if the sender had not trusted the receiver in the first place.

This game provides an easy way of measuring trust and trustworthiness. Of course, this game excludes a number of aspects that would characterize transactions in real-life such as communication, word-of-mouth, face-to-face interaction, handshakes, promises and such. But that is the beauty of this game. It tries to measure trust in a purely abstract way. The factors mentioned above would most likely lead to *increased* trust. But if we can document the existence of trust in this very abstract and context-free situation, then we can really claim that trust is a *primitive* in many human transactions. We can always add layers of complexity once we know what happens in the simplest possible (and most abstract) scenario.

The game designed by Berg and her colleagues is a simplified version of another game first studied by Colin Camerer of Caltech and Keith Weigelt of New York University in 1988. Camerer and Weigelt's game is formulated in terms of an entrepreneur who approaches a bank for a loan. The bank is the sender in their game and can choose to lend money or not. If the bank does make a loan, then the entrepreneur (who is analogous to the receiver) decides whether to repay the loan with interest or renege. Repaying the loan makes both parties better off compared to the situation where the bank does not make the loan at all. However, in this experiment the entrepreneur can be one of two "types". With some chance, he/she is an "honest" type who prefers to pay back the loan with interest thereby making both parties better off. But with some chance, the entrepreneur is "dishonest" and prefers to renege and run off with the money, making him/her better off at the expense of the bank, whose trust is exploited. While the bank does not know for certain which entrepreneur is honest or dishonest, the bank does know the probability of each type. For instance, the bank might know that there is a 1/3 chance that the entrepreneur is honest and 2/3 chance that he/she is dishonest, etc. The Camerer and Weigelt game and the corresponding analyses are more complex than its simplified version studied by Berg and her colleagues.

In the Berg et al. game, if the sender sends any money to start with, then we can say that the sender has decided to trust the receiver and the *amount sent* can be used as a measure of the sender's trust. Similarly, if the receiver sends back an amount that makes the sender and the receiver both better off then we can say that the receiver is being trustworthy and use the *amount returned* as a measure of the receiver's reciprocity. Very often, rather than using the absolute amount sent back by the receiver, I will use the percentage of the total sent back. This is because, as you will soon see, different receivers receive different amounts. So, for instance, the receiver who receives $15 and sends back $7.50 (i.e., 50% of the amount that he received) is actually being more trustworthy than a receiver who receives $30 but sends back $10 (i.e., 33% of the total amount that he received), even though in absolute amounts, the first receiver is sending back less than the second − $7.50 as opposed to $10, respectively.

Berg and her colleagues recruited 64 participants to take part in this game and divided them into 32 pairs of senders and receivers with each participant getting $10. They also implemented a complex double-blind protocol where the experimenter could not observe what individual senders or receivers were doing. Thus, all decisions taken by senders and receivers were completely anonymous with respect to other participants and with respect to the experimenter. What happened? Remember that from the perspective of pure self-interest, we expect the sender to send nothing and if the senders do send something then we would expect the receivers to return nothing.

In Figure 9.2, I show the amounts sent by the various senders. The data are arranged in descending order by the amount sent and the senders have been re-labelled accordingly. These participant numbers are different from the actual numbers assigned to them in the original study. Out of the 32 senders, five senders (senders 1 through 5 located at the extreme left of the chart) sent all $10, sender 6 sent $8, senders 7, 8 and 9 sent $7 each, senders 10 through 14 sent $6 each, the next six senders (15 through 20) sent $5 each, senders 21 and 22 sent $4 each, senders 23 through 26 sent $3 each, senders 27 and 28 sent $2 each and senders 29 and 30 sent $1 each. Only two out of 32 senders (senders 31 and 32 located at the extreme right of the chart) sent nothing. Thus, 30 out of 32 senders sent positive amounts and 20 out of 32 senders (63%) sent $5 or more. This seemed to suggest that a majority of the senders were willing to repose substantial amounts of trust in strangers.

Was their trust reciprocated? The answer here is more complicated and the answer is yes and no. In many cases, the trust of the senders was reciprocated, and both the sender and the receiver of the pair were better off than if the sender had not trusted at all. But this was not always true, and, in some cases, the sender was exploited with the receiver expropriating the entire surplus created, returning little or nothing to the sender.

I show the behaviour of the receivers in Figure 9.3. Once again, the receivers have been arranged in descending order according to the total amount they received and have been labelled accordingly as well. Remember that there were five senders who sent all $10 and

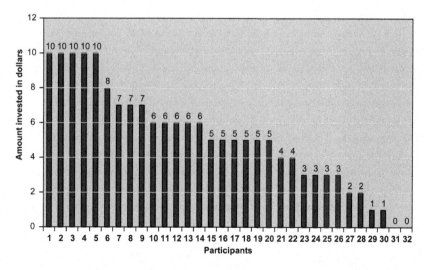

Figure 9.2
Amounts sent by various senders in the Berg et al. (1995) trust game. Re-created on the basis of data in the original study

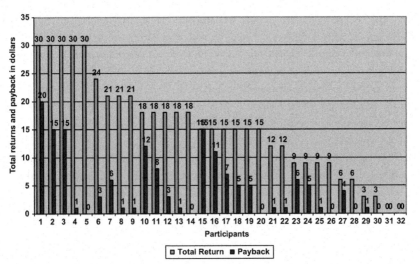

Figure 9.3 Responder behaviour in the Berg et al. (1995) trust game. Re-created on the basis of data in the original study

any amount sent by the sender is tripled by the experimenter. Thus, there were five receivers who received $30. I have labelled these five receivers as receivers 1 through 5. Of these five, receiver 1 sent back $20. This meant that the sender and the receiver in this pair ended up with exactly $20 each. Receivers 2 and 3 sent back $15. Remember the receiver got $10 at the beginning of the game. This meant that in each case, the sender in the pair ended up with $15 while the receiver ended up with $25. The receivers made out better than the senders, but the senders still ended up with $5 more – $15 as opposed to $10 – than if they had not trusted the receiver at all. But receivers 4 and 5 were not nice. Receiver 4 sent back a dollar only, meaning the sender ended up with a dollar while the receiver ended up with $39. Receiver 5 sent back nothing, meaning the paired sender ended up with nothing while receiver 5 ended up with $40. Other receivers sent back various amounts. Thus, while it is true that many receivers did not reciprocate, many others did, and the level of reciprocity exhibited exceeded what self-interest-based predictions would have held. Senders who sent $5 or more on average made a profit on the amount sent. Investments of $5 had an average payback of $7.17, while investments of $10 had an average payback of $10.20.

Just as Güth and his colleagues did with the ultimatum game, Berg and her colleagues were aware that the decisions of the participants to trust or reciprocate may be caused by mistakes or lack of comprehension of the instructions. So they decided to run a second experiment called the *social history* experiment, where the first experiment described above is the *no history* experiment. In the social history experiment, they recruited 56 participants (28 pairs) who had *not* participated in the previous no history experiment and had them take part in the same game with one difference. Each participant in the social history treatment was given a report summarizing the decisions of the 32 pairs in the no history experiment.

Suppose that, in the first experiment, senders failed to anticipate that the receivers had no incentive to return any money. Then, providing the history of prior plays might make the senders in the second experiment more aware that some of the receivers in the first experiment did not reciprocate and this may make the senders in the second experiment leery of sending money. Alternatively, the senders in the social history treatment may focus on the positive net returns of $5 and $10 investments. This could result in an increase in trust and more decisions to send either $5 or $10. The outcome of the social history experiment was broadly similar to the no history one. Only three out of 28 senders sent nothing. Thirteen out of 24 receivers who received a positive amount returned more than the paired sender sent, resulting in positive net returns for both. Investments of $5 had an average payback of $7.14 while investments of $10 had an average payback of $13.17. In fact, the participants in the social history treatment seemed to exhibit slightly higher levels of trust and reciprocity than the no history participants. Thus, history, rather than teaching the participants the folly of being trusting and trustworthy, seemed to have reinforced both of these responses.

So, a number of senders seem to believe, like Ralph Waldo Emerson: "Trust men and they will be true to you; treat them greatly and they will show themselves great".

IS TRUST NOTHING BUT ALTRUISM? HOW ABOUT RECIPROCITY?

As with the ultimatum game results, the question arose: was the decision by the senders to send money in this game motivated by a desire to share rather than based on expectations of reciprocation as would be required if these transfers were motivated by trust? Similarly, was the decision by some of the receivers motivated by generosity rather than reciprocity?

Berg and her colleagues had anticipated and pre-empted this potential criticism by giving $10 to both the sender and the receiver. Think about this for a minute. Suppose senders do care about an equitable distribution. Should they then send money? Not necessarily, because even if they did not send anything, unlike the dictator or ultimatum games, the receiver does not go home with nothing. Both have $10 and even in the absence of a transfer from the sender to the receiver, each would still end up with $10 – a perfectly equitable distribution. There is one catch though. In this game, each dollar sent gets multiplied. Thus, if a sender cares about *joint* welfare – that is, the benefit to the sender and the receiver taken together – then she may still send money, because each dollar sent will generate $3 for the receiver. The sender is worse off by a dollar but the receiver is better off by three times that amount, so, collectively, the two are better off. Thus, senders may send money even in the absence of trust if the senders have *other-regarding preferences*, where they care about the welfare of the receiver (or the joint welfare), rather than only *self-regarding* preferences, where they care only about their own monetary pay-offs.

James Cox of the University of Arizona suggested that the original Berg, Dickhaut and McCabe experiments do not allow one to distinguish between transfers resulting from trust and transfers resulting from other-regarding preferences; neither does their design distinguish between receiver reciprocity and returns resulting from other-regarding preferences. Cox designed an experiment which involved each participant taking part in (1) the Berg–Dickhaut–McCabe investment game; (2) the dictator game studied by Forsythe and others earlier in this book[2] and (3) a *modified dictator* game. You already know how the Berg–Dickhaut–McCabe investment game and the dictator game works. Cox argues along the following lines: suppose we compare the amounts sent by the senders in the trust game with the amounts sent in the dictator game. In the trust game, there is the possibility of getting a return from the receiver and, therefore, the possibility of making net gains, but, in the dictator game, there is no possibility of getting a return from the receiver. Thus, any transfers made in the dictator game must be motivated by other-regarding preferences only, whereas transfers in the investment game can be made either due to trust or due to other-regarding preferences. Thus, if the amounts sent in the investment game exceed those sent in the dictator game, then the additional amount must be due to trusting motivations.

Cox's third treatment – the modified dictator game – is complicated, so I will provide a brief sketch of how this game works. Suppose that, in the investment game, we have two pairs – (1) Bonnie and Clyde and (2) Thelma and Louise, with Bonnie and Thelma as the senders and Clyde and Louise as the receivers (mnemonic: the first person of the pair is the sender while the second person is the receiver). Suppose that in the investment game, Bonnie sends Clyde $4 out of $10, while Thelma sends Louise $7 out of $10. This implies that Bonnie has $6 left while Thelma has $3 left. On the other hand, since the amount sent is tripled, Clyde receives $12 while Louise receives $21. What Cox does at this point is to set up the modified dictator game.

Suppose, in this modified dictator game, we have two pairs as well – (1) Frankie and Johnny and (2) Butch and Sundance. Then he gives the two senders, Frankie and Butch, the amounts that the two senders, Bonnie and Thelma, kept for themselves. That is, Frankie gets $6 (what Bonnie had) while Butch gets $3 (the amount that Thelma had). And he gives the two receivers, Johnny and Sundance, the amounts that Clyde and Louise got, which are $12 and $21, respectively.

Then he asks Johnny and Sundance to play a dictator game with these two amounts ($12 and $21 respectively) and asks them if they wish to send any money to Frankie and Butch, respectively. The idea is this: since, in this modified dictator game, the proposers (or senders), that is, Frankie or Butch, did not really send anything, the receivers cannot be motivated by positive reciprocity, that is, a need to repay a friendly action by the sender. Thus, if the receiver sends any money to the sender in this modified dictator game, that decision must be motivated by other-regarding preferences rather than reciprocity. In contrast, in the investment game, the receiver can be motivated to return positive amounts by reciprocity or by unconditional other-regarding preferences. Thus, if the *amounts returned* in the investment game exceeds those *sent* in the modified dictator game, then *that excess* must be motivated by reciprocity on top of any altruistic tendencies. Table 9.1 explains the structure of Cox's modified dictator game.

Table 9.1 Cox's (1994) modified dictator game

First dictator game with two pairs {Bonnie and Clyde} and {Thelma and Louise}	
Allocator Bonnie (endowment of $10) keeps $6 and sends $4 to paired receiver Clyde	Allocator Thelma (endowment of $10) keeps $3 and sends $7 to paired receiver Louise
Receiver Clyde gets tripled amount of $12	Receiver Louise gets tripled amount of $21
Clyde has no further decision to make	Louise has no further decision to make
Second (subsequent) dictator game with two pairs {Frankie and Johnny} and {Butch and Sundance}	
Allocator Frankie gets $12 (same as Clyde) Frankie decides whether to send any money to Johnny	Allocator Butch gets $21 (same as Louise) Butch decides whether to send any money to Sundance
Receiver Johnny (endowment of $6; same as amount kept by Bonnie)	Receiver Sundance (endowment of $3; same as amount kept by Thelma)
Johnny has no further decision to make	Sundance has no further decision to make

Cox finds that participants are motivated by both sets of factors (1) altruistic other-regarding preferences as well as (2) trust and reciprocity. Average transfers in the investment game ($5.97 out of $10.00) are higher than the average transfers in the dictator game ($3.63 out of $10). This shows that participants are motivated by trust over and above any other-regarding preferences. The average amount returned in the investment game ($4.94) is also higher than those transferred in the modified dictator game ($2.06), providing evidence that reciprocity and a desire to reward the sender's trust play a role over and above any altruistic tendencies.

Nava Ashraf, Iris Bohnet and Nikita Piankov, at Harvard's Business School, also examine this issue of trust and reciprocity in an ambitious project with participants from South Africa, Russia and the US, using an approach similar to the one adopted by Cox. They also look at the Berg–Dickhaut–McCabe investment game and the dictator game, but, rather than using Cox's modified dictator game, they look at the *triple dictator game*. In the dictator game, if the proposer gives \$X to the responder then the proposer gets \$(10 − X) while the responder gets \$X. The triple dictator game is similar, except in this game, the amount (\$X) given to the responder is *tripled* by the experimenter so that the proposer gets \$(10 − X), as in the dictator game, but the responder gets \$3X. The responder does not have to make a decision, that is., the responder does not have to send any money back.

The similarity between the investment game and the triple dictator game is that in both games, the amount sent is tripled. The difference is that, in the trust game, the sender can hold expectations of getting money back and thereby making a profit, while, in the triple dictator game, there is no possibility of any money being returned. Suppose "S" denotes the amount sent in the investment game and "R" denotes the amount returned by the receiver. Ashraf and her colleagues measure trust by looking at the *amount of money sent* in the investment game (S) and measure reciprocity by looking at the *proportion of money returned* by the receivers out of the tripled amount received (R/3S). They argue as follows.

First, if senders are motivated by trust, then the amount sent (S) should be related to the expected return from the receiver (R/3S). But if the senders are sending money because they have other-regarding preferences and realize that $1 sent creates a surplus by generating $3 for the receiver, then the amount sent in the investment game should be related mostly to the *amount sent in the triple dictator game* rather than the *amount expected back from the receiver in the investment game*.

Second, if receivers are motivated by reciprocity, then the proportion of money returned, R/3S, would depend more on 3S (triple the amount sent). But if receivers are motivated by altruism, then R/3S would be related more to *money sent in the dictator game* rather than *money received in the trust game*. As in Cox's study, these researchers also find substantial evidence in support of the trust and reciprocity hypothesis, though they do report that there is some evidence of both senders and receivers being motivated by other-regarding preferences.

THE ROLE OF EXPECTATIONS IN THE DECISION TO TRUST

Because trust is so fundamental to so many transactions – and betrayal of that trust could cause psychological and financial trauma – it is important that we make sure that behaviour in the investment game does indeed reflect a willingness to trust strangers. The two studies discussed above suggest that both trust and other-regarding preferences matter. But what if people are mostly motivated by a desire to share and to a lesser extent by trust? In that case, we might be barking up the wrong tree if we put too much emphasis on trust.

Uri Gneezy, Werner Güth and Frank Verboven attempted to understand the behaviour of the senders by having people take part in a trust game where they systematically varied the amount that the receiver could return. In this study, amounts sent were only doubled rather than tripled. So, if the sender sent $10 then the receiver got $20. In one treatment, the receiver could return only up to $2, regardless of the amount that he/she received from the sender. In the second treatment, he/she could return up to $10. In this second treatment then, the receiver could at least make a full repayment of any amount sent even if he/she did not or could not guarantee a positive net return to the sender (in those cases where the sender sent all $10 to the receiver). In the third treatment, he could return as much as $18 and could, therefore, give back a positive net return to the sender for any amount sent.

If the senders in this game are motivated purely by a desire to share, then the amount that the receiver can repay should not matter and should not have an impact on the amount sent. On the other hand, if senders are motivated by expected reciprocation on the part of the receivers, then we would expect them to send more when higher repayments are possible. This conjecture is borne out. The average amount sent when the receiver can repay only $2 is $2. But this amount is significantly higher when the repayment amount is $10 or $18. When receivers can repay up to $10, the average amount sent is $6.50, while for repayments of $18 the average amount sent is $5.63. These two amounts are not statistically different. The reason why the amount sent when the upper bound on repayment is $18 is not different from when the upper bound on repayment is $10 is probably that senders did not expect the receiver to send back much more than $10 even with a higher repayment amount and so the raising of the upper bound from $10 to $18 did not influence decisions much.

Andreas Ortmann, John Fitzgerald and Carl Boeing at Bowdoin College in Maine decided to take a different approach. They start by replicating the findings of the original Berg, Dickhaut and McCabe study, but then introduce a number of modifications that might help explain whether transfers are in accordance with the trust and reciprocity hypothesis.

They employ five treatments. The first is a baseline no history treatment which is exactly the same as, and designed to replicate, the no history treatment in the original Berg, Dickhaut and McCabe study. The second treatment is a social history treatment, which again is similar to the social history treatment in the Berg, Dickhaut and McCabe study and replicated that study's social history treatment by presenting the results from the baseline no history treatment to the participants. In the third treatment, besides presenting the participants with the values of previous investments and returns in a table (as in the Berg, Dickhaut and McCabe study), Ortmann and his colleagues furnished *in addition* a version of the graph shown in Figure 9.3, that is, the graph which shows the different amounts received by the receivers and the amounts they returned. In the fourth treatment, they use the baseline no history treatment but then also ask the senders to fill out a questionnaire prior to making a decision about sending money. The questionnaire is designed with two specific purposes. First, it was to ensure that senders understood the design and considered their decisions carefully before making them. Second, it was to help participants determine how much to invest by having the senders ponder the consequences of their decisions before they made them, thus reducing the potential for confusion. Specifically, the senders were asked the following questions. (a) How much money do you think you will send? (b) How much money will your paired receiver receive if you send this much? (c) How much money do you think will be returned to you? (d) How much money would you return if you were the receiver? The researchers thought that this fourth treatment (which should prompt strategic reasoning) would lead to significant drops in both the amounts sent and, consequently, the amounts returned. In a fifth and final treatment, they not only have the senders fill out the questionnaire but also present them with a version of Figure 9.3 showing the various amounts returned by the receivers.

Surprisingly, none of these manipulations make any difference. Across the different treatments the average amounts sent by the senders are not statistically different. Table 9.2 presents the average amounts sent out of the initial endowment of $10. The authors end by saying that their findings suggest that the original Berg, Dickhaut and McCabe results are quite robust. Even a presentation mode which focuses on relative, rather than absolute, returns, coupled with questionnaires designed to induce strategic reasoning, does not get rid of trust among the senders.

Ananish Chaudhuri at the University of Auckland and Lata Gangadharan at the University of Melbourne also home in on the role of expectations using 100 participants at the University of Melbourne. In their study, participants play both roles – that of the sender and of the receiver – in the investment game but with different partners in each role. Participants also play the dictator game. Like the Ortmann, Fitzgerald and Boeing study, they also decided to prompt strategic reasoning by (1) asking each sender in their experiment whether he/she expected anything back from the receiver he/she is paired with, and if he/she did, how much he/she expected to get back; (2) but, on top of that, they also asked the senders to write down (using free-form responses) their motive in sending money to the receiver.

Chaudhuri and Gangadharan find that the amount of money expected back from the receiver plays a major role in influencing the amount of money that is sent. Given that each dollar sent by the sender to the receiver in the trust game is tripled, the sender is at least as well off or better off if the receiver returns exactly one-third or more of this tripled amount respectively. For returns of less than a third, the sender is worse off.

There is a significant difference in the behaviour of those who expect less than one-third and those who expect more. There are 44 participants who expect to get back *less than*

Table 9.2 Average amount sent across various treatments in Ortmann et al. (2000)

	Number of pairs	Average amount sent(Out of $10)
Berg, Dickhaut and McCabe study		
1. No history treatment	32	$5.20
2. Social history treatment	28	$5.40
Ortmann, Fitzgerald and Boeing study		
1. No history treatment	16	$4.40
2. Social history treatment	16	$4.70
3. Social history plus graph	24	$4.70
4. No history plus questionnaire	12	$5.80
5. Social history plus graph plus questionnaire	16	$5.50

Source: Created on the basis of data provided in the original study

one-third of what the receiver gets and these participants on average sent $2.14 out of $10. The modal amount, sent by 18 out of these 44 participants, is $0. On the other hand, of the 37 participants who expected to get back *more than* one-third, the average amount sent is $6.05. There are 17 participants who expected to get back exactly one-third and these participants on average sent $5.41. Of the 54 participants who expect to get back at least one-third or more, the modal amount sent is $10, with 17 out of 54 participants sending all of their initial endowment. (Two participants did not respond to this question.)

The amount that the sender sends to the paired receiver is positively correlated with the sender's expectation about the per cent amount that the receiver will return (i.e., the sender's expectations about the receiver's reciprocity). Chaudhuri and Gangadharan also look at the free responses provided by the senders about what motivated them to send money (or not) to their paired receiver in the trust game and find that a majority of responses exhibit an explicit recognition of the role of trust in generating positive net returns for both the sender and the receiver. An example of such responses is the following:

> I want the $10 but we could both make more if we work together and split the $30 and make $15 each. This is a total risk because it would be tempting for the other person to keep the $30. I am hoping that an obvious gesture of generosity will get me some money back, $10 at least.

This participant sent her entire endowment of $10 to the paired receiver.

Chaudhuri and Gangadharan also find that the amount of money received by the receiver from the paired sender and the proportion of the tripled amount that the receiver sends back are closely related. This implies that when the receiver receives a larger percentage of the initial endowment of the sender, the receiver responds by returning a larger percentage as well. On the face of it, then, these results suggest – as Ortmann and his colleagues point out – that "trust may be a primitive that participants use as guiding behavioural instinct in unfamiliar situations."

IS A TRUSTING DECISION ANALOGOUS TO A RISKY ONE?

Any time the sender in the investment game decides to repose trust on the receiver, that is, whenever someone decides to trust a stranger, he/she is implicitly taking a chance. There is some chance that the recipient of that trust will turn out to be trustworthy and repay that trust, making both parties to the transaction better off. But there is also a chance that the receiver will renege and take the entire amount, leaving the trustor worse off than if he/she had not trusted at all. Thus, the decision to trust *may* be thought of as being similar to buying a lottery ticket. With some chance, you will make a lot of money, but with some chance, you will earn nothing and lose the amount you spent buying the ticket(s). Do people who are confronted with a situation where they have to repose their trust in a stranger behave as if they are essentially buying a lottery ticket? By and large, the answer turns out to be in the negative. The mental algorithm that is called upon when asked to repose trust in a stranger seems to be substantially different from the one that is called upon when people buy a lottery ticket.

One of the early attempts to disentangle trust from risk was undertaken by Chris Snijders and Gideon Keren. They look at a simpler version of the Berg–Dickhaut–McCabe investment game. In the Snijders–Keren version of the game, the sender has two options – (1) to send all $10 so that the receiver gets $30 or (2) to send nothing.[3] If the sender chooses the second option (which is similar to the sender's decision to send nothing in the investment game) then both the sender and the receiver end up with some default amount. For the sake of convenience, let us say this sum is $10. So, in the absence of trust, each party gets $10. However, if the sender does decide to trust and send money (which means sending all $10), then the receiver is restricted to two options as well. He/she can *reciprocate* (Snijders and Keren use non-emotive words like "send money" or "send money back" rather than loaded terms like "trust" and "reciprocate") in which case, say, each party gets $20. Or he/she can *betray* the sender's trust, in which case the sender gets $0 and the receiver gets $40.

In this case, the sender's decision to send the $10 to start with essentially implies that there are two possible outcomes – (1) a return of $20, that is, a gain of $10, or (2) a return of $0, that is, a loss of $10. The potential risk associated with the decision to send all $10 can be manipulated by changing the potential amounts that the receiver can send back. For instance, suppose the choices are less stark in that the two options for the receiver are (1) send back $10 out of $30 and keep $20 and (2) send back $20 out of $30 and keep $10. Here, the sender is guaranteed that he/she will *not* lose any money, even if he/she does not make a positive net return. In this case, then, the sender is looking at two possible outcomes – (1) a loss of $0 or (2) a gain of $10, that is, no chance of making a loss. Therefore, a sender may be much more inclined to send money in the second scenario compared to the first. Thus, by changing the amounts that the receiver can send back and, consequently, the potential gains and losses to the sender, one can see what kinds of changes there are in the sender's decision to send money. Snijders and Keren went on to suggest that the potential gains and losses and *the risks associated with those* seem to matter a lot in the senders' decisions to send money.

But a number of studies since then have questioned this finding. Iris Bohnet and Richard Zeckhauser of Harvard Kennedy School argue that one drawback to the conclusions reached by Snijders and Keren is that they try to evaluate people's attitudes towards risk within the context of the investment game itself, whereas a better option would be to evaluate this using a different task. Bohnet and Zeckhauser have participants take part in three different games. First, they play the binary choice version of the investment game where the sender has two options, as in Snijders and Keren.

Next, they take part in a second game where the senders are essentially making a lottery choice. They are posed the following question: suppose they send all $10 and there is some chance that they will get back $20 (i.e., gain $10) and some chance that they will get back $0 (i.e., lose $10). *Senders are asked to state under what circumstances they would be willing to send $10.* Would they do it if the chance of getting back $20 is 50% and getting back $0 is 50% (which implies an *expected* return of $10)? How about if the chance of getting back $20 is 60% or 70% and so on?

The researchers had already decided the actual chance of getting back $20 prior to the beginning of the experiment. *Suppose the chance of getting back $10 and thereby making an extra $10 is 50% and the chance of getting back nothing is 50%.* Every participant who states that he/she is willing to send all $10 as long as there was a 50% chance of getting back $20 then plays this game. If he/she stated that he/she would not send any money unless the chance of getting back $20 was *more than 50%*, then he/she did not have to play the lottery game and simply kept the initial endowment of $10.

However, one issue with the lottery game is that this is an individual decision-making game where there is no receiver, while in the investment game there is a sender and a receiver, and we have seen that often the senders do care about what happens to the receiver. Thus, Bohnet and Zeckhauser have their participants take part in a third game – the *risky dictator game*. The risky dictator game is similar to the lottery choice game. But now, if the sender sends any money and the chance outcome is such that both the sender and the receiver receive a positive net return, then the passive responder of this dictator game also gets some money. So, for example, if the chance outcome is such that the sender gets $20 and the receiver gets $20, then the passive responder in this dictator game will actually be given $20.

Bohnet and Zeckhauser find that sender behaviour is indeed different in the investment game compared to the lottery choice game or the risky dictator game. People are much less willing to send money and take the chance of being exploited in the investment game while their behaviour in either the lottery choice game or the risky dictator game are not different. Bohnet and Zeckhauser comment: "Our results suggest that the decision to trust is influenced by more than just risk ... They behave as though there is a *betrayal cost* above and beyond any dollar losses" (emphasis in the original).

Catherine Eckel and Rick Wilson also examine this relationship between trust and risk. Eckel and Wilson recruit participants at two different locations – Virginia Polytechnic (in Blacksburg, Virginia) and Rice University (in Houston, Texas) – to undertake four different tasks. (1) They play the trust game where one member of the pair is in Virginia while the other member is located in Houston. This made it extremely unlikely that members of the pair would ever run into one another. (2) They fill out a 40-question psychological survey called the Zuckerman Sensation Seeking Scale which is designed to elicit participants' preferences about seeking out novel and stimulating activities. The survey asks participants to choose their preferred option from a pair of statements about risky activities. For example, one pair of statements is: Option 1: *skiing down a high mountain slope is a good way to end up on crutches*; or Option 2: *I think I would enjoy the sensations of skiing very fast down a high mountain slope*. (3) They are also asked to choose their preferred option from a series of ten lotteries, each of which offer two alternatives, such as the following: Option 1: (i) *10% chance of getting $2 and 90% chance of getting $1.60* or (ii) *10% chance of getting $3.85 and 90% chance of getting $0.10*; Option 2: *20% chance of getting $2 and 80% chance of getting $1.60* or (ii) *20% chance of getting $3.85 and 80% chance of getting $0.10*, and so on. (4) Then they are asked to make another risky choice where they could choose to get $10 for certain or they could choose a lottery which would pay $0 or $5, or $10 or $15 or $20 with 10%, 20%, 40%, 20% and 10% chance, respectively. The participants get paid $5 for filling out the survey and also get paid depending on their choices in the two lotteries.

What Eckel and Wilson find is that none of the three risk measures (neither the Zuckerman Sensation Seeking Scale nor the two lottery choices) has any significant correlation with the decision to send money in the trust game (i.e., the decision to trust). While it seems to be a logical inference that the decision to trust a stranger may be caused by the same mental processes that allow or induce people to engage in risky gambles, the results presented above seem to suggest that there is little evidence that the decision to trust is perceived in the same way as a risky choice.

Michael Kosfeld, Marcus Heinrichs, Urs Fischbacher and Ernst Fehr at Zürich and Paul Zak at Claremont Graduate University adopt an extremely novel approach towards testing the relation between trust and risk. They look at a slightly modified version of the investment game where both the sender and the receiver have $12 each. (These researchers utilize a fictitious experimental currency which is converted into cash at the end of the session. For the sake of simplicity and convenience, I will stick to the dollar notation.) The sender has four options regarding the money he/she can send. Specifically, he/she can send $0, $4, $8 or $12. This amount is tripled, which means that the receiver will get $0, $12, $24 or $36, respectively. The receiver can then send back any amount up to the maximum received. For instance, if the sender sends $8 then the receiver gets $24 and he/she can return any amount between $0 and $24.

In a second treatment, the sender faces the same choices as in the investment game except a random mechanism, rather than a human being, decides how much money the sender will get back. Thus, this second treatment is analogous to participating in a lottery with good and bad outcomes both possible. These researchers implement a double-blind protocol where the experimenter is unaware of the decisions made by individuals and the decisions could not be traced back to the individual decision makers. Here is the novel part of this study. In both the investment game as well as the lottery choice game, some of the participants receive a single intranasal dose of oxytocin while the rest receive a placebo. (Participants in the oxytocin group receive three puffs per nostril of Syntocinon spray manufactured by Novartis.) Oxytocin is a neuropeptide which plays a central role in social interactions. Besides its well-known physiological functions in milk-letdown and during labour, oxytocin receptors are distributed in various brain regions associated with pair bonding, maternal care, sexual behaviour and the ability to form normal social attachments.

There are 58 senders in the trust game – half of them were administered oxytocin while the other half received a placebo. The data show that oxytocin increases senders' trust considerably. Out of the 29 senders who received oxytocin, 13 (45%) showed maximal trust by sending their entire endowment to the paired receiver. However, in the placebo group, only six out of 29 (21%) did so. The average transfer in the oxytocin group is $9.60, which is significantly higher than that in the placebo group ($8.10). The median transfer in the oxytocin group is $10 while the median for the placebo group is $8.

There are 61 participants who took part in the lottery choice game: 31 in the oxytocin group and 30 in the placebo group. There are no significant differences in behaviour between these two groups. The average or median amount sent by those in the oxytocin group is not different from that sent by the participants in the placebo group. Thus, administration of oxytocin leads to increased trust in the investment game but does not affect behaviour in the lottery choice game suggesting, yet again, that the decision to trust is fundamentally different from the decision to accept a risky gamble.

DO TRUST AND TRUSTWORTHINESS GO TOGETHER?

In most studies of trust, there is the implicit assumption that trust and trustworthiness must be similar psychological constructs, meaning that a person who is trusting of another would, when given the opportunity, also reciprocate the trust of others. Surprisingly, this turns out not to be true – those who trust do not necessarily reciprocate. Chaudhuri and Gangadharan were well placed to investigate this issue because, in their study, each participant played once as the sender (which generates a measure of that participant's level of trust) and once as the receiver (generating a measure of that person's trustworthiness).

Chaudhuri and Gangadharan define a participant as "trusting" if he/she sent *exactly 50% or more* of his/her initial endowment of $10 in the investment game (i.e., $5 or more). If he/she sent *less than 50%*, then this participant is labelled "non-trusting". Then we can see if the participants classified as "trusting" using this definition exhibit greater reciprocity than the "non-trusting" participants. It turns out that the answer is no. Using the 50% cut-off, there are 58 participants who are non-trusting (sent less than 50%) and 42 trusting (sent exactly 50% or more). The non-trusting participants returned, on average, 18% of the amount they received while the trusting participants returned 16%. This difference is not significant and the result does not change when they try alternative definitions of "trusting".

The people who trust but do not reciprocate seem less motivated by pure trust, but, rather, are interested in exploiting the trust and trustworthiness of others in increasing their own pay-off. It appears that this group of participants engage in the following course of action. As the sender, they repose trust on the other player, hoping for reciprocity from him/her and, consequently, a bigger pay-off. However, as the receiver (and the recipient of a trusting move from the paired sender) they choose not to reciprocate and choose to appropriate the entire (or most of the) surplus created by the sender's trusting act, thereby grabbing a much larger pay-off.

The above evidence suggests that while a large majority of participants in this game exhibit trust, not all of them necessarily reciprocate trust when they have the opportunity to do so. Thus, many participants, while trusting, may not be trustworthy. How about those who do reciprocate trust? Do they also trust more? The answer turns out to be an emphatic yes. Suppose a participant is "trustworthy" if he or she returned *at least one-third or more* of any amount offered to them. There are 27 such participants. The remaining 55 who returned *less than one-third* are deemed "less trustworthy". It turns out that the 27 "trustworthy" participants, in their role as the sender, send on average $5.33 out of $10, which is higher than the $3.82 on average sent by the remaining 55 "less trustworthy" participants.[4]

One interesting insight arising from the Chaudhuri and Gangadharan study is the dissonance between trust and reciprocity in that those who trust are not necessarily trustworthy, but the trustworthy people are more trusting. Chaudhuri and Gangadharan go on to argue that what many prior studies have interpreted as trust has two distinct components. One is being both *trusting* and *trustworthy* in the sense of possessing a general social orientation towards others, while the other – a predilection for trust with no associated desire to reciprocate – has an implicit element of *opportunism* associated with it. The former component is definitely a desirable quality but the latter probably not. The noted Harvard sociologist Robert Putnam, in his book, *Bowling Alone: The Collapse and Revival of American Community*, comments:

> Other things being equal, people who trust their fellow citizens volunteer more often, contribute to charity, participate more often in politics and community organizations, serve more readily on juries, give blood more frequently, comply more fully with their tax obligations, are more tolerant of minority views, and display many other forms of civic virtue.

But when it comes to the idea of social orientation – as in this quote from Putnam for instance – it is trustworthiness that is more important and relevant, rather than trust. If one is trustworthy, then one is definitely trusting, but a trusting individual is not necessarily trustworthy. In this particular quote, Putnam's use of the word "trust" should be interpreted as "trustworthiness".

DOES TRUST PAY?

Earlier, I discussed the work by Andreas Ortmann and his colleagues in replicating the Berg et al. trust game results. Ortmann and colleagues find that multiple different ways of presenting the trust game do not make a difference and that participants exhibit significant amounts of trust under the various different presentations. This prompted these researchers to conclude that trust is a "primitive". But, while it is clear that participants exhibit significant amounts of trust, the question remains, does this trust pay? Does Valjean follow the straight and narrow path following Monsignor Myriel's act of trust? In trust games of the Berg et al. type, do the senders end up being better off? Do they make more than their original endowment of $10?

In the original Berg et al. study, the senders, on average, keep $4.84 and send $5.16 to the paired receivers. This implies that the receivers received, on average, the tripled amount of $15.48. But, on average, the receivers returned $4.66 and kept $10.82. This means that the receivers, on average, ended up with $20.82; the original endowment of $10, since both the sender and the receiver received an initial endowment of $10, plus the $10.82 they keep from the triple amount received. But how much do the senders make on average? If they keep $4.84 on average and receive $4.66 back from the receivers on average, then, on average, senders make only $9.50, a loss of $0.50 (5%) since they would have made $10 if they simply hung on to their initial $10 endowment. Matters did improve somewhat in the second social history treatment. Here, on average, senders sent $5.36, implying that they kept $4.64. The average return out of the tripled amount received by the receivers was $6.46. So, on average, the senders made $11.10, a return of 11%. But, by and large, prior experimental studies document that, on average, acts of trust do not pay off. Sender earnings, following an act of trust, are typically less than what would have been the case had he/she not extended trust in the first place. So much so that in surveying this literature for his book, *Behavioral Game Theory*, Colin Camerer of Caltech comments: "The fact that the return to trust is around zero seems fairly robust." Similar arguments have been made by others, such as Ashraf, Bohnet and Piankov.

Should we then conclude that the Berg et al. trust game is ill equipped to measure trust? And, in that context, is trust a bad investment? Will reposing trust in unknown strangers typically lead to losses? Or, could it be that the absence of extra returns to trust is an artefact of the way the instructions are framed? Richard Cookson of York University writes:

> Experimental economists typically devote a great deal of effort into investigating complex variations in strategy sets ... in order to test competing theories. By contrast, rather less time and effort is spent on investigating simple variations in how those strategy sets are described to subjects.

Noel Johnson of George Mason and Alexandra Mislin of American University undertake a meta-analysis of trust games involving 162 replications of the Berg et al. game to identify factors affecting behaviour. But almost all of these change various parameters of the game, such as: whether (i) the receiver receives an endowment or not (amount sent is lower with receiver endowment); (ii) subjects are paid for each round or for a randomly chosen round (the latter payment scheme reduces trust); (iii) the amount sent is doubled or tripled (receivers reciprocate less when amount is tripled) and (iv) whether subjects play one role or both roles (there is less reciprocity when participants play both roles). One manipulation that may be considered as a framing effect is whether players play against another human or a computer. The former leads to greater trust (though the effect is only marginally significant).

But, by and large, the majority of replications do not focus on alternative ways of presenting the game. Cookson suggests that presentational details (essentially, how the game is framed and explained to participants) matter, particularly when discussing generalizability of results from one experiment to another or to non-experimental settings. Interpretation of experimental results may depend crucially on how participants perceive the game and whether they and the experimenter attach the same meanings to the relevant actions in the strategy sets. Martin Dufwenberg of the University of Arizona and his colleagues say that framing may play a pre-eminent role in psychological games, where pay-offs depend on both actions and beliefs; if and when framing changes beliefs, actions may change as well.

Lee Cronk, an anthropologist at Rutgers University, looks at such framing effects in the Berg et al. trust game played by Maa speaking pastoralist Maasai in Kenya. In a control treatment, subjects play the game with neutral instructions. The experimental treatment utilizes a framing that invokes *osotua*, which literally means "umbilical cord" but refers to *gift-giving relationships based on obligation, need, respect, and restraint*. The results suggest that, compared to games with neutral framing, in the "osotua" frame, there is reduced trust (measured by average amount sent by senders) and reciprocity (measured by average proportion returned by receivers). Senders also expect lower returns in the "osotua" frame. Cronk suggests that the "osotua" framing seems to have shifted game play away from the logic of investing and towards mutual obligations to respond to genuine needs. Since the perceived need is assessed to be less in the framed game, transfers are also lower.

Ananish Chaudhuri, Sherry Li and Tirnud Paichayontvijit of Auckland look at the impact of framing. They run five different treatments; two of them are identical to the original Berg et al. protocol except in one case (the *private knowledge* treatment) the instructions are provided to the participants on their computer screens, while in the second (*common knowledge* treatment) the instructions are provided on-screen but also read out loud for everyone to hear.[5] The main manipulation is a *context treatment*, designed to provide an explanation of the game, in order to make sure that the participants in the game interpret the nature of the game in the same way as the experimenter; that is, the participants also understand that the game is about trust and reciprocity. This aim is achieved by adding the following to the standard instructions for the game.

One way to think about this situation is as follows: the receiver has no incentive to send any money back to the sender because the round ends immediately after that. Anticipating that, the sender should hang on to his $10.00 and send nothing to the receiver. This means they will both end the round with $10.00 each.

But suppose the sender decides to transfer $10.00 to the receiver. Then the receiver will get $30.00. If the receiver sends back an amount more than $10.00 then it is easy to see that both the sender and the receiver can make more money than if they simply hung on to their $10.00 in each and every round.

In two additional treatments, the researchers explicitly add the words "trust" and "trustworthy" and counterbalance the design by changing the position of the two above paragraphs.[6] (These two treatments are referred to as *context-loaded A* and *context-loaded B*, respectively, where loaded framing means the use of emotive language rather than neutral language.) In one presentation, the explanation with regard to the Nash equilibrium prediction appears first, while, in a different presentation, the explication of the role of trust and reciprocity (and the fact that participants can both be better off as a result) appears ahead of the self-interest-based explanation in line with the equilibrium prediction. Each participant is assigned the role of a sender or a receiver. These roles are fixed for the entire experiment. Senders and receivers play for ten rounds and are randomly re-matched from one round to the next. Figure 9.4 shows what happens to the average amount sent across the five different treatments. Averaged over all ten plays of the game, the amount is smallest ($2.56 out of $10, or 26%) in private knowledge and largest ($6.75 or 67.5%) in context-loaded B.

Did trust pay? Before I answer the question, in Figure 9.5 I show the average proportion returned in each treatment, once again averaged over all ten plays of the game. Bear in mind that, in order for trust to pay, on average, paired receivers must return at least one-third of the tripled amount. If the average return is less than a third, then, on average, trust will not

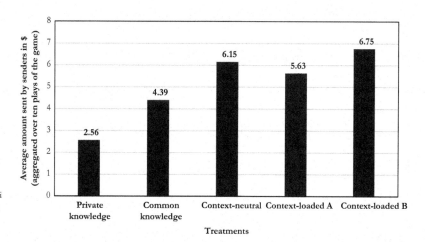

Figure 9.4
Average amount sent across the five different treatments in Chaudhuri et al. (2016). Re-created on the basis of data in the original study

235

pay. But if the average return is more than a third, then it will. As Figure 9.5 shows, the average returns in the three context treatments are greater than a third (more than 33%). This implies that the average returns to the senders in all three context treatments will be higher than if they simply hung on to their initial endowments.

Clearly, trust will pay in the three context treatments. Table 9.3 makes this clear. Sending nothing means that the sender earns $10 by keeping the entire endowment. However, aggregated over the five treatments, the average earning when sending all $10 is $11.62, a return of 16.2%. However, there are wide variations in these earnings. To study this in detail, we can look for the modal transfer (i.e., the transfer made most often or with highest frequency) in each treatment. In the private knowledge treatment, the modal transfer is zero. In fact, in this treatment, sending all $10 results in a large loss (of about 35%), with an average return of $6.54. There are two modes in the common knowledge treatment: $0 and $10. When the senders sent $10, there is an approximately 9% return, with average returns of $10.87. But in the three context treatments, the modal transfers are always $10 and the returns are much larger, with average returns of $12.84 (28%) in context-neutral, $12.52 (25%) in context-loaded A and $11.41 (14%) in context-loaded B.

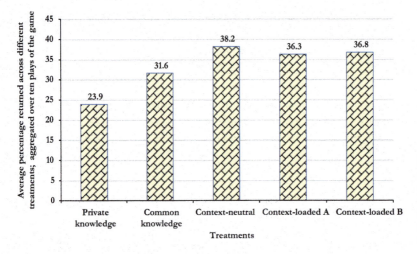

Figure 9.5
Average proportion returned across the five treatments in Chaudhuri et al. (2016). Re-created on the basis of data in the original study

Table 9.3 Modal transfers, earnings and returns across different treatments in Chaudhuri et al (2017)

Treatments	Private knowledge	Common knowledge	Context-neutral	Context-loaded A	Context-loaded B
Modal transfer	$0	($0) [$10]	$10	$10	$10
Percentage of total transfers	50%	(22%) [22%]	33%	39%	32%
Average earning from modal transfer	$10	($10) [$10.87]	$12.84	$12.52	$11.41
Returns to trust	0%	(0%) [9%]	28%	25%	14%

This suggests that when the underlying contingencies implicit in the transaction are made clear to subjects in the three context treatments and all participants interpret the game in the same way and this interpretation coincides with that of the experimenter, trust does pay. The returns to trust are statistically and economically larger and more dramatic than those in the Berg et al. social history treatment. Furthermore, it is noteworthy that providing context leads to a pronounced shift in the amount transferred towards $10, and this, in turn, generates returns to the tune of 14% to 28%. It also appears that explicit use of loaded terms, such as "trust" and "trustworthiness", is not essential; provided the right framing, subjects seem quite capable of inferring the strategic imperatives, even without resorting to emotive words. Relatively neutral cues, as long as they are enough to generate a common interpretation of the game, can promote both trust and trustworthy behaviour.

CASE STUDY 9.1 THE NEUROECONOMICS OF TRUST AND RECIPROCITY

When we trust someone and that trust is betrayed, we feel "cheated" and often want to lash out to punish the "cheater". Dominic de Quervain, Ernst Fehr and other colleagues decided to use positron emission tomography (PET) scans to see what happens inside our brains if that cheating is intentional as opposed to unintentional. What if the punishment is costly or free? What if the punishment is real or symbolic? How does our brain respond?

Participants were endowed with 10 monetary units (MU) each, which were redeemable for cash at the end of the experiment. The sender can either keep all 10 MU or send all of it to a receiver. Any amount of money sent is quadrupled, that is, multiplied by four as opposed to the usual multiplier of three in the Berg et al. trust game. So, if the sender sends 10 MU, then the receiver gets 40 MU and ends up with 50 MU, including the 10 MU the receiver was endowed with in the beginning. The receiver can choose one of two responses: (i) a "trustworthy" response of returning 25 MU, such that sender and receiver end up with 25 MU each or (ii) an "untrustworthy" response of keeping all the money, in which case the sender ends up with nothing and the receiver gets 50 MU. Each sender plays multiple receivers.

Senders are allocated 20 points to punish receivers in the event of untrustworthy behaviour. Each point sent in punishment reduces the receiver's pay-off by 2 MU; so, if the sender sends 20 points then it will cost the receiver 40 MU. Senders are also asked to rate the perceived unfairness and desire to punish on a seven-point scale from −3 to +3.

Untrustworthy behaviour by the receiver can be "intentional (I)" (decided by the receiver) or "non-intentional (N)" (decided by chance), and punishment can be costly, free or symbolic. There are four conditions: (i) untrustworthy behaviour by the receiver is intentional and punishment is costly (IC); (ii) untrustworthy behaviour by the receiver is intentional and punishment is free (IF); (iii) untrustworthy behaviour by the receiver is intentional and punishment is symbolic (IS); and finally (iv) untrustworthy behaviour by the receiver is non-intentional (decided by chance) and punishment is costly (NC).

PET scans taken during the play of the games show that in those cases where senders are able to punish the receivers for their untrustworthiness, there is significant activation in the caudate nucleus (a part of the dorsal striatum). In animals (e.g., rats and monkeys) the caudate nucleus has been implicated in the processing of reward. Neuroimaging studies that investigate reward processing also report caudate activation. Figure 9.6 shows the degree of perceived unfairness and the desire to punish across the four treatments.

Clearly, then, trustors are keen to punish untrustworthy behaviour and punishment seems to provide psychological rewards. But a question remains: do those who punish more feel more satisfaction? Or, are those who anticipate greater satisfaction from punishment willing to invest more money in punishment? The authors report that those who spent more money for punishment even when punishment is costly (and untrustworthy behaviour is intentional) exhibit higher caudate activation, meaning that the act of punishment was rewarding. Next, the authors look at people who choose the maximum punishment amount when punishment is free (and cheating is intentional). Suppose the second of the two above hypotheses is correct, that is, that people who expect to get more satisfaction from punishment are willing to spend more money to punish. Then we would expect to see that the people who choose the maximum amount of punishment when punishment is free will also be willing to punish more, even when punishment is costly. It turns out that those subjects who chose the

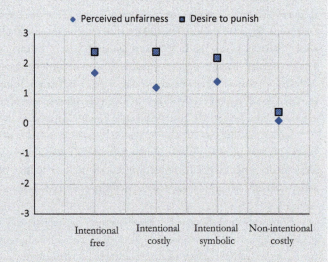

Figure 9.6
Perceived unfairness and desire to punish across the four treatments in de Quervain et al. (2004). Re-created on the basis of data in the original study

maximal punishment of 20 MU (meaning a loss of 40 MU for the punishment recipient) in IF also chose to spend more in the IC condition. These results suggest that the observed activations in the dorsal striatum reflect expected satisfaction from punishment, which is consistent with the view of the dorsal striatum as a key area involved in goal-directed, rewarding behaviour.

CONCLUDING REMARKS

The economist Paul Seabright of the University of Toulouse, in his book *The Company of Strangers: A Natural History of Economic Life*, points out that the decision to trust strangers and to reciprocate others' trust is crucial to exploiting the benefits of a sophisticated division of labour among large groups of humans; notions of trust and reciprocity are, therefore, fundamental to economic life. A large number of transactions in day-to-day life – particularly more anonymous ones such as those conducted via the internet – would never take place if people were myopically self-interested and opportunistic. This is because many economic transactions are not simultaneous. Sometimes the buyer pays first and then the seller sends the good, or the seller sends the good first and then bills the buyer later. This, in turn, requires the more vulnerable party to repose trust in the less vulnerable one. What makes trusting strangers – and thereby making one's own self vulnerable to exploitation – a reasonable thing to do? Seabright argues that this is because we have created structures of social life in which such judgements of trust make sense and these structures work because they fit in well with our natural dispositions.

Trusting actions are not naïve and are predicated upon expectations of reciprocity on the part of the trustee. Neither of these two dispositions – trust or reciprocity – could support cooperation without the other. Those who trust naïvely, without any calculation of expected reciprocity, would be easily exploited. On the other hand, those who engage in calculated and strategic trust without any tendency to reciprocate others' trust would be too opportunistic and it is unlikely that they will be trusted too often.

We have seen in the preceding pages that trust seems to be a "primitive" and is robust to multiple different ways of presenting the game. We saw that trusting and reciprocal decisions are not the same as, and more nuanced than, altruistic acts, and that decisions involving trust are predicated on expected reciprocation. We also discussed that the decision to trust is qualitatively different from decisions under risk and learned that when it comes to making trusting decisions, there seem to be at least two types: (1) a type that typically trusts and reciprocates trust; for whom trust and reciprocity is a general social orientation towards others. But (2) there is also a type of person that tends to trust as a calculated gamble, but also tends not to reciprocate. It is possible that the latter type may benefit in the short run by exploiting the reciprocity of others, but in the longer term, it is probably the former type who will be better able to reap the benefits of complex exchanges and the division of labour among disparate groups of strangers.

Finally, we discussed the fact that, at times, the absence of returns to trust using the trust game may result from different interpretations of the game by the experimenter and the participants. However, relatively neutral cues designed to explain the underlying context of the game and, thereby, create a common understanding, results in higher levels of trust and reciprocity and significant returns to trust. In the next chapter, I discuss the implications of these findings for a variety of economic transactions with particular emphasis on personnel management and agency relationships.

The insights from this chapter can be summed up very nicely in the following anecdote told by Robyn Dawes (of Carnegie Mellon) and Richard Thaler:

> In the rural areas around Ithaca it is common for farmers to put some fresh produce on the table by the road. There is a cash-box on the table, and customers are expected to put money in the box in return for vegetables they take. The box has just a small slit, so money can only be put in, not taken out. Also, the box is attached to the table, so no one can (easily) make off with the money. We think that the farmers have just about the right model of human nature. They feel that enough people will volunteer to pay for the fresh corn to make it worthwhile to put it out there. The farmers also know that if it were easy enough to take the money, someone would do so.

NOTES

1 Actually, they called them players in Room A and players in Room B, respectively. But, rather than using the different terms used by different researchers, I am going to use the terms "sender" and "receiver" consistently.
2 Remember that the dictator game is the one where the proposer is given a sum of money (say $10) and asked to suggest a split of this amount between him/her and the responder, except that the responder has no say in the matter and has to accept any offer that the proposer makes to him/her, which could be zero dollars. In the event that the proposer gives $X to the responder, the proposer gets $(10 − X) while the responder gets $X.
3 Snijders and Keren use different amounts. I will use $10 or $20 for the sake of simplicity, convenience and in order to keep parity with my discussion of the investment game above. This will make it easier to follow my arguments.
4 A sharp reader might notice that 27 and 55 add up to 82 rather than 100, which is the number of participants in this particular study. This is because there were 18 receivers in this study who received nothing from the sender. And, therefore, these 18 receivers had no decision to make regarding how much to send back. These 18 people are excluded from the discussion on the amount returned, leaving only 82 observations.
5 There is evidence that reading instructions out loud makes a difference. For one thing, now everyone is sure that everyone else has received the exact same instructions, since they all heard it being read out loud. There is also evidence that people process visual and auditory (or visual as opposed to visual and auditory) stimuli differently. This is typically why attending lectures is usually more useful and results in better performance than simply reading the book or even listening to lecture recordings.
6 One way to think about this situation is as follows: the receiver has no incentive to send any money back to the sender because the round ends immediately after that. Anticipating that, the sender should hang on to his $10 and send nothing to the receiver. This means they will both end the round with $10 each.

But suppose the sender decides to trust the receiver by sending $10. Then the receiver will get $30. If the receiver behaves in a trustworthy manner and sends back an amount more than $10, then it is easy to see that both the sender and the receiver can make more money than if they simply hung on to their $10 in each and every round.

10 Trust and trustworthiness in markets

In this chapter, I:

- *Continue the discussion about trust and trustworthiness by looking at their impact on various market transactions;*
- *Examine their role in personnel management and labour contracts and discuss how outcomes may differ from the predictions based on self-interest;*
- *Explore the role of trust and trustworthiness as embodied in notions of "social capital" and their impact on economic growth and development;*
- *Extend the discussion of trust-based motivations to look at the more general issue of extrinsic and intrinsic incentives in a variety of economic transactions ranging from climate change to providing micro-credit to small lenders.*

INTRODUCTION

In the previous chapter, I discussed how notions of trust and reciprocity, as distinct from any notions of altruism, play a role in economics, particularly in situations of bilateral bargaining. In this chapter, I extend this discussion to a range of wider applications.

Let us take the example of the owner of a café hiring a manager to run the place. The owner obviously wishes the place to do well and sell lots of coffee and pastries so that he/she can turn a profit. In order for that to happen, the manager needs to work hard. But if the manager does not get a share of the profit generated by the business (suppose the manager gets a fixed salary), then the manager may not have much of an incentive to work hard. Hard work requires effort and while the manager's hard work will make more money for the owner, it may not necessarily benefit the manager. Thus, if the manager is paid a fixed wage, then he/she is better off not putting in much effort at all. If business is bad then he/she can blame it on bad location or hot weather. (Manager to owner: "It's been so hot lately; no one's drinking coffee, Boss. What we really need is a liquor licence so that we can sell beer and mixed drinks.") The problem is that if business is bad, the owner cannot be sure whether that is really due to the location or the weather or whether it is because the manager is lazy or rude to the customers and provides bad service. In order to find that out, the owner will have to continually supervise or monitor the manager, but, in that case, the owner might as well run the place on his/her own. But the owner may have other businesses or other things to do with his/her time, making it impossible for him/her to spend all his/her time supervising the manager. In cases like this, it gets difficult to achieve much in the absence of some amount of mutual trust between the employer and the worker.

In 2015, Afzaal Deewan and his partner, Natalie, set up the restaurant Der Wiener Deewan, serving buffet-style Pakistani food on Liechtensteinstrasse in Vienna. But the restaurant came with a twist. The owners decided to do away with prices! Instead, their motto was "eat all you want, pay as you wish". At the conclusion of the meal, patrons can pay based on what they thought their meal was worth. Self-interest would suggest that unless there are people who live close by and intend to engage in repeat business, many others, particularly visitors to the city who are unlikely to go back, should eat a lot and only pay a small amount. Soon, the restaurant should be struggling. But, contrary to what we may think, the restaurant has been thriving. In this chapter, I look at multiple examples of such behaviour that rely on mutual trust and reciprocity even in the absence of any formal compliance mechanism.

TRUST AND TRUSTWORTHINESS IN AGENCY RELATIONSHIPS

The previous example is referred to as an "agency problem" (or, in the parlance of the economist, a "principal-agent" problem). An agency problem arises in many, if not most, employment relationships. Besides the example alluded to above, other examples include: a landowner hiring a worker to work the land; shareholders of a company hiring a CEO; the state or national government hiring a director to head a state-run enterprise. The crux of the problem is similar in all these cases: the goals of the owner (principal) and the worker (agent) are often not aligned in the sense that the worker may have objectives that are very different from those of the owner.

Faced with an agency problem like this, economists suggest that one must provide the proper incentives (carrots and sticks) to the employee, in order to get him/her to perform his/her duties satisfactorily. The carrots may include wages, salaries, performance-based bonuses, commissions and the possibility of promotions, while the sticks include rebukes, bad reports (making later promotions more difficult), fines, penalties, demotions and, of course, termination. In fact, the view that incentives are crucial to achieving optimal outcomes in employment relationships is fundamental to economic thinking. And while economists often disagree over a number of issues, there is broad agreement about the need for designing proper incentive schemes for employees. So much so that N. Gregory Mankiw, who is the author of one of the most (if not *the* most) popular textbooks for undergraduates in economics, provides a list of ten fundamental principles that most economists agree on; number four on that list is: *People respond to incentives.*

This, in turn, leads to the following dictum: employment relationships must be governed by explicit contracts which are incentive compatible, meaning that they must clearly specify the incentives involving the rewards for performing well and the punishments for performing poorly. In the absence of a well-designed, incentive-compatible contract providing both carrots and sticks, employees have no incentive to work hard and will inevitably shirk, leading to lower profits for the owner. While most economists will readily agree about the importance of incentives, there is mounting evidence now that economists may be over-emphasizing the need for explicit incentives. Often, a system of implicit contracts essentially relying on the mutual trust and reciprocity between owners and workers performs as well as a system based on explicit incentives specifying rewards and punishments.

This, however, is not a new idea and has been around for a while; at least since the economist George Akerlof of Berkeley proposed the idea of labour contracts as "gift exchange" in the early 1980s. Akerlof built his arguments on the basis of a study done in the mid-1950s by the sociologist George Homans, who focused on the behaviour of "cash posters" at Eastern Utilities located in the east coast of the United States. Homans looked at a group of ten young women whose job it was to record customers' payments on ledger cards at the time of receipt. The company's policy for such cash posting was 300 per hour. Careful records were kept of the speed at which various workers worked and those who fell below the quota received a mild rebuke from the supervisor. What Homans found was that the average number of cash postings per hour was 353, 18% greater than the required number set by the employer.

Standard economic theory has a hard time explaining (1) why the faster cash posters did not reduce their speed to just meet the required standard of 300 and (2) why the firm did not increase the speed expected of the faster workers. All cash posters were paid the same hourly wage rate and it was not the case that the faster workers could expect to earn more in the form of performance bonuses. If and when the workers got promoted, it was to a job that brought with it more responsibility but still paid the same wage. Furthermore, workers quit their jobs quite frequently (in most cases to get married) and, thus, the length of the firm–employee relationship was not particularly long; so, the scope for generating long-term feelings of loyalty was limited. Since the hourly wage was fixed and did not depend on effort, and the reward of future promotions was rarely a consideration, economic theory suggests that the workers should adjust their work habits to just meet the quality standard set by the company. But it was obvious that the workers were putting in effort far in excess of what was expected of them.

This led George Akerlof to propose a new model of employment relationships based on "gift exchange" between the employer and the employee. According to Akerlof, as part of their interactions, employees acquire sentiments for each other and also for the firm. As a consequence of sentiment for the firm, the workers derive utility (satisfaction) from an exchange of "gifts" with the firm where the level of satisfaction depends on the norm of gift exchange. On the worker's side, the "gift" given is work in excess of the minimum work standard; on the firm's side, the "gift" given is wages in excess of what these women could receive if they left their current jobs. When firms pay their workers a wage that exceeds what those workers could earn in an alternative job, or a wage that exceeds the wage dictated by the forces of demand and supply in the market for labour, economists call that an *efficiency wage*. Such efficiency wages are used in many industries to (1) create loyalty on the part of the employee; (2) prevent workers from quitting (because the alternative jobs may pay a much lower wage) and (3) attract better skilled workers. Akerlof argues, on the basis of findings in the sociology literature, that workers' efforts are often determined by the prevailing norm in the work group and may not be determined solely by the wage paid.

This, in turn, has important and somewhat counter-intuitive implications for the market for labour. Classical economic theory assumes that the wage rate in the market for labour is determined by the interaction of the demand for labour coming from businesses and the supply of labour coming from workers. As long as a firm is willing to pay this market-determined wage, it can hire as many workers as it wants. If the firm is unwilling to offer the market wage, then it will be unable to hire any workers. But if the gift-exchange model of business–worker interaction is correct, then firms may very well find it advantageous to pay a wage in excess of that which they have to pay in order to hire labour, and, in return, workers may respond by putting in effort that is in excess of what they have to provide.

In terms of gift exchanges in the labour market, this means that the worker who does no more than the minimum required to keep his/her job may at least suffer from a slight loss of reputation; reciprocally, the firm that pays its workers the bare minimum necessary to retain them will also lose some reputation. In the standard economic model, a profit-maximizing firm never chooses to pay more than the market-clearing wage because there is no advantage to doing so. In the gift-exchange model, however, the firm finds it advantageous to pay a wage in excess of the one at which it can acquire labour, because there are benefits from paying a higher wage.

Truman Bewley of Yale University has done extensive work in the area of labour contracts and finds that the gift-exchange model does indeed apply to real-life labour management practices. In a study based on interviews with 246 company managers and 19 labour leaders in the North-Eastern United States during the early 1990s, when unemployment was high due to a recession, Bewley found that the managers of most enterprises were reluctant to enact a reduction in wages even though, given the extensive unemployment, they could have easily afforded to hire workers at lower wages. The primary resistance to wage reduction comes from upper management and not from employees. Bewley suggests that the main reason for avoiding pay-cuts is that such pay-cuts hurt morale. Bewley comments:

> Morale has three components. One is identification with the firm and an internalization of its objectives. Another is trust in an implicit exchange with the firm and with other employees; employees know that aid given to the firm and to co-workers will eventually be reciprocated ... The third component is a mood that is conducive to good work. ... Managers are concerned with morale because of its impact on labor turnover, recruitment of new employees and productivity. ... The morale of existing employees is hurt by pay cuts because of an insult effect ... Workers are used to receiving regular pay increases as a reward for good work and loyalty and so interpret a pay cut as an affront and a breach of implicit reciprocity ... Resistance to wage reduction and the need for internal pay equity stem from ideas of fairness that usually refer to some reference wage. The reference wage for pay cuts is the previous wage.

While there seems to be ample evidence to support Akerlof's idea of gift-exchange such as the Homans study of cash-posters at Eastern Utilities, still, these are non-replicable one-off observations. Ernst Fehr at the University of Zürich along with his collaborators, Simon Gächter, Urs Fischbacher, Georg Kirchsteiger, Arno Riedl, Klaus Schmidt and Alexander Klein, among others, set off on an ambitious research project to test the validity of the gift-exchange model in employment relationships using a series of well-crafted experiments. Once again, the big advantage to these experiments was the fact that Fehr and his associates could change the experimental design in a number of ways to understand what the impact is on behaviour. This allows for teasing out the effects of various causal factors on the efficacy of employment contracts.

Fehr and his associates examine these issues at length using a variety of different set-ups. In the interests of convenience and simplicity, I am going to discuss the findings of their experiments using a uniform language even though the presentation of the actual game varies between different papers. The basic idea is to look at an employment relationship between firms and workers. Participants are assigned to the role of a firm or a worker at the beginning of the session and these roles remain unchanged for the entire time. The worker needs to expend effort to produce an output which is turned over to the firm. Effort imposes costs (possibly psychological) on the worker. The higher the effort, the greater the output produced. But higher effort also imposes a larger cost on the worker. Fehr and his associates impute a monetary value to this cost. The firm sells the output and earns revenue. The worker is paid a wage. The firm's profit is the difference between the revenue that it earns and the wage that it pays the worker. The worker's profit is the difference between the wage and the (monetary) cost of his/her effort.

Needless to mention, the firm is better off the higher the effort put in by the worker, since that generates a higher output and, consequently, higher sales revenue for the firm. However, since effort is costly, putting in more effort imposes a larger cost on the worker; therefore, if he/she is paid a fixed amount of money for his/her effort, then the worker is better off putting in low effort. Thus, there is a dichotomy between the goals of the firm and those of the worker. The firm wants the worker to work hard and put in a lot of effort, which will create a larger output and more revenue. The worker on the other hand, has little incentive to do so if he/she is paid a fixed amount, and should put in the smallest amount of effort that he/she can get away with (one that will not get him/her fired from the job).

In most of their settings, for the sake of simplicity, one firm can hire only one worker at a time but usually there are more workers than there are firms, implying that some workers will be unemployed in a given round. This gives the firms more market power in the sense that, given the competition between workers for jobs, the firm can get away with paying a low wage and asking for a large effort in return. Some workers might balk at offers paying a low wage and asking for high effort, but the alternative is to turn down the offer and earn nothing. Faced with the prospects of making no profit or making a small profit, some workers might easily prefer the latter option, especially if they think that someone else might take the firm up on its offer if they do not. However, firms and workers are randomly re-matched from one round to the next, making it extremely unlikely that the same firm and the same worker will interact more than once. This has the effect of making each interaction a one-off encounter. Given that there is little possibility of the same firm and the same worker meeting again in the future, there is an enhanced incentive for both the firm and the workers to behave in a self-interested way and focus narrowly on maximizing their earnings on a round-by-round basis without worrying about the possibility of future retaliations by one party or the other.

Ernst Fehr, Georg Kirchsteiger and Arno Riedl undertook one of the first experimental tests of the gift-exchange model. Their starting point was this: if firms and workers all act according to the laws of economics, then what we would expect to see in any labour market is that firms will pay their workers the market wage as determined by the demand and supply of labour. Workers, in turn, will put in the bare minimum effort that is required in order to keep their jobs. They designed an experiment where, in the first stage, firms make wage offers to workers. Workers can either accept or reject a particular wage offer. If the worker accepts, then the worker can respond with an effort level. In the experiment, the workers have no monetary incentive to choose anything greater than the minimum possible effort level and, anticipating that, the firms have no incentive to offer anything other than the market-clearing wage as determined by the demand and supply of labour. On the other hand, if the gift-exchange model is a good predictor of actual behaviour, then we would expect to see firms routinely offering a wage that is greater than the minimum they need to offer and workers in turn reciprocating with effort levels that are in excess of the minimum required.

Fehr, Kirchsteiger and Riedl's results are strongly supportive of the gift-exchange model. They find that, on average, firms offer wages which are considerably higher than the market-clearing wage even though they do not have to, especially in light of the fact that there are more workers than jobs and, therefore, workers should be willing to work for relatively low wages. Workers, in turn, respond with effort levels which are four times those of the predicted effort level.

Furthermore, they find that, on average, worker effort is increasing in the wage offered; that is, when the firms offered the workers a higher wage (which is analogous to a trusting move, since the worker can simply take the wage and put in the lowest possible effort in return), the workers reciprocated with higher effort levels. Fehr, Kirchsteiger and Riedl conclude that fairness considerations do prevent wages from declining to the market-clearing level. This is surprising because, given that there are fewer jobs than there are workers (and, therefore, some workers would be unemployed in any given round), we would expect that workers, in competing against each other for scarce jobs, would put downward pressure on the wage, driving it down to the market-clearing level. But, clearly, this is not what happens and firms continue to pay higher wages than they need to in order to attract workers. Firms anticipate worker reciprocity – that offering a higher wage will elicit higher effort.

In a follow-up study, Ernst Fehr and Simon Gächter allow the firms to offer two types of contracts: (1) a trust contract; here, the firm offers a fixed wage to the worker and asks for a certain amount of effort in return. This is similar to the wage offers in the Fehr, Kirchsteiger and Riedl study. The worker, if he/she accepts the contract, can take the wage and decide how much effort he/she wishes to put in. He/she is under no compulsion to put in the amount of effort requested by the firm, since the firm has no opportunity to penalize the worker in any way and cannot retaliate against the worker in a future round since it is extremely unlikely that they will interact more than once. Thus, the effort desired by the firm of the worker is more in the nature of a request (or moral suasion) and the worker is under no compulsion whatsoever to abide by this request. Again, following the tenets of classical economic theory, in this scenario, where the firm is offering the worker a fixed wage and the worker can provide any effort in return (regardless of the effort that the firm asks for), the worker has no explicit incentive to put in anything more than the minimal effort and we would expect the worker to do exactly that: take the wage and put in the smallest possible effort. Thus, the trust contract provides only an implicit (or an intrinsic) motivation to the worker by reposing trust on the worker and appealing to his/her reciprocity, but does not have any explicit incentives built into it.

(2) Alternatively, the firm can offer the worker an incentive contract. Here, the firm offers the worker a wage and asks for a desired level of effort as in the trust contract; but, in addition, the firm can choose to monitor the worker and if the worker does not put in the requisite effort level, then the firm can penalize the worker by imposing a monetary fine (which could be a salary deduction) payable to the firm in the event of non-compliance. (Consequently, in what follows, I will often refer to the incentive contract as a "penalty contract" to make explicit the reliance on a monetary fine in the event that the worker is found to be shirking.) Monitoring imposes a cost on the firm because the firm has to invest money into installing a monitoring technology (such as closed-circuit cameras or random visits by supervisors to check on the workers). Furthermore, the monitoring is not perfect in the sense that there is a chance that the monitoring technology will pick up when a worker is shirking and penalize him/her, but there is also a chance that the shirking will go undetected. However, by suitably choosing the values of the wage to be paid to the worker and the penalty imposed, the firm should be able to provide the right incentives to the worker to put in more than the minimum effort. This is the more traditional approach of providing explicit carrot-and-stick based incentives, and this explicit incentive contract is expected to induce the worker to put in more effort than the (implicit) trust-and-reciprocity based contract.

Before I turn to discussing the results from this study, I want to point out one thing. In this line of research, a key metric is the *rent offered* in a contract. Rent is a measure of how generous (or not) the offered contract is and the meaning of rent here is different from its everyday meaning. In economics, rent is the difference between what one actually earns and what one could potentially have earned from the next best available option.[1] In the context of research discussed here, the worker's outside option is typically set to zero (without loss of generality). This means that if the worker does not accept the contract offered by the employer, then he/she gets nothing; or, in reality, he/she will just get the show-up fee for the study. This is a trivial assumption because we can always pay the worker a small amount even for rejected contracts. But the crucial point is this: a self-interested employer has no incentive to pay positive rents to a worker; he/she should pay only what the worker could earn in the best available alternative. Whatever the wage in that alternative is, the employer should pay that or possibly a little more. In this context, we have set the alternative pay-off to zero. This means that the employer should reimburse the worker only for the cost of his/her effort (or possibly a little more, but not much). So, wage paid should be roughly equal to the cost of effort and, therefore, the magnitude of any rent conceded should be equal or close to zero. This should be particularly true in trust-based contracts where the employer has no enforcement mechanism at his/her disposal to ensure worker compliance. The employer is free to offer higher wages (and rents) and we would expect the worker to accept this thankfully, but, in the absence of any compliance mechanism, we would not expect any increase in effort level. In Figure 10.1, I show what happens to the rent offered in experiments such as these, where rent is defined as the difference between the wage offered and the cost of effort, with the assumption that the rent paid should be small. This figure is from a replication I did (along with Amy Cruickshank and Erwann Sbai of Auckland), of the work of Fehr and his colleagues. The set-up is identical to the other studies except we were more interested in looking for gender differences in behaviour, as both employer and employee. I have not discussed gender issues in this book and so the rest of the work is not germane to this topic.

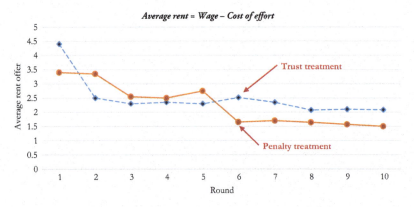

Figure 10.1 Average rent offered in trust and penalty treatments. Re-created on the basis of data in Chaudhuri et al. (2015)

The dashed line with diamonds shows the average rent offered in the trust treatment, while the solid line with circles shows the same for the incentive (penalty) treatment. What is noteworthy is that employers routinely offer large rents in both sets of contracts, trust-based or incentive-based, and even though there is some tendency for this rent to decrease over time, even by the last round the amount of rent offered is significantly greater than zero. And, while the differences between the two sets of contracts are not pronounced, if anything, the trust-based contracts offer higher rent than the penalty-based contracts.

Fehr and Gächter made a series of surprising discoveries. First, on average in the trust-based contracts, firms offer higher wages (and higher rents) and ask for higher effort from the workers compared to the incentive (penalty) contract. Second, the effort level put in by the workers under an incentive contract is lower than that put in by the workers in the trust contract. This finding is driven by the fact that even with explicit fines for non-compliance, a number of workers shirk given that the monitoring technology is imperfect and does not catch shirking with 100% accuracy. Voluntary cooperation, as measured by the excess of effort provided over the amount requested from the worker, is higher under a trust contract compared to an incentive contract, meaning that under trust contracts that offer higher rents, workers routinely provided more than the minimal amount of effort required of them, while under incentive contracts few workers did so. This suggests that the provision of explicit penalties in the contract might have led to a reduction in voluntary cooperation among the workers. Under trust-based contracts, an increase in the wage (and rent) offered elicited much higher effort levels from the workers, and overall, contracts that relied on mutual trust and reciprocity among firms and workers led to higher earnings for both parties involved compared to incentive contracts. Figure 10.2 shows the effort demanded and the actual effort provided in the trust-based and penalty-based contracts. Once again, the dashed lines relate to the trust-based contracts while the solid lines refer to the penalty-based contracts. What stands out is that employers ask for much higher effort and, in general, obtain this in the trust-based contracts. This is surprising, given the lack of any enforcement mechanism in this treatment, and one must conclude that this is being driven by mutual trust and reciprocity; the employer pays higher rent than he/she needs to and the worker responds with higher than minimal effort.

In another study, Fehr, Gächter and Kirchsteiger add a third stage to the employment contract. In the first stage, the firm offers a contract to the worker. In the case of a trust

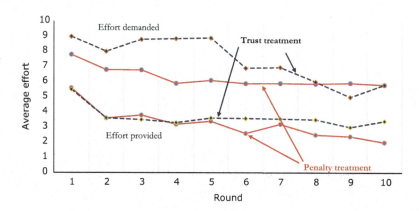

Figure 10.2 Effort demanded and actual effort provided in the trust and penalty treatments. Re-created on the basis of data in Fehr and Gächter (2002b)

contract, this consists of a wage offer and a suggested effort level. In the case of an incentive contract, this consists of a wage, a suggested effort level and a pre-specified fine payable by the worker to the firm in the event that the worker is caught shirking and providing less than the effort asked for. Once again, the monitoring is imperfect and the worker may or may not get caught shirking. In the second stage, the worker decides whether to accept the wage offer or not, and if he/she does accept the wage, then he/she decides what amount of effort to put in. As in the Fehr and Gächter study, the worker has no incentive to provide anything greater than the minimal effort under a trust contract, while with an incentive contract, by appropriately choosing the values of the fine and the chance of getting caught, the firm can guarantee that the worker will provide higher effort.

Fehr, Gächter and Kirchsteiger add a third stage, where the firm gets to see the effort level chosen by the worker in the second stage and whether this effort is greater than, equal to, or less than the effort level demanded by the firm. After observing the worker's effort, the firm can decide to either further punish the worker over and above the fine (in those cases where the effort level is less than the effort demanded), or reward the worker with a bonus (in those cases where the effort level is greater than the effort demanded). However, both the reward and the punishment impose a monetary cost on the firm, in the sense that it has to dip into its profit if it wishes to reward or punish the worker. Keep in mind that all of these are one-off interactions with very little possibility of the two parties meeting in the future.

In the third stage, the firm has no incentive to spend money to reward or punish the worker for effort provided. Suppose the worker shirked and caused the firm to lose money. It still does not make sense for the firm to lose more money by punishing the worker, because the firm is not going to interact with this particular worker again. So, the firm might as well swallow its loss and its pride and move on to the next interaction. Similarly, there is no incentive for the firm to reward the worker even if the worker provided more effort than asked for. The worker has already been paid a wage and the worker has no way of compelling the firm to pay a bonus. The firm does not care if the worker is disgruntled because the firm is not going to interact with this particular worker again and so, even if the worker is unhappy, it will not affect the firm in future interactions.

Surprisingly (or maybe not so surprisingly), Fehr and his associates find that in about 50% of cases where the worker shirked in stage two, the firm punished those workers in stage three, even though this punishment imposed monetary costs on the firm and did not generate any future benefits such as an enhanced reputation for toughness since the same two parties were not going to interact any more. Moreover, in about 50% of cases where the worker simply provided the effort level called for (or in those few cases where the worker provided effort in excess of that demanded), the firm actually rewarded the worker with a bonus even though the firm did not have to do so and the reward was monetarily costly for the firm. While the firms have no incentive to either reward or punish in the third stage and the presence of the reward/punishment opportunities should not make any difference whatsoever, still the mere fact that such an opportunity to reward/punish does exist leads to firms demanding much higher effort in this treatment and workers also responding with high effort. Figure 10.3 makes clear how much of a difference, in terms of effort demanded and provided, is made by the addition of two-sided reciprocity; from both the worker's side and the employer's side. In this figure, *WRT* or *weak reciprocity treatment* refers to the contract where there is no third stage with the possibility of rewards/punishments, while *SRT* or *strong reciprocity treatment* refers to a contract where, based on the worker's effort in the second stage, the employer has the option of rewarding/punishing the worker in the third and final stage.

Fehr and his associates go on to argue that such high wage–high effort strategies are better from the point of view of both the firms and workers and that mutual trust and reciprocity between firms and workers lead to better outcomes for them. They suggest that:

> exclusive reliance on selfishness and, in particular, the neglect of reciprocity motives may lead to wrong predictions and to wrong normative inferences. We argue that reciprocal behaviour may cause an increase in the set of enforceable contracts and may thus allow the achievement of nonnegligible efficiency gains.

The idea of gift-exchange between employers and workers might sound great in theory, but does it really work as a business practice? Does it reduce employee turnover? Do the firms that implement such a model do better or worse than firms that rely on traditional command-and-control type systems? James Baron and Michael Hannan of Stanford University

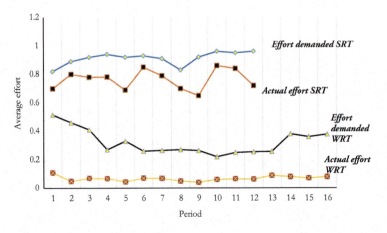

Figure 10.3 Effort demanded and actual effort provided in SRT and WRT. Re-created on the basis of data in Fehr et al. (1997)

250

and Diane Burton of MIT, working under the aegis of the Stanford Project on Emerging Companies (SPEC), examine the impact of organizational practices on employee turnover in a sample of high-technology start-ups in California's Silicon Valley. Baron and his colleagues ask the question: given that different high-tech start-ups in Silicon Valley seem to have implemented distinctive types of contractual relationships between the owner(s) and the workers, what are the implications of these human resource practices on the propensity of employees to quit?

Baron and his colleagues approached 376 firms that were founded in the 1990s and have at least ten workers. Of these, 173 firms agreed to participate in the study. Trained MBA and doctoral students conducted semi-structured interviews with the CEO of the company. The CEO was asked to identify the founder (or member of the founding team) best equipped to provide information about the firm's origins and the best informant regarding human resource management practices in the organization. The individuals concerned were requested to fill out surveys prior to being interviewed. The researchers found that one aspect of the employment relationship which loomed large in the organization of many start-ups was attachment.

The founders articulated a number of different bases of employee attachment, which the researchers broadly classify into three categories: love, work and money. Some founders wished to create a strong family-like feeling and an emotional bond between the workers and management on the one hand, and between the workers themselves on the other, that would inspire superior effort and increase retention of highly sought employees, thereby avoiding the frequent quits among workers that plague many of these start-ups. What binds the worker to the company in this framework is a sense of belonging and identification with the company – consistent with the model of gift-exchange discussed above. Some founders wished to stimulate their workers by providing the opportunity for interesting and challenging work. Finally, others considered the employment relationship as merely a simple exchange of labour for money. As for coordinating and controlling the actions of workers, there seemed to be two approaches – one involving informal control through peers by creating a particular organizational culture, and the other espousing a more traditional view based on formal carrot-and-stick based procedures and systems.

Based on their extensive surveys and interviews, the researchers classify the organizational structures of the high-tech start-ups into five separate models (albeit with some degree of overlap between them): (1) the engineering model, which involves attachment through challenging work, peer group control and selection based on specific task abilities; (2) the star model, which creates attachment based on challenging work, reliance on autonomy and professional control, and selecting elite personnel based on long-term potential; (3) the commitment model, which entails reliance on emotional–familial relationships based on mutual trust and reciprocity between management and workers and among workers themselves; (4) the bureaucracy model, which involves attachment based on challenging work, but worker selection based on qualifications for a particular role and formalized control; and finally (5) the autocracy model, which relies on employment premised on monetary considerations, control and coordination through close personal oversight and selection of employees to perform pre-specified tasks. In the context of our earlier discussion, the commitment model is the one which most closely resembles the gift-exchange model while the autocracy model and, to a lesser extent, the bureaucracy model are the ones that most closely approximate the classical economic approach to employment relationships. If you accept the tenet that it is essential to provide workers with explicit and extrinsic motivations in order for them to put in high effort, then the organizations relying on the commitment model should perform worse than the ones using the autocratic or bureaucratic models.

What Baron and his colleagues find is that the main contrast in human resource practices is between the autocratic model, which exhibits the highest rates of employee turnover, and the commitment model, which displays the lowest rates. Furthermore, firms whose CEOs rely on either the autocratic or the bureaucratic model experience far greater turnover than the firms which implement the commitment model. Employee turnover is, after all, only one metric of how a firm is doing, and possibly more important than employee turnover is the issue of firm profitability, though excessive turnover might have a disruptive influence and reduce profitability. Baron and his colleagues therefore decided to look at how these various models perform in terms of "one compelling indicator of performance": revenue growth. Given that young high-tech start-ups incur significant set-up costs which might dampen profitability, an ability to increase the revenue flow is a good indicator of later success. Baron and his colleagues find that there is a strong negative relationship between employee turnover and revenue growth, implying that firms which experience excessive labour turnover (such as the ones relying on the autocratic or bureaucratic models) also experience much slower revenue growth compared to firms which manage to retain their workers (such as the ones which implement the commitment model).

FURTHER ECONOMIC IMPLICATIONS OF FAIRNESS AND TRUST

At the end of the day, a fundamental preoccupation of economists is the betterment of people's lives, which involves addressing issues of economic development. Economists usually stress the importance of markets, legal and political institutions and a system of formal rules and laws governing economic activity for successful economic development. This traditional approach does not make allowances for the role of fairness or social norms in the process of development. But, over the previous few chapters, I have shown that informal social rules or norms of behaviour, embodied in things such as the decision to trust strangers or reciprocate others' trust, are equally, or more, important. At the very least, economists and policy makers need to be aware of the role that such social norms play because ignoring them can often lead to unintended consequences causing more harm than good.

In his book *Globalization and its Discontents*, the 2001 Economics Nobel Laureate, Joseph Stiglitz, points out that one reason policies espoused by international agencies, such as the International Monetary Fund (IMF), have often been controversial is due to an excessive emphasis on "market fundamentalism", the view that open and free markets are the panacea for all the ills of less developed economies. No serious economist will ever suggest that free markets are undesirable, but what needs to be understood is that the success of reforms is often dependent upon the sequencing of such reforms and also on local norms and conditions. External regulations imposed by central governments or international agencies which completely disregard local community-based initiatives might exacerbate problems rather than alleviate them. I end this chapter with some relevant examples.

THE GRAMEEN BANK EXPERIENCE

A pervasive problem in less developed countries (or even for the less well-off in some developed countries) is the lack of credit; that is, an inability to borrow money to finance entrepreneurial activities. Let me stick with the problems of the less developed world for now. In rural areas of these countries, there are people who are engaged in agriculture or handicrafts and often work for others for a pittance. Some of them might be able to work on their own – till their own land or start their own basket-weaving or wood-carving enterprise. Most such activities, however, require some start-up money, typically amounts that would be considered embarrassingly small by those of us who are used to a first-world lifestyle. Yet, even these very small amounts of money pose an insurmountable barrier to these people. Formal banks are unwilling to lend money to them because they rarely have any collateral that they can pledge against that loan.

The recourse is often to borrow money from local money-lenders, who typically charge exorbitant interest rates, sometimes 100% or more. This, in turn, often forces the borrower into life-long debt that they struggle to pay off year after year. It is not difficult to understand the reluctance of banks to lend money to the rural poor because it is difficult for the banks to monitor these loans. For instance, when a debtor comes in and says that he/she is unable to repay the loan because of reasons beyond his/her control such as floods, droughts or pestilence, the bank manager often is not well placed to corroborate this story. As a result, default rates are high and many rural credit schemes have a poor track record of loan recovery. Economists had been aware of this problem faced by the rural poor, but the first truly innovative solution was offered by an enterprising economist named Muhammad Yunus, who, in the early 1980s, started an enterprise named Grameen Bank (Grameen means "rural" in Bangla, the language spoken in Bangladesh).

The Grameen Bank makes small loans to the rural poor without requiring any collateral. Borrowers must belong to a "solidarity group" typically consisting of five members. One member of the group receives a loan and must repay it before another member can receive a loan. The group is not required to give any guarantees for a loan to one of its members. Repayment responsibility rests solely on the individual borrower, while the group's job is to ensure that the borrower behaves in a responsible way. The vast majority of Grameen Bank loans are given to women on the basis of prior evidence that money lent to women is used more effectively. The system essentially relies on two principles: (1) *peer monitoring*, where members of the group who live in the same village monitor the debtor and make sure that the money is spent on productive activities and not on alcohol or cigarettes; and (2) *mutual trust and reciprocity* between the bank and the borrowers on the one hand, and between the group members on the other hand. Prior to getting a loan, group members have to pledge to uphold a number of values and principles which include:

> (1) We shall not inflict any injustice on anyone; neither shall we allow anyone to do so. (2) We shall collectively undertake bigger investments for higher incomes. (3) We shall always be ready to help each other. If anyone is in difficulty, we shall all help him or her. (4) We shall take part in all social activities collectively.

Grameen Bank's track record has been notable, with loan repayment rates of close to 100%. More than half of its borrowers in Bangladesh (close to 50 million) have risen out of acute poverty thanks to these loans, as measured by standards such as having all children of school age in school, all household members eating three meals a day, a sanitary toilet, a rainproof house, clean drinking water and the ability to repay a loan of 300 taka (around US $4.50 at the exchange rate prevailing in mid-2008) per week. In 2006, Muhammad Yunus and the Grameen Bank together were the recipient of a Nobel Prize "for their efforts to create economic and social development from below". But, probably reflecting the fact that Yunus' ideas are radical and not entirely commensurate with mainstream economics, the award given was the Nobel Peace Prize rather than the Nobel Prize in Economics.

Dean Karlan, of Yale University, provides an excellent illustration of the role that economic experiments can play in policy making. In the early 2000s, while working on his doctoral dissertation at MIT, Karlan travelled to Peru to look at participation in a microcredit association called FINCA (Foundation for International Community Assistance). He had 397 pairs of participants take part in a slightly modified version of the Berg–Dickhaut–McCabe investment game and then also looked at the behaviour of these participants in terms of their involvement in the credit association. He finds that participants who behave in a trustworthy manner in their role as the receiver in the investment game (that is, those who return at least as much as they are sent by the sender so that the sender did not lose money) are also *more likely* to repay loans, *more likely* to engage in greater voluntary saving and *less likely* to drop out of the credit programme.

EXTRINSIC INCENTIVES CAN CROWD OUT INTRINSIC MOTIVATIONS

In Chapter 9 and earlier in this chapter, while discussing the role of trust and trustworthiness in economic transactions, I mentioned that economists typically emphasize the need and importance of explicit and extrinsic incentives, in order to motivate people to take the appropriate course of action (such as inducing workers to put in the desired level of effort). But I also pointed out that, at times, mechanisms that rely on mutual trust and reciprocity and moral suasion among socially connected groups of people can do at least as well as, if not better than, mechanisms that rely on explicit carrots and sticks. Here are some more examples of situations where externally provided carrots and/or sticks achieve inferior outcomes compared to approaches that appeal to people's sense of fair play and civic mindedness.

Bruno Frey and Felix Oberholzer-Gee at the University of Zürich look at people's responses to what are called NIMBY (Not in My Backyard) problems. This refers to a community's willingness, or lack thereof, to accept the location of noxious or undesirable facilities (such as nuclear power plants, prisons, airports, electrical pylons, chemical factories, etc.) in their neighbourhoods. One response by governmental agencies in such cases is to offer financial compensation to communities in return for their willingness to accept such facilities. Frey and Oberholzer-Gee argue that, in some cases, offering an external incentive, such as monetary payments, may actually be counter-productive because such incentives partially destroy or *crowd out* any intrinsic motivation that the community may have felt in accepting the facility. Consequently, such monetary incentives may become less effective, and in some instances may lead to a *lower* willingness to accept the facility in question. If a person derives intrinsic benefits by behaving in an altruistic manner or doing his/her civic duty, then paying him/her for this service may reduce his/her intrinsic motivation to do so.[2]

Frey and Oberholzer-Gee conjecture that if local residents perceive it as their civic duty to accept a NIMBY project, introducing monetary compensation may reduce support for the noxious facility. In early 1993, the researchers hired a professional survey institute to approach 305 residents of two communities in central Switzerland to inquire about their willingness to accept the placement of a nuclear waste repository in their locality. The first question asked of all respondents was:

> Suppose that the National Cooperative for the Storage of Nuclear Waste (NAGRA), after completing exploratory drilling, proposes to build the repository for low- and mid-level radioactive waste in your hometown. Federal experts examine this proposition, and the federal parliament decides to build the repository in your community. In a town hall meeting, do you accept this proposition, or do you reject this proposition?

Fifty-one per cent of respondents said that they would vote in favour of having the nuclear waste repository in their community, 45% opposed the facility, while 4% did not care.

Next, the researchers repeated the exact same question, asking the respondents whether they would be willing to accept the construction of a nuclear waste repository if the Swiss Parliament offered to compensate all the residents of the community that accepted the nuclear storage facility. The initial amounts offered to respondents were (i) $2,175 per individual per year or (ii) $4,350 per individual per year or (iii) $6,525 per individual per year. Surprisingly, while 51% of the respondents agreed to accept the nuclear waste repository when no compensation was offered, the level of acceptance *dropped* to 25% when compensation was offered. However, the exact amount of the compensation did not appear to have a significant effect on people's acceptance levels. Everyone who rejected the first compensation was then made a better offer, thereby raising the amount of compensation from $2,175 to $3,263, from $4,350 to $6,525, and from $6,525 to $8,700. Despite this marked increase, only a single respondent who declined the first compensation was now prepared to accept the higher offer.

To further test the crowding-out effect, Frey and Oberholzer-Gee conducted an identical survey in six communities in north-eastern Switzerland designated as potential sites for a second Swiss repository, a facility for long-lived, highly radioactive wastes. Two hundred and six interviews were conducted in these communities using procedures identical to the first survey. Here, 41% of respondents stated that they would vote for the high-level radioactive waste facility, 56% would have voted against it, and 3% did not care. When community members were offered compensation, the level of acceptance *dropped* to 27%. As before, offering higher amounts did not lead to significant changes in the level of support. These findings are not unique to Switzerland. Howard Kunreuther (of the Wharton School at the University of Pennsylvania) and Douglas Easterling (of Wake Forest) have undertaken significant work in this area along with other collaborators. Their group carries out a survey regarding the location of a nuclear waste facility in Nevada, USA and find that increased tax rebates failed to elicit increased support for such a facility. Other researchers have reported similar findings: that support for noxious facilities often decline when people are offered compensation.

One possibility as to why citizens' acceptance levels decline when offered compensation is that the offer of a generous compensation might be taken as an indication that the facility is more hazardous than they previously thought. A higher compensation then might indicate higher risk associated with the facility, which in turn leads to a lower level of acceptance. Frey and Oberholzer-Gee test this by directly asking respondents whether they perceived a link between the size of the compensation and the level of risk. Only 6% agreed with this connection, which indicates that it is not the perception of higher risk with higher compensation that is driving these responses.

Frey and Oberholzer-Gee conclude by commenting

> where public spirit prevails, using price incentives to muster support for the construction of a socially desirable, but locally unwanted, facility comes at a higher price than suggested by standard economic theory because these incentives tend to crowd out civic duty. ... These conclusions are of general relevance for economic theory and policy because they identify a particular limit of monetary compensation to rally support for a socially desired enterprise. The relative price effect of monetary compensation is not questioned in any way, but this measure becomes less effective when crowding-out is considered.

INTRINSIC MOTIVATIONS, SUSTAINABILITY AND CLIMATE CHANGE

While Frey and Oberholzer-Gee use surveys, Juan Camilo Cardenas (of the Universidad Javeriana) and John Stranlund and Cleve Willis (of the University of Massachusetts, Amherst) provide experimental evidence of the same phenomenon. Cardenas and his colleagues carry out their experiments in the three rural villages of Circasia, Encino and Finlandia in Colombia. Of these, Encino is located in the eastern Andean region while Circasia and Finlandia are located in the Quindio coffee region of the mid Andes. These locations were chosen because they each have predominantly rural populations with significant interest in local natural resources and environmental quality. Their experiments are designed to approximate an environmental quality problem that villagers in developing countries routinely face.

Specifically, participants were asked to decide how much time they would spend collecting firewood from a surrounding forest, given that the collection of firewood has an adverse effect on the water quality of the region due to soil erosion. Next, the researchers confront their participants with a government-imposed quota on the amount of time that can be spent collecting firewood. The quota, however, is enforced imperfectly, in the sense that there is only a small chance that someone exceeding the quota would be detected and punished, which is typical of such command-and-control environmental problems in rural areas of less developed countries. Thus, the participants are essentially confronted by a social dilemma which is very similar to the ones that they face in their day-to-day lives. What Cardenas and his colleagues find is that the outcome, in terms of time spent collecting firewood, was *worse* in the presence of the imperfectly enforced government-imposed regulation, because, when confronted with the external regulation, the behaviour of the participants became significantly more self-interested, while, in the absence of any regulatory control, their choices were more group-orientated.

Cardenas and his colleagues have their participants take part in two treatments of their experiments whose design is very similar to the public goods (or social dilemma) games that I talked about earlier. One hundred and twelve participants are divided into 14 groups with eight members in each group. All groups play a number of initial rounds of the game without any regulation and without being able to engage in any communication with fellow group members. Seventy-two of those 112 participants (nine groups) then play additional rounds of the game in which they are allowed to communicate with their group members between each round. The remaining 40 participants (five groups) go on to play additional rounds, where they do not have any communication opportunities but instead face a regulation, which stipulates that they should not spend more than a particular amount of time collecting firewood. They are told that once each group member had made a choice regarding how much time to spend in this activity, there was a small chance that one group member would be selected for an audit to verify compliance with the rule. Specifically, after each group member had decided, a die would be rolled and an audit would take place only if an even number, that is, two, four or six, came up. If an audit was to take place, then a number between one and eight would be drawn from a hat to indicate which particular member out of the eight group members would be audited. There was thus a 1/16 (approximately 6%) chance of being detected and penalized in the event of non-compliance.

Cardenas and his colleagues find that when participants do not face any external restrictions and cannot communicate with each other, their decisions tend to be neither purely self-interested nor commensurate with what would maximize the group interest. This is in keeping with other studies that look at behaviour in social dilemmas. When there is no regulation, but participants are allowed to communicate with group members between rounds, individuals make more efficient choices, that is, choices that generate more social welfare. But, surprisingly, regulatory control caused subjects to tend, on average, to make choices that were much more self-interested than in the other two cases. Consequently, average individual earnings under regulation were lower than in the absence of such regulation, and much lower than the earnings of those subjects who were simply allowed to communicate with each other, in spite of the fact that the regulatory institution was designed to induce more efficient choices.

Cardenas, Stranlund and Willis conclude:

Economic theory will be a poor guide for designing environmental policies if it does not allow for other-regarding motivations, or if it fails to recognize that these motivations are not fixed with respect to institutional arrangements. Recognizing ... the balance between self-interested and group-regarding behaviour when it occurs will have profound implications for nearly every aspect of environmental policy design and evaluation.

Once again, the above suggests that there is considerable experimental, as well as survey-based, evidence that external incentives may crowd out intrinsic motivations and, therefore, may be detrimental to successful collective action. Does this work in real life? Elinor Ostrom[3] and her colleagues associated with the "Workshop in Political Theory and Policy Analysis" at Indiana University have collected thousands of written cases about resources managed by local users of fisheries, irrigation systems and grazing lands. In Nepal, they have collected data about the rules and general management strategies used to manage over 200 irrigation systems. Some of these are managed by government agencies (agency managed irrigation systems or AMIS) while some are managed by the farmers (farmer managed irrigation systems or FMIS). Ostrom and her colleagues find that compared to AMIS, FMIS are able to achieve a higher agricultural yield, more equitable distribution of water and better maintenance of the irrigation systems. There are striking differences in the way the two systems are managed. Under AMIS, infractions are recorded by government officials, while under FMIS, they are recorded by the farmer monitors. Furthermore, the AMIS tend to rely more on fines for infractions than the FMIS do. Rules and quotas are followed 65% of the time in FMIS compared to only 35% of the time in AMIS. Thus, rules and sanctions designed by the farmers themselves tend to be more effective than those imposed by government officials.

EXTRINSIC INCENTIVES AND CROWDING OUT OF INTRINSIC MOTIVATIONS

A fascinating example of the detrimental effects of external intervention comes from Uri Gneezy and Aldo Rustichini's study of ten private day-care centres in Haifa, Israel. The day-care centres are all located in the same part of town and there are no obvious locational or other differences among them. The owner of the day-care also acts as the principal. These day-care centres operate between 7:30 a.m. and 4:00 p.m. during weekdays. If a parent does not pick up his or her child by 4:00 p.m. then a teacher has to stay back with the child. This is inconvenient for the teacher, who does not get any additional financial remuneration for staying beyond the usual operating hours. Teachers typically rotate this task, which is considered part of their duties, a fact that is clearly explained at the time a teacher is hired.

Gneezy and Rustichini had their research assistants approach the principal of each of these ten day-care centres. The principals were requested to participate in an academic study about the influence of fines. Each principal was promised that, at the end of the study, he/she would receive coupons with a value of 500 Israeli new shekels (ILS) for buying books.[4] The study lasted 20 weeks between January and June 1998. In the first four weeks, Gneezy and Rustichini simply recorded the number of parents who arrived late each week. At the beginning of the fifth week, they introduced a fine in six of the ten day-care centres. The announcement of the fine was made with a note posted on the day-care centre's bulletin board, which is usually the means via which important information and announcements are conveyed to the parents. The announcement specified that the fine would be 10 shekels for a delay of 10 minutes or more. The fine was per child. Thus, if a parent had two children in the centre and arrived late to pick them up, then that parent had to pay 20 shekels. These fines would be added to the usual monthly payments made by the parents. At the beginning of the 17th week, the fine was removed with no explanation. Notice of the cancellation was posted on the same bulletin board. If parents asked about the removal of the fine, the principals were instructed to inform them that the fine had been a trial for a limited time and that the results of this trial were being evaluated.

Figure 10.4 indicates the rather dramatic impact of the fine. The solid line with stars shows the average number of parents coming late per week, before and after the introduction of the fine, at the six day-care centres where the fine was introduced. The broken line with

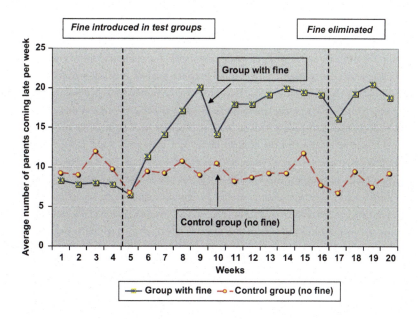

Figure 10.4 Impact of fines in the day-care centres. Re-created on the basis of data in Gneezy and Rustichini (2000a)

circles shows the average number of parents coming late per week at the remaining four day-care centres where no fines were in place.

Two things are obvious from this figure. (1) In the six day-care centres where the fine is introduced, there is a dramatic *increase* in the number of parents arriving late in the first three–four weeks after the fine is put in place. The rate finally settled at around 20 late arrivals per week, a level that was higher than, and about twice as large, as the initial one. There is no noticeable change in the number of parents arriving late at the other four day-care centres where no fine is imposed. (2) In the six day-care centres where the fine is introduced, the number of parents arriving late continues to be high and remains considerably above their pre-fine levels *even after the fine is withdrawn* at the beginning of the 17th week.

Thus, the introduction of an explicit incentive in the form of a fine imposed on parents arriving late seems to have exacerbated the problem of late arrivals rather than alleviating the problem. How can we explain this rather counter-intuitive phenomenon? Here is how Gneezy and Rustichini interpret the behaviour of the parents. Prior to the introduction of the fine, parents probably regarded the action of a teacher who stayed behind with a child as an act of generosity.

They may have thought: "The contract with the day-care centre only covers the period until four in the afternoon. After that time, the teacher is just a nice and generous person. I should not take advantage of her patience." The introduction of the fine changes the perception into the following: "The teacher is taking care of the child in much the same way as she did earlier in the day. In fact this activity has a price (which is called a 'fine'). Therefore, I can buy this service as much as needed." Parents feel justified in their behavior by a social norm that states, approximately: "When help is offered for no compensation in a moment of need, accept it with restraint. When a service is offered for a price, buy as much as you find convenient." No guilt or shame … can be attached to the act of buying a commodity at will.

Further experimental evidence about the downside of external incentives comes from the work of Ernst Fehr and Bettina Rockenbach. Fehr and Rockenbach had 238 participants take part in the Berg–Dickhaut–McCabe investment game. The sender and the receiver have $10 each. The sender can send any or all of this $10 to the receiver. Any amount sent to the receiver is *tripled* by the experimenter. The receiver is then given the option of keeping all the money given to him/her or sending some back to the sender. The game ends at that point.

Fehr and Rockenbach look at two treatments. The first treatment is the *trust* treatment; this is almost identical to the original investment game and works mostly in the way described above, except that, if the sender does transfer any money to the receiver, then the sender is asked to specify a "back-transfer"; that is, the sender is asked to specify an amount he/she would like the receiver to return. For instance, suppose the sender sends $5. In that case the receiver would be given $15. Then the sender can specify a back-transfer of any amount between $0 and $15 (that is, any amount less than or equal to the maximum amount received by the receiver). In the trust treatment, the receiver is under no compulsion to adhere to this desired back-transfer and can return any amount, which can be less than what the sender asked for.

The second treatment is the *incentive* treatment. This is similar to the trust treatment except, here, in addition to specifying a desired back-transfer, the sender can also *choose* to impose a fine of $4 on the receiver if the receiver returns an amount which is less than what the sender asked for. However, the sender can decide *not* to impose the fine, even though the option is there.

Fehr and Rockenbach find, in keeping with prior studies, that senders choose to trust the receivers and transfer non-trivial amounts and receivers reciprocate that trust by returning money. But, surprisingly, across all transfers by the sender, the receivers return *more* money when the sender had the option of imposing a fine but chose not to do so, and the receivers return *much less* when the sender imposes the fine at the outset. On average, the receivers return 41% of the tripled amount received in the trust treatment (where no fine is available to the sender), 30% of the tripled amount in the incentive treatment where the sender chooses to impose the fine and 48% of the tripled amount in the case where the sender could have imposed the fine but chose *not* to do so.

If we look at the amount of money returned by the receivers as a proportion of the back-transfer that the sender specified, then we find that, on average, the receivers return 74% of the desired back-transfer in the trust treatment (where no fine is available to the sender), 55% of the desired back-transfer in the incentive treatment where the sender chooses to impose the fine and 74% of the desired back-transfer in the case where the sender could have imposed the fine but chose *not* to do so.

TRUST AND GROWTH

In previous chapters, I have discussed how mutual trust and reciprocity among members of a community can create social connections that might enable those communities to achieve successful collective action which would be difficult to attain in the absence of such social ties. The all-encompassing phrase that is often attached to such social networks based on mutual trust and reciprocity among citizens is *social capital*. Traditionally, economists have tended to emphasize the importance of physical and human capital as prerequisites for successful economic development.[5] But more and more economists are beginning to realize that such intangible things as the degree of trust exhibited by a country's citizenry – trust in their governments, in the country's legal and political institutions, indeed, trust among themselves – also play a crucial role. In fact, in the absence of such mutual trust and reciprocity, economic development may falter, even with adequate supplies of physical and human capital.

Stephen Knack and Phillip Keefer of the World Bank and Paul Zak of Claremont Graduate University have undertaken extensive work looking at the relationship between a country's level of trust and that country's economic performance for 29 market based economies surveyed during the early 1980s and the early 1990s.[6] They report that social capital matters for economic performance. These researchers focus on the role of trust and that of civic cooperation among citizens. The question used to assess the level of trust in a society is: "Generally speaking, would you say that most people can be trusted, or that you can't be too careful in dealing with people?" They use as their indicator of trust, the percentage of people in each country who say that "people can be trusted".

To get a measure regarding norms of civic cooperation, they use responses to questions about whether each of the following behaviours "can always be justified, never be justified or something in between": (1) claiming government benefits which someone is not entitled to; (2) avoiding a fare on public transport; (3) cheating on taxes given the chance; (4) keeping money that someone has found; and finally, (5) failing to report damage one has done accidentally to a parked car. Suppose respondents answer these five questions by choosing numbers on a numeric scale such as 1 (always justifiable) to 10 (never justifiable). These numerical responses can then be used to construct a quantitative measure of the degree of civic cooperation which exists in that society, with higher numbers (closer to 10) indicating greater degrees of civic cooperation.

For the 29 countries mentioned above, Knack and his colleagues look at the relationship between rates of growth in per capita income on the one hand and their measures of trust and civic cooperation on the other. They find that trust and norms of civic cooperation have a strong influence on the rates of growth of per capita income. Countries whose citizens exhibit higher levels of trust and civic cooperation experience faster economic growth, and this effect of trust and cooperation on growth is more pronounced for less developed countries than for more developed countries.

Knack and his colleagues explain their findings by suggesting that this is mostly because individuals in higher-trust societies spend less to protect themselves from being exploited in economic transactions. Written contracts are less likely to be needed and litigation may be less frequent. Individuals in high-trust societies are also likely to divert fewer resources to protecting themselves – through arbitrary tax payments, bribes, or private security services and equipment – from unlawful or criminal violations of their property.

Low trust can also discourage investments and innovation. If entrepreneurs must devote more time to monitoring possible malfeasance, they have less time to devote to innovations in new products and processes. Societies characterized by high levels of trust are also less dependent on formal institutions to enforce agreements. Thus, informal credit markets based on strong interpersonal trust (such as the one implemented by the Grameen Bank) can facilitate investments in situations where bank loans are unavailable. Government officials in higher-trust societies are perceived as more trustworthy and their policy pronouncements as more credible. This, in turn, often triggers greater investment and other economic activities. Finally, trusting societies not only have stronger incentives to innovate and to accumulate capital, investments in citizens' health, education and welfare are more likely to yield higher returns in these countries.

CONCLUDING REMARKS

In the preceding pages, I have provided evidence that social norms and such norm driven behaviour, as embodied in the decision to trust strangers and to reciprocate others' trust (often collectively referred to as social capital), have a profound influence across a wide range of economic transactions. Such norms have enormous ramifications, including an impact on the growth and development of societies as a whole.

I have argued that, contrary to the usually held view in economics that eliciting effort for workers requires explicit carrot and sticks, similar goals may be achieved on the basis of mutual trust and reciprocity between workers and employers. In many cases, this has implications for worker turnover and profitability of organizations. One immediate outcome of the reliance on the pure self-interest model of human behaviour is the emphasis on the use of explicit/extrinsic motivations in employment contracts. As I have argued above, and as Bruno Frey of the University of Zürich points out in his book, *Not Just for the Money*, there are many cases where such explicit carrots and sticks are useful, and indeed necessary, to elicit effort from workers or ensure compliance with the desired course of action. But in many cases – and I have identified quite a few above, including Frey's own results on the location of noxious facilities – this reliance on explicit incentives can be counter-productive and detrimental because they crowd out intrinsic motivations and one's latent desire to do the right thing even without any financial incentives to do so. It is important to bear in mind the results of this line of research when designing economic policies, because ignoring them may lead to large welfare losses.

I will end with yet another Covid-19 story. In mid-2020, as part of its ongoing effort to prevent community transmission, the New Zealand government decided that all arrivals to New Zealand will be required to spend 14 days in quarantine. As the costs of such quarantine mounted, the government decided that all returnees, which were almost exclusively New Zealand citizens living overseas, will have to pay for the cost of their own quarantine. This was controversial, both legally and morally, since the right to return to one's homeland is part of the compact between a state and its citizens. Tensions heightened when some returnees breached quarantine. In one case, a woman who broke out of quarantine to attend her father's funeral was sentenced to two weeks in prison! Of course, when this happened, everyone focused their attention on the few rule breakers rather than the thousands who willingly complied.

Based on the evidence presented above, I argued in print and electronic media that a more efficacious policy would have been to ask people to self-isolate for two weeks as was required during the early part of the pandemic. Like Scandinavian countries, New Zealand is a high trust society and most people would have willingly self-isolated when asked to do so.

The government could always reserve the right to prosecute those who violated this via contact tracing and other means as was being done by the government of Taiwan. As Cardenas and his colleagues argue above, people are much more likely to behave in a group-minded way when we appeal to their goodwill. But forcing compliance on the basis of punishments makes people more self-regarding and can be counter-productive. The evidence presented in this chapter and the previous one suggests that this model of humanity based on mutual trust and reciprocity (particularly in societies that display high levels of social capital) actually yields better outcomes than one which proceeds to implement policy on the basis of general mistrust. Unfortunately, my arguments fell on deaf ears. But my hope is that those of you who read this and find this evidence compelling will take a more nuanced view when designing policy in the future.

NOTES

1 By this measure, top professional athletes receive a large amount of rent because there is a large difference between the amounts they actually earn and what they could potentially have earned in another occupation if they had failed to reach the top of their respective fields. The top 50 or even the top 100 tennis players in the world earn a lot (many of this coming from appearance fees in smaller tournaments around the world, even in the absence of actual tournament wins). But for those beyond the top 100, earnings tend to be meagre. The same is possibly true for CEOs, who make significantly more than the second in command. One explanation of this is that these are tournaments and the prize for winning is large enough in order to motivate everyone to work hard in order to achieve that ultimate prize.
2 In the early 1970s, Richard Titmuss claimed that while a lot of people are willing to donate blood voluntarily, paying people to donate blood actually leads to reduced blood donation. Many voluntary donors are turned off by such payments since these payments (possibly) reduce the donor's option of indulging in the "warm-glow" of altruistic feelings. When an external motivation is seen to be controlling, it might destroy or reduce an internal motivation to do something out of a sense of altruism.
3 Elinor Ostrom was the first woman to receive the Nobel Prize in Economics in 2009. She passed away in 2012.
4 At the time of this study during the first half of 1998, one US dollar was approximately equal to 3.7 shekels.
5 The phrase "physical capital" refers to investments in entities such as machines, factories and infrastructure, such as roads, bridges and highways. "Human capital" refers to investments in health, education and skills of citizens.
6 The countries included are Argentina, Australia, Austria, Belgium, Brazil, Canada, Chile, Denmark, Finland, France, Germany, Iceland, India, Ireland, Italy, Japan, Mexico, the Netherlands, Nigeria, Norway, Portugal, South Africa, South Korea, Spain, Sweden, Switzerland, Turkey, the United Kingdom and the United States of America.

11 Cooperation in social dilemmas

In this chapter, I:

- *Introduce the public goods game, at times referred to as a voluntary contributions mechanism, as a model for problems of collective action;*
- *Show that people are more cooperative than would be suggested by models based on self-interest and, therefore, people are much better at solving collective action problems than we would think;*
- *Demonstrate that, confronted with a collective action problem, often called a social dilemma, the behaviour of a plurality (if not a majority) of people depends crucially on their beliefs about other members of the group; if people believe that others would cooperate, they do so too;*
- *Explain that while social dilemma problems are essentially prisoners' dilemma games, albeit with multiple players, it is possible to transform this to a stag-hunt type coordination problem, where everyone cooperating can be a perfectly rationalizable Nash equilibrium.*

AN EXAMPLE OF A SOCIAL DILEMMA

Close to where I live in the city of Auckland is a playground for small children called "Little Rangitoto Reserve". When my daughters were little, we used to go there often. From what I understand, the equipment in this playground – the slides, the swings, the jungle gym and the monkey-bars – were not provided by the Auckland City Council but were, rather, bought by local residents on the basis of voluntary contributions. On the face of it, this is probably not surprising to any of you, since you may have experience with similar such ventures or others which rely on voluntary charitable contributions for a good cause. It happens all the time and, as a result, we tend to forget that this is actually quite an accomplishment.

I alluded to this park example back in Chapter 6 on strategic thinking. But it has been a while and so, let me go ahead and explain this once more. Suppose you want to build a similar public park in your neighbourhood and you decide to approach local households for a certain contribution. Not everyone in the neighbourhood has to contribute for the park to be built. As long as some of the families contribute, you will have enough money for the park. What are the chances that you will be able to raise enough money? The chances are actually good, but there is an inherent social dilemma here. For the time being, suppose (as economists often tend to do) that, by and large, people are self-interested and care (mostly) about their own welfare. It is obvious that if everyone does chip in with a contribution then the park will be built and everyone in the neighbourhood can take their children there. Collectively then, we will all be better off if everyone cooperated.

But let us think for a minute about an individual (who cares primarily about his/her own well-being and those of his/her close ones) trying to decide whether to contribute or not. Suppose he/she does not contribute any money to the pot and the park is not built. Then he/she is not better off but he/she is not worse off either, since there was no park there before and there will not be one in the future. But suppose he/she does not contribute, but enough money is raised to build the park. Now a park is quite different from (say) a health club because, once the park is built, it is extremely difficult to keep anyone out regardless of whether he/she has paid or not. Typically, you cannot really have a membership for a public park. So, even if someone has not paid, this person cannot be prevented from going to the park once it is built. Thus, he/she has not contributed anything but still gets to enjoy a walk in the park with his/her child or his/her dog. This person is then better off, since he/she has not paid anything out of his/her own pocket but still gets to enjoy the open air of the park and the verdant surroundings. Whether the park is built or not – for an individual who cares primarily about his/her own self-interest – the practical course of action is to not contribute any money.

If you recall our discussion on strategic thinking from Chapter 6, you will quickly realize that this situation is essentially the same as a prisoners' dilemma game. Everyone is collectively better off if everyone contributes (and the park is built), but, from a purely individualistic and self-interested point of view, it is rational to withhold contribution. If the park is not built, then you are no worse off, but if it is built, then you are better off. But if everyone thought this way, then no one contributes and nothing is accomplished. Economists refer to this type of behaviour as *free-riding* – taking advantage of other people's contributions. This is the same story that we discussed in Chapter 6 regarding the behaviour of Yossarian, who never helped in building the officers' club but went there often once it was built.

Economists refer to a public park as a *public good*. A public good is one whose consumption is *non-rival* and *non-excludable*. A good is non-rival in consumption when the use of the good by one individual does not prevent other individuals from using (consuming) the same good. Non-excludable means that once the good (the park) is provided, no one can be excluded from the consumption of the good, even if that person did not pay for its provision.

Examples of public goods include: clean environment, national defence, the police, the fire service, highways, public parks, public libraries, public hospitals and so on. Of course, some of these are more excludable than others. No one can be prevented from enjoying the benefits of clean air. Similarly, if the army goes to war, it does so for every citizen, regardless of who paid their taxes or not. If your house is on fire, the firemen will show up and fight the fire without asking whether your taxes are up-to-date or whether you contributed when they held a bake sale at the fire station last month. But the more drivers there are on the highway to the beach on a sunny summer weekend, the slower the progress. Some people might look at the traffic and decide not to go out at all. In this case, the ones who decide to stay home are excluded at the expense of those who are on the road. Thus, highways are more excludable and, in one sense, less of a public good than the environment.

So, the question we are interested in answering is: what motivates people? Who contributes? Who does not? Why do the ones who contribute, do so, and those who do not, do

■ Cooperation in social dilemmas

not? Because what we are essentially dealing with here are people's in-built preferences and their beliefs; naturally occurring field data is of not much benefit to us since they do not really allow us to peer inside people's minds. We could certainly use survey questionnaires. We could ask people what motivated them to undertake a particular action. But the problem is that there is no guarantee that they would give you truthful responses. Someone who did not contribute when nobody could see that decision might very easily feel embarrassed to admit that in public.

Economists studying this problem designed an excellent game which simulates this decision-making situation. This is how the game goes. A group of four participants are gathered in a room. They are each given a sum of money (say $5) and they are told that each member of the group can allocate this money between a private account and a public account. Money allocated to the private account remains unchanged and is theirs for good. However, any amount contributed to the public account is multiplied by a factor greater than 1 (say 2) by the experimenter. This multiplied amount is then distributed equally between the four group members. Thus, any contribution made by an individual to the public account generates a positive externality in the sense that it yields a return to other members of the group who may not have contributed anything to the public account. Figure 11.1 provides details of this game.

The socially optimal (or socially desirable) outcome in this game is for every player to contribute their entire amount to the public account. In this case, total contributions to the public account amount to $20, which, given a multiplier of 2, is doubled to $40 by the experimenter. Redistributed equally among the group members, this nets each person $10. Each member then gets a 100% return on his/her initial investment. However, individual rationality suggests a different course of action. Think about an individual player trying to decide how much to contribute. If this individual contributes $1 and no one else contributes anything, then the $1 is doubled to $2. Distributed equally between the four players, this gives each player $0.50. The player who contributed is worse off (incurs a 50% loss on

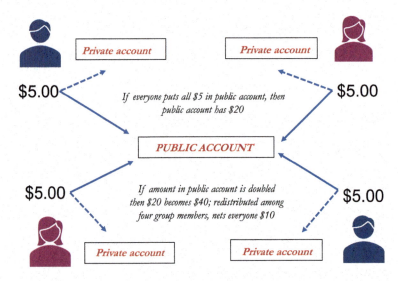

Figure 11.1
Structure of the public goods game

his/her investment) while every other player is better off at the expense of the player who contributed. Thus, if a player does not contribute, then he/she is no worse off if no one else contributes, but he/she is actually better off if some others contribute. This tension between contributing to the public good and free-riding on others' contributions poses a *social dilemma* which has been studied extensively by both economists and psychologists.[1]

John Ledyard of Caltech, who has done extensive work in the area, points out that some of the most fundamental questions about the organization of society centre around the issues raised by the presence of public goods and the consequent social dilemma posed above. How well do current political institutions perform in the production and funding of public goods? How far can volunteerism take us in attempts to provide efficient levels of public goods? At a more basic level, contributions to public goods raise fundamental questions about whether people are generally selfish or cooperative.

Economic theory, based on the assumption of a rational *homo economicus*, suggests that, faced with a situation like this, every rational self-interested player will engage in strong free-riding behaviour by not contributing any money to the public pool at all, just like Yossarian in *Catch-22*. But now we have access to economic experiments and can see what people do when confronted with this particular situation.

A lot of the early work in this area was undertaken by Mark Isaac at the University of Arizona, James Walker at Indiana and Charles Plott at Caltech, along with their collaborators Arlington Williams, Susan Thomas, Oliver Kim and Kenneth McCue. These researchers found that if you get a group of people together – they could be perfect strangers, friends or acquaintances – there is a remarkable regularity to behaviour. Total contributions to the public pool always tend to be between 40% and 60% of the maximum possible. That is, if the maximum total contribution is $20, then contributions usually average between $8 and $12. This does not imply that every group member contributes between 40% and 60%. Rather, some contribute 100% while others contribute nothing. And this behaviour seems to be robust in the sense that the behaviour is remarkably similar across various countries and cultures.

What happens if you had the same group of people play the game more than once, that is, suppose you asked them to continue playing for ten rounds? In each round they have a sum of money (say $2) and they have to make the decision regarding how much to contribute to the public account over those ten rounds. (So that, if they simply held on to the $2 in each round, they would end up making $20.) What happens in that case is shown in Figure 11.2. Contributions typically start between 40% and 60% and then decline over time with the average contribution falling lower and lower, though the contributions never reach zero even if people play for as many as 50 or 60 rounds. Some people contribute nothing and free-ride for the entire time, while others start by contributing a lot (100% or close to it) and then reduce their contribution over time.

There are a number of puzzles here. Why do some people contribute, while others do not? Why do some people cooperate at the beginning and free-ride later? If they are going to free-ride, why do they not start to do so immediately? We have already argued that free-riding is the self-interested course of action in this game. So, maybe that is easier to understand – why people free-ride. They are self-interested and wish to maximize their own monetary gains at the expense of others. But what can we say about those participants who

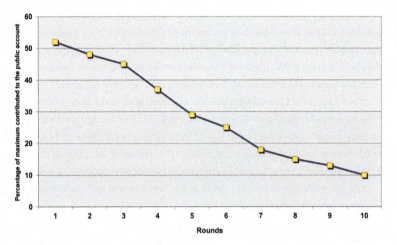

Figure 11.2 Pattern of decaying contributions in public goods games

contribute a lot? Are they being purely altruistic? That is, do they contribute because they care about the welfare of others? The easy way out would be to say: why is this surprising? Of course, there are different types of people in the world. Some of us are generous and care more about cooperating with others while some of us care less (like the Cyclopes in *The Odyssey*):

> And we come to the land of the Cyclopes, a fierce, lawless people who never lift a hand to plant or plough but just leave everything to the immortal gods. ... The Cyclopes have no assemblies for the making of laws, nor any established legal codes, but live in hollow caverns in the mountain heights, where each man is a lawgiver to his own children and women, and nobody has the slightest interest in what his neighbour decides.

ARE SMALLER GROUPS BETTER AT ADDRESSING COLLECTIVE ACTION PROBLEMS?

Before we start to look for explanations for the pattern of decaying contributions, let us address another issue that often comes up. Intuitively, at least, it appears that problems of collective action should be exacerbated as the group size grows larger. Surely, if sustaining cooperation is difficult in this game with two or four people, it will become even harder with more people. Mark Isaac of Arizona and Jimmy Walker of Indiana look at this issue and the answer turns out to be negative; larger groups are not less cooperative than smaller ones. Before I discuss the findings of Isaac and Walker, I need to explain what is meant by the *marginal per capita return* (MPCR) in a public goods game, since this will play a major role in the results to be discussed.

Think about the public goods game with four people discussed earlier in the chapter. If and when a participant puts $1 into the public account and no one else puts in anything, the $1 is doubled to $2. When this $2 is redistributed among the four group members, each member receives $0.50. So, effectively, the participant who put in the dollar gets $0.50 back. This amount, 0.50, is defined as the marginal per capita return. The idea is that if the MPCR is 0.5, then if and when someone puts in a dollar and no one else does, the person contributing can expect to make $0.50 per dollar contributed. If there are five group members and each dollar is doubled and redistributed, then the per capita return will be 0.40 ($2/5). If there are ten group members, then the per capita return will be 0.20 ($2/10) and so on. On the other hand, if there are four group members but each dollar contributed is multiplied by three, then the marginal per capita return is 0.75 ($3/4).

The point is this: pure self-interest suggests that group members should contribute nothing to the group account; however, clearly this is not what happens; most people contribute something. Below, we will see that a crucial feature in deciding whether to contribute or not is the beliefs that people possess about their group members. But assuming that each player has some expectation that others will contribute something rather than engaging in complete free-riding, each player is more likely to contribute when the MPCR is high than when it is low. For instance, if the MPCR is only 0.20 (where there are ten group members and contributions are multiplied by 2), then a group member will be less likely to contribute than if the MPCR is 0.80 (where there are ten group members also but contributions are multiplied by 8). In the first case, if no one else contributes, then the contributor will get back $0.20 on the dollar and experience a loss of $0.80 per dollar contributed, while in the second case, the loss is only $0.20 per dollar contributed. In general, then, if there are n members in a group and each dollar contributed is multiplied by m, then the MPCR = m/n.

Isaac and Walker looked at two issues: first, are contributions higher or lower when the MPCR goes up? I have argued immediately above that we expect a higher MPCR to lead to higher contributions. Second, are contributions higher in small groups as opposed to larger groups? In order to look at this, Isaac and Walker use two different values of the MPCR, 0.3 and 0.75, and they look at two different group sizes, groups of four and groups of ten. This leads to a 2 × 2 design. Table 11.1 explains that 4 and 10 refer to the respective group sizes while L or H refer to the MPCR, 0.30 or 0.75. Comparing 4L with 4H tells us what happens to levels of cooperation when the group size is small but the MPCR is increased from 0.3 to 0.75. Comparing 10L and 10H tells us the effect of increasing the MPCR when the group size is large. Similarly, comparing 4L and 10L tells us what happens when the group size increases while the MPCR is held constant at the low value of 0.3. Finally, the 4H and 10H comparison tells us the effect of increasing group size when the MPCR is held constant at the high value of 0.75.

Figure 11.3 shows the results. Not surprisingly, and in keeping with prior findings, contributions decay over time in all treatments. Also, possibly not surprisingly, contributions are higher with MPCR of 0.75 as opposed to MPCR of 0.3. This is true of both groups of four (shown with solid black lines) and ten (dashed black lines). Both groups are more cooperative at a higher value of MPCR. What is possibly surprising is the effect of group size. It is clear that larger groups are no less cooperative than smaller ones. When the MPCR is high (0.75),

Table 11.1 Interaction of group size and MPCR in Isaac and Walker (1988b)

	Group size = 4	*Group size = 10*
MPCR = 0.3	Treatment 4L	Treatment 10L
MPCR = 0.75	Treatment 4H	Treatment 10H

■ Cooperation in social dilemmas

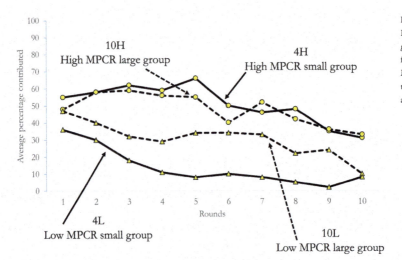

Figure 11.3
Results from the public goods game with different group sizes and MPCRs. Re-created on the basis of data in Isaac and Walker (1988b)

groups of ten seem to be as cooperative as groups of four. But when the MPCR is low, groups of ten appear to be more cooperative than groups of four.[2]

Why is it that larger groups are not less cooperative? We would normally expect that as groups become larger, it would be easier to free-ride because free-riders may be noticed less. But equally, when groups become large, the degree of monitoring of members is also higher. When there are four members in the group, there are three pairs of eyes watching you, while, with ten members, one is being watched by nine pairs of eyes. It is possibly this priming effect of being watched by more people if one is caught free-riding that leads to lower free-riding in larger groups. Indeed, there is a literature in network architecture that suggests this to be the case. In the set-ups we have discussed, the network is complete, in the sense that each player can observe and, in turn, be observed by, every other player. Instead, one can have incomplete networks, where, say, players are arranged in a circle and each player can observe and be observed by only their two immediate neighbours. Evidence suggests that the level of cooperation goes down in such incomplete networks where the degree of monitoring of each player's actions is lower. There is a large literature on such network architecture. I will briefly discuss aspects of this in the next chapter.

ARE CONTRIBUTIONS CAUSED BY CONFUSION ON THE PART OF THE PARTICIPANTS?

The pattern of decaying contributions shown in Figure 11.2 needs answers to two questions: first, why do the contributions decay over time? If people wish to free-ride, why don't they start from the very beginning? If they wish to cooperate, why don't they keep cooperating over time? Given that this decay phenomenon has been replicated in numerous experiments with different parameters and subject pools, it seems quite robust. Most groups have a hard time sustaining cooperation over time. This leads to the second question: what kinds of interventions would it take to sustain cooperation over time? I address the first of these questions in this chapter. I will discuss the second in Chapter 12.

One possible explanation for why these contributions decay over time is this: when you bring participants into a laboratory and ask them to play this game for money, the situation confronting those participants is relatively novel. The instructions they are given are often phrased in abstract terms and do not use emotive terms such as contributing to charity. Thus, it might take people some time to understand what real-life situation this game corresponds to. People might contribute in the beginning before they really understand the incentive structure of the game, but, as comprehension dawns, they realize that the rational thing to do would be to free-ride and they start to do so, which leads to the resulting decay in the contributions to the public account. Different people may come to this realization at different times, which explains the slow decay in contributions rather than a sudden swift drop. We will call this the *learning* hypothesis, that is, participants do not figure out that they should free-ride straight off the bat, but "learn" to do so over time as they gain familiarity with the situation.

A group of economic theorists – David Kreps, Paul Milgrom, John Roberts and Robert Wilson – suggested an alternative hypothesis and a more complex explanation to this phenomenon. They posited the following: suppose there are two types of people – sophisticated ones and unsophisticated ones. The former types all realize that the rational course of action in this game is to free-ride, while the latter types do not. Because the unsophisticated players do not understand that they should free-ride, they contribute to the public account. The sophisticated ones realize that they should free-ride but they also realize that if they do so from the very outset, then the unsophisticated players will look at what they are doing and figure out the incentives to free-ride as well. Thus, the sophisticated players may decide to mimic the unsophisticated ones at the beginning and contribute to the public pool so as to not alert the unsophisticated players to the possibility of free-riding. Once the unsophisticated players have been lulled into a sense of security that others in the group will also contribute, the sophisticated ones start to free-ride on the contributions made by the unsophisticated ones. This guarantees the sophisticated players a higher monetary return than if they had started to free-ride from the very beginning and induced the unsophisticated players to free-ride as well. Let us call this the *strategies* hypothesis.

Are these conjectures correct? How should one test them? This is another example where survey questionnaires or field data are not of much assistance at all. James Andreoni, of the University of Wisconsin, came up with an ingenious way of putting these conjectures to the test. Andreoni recruited 70 participants to play the public goods game in groups of five for ten rounds. In each round, a participant had 50 tokens. And in each round, participants could divide their tokens between a private account and a public account. Tokens kept in the private account were worth one US cent each. Total tokens placed in the public account were multiplied by 2.5 and redistributed equally among the five participants, giving each of them 0.5 cents. This implied that a single token contributed to the public account by any participant generated a return of 0.5 cents for each of the other group members, regardless of whether they had contributed anything to the public account or not.

Andreoni looked at the effect of two different treatments. In the *strangers* treatment, 40 participants were randomly assigned (by a computer) to one of eight groups containing five participants each. These participants were told that they would play the game exactly ten times, but that after each repetition, the composition of the group would change in an

■ Cooperation in social dilemmas

unpredictable way with the computer randomly re-assigning participants to groups. While participants knew that they would be re-assigned, they never learn the identity of the other four members of the group in any round. This random re-assignment of participants to groups severely limits the gains from playing strategically. In a second *partners* treatment, 30 participants were formed into six groups of five. They played the exact same game as those in the strangers treatment, except here, the composition of the groups remained unchanged for the entire time.

These two treatments are designed to test the strategies hypothesis in the following way: suppose a participant is initially investing a certain amount of tokens into the public account. This participant experiences an epiphany in a particular round t and realizes that the rational thing to do would be to free-ride in this game. If this participant is in the partners treatment and is interacting with the same group of participants over and over again, then he/she might have an incentive to continue to cooperate and contribute to the public account so as to not alert those players who may not have figured out the free-riding strategy. But if this person is in the strangers treatment, then he/she is interacting with different people in each round and, therefore, each round in this treatment is analogous to a one-off interaction. There is no benefit to engaging in strategic behaviour here – such as mimicking the behaviour of unsophisticated participants or sending signals about one's cooperativeness – because you are not going to interact with them in the future. Thus, once you figure out that the rational course of action is to free-ride, in the strangers treatment you might as well start engaging in this behaviour from that point onwards, because in every round you are interacting with a different group of participants. This then implies that we should expect to see greater cooperation – and higher contributions to the public account – in the partners treatment compared to the strangers treatment.

In order to isolate the learning hypothesis, Andreoni decided to include a *surprise restart*. After the participants had finished interacting for ten rounds, he told them that there was time to play a few more rounds where they could earn additional money. He then had them participate for *three more* rounds. The idea here is this: if the decay in contributions is due primarily to participants gradually figuring out the rational strategy that they should free-ride, then once they learn to free-ride, they should continue to do so even after the restart. Therefore, the restart should not change behaviour in any way. Contributions should continue to exhibit the same pattern of decay even after the restart. But if not, then this might imply that learning alone cannot explain the pattern of decaying contributions.

The results were surprising and did not provide corroboration for either the strategies or the learning hypothesis. First, by and large, contributions were higher in the strangers treatment compared to the partners treatment. Second, the extent of free-riding was greater in the partners treatment also. Both of these contradicted the strategies hypothesis. What was even more striking was the fact that, following the restart, contributions jumped up in both the partners and the strangers treatments, which contradicted the learning hypothesis. In Figure 11.4, I show the pattern of contributions during the initial ten rounds and then for the three additional rounds after the restart. For the first ten rounds, the contributions show the familiar pattern of decay that we saw in Figure 11.2, but, contrary to the strategies hypothesis, the contributions by strangers are almost always greater than those by partners.

Cooperation in social dilemmas

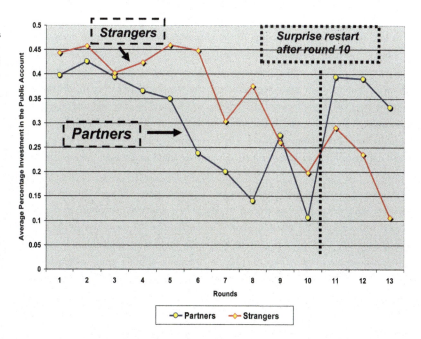

Figure 11.4
Pattern of contributions in the public goods game with partners and strangers and a surprise restart. Re-created on the basis of data in Andreoni (1988)

After the restart, contributions *increase* in round 11, contradicting the learning hypothesis, and this increase is more pronounced for the participants in the partners treatment.

Subsequently, a large number of researchers in both the US and in other countries around the world replicated Andreoni's experiment. Rachel Croson of the University of Pennsylvania and James Andreoni provide a comprehensive overview of this work and discuss nine papers that use this partners versus strangers paradigm. Out of those nine studies, two were cross-cultural studies looking at behaviour of participants in more than one country. One of these was an ambitious study carried out by Jordi Brandts, Tatsuyoshi Saijo and Arthur Schram comparing the behaviour of participants in four different countries – Japan, the Netherlands, Spain and the USA. The other, by Roberto Burlando and John Hey, compared the behaviour of participants in the UK and Italy. Thus, these nine studies analyse differences in behaviour among thirteen separate groups of participants. The results are mixed. In five out of thirteen groups of participants, partners contribute more than strangers; in four cases, the strangers contribute more, while, in the remaining four cases, there is no difference in contributions between partners and strangers.

One thing that is common to many of these studies is that they all report the surprise restart effect and the effect is always stronger for partners than for strangers. Richard Cookson of York (whose work I alluded to in Chapter 9 about framing effects in trust games) finds that the restart effect happens even if the game is restarted as many as four times. I will have a little more to say about the restart effect and the causes behind it later in this chapter.

LOOKING FOR ALTERNATIVE EXPLANATIONS

So, neither the strategies nor the learning hypothesis was able to provide a satisfactory explanation to the questions that we posed above. Three Swiss researchers at the University of

Zürich – Urs Fischbacher, Simon Gächter and Ernst Fehr – designed an ingenious experiment to test an alternative explanation to the phenomenon of contributions decay in the game. They recruited 44 participants and then divided them into 11 groups of four. Each participant plays only once, which generates 44 independent observations. The participants took part in a public goods game very similar to the one described earlier in this chapter. Participants are given an endowment of 20 tokens which could be allocated to a private or a public account. Tokens allocated to the public account are multiplied by 1.6 and redistributed equally among the group members. The participants were provided with the instructions and ten control questions to practise, so that they could understand the mechanics of the game.

Participants were then asked to fill out two separate forms – first, an "unconditional" contribution form where participants had to decide how much to contribute to the public account without knowing anything about the contributions of the others in the group. Following that, they were asked to indicate how much they would contribute for each one of 21 possible average contributions (0, 1, 2, ..., 20 tokens) of other group members. One member of the group, picked randomly, had to play the game according to the conditional contribution schedule while the other three were free to make unconditional contributions. This induces participants to take the conditional cooperation questionnaire seriously because everyone realizes that some of them will have to abide by their responses on this form.

Fischbacher et al. find that (1) 50% of the participants are conditional co-operators; these participants increase their contributions with an increase in the average contribution in the group. If these participants exactly matched the group average, then their contribution profile would coincide with the 45° line. That is not the case, and the contribution profile of the conditional co-operators lies slightly below the 45° line pretty much for all contribution levels, indicating that there is a bit of a self-serving bias among the conditional co-operators. (2) 30% of the participants are free-riders; (3) 14% of the participants have a hump-shaped contribution pattern. The contribution of participants in this group increases as the group average increases up to an average of ten tokens (50% of the initial endowment), but once the average group contribution exceeds ten tokens, their contributions decline with increasing group average.[3] (4) Finally, 6% of participants behaved in ways that could not be readily categorized. Given that the majority of participants are conditional co-operators, who are willing to contribute more if others do so too, average group contribution increases with an increase in the average belief about others' contributions. That is, as long as others contribute more, the group as a whole will also contribute more *on average*. In Figure 11.5, I provide an overview of their results, except I have split out the conditional co-operators into two groups: *strong conditional co-operators*, whose contributions are strongly positively correlated with the expected contribution of group members, and *weak conditional co-operators*, whose contributions show weaker correlation. Fischbacher et al. put these two types into only one category that they called conditional co-operators.[4]

Fischbacher and his colleagues go on to provide a rationale for why contributions fall off over time. They suggest that any heterogeneous group of participants consists of conditional co-operators and free-riders. Those conditional co-operators who possess optimistic beliefs about their peers and believe that their peers will contribute to the public account start out by contributing to the public account as well. But, over time, they begin to realize that

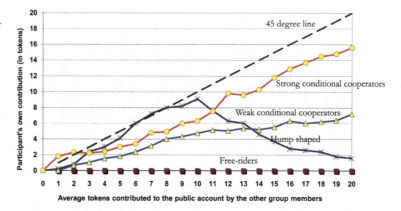

Figure 11.5 Contribution patterns of different types of participants from Fischbacher et al. (2001). Re-created on the basis of data in the original study

not everyone in the group is like them and that some people in the group are free-riders. In response, over time, the conditional co-operators reduce their contributions too, leading to the decaying pattern in contributions.

There is yet another reason why contributions may decay. Notice from Figure 11.5 that even if all players are strong conditional co-operators, and they are willing to contribute more if they expect other players to contribute more, the match in contribution from the conditional co-operators is not quite dollar for dollar. If conditional co-operators matched others' expected contributions dollar for dollar then their contribution profile should coincide with the 45° line, but it does not. The contribution profile even for strong conditional co-operators falls a little below the 45° line. Fischbacher et al. called this conditional cooperation but with a *self-serving bias*.

Further corroboration of this idea – that decaying contributions result primarily from reduced contributions by co-operators – comes from a study by Anna Gunnthorsdottir (of the Australian Graduate School of Management), Daniel Houser and Kevin McCabe (both of George Mason University). Here is what Gunnthorsdottir and her colleagues did. They recruited 264 participants at the University of Arizona to take part in a public goods game. There are 12 participants in each session who are formed into groups of four and interact for ten rounds. Participants are assigned to one of two treatments. In the baseline, or control, condition, the assignment of participants to groups is random. Groups are re-formed at the end of each round but, in the control condition, this regrouping is done randomly so that each participant has an equal chance of ending up in a group with any three other participants.

However, there is also an experimental *sorted* condition. Here, in each round, after participants have made their decisions, the four highest contributors to the public account are placed into one group; the fifth to eighth highest contributors are placed into the second group and so on. Participants are not told the exact mechanism by which the groups are formed, but might be able to deduce this by observing the pattern of contributions to the public account.

It will probably not come as a surprise to you that when the more cooperative types are sorted into the same group, they manage to sustain higher levels of contribution compared to the randomly formed groups. In the treatment where the groups are formed randomly, one observes the usual pattern of decay, but there is considerably less decay in contributions in the sorted treatment where the like-minded participants are grouped together.

However, the innovative part of this study – and the one that is immediately relevant for our purposes – arises from its analysis of how the behaviour of those with a more cooperative disposition differs from those who are less cooperative. Gunnthorsdottir and her colleagues start from the premise that a person's initial contribution to a public good is a useful and reliable measure of his or her cooperative disposition. Using first-round contributions only, Gunnthorsdottir and her colleagues classify participants into two categories: those who contribute 30% or less of their endowments are labelled "free-riders", while the rest are labelled "co-operators". This classification is done only once and is not changed during the session.

Gunnthorsdottir and her colleagues find that when the co-operators are grouped together with other co-operators in the sorted treatment, they manage to sustain high contributions throughout. Moreover, the contributions of the co-operators in the sorted treatment always exceed those in the random treatment. This is due, in large part, to the nature of the interaction that they encounter. In the sorted treatment, the co-operators realize, by observing the average group contribution, that they are interacting with other co-operators and the cooperative nature of their shared history makes them much more inclined to cooperate. However, in the control treatment, where groups are formed randomly and co-operators interact with free-riders frequently, there is no such shared history of cooperation over time; here the co-operators reduce their contributions over time, sometimes quite rapidly so.

In fact, by comparing separately the contributions of the co-operators and the free-riders in the random treatment (which exhibits the familiar pattern of decaying contributions), Gunnthorsdottir and her colleagues discover that the decay in contributions in this treatment results primarily from a decay in the contributions of the cooperative types. Based on these findings, it is likely that the familiar pattern of decay in contributions that we observe in the public goods experiments (where the usual practice is to form groups randomly) arise primarily from a loss of faith on the part of co-operators who start out with high contributions but are disillusioned over time, resulting in a reduction in contributions over time.

Subsequently, a number of other researchers have replicated this finding, that when it comes to such social dilemmas, the majority of people are neither purely self-interested free-riders nor are they incurable optimists wearing rose-tinted glasses. But, rather, they are astute individuals who either possess or form beliefs about how their peers will behave and then behave accordingly. If they think their peers will cooperate, then so will they, if not, then they will not cooperate either. Claudia Keser and Frans van Winden, at the University of Amsterdam, also examine this phenomenon and classify participants in their study according to how they responded to the *average group contribution* in the previous round. In keeping with the notion of conditional cooperation, around 80% of their participants respond to the information about group average by changing their own contributions in the next round. Those who are above the average in one round decrease their contributions in the following round and those who are below the average increase their contributions. (Keser and van Winden were probably the first experimental economists to formally use the term "conditional cooperation".)

Ananish Chaudhuri and Tirnud Paichayontvijit analyse the behaviour of 88 participants and find that 62% of them are conditional co-operators while only 16% are free-riders. Around 9% of the participants show the familiar hump-shaped contribution pattern. Furthermore, they find that when participants are provided with information about the presence of other conditional co-operators in the group, their contributions to the public account increase, but, more importantly, this increase is most pronounced for the conditional co-operators themselves. This, in turn, suggests that one way of getting people to cooperate more would be to foster more optimistic beliefs, because those who think that their peers will cooperate are themselves willing to cooperate. Thus, you may have a group of conditional co-operators but they may not necessarily cooperate until they are convinced that others will cooperate as well. Thus, often the key issue is to convince these people of the existence of other co-operators in the group in order for cooperation to take root.

Before moving on, I should point out that social psychologists have been writing about the phenomenon that beliefs about others' actions affect behaviour in social dilemmas before economists started doing so, even though the psychologists may not have actually used the term "conditional cooperation" and typically do not focus on its economic implications. One of the earliest studies on the topic was carried out by Harold Kelley and Anthony Stahelski, of the University of California, Los Angeles in 1970. Kelley and Stahelski look at how participants' beliefs affect cooperation in the prisoner's dilemma game. There is a large literature in social psychology, including the Kelley and Stahelski study and a number of others that followed, looking broadly at issues of cooperation and selfishness, often using the prisoner's dilemma game.[5]

DO PARTICIPANTS DISPLAY A HERD MENTALITY?

The concept of conditional cooperation was a radically new one which not only provided a new way of thinking about cooperation in social dilemmas but also, as we will see below, provided ideas about how we could enhance cooperation among humans in such dilemmas. But there was one question mark. There is evidence that people often love to conform because non-conformity is (psychologically) painful. Suppose someone asks you: "how much will you contribute to the public good out of your 20 tokens, if others in the group contribute 18 tokens (90%)?" You might very easily respond that you will contribute 90% or close to it also; not because that is what you *want* to do, but because that is what *you think you ought to do* so that you can conform with the rest of the group.

In Chapter 3, we discussed the notion of "priming" and I presented a brief overview of the work of Solomon Asch. Here, participants are shown three lines and asked to say which one is the shortest or longest. There is a clear choice, but unbeknown, to the participant, everyone else in the room is a confederate of the experimenter who all provide the same incorrect answer. The question is: faced with this overwhelming majority of people who clearly seem to believe that their incorrect answer is actually correct, does the participant stick with the obviously correct answer or does he/she go with the "herd" to avoid the psychological cost of non-conformity?

By and large, follow-up studies on conditional cooperation suggest that conformity, or herd mentality, is not the primary driving force behind the phenomenon of conditional cooperation. Robert Kurzban, at the University of Pennsylvania, and Daniel Houser, at George Mason, explore the heterogeneity in types by having 84 participants take part in a series of public goods games played over a number of rounds. In each game, participants are randomly formed into groups of four. Each participant has 50 tokens and all participants simultaneously decide how to allocate their tokens between a private or a public account. In each game, this is followed by a number of rounds, each of which proceeds as follows: first, one player in each group is provided with the current aggregate contribution to the public account and is afforded an opportunity to change his/her allocation to the two accounts. Then the next player is given the same opportunity, and so on. Each game proceeds round by round with each participant getting at least one chance to change his/her mind, and the game ends at a point unknown to the participants. Pay-offs to participants in each game are determined by the final allocation of tokens between the private and public accounts at the point where the game ends. Each experimental session contains at least seven games involving the initial simultaneous contribution decision followed by multiple rounds where the participants are given the chance to change their allocations.

This repeated elicitation of information regarding how much each participant wishes to contribute to the public account guarantees two things: (1) by allowing the participants to think about their answers multiple times, it enables participants to learn about the problem and avoids the possibility that contributions are the results of mistakes rather than deliberate acts; (2) the fact that participants are allowed to make their choices anonymously and are provided multiple opportunities of changing their mind reduces the possibility of conformity playing a major role. After all, a participant might choose to conform to what the rest of the group is doing the first time or the first few times, but it is likely that if a participant does not wish to conform, then, after the first few attempts, he/she will assert his/her true preferences, especially when participants are told that *they can change their mind if they wish to do so* and when *they can see others doing so*. At the very least, the multiple elicitations of responses, under conditions of anonymity, should strongly attenuate any latent desire towards conformity.

Kurzban and Houser rely on a procedure similar to the one followed by Fischbacher, Fehr and Gächter discussed above. Like Fischbacher and his colleagues, Kurzban and Houser also look at how contributions vary with a change in the *average* group contribution. They base their inferences about a participant's type by drawing a graph of the participant's contributions against the average contribution to the public account that this participant observes before making his/her own contribution. Contributions by co-operators lie well above the 45° line on this plot. Contributions by the conditional co-operators cluster around the 45° degree line, while contributions by the free-riders are small, regardless of the contributions of the others. Using this approach, Kurzban and Houser classify 53 out of 84 participants (63%) as conditional co-operators, 17 participants (20%) as free-riders and 11 participants (13%) as co-operators. The remaining three participants could not be classified into any of the above three categories. The authors find that these classifications are stable by having participants take part in three additional games and show that those classified as free-riders contribute less on average than their peers, co-operators more, and conditional co-operators about the same as their group average. Furthermore, groups that consist of more co-operators, on average generate higher contributions.

TURNING THE PRISONER'S DILEMMA INTO A STAG HUNT GAME

In 1993, Matthew Rabin, of the University of California at Berkeley, wrote a paper titled "Incorporating fairness into game theory and economics", where he provided a different explanation behind the behaviour in the public goods game. He suggested that people approach the game differently from what was thought before. He argued that, essentially, people saw this game as one which required coordinated action on the part of the participants and that there were multiple possible outcomes. In one outcome or in one group, participants may succeed in generating an implicit and virtuous norm where everyone manages to coordinate their actions so that everyone chooses a high contribution to the public account. This is certainly the most desirable outcome from society's point of view. But it is also possible that, at times, participants may not be able to coordinate their actions to reach this socially desirable outcome and might end up choosing low contributions. Choosing low contributions becomes a "bad" equilibrium where everyone realizes that, collectively, they have not managed to reach the socially desirable outcome, but once they have all coordinated their actions to choose low contributions, no one wants to increase his or her contribution unless everyone else increases their contributions at the same time. For instance, as we discussed earlier with regard to the ultimatum game in Chapter 7, the Lamalera and Ache seemed to have evolved a norm of making generous offers in the ultimatum game while the Machiguenga seemed to have evolved a norm of low offers which are routinely accepted by the responders.

Thus, Rabin suggested that actual behaviour is far more nuanced than it appears at first sight and the motivations behind that behaviour are also quite complex. In the context of prisoner's dilemma-type games, which pose a conflict between cooperation and self-interest, Rabin argued that if each player cares about the other and assumes that the other player does the same, then the players may collectively be able to achieve mutual cooperation. In a way, Rabin's argument anticipates the idea of *conditional cooperation* in the sense that what they contribute depends crucially on what they believe other members of the group will contribute. Those with optimistic beliefs, that is, those who believe that their peers will be generous and contribute to the public account, start out by contributing a lot as well. These optimists essentially try to coordinate their actions to reach the socially desirable outcome of high contributions. But those who believe that others will contribute little, respond in kind and aim for the outcome where everyone is either free-riding or close to it. Thus, people are neither purely altruistic nor purely free-riders (of course, there are some who *are* altruists and some who will *always* free-ride), but, rather, a majority of people behave according to their perceptions of their group members.

Figure 11.6 highlights Rabin's arguments. Remember that the public goods game is essentially a multi-person version of the prisoner's dilemma game, where free-riding is the dominant strategy leading to a Nash equilibrium, while mutual cooperation is the social optimum but not part of the profile of equilibrium actions. Rabin posed his theory in terms of the simpler prisoner's dilemma version of the game. The top panel of Figure 11.6 shows the generic form of the prisoner's dilemma game where free-riding is the dominant strategy. But now suppose each player cares about the other and gets an additional psychological pay-off of δ if they both choose to cooperate. Further suppose that δ equals 2. The new pay-off matrix is shown in the bottom panel of Figure 11.6. What this does is transform the prisoner's dilemma game into a stag hunt game with two equilibria: one where both players cooperate and receive $5 each, and a second where both defect (and receive $2 each) but, and this is the important point, the equilibrium where both players cooperate is now the pay-off dominant equilibrium. This means that in the presence of reciprocal motivations on the part of both

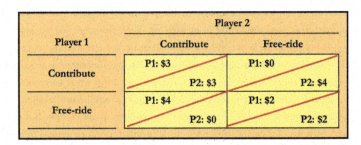

Figure 11.6
Pay-off matrix of the generic prisoner's dilemma game and of a modified version of the game in Rabin (1993)

players, mutual cooperation can emerge as an equilibrium and can, in fact, be a pay-off dominant outcome making it a relatively more attractive option. Rabin, thus, provides a perfectly reasonable explanation of how one can and should expect to see cooperative behaviour in the public goods game in the presence of mutual trust and reciprocity.

If players' beliefs about each other's future actions and the degree of reciprocal altruism can transform a multi-person prisoner's dilemma game into a coordination problem where mutual cooperation is the pay-off dominant outcome, then this ascribes a crucial role to those beliefs in mitigating free-riding behaviour. In turn, this has another significant implication about the pattern of decaying contributions over time. Earlier, we argued that the pattern of decay comes about due to interaction between conditional co-operators and free-riders. Conditional co-operators start out expecting others to contribute, but, over time, realize that others are not.

The decay in contributions is also possible even if the majority of participants are conditional co-operators (with a few free-riders) but they differ in their beliefs about their peers. Consider a group of three participants – two conditional co-operators and a free-rider. A conditional co-operator who believes that his/her peers will contribute a lot – say 80% or more – to the public account will also do the same. Suppose the first contributor contributes 70% of his/her initial endowment to the public account. But another conditional co-operator might easily possess pessimistic beliefs about fellow citizens and start out contributing only 20% of his/her endowment to the public account. The free-rider contributes nothing to the public account. The average contribution in this group, then, is 30% of the maximum possible. This would then induce the first, optimistic, conditional co-operator to revise his/her beliefs downwards and reduce his/her contribution in subsequent rounds. Of course, this should also induce the pessimistic conditional co-operator to revise his/her beliefs upwards and increase his/her contribution in future rounds. But it seems to be the case that the disillusionment of the optimist and the consequent reduction in this disgruntled person's contribution far exceeds any increase in contributions from the pessimist, leading to a decaying pattern of contributions.[6]

Experimental support for this conjecture came from work undertaken by Ananish Chaudhuri, Tirnud Paichayontvijit and Alexander Smith. They carry out a standard linear public goods game where participants are first classified into three categories on the basis of their prior beliefs. The belief elicitation process is incentivized so that participants have an incentive to report their beliefs truthfully. The three categories are: *Optimists*, those who expect others to contribute 70% or more; *Realists*, those who expect others to contribute between 40% and 60%, and finally *Pessimists*, who expect others to contribute 30% or less.[7] Research undertaken by others, including Umut Ones and Louis Putterman, show that such initial beliefs can be highly stable over time. So, classifying players into categories like this and then following the actions of those so classified can be a meaningful exercise.

Chaudhuri and his colleagues undertake a number of different treatments, in each of which participants interact in fixed groups of four for 24 rounds. In one of those treatments, participants play the game for 24 rounds and do not learn anything about the contributions of others or their own earnings until the very end. They find that, in this situation, contributions for the different treatments show little signs of decay, whether in the aggregate or for the individual groups of optimists, realists and pessimists. Figure 11.7 shows the results broken up by the three different categories. Those who expect their peers to contribute 70% or more to the public account, contribute 70% or more *on average* for the entire set of 24 rounds. Those who expect the members of their group to contribute between 40% and 60%, contribute between 40% and 60% themselves for the entire time, and those who expect others to contribute less than 40%, also contribute less than 40% for the whole session.[8]

It seems that, in keeping with the Rabin conjecture, the players are behaving as if they are playing a stag hunt type coordination game with three different equilibria: one with high contributions, one with medium contributions and one with low contributions. Each group is influenced by their initial beliefs about their peers and, in the absence of any information as

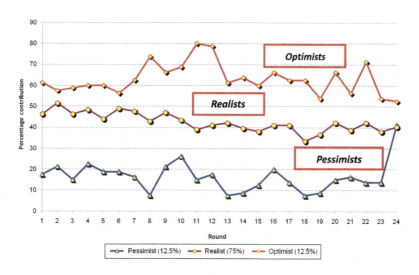

Figure 11.7 Contributions in the public goods game broken down by optimists, realists and pessimists. Re-created on the basis of data in Chaudhuri et al. (2017)

to what others are doing, each group persists in contributing that amount which is commensurate with their beliefs. This also lends further credence to the arguments by Fischbacher, Fehr and Gächter that the decay in contributions arises from the fact that conditional cooperators reduce their contributions over time as they begin to realize that there are others in the group who are either contributing less or completely free-riding.

But Chaudhuri et al. show something else. In other treatments where participants do get to see what others are doing, they replicate the usual pattern of decaying contributions, but with one twist. As noted above, each of the three groups is essentially trying to coordinate to a level of contribution that they think will be matched by others. Over time, the contributions from realists stay relatively stable with small declines because, by and large, they are close to the group average and do not need to make large adjustments. The movements come primarily from the optimists and the pessimists. Over time, the optimists move down while the pessimists move up. But, then, why do contributions decay? Because the reduction coming from optimists over time far exceeds any increase from pessimists.

This is intuitive, but an excellent explanation for this difference in behaviour for optimists and pessimists comes from Ernst Fehr, of Zurich, and Klaus Schmidt, of Munich. Fehr and Schmidt argue that people care about two things; certainly, they care about their own pay-off. But, on top of that, people care about how they are doing vis-à-vis others in the group; that is, they also care about equity or lack thereof. This is not surprising, given our discussion about the results from the ultimatum game in a previous chapter. But people actually care about two types of inequity: (i) *advantageous inequity*; this is where someone receives more and is better off than others on average; (ii) *disadvantageous inequity*, where someone receives less and is worse off than others on average. Advantageous inequity (where we are better off than others) leads to feelings of "guilt", while disadvantageous inequity, which makes us worse off than others, leads to "envy". Fehr and Schmidt argue that envy is a more powerful motivator than guilt. How does this relate to the optimist–pessimist story?

Optimists, in general, are contributing more than the average. This implies that, on average, they are taken advantage of and end up earning less than the average. So, optimists feel envy. Pessimists, on the other hand, are contributing less than the average and reaping the benefit of others' contributions. They are making more than others, on average. So, pessimists feel guilt. Both of these emotions lead to adjustments in contributions; downward for the optimists and upward for the pessimists. But envy is more powerful than guilt. So, optimists adjust downward a lot more than pessimists do upward, and the net result is a steadily decaying profile of contributions.[9]

CONCLUDING REMARKS

The applications of the ideas conveyed in this chapter relating to the tension between cooperating for the common good and free-riding in individual self-interest will be obvious to readers. They range from voluntary contributions to charity, to the provision of local and national public goods, to controlling environmental pollution and guaranteeing cleaner air, to protecting over-fishing and over-grazing of public lands. Most readers will be able to think of one or more examples of such social dilemmas that they have first-hand experience with, where they either managed to resolve the dilemma by fostering successful cooperation or failed to do so because of free-riding on the part of one or more members of the group. We are all part of a community: groups, tribes, clans, states, *homo sapiens* ... . John Donne wrote in 1623:

> No man is an island, entire of itself; every man is a piece of the continent, a part of the main; if a clod be washed away by the sea, Europe is the less, as well as if a promontory were, as well as if a manor of thy friend's or of thine own were; any man's death diminishes me, because I am involved in mankind, and therefore never send to know for whom the bell tolls; it tolls for thee.

In the autumn of 2003, New Zealand was faced with an acute shortage of power. The country relies primarily on hydro-electric power and a very dry summer had led to a depletion of the water reservoirs. Faced with this crisis, the government made a public appeal to households and businesses to reduce their power consumption as much as possible. Now, from the point of a view of an economist, an appeal like this is doomed to failure. Because not everyone has to reduce consumption; as long as some do, the power crisis could be averted. Thus, if my neighbour cuts down on his/her consumption, I do not have to do so, and I can free-ride on his/her frugality. Therefore, everyone has an incentive to free-ride by not reducing his/her own consumption as long as enough others reduce theirs. But if everyone reasons along those lines, then no one will conserve power and there will certainly be a shortage. To my surprise, the crisis was averted. People voluntarily reduced consumption. Restaurants in Auckland turned off their lights and started serving dinners by candle-light. Some restaurants reported that this made the dinners a much more intimate and romantic affair and seemed to have added to the diners' enjoyment. As I write this book in the middle of 2020, we are faced with another drought due to a long rainless summer. Auckland City has asked citizens to voluntarily reduce water usage. The results are not in yet, but on the basis of past experience and the results presented in this chapter, I am hopeful that we will be able to achieve the necessary reductions.

The issues and findings in this area have implications far beyond economics and go to the heart of the problem of evolution itself. Cooperation, or altruistic behaviour, is an evolutionary puzzle. In the context of evolution, an organism or individual that does engage in altruistic behaviour effectively reduces its chances of reproductive success at the expense of those who engage in selfish behaviour. If you give up your share of the food or readily share the spoils of your hunt or even put your life on the line for another (members of your clan/tribe/ethnic group/country), then you are making yourself potentially worse off, while another person who behaves in a self-interested manner and exploits your altruism gains at your expense. There are many examples of cooperation, not only among humans but also among other life-forms, where some organisms exhibit strategies that favour the reproductive success of others, even at a cost to their own survival and/or reproduction.

Here are some examples: (1) insect colonies, with sterile females acting as workers to assist their mother in the production of additional offspring; (2) alarm calls in squirrels or birds; while this may alert group members of the same species to the presence of a predator, they draw attention to the caller and expose it to increased risk of predation. The puzzle here is this: if some individuals are genetically predisposed to behave in an altruistic manner to the benefit of others, then this behaviour reduces the reproductive fitness of the altruistic individual, and such an "altruistic" gene, *if it exists*, will surely die out over time. Therefore, via the process of natural selection, a gene that codes for a particular trait which increases the fitness of the individual carrying that gene should increase in frequency within the population over time; conversely, a gene that lowers the individual fitness of its carriers should be eliminated. The issue of cooperation is one which has received enormous attention from all types of social scientists, including economists, and is fraught with controversy. The two most popular and well-accepted theories explaining cooperation among organisms are (1) the theory of kin selection proposed by William Hamilton in 1964 and (2) the theory of reciprocal altruism proposed by Robert Trivers in 1971.

William Hamilton, writing in the *Journal of Theoretical Biology*, provided one explanation for the persistence of cooperative behaviour. Hamilton argued that a gene leading to behaviour which increases the fitness of relatives but lowers that of the individual displaying the behaviour may nonetheless proliferate within the population, because relatives often carry the same gene. This theory came to be known as the theory of *kin selection*, though the phrase itself was coined by John Maynard Smith. The noted biologist, J. B. S. Haldane is supposed to have said: "I would lay down my life for two brothers or eight cousins". Haldane's remark alludes to the fact that if an individual loses its life to save two siblings or eight cousins, it is a "fair deal" in evolutionary terms, as siblings share 50% of their genes while cousins share 12.5%.

The theory of reciprocal altruism, proposed by Robert Trivers, suggests that altruistic behaviour can take on a conditional aspect whereby an organism acts generously and provides a benefit to another without expecting any immediate repayment. However, this initial act of altruism must be reciprocated by the original beneficiary at some point in the future. Failure to reciprocate on the part of the beneficiary will cause the original benefactor to not engage in such altruistic acts in the future. In order for the altruist not to be exploited by non-reciprocators, we would expect that reciprocal altruism can only exist in the presence of mechanisms to identify and punish "cheaters". An example of reciprocal altruism is blood-sharing in vampire bats. Bats who manage to get enough blood feed regurgitated blood to those who have not collected much, knowing that they themselves may someday benefit from a similar donation; cheaters are remembered by the colony and ousted from this collaboration.

However, the evidence that I have presented in the earlier part of this chapter suggests that, across a variety of economic transactions, humans routinely cooperate with genetically unrelated strangers, often in large groups, with people they will never meet again and when reputation gains are small or even absent. People not only routinely contribute to charity; they also give blood and donate organs – often to complete strangers. Thus, socio-biological theories such as kin selection or reciprocal altruism may not be able to explain large patterns of human cooperation.

The extensive work done by Ernst Fehr at the University of Zürich and his many collaborators, including Simon Gächter, Urs Fischbacher, Armin Falk, Klaus Schmidt, Herbert Gintis, Samuel Bowles and Robert Boyd, suggest an alternative theory of cooperation which they label "strong reciprocity". This is defined as the predisposition to build virtuous norms of cooperation and to punish (at personal cost, if necessary) those who violate cooperative norms even when it is implausible to expect that those costs will be recouped at a later date.

They argue that strong reciprocators are conditional co-operators (who behave altruistically as long as they believe that others will do so as well) and *altruistic punishers* (who apply sanctions to those who violate implicit social norms, even at a personal cost to themselves). We will have a lot more to say about such altruistic punishers in the next chapter.

Furthermore, a group consisting of a majority of co-operators will typically outdo groups consisting predominantly of free-riders, and, as long as the co-operators engage in assortative matching (i.e., they mate with their own type), the co-operative gene can proliferate in the population. While such group-selectionist arguments have been controversial in biology, given the ability of humans to create culturally evolved norms of cooperation, group selection may be more plausible among humans than in non-human primates.

This line of research on strong reciprocity can provide a new understanding of cooperation and the formation of virtuous norms. What this line of research suggests, then, is that socially connected communities may be able to achieve more cooperation than the standard economic view would suggest. What this also suggests is that, in many instances, communities may be able to provide local public goods on the basis of their own resources rather than waiting for government intervention. I hasten to add that I am no neo-liberal who believes that government is bad, full stop. I firmly believe in the virtues of the welfare state and the role of the government in providing a social safety net.

However, we also need to realize the limits on the ability of governments to promote social welfare. Collective action for the common good is not as insurmountable a problem as we (economists) often suppose it to be, and communities can adopt innovative approaches – based on networks, communication, punishments or social ostracism – in order to generate norms of cooperation on their own. What seems absolutely crucial to successful cooperation is the creation of optimistic beliefs about the actions of our peers. More importantly, a majority of people are willing to cooperate as long as enough others do; they just need to be made aware of the fact that there are others like them. This seems to be the key to generating the requisite optimistic beliefs that can lead to successful collective action.

NOTES

1. The version of the public goods game I have described here is due to John Ledyard of Caltech. This particular game is more specifically referred to as a "linear public goods game". This is because any contributions to the public account here generates a positive externality for all group members. One can also think of "threshold public goods games", where there is a positive externality (say, the park is built) only if contributions reach a certain threshold; otherwise, contributions may be refunded or lost. It is also the case that, in the linear public goods game, the socially optimal outcome is full contribution, while contributing nothing (complete free-riding) is the individually rational course of action and leads to the Nash equilibrium. There may be other public goods games where the Nash equilibrium is in the "interior", implying that the Nash equilibrium involves contributing something rather than nothing. I am going to confine attention to the linear public goods game since the game is very simple and makes all the points I need to make. There is no loss of generality in studying the simpler game and all the points that apply to this game will mostly apply to all the other more complex formulations of the game.
2. Along with Arlington Williams, of Indiana, Isaac and Walker later went on to look at cooperation levels in groups of 40 and 100 and found that these groups were actually more cooperative than groups of four or ten; most likely for the monitoring effect I will allude to immediately below.

3 The hump-shaped contributors show up in most studies that examine the phenomenon of conditional cooperation except that they are always a small minority. This group appears to think along the following lines: as long as the group contribution is low, they are willing to pitch in and help out; but, beyond a point, where the group contribution is relatively high, they feel that there is no longer any need for them to contribute and so they bail out and prefer to keep their endowments.

4 By looking at the data for individual participants in the Fischbacher et al. (2001) study, one can distinguish between strong and weak conditional co-operators. The contribution profile for both are positively sloped in that contributions increase in the expected contribution of group members but the profile for strong conditional co-operators has a greater slope than the one for the weak conditional co-operators.

5 It is also the case that, in 1984, Bob Sugden, of East Anglia, had put forward a theory of voluntary provision of public goods on the basis of mutual reciprocity among participants. Sugden's idea of reciprocity is essentially a precursor to the idea of conditional cooperation. In a paper published in 2007, Rachel Croson provides experimental support for Sudgen's concept of reciprocity. (Hat tip to Simon Gächter for pointing out that research on conditional cooperation in social psychology predates that in economics, and to Abhi Ramalingam for reminding me to connect conditional cooperation to Sudgen's work.)

6 I am going to side-step the issue of where these beliefs come from in the first place. They could be the product of nature or nurture (upbringing and socialization). This discussion is beyond the scope of the current volume.

7 Each participant has an endowment of ten tokens in each round and contributions can only be in whole tokens. So, 70% implies contributing seven tokens or more.

8 This figure shows a significant "end-game" effect for the pessimists whose contribution in the very last round shows a sharp upward spike. Such end-game effects are commonplace in public goods experiments and will be discussed more in the next chapter. What is noteworthy is that the change in contribution is in the "wrong direction". If people are more likely to free-ride in the very last round, then we would expect a sharp drop in contribution. But for the optimists and realists there is no such drop-off and for the pessimists there is actually an increase, contrary to the Nash equilibrium prediction.

9 In a follow-up study with the same classification of participants into optimists, realists and pessimists, Chaudhuri revisits the issue of multiple surprise restarts along the lines of Richard Cookson, who showed that contributions jump up even with as many as four restarts. Except, Chaudhuri wanted to see who was responsible for this increase: optimists, realists or pessimists. Chaudhuri implements three restarts and finds contribution jumps in each case. While not all of the differences are significant, the most pronounced jumps come from the optimists and is driven primarily by the fact that, following each restart, there is a renewed sense of optimism among the optimists, who believe that after the restart group members will contribute more. Echoing earlier results, the renewed optimism and restart effect is most pronounced with partners matching, where group composition is fixed over time, as opposed to strangers matching, where participants are randomly re-matched from one round to the next.

12 The carrot or the stick

Sustaining cooperation in social dilemmas

In this chapter, I:

- *Extend the discussion from the previous chapter, to explore ways of sustaining cooperation in social dilemmas;*
- *Discuss how cooperation can be sustained via the use of altruistic punishments where participants punish others for free-riding, even when such punishment is costly and does not confer future benefits;*
- *Explore factors that affect the efficacy of such punishments, including the potential costs and benefits of implementing them and the time horizon during which these interactions play out;*
- *Examine other non-punitive mechanisms for fostering cooperation over time; such may include forming groups sorted on the basis of their cooperative tendencies as well as various other measures of moral suasion.*

INTRODUCTION

In Chapter 11, I argued that in a variety of social dilemmas, people behave as conditional co-operators who decide whether to cooperate or not depending on their beliefs about their peers. In this chapter, I will show how conditional co-operators are often able to sustain norms of cooperation sometimes via the use of costly punishments and sometimes via the use of other mechanisms such as communication, expressions of disapproval, assortative matching and advice giving. The noted political scientist Robert Axelrod, of the University of Michigan, suggests that virtuous social norms can be sustained by (1) *deterrence*, which relies on punishment of those who deviate from the expected course of action or (2) *internalization*, where a norm becomes so entrenched in a society that violating it causes psychological discomfort. This is what I turn to next.

SUSTAINING SOCIAL NORMS BY PUNISHING FREE-RIDERS

Throughout the 1990s and early 2000s, Ernst Fehr and Simon Gächter, at the University of Zürich, had been thinking about and studying the problem of sustaining cooperation in social dilemmas. They had already found that a majority of people were conditional co-operators who behaved in accordance with their beliefs about their peers and were often successful in sustaining cooperation. They now made another startling discovery. They found that conditional co-operators are also "altruistic punishers", that is, conditional co-operators are willing to apply sanctions to those who violate implicit social norms even when such punishments impose a substantial pecuniary cost on those meting out that punishment.

Fehr and Gächter recruited participants to play the public goods game. One set of participants played the game in groups whose composition remained unchanged for the entire 20 rounds. This is the "partners" treatment. In another treatment, participants are randomly re-matched at the end of each round, exactly as in Andreoni's study. This is the "strangers" treatment. In each treatment, participants play for 20 rounds – the first ten rounds without any punishment possibility and then the next ten rounds with punishment. Participants are placed into groups of four. In each round, a participant has 20 tokens which can be allocated between a private and a public account. Total tokens contributed to the public account are multiplied by 1.6 and then redistributed equally among group members. A participant's earning in any round is the sum of the tokens allocated to the private account plus the returns from the public account. At the end of the experiment, tokens are redeemed for cash. During the first ten rounds, in each round, participants only decide how to allocate 20 tokens between the two accounts.

The second set of ten rounds has two stages in each round. In the first stage, participants play the exact same public goods game where they decide how to allocate tokens between a private and a public account. In the second stage, participants get to see the contributions of other group members (without learning their identities) and can then choose to punish the other group members. Participants can allocate up to ten punishment points in each round and each punishment point reduces the punished participant's pay-off by a certain amount. For the sake of simplicity, let us assume that for every $1 given up by a punisher, the pay-off to the punishment recipient is reduced by $3.[1] So, the punishment is costly to the punisher in that the cost of the punishment points is subtracted from the earnings of the punishing participant, but these punishment points lead to a greater reduction in the monetary pay-off of the person being punished.

Fehr and Gächter conjecture – along the lines of Andreoni – that participants in the strangers treatment will not engage in punishment, since with random re-matching at the end of each round, the value of signalling and reputation formation via punishment of free-riders is minimal, especially given that such punishment imposes a pecuniary cost on the punisher. Therefore, the Nash equilibrium of this game is for no one to punish, and, anticipating that, for everyone to free-ride. However, in the partners treatment, there are benefits to building up a reputation by punishing free-riders. A participant who is punished might think that there are punishers in the group and, hence, might be less inclined to free-ride and thus, in fixed groups, the availability of punishment might lead to higher contributions to the public good.

Fehr and Gächter observe significant amounts of punishment under both conditions. The availability of punishment raises contributions significantly in both treatments, but the impact is more pronounced in the partners treatment than in the strangers treatment. In fact, in the partners treatment, contributions approach 100% of the social optimum (of full contribution) in the later rounds. Figure 12.1 provides an overview of average contributions in the two treatments with and without punishments. Across all rounds, the average contribution to the public good in the absence of punishment is 19%, while, once punishments are allowed, contributions average 58%.

Figure 12.1
Average contributions in the partners and strangers treatments with and without punishments. Re-created on the basis of data in Fehr and Gächter (2000)

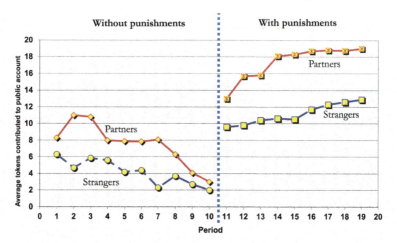

Remember that in typical public goods experiments, contributions show a familiar pattern of decay over time. However, once participants are allowed to punish one another, in both the partners and the strangers treatment, contributions exhibit an increasing profile. The average contribution in the last round without punishments is 10% (significantly lower than the average of 19% across all rounds), but with punishments, the average last round contribution is 62%, which is higher than the average across all rounds of 58%. Fehr and Gächter also found that punishments were primarily aimed at those who contributed less than the group average in any round, and the further below the group average was the participant's contribution, the greater was the magnitude of the punishment handed out to this participant.[2, 3]

While the papers by Fehr and Gächter show that costly punishments can indeed raise contributions to levels above those attainable in the absence of such punishments, in those studies, the participants do not get to choose whether punishments are available or not. Three German researchers, Ozgur Gürerk, Bernd Irlenbusch and Bettina Rockenbach analyse contribution behaviour in a public goods game where participants can *choose* to be in either a sanctioning environment (i.e., one which allows participants to punish their group members) or a sanction-free environment.

Each round of this experiment consists of multiple stages. In stage 1, participants have an opportunity to choose to be in either a *sanctioning* or a *sanction-free* institution. In stage 2, participants participate in a linear public goods game. The round ends here for participants who chose to be in the sanction-free institution. Participants who chose to be in the sanctioning institution continue to stage 3, where they can allocate either positive or negative sanction points to other members. A positive sanction (actually a reward) awards the recipient one token and costs the sender one token. A negative sanction (a punishment) costs the recipient three tokens and costs the sender one token. Participants receive feedback on earnings at the end of the round. The experiment consists of 30 rounds and participants are randomly re-matched at the end of each round. This is a between-subjects design, and, in each round, once participants choose to be in a particular institution, they do not learn the results of the other institutions.

■ The carrot or the stick

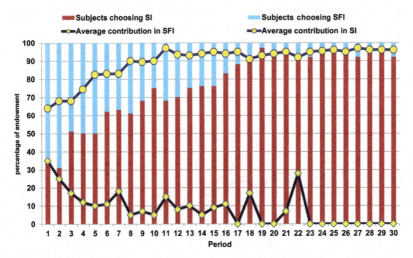

Figure 12.2
Contributions in and subjects' choices of sanctioning and sanction-free institutions. Re-created on the basis of data in Gürerk et al. (2006)

In the first round of the game, a majority (63%) of the participants chose to be in the sanction free institution (SFI) rather than the sanctioning institution (SI). Participants who do choose to be in the SI, however, contribute on average 64% to the public good, which is significantly higher than the 37% contributed by those who chose to join the SFI. Over time, the SI becomes the predominant institution and, eventually, close to 100% of participants choose the SI. By round ten of the 30-round interactions, contributions in the SI increase to 90% and continue to go up from there. In contrast, contributions in the SFI decrease to zero. Averaged across all rounds, contributions in the SI are 91%, significantly higher than the 14% in the SFI.

Moreover, not only do more and more participants migrate from the SFI to the SI over time, migrating participants engage in high levels of cooperation and also very quickly adopt the prevailing SI norm of punishing low contributors. Over time, as the amount of free-riding falls away to zero and the need for punishment diminishes, the difference in pay-offs between high contributors who do not punish free-riders and high contributors who do punish becomes smaller, suggesting that "selection pressures" against strong reciprocators become weaker over time. Figure 12.2 shows the evolution of subjects' choice of institutions and contributions over the 30 periods of interaction. The average contributions in both institutions over time are measured as the percentage of the endowment contributed to the public good.

ON THE COST EFFECTIVENESS OF COSTLY PUNISHMENTS

Nikos Nikiforakis (of the University of Melbourne at the time) and Hans-Theo Normann (of Düsseldorf) found the results with regards to altruistic punishment compelling but were plagued with one unanswered question. It was clear that the use of costly punishments led to higher levels of contributions. But, at the end of the day, it is not primarily the contributions to the public account that we care about, but, rather, the returns from the public account. In other words, suppose we all contribute all our endowments to the public account but at the same time also spend a lot of money to punish each other in order to make sure that everyone contributes. In this case, the returns from the public account may be high but we have also wasted a lot of resources in punishing one another. So, rather than focusing on contributions, we need to focus on *efficiency*. Suppose there are no punishments and everyone contributes their entire endowment to the public account, so that the public account consists of the maximum possible amount, which is redistributed among group members. This is the socially optimum outcome and, in this case, we can say that it is also the *efficient* outcome. So, if everyone has $5 and contributes the whole thing to the public account, then the latter has $20. This is doubled to $40, and, when redistributed, nets everyone $10. In this case, we have achieved the efficient outcome, a 100% return on investment. But suppose, in order to achieve this outcome, players have ended up spending $4 on either punishing another or getting punished or both, then each player is left with only $6, which is only a 20% return.

So, according to Nikiforakis and Normann, the question is: are the returns still high when we subtract the cost of punishing and/or being punished? To calculate efficiency, we need to look at four things: money allocated to the private account; returns (if any) from the public account; the cost of punishing others; and finally the cost incurred if one is punished by others. In order for social welfare to be high, it must be the case that participants are better off after we have taken all of these costs into account. Moreover, what we ideally want to see is efficiency in the presence of punishment opportunities being actually higher than in the absence of punishments. For instance, if there are no punishment opportunities, then people may free-ride more. But, if the cost of punishing one another is so high that net efficiency is actually lower even with higher contributions, then we have not actually managed to improve matters much.

Nikiforakis and Normann suggest that the ability of costly punishments to sustain high contributions to the public good depends crucially on the effectiveness of that punishment, that is, the factor by which each punishment point reduces the recipient's pay-off. They look at four different experimental treatments where each punishment point meted out costs the punisher one experimental currency unit (ECU). But, in treatment 1, each point reduces the punishment recipient's income by one unit, in treatment 2 by two units, in treatment 3 by three units and, finally, in treatment 4 by four units. There is also a control treatment where no punishment mechanism is available. Participants are placed into groups of four and play for ten rounds in a partners protocol. In order to prevent reputation formation, given fixed groups, participant identification numbers are changed randomly from one round to the next.

The authors find that there is a monotonic relation between the effectiveness of the punishment and mean contributions; as the effectiveness goes up, so does the mean contribution. Average contributions range from 9% in the control treatment to 33% in treatment 1, 57% in treatment 2, 87% in treatment 3 and 90% in treatment 4. However, the effectiveness of the punishment matters, in that it is only in the two "high" punishment treatments, where each punishment point costs the recipient either three or four currency units, that contributions actually increase over time, as in the original Fehr and Gächter (2000) study. Contributions in the other less effective punishment treatments show the familiar pattern of decay.

Furthermore, higher contributions sustained on the basis of punishments do not necessarily translate into higher efficiency. Compared to the control treatment, it is only in treatment 4 (where the punishment inflicts the maximum penalty on the recipient) that average earnings are consistently higher. So, it appears that the mere existence of punishment may not always be sufficient to enhance cooperation. In order for punishment to truly make a difference, it must inflict a penalty that is substantially higher than the cost of meting out that punishment. Figure 12.3 summarizes the role of punishment effectiveness on efficiency. It is only when the punishment has maximum effectiveness, depicted by the line with circles labelled "treatment 1:4", that it leads to significant gains in efficiency compared to the control treatment.

In Chapter 11, we explored the issue of what happens to cooperation when groups become larger. At the time, we saw that larger groups were no less cooperative than smaller groups and may possibly be more cooperative. I also argued that a crucial feature is the degree of monitoring; can each player see the decisions of all other players or only some of the other players; that is, is monitoring of players full or only partial? Jeffrey Carpenter, of Middlebury College, decided to extend this line of work to the issue of punishment effectiveness by asking what happens to monitoring of free-riders and punishment as the group size becomes bigger. On the one hand, as groups grow, it becomes harder for each individual to monitor others and, as a result, free-riding might become more prevalent as punishment becomes less of a deterrent. On the other hand, in larger groups there are more people monitoring each free-rider, so that free-riders might actually receive more punishment in total compared to smaller groups.

Carpenter looks at both the effect of the *group size*, as well as the *monitoring fraction*, which refers to the fraction of the group each agent can monitor. There are two group sizes, five and ten, two values of the MPCR, 0.375 and 0.75 and four possible types of monitoring: (1) *no monitoring*; (2) *full monitoring*; (3) *half monitoring* and (4) *single monitoring*. In the no monitoring treatment, agents see what others contributed but cannot punish them. In full monitoring, agents can punish any and all other group members as long as they have the resources to do so. In half monitoring, agents can punish that half of the group which is

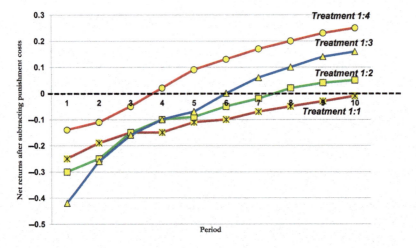

Figure 12.3 Role of punishment effectiveness on efficiency. Re-created on the basis of data in Nikiforakis and Normann (2008)

located closest to them on a circle, and finally, in single monitoring, they can punish only one other group member.

The punishment mechanism is the same as that used in Fehr and Gächter. For either value of the MPCR, contributions in the five-person groups with either full or half monitoring start at about 55% and remain stable around that mark for the duration of the session. For the ten-person groups, with either full or half monitoring, contributions start at the same level but then show a clearly increasing profile, reaching almost 100% contribution in the last three rounds of interaction. In both five- and ten-person groups, especially with MPCR = 0.75, there is a clear bifurcation, with contributions showing an increasing profile with either full or half monitoring on the one hand, and a decaying pattern with single or no monitoring on the other.

THE POSSIBILITY OF "PERVERSE" PUNISHMENTS

The above discussion suggests that costly monetary punishments of free-riders can sustain high levels of contribution to the public good but that the efficiency implications are somewhat ambiguous. Punishments can result in higher efficiency but, in order to do so, they must be cost effective. It must be possible to mete out hefty punishment relatively cheaply. In terms of our experimental set-up, this means that the cost–benefit ratio of punishments must be at least 1:3 that is, each $1 given up in punishment cost must reduce the pay-off to the punishment recipient by $3 or more, in order for punishment to be effective. If the cost–benefit ratio is lower, say 1:2 or less ($1 of punishment cost reduces the pay-off to the recipient by $2 or less), then efficiency is actually lower than would be the case in the absence of any punishment opportunity.

Nikos Nikiforakis, who was keenly interested in such issues of punishment and retribution, added another note of caution about the salutary effects of punishments. He shows that if one allows the possibility of counter-punishments by punished free-riders, co-operators are less willing to punish. He finds that punishments are often "perverse" or "anti-social" in nature in the sense that those who free-ride often punish those who cooperate. I will explain the thinking behind such perverse punishments shortly. In what follows, I will stick to the terms "antisocial" punishment to indicate punishment of high contributors and "pro-social" punishment to indicate the more usual punishment of free-riders by co-operators.

Nikiforakis looks at two different punishment mechanisms. The *punishment* treatment is similar to the 1:3 protocol discussed above. The other treatment, which is the primary focus of this study, adds a third *counter-punishment* stage following the second punishment stage to each round. At the beginning of this third stage, each participant is informed about the number of punishment points assigned to him/her by his/her group members and is given an opportunity to assign counter-punishment points to those participants in turn. These costs work cumulatively. A participant's final earnings in a round in this third treatment is his/her earnings from the public goods game in stage 1 minus all the income reductions caused by the punishment points assigned to this participant by others and those assigned by the participant to his/her peers over the two stages of punishment and counter-punishment.

A crucial feature of this study is that only those participants who are actually punished in stage 2 are allowed to engage in counter-punishment and they can only punish those who punished them in the first place; moreover, a participant must have a positive account balance in order to carry out any counter-punishment and these must be carried out in the stage immediately following the punishment. This is a within-subjects design with both fixed groups and random re-matching. Participants interact for 20 rounds in two blocks, which are counter-balanced.[4] In one of those blocks, participants play the standard public goods game, while, in the other block, they have the opportunity to either engage in punishment or both punishment and counter-punishment.

Nikiforakis finds that individuals in the punishment treatment are significantly more likely to contribute to the public account compared to those in the counter-punishment treatment, where contributions show the familiar pattern of decay. The counter-punishment treatment also leads to lower average earnings (lower average efficiency) compared to *both* the punishment treatment and the control treatment. In looking at why the counter-punishment treatment does worse than the punishment treatment, the author finds that participants in this treatment engage in substantial amounts of antisocial punishment which can be attributed to one of two factors or a combination of those. One is the anticipation by some free-riders of the forthcoming punishment from co-operators and the formers' willingness to retaliate those sanctions. Here, participants use counter-punishments strategically to signal that future sanctions will not be tolerated, and this is especially true in fixed groups, which afford scope for such signalling. The second factor is the desire to avenge sanctions meted out to them in previous periods. In fact, participants in the counter-punishment treatment are 15% less likely to punish free-riding compared to the punishment treatment, mostly because co-operators anticipate that this might in turn lead to antisocial punishment and wish to avoid that.

However, three researchers at Brown University, Matthias Cinyabuguma, Talbot Page and Louis Putterman, suggest that the specific mechanism for implementing counter-punishments might make a big difference to their eventual impact. In the Cinyabuguma et al. study, participants do not learn the identity of those who punished them. This makes it impossible to engage in targeted revenge. Instead, each participant is told the pattern of punishing high, average and low contributors in the group in the first stage and then that participant can decide who to counter-punish, that is, whether to engage in counter-punishment of pro-social or antisocial punishers.

Contrary to Nikiforakis, who found that contributions and earnings in the treatment with counter-punishment were lower than that in the punishment treatment, Cinyabuguma et al. find that the availability of counter-punishment does not reduce either contributions or earnings to levels lower than those achieved in the punishment only treatment, at least not significantly so. It is conceivable that this is due mostly to the design differences between the two studies. The opportunity to engage in counter-punishment, then, seems to have a very different impact depending on its exact implementation.[5] So, whether and to what extent punishments enhance efficiency then depends rather crucially on whether targeted retribution is possible (as in Nikiforakis) or not (as in work by Cinyabuguma and his colleagues).

Simon Gächter had been working and thinking about justice and punishment for a long time. Now, along with colleagues Benedikt Herrmann and Christian Thöni, he embarked on an ambitious cross-cultural project to try and understand the nature of pro-social and antisocial punishments by comparing the behaviour of undergraduate students across 16 different

Figure 12.4
Pro-social and antisocial punishments across different societies. Re-created on the basis of data in Herrmann et al. (2008)

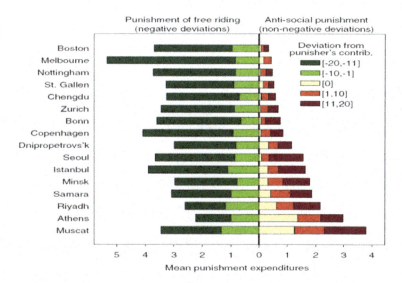

locations using a between-subjects protocol.[6] The incidence of antisocial punishments is the lowest among the participants from Western industrialized nations, where the bulk of the previous experimental data comes from. This, in turn, suggests that the evidence in favour of the cooperation-enhancing role of punishments that comes from prior experiments run in Western societies may actually be over-estimating the efficacy of such punishments, and, in other societies, the presence of antisocial punishments may actually have a large detrimental role.

Different participant pools reacted very differently to the punishment received. In only 11 out of 16 societies, those punished in one round for contributing less than the group average increased their contribution in the next round and the extent of the mean estimated increase per punishment point received varies considerably. Thus, punishment did not have an equally strong disciplinary effect on free-riders in all participant pools in increasing their cooperation, and, in some societies, punishments did not increase cooperation at all. Figure 12.4 summarizes the nature of pro-social and antisocial punishments across these diverse societies. The authors went on to suggest that antisocial punishments are more prevalent in societies which are characterized by (1) a lack of strong social norms of civic cooperation as expressed in people's attitudes towards tax evasion, abuse of the welfare system or dodging fares on public transport and (2) weak law enforcement.[7]

ARE PUNISHMENTS MORE EFFECTIVE IN THE LONG RUN?

Joe Henrich of Harvard and Rob Boyd of UCLA suggest that punishments take time to put down roots but, once embedded, they are more effective over a longer time horizon. Suppose being punished is sufficiently costly so that co-operators have higher pay-offs than defectors. Then, a second-order free-rider who cooperates but does not punish free-riders will achieve a higher pay-off because they avoid the punishment cost. But if defections do not pay, then such defections will occur rarely and by mistake; so, over time, such defections become less

■ The carrot or the stick

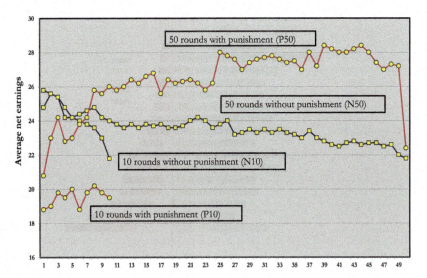

Figure 12.5
Effectiveness of punishments over the long horizon. Re-created on the basis of data in Gächter et al. (2008)

frequent, and as we ascend higher orders of punishing, the difference in pay-offs between punishers and second-order free-riders will start to approach zero. Over time, a process of conformist transmission should tilt the scales away from free-riding toward cooperation. This implies that, over a long horizon, the threat of punishment will be enough to sustain cooperation without much actual punishment being carried out.

Experimental evidence for this conjecture came from Simon Gächter, Elke Renner and Martin Sefton, of the University of Nottingham. They examine, using a between-subjects design, whether the duration of interaction affects the efficacy of punishments by looking at two different punishment treatments, one which lasts ten rounds (treatment *P10*) and the other which lasts 50 rounds (treatment *P50*). There are also two control treatments without any punishment opportunities, one lasting ten rounds (treatment *N10*) and the other lasting 50 rounds (treatment *N50*). Here, each punishment point costs the punisher one token but reduces the punished participant's pay-off by three tokens. What is particularly striking in this study is that per period contributions in the *P50* treatment are 25% higher than those in the *P10* treatment and 50% higher than those in the *N50* treatment. Average net earnings are significantly higher in the *P50* treatment compared to the *N50* or *P10* treatments. Finally, towards the later stages of the *P50* treatment, cooperation seems to become stabilized without much actual punishment being meted out, which results in punishment costs becoming negligible, resulting in higher earnings in this treatment. Figure 12.5 shows the results for this study. You may recall our discussion about end-game effects from Chapter 11. Note the pronounced end-game effect in the 50-round game with punishments, where there is a sharp drop in contributions in the final round.

THE "VERDICT" ON COSTLY PUNISHMENTS

The evidence on costly punishments suggests that providing participants with the opportunity to engage in such punishment of group members can usually help sustain high levels of contributions. But this finding is subject to at least three caveats. First, there is the problem that the punishment itself creates a second-level public good; those who are willing to mete out costly punishment must not only punish free-riders but also those non-punishers who might contribute but do not punish free-riders and, hence, free-ride on others' punishment and so on. In the words of Robert Axelrod, of Michigan, this requires the creation of "meta-norms" of punishment. I say more on this topic shortly below.

The second problem has to do with the issue of antisocial punishments. The presence of such antisocial punishments may result not only in no increase in cooperation, but also seriously reduce efficiency compared to control treatments with no punishment. The cooperation enhancing effect of punishments seems more prominent in particular participant pools, especially in Western industrialized societies. Also, the exact nature of counter-punishment matters. If participants are only allowed to engage in pro-social punishments but not in targeted revenge, then this could be welfare improving. However, if we allow for both anti-social and "norm enforcing" (pro-social) punishments, then the net effect is detrimental to cooperation because the increase in cooperation caused by norm enforcing sanctions does not fully offset the contribution reducing effect of antisocial punishments.

The third problem is that the efficiency implications of costly punishments are not clear cut. By and large, across the majority of studies cited above, efficiency is actually lower in treatments with punishment compared to control treatments without punishment. The ability of punishments to enhance *efficiency* seems to depend crucially on the cost-effectiveness of the punishment and on the time horizon for interaction. It is only when the punishment is *low cost* and *high impact* that it also leads to an increase in efficiency over and above any increase in contributions. Interactions also have to be sufficiently long-lived so that, over a long time horizon, the threat of punishment is enough to sustain cooperation without much actual punishment having to be meted out.

SUSTAINING COOPERATION VIA MEANS OTHER THAN PUNISHMENTS

The work of Fehr and Gächter and others, discussed above, showed that conditional co-operators are often willing to engage in costly punishment in order to deter free-riding and maintain virtuous norms of cooperation. This is in keeping with the injunction in Leviticus (24: 19-20): "And if a man injures his neighbor, just as he has done, so it shall be done to him: fracture for fracture, eye for eye, tooth for tooth; just as he has injured a man, so it shall be inflicted on him."[8] But, as Robert Axelrod points out, the existence of punishment creates a secondary social dilemma. If one member of the group engages in costly punishment of a free-rider, then another group member can free-ride on the first person's punishment. So, I may not necessarily be free-riding but I may not wish to take the time and effort to punish those who are. I am bothered by the litter and the graffiti and the loud music at block parties and drunken brawls at the neighbourhood bar, but I might leave it to my neighbour to go around and knock on doors at the city council or meet the local councillor to do something about it. In this case, I am free-riding on the fact that my neighbour is willing to take the time and trouble to tackle these problems. But then, if some people are willing to punish while others are not, we need a second set of punishments for the non-punishers! Now we need to punish the non-punishers because unless all conditional co-operators are willing to punish, cooperation may unravel.

So, a norm of cooperation and punishment of free-riders is no longer enough, we now need meta-norms; punishments of non-punishers and then punishments of those who do not punish non-punishers and so on. But this may imply that "an eye for an eye makes the whole world blind"; a quote that is generally attributed to Mahatma Gandhi. Thankfully, however, while such costly punishments are indeed extremely successful at deterring free-riding, it turns out that conditional co-operators do not need to rely on costly punishment exclusively in order to achieve this goal but can resort to various other mechanisms to sustain cooperation as well. The studies that look at non-punitive measures can be broadly classified into (1) those that attempt to foster cooperation among participants without making any attempt to sort them and (2) those that try to form sorted groups on the basis of similarity of behaviour or preferences.

These are essentially means of appealing to human goodwill. Or, in the words of Portia from *The Merchant of Venice*[9]:

> The quality of mercy is not strained.
> It droppeth as the gentle rain from heaven
> Upon the place beneath. It is twice blest:
> It blesseth him that gives and him that takes.

SUSTAINING COOPERATION IN NON-SORTED GROUPS

One obvious mechanism to promote cooperation is to allow for communication among participants. Mark Isaac of the University of Arizona and James Walker of Indiana University look at the role of communication in fostering cooperation. They have participants play the public goods game in groups of four. In one treatment, participants play the game for ten rounds without any communication opportunities. Then they play for another ten rounds where they are allowed to engage in free-form communication about all aspects of the problem at hand at the beginning of each of those ten rounds. In a second treatment, they are allowed to communicate prior to each round for the first set of ten rounds but then no communication is allowed for the second set of ten rounds. Figure 12.6 illustrates the results.

When the participants start with no communication in the initial set of ten rounds (top panel of Figure 12.6), contributions start at around 45% and show the familiar pattern of decay from then onwards. However, once communication is allowed during the second set of ten rounds, contributions jump up to 60% in round 11 and exhibit an increasing profile for the remaining rounds, reaching 100% in round 18 and averaging greater than 90% in the last three rounds. In the treatment where participants start with communication (bottom panel of Figure 12.6), contributions start at 100% in round 1 and hover around 90% for rounds 2 through 6 before stabilizing at 100% for the last four rounds. Surprisingly, participants manage to sustain this high level of cooperation even after they are prevented from communicating. Contributions stay at, or close to, 100% for the next seven rounds, finally dropping down to around 80% for the last three rounds.

Figure 12.6
Effects of communication in the public goods game. Re-created on the basis of data in Isaac and Walker (1988a)

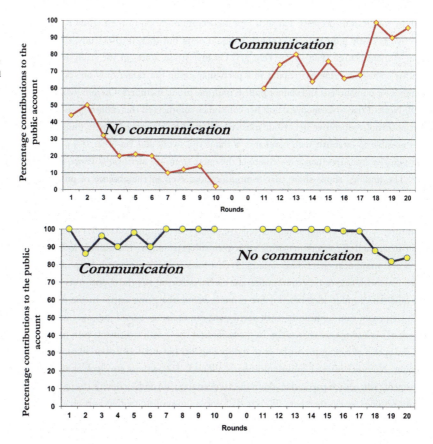

One might think that the primary role of communication is to foster a feeling of community and belonging and, thus, any type of communication might enhance cooperation. But Robyn Dawes, Jean McTavish and Harriet Shaklee showed that in order to be effective, such communication must allow participants to talk extensively about the actual dilemma facing them. Irrelevant communication, where participants are allowed to talk about everything else other than the problem facing them, is not as successful in fostering cooperation and deterring free-riding.

Elinor Ostrom, James Walker and Roy Gardner of Indiana University also corroborate this finding vis-à-vis the effectiveness of communication in a common pool resource extraction game. The common pool resource extraction game is similar to the public goods game but, rather than contributing to a public account, participants are asked to make withdrawals from a common pool. The optimal outcome is achieved when everyone abides by a pre-assigned quota of extraction, but each individual has an incentive to exceed the quota because, if every other participant abides by the quota, then the person engaged in over-extracting (analogous to free-riding in the context of the public goods game) is strictly better off. This game simulates a number of real-life dilemmas such as over-fishing in lakes, rivers and oceans, over-grazing on public land as well as environmental pollution.

They look at both communication and costly punishments and find that when participants are allowed to engage in communication at the beginning of each round for multiple rounds, withdrawals decrease and such repeated communication in their study is almost as effective as costly punishments. Though I should point out that, in this study, the punishment is more benign than in the Fehr and Gächter study, since, in the study by Ostrom and her colleagues, each participant in a particular group can target only one other group member for punishment and cannot punish multiple group members. Ostrom (who won the 2009 Nobel Prize in Economics) and her colleagues commented that, contrary to the belief that norms of cooperative behaviour must be enforced by the sword (costly punishments), it is possible to establish such covenants without the sword and via other less punitive or non-punitive measures (hence my choice of the quote from *The Merchant of Venice*, above).[10]

The findings above show that communication, even in the absence of punishment, can improve cooperation. Since there are no enforcement costs here, higher contributions also imply higher efficiency. Olivier Bochet, Talbot Page and Louis Putterman extend this literature by directly comparing the relative efficacy of communication vis-à-vis punishment in sustaining cooperation using a between-subjects design. The authors look at three types of communication; (1) face-to-face, (2) chat-room and (3) numerical cheap talk. In the treatments with face-to-face communication, each participant has the opportunity to talk to the other three group members for five minutes before the game starts. In the treatments with chat-room communication, each participant can exchange verbal messages with group members via a computer chat-room. In the numerical cheap talk treatment, each participant has the option of typing in a number to indicate his/her potential contribution to the public account. No other form of communication is allowed. The authors also look at three more treatments where each particular communication strategy is combined with the opportunity to punish one's group members. It costs 0.25 tokens to punish another participant by one token, implying a cost–benefit ratio of 1:4. There is also a punishment-only treatment which only allows for punishment of group members but no opportunity to communicate.

The main insight from this study is that once face-to-face communication is allowed, average contributions jump up to 96% of the maximum, which is significantly higher than those in the control and the punishment-only treatments. Given the already high contributions in the face-to-face condition, allowing punishments on top of that leads to only a small increase in average contributions to 97%. The chat-room communication with punishment does almost as well as the face-to-face treatment and gets average contributions of around 96%, while the chat-room communication without punishment does not do as well, with contributions averaging 81%. However, both versions of the chat-room treatment do better than either the control or the punishment-only treatment. Unlike the other communication treatments, the numerical cheap talk treatment with or without punishments does not exhibit either higher contributions or higher earnings as compared to either the control or the punishment-only treatments.

A group of researchers that includes David Masclet and Marie-Claire Villeval, both of the University of Lyon, and Charles Noussair and Steven Tucker, both at Purdue University, were intrigued by the Fehr and Gächter results about costly punishment and decided to extend this work by looking at the impact of non-monetary punishments and whether such punishments, such as expressions of disapproval, can also enhance cooperation. They look at two treatments. The first monetary punishment treatment works in the same way as in most other studies discussed above. In the non-monetary punishment treatment, participants are given the opportunity of expressing approval or disapproval of the actions of other group members, but approval or disapproval does not have any pecuniary impact on anyone's pay-offs. As in the monetary punishments treatment, each participant can assign between zero and ten points to another participant, where zero indicates no disapproval and ten indicates maximum disapproval.

Each session of this study consisted of 30 periods, divided into three segments of ten periods each. During each ten-period segment, participants did not know whether the experiment would continue beyond that segment or not. However, they knew the segment length and that each period during the segment would proceed in an identical manner. The first ten periods were played without any punishment opportunities. A monetary or non-monetary punishment was introduced at the end of the tenth period and remained in force until period 20. After that, participants reverted to the baseline treatment as in the first ten periods and played another ten periods with no punishment opportunities. The authors also compare the performance of fixed groups (partners) versus randomly re-matched groups (strangers) in both the monetary and non-monetary punishments environment.

These researchers find that both monetary and non-monetary sanctions initially increase contributions by a similar amount, but that, over time, monetary sanctions are more effective and lead to higher contributions than non-monetary sanctions. Furthermore, and not surprisingly, they find that non-monetary sanctions are more effective in the partners treatment as opposed to the strangers treatment. The authors also find that the average earnings of participants are higher with either monetary or non-monetary punishments compared to the situation where no sanctions are available.

Ananish Chaudhuri and Tirnud Paichayontvijit of Auckland extend this work on the role of communication in social dilemmas. In the parlance of economics, such messages or announcements promising cooperation are nothing but "cheap talk", in the sense that these are completely non-binding and unenforceable, even though clearly they seem to make a difference in terms of enhancing cooperation. Chaudhuri and Paichayontvijit provide a different perspective on the Gächter et al. results that punishments are more effective in the long run. In this study, participants play the linear public goods game for 30 rounds. In one treatment, they can engage in costly punishment along the lines of previous studies. In another treatment, periodically, the experimenter reads aloud an exhortative message asking everyone to contribute to the public account since everyone is better off if everyone contributes his/her entire token endowment to the public account. This exhortative message can be thought of as being similar to public service messages or advertisements. Finally, a third treatment combines messages with a surprise restart. For each of these treatments, they also look separately at behaviour when group composition is fixed (partners) and when group members are randomly re-matched from one round to the next (strangers). Their results suggest that messages appealing to human goodwill can be quite effective in enhancing cooperation compared to punishments, even with a moderately long horizon. Punishments have much greater impact in the partners protocol than with the strangers one. The authors conclude:

> It is clear that there will always be some time horizon for which punishments will outdo other mechanisms in terms of efficiency. But the efficiency enhancing properties of punishments take time to get established and appeals to human goodwill have a much more immediate impact and outdo punishments for extended periods. ... But, the question is not

so much whether punishments are sufficient to deter anti-social behavior. Of course, they are. However, it is possible that, at times and across a range of social dilemmas, especially in the context of anonymous short-lived interactions, more benign mechanisms may achieve similar goals, at a lower social cost.

COOPERATION IN SORTED GROUPS

In many of the things we do in life, we actually *choose* the people we wish to interact with. We decide who to invite to our parties and camping trips; who to watch the Super Bowl or the World Series of baseball or the Rugby World Cup with; we join book clubs and bridge clubs and political parties; we become involved with voluntary associations such as Rotary Club or Amnesty International. Sustaining cooperation in such sorted groups might prove to be less of a challenge. Such sorting may be (1) *exogenous* (undertaken by the experimenter on the basis of a pre-determined rule which may or may not be known to the participants) or (2) *endogenous* (allowing participants to form groups or leave groups on their own accord).

Exogenously sorted groups
Anna Gunnthorsdottir (of the Australian Graduate School of Management at the University of New South Wales), Daniel Houser and Kevin McCabe (the latter two at George Mason; we have already met McCabe as one of the creators of the paradigmatic trust game) investigate this issue by sorting cooperative contributors in the same group. Each session comprises 12 participants. Participants are grouped into four where they play ten rounds of a public goods experiment with three possible values of the MPCR: 0.3, 0.5 and 0.75. The authors look at two different grouping rules: (1) participants are *randomly re-matched* into different groups at the end of each round (*random* treatment) and (2) participants are *sorted* into groups depending on their contribution at the end of each round (*sorted* treatment). The four participants who contribute the most to the public account are placed into one group; the fifth to eighth highest contributors are placed into another group; and the four lowest contributors are placed in the third group. Hence, the grouping is dependent on the contribution in the current round. To avoid strategic behaviour, participants are not informed about how the groups are formed. For a given value of the MPCR, contributions among the sorted groups are always greater than among randomly formed groups. Also, the decay in contributions is much slower among sorted groups compared to the randomly formed groups, with little or no decay in the two sorted treatments with MPCR = 0.5 and MPCR = 0.75.

The authors define "free-riders" as those who contribute 30% or less of their endowment to the public account in the first round. The rest are defined as "co-operators". Within each MPCR, by round four at the latest, contributions by co-operators in the sorted treatment exceed contributions by co-operators in the random treatment. Since the sorted treatment reduces the number of interactions between co-operators and free-riders, the authors conclude that higher contributions by the co-operators in this treatment are due primarily to the more efficacious nature of their prior interactions and the exposure to a history of cooperative interactions. On the other hand, the decay in contribution in the random re-matching treatment is due almost entirely to the reduction in contribution by the co-operators who experience much greater interaction with free-riders.

In a study by Simon Gächter and Christian Thöni (of Lausanne), participants first take part in a "ranking experiment" which consists of playing a one-shot linear public goods game with an MPCR of 0.6 in randomly formed groups of three. Participants did not receive any information about the contribution of other group members or their earnings at this point. Following this, participants take part in the main experiment, which consists of playing a ten-period repeated linear public goods game.

For the main experiment, the three highest contributors in the ranking experiment are put together in one group, the next three in the second group and so on till the three lowest contributors, who form the last group. Participants get to know how these groups are formed and are also informed of how much their *new group members* contributed in the ranking experiment. There is also a control treatment, where the groups are formed *randomly* and has nothing to do with what the participants contributed in the ranking experiment. The authors also combine the two grouping protocols with the opportunity to punish group members. This then gives rise to four separate conditions: (1) sorted no punishment; (2) random no punishment; (3) sorted punishment; and (4) random punishment.

Sorting people into groups based on their performance in the ranking exercise led to a substantial increase in contributions. Even without any punishment opportunities, the top third of contributors in the sorted groups contribute significantly more than the most cooperative third in the randomly formed groups, with average contributions of 70% of the social optimum among sorted groups and only 48% of the social optimum among random groups. Not only that, the three highest contributors in the sorted groups achieved the same level of contribution as the most cooperative third of randomly formed groups, even when the latter had a punishment option at their disposal. The availability of a punishment opportunity does not make a difference in sorted groups since the three highest contributors in the treatment with sorting but no punishment manage to sustain the same level of cooperation as those in the treatment with sorting and punishment.

Angela de Oliveira, Rachel Croson and Catherine Eckel also engage in exogenous sorting, but, in their study, some participants are explicitly informed about the type of the other group members while others are not. So, the focus is on the role of information regarding the type of group members. Participants first play a one-shot public goods game where they are categorized either as "conditional co-operators" or as "selfish" using the same approach as in the original Fischbacher, Gächter and Fehr study on conditional cooperation. Then, on a different day, they take part in a linear public goods game repeated for 15 rounds. Participants are placed into groups of three, where the groups can be (1) homogeneous, consisting of either all conditional co-operators or all selfish players or (2) heterogeneous, consisting of two players of one type and one of the other. In the *known distribution* treatment, participants are explicitly told about the composition of the group prior to starting the experiment, while in the *unknown distribution* treatment they are not given this information. In both treatments, the participant knows his/her own type. The composition of the groups remains unchanged for the duration of the session.

There are two important insights coming out of this study. First, not surprisingly, contributions in groups with three conditional co-operators are significantly higher than in those with two conditional co-operators or one. But, more importantly, contributions in groups with three conditional co-operators are higher when the distribution is *known* as opposed to when it is *unknown*. This suggests that the mere presence of conditional co-operators (which can conceivably be inferred from the contribution patterns) is not enough; conditional co-operators need to know that there are no selfish types in their group for them to sustain cooperation. This latter finding echoes the results reported by Ananish Chaudhuri and Tirnud Paichayontvijit (from Chapter 11) that conditional co-operators cooperate more when they are made aware of the presence of other conditional co-operators.

Endogenous sorting of participants
Talbot Page, Louis Putterman and Bulent Unel adopt an approach that is similar to Gächter and Thöni above, except that, in Page et al., participants can choose who they want in a group with them. There are 16 participants in each one of sixteen sessions. At periodic intervals during a session, each participant is shown a list, without other identifying information and in a random order, of each of the other 15 participants' average contribution to the public account up to that point. Participants are then given the opportunity to express a preference among possible future partners by ranking them. The four individuals with the highest rank are then put together in the same group, followed by the next four and so on. Here, the group size is always equal to four, except participants get to choose which group they wish to belong to.

After new groups are formed, participants resume play without information about whom they have been grouped with, though they could possibly infer this by observing the contributions of group members. The authors also look separately at a punishment treatment and a combined treatment with regrouping and punishment. Regrouping leads to significant increases in contribution to the public good compared to the control treatment. Moreover, average contributions in the regrouping treatment are about the same as in the punishment treatment (about 70% of the social optimum on average). Thus, the participants' abilities to influence who they are grouped with has a demonstrable positive effect on cooperation and efficiency in this study.

Gary Charness and Chun-Lei Yang undertake a more elaborate investigation where participants are not only free to leave their current groups, but can also vote to expel group members. However, here, the expulsion vote is less punitive because expelled members are free to join other groups or remain as "singles" with the same endowment. Thus, expulsion need not imply a reduction in pay-off. Beyond this, there are also opportunities for mergers among groups as a whole. There are two experimental treatments and a control treatment, each consisting of two blocks of 15 rounds each.

The main focus of interest in this study is their treatment 2, where nine people in a "society" are placed into three groups of three participants each and play a public goods game for 15 rounds. The social value of an allocation to the public account depends on the group size, and the greatest group returns are achieved by forming a "grand coalition" where all nine members of the society belong to the same group. After the first three periods, participants learn about the average contribution of each other individual in their society (by identification number only) for those three periods. At that point, participants can choose to either exit the group or vote to expel other group members. Groups are allowed to merge as well. After the end of the first segment of 15 rounds, groups are re-formed and play a second set of 15 rounds which proceed along similar lines.

Clearly, endogenous group formation enhances contributions to the public good in comparison to exogenously formed groups, as in the control treatment. While the contribution rate in exogenously formed groups in a control treatment steadily decline to around 25% of the social optimum, in endogenously formed groups the rate increases to above 95% in the later periods. The most commonly occurring group composition in this treatment is, in fact, the grand coalition of all nine members of the society belonging to the same group, followed by 8-1 and 7-2 splits, respectively. These larger groups tend to be quite stable over time. The authors also find that participants are less likely to exclude another group member the higher that member's contribution vis-à-vis the group average, and that individuals/groups are more likely to merge with another group when that latter group is larger and achieves higher average contributions vis-à-vis the contributions in the former group. Given the ability to sort co-operators in this treatment, profit-maximizing participants find that it pays to cooperate, given that they manage to belong to groups where others also contribute.

AN INTERGENERATIONAL APPROACH TO COOPERATION

Ananish Chaudhuri, Pushkar Maitra (of Monash University) and Sara Graziano (of Wellesley College) were interested in studying how norms of cooperation might be transmitted from parents to their progeny. After all, we are always telling our children to play fair, wait their turn on the playground and to share their toys with others. While we face many social dilemmas in real life, we rarely confront them in a vacuum. When faced with such situations, we often have access to the wisdom of family or friends who may have prior experience with a particular situation and might be able to give us advice regarding how to address a particular issue. In the US, your friends will tell you that you should tip 15% in restaurants and people will think you are a cheapskate if you don't. But in New Zealand or Australia, you are not supposed to tip at all and people will get mad if you do. "You are ruining things for the rest of us", they will tell you down under.

Chaudhuri and his colleagues conjecture that playing a public goods game where each group of participants, after their turn is over, can leave advice to the succeeding group, might, over time, lead to the evolution of norms of cooperation, with later generations not only achieving higher levels of contribution but also managing to mitigate problems of free-riding. Norms or conventions of behaviour that arise during one generation may be passed on to the successors.

In this study, participants in one generation leave advice for the succeeding generation via free-form messages. Such advice can be *private knowledge* (advice left by one player in one generation is given only to his/her immediate successor in the next generation), *public knowledge* (advice left by players of one generation is made available to all members of the next generation) and *common knowledge* (where the advice is not only public, but also read aloud by the experimenter). Contributions in these advice treatments are compared to those in a control (no advice) treatment where participants play the usual public goods game without any advice. Participants play in groups of five for ten rounds. Each participant has ten tokens per round and can allocate tokens to a private account or a public account. Tokens contributed to the public account are doubled and redistributed equally. However, each participant in one generation is connected to another participant in the immediately succeeding generation and each participant in a previous generation earns a second payment which is equal to 50% of the earnings of his/her successor in the next generation. This second payment provides an incentive to participants to take the advice-giving part seriously.

Chaudhuri and his colleagues – using data gathered in Auckland (New Zealand), Calcutta (India) and Wellesley (Massachusetts, USA) – find that such passing of advice from one generation to the next is indeed successful in enhancing cooperation and reducing free-riding, but only when the advice passed from one generation to the next is common knowledge (i.e., the advice left by players of one generation is made available to all members of the next generation and this advice is also read aloud by the experimenter). They find that average contributions in the common knowledge of advice treatment are significantly higher than in the other treatments, including the control (no advice) treatment. To a large extent, the high contributions in the common knowledge of advice treatment are driven by strongly exhortative advice. In the common knowledge treatment, especially in the later generations, the advice is very strong, with literally every participant exhorting their successors to contribute *"all ten (tokens) all the time!"* This exhortative advice in turn influences behaviour through its impact on the beliefs that participants hold. The authors also collected data on the beliefs that participants held about what their peers will do (using incentivized belief elicitations) and find that when the advice from a previous generation is common knowledge, subjects are more optimistic about the cooperativeness of their group members.

CONCLUDING REMARKS

In this chapter, I have addressed the issue of sustaining cooperation in social dilemmas. I started the chapter by showing how cooperation can be sustained via the use of altruistic punishments. I then went on to discuss some limitations of such punishments. These include the fact that punishments create a second-level public good requiring, in the words of Robert Axelrod, "meta-norms of cooperation". I also showed that the efficiency implications of punishments can be ambiguous. This may depend crucially on the cost–benefit ratio and the length of the time horizon. Finally, I showed how the presence of "anti-social" punishers can reduce the efficiency of punishments.

I provided evidence that, in the presence of conditional co-operators, contributions to the public good can be sustained by means other than monetary punishments. These may include non-monetary punitive measures such as expressions of disapproval or social exclusion. They could also include other interventions, such as different types of communication, including advice giving from one generation to the next and assortative matching of like-minded participants. In some cases, such assortative matching is achieved exogenously with the experimenter sorting participants into groups based on similarities in their behaviour or preferences. In other cases, participants left to themselves can form cooperative groups endogenously and can sustain cooperation either via expulsion of free-riders or via leaving less cooperative groups for more cooperative ones.

We now have a fairly clear picture of the preference heterogeneity among participants and the preponderance of conditional co-operators. We also have a good idea of how we can go about creating institutions – particularly those relying on costly punishments – that exploit such conditional aspects of behaviour to sustain cooperation. What, then, are potentially fruitful avenues of further exploration? One obvious way forward is to apply the lessons learned to "field" settings in designing institutions that deal with social dilemmas. The possible applications are numerous, including charitable contributions, tax compliance, managing natural resources, labour relations, legal enforcement and others, possibly unexplored as of yet. It is also clear that there will continue to be substantial contributions to this literature from a neuroeconomic perspective, especially in terms of understanding the motives behind, and the neural pathways involved in, altruistic punishments and norm compliance.

Finally, this line of work is expanding upon traditional socio-biological theories of human cooperation with their emphasis on individual selection, such as kin selection (as in William Hamilton's 1964 work), reciprocal altruism (proposed by Robert Trivers, 1971) or costly signalling (Zahavi and Zahavi, 1997). In fact, the emerging literature on "strong reciprocity" (as discussed in the book *Moral Sentiments and Material Interests*, edited by Herb Gintis, Sam Bowles, Rob Boyd and Ernst Fehr), argues that the presence of *homo reciprocans* – conditional co-operators who are willing to punish free-riders even if such punishment is costly to the punishers and confer no future benefits – may be the primary driving force behind sustaining cooperation in a variety of social settings. These insights seem to provide new evidence in favour of multi-level selection as well as gene-culture co-evolution (for instance, in Peter Richerson and Rob Boyd's 1985 book, *Not by Genes Alone*, or Eliot Sober and David Sloan Wilson's 1998 book *Unto Others*) as opposed to selection at the level of the individual.

In recent times, a group of researchers led by Quentin Atkinson at the University of Auckland have extended this line of work to study the evolution of political ideology.[11] Research conducted in the second half of the 20th century and the first decade or so of the 21st century suggests that political attitudes and values around the globe are shaped by two ideological dimensions, typically referred to as economic and social conservatism (the converse being economic and social progressivism). However, it remains unclear why this ideological structure exists. Atkinson, along with his collaborators Scott Claessens, Chris Sibley and others, show that there is a striking concordance between these dual dimensions of ideology and independent convergent evidence for two key shifts in the evolution of human group living. First, humans began to cooperate more and across wider interdependent networks. Second, humans became more group-minded, conforming to social norms in culturally marked groups and punishing norm-violators. They propose that fitness trade-offs and environmental pressures leading to differential expressions of inherent preferences have maintained variation in these two predispositions: willingness to cooperate and conform within modern human groups, naturally giving rise to the two dimensions of political ideology. Atkinson et al. use a series of behavioural decision-making games like the ones discussed in this book to provide insights into the biological and cultural basis of political ideology and their evolution.

NOTES

1   This is not quite accurate for the original study but for reasons that will become clear shortly, a large number of subsequent papers have tended to adopt this punishment structure; for each dollar given up by a punisher, the punishment recipient's pay-off is reduced by $3. I am not doing too much injustice to the original Fehr and Gächter study by making this assumption.

2. In a later study, Fehr & Gächter extend their exploration to a within-subjects design except with random re-matching in all sessions. In one treatment, participants play six rounds without a punishment option followed by another six rounds with the punishment option. This sequence is reversed in the second treatment. Here, each token of punishment reduces the earnings of the punished participant by three tokens. Since participants are randomly re-matched at the beginning of each round, theories of reciprocity or costly signalling cannot explain cooperation and punishment in this environment. The authors suggest that punishment in this context is truly "altruistic", in the sense that this punishment is costly to the punisher but does not generate any immediate benefits for the current group members since groups are randomly reconstituted at the end of each round. The results show that 84% of participants punish at least once. Punishments appear to be triggered by negative emotions, given that 74% of punishment is imposed by participants who contribute higher than the group average on those who contribute lower than the group average.
3. Studies implementing a punishment mechanism fall into one of two categories. Either they use a "within-subjects" design where the same participant takes part in two treatments: an experimental treatment with a punishment option and a control treatment without punishment. Others use a "between-subjects" treatment where some participants take part in treatments with punishment while others take part in a control treatment without. In what follows, every time I say that this is a "between-subjects" treatment, it will imply that besides the experimental treatments, one set of participants always take part in a control treatment, where no punishment opportunity is available.
4. This means that participants do not all face the treatments in the same order. Some may face one treatment first while others take part in a different treatment first.
5. In fact, in a follow-up study with Arhan Ertan, Page and Putterman allowed their participants to vote on who should be punished – those who contribute less than, equal to or greater than the group average contribution. The authors find that there are no groups where a majority voted to allow punishment of participants who contribute more than the group average. This ruled out the possibility of "antisocial" punishments.
6. These locations are: Athens, Bonn, Boston, Chengdu, Copenhagen, Dnipropetrovs'k, Istanbul, Melbourne, Minsk, Muscat, Nottingham, Riyadh, Samara, Seoul, St. Gallen and Zurich. Henrich et al. (2010) point out that most people are not WEIRD (meaning Western, Educated, Industrialized, Rich and Democratic). Yet, the participants in the vast majority of studies, including those cited in this article, come from that somewhat unusual pool. Hence, the extent to which these results are applicable to those who are not WEIRD is open to debate.
7. The rule of law indicator is based on a number of variables that measure "the extent to which agents have confidence in and abide by the rules of society, and in particular the quality of contract enforcement, the police, and the courts, as well as the likelihood of crime and violence" (Herrmann et al., 2008, p. 1366).
8. Leviticus 24:19-20. (New American Standard Bible).
9. *The Merchant of Venice*, Act 4, Scene 1.
10. Elinor Ostrom (or "Lin" to her many students, collaborators and admirers) passed away in 2012. Ostrom was primarily a political scientist but is probably best remembered for her tremendous contribution toward conserving common pool resources using insights from behavioural economics. She was working on issues of sustainability and climate change long before these issues became fashionable and mainstream.
11. Other members of this group are Ananish Chaudhuri, Scott Claessens, Kyle Fischer, Guy Lavender-Forsyth and Chris Sibley.

13 I will if you will

Resolving coordination failures in organizations

In this chapter, I:

- *Describe coordination problems that give rise to multiple equilibria;*
- *Explain how and why such coordination problems arise in everyday life;*
- *Define two different types of coordination problems; those where the equilibria are pay-off ranked, in the sense that one equilibrium yields a higher pay-off to all players, and those where there is no such ranking among the equilibria;*
- *Show that a crucial feature of resolving coordination problems is the creation of appropriately optimistic beliefs regarding the actions of one's peers;*
- *Discuss applications of such coordination problems to economics.*

COORDINATION FAILURES IN REAL LIFE

The next time you fly somewhere and you are waiting to board your plane, take a look outside at the waiting aircraft. Most of us do not really appreciate this, but there is frenzied activity going on. The pilot and co-pilot are carrying out pre-flight checks; baggage handlers are unloading the baggage from the inbound flight and loading the baggage for the outbound passengers; one group is cleaning the cabin and the toilets; another is loading the fuel; yet another is loading the food containers. The only way the plane will get off on time – and the percentage of on-time departures is an important measure of how well an airline is performing – is if all these groups manage to successfully *coordinate* their actions and work at the same pace; if even one group lags behind the others, the plane will be delayed.

Delays, even small ones, in one flight taking off – especially at large and busy airports such as Frankfurt, New York or Singapore – often have a ripple effect on flights later in the day with all flights getting progressively more delayed as the day wears on. Thus, on-time departure of a flight requires a disparate number of people to coordinate their actions.

To most of us, this seems like a trivial issue – after all, planes take off on time more often than they are delayed. But getting a large group of agents to successfully coordinate their actions actually poses a non-trivial challenge for many organizations. Continental Airlines, for instance, ran into trouble in the 1980s due to its failure to resolve such coordination problems in a satisfactory manner. Since deregulation of the airline industry in the United States in 1978, over the next decade or so, Continental typically averaged last among the ten major domestic airlines in on-time arrival, baggage handling and customer complaints and filed

■ I will if you will

twice for bankruptcy, once in 1983 and then again in 1990. I will have more to say about the experiences of Continental Airlines shortly.[1]

Coordination problems are not restricted to airlines only, but arise in a variety of organizations and across a number of different contexts. Such coordination problems arise in any industry that is engaged in team production along an assembly line, such as in steel mills and automobile factories. The next time you take the children to McDonald's or Burger King (or even if you sneak in surreptitiously on your own to get your burger fix), take a look behind the counter. There is an immense coordination problem being addressed there. In order to get a burger from the person who is frying them to the person who puts them inside the buns to the person who puts on the cheese, onions and pickles and wraps them to the person at the front of the store who finally hands it over to the customer, a complex coordination problem has just been addressed where success depends on how quickly one can get the burger to the customer and reduce the time people are waiting in line.

A similar coordination problem arises, for instance, in deciding whether to join a protest against an unpopular regime or not. Here, I wish to join the protest if, and only if, I am convinced that another person or group of people will also join in. The probability of being beaten up by the police or getting arrested is much lower if there are thousands of protesters than if there are only a handful. Thus, I want to join the protest only if enough others join also. The desire on the part of participants in such situations to undertake a course of action only if enough others do the same often means complete lack of coordination and unsuccessful outcomes; but if and when participants do manage to coordinate their actions, they can also achieve enormous success.

CASE STUDY 13.1 PROTESTS, PCS, BUYING GROCERIES AND STOPPING AT GREEN LIGHTS

As the late and unlamented dictator of Romania, Nicolae Ceauşescu, found out in December 1989, coordinated actions among protesting citizens can be a very powerful tool in bringing down an unpopular regime. Within a span of about ten days in December 1989, Ceauşescu and his wife Elena went from being absolute rulers of a nation to their execution by firing squad in Targoviste, Romania, due in large part to massive and coordinated protests across the nation.

Here are a number of other situations where coordination issues are important. If you are sitting next to a computer, look over at the keyboard. The keyboard that the overwhelming majority of us use is called the QWERTY keyboard. It takes its name from the first six letters located to the left of the keyboard's first row of letters. The QWERTY design was patented by Christopher Sholes in 1874 and sold to Remington in the same year, when it first appeared in typewriters. This is, in fact, the only keyboard that most of us have ever encountered. The original design of the keyboard had the characters arranged alphabetically, set on the end of a metal bar which struck the paper when the appropriate key was pressed. However, when someone typed at speed, the bars attached to letters that lay close together on the keyboard tended to stick to one another, forcing the typist to manually disentangle the bars. This prompted Sholes to split up the keys for letters commonly used together to speed up typing. But this also had the unintended consequence of making the QWERTY keyboard less efficient. There exists another keyboard called the DVORAK keyboard which is simpler and makes for faster typing. But we seldom see these keyboards around. Why? Because moving from the QWERTY keyboard to the DVORAK keyboard would require massive coordination between users and producers of keyboards; people who have already spent time and effort learning QWERTY will be willing to learn DVORAK if, and only if, enough others are doing so and these keyboards are available widely; but producers will only produce the keyboard if, and only if, there are enough users and, therefore, demand for these keyboards. A move to DVORAK then requires a simultaneous switch by users and producers.

Similarly, should an organization invest in Macs or PCs? I want to be proficient in using PCs if everyone around me is using PCs, but if everyone uses Macs, then I am better off with a Mac. But if I have spent an awful amount of time learning how to use a PC and then find that everyone around me is using a Mac, then I have a problem and am better off switching to a Mac also, but the switch is costly in terms of time and effort.

These days, when we go to the supermarket for groceries, we take the barcode on products as given and do not give it a second thought. These barcodes make paying for things a lot easier since it prevents the person at the check-out counter from having to look up the price all the time. But the implementation of these barcodes required the resolution of a complex coordination problem; it was expensive to install barcode scanners and supermarkets were willing to do so if, and only if, producers were going to invest in the technology that put barcodes on their products; but producers would be willing to put the barcodes on only if enough supermarkets had barcode scanners.

A classic example of a pure coordination problem arises from which side of the road to drive on. Americans and people in Western Europe drive on the right; the British and people of former British colonies like India, New Zealand and Australia drive on the left; confusion reigns when American tourists visit New Zealand and vice versa.

Following the Cultural Revolution of 1966, Chairman Mao of China urged thousands of students, who came to be known as Red Guards, to change old customs, habits, culture, and thinking. It is said that some Red Guards tried to force traffic to *stop* at green lights and *go* on red, red being the colour of the revolution which symbolized progress. This attempt at breaking down the existing convention did not achieve much success!

Along similar lines, while electronic appliances in most parts of the world run on 220 volts, those in the US run on 110 volts. This makes US electronic appliances unusable in other parts of the world. (My wife and I brought over a bunch of electronic goods when we moved from the US to New Zealand and tried to run them using voltage converters for a while; it was not long before they all burned out!)

■ I will if you will

The primary insights from these stories are: first, in most of these cases, coordinating to some outcome is more desirable than *not* coordinating at all. So, it would be better if we all drove on the left and used 220 volts. This would impose a cost on those who would need to get accustomed to the new system but, in the long run, this would aid coordination and eliminate the confusion that now exists.

Second, the fundamental strategic problem created by issues of coordination is very different from the social dilemmas that we encountered in earlier chapters. A coordination problem is *not* a social dilemma like the prisoner's dilemma. In deciding whether to work on the officer's club or not, Yossarian is always better off if he shirks and lets Nately do all the work. But when it comes to undertaking coordinated actions, this is no longer true. Now it makes sense for Yossarian to work if he thinks Nately will work as well but to shirk if he thinks Nately will shirk; Yossarian would like to join the demonstration if Nately does so and vice versa; Yossarian would like to drive on the left if Nately does so and Yossarian would like to use a PC if Nately is using a PC and so on.

There is no longer a *unique* strategy for Yossarian as there was in the prisoner's dilemma game; now Yossarian is better off if he does what Nately is doing, but how do they make sure that they both do the same? How do I know for sure that other people will show up at the demonstration? Or, in a more general setting, how do the groups at Continental Airlines go about coordinating their actions? Moreover, in many of these cases, there is more than one feasible outcome, such as Yossarian and Nately both deciding to work or both deciding to shirk; Yossarian and Nately both showing up with placards at the demonstration or both

Della's strategy	Jim's strategy	
	Sell watch	Don't sell watch
Sell hair	Della's profit = $0 Jim's profit = $0	Della's profit = $3 Jim's profit = $5
Don't sell hair	Della's profit = $5 Jim's profit = $3	Della's profit = $0 Jim's profit = $0

Hunter 1	Hunter 2	
	Hunt stag	Hunt rabbit
Hunt stag	1's profit = $8 2's profit = $8	1's profit = $0 2's profit = $5
Hunt rabbit	1's profit = $5 2's profit = $0	1's profit = $5 2's profit = $5

Figure 13.1
Pay-off matrices for the battle of the sexes game and the stag hunt game

312

staying home; the groups at Continental all working quickly to get the plane off the ground at the designated time or all of them taking their own sweet time leading to massive delays and dissatisfied customers.

I introduced such coordination problems in Chapter 6, where I discussed issues of strategic thinking. There, I introduced two different types of coordination games, where the incentives were different. In the battle of the sexes game played by Della and Jim (from O. Henry's *Gift of the Magi*), there were two equilibria; one yielded a higher pay-off to Della and the other yielded a higher pay-off to Jim. The other one was the stag hunt game, which also had two equilibria, but one of them was pay-off dominant, in the sense that both players received a higher pay-off if they managed to coordinate to this equilibrium, as opposed to a secure or risk dominant equilibrium, which yielded a lower but guaranteed minimum pay-off. I reproduce the two games in Figure 13.1 to remind readers and as a segue to the rest of the discussion for this chapter. The top panel of Figure 13.1 shows the battle-of-the-sexes game, while the bottom panel shows the stag hunt game. I have highlighted the equilibria in each case, though I expect most readers will recall much of this from our previous discussion.

EXPERIMENTAL EVIDENCE ON COORDINATION FAILURES

So, how do people do when confronted with one of the coordination problems described above? How should we go about trying to understand how good or bad people are in coordinating their actions? One immediate thought that comes to mind is to look at organizations that deal with problems like these on a regular basis. You could go to an automobile manufacturing factory or a steel mill and observe how their workers perform along an assembly line. Or you could spend time at an airline hub such as Atlanta for Delta or Singapore for Singapore Airlines and see how these companies go about getting their workers to coordinate their actions to ensure smooth landings and take-offs. This would, and certainly does, yield valuable information. But, at the end of the day, the data that you get might tell you a lot about the operations of the company in question, but it may not be easy to extrapolate from that to the operations of other companies. This is because each organization has its own culture and its own set of rules and goes about addressing their problems in their own unique ways. It is often difficult to isolate the fundamental problem from the rules, conventions and shorthands that organizations have evolved in order to solve that problem.

Experiments provide an alternative. It is possible to take the underlying problem and its incentive structure and design a suitable experiment. The sterile atmosphere of the laboratory and the use of neutral context-free language certainly sacrifice a lot of reality but there are some benefits as well. First, it allows us to study the problem in the absence of any intervention whatsoever and, thereby, gain an understanding of what happens in the absence of any rules or conventions already in place. Because of these conventions and cultures that organizations develop to deal with coordination problems in real-life, operations in these organizations are likely to be much less dysfunctional than suggested by laboratory experiments. But the experiments can establish a lower bound on how bad the problem can be or what a new organization starting out might expect to encounter.

Second, experiments can also provide valuable pointers regarding how to address these issues. Because you can make small changes to the experimental design in order to tease out differential responses to those changes, you can see which interventions do better than others. Thus, you can use the experiments as a "wind-tunnel" where you can test various recommendations and see which ones work well and which don't; it would be very expensive to implement a set of policies at the company level only to find out that they are completely ineffective or, worse yet, provide perverse incentives to workers.

Third, the insights gained from experiments can complement what you learn via your field studies and, at the same time, might also provide ideas and directions for changes that might lead to greater coordination and efficiency. Experiments not only provide you a mechanism to get a better handle on the underlying problem, but can also provide you with a relatively inexpensive way of figuring out how you might be able to implement policies that help workers coordinate their actions.

In the late 1980s, a group of researchers – Russell Cooper, Douglas DeJong, Robert Forsythe and Thomas Ross – at the University of Iowa embarked on an ambitious project to understand problems of coordination failure. They decided to look at both the battle of the sexes game as well as the stag hunt game. They essentially ask two questions: (1) how well do people manage to coordinate their actions in these games? (2) if they do not manage to coordinate, then what mechanisms or interventions might help them to achieve greater coordination?

Let me start with the first question. They had 99 advanced undergraduates and MBA students participate in the battle of the sexes game and 275 advanced undergraduates and MBA students participate in two different versions of the stag hunt game. They designed a set of appropriate games which preserved the incentive structure of the two different problems. The games looked similar to the ones I have described in Figure 13.1 except the strategies for the two players were given non-emotive labels such as "Top" and "Bottom" for one player and "Left" and "Right" for the other. The participants played a number of times, and, at the end of each round, they were randomly re-matched so that they usually did not play another player more than once. In any case, all interactions were carried out via computers so that no one ever learned the identity of the player he/she was paired with.

When Cooper and his colleagues looked at behaviour in the battle of the sexes game, they found, possibly not surprisingly, large scale coordination failure. The players managed to coordinate to one of the available equilibria in only 48% of the total interactions and failed to coordinate, thereby earning zero for both players, in 52% of interactions. Needless to mention, most of this coordination failure is caused by each player going for his or her most favoured outcome; that is, Pat choosing to buy a ticket to the opera while Chris buys a ticket to the ballgame. This suggested that, when faced with a problem like this, people like Pat and Chris would spend many anniversaries doing something on their own![2]

But even more surprising was the behaviour in the stag hunt game. In this game, the pay-offs that players get are common knowledge in that it is immediately apparent to both players that they are both better off if they cooperate (and hunt the stag) rather than act on their own (and hunt the rabbit). Yet, in the experiments run by Cooper's group, there were massive coordination failures. The vast majority of their participants failed to coordinate to the pay-off dominant outcome, choosing the secure outcome instead. In one version of the stag hunt game, where each player had to choose one of two strategies, more than 80% of their participants chose the secure strategy of hunting a rabbit that led to the secure outcome. In another version of the game, where each player had a choice of one of three strategies, the lack of coordination was even starker. In the second game, Cooper and his colleagues found that out of 330 choices made by the participants, only five were ones commensurate with the pay-off dominant outcome and the remaining 325 were strategies that led to the secure (and lower pay-off) outcome.

In fact, Cooper et al. find that the presence of dominated strategies and the pay-offs that result from the play of those dominated strategies make a significant difference to the degree of coordination success. Consider the two games shown in Table 13.1. On the face of it, it looks as if both these games have three Nash equilibria: {1, 1}, {2, 2} and {3, 3}. But this is incorrect. If you look closely, you will see that Strategy 3 is dominated by Strategy 1 for both players. Consider the row player. If the column player chooses Strategy 1, then the row player gets $35 from playing Strategy 1 as opposed to $0 from Strategy 3; if column player chooses Strategy 2, then row player gets $35 from Strategy 1 and $0 from Strategy 3. Finally, if column player selects Strategy 3, then row player gets $70 from 1 and $60 from 3. In each case, the pay-off from Strategy 1 is strictly higher than the pay-off from Strategy 3. An exact same argument is applicable for the column player. This implies that Strategy 3 is strictly dominated for both players. If we eliminate this dominated strategy, then the remaining game becomes a standard 2×2 stag hunt game with two equilibria; a pay-off dominant equilibrium at {2, 2} yielding $55 for each player and a risk-dominant equilibrium {1, 1} where each player gets $35.

It is worth noting that the choice of Strategy 3 by each player results in each getting $60, which is higher than the $55 that they get in the pay-off dominant equilibrium. So {3, 3} can be thought of as a joint maximum but attaining this requires players to play a strictly dominated strategy, which would potentially require an even greater feat of coordination.

The final interesting thing about the two games in Table 13.1 is what happens if players fail to coordinate. First look at Game 1. Suppose row player chooses Strategy 2 in order to coordinate to the pay-off dominant outcome at {2, 2} while column player wishes to reach the {3, 3} outcome that leads to maximum payoff for both. So, column player chooses the dominated Strategy 3. This means that the players will end up at {2, 3} and each earn nothing. (Remember that because the game is symmetric, arguments that apply to row player apply with equal force to column player.) But, if we now look at Game 2, we find that in that game, the threat of getting nothing from mis-coordinating to {2, 3} has been removed for row player. Here, row player gets $100 while column player gets nothing.

Table 13.1 Two stag hunt games, each with a dominated strategy, leading to different results

Game 1
Row player

	Column player		
	1	2	3
1	$35, $35	$35, $25	$70, $0
2	$25, $35	$55, $55	$0, $0
3	$0, $70	$0, $0	$60, $60

Game 2
Row player

	Column player		
	1	2	3
1	$35, $35	$35, $25	$70, $0
2	$25, $35	$55, $55	$100, $0
3	$0, $70	$0, $100	$60, $60

Now, normally, game theory suggests that the pay-offs in those cells that are not part of any equilibrium should not matter at all in terms of player choices. In economics and other sciences, the fancy term for this concept is *independence of irrelevant alternatives*. This means that irrelevant alternatives should make no difference to our choices. In this specific case, this means that what happens when players select a dominated strategy should have no influence on the outcome of the game. This is because we assume that players will start to play the game by ruling out the dominated Strategy 3. This leaves them with only Strategies 1 and 2, and rational players should have no difficulty in coordinating to the {2, 2} pay-off dominant equilibrium.

But, as we know well now, irrelevant alternatives and dominated strategies do matter. Not surprisingly, Cooper et al. find that in Game 1, where the penalty for mis-coordination is getting $0, the majority of players end up coordinating to the risk-dominant {1, 1} equilibrium. But in Game 2, where this penalty is no longer present, players find it easier to coordinate to the pay-off dominant {2, 2} equilibrium. Cooper et al. explain these results by suggesting that in both games, players place positive probability on some others playing the dominated (but cooperative) Strategy 3, which is not surprising in light of what we have discussed earlier in terms of human cooperation. But, in doing so, the pay-off that arises when players fail to coordinate and end up at outcomes like {2, 3} has a crucial impact on which equilibrium is selected. I will have a bit more to say about this when I talk about the role of communication in such games.

THE MINIMUM EFFORT COORDINATION GAME

An even more dramatic example of people's inability to coordinate their actions so as to achieve the maximum pay-off came from a group of researchers at Texas A&M University around the same time in the late 1980s. John van Huyck, Raymond Battalio and Richard Beil looked at a more elaborate version of the stag hunt game. Their set-up actually better represents the coordination problems faced by groups in organizations like those working on getting the plane off the ground. Van Huyck and his colleagues called their game "the minimum effort game".

In their game, players in a group have to pick numbers between 1 and 7. The choices are made without any communication or interaction of any kind. The money that each person earns depends on two things: (1) the number picked by that person and (2) the *lowest number picked by someone in the group*. If everyone picks 7, each player earns $1.30. If they all pick 6, each player earns $1.20; if they all pick 5, each earns $1.10; and so on down to the case where each player earns $0.70 if everyone picks 1. But here is the catch. Because the payoff depends not only on your own choice (or your own effort level), but on the lowest number picked by a group member (i.e., the lowest effort exerted in the group), even if it is only one person picking that low number (low effort), choosing higher numbers is risky. If you pick a high number while someone in the group picks a low number, then you get next to nothing. For instance, suppose you pick 7 while someone in the group picks 1, then you get only $0.10. This essentially means that being away from (above) the lowest number picked by the group yields little money. If everyone but one person in the group picks 7 while that last person picks 1, then the people picking 7 all earn $0.10 each while the person picking 1 earns $0.70.

The person picking the lowest number has a lot of power to hurt those who are taking the risk of choosing higher numbers. Table 13.2 shows the pay-off matrix for this game.

This is similar to the example of the plane taking off on time. In the case of the aeroplane, even if every group but one works quickly and completes their task in the recommended time while one group dawdles, the plane will not take off on time and the effort put in by the conscientious workers is wasted. Similarly, if you think of mountain climbing, even if all but one of the mountain climbers are making steady progress, the one straggler – the weak link – can hold up progress.

Players in such minimum effort games therefore face two challenges. The first is to coordinate their actions to one number between 1 and 7. This is because if everyone else is picking 1 then you don't want to pick anything higher because it will cost you money. But second, you want the group to collectively coordinate and pick the highest number possible because that yields the highest pay-off to each player. So, each player is better off and makes the most money if they all pick 7 (analogous to everyone working hard).

But as I mentioned before, even if every player except one chooses 7 while that one straggler chooses 1, then that person choosing 1 – the lowest number or effort level – can hurt the others badly and slow down progress. So, if you are not convinced that everyone in the group will choose 7 and you have even the slightest doubt that someone in the group might actually choose 1, then you might want to be risk averse and choose 1 as well. By choosing 1, you will guarantee that your choice is the minimum in the group. If everyone reasons along the same lines, then they will choose 1 as well. And at that outcome, you are guaranteed to earn $0.70. Higher choices are more lucrative as long as everyone chooses high, but in the absence of any communication with others or commitments from them, higher choices bring with them the risk of a lower pay-off and the further away you are from the person choosing the lowest number, the worse off you are! This then suggests that if you are not certain that others will pick high numbers, then the secure course of action would be to choose 1, thereby guaranteeing a pay-off of $0.70. So, everyone picking 1 emerges as the secure option in this game. This is not all that different from the stag hunt game. Everyone picking 7 is analogous to the hunters cooperating to hunt the stag, while everyone picking 1 is similar to each hunter going off on his/her own to hunt the rabbit.

Van Huyck and his colleagues recruited 107 participants who took part in seven groups. There were four groups of 16 players each, two groups of 14 each and one group with 15 players. The group members interacted for ten rounds, picking a number in each of those

Table 13.2 Pay-off matrix: Van Huyck et al. (1990) minimum effort coordination game

		\multicolumn{7}{c}{*Smallest value of effort chosen in the group*}
		7	6	5	4	3	2	1
Value of effort chosen by a player	7	1.30	1.10	0.90	0.70	0.50	0.30	0.10
	6	---	1.20	1.00	0.80	0.60	0.40	0.20
	5	---	---	1.10	0.90	0.70	0.50	0.30
	4	---	---	---	1.00	0.80	0.60	0.40
	3	---	---	---	---	0.90	0.70	0.50
	2	---	---	---	---	---	0.80	0.60
	1	---	---	---	---	---	---	0.70

ten rounds. At the end of each round, the participants are informed about the lowest number picked by someone in the group but not who picked that number. They also did not learn what the other group members chose. Thus, it is entirely possible that many, if not most, in a group could have chosen 7 while maybe only one player chose 1. At the end of the round, the players only learn that the lowest number picked in the group was 1. Since each player's pay-off depends on his/her choice and the lowest number picked, each player can figure out how much he/she earned in a particular round once told about the lowest number chosen. The composition of the group remained unchanged for the entire time, so the same group of people interact with one another over and over again, which is probably closer to what happens in real life.

Remember that each player earns $1.30 if they all choose 7 while each gets $0.70 if they all choose 1. Thus, in each round, the pay-off to coordinating to the pay-off dominant outcome is almost twice that of coordinating to the secure outcome. The instructions are read out loud and make this fact common knowledge among the participants. In Table 13.3, I show a typical pattern of choices in a group of 16 playing the game for ten rounds. In the first round, eight people picked "7" and 13 out of 16 people picked "5" or more; no one picked "1" and the minimum number chosen was "2". But, over time, there is an inexorable move toward picking smaller numbers, such that by round ten, 13 out of 16 players picked "1". The minimum chosen was "2" for the first three rounds and "1" for the remaining 7 rounds.

The behaviour of the group members – and the failure to coordinate to the pay-off dominant outcome – is quite striking! Table 13.4 shows the minimum number that the seven groups managed to coordinate to. As can be seen from this table, none of the groups managed to coordinate to any number higher than 4. Only two groups – Groups 3 and 4 – managed a minimum of 4, but that too for only the first round. Moreover, none of the seven groups managed to keep the minimum above 1 for more than three rounds. By round four, at least one person in each and every one of these seven groups chose 1. Furthermore, in most groups, by the end of round ten, the majority of the group members were choosing 1. In Groups 1 and 2, which had 16 players each, 13 out of 16 players chose 1 in round ten. In Group 4 which had 15 players, 13 of them chose 1 in round ten. Thus, these players were, by and large, coordinating their actions, no doubt, but they were coordinating to the outcome that was the worst possible in terms of the pay-off that they earned. The failure to coordinate

Table 13.3 Typical pattern of effort choices by individuals within groups in Van Huyck et al. (1990) minimum effort coordination game

					Rounds					
Number chosen	1	2	3	4	5	6	7	8	9	10
7	8	1	1	0	0	0	0	0	0	1
6	3	2	1	0	0	0	0	0	0	0
5	2	3	2	1	0	0	1	0	0	0
4	1	6	5	4	1	1	1	0	0	0
3	1	2	5	5	4	1	1	1	0	1
2	1	2	2	4	8	7	8	6	4	1
1	0	0	0	2	3	7	5	9	12	13
Average chosen	5.81	4.25	3.88	2.88	2.19	1.75	2.06	1.5	1.25	1.56
Minimum chosen	2	2	2	1	1	1	1	1	1	1

Table 13.4 Typical pattern of minimum effort choices across all groups in Van Huyck et al. (1990) minimum effort coordination game

	Rounds									
	1	2	3	4	5	6	7	8	9	10
Groups										
1	2	2	2	1	1	1	1	1	1	1
2	2	1	1	1	1	1	1	1	1	1
3	4	2	2	1	1	1	1	1	1	1
4	4	2	3	1	1	1	1	1	1	1
5	3	2	1	1	1	1	1	1	1	1
6	1	1	1	1	1	1	1	1	1	1
7	1	1	1	1	1	1	1	1	1	1

to the pay-off dominant outcome where everyone chose 7 and earned $1.30 in each round is evident.

To what extent is the lack of successful coordination dependent on the size of the group? The groups that Van Huyck and his colleagues used were relatively large, consisting of 14 to 16 people. Would smaller groups do better? Van Huyck and his colleagues repeated the same game, but this time with only two players in each group and found that these two participants manage to coordinate to the pay-off dominant outcome of both choosing 7 most of the time. So, coordination failure was not a concern in two-person groups. Thus, the failure to successfully coordinate seems to be a problem of large groups. But exactly how large is "large"? The answer came from Marc Knez of the University of Chicago and Colin Camerer of Caltech who had participants in their experiment take part in a variant of the minimum effort game in groups of three. The three-player groups were not very successful in achieving coordination to the pay-off dominant outcome. Thus, groups of three appear to be large enough for coordination to break down, and larger groups are expected to do worse.

A number of subsequent studies replicated this inability of groups to coordinate to the pay-off dominant outcome and it became clear that these results were robust and not unique to the experiments carried out by Cooper and his colleagues or Van Huyck and his colleagues. Economists have great faith in the rationality of economic agents and their ability to seek out opportunities that yield the most money. Needless to mention, the results reported by Cooper and his colleagues or Van Huyck and his colleagues came as an enormous surprise to most economists. Prior to the publication of these results, economic theorists had argued that, when confronted with a stag hunt type problem, rational economic agents would be able to use their powers of deductive reasoning to figure out that they should coordinate to the pay-off dominant outcome; after all, that was the outcome that yielded the most money.

These results disproved that conjecture. They suggested that, in the absence of any intervention, such as some sort of rules or conventions or the possibility of communication with other group members and the opportunity to make commitments, reasonably intelligent people may find it extremely difficult to coordinate to the pay-off dominant outcome. Van Huyck and his colleagues, however, argued that this was not necessarily a failure of deductive reasoning in the sense that it was not the case that people were unable to figure out that they would make more money if they all chose 7 and coordinated to the pay-off dominant outcome. Rather, the failure to reach the pay-off dominant outcome was caused by *strategic uncertainty*; that is, people are reluctant to choose high numbers because they are not absolutely convinced that everyone else in the group will do the same. So, in a way, this comes down to a question of trust after all. A particular member of the group is perfectly willing to work hard as long as he/she knows that he/she can trust his/her peers and is convinced that they will work hard as well. But any doubt in the minds of the group members, even if small, that at least one person in the group might end up choosing 1, leads them to choose 1 as well, and thereby destroys the possibility of coordinating to the pay-off dominant outcome. The key issue, then, is to create the appropriately optimistic beliefs in the minds of the participants that fellow group members will all choose the strategy that is commensurate with the pay-off dominant outcome.

As I pointed out above, this does not suggest that most groups or organizations are really this bad at coordinating the actions of group members. In fact, most are rather good at addressing such problems. But what these results do suggest unambiguously is that: (1) strategic uncertainty about the actions of other group members loom large in such situations and (2) in the absence of judicious interventions designed to mitigate problems of coordination failure, this strategic uncertainty can lead to massive coordination failures and some seriously sub-optimal outcomes. This, in turn, led to attempts to understand what form those interventions should take and an analysis of interventions that work better than others. That is what I look at next.

But before that, I need to point out the following. In discussing interventions that facilitate coordination, I am going to focus to a large extent on coordination in stag hunt games. This is for two reasons. First, the kind of problems that are encapsulated by the battle of the sexes game – such as the adoption of standards such as keyboards, operating systems, television broadcasting systems, electrical power, which side of the road to drive on, and so on – are often extremely history dependent. That is, a particular standard was adopted due to a historical accident or because somebody invented or discovered something first, and that initial incident to a large extent dictated the course of events to follow.

This is like rain falling on one of two sides of a continental divide, a line of elevated terrain. Drops of rain falling on one side of the divide will eventually travel to one ocean or body of water, while other drops falling in close proximity but on the other side of the divide will usually travel to another ocean or body of water, generally on the opposite side of the continent. Thus, once one person or a group starts using QWERTY, others start to use it too; film studios follow the leader and set up around Hollywood; start-up dotcoms congregate around Silicon Valley while other high-tech firms gravitate towards Route 128 in Massachusetts. But this also implies that once players, groups and organizations are locked into one of these choices, it is difficult to induce the parties involved to change their strategy and move to a different outcome. As a result, resolving coordination failures in such circumstances is more difficult (and maybe of less immediate relevance).

Second, and quite possibly as a result of the first difficulty, there has been more work trying to understand how to facilitate coordination in stag hunt games rather than battle of the sexes games. Moreover, the stag hunt game is more relevant to the problems faced by many organizations and, therefore, economists have spent more time trying to understand how to resolve coordination failures in such cases.

TALK IS CHEAP; OR IS IT? USING COMMUNICATION TO RESOLVE COORDINATION FAILURES

So, the question is: how do we get people to coordinate their actions to one of the available equilibria in a coordination game; or, put differently, how do we prevent people from failing to coordinate and ending up at a bad outcome? One obvious answer is to allow people to communicate. It is true that in the sterile, context-free environment of the laboratory people are not very successful in using deductive principles to coordinate their actions. But people who confront these problems in their day-to-day lives are colleagues and co-workers who chat with one another over coffee and around the water-cooler. This ability to talk with other members of the group should surely suffice to remove any strategic uncertainty that causes such massive coordination failures in the laboratory.

If you talk to economists, you will often hear the refrain that "talk is cheap". What they mean by this is that in a variety of contexts involving strategic decision making, people can promise that they will behave in a particular way – act fair or be cooperative – but there is nothing to prevent them from reneging on that promise when it comes time to make the actual decision, especially if they will be monetarily better off by doing so. Thus, the "talk is cheap" argument essentially inveighs against the possibility of binding commitments because in many situations it is difficult to enforce the promise *ex post*, thereby leaving open the possibility of opportunistic behaviour later on in spite of any promises made earlier. And if someone cannot be held to his/her promise, then the promise, or the talk, may not be a good indicator of future behaviour. However, as I have argued in previous chapters, in a wide variety of circumstances people's behaviour is far less opportunistic than is suggested by economic theory. Many – if not most – people probably feel an ethical compunction against violating a promise made in good faith and, therefore, we should expect that such promises will have an impact. I alluded to the efficacy of cheap talk messages in Chapter 12 as well, where we discussed the role of communication in fostering cooperation.

Cooper and his colleagues at Iowa were quickly on to this problem. They decided to see what happens when players are allowed to communicate in (1) the battle of the sexes game and (2) the stag hunt game. One question here was how to structure this communication. After some deliberation, Cooper and his colleagues decided that they were going to have their participants make a short announcement, rather than engage in unstructured and free-wheeling conversations. This was primarily because it is often difficult to extract the essence of what exactly is said during such free-wheeling conversations. People can often be imprecise and might make different – and even contradictory – statements, so that it is hard to know what course of action a particular participant is really advocating. This can also lead to a loss of experimental control. The advantage of structured statements – such as "I will choose to hunt the stag" – is that they are usually less ambiguous and indicate the participant's desired course of action clearly.

Cooper and his colleagues also decided to look at two different types of communication where: (1) only one of the two players could make an announcement and (2) both players could make announcements. The players also had the option of choosing to remain silent. The results are not surprising, or may be surprising only to economists, who are sceptical of "cheap talk" announcements. Cooper and his colleagues first looked at the battle of the sexes game. When only one of the two players could make an announcement, he/she, of course, almost always announced that he/she was going to play the strategy that yielded a higher return to him/her (so Pat says "Opera" while Chris says "Baseball"), but once that announcement was made, coordination followed in close to 100% of cases. Out of 330 outcomes that Cooper and his colleagues observed, there were only 16 times that the players failed to coordinate to one of the equilibria.

However, when they turned to the case where both players could make announcements, the result was not as satisfactory. Now there were a lot more disequilibrium outcomes, owing, in large part, to the fact that each player now tended to announce that he/she will play the strategy that would yield him/her the higher pay-off. However, what these results clearly demonstrated was that, contrary to the supposition of economists, non-binding "cheap talk" messages can be very effective in fostering coordinated behaviour.

As I note above, to economists, the more interesting coordination problem is the stag hunt game, where players need to coordinate to the pay-off dominant outcome. Cooper and his colleagues decided to look at two different stag hunt games: (1) one where players could choose one of two strategies and (2) a more complicated game where players could choose one of three strategies. As before, they allowed for (1) "one way" announcements, where one of the two players could make a statement regarding his/her strategy choice and (2) "two way" announcements, where both players could make announcements.

When only one of the two players could make an announcement, that certainly led to more coordination than in the absence of any announcement, but it did not lead to as much coordination as one would expect. In about 13% of cases (21 out of 165) the player making the announcement actually chose to say that he/she would play the secure strategy of hunting rabbit. But even though in the majority of cases (144 out of 165, or 87%) the announcement was "hunt stag", still, this led to coordination to the pay-off dominant outcome of both players choosing to hunt stag in only about 60% of cases. In 51 cases (35%), players still ended up at one of the disequilibrium outcomes following a promise to hunt stag by one of the players. This was surprising and suggested that one-way announcements are not that effective in removing the strategic uncertainty from the minds of players that both players will indeed choose to hunt stag following the announcement.[3]

However, once Cooper and his colleagues allowed *both* parties to make announcements, coordination improved dramatically. In 95% of cases, each player chose to announce that he/she would hunt the stag. In 91% of those cases the players managed to coordinate to the pay-off dominant outcome. Thus, allowing both players to make an announcement seemed to guarantee two things: (1) both players would overwhelmingly announce playing the strategy that would lead to maximum pay-offs and (2) that this, in turn, would indeed lead to coordination to this outcome.

Van Huyck and his colleagues were also exploring the role of communication in fostering greater coordination among groups and decided to take a slightly different tack. They came up with a deceptively simple idea but one which performed extremely well. They decided that, rather than ask *participants* to make public announcements, they were going to have an external arbiter make the announcement. The external arbiter's role was simply to point out to the players that they would be far better off monetarily if they managed to coordinate to the pay-off dominant outcome, and, therefore, it was in their best interest to choose the strategy which led to this outcome. Of course, participants were free to completely disregard this announcement and choose whatever strategy they wanted. Van Huyck, working with Ann Gillette and Raymond Battalio, showed that a simple announcement instructing the participants to choose the strategy commensurate with the payoff dominant outcome led to coordination to this outcome in close to 100% of cases.

In case you are wondering about how one goes about making such public announcements to foster coordination, Michael Suk-Young Chwe of UCLA points out that organizations rely on such public announcements all the time. Often this might take the form of relying on television advertisements during widely watched events. In the United States, for instance, the event with the highest viewership is the Super Bowl, the championship game of the National Football League. Chwe points out that the most recent trend in television advertising during the Super Bowl is the appearance of advertisements for websites. During the 1999 Super Bowl, HotJobs.com spent nearly half of its yearly revenues on a single advertising spot and Monster.com bought two slots. These are both job listing sites and their growth is essentially a coordination problem. An employee wants to look for a job on one of these websites only if he/she knows that employers are also looking there and an employer will list his/her jobs only if he/she can be sure that enough prospective applicants will be searching this site for jobs.

In his book *Rational Ritual: Culture, Coordination and Common Knowledge*, Chwe writes:

Because each individual wants to participate only if others do, each person must also know that others received a message. For that matter, because each person knows that other people need to be confident that others will participate, each person must know that other people know that other people have received a message, and so forth. In other words, knowledge of the message is not enough; what is also required is knowledge of others' knowledge, knowledge of others' knowledge of others' knowledge and so on – that is "common knowledge". To understand how people solve coordination problems, we should thus look at social processes that generate common knowledge.

However, things got murky in a hurry when Cooper and his colleagues looked at more complicated games that allowed people to choose from more than two strategies, that is, games that allowed people more than two choices such as the minimum effort game studied by Van Huyck and his colleagues, where participants had to choose one of seven available strategies, or the games shown in Table 13.1, where the players need to choose one out of three strategies. When Cooper and his colleagues looked at the more complicated games with three strategies for each player, they discovered that players found it more difficult to coordinate to the pay-off dominant equilibrium, owing, in large part, to the fact that now players often announced very different strategies. Actually, in this case, players had an easier time when only one player was allowed to make an announcement. When only one player could make a promise, this player chose to announce the strategy "hunt stag" in 118 out of 165 (72%) cases and out of those 118 cases, the players managed to coordinate to the pay-off dominant outcome 111 times.[4]

But confusion reigned once both players were allowed to make announcements. When both players announced their desire to "hunt stag", this was generally followed by both players coordinating to the pay-off dominant outcome. But the problem was that in over one half of the cases, the players announced their desire to choose a strategy that was different from "hunt stag". In fact, a whopping 25% of the announcements were that the player concerned was going to "hunt rabbit". Needless to mention, the fact that players often announced their desire to play strategies other than "hunt stag" meant that coordination to the pay-off dominant outcome was harder to achieve in this more complicated game.

This is partly because now players have to solve *two* coordination problems rather than one. Put another way, they now need to solve two successive coordination problems, where the success in the second game depends on success in the first game. Now, they first have to coordinate on a message, such as Strategies 1, 2 or 3, as in the games shown in Table 13.1. Once they have managed to do that, and if they have managed to do that, then they need to actually coordinate on those announced strategies. This is not easy. As we discussed above, row player may believe it will be self-evident to everyone that Strategy 3 is dominated and the rational thing to do is to coordinate to the pay-off dominant {2, 2}. So, row player announces "2". Column player, meanwhile, thinks that it should be obvious that players should choose "3", since this maximizes pay-offs for both players even if it involves the play of a dominated strategy. (After all, we do know already that a lot of people choose to "cooperate" in social dilemma games, even though free-riding is the dominant strategy.) So, column player announces "3". Now, it also matters crucially as to what the pay-off is in the {2, 3} cell. If the pay-off is {$0, $0} as in Game 1 of Table 13.1, then, following these announcements, neither player wishes to end up in that cell. If this was Game 2, where {2, 3} yields $100 for row player but $0 for column player, following a {2, 3} announcement, row player may still want to play Strategy 2, but column player no longer wishes to play Strategy 3. So, what do they do? Does row take column's word and move to "3" or does column take row's word and move to "2"? If they both move in order to avoid the {2, 3} outcome, then it is likely that they will end up at another disequilibrium outcome of {3, 2}. This is good for column player, who gets $100, but is terrible for row, who gets nothing.

The result obtained by Cooper and his colleagues that announcements did not work so well in games where players could choose one of three strategies was corroborated by Jordi Brandts of the Centre for Economic Analysis in Barcelona and Bentley McLeod of the University of Montreal. They also found that recommending a particular strategy to the players (along the lines of Van Huyck, Gillette and Battalio) did not do all that well in getting players to coordinate their actions in more complicated games where the pay-off dominant outcome was also risky, in the sense that failure to coordinate to the outcome could result in a bad outcome (little money) for the players.

Andreas Blume of Pittsburgh and Andreas Ortmann of Charles University in Prague looked at the impact of communication in the minimum effort game, where players are asked to choose a number between 1 and 7. They had 12 groups play the game. Each group had nine players and played for eight rounds with the composition of the group remaining unchanged for the entire time. Four of these groups played the minimum effort game without any communication opportunities, while the other eight groups could communicate. Following the lead of Cooper and his colleagues, Blume and Ortmann had participants make a single public announcement rather than engage in unstructured conversation. In each of the eight rounds, there are two stages. In the first stage, players can send messages to one another indicating what number they are going to choose in the second stage. Thus, in Stage 1, a player might say "I will choose 7" and this message is conveyed to the other members of the group via their computer screens. Once all players have had an opportunity to send a message, the experiment moved on to the second stage, where the participants made actual number choices. The first stage messages are "cheap talk" because the players are not making binding commitments. A player can say that he/she will choose 7 in Stage 1, but then he/she is free to change his/her mind and choose a different number in Stage 2 and no one can force him/her in the second stage to choose the number he/she said he/she would choose.

Blume and Ortmann found two things. First, and not surprisingly, the ability to send messages helps coordination. Thus, groups who can send messages to one another manage to coordinate much better than the groups who have no such opportunity. But second, and surprisingly, groups still find it difficult to coordinate to the pay-off dominant outcome consistently. Out of the eight groups that had the opportunity to communicate, there was only one group where the participants consistently chose 7 for all eight rounds. The other groups achieved various degrees of success but none of them could manage to sustain the all-7 outcome for the entire eight rounds.

These results suggest that: (1) coordination problems in real life need not pose as much of a challenge as suggested by the early laboratory experiments which used context-free language and did not allow the participants any opportunity to communicate. (2) In real life, subjects might be able to resolve such coordination issues by simply talking to their group members in some form or another. (3) But, at the same time, these experiments also suggest that getting participants to consistently coordinate to the pay-off dominant outcome is harder than one would suppose. Bilateral or multi-lateral communication, while certainly useful and enabling greater coordination than would be possible in the absence of any communication, still does not seem to succeed in getting participants to coordinate to the pay-off dominant outcome consistently, especially if (1) the game is complex, allowing players more than two strategy choices and (2) if the game involves a large number of players, where "large" means three or more group members.

In a way, the fact that participants did not manage to do well with multi-lateral messages may not be that surprising. The primary point here is to reduce the amount of strategic uncertainty so that everyone is convinced that everyone else will choose to hunt a stag. So, when only one person can make an announcement and says "I am off to hunt a stag", it may be easier for others to coordinate their actions compared to when everyone can talk all at once. If everyone can send a message, that might effectively create a *two-tiered* coordination problem. Now everyone must first coordinate to the *same message* and having successfully done so – which is not guaranteed by any means – they must then go on to successfully coordinate on the *same action*. Too many message options do not seem conducive to greater coordination.

This, in turn, led researchers to start thinking of other ways besides communication to foster coordination in organizations. In what follows, I examine these different approaches. I would like to remind you once more that, below, I will confine my attention to stag hunt type games for reasons I outlined earlier.

MONEY TALKS: THE ROLE OF INCENTIVES

Most economists believe that a wide variety of economic problems can be resolved by providing the right incentives. So, the obvious question is: could we improve coordination in organizations by providing an incentive to the workers to efficiently coordinate their actions? And if so, what form should those incentives take?

Jordi Brandts of the Institute of Economic Analysis at Barcelona and David Cooper (then at Case Western's Weatherhead School of Management, now at Florida State) set out to understand coordination problems, particularly in the context of economic organizations, and designed a set of experiments that simulated the inner workings of a firm. In order to add more reality to their set-up, they moved away from the standard economic practice of using non-emotive and context-free language and chose to provide instructions using more realistic language. They took the minimum effort game studied by Van Huyck and his colleagues and changed it into a "corporate turnaround game". In this game, participants were referred to as "employees" who work for a "firm". Each firm has four workers and one manager. The workers can choose one of five numbers – 0, 10, 20, 30 or 40 – which is tantamount to choosing how many hours to work during the week. Choosing "0" means not doing any work at all while choosing "40" means putting in a 40-hour work week. The pay-off dominant outcome is the one where all the workers choose to work for 40 hours a week while the secure outcome is the one where they all slack off and choose 0. There are a total of 60 firms with 240 workers over two locations – Barcelona and Cleveland.

The manager's aim is to get the workers to coordinate to the pay-off dominant outcome by choosing appropriate incentive bonuses. Workers' salaries depend on a fixed wage *and* an incentive bonus rate which pays them an amount that depends on what the minimum hours of work chosen (by someone in the group) is. The total bonus that the workers can earn is obtained by taking the minimum hours worked by a member of the firm and multiplying it by a constant amount, the bonus rate. Thus, the corporate turnaround game preserves the features of the minimum effort game because one worker choosing to loaf around can lower the minimum effort for the group as a whole and lead to a lower bonus amount for everyone involved, including those who are working much harder. This also implies that if even one person in the group chooses to put in zero effort, then the effective bonus for the group as a whole is zero. But if the minimum number of hours is greater than zero, then the workers all get an appropriate bonus depending on the minimum hours and the bonus rate.

The participants play the game for 30 rounds in three blocks of ten rounds each. The composition of the firm remains unchanged for the entire 30 rounds. This implies that the same four workers interact with each other for the entire duration, allowing them to build trust and develop a feeling of community. Furthermore, in real life it is often the case that most groups facing such coordination problems are fixed in nature in that it is the same people interacting with each other for long periods of time. But, at the same time, the fixed nature of the grouping might also exacerbate problems of history dependence, that is, once a group has fallen into the low or no coordination trap, they may find it more difficult to climb out of that if they are interacting with the same people over and over again.

In the first study that Brandts and Cooper carry out, the manager plays a passive role and the magnitude of the incentive bonus is actually predetermined for each ten-round block. In each case, the bonus is set at a very low level for the first block of ten rounds. Brandts and Cooper do so deliberately because they *want* the workers to be unsuccessful in their attempts to coordinate. That is, they want the workers in each firm to end the first block of ten rounds choosing low numbers close to zero so that each firm is experiencing serious coordination failures at the end of those ten rounds. The reason they do so is this: if the firms do not experience coordination failure then there really is no problem left to solve. It is only when firms are experiencing coordination failures that one can study whether changing the incentives has an impact on enabling workers to achieve greater coordination. So Brandts and Cooper essentially want to establish a history of coordination failure during the first block of ten rounds and then see if increasing the incentive bonus rate can get people to break out of this and achieve greater coordination.

By setting the bonus rate quite low, Brandts and Cooper do successfully trap these firms into pervasive coordination failures. During the first block of ten rounds, the minimum effort chosen is indeed quite low and is zero for 71% of effort choices. The average minimum across all firms and aggregated over all rounds is only 5.71 during the first block of ten rounds. That is, averaged across all firms and over the first ten rounds, the minimum amount of work put in by the workers is about 5.71 hours per week. Most firms are experiencing serious coordination failures, with multiple workers choosing to shirk completely and put in zero hours per week. Out of 45 firms with a minimum effort of zero in round ten, 43 have more than one employee choosing zero and 26 have all four employees choosing zero.

The question is: can increments in the bonus rate induce the workers to break out of this coordination failure trap and move them towards working harder? The answer turns out to be a resounding yes, but with a twist. Brandts and Cooper look at three possible increments in the bonus rate: (1) where the bonus rate is increased by 33%; (2) where it is increased by 67% and (3) where it is raised by 133%. What Brandts and Cooper find is that increasing the bonus rate has a large positive impact on coordination. The average effort levels forthcoming are much higher when the bonus rate is raised, but, strangely enough, the actual increase in the bonus rate does not seem to matter. While all three increments led to higher effort, the 133% increase does not improve performance any more than the 33% increment does! So, employees seem to react to a higher bonus, but, beyond a point, the actual increment becomes secondary as long as they *are* rewarded for working harder. Of course, given that there is an upper bound on work effort, there is a limit to how much of an improvement a bonus can elicit, no matter how high that bonus is.

There are a number of other interesting findings. Once the bonus rate is increased and the employees were being rewarded for working harder, most workers did increase their effort up from zero. But a bifurcation emerges over time. In some groups, the employees who have moved to higher effort levels drag their more recalcitrant compatriots up with them, but in other groups, the laggards, who do not increase their work effort, ultimately discourage the others who are trying, and the hard workers in turn eventually respond by lowering their work effort also. Thus, at the micro-level, the impact of higher bonuses is not the same for every firm – it works better for some than it does for others.

To an extent, whether the bonus works well or not depends on the presence of "strong leaders" – workers who respond to an increase in the bonus by sharply increasing their work effort. The more strong leaders there are in a particular group, that is, the more people there are who increase their work effort significantly following an increment, the better the firm does at raising its average productivity. I will come back to this point shortly below.

Brandts and Cooper also find that once the firm has managed to break out of the low effort trap, reducing the bonus rate does not hurt. This is good news for the firm because paying the bonus is costly and has implications for the firm's bottom line. So, it seems that all the workers need is a temporary crutch. Once the higher bonus reduces strategic uncertainty and enables them to improve their productivity, they can manage to remain coordinated even if the bonus is reduced later on.

Finally, Brandts and Cooper ask: does it matter how long a firm has experienced a lack of productivity and low morale? Is it more difficult to turn around firms that have been mired in a low productivity trap for a much longer time? The answer, not surprisingly, turns out to be yes. When the coordination problems have persisted for a longer time, the bonus is less effective. When the bonus is introduced earlier, a number of employees – the leaders – increase their effort and persist there, and eventually they drag the laggards up to higher effort levels as well. But when the coordination failure problems have been allowed to fester for a longer time and the bonus is introduced later, the leaders do increase their effort levels in response but give up soon and reduce their effort when others do not follow suit quickly. It appears that a long history of coordination failures breeds much greater pessimism even among the more dynamic leaders who do respond positively to the increased incentives.

In a follow-up study, Brandts and Cooper bring a fifth participant into each firm – the manager. While, in the previous study, the bonus rate was predetermined for each block of ten rounds at a time, now, the manager has discretion from round to round as to what bonus he/she wants to pay the workers. Furthermore, the manager can also send messages in an attempt to exhort the workers to expend greater effort. A "firm" now consists of four workers and one manager who interact for 30 rounds with the composition of the firm remaining unchanged for the entire duration. For the first ten rounds, the manager is purely passive and does not take any part in the proceedings. Once again, the aim here was to get the workers in the firm to fall into a low (or no) coordination trap and then have the manager come in and try to improve coordination by the judicious use of messages and/or bonuses. So, the manager plays an active role for the last 20 rounds. In each round, the employees choose an effort level between 0 and 40, as in the previous study. The manager gets to see only the *minimum* effort put in and not the effort put in by individual workers; so, in a sense, the manager cannot distinguish who is working hard and who is not but can make out if the assembly line is moving along quickly or not. (The participants in this second study are actually getting less feedback than in the former study, which makes resolving coordination problems more difficult.) Once the manager takes over, he/she can use a mixture of performance bonuses based on increased effort as well as exhortative messages in an attempt to foster greater coordination.

Brandts and Cooper find, again not surprisingly, that the use of a mixture of exhortative messages and appropriate performance bonuses are indeed successful in improving coordination and productivity. But the surprising result is that communication – the ability to send messages – seems to be a more effective tool than the payment of performance bonuses alone. Here is how Brandts and Cooper see it:

> Our results emphasize the importance of communication. As the available avenues of communication increase, both employees' effort and managers' profits increase. Communication is a more effective tool for increasing manager profits than financial incentives. ... This is the central result of our paper – for managers attempting to overcome a history of coordination failure, it's what you say, not what you pay, that largely determines your success. While

managers try a wide variety of communication strategies, including complex multi-round plans, the most successful communication strategy is quite simple: explicitly request that all employees choose a high effort level, emphasize the mutual benefits of coordinating at a high effort level, and assure the employees that they are being paid well (although it is not necessary to actually pay them well). In other words, managers succeed in this environment by acting as good coordination devices.

The reason why good communication is a more profitable strategy is not hard to see. Messages cost far less than incentive bonuses! Therefore, if you can improve performance using suitably exhortative messages, then that improves your profitability far more than when you actually have to pay your workers more in order to motivate them. Does this mean incentive bonuses are not important and simple "cheap talk" messages (a deft "attaboy" here or a pat on the back there) are good enough to improve performance in firms mired in low productivity? Not so, suggest Brandts and Cooper. They go on to add that financial incentives are important but *in conjunction* with appropriately exhortative messages. Simply raising incentives is poor managerial strategy; it is essential to reinforce the financial incentives with messages providing the insight that everyone is better off when everyone works harder. In that sense, Brandts and Cooper's findings add weight to the results of Van Huyck, Gillette and Battalio, who also looked at the efficacy of messages announced by an external arbiter. The combination of incentive bonuses and messages together seems to be a better coordination device and is better able to reduce strategic uncertainty among the participants.

The previous study looks at whether managers can make a difference; but the "manager" in this study is, after all, an undergraduate student who has little, if any, real managerial experience. The way to see if managers can really make a difference in getting their workers to coordinate would be to look at real-life managers. If getting employees to work in a coordinated manner is a central issue in many organizations, then successful managers should be good at figuring out how to resolve such coordination failures. This could be for two reasons. First, it is those who are better at motivating their workers that eventually beat out others and rise to top management positions. Second, the fact that they are in managerial positions also implies that they have greater experience dealing with problems of coordination failures and this, in turn, gives them valuable perspective and knowledge into what policies work better than others.

This is what David Cooper proceeded to study next. (This is another example of how experimental economists are increasingly drawing their participants from outside the usual pool of students.) But how do you get real managers to come to a laboratory and take part in this game? The Executive MBA programme at the Weatherhead School provided a solution. The participants in the Executive MBA programme are all experienced and successful mangers, with at least ten years of work experience, including five years in a managerial role. Cooper finds that the experience of managers does matter in that when the members of the Executive MBA programme are placed in the role of the manager in the corporate turnaround game, they are able to overcome a history of coordination failure much faster than students playing the role of the manager. This superior performance is not driven by paying more money to the workers, but by sending more effective messages that work better in motivating workers.

In order to understand which communication strategies work better, Cooper takes the various messages sent and puts them into appropriate categories: for instance, there is a category for "ask for effort". Under this category, there are three sub-categories: "polite", "rude", and "specific effort level". What Cooper finds is that professional managers are far more communicative than student managers and have a better intuitive feel for what kinds of messages would do better in reducing strategic uncertainty among employees. It is not so much that the "real" managers say things that are different from what the "student" managers say. Rather, the "real" managers say the right things more frequently. For example, professional managers are far more likely to ask for a specific effort level and more likely to offer encouragement to workers. One striking difference is that professional managers are six times more likely than student managers to make explicit references to *trusting* one's fellow workers.

Cooper adds:

To understand why this particular communication strategy works, recall that coordination is largely a problem of beliefs. Communication correlates beliefs, leading to the correlation in actions ... With a good communication strategy, the manager creates common beliefs that most employees will be choosing high effort levels. This is most obvious when a manager asks employees for a specific effort level ... More subtly, pointing out the mutual benefits of successful coordination ... creates expectations that all employees will select high effort levels in order to enjoy higher payoffs, making it safer for any one employee to increase his effort level.

WHEN IN ROME ... CREATING CULTURE IN THE LABORATORY

Two themes emerge from our discussion so far. First, in the absence of any communication or other interventions and in the stark context-free laboratory settings, participants often find it difficult to coordinate their actions. Second, a number of interventions, such as various types of communication mechanisms or performance bonuses, can help alleviate this problem to a large extent if not completely. Turning towards the real world, while large-scale coordination failures are a reality in many organizations, yet many others do seem to address these issues adequately. At the very least, many organizations are not as dysfunctional as the laboratory worst case scenario and many of them do manage to do well in resolving these issues.

How do they do it? It is very likely that they rely on a combination of approaches like the ones suggested above, but there may be yet another option for fostering coordination: a process of acculturation of new workers. Corporations engage in a wide variety of exercises in an attempt to build trust and promote teamwork among workers. These include mentoring of junior recruits by more senior members of the firm; sometimes they involve going on retreats, including rock-climbing or white-water rafting in teams which force team members to rely upon and support one another and build trust among teammates.

Roberto Weber of Carnegie Mellon University decided to see if a process of acculturation can help workers learn to coordinate their actions better. We already know that, typically, a small group (say, two players) finds it easier to coordinate actions. It is when the groups start to become large that the problems creep in. Yet, in real life, many large firms and organizations do manage to get their workers to coordinate their actions. Weber conjectures that this might be due to the fact that the founding members of a firm, who are a small group to start with, manage to resolve coordination problems and, in doing so, they manage to establish a set of rules or norms of self-governance. As the group grows, new entrants are exposed to, and acculturated into, these "good" norms and manage to sustain the norms of coordination that are already established. So, the idea is to start small, establish a norm of coordination early on (which is easier in small groups), and grow slowly, while exposing new members to the already established norms and expecting them to adhere to it. This should allow organizations to grow but still remain coordinated.

Weber uses the minimum effort game originally studied by John Van Huyck and his colleagues in order to see if he could indeed get small groups to first manage to coordinate their actions and then grow larger while maintaining that coordination. I would like to remind you that in the minimum effort game, each participant picks a number between 1 and 7 and the pay-off he/she gets depends on the number he/she picks and the smallest number picked by someone in the group. However, everyone is better off and gets the maximum pay-off if all group members manage to coordinate their actions to choose 7.

Weber looks at three treatments: (1) a control treatment, where a group of 12 players play the minimum effort game for 12 periods; (2) a "history" treatment, where each group starts out with two players; the rest of the group initially do not participate but only observe what the initial players are doing; every few rounds one person is added to the group and starts to play the game with the ones who were playing before so that all 12 players are participating for the last few rounds. (On a few occasions, Weber added more than one person at the same time, but that was the exception rather than the rule.) Weber comments that this history condition serves as a "simple metaphor for the extensive training, socialization and acculturation often required of new entrants to a firm or country". Finally, (3) there is also a "no history" treatment which is similar to the "history" treatment in that players are added, usually one at a time, except, unlike the "history" treatment, these new entrants do not get to see what happened prior to their entry into the game and, therefore, have no history to fall back upon. There were five "control" groups with 12 players in each for a total of 60 participants; nine groups in the "history" treatment, each with 12 players for a total of 108 participants and three groups of 12 each (36 players) in the "no history" treatment. The composition of these groups remains unchanged for the duration of the session.

Weber demonstrates a strong regularity that this process of slow organizational growth while exposing the workers to "history" – a shared norm of coordination – does often lead to large groups of 12 efficiently coordinating their actions; that is, all members of the group manage to choose 7 for multiple periods at a stretch. In three of nine groups, the minimum remains at 7 throughout the growth process even when all 12 players are participating. In another group, players choose 5 throughout the growth process. Overall, in five out of nine groups, the full group of 12 manages to sustain coordination to a minimum higher than 1 for all rounds. This is in sharp contrast to what happened in Van Huyck, Battalio and Beil's study where, by round four in any group, the minimum had dropped down to 1.

Not all groups that get to see the prior history do well. In four groups, by the time the group reaches its full size of 12, the minimum had dwindled down to 1. However, it is equally true that the groups which play with history do manage much better coordination than either the control groups or the groups which do not get to see history. Weber's results suggest that efficient coordination can be achieved if groups start out small, grow slowly and expose new members to the already established norm of coordination during this growth process. If this history is not available, then efficient coordination is not possible.

Ananish Chaudhuri at the University of Auckland, Andrew Schotter at New York University and Barry Sopher at Rutgers University take Weber's idea of acculturation further by designing an elaborate experiment where new entrants can not only observe the history of what happened before their arrival, but can also receive advice from their predecessors. Andrew Schotter and Barry Sopher were already engaged in an elaborate research project trying to understand the evolution of norms and conventions in various economic transactions. They argued that socialization and cultural influences have enormous impact on all aspects of human behaviour, including economic interactions. Norms or conventions of behaviour that arise during one generation may be passed on to the successors in following generations. Such norm-driven behaviour may help sustain higher levels of cooperation in many social dilemmas than is predicted by gene-based economic or evolutionary theory, such as the theory of reciprocal altruism or the theory of kin selection that I discussed at the end of Chapter 12.

In order to examine the evolution of social norms, Schotter and Sopher had designed an innovative "intergenerational framework". Here, a sequence of participants play a variety of games (such as a battle of the sexes game or an ultimatum game) for a number of periods and are then replaced by new players, who continue the game in their role for a similar length of time. Players in one generation can communicate with their successors in the next generation and advise them on how to play the game. Norms developed during one generation can be passed on in the history of human societies via word-of-mouth transmission of knowledge and experiences. In addition, players in each generation care about the succeeding generation in the sense that each player's pay-off depends on not only the pay-offs achieved during his/her own generation, but also on the pay-offs of his/her children in the next generation. Thus, each generation has a direct monetary stake in what happens in the next generation.

The idea is to study how such advice left by people who have experience with the problem at hand creates norms of behaviour which help resolve social dilemmas or problems of coordination. After all, we ask for advice in so many things that we do: when we choose a doctor or a dentist or a car mechanic or a school for our child, or when we buy a house or a car or pick a mutual fund. Therefore, it stands to reason that when we encounter a problem for the first time, we may not be in a complete vacuum; there may be, and usually are, others around who already have some experience and can advise us regarding the appropriate course of action. This is Weber's idea of acculturation of new entrants into the mores and culture of the new organization or country.

Chaudhuri, Schotter and Sopher decided to apply this idea of generations of players leaving advice for their successors in order to see if that could help resolve problems of pervasive coordination failure. Like Weber, they also look at the minimum effort game of Van Huyck and his colleagues, but their design is more elaborate than Weber's. In the experiments carried out by Chaudhuri and his colleagues, there are eight players in a group and each group constitutes a generation. Each group plays the minimum effort game for ten rounds and the composition of the group remains unchanged for the entire duration.

Chaudhuri and his colleagues look at the impact of both history and advice. In one treatment, subjects in each generation leave advice "privately", in the sense that a player in one generation leaves advice to only his/her *own* successor in the next generation; here, members of each generation get one piece of advice from their immediate predecessors. In a second treatment, advice is combined with history, in that members of each generation not only get a piece of advice from their immediate predecessors, but can also get to see the history of prior interactions, that is, they can see what happened in their parents' generation and their grandparents' generation, etc. In a third treatment, the advice is "public"; here, the advice from the members of one generation is made available to *all* the members of the next generation. But the public advice is provided in two different ways: (1) for some participants, the advice from a previous generation is typed up on a sheet of paper and given to members of the current generation; each member of the current generation knows that each of them is looking at a sheet with the exact same information on it, eight pieces of advice written by their immediate predecessors. (2) But for some others, this advice is not only distributed on sheets of paper but is also *read aloud* by the experimenter (actually a research assistant) prior to the beginning of the session. In these public advice treatments, participants are not shown the history of prior plays. As always, the behaviour of the participants who get advice and/or get to see the history of prior interactions is compared to the behaviour of a control group of participants who play the same game with no advice nor history.

Chaudhuri and his colleagues conjecture that allowing participants to leave advice to their successors using such an intergenerational design might, over time, enable future generations to achieve efficient coordination. A generation that failed to resolve the underlying coordination problem might advise the next generation accordingly by writing advice that suggested "do as we are telling you to do, not as we did", and such advice, if followed, might lead to a convention selecting the pay-off dominant outcome.

Chaudhuri and his colleagues, however, go one step further and also collect data on the beliefs that people hold. Remember, I said at the outset that often the fundamental reason behind the lack of coordination success is *strategic uncertainty*; uncertainty regarding the actions to be taken by others. Mechanisms or processes that create more optimistic beliefs will be more successful in resolving coordination problems. It is likely that the interventions which succeed do so by creating appropriate beliefs, but it is still important and instructive to actually look at those beliefs and how they are affected by different institutions.

Chaudhuri and his colleagues find that, while the availability of advice does help considerably in resolving coordination failures, the manner in which this advice is distributed is of crucial importance. When advice from one generation to the next is private, so that a parent advises his or her offspring alone, this advice does not help coordination at all, mostly because the advice here tends to be pessimistic, suggesting that participants stick to the strategy that leads to the secure outcome. A lot of the advice here takes the following form: "Pick 1 in all the rounds. You could bet that everyone may pick 7 but they will not. Always pick 1." Or words to that effect.

Contrary to Weber's finding that history helps if the group starts small and grows slowly, Chaudhuri and his colleagues find that history is not very helpful for groups that are already large. In fact, they find that advice is more useful and facilitates greater coordination than history does. Strangely enough, if participants receive pessimistic advice, then they are most likely to end up at the "bad" secure outcome even if they can see that their predecessors were relatively successful in achieving coordination via the history of prior plays. In this sense, "good" history does not help if the advice left is "bad", and "good" advice (even if coupled with "bad" history) works better than "good" history.

In order for advice to help people coordinate their actions, this advice (1) must be distributed publicly in the sense that the advice from all members of one generation must be made available to all the members of the next generation and (2) must also be *read out loud*. Thus, each and every member of a group must know that everyone else is receiving the exact same information (message) and, furthermore, each person must be convinced that each of them has heard this message being read out loud. Therefore, it must be common knowledge that everyone has received the same message. It is only when the message is made public and also read out loud, making it common knowledge, that the participants consistently choose 7 in the minimum effort game and manage to coordinate to the pay-off dominant outcome. The nature of the advice when it is public is also qualitatively different from when it is private. A typical example is: "Pick 7 every time, *every time*. If everyone picks 7 every time, everyone will make the maximum per round, $1.30 × 10 $13.00) ... Don't be stupid. Pick 7."

There is one twist to this finding. If the message being given to the subjects is very strong, in that every member of one generation urges their successors to choose 7 all the time, as in the strongly exhortative message given above, then the message will foster coordination even if it is *not* read out loud, as long as it is distributed in a public manner so that everyone knows that everyone else is reading the same message. But if there is even a small amount of equivocation in one or more of the pieces of advice given, then, in order for efficient coordination to occur, these messages must be public and also read out loud.

Why does advice – particularly strongly exhortative advice – have such a positive impact on behaviour? One way that advice can foster coordination is via the creation of more optimistic beliefs. I have argued above that the problem here is essentially one of trust. In order to choose the strategy that leads to the pay-off dominant outcome, each and every subject must be convinced that their group members are also going to choose the same strategy. Even a small modicum of doubt regarding the choices of others is often enough to destroy any possibility of successful coordination. The role advice plays, or can play, then, is to remove or reduce that doubt about the strategy choice of other players. Does it do so? Chaudhuri and his colleagues were uniquely placed to answer this question because they had actually collected data on those beliefs.

At the beginning of the experiment, Chaudhuri and his colleagues provided their participants with the instructions to the experiment. Then the participants receive the advice and, depending on the treatment, the history, from the previous generation. This advice could be private or public. After this, and before commencing the actual game, these researchers asked the participants to state what they expected each and every member of the group to choose in the first round of the ten-round session. Participants are actually paid on the basis of how accurate their predictions are. Therefore, they have an incentive to think about their predictions carefully and make accurate predictions. Chaudhuri and his colleagues found that most of their treatments involving history and/or advice did *not* completely remove the doubt that someone would choose 1. In all these treatments, participants thought there was a positive, albeit small, chance that someone in the group will choose 1. This very small amount of doubt was enough to destroy successful coordination and made certain that, in short order, participants fell into the coordination failure trap of the majority, if not all, choosing 1. The one treatment where this doubt was removed was when the advice was public and read out loud. Here, finally, participants were convinced that no one in the group would choose 1. These optimistic beliefs led participants to choose 7 consistently in this treatment.

In order to successfully coordinate their actions, players need to possess appropriately optimistic beliefs about each other's actions and their beliefs about others' beliefs and so on. When advice is private or less than common knowledge, players' beliefs are not sufficiently optimistic. But when the advice is made common knowledge by making it public and also read aloud, each subject reads and hears the same information and knows that everyone else is also reading and hearing the same message. This finally succeeds in creating an atmosphere where players feel sufficiently bold to start by choosing 7 and then go on to establish a norm of coordination based on that auspicious start.

FROM THE LABORATORY TO THE REAL WORLD: DO THESE INTERVENTIONS WORK? THE STORY OF CONTINENTAL AIRLINES

Our discussion up to this point should have convinced you of two things: (1) in stag hunt-type coordination problems, participants often find it difficult to coordinate to the pay-off dominant outcome; but (2) a number of relatively easy interventions such as communication among participants, advice from people who have prior experience in the matter, acculturation into the norms of the relevant group or incentive bonuses, seem to be quite successful in facilitating coordination. The big question is: these interventions seem to work well in the relatively sterile atmosphere of the laboratory, but will they still work out there in the real world?

Marc Knez and Duncan Simester (both of MIT) decided to see if the interventions work by looking at how Continental Airlines managed to turn things around in the mid to late 1990s. I mentioned before that the operations of an airline require extensive coordination and have a "weak-link" structure in that the performance of the organization as a whole is crucially dependent on the performance of component units. One sluggish worker or group can slow things down and hurt the organization even if everyone else is working at speed. Therefore, the overall performance of the organization is determined to a large extent by the performance of the slowest or worst-performing entity within the organization. This, in turn, implies that the benefits to the organization from getting all the groups and workers involved to coordinate their activities are immense. The operations of an airline company can tell us a lot about the success, or lack thereof, of various interventions in facilitating successful coordination.

Prior to 1995, Continental was one of the worst performing airlines in the industry. Following deregulation of the airline industry in the US in 1978, Continental had declared bankruptcy twice, once in 1983 and again in 1990, and, on average, was ranked last among the ten major domestic airlines in important measures of performance such as on-time arrival, baggage handling and customer satisfaction. At the end of 1994, a new senior management team was brought in to address the myriad problems Continental was facing. The new team introduced the "Go Forward Plan". This plan had three important components:

(1) changing airport managers; (2) improving the flight schedule and (3) introduction of a *group incentive scheme* that paid a *monthly bonus* if a firm-wide on-time performance goal was met. The bonus scheme announced on 15 January 15 1995 promised $65 to every hourly employee, including part-time employees, in every month that Continental's on-time performance ranked within the top five in the industry. In 1996, the scheme was modified, paying $65 per month in months when Continental ranked second or third in on-time performance and $100 if it ranked first.

After reporting net losses of $125 million in 1992, $199 million in 1993 and $613 million in 1994, Continental reported a net profit of $224 million in 1995. This grew to $319 million in 1996 and $385 million in 1997. These profit increases were accompanied by improvements in other measures of performance, such as on-time arrival and departure. Continental's senior management attributed much of the success to the new bonus scheme, which resulted in an increase in employee effort as well as mutual monitoring of co-workers and a reduction in employee turnover and the number of people taking days off due to sickness. Furthermore, the bonus scheme was self-funding. After the introduction of the scheme, fewer Continental customers missed connections and had to be re-accommodated on other flights, while other airlines now increasingly used Continental to re-assign their customers with missed flights.

But, in addition to the financial incentives provided for improvements in performance, the new management also adopted other new policies, which included the introduction of bulletin boards and a quarterly employee magazine, regular voice-mail and video statements from the CEO and increasing visibility and accountability of senior managers. These additional steps also contributed significantly to the turn-around.

At the time, Continental had approximately 35,000 employees who, individually, had a negligible influence on overall performance. Moreover, the employees were geographically dispersed, restricting (or preventing) direct interaction between workers and direct observations of each other's actions. How and why did the policies implemented by the new management team – including the bonus and other devices, such as the use of bulletin-boards and public announcements from the CEO – impact performance? Knez and Simester argue that, to a large extent, the interventions improved performance by increasing the level of *mutual monitoring* among the workers. Continental's adoption of the incentive schemes raised *expectations* that other groups – whether at the same airport or different ones – were improving their on-time performance as well, and this enhanced expectation enabled workers to coordinate their actions.

The performance bonus was not targeted towards particular employees but was based on coordinated actions by many workers. Therefore, the choice of low effort by any one worker or group not only reduces the chances of that group getting the bonus, but also reduces the chances of all other groups whose performance depends on the one group lagging behind. This creates an incentive for employees to monitor each other's efforts and encourage lagging colleagues to work harder. This can take two forms: (1) peer pressure on those who are not putting in the required effort coupled with (probable) feelings of shame on the part of the laggard; (2) reporting low effort on the part of some workers to management. Because workers in many groups work closely with one another in pushing out or waving in aircrafts, loading and unloading baggage, etc., they are well placed to see how hard someone is working.[5]

Such mutual monitoring took a variety of forms and included employees being summoned from the break-room by colleagues or employees being chastised for leaving their stations. Employees also began to contact colleagues who had called in sick to ask if assistance was needed and also to monitor if the absences were legitimate or not. When Knez and Simester asked Continental's CEO why the bonus was offered to all workers and not merely the ones who did improve their performance, he responded that this was done to impress upon all workers that improvements would require effort and commitment from everyone, not just a key few. Thus, the focus was squarely on creating more optimistic expectations and changing overall employee behaviour. Continental used a judicious mix of financial incentives as well as good communication strategies and exhortative messages to turn things around, exactly as suggested by some of the papers I have cited above.

FROM THE REAL WORLD, BACK TO THE LABORATORY: ARE YOU PARTNERS OR STRANGERS?

Many of the coordination problems that arise in real life involve people and groups who interact with one another repeatedly. The people who work at Continental or at a steel mill or work along the assembly line of a car manufacturing company are essentially interacting with the same group of people over and over again. Therefore, they usually know each other well. This also makes it easier to monitor the work of others and figure out when someone is not putting in the requisite work, is spending too much time in the break-room or is calling in sick under false pretences. We have already seen that, even among people who interact with each other on a daily basis, the problems of coordination failure can be severe. The majority of the studies that I have discussed above (with the exception of the work done by Russell Cooper and his colleagues at Iowa), and especially all the ones that looked at how to improve coordination in large groups using the minimum effort game, have done so using groups whose composition remains fixed over time. This focus on fixed groups is understandable, given that many of these problems are essentially problems faced by groups whose members interact repeatedly over time.

But it is not the case that all coordination problems are faced by groups whose composition remains relatively stable over time. There are a number of instances where group membership changes frequently. The Internal Revenue Service (IRS) in the US or tax agencies in other countries routinely hire additional temporary workers right around the deadline for filing taxes. Similarly, immigration agencies in many countries will take on additional temporary workers when faced with a sudden influx of applications. The Post Office will hire additional workers to tide them over the rush of the holiday season. The turnover rate of workers at most fast-food outlets is very high, meaning that there are workers coming and going frequently. All these enterprises are also called upon to resolve demanding coordination problems.

But the nature of their problem differs in that members of these groups are not as close-knit as those working for companies where the group composition is relatively stable over time. If we think of the group members at Continental as "partners", the workers at McDonald's or the IRS are often "strangers"; people who work together for relatively short periods of time and then disperse with not enough time to build lasting relationships. So, how do these strangers perform when it comes to taking coordinated actions?

There are two ways this can go: (1) the ability to interact repeatedly with the same people and the possibility of forming long-term relationships can make it easier to establish trust; this, in turn, can help coordination by creating optimistic beliefs about the actions of fellow group members. If this is true, then fixed groups should be better able to coordinate their actions compared to groups which are short-lived. (2) However, one cannot rule out the possibility that fixed groups may encounter more problems. In groups where the composition is fixed, initial acts of bad faith such as providing low effort may tend to fester and the group might end up in a cycle of recriminations like a bad marriage, where the group gets caught in a low-effort outcome. With no new blood coming in, no one can quite find the energy to break out of this cycle. In this case, short-lived groups may actually do better. With the composition of the group changing frequently, new people with no baggage or ill feelings from previous interactions come in and bring new optimism and expectations. This might enable these groups to do better in coordinating their actions.

It turns out that it is the former conjecture that is proved correct. One of the first studies to explicitly look at this issue was done by Kenneth Clark of Manchester and Martin Sefton of the University of Newcastle upon Tyne in the late 1990s. They had 160 participants take part in a simple stag hunt game. Participants are formed into pairs and play a game where each player can choose one of two strategies. The game has two equilibria – one pay-off dominant and the other secure.

Each session consists of 20 participants. Ten of them are sent to one room while the other ten are sent to a different room. People in one room are always paired with the people in the other room. In one treatment, subjects are in "fixed" groups. Here, the same two participants (located in separate rooms) play against one another ten times in a row. In a "re-matching" treatment, each participant plays ten times, but each time with a different participant who is always in the other room. Thus, in the first treatment, since the participants are interacting repeatedly, they have greater opportunity to build trust and establish a reputation for behaving in a particular way. They have the option of using conditional strategies of the following type: *I am going to start by putting in high effort because I expect you to do the same; if you do not then I will stop working hard as well and we will both be worse off.* These types of conditional strategies, using the early rounds to build a relationship, might encourage people to choose the more risky strategy of hunting stag early on and then go on to build on that early cooperation. Participants who do not have this opportunity and are continually being thrown into new relationships would have a hard time establishing trust.

Clark and Sefton find that more participants choose the riskier stag hunt strategy in fixed groups. They have 200 observations for the game played in each treatment: fixed pairings and re-matched pairings. Participants in fixed pairings manage to attain the pay-off dominant outcome 116 out of those 200 times, while, in re-matched pairings, this happens only four out of 200 times. People in the fixed pairings also managed to coordinate their actions, either to the pay-off dominant outcome or the secure option, more often. These participants ended up at a disequilibrium outcome in only 17% of cases, while the participants who were re-matched at the end of each round found it more difficult to coordinate and ended up at disequilibrium outcomes in 30% of cases.

If participants playing as partners in fixed pairings do better in this game, then it is conceivable that the same would be true for the more complex minimum effort game which captures the nature of the interaction in many corporations. That is exactly how it turns out. Ananish Chaudhuri and Tirnud Paichayontvijit at the University of Auckland have 208 participants take part in a slightly modified version of the minimum effort game. They ask two questions: (1) do groups which experience greater turnover fare worse in coordinating their actions? And (2) if that is the case, then what kinds of interventions work for these groups? Do the ones that work for fixed groups also work for groups whose composition changes frequently?

Participants are formed into groups of five and play for a number of rounds. There are two matching protocols: in one treatment, this grouping is "fixed" in that the composition of the group remains unchanged and the same five participants interact with one another for the entire time. In a second treatment, participants are re-matched at the end of each round. Here, each session typically has 20 participants and, at the beginning of each round, these participants are randomly formed into groups of five using a computer programme. This makes it unlikely that the same group of five will interact more than once. Remember that in this game, the best outcome is when all members of the group choose 7, which yields the maximum money to each participant and corresponds to the pay-off dominant outcome.

In each matching protocol, groups first play five rounds without any intervention. There are five players in each group and one play of the game in any particular round is generated once all five members of a group have made an effort choice. This gives Chaudhuri and Paichayontvijit 120 observations in the random matching protocol and 75 observations in the fixed matching protocol. Exactly as in the Clark and Sefton study, groups whose composition remains unchanged over time are far better at taking coordinated actions compared to groups whose members are re-matched at the end of each round. When these researchers looked at the proportion of cases where the smallest number chosen in the group was 1, they find that, for the fixed groups, the proportion of cases where the group minimum is 1 is relatively stable and hovers around 10%. The situation is radically different among the randomly re-matched groups. Here, the proportion of groups ending up at the minimum possible effort level increases from 27% in round 1 to 50% in both rounds 4 and 5.

Given this lack of coordination success on the part of the re-matched groups, the next question was: what kinds of interventions work better for these groups? Chaudhuri and Paichayontvijit look at two different kinds of interventions: (1) an *announcement* (essentially a recommendation from an external arbiter) along the lines of Van Huyck, Gillette and Battalio and (2) an *incentive bonus* along the lines of Brandts and Cooper. The announcement takes two forms: (1) *Public*, where the message is printed out on a sheet of paper and given to everyone; everyone knows that everyone else is receiving the exact same message (think of this as posting messages on a public bulletin board); and (2) *Common knowledge*, where, in addition to handing out the sheet with the message, an assistant reads the message out loud for everyone to hear. (Think of this as videos with exhortative messages played to all members of a group at the same time.) The bonus works a little differently than in Brandts and Cooper. In Brandts and Cooper, the bonus depends on the minimum amount of work hours chosen and workers get a bonus as long as the minimum is higher than zero; of course, the highest bonus is received when they choose to work the maximum of 40 hours (analogous to choosing 7 in the minimum effort game). In Chaudhuri and Paichayontvijit, the bonus is given in every round that the group manages to coordinate to 7, that is, all group members

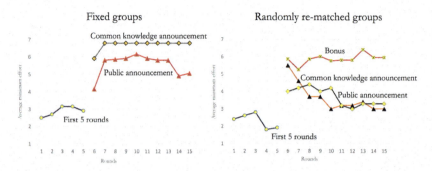

Figure 13.2 Announcements and bonuses with fixed and randomly re-matched groups in the minimum effort game. Re-created on the basis of data in Chaudhuri and Paichayontvijit (2010)

choose 7. There is no bonus for coordinating to anything less than 7, unlike in the Brandts and Cooper study. This is similar to Continental's policy of paying a $100 bonus for coming first, or paying $65 for coming second or third, but a fourth place finish or worse yields no bonus at all. For reasons that will become clear below, the bonus treatment is implemented only for the strangers matching protocol.

Figure 13.2 shows what happens in this study. Chaudhuri and Paichayontvijit find that when the composition of the group remains fixed over time, a common knowledge announcement exhorting everyone to choose 7 and pointing out the benefits of doing so is enough to get consistent coordination to the pay-off dominant all-7 outcome. However, the same announcement (whether public or common knowledge) enjoys limited success when the groups are short-lived and participants are randomly re-matched at the end of each round. Here, the intervention that ultimately gets players to coordinate to the pay-off dominant outcome (or close to it) is the payment of an incentive bonus and a public announcement of that bonus; short of that public announcement and the payment of a performance bonus, these groups are not very successful in coordinating their actions. This suggests that groups which experience frequent turnover are much more prone to pervasive coordination failures; communication alone may no longer suffice in resolving these failures but needs to be accompanied by financial carrots in the form of performance bonuses.

CONCLUDING REMARKS

Michael Kremer, an economist at Harvard University (who won the Nobel Prize in 2019), points out a dramatic and ultimately heart-rending story of coordination failure. On 28 January 1986, the space shuttle Challenger exploded 73 seconds into its flight after an O-ring seal in its right solid rocket booster failed at lift-off. This, in turn, led to structural failures and eventually, aerodynamic forces broke up the shuttle. The shuttle was destroyed and all seven crew members were killed. While the thousands of components of the space shuttle were fine, the shuttle blew up because an O-ring, a relatively minor component, did not work properly.

Kremer uses this example to argue that in a variety of economic contexts, coordinated action is prevented by seemingly minor glitches or small degrees of uncertainty. He goes on to use the experience of the space shuttle Challenger and the failure of the O-ring to propose that extensive coordination failures might be at the heart of under-development in many countries. Here, countries may be caught in a low-level equilibrium "trap" when development requires the simultaneous industrialization of many sectors of the economy but no sector can break even by industrializing alone. Successful development, then, might require a "big push", needing coordinated action by different sectors of the economy. Similarly, in a macroeconomic context, an economy can get trapped in an under-employment equilibrium during recessions. In such instances, no firm wishes to expand production unless it can be assured that others will do so, yet not doing so leads to an outcome that is worse for everyone concerned.

The available evidence suggests that, in most of these cases of coordination failure, the primary source of the problem is strategic uncertainty about others' actions. I do not wish to adopt the risky strategy that could lead to the pay-off dominant outcome until and unless I am convinced that others in my group will do the same. And until I acquire that trust in my peers, we might be doomed to be caught in a low (or no) coordination trap. To a large extent, resolving such coordination failure problems boil down to the creation of appropriately optimistic beliefs that others in the group will choose the more risky stag hunt strategy as well.

The exact mechanism of creating those beliefs will depend on the particular problem at hand and could involve the use of good communication strategies, such as exhortative messages via bulletin boards or television advertisements; sometimes they might require monetary incentives; at times, the monetary incentives might need to be reinforced by congratulatory messages; other times, one might need extensive acculturation and socialization of new entrants. Whatever the nature of the intervention, it will almost always require social processes that generate common knowledge by putting the information in the *public* domain so that everyone is convinced that everyone else is getting the exact same message and feels emboldened to act so as to coordinate their actions. A shared comprehension of the message is crucial to achieving successful coordination.

NOTES

1 Continental Airlines is no longer in existence, having merged with United in 2010. The combined entity is known as United Airlines.
2 This example refers to Chapter 6, the section headed "Men are from Mars and Women are from Venus".
3 It is worth iterating here that I am often going to use the phrase "hunt stag" to refer to the pay-off dominant strategy. I think that in the context of the discussion it will be obvious to readers that this is what "hunt stag" means. This is also a simply mnemonic device that immediately reminds the reader about the nature of the incentives underlying these games.
4 As noted earlier, I am using "hunt stag" as a shorthand for the pay-off dominant strategy. In some of these games there are more than two strategies but there is always a pay-off dominant equilibrium that comes about when each player choose the pay-off dominant strategy ("hunt stag") commensurate with this equilibrium.
5 Note the similarity here with the group lending policy and peer monitoring implemented by the Grameen Bank of Bangladesh. We discussed this back in Chapter 10.

14 Behavioural analyses of markets

In this chapter, I:

- *Provide an overview of the workings of the market system, including the concepts of demand, supply, equilibrium price, consumer surplus and producer surplus;*
- *Show that markets may take various different forms with differing rules and institutions;*
- *Explore the implications of different market structures for the prices that prevail in those markets and for consumer and producer surplus;*
- *Revisit the role of fairness in determining market outcomes;*
- *Examine the role of price controls within these market institutions.*

INTRODUCTION

I started working on this book in the early part of 2020 when the world was going through the COVID-19 pandemic. Within a matter of months, if not weeks, the Dow Jones Index (and others such as S&P 500) tumbled as share prices fell with panicked investors selling off shares that they expected to lose value. As international travel came to a standstill, demand for airline tickets fell and so did prices as airline companies started offering deals to attract flyers. With tourism non-existent, the price of hotel rooms fell and, with more and more people not driving during stringent lockdowns, the demand for fuel fell, leading to a sharp drop in petrol prices. By May of 2020, nearly 40 million people had filed for unemployment in the US as businesses stopped hiring. Almost everyone has an intuitive understanding of why these things happened. They are all attributable to the workings of the market system via demand and supply. Since businesses were not hiring, the supply of workers (or labour) far exceeded the demand, leading to large scale unemployment. As people drove less, there was less demand for petrol, leading to a fall in price. Most investors wanted to sell off their shares with few willing to buy, leading to a steep fall in the price of shares.

Demand and supply are two frequently used words in economics. In fact, most people think that demand and supply constitute the bulk of economics. The next time you are at a social gathering and you tell people that you are studying economics, sooner or later, someone will say something along the lines of: "It's all demand and supply, right?" At this point, you will also realize that this is partly, but not entirely, correct. After all, we are in Chapter 14 of the book and the words demand and supply have appeared only infrequently in the previous chapters. So, there is a lot more to economics than demand and supply. But it is true that the notions of demand and supply and the workings of the market system are an integral part of the study of economics. So, in this chapter and the following one, I will talk about markets and see what behavioural economics has to say about this.

Economists of all stripes believe that, as far as practicable, matters should be left to markets. As the proverbial saying goes: markets may be a bad way of organizing trade and exchange but everything else (such as planned economies) are worse. In fact, it is probably fair to say that whenever non-economists hear the term "markets", a furrow appears in their brows as if there is something distasteful about the entire notion. But, as I hope to convince you, the distrust in markets is misplaced. Much of this reservation relies on assumptions about certain types of market failures. For example, markets are not very good at dealing with externalities such as pollution, which, in turn, requires some government regulation. Markets are often not competitive and confer excessive "market power" to one group to the detriment of the other. I will explain shortly what this means. But, as I pointed out earlier, markets also have a humanizing effect on behaviour in the sense that when we look at small-scale societies, the ones who are more integrated in market economies tend to behave more in accordance with norms of fairness.

DEMAND

I am huge fan of Leonard Cohen, who passed away in 2016. Thankfully, a few years before that, Cohen performed two sold-out concerts on back-to-back days in Auckland. I managed to grab two tickets for my wife and I for what turned out to be one of the most enduring experiences in my life. But, enough about my admiration for Leonard Cohen. Let us talk about all the other fans, what they did and the prices they were willing to pay for those tickets. Figure 14.1 shows a hypothetical structure of the demand for Cohen's concert. Obviously, there are many fans of Cohen but these fans differ in the degree to which they like him, the amount of money they are willing to shell out for a concert (probably depending on how much money they make and what else they have planned for in terms of entertainment), the number of tickets they are willing to buy (whether only for the parents or for the children too), etc.

In looking at the demand for this concert, we will put the price on the Y-axis and the quantity on the X-axis. There is no compelling reason for doing this. This is more of a convention and, as we will see soon, this makes other calculations easier. Let us say that there is

Figure 14.1
Step-like demand function

some price $P1 (say $500), such that if the price is above $P1, no one is willing to buy any tickets. But at $P1, some people like me and some others are willing to buy as many as Q1 tickets. So, if the concert organizers decided to charge everyone $P1, they will be selling Q1 tickets. But, if the concert organizers decided to charge everyone $P2 (say $400), then the Q1 people who were willing to pay $P1 ($500) will still be willing to buy since they were willing to pay more in any case. In addition, some more people will now be willing to buy. For instance, at price $P2, I might buy tickets not only for my wife but also for my two daughters. It is important to note an assumption here. If the concert organizers drop the price to $P2, then they need to do this for everyone, so that even those who were willing to pay $P1 will now pay the lower price of $P2.[1] So, when the price drops to $P2, there are more buyers willing to buy and the total number of tickets sold goes up to Q2. If the price is even lower, say $P3, then the quantity of tickets sold will go up to Q3 and so on.

This generates the step-like demand shown in the left-hand panel of Figure 14.1 and is the demand for this particular Leonard Cohen concert. One key feature is that there is a negative relationship between price and quantity: if and when the price drops, more people are willing to buy tickets, and so, at lower prices, more tickets will be sold. The step-like function shows the demand for Leonard Cohen concert tickets at various prices. Working with a step-like function like this is not easy. So, we can approximate this with a straight line, that we will call the *demand curve*.[2] Clearly, on the left-hand panel, the quantity steps at each price point are quite wide and the straight-line approximation is not very accurate. But, if the market was "thicker", in the sense that I looked at lots of price–quantity configurations close to one another, as in the right-hand panel of Figure 14.1, then my straight-line approximation is not that far off the mark. I am certainly sacrificing some accuracy, but, in return, I am gaining tractability, since working with a smooth straight-line demand curve is a lot easier than working with a step-like one.

In fact, this straight-line approximation of demand lies at the heart of demand estimation. If you were running a business and wanted to estimate the demand for your product, then you would undertake a similar exercise. You could start with a market survey or get hold of some historical price–quantity data. Typically, you want to know about more things than only price, such as income levels in the market where you wish to sell your good or the prices of goods that are complements to, or substitutes for, your good.[3] Once you have gathered all of this data, you will typically need to run a multi-variable regression connecting the demand for your good with the price of the good and all of the other variables. The regression analysis will give you a straight-line (or affine) relationship between the quantity of the good and its price along with the other variables. Typically, we then say that *ceteris paribus* (meaning "holding other things constant", that is, if everything other than the price of the good, such as income or prices of other goods, were to be held constant), we can express the quantity of the good as a function of its price (demand curve) or we can express the price as a function of quantity (inverse demand curve). We will typically use the latter formulation even though I will take the liberty of calling this the demand curve.

Along a demand curve then, price and quantity are negatively related. If the price is higher (lower), then the quantity bought will be lower (higher), resulting in movement from one point to another on the demand curve. This is typically referred to as movement along the curve or, more specifically, changes in quantity demanded. But there are other factors

Figure 14.2 Shifts in demand

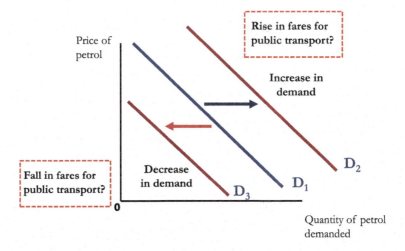

that may affect the demand for a good. For instance, if the price of petrol increases, then more people may decide to take public transport, thereby increasing the demand for the same. If the price of coffee beans increases, then this will lead to a reduced demand for coffee, but, equally, this will also lead to a decrease in demand for coffee creamers. These changes are usually referred to as shifts of the demand curve as a whole or, more specifically, a change in demand. The idea being that these changes are being driven by something other than the price of the good. So, when coffee prices go up, people will buy fewer coffee creamers, even if the price of coffee creamers has not changed.

Figure 14.2 illustrates such a shift in demand. Here, I have drawn a downward-sloping demand curve for petrol. When petrol prices rise (fall), people buy less (more) petrol. But, even if the price did not change, another factor, such as the fares on public transport, may impact the demand for petrol. For example, if it became really cheap to take the bus/train/subway to work, and/or the price of parking in downtown Auckland went up a whole lot, a bunch of people may decide to drive less to work. This reduces the demand for petrol even though the price of petrol has not changed. A similar effect in reverse happens if, say, public transport fares went up a lot. People who were taking public transport may decide that it is cheaper and more convenient to drive to work. This will increase the demand for petrol, in spite of the fact that petrol prices have not changed.

SUPPLY

Obviously, if we as consumers demand to buy a variety of goods, there must be a corresponding supply of these goods. Just as we did in the case of demand, we can think of supply as a step-like function also. Figure 14.3 illustrates a typical supply function. An intuitive way to think of this is: different sellers have different costs of producing their goods. Therefore, the price they are willing to accept for their goods reflects their underlying cost structure. So, if the market price happens to be $P1, then only Seller 1 is willing to sell anything at this price, since this is the only seller whose costs are low enough to make it profitable to sell at this price. Say this seller's cost is a fraction (say, $0.50) less than $P1, so, if push comes to

■ Behavioural analyses of markets

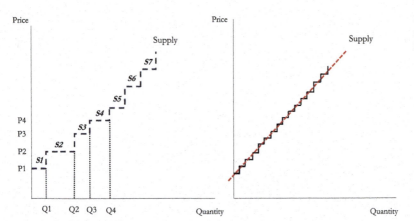

Figure 14.3
Step-like supply function

shove, this seller is willing to accept $P1 and make a profit of $0.50 per unit. Of course, he/she would like to get more, but clearly, there must be some price that makes it worth his/her while to sell at that price. So, this is the minimum price he/she is willing to accept for his/her good. For now, we will assume that production and sale are the same thing; each producer has a finite capacity and as long as the market price makes it profitable to sell, this seller sells everything until he/she is out of stock.

If the market price was higher at $P2, then a second seller finds it profitable to sell since he/she has costs that are less than $P2. At $P2, it is still profitable for the first seller and so that total quantity available for sale in this market increases to Q2. If the price was higher at $P3 (or $P4), then more sellers enter the market and the total quantity available for sale increases to Q3 (or Q4). It is absolutely fine if the cost of production for all sellers is the same; say, everyone has the same cost as Seller 1 and they are all willing to accept $P1 as their minimum acceptable price. In this case, the supply curve becomes a horizontal straight line at the price $P1. This may happen but it is more general to assume that different sellers have different costs, generating the step-like supply function. We will discuss situations below where the supply curve is horizontal and I will show that the basic intuitions remain unchanged. And, as in the case of demand, if the market is "thick" with lots of sellers at different cost/price points, then we can easily approximate the step-like function with a straight line, without sacrificing too much in the way of accuracy.

As opposed to demand, the supply curve is upward sloping, simply because when the market price rises, more and more sellers enter the market with their goods and so the quantity supplied increases. Along the supply curve, then, when the price rises, quantity also rises. This is the movement along the curve; if market price is higher (lower), more sellers want to sell and so the quantity available for sale is higher (lower). And, just as in the case of demand, other factors, besides price, may shift the supply curve. For example, if there is war in the Middle East where the bulk of our oil comes from, cutting off supply lines, then the supply of petrol goes down (shift to the left), regardless of the price. Similarly, if the members of the Organization of Petroleum Exporting Countries (OPEC) each individually decide to produce a lot more than their quota, then the supply of petrol will increase (shift to the right), regardless of oil prices. Figure 14.4 illustrates these shifts.

346

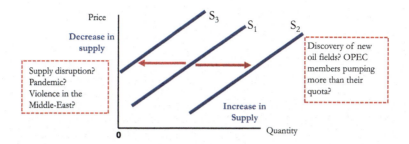

Figure 14.4
Shifts in supply

THE THEORY OF COMPETITIVE EQUILIBRIUM

The most common paradigm of market interactions that we teach students of economics is the perfectly competitive market. A perfectly competitive market is characterized by being "thick", that is, lots of buyers and sellers. Each individual buyer's demand or individual seller's quantity available for sale is small compared to the total demand and supply in the market. As a result, neither the buyer nor the seller has any "market power", meaning that an individual buyer or seller's decision to buy or sell (or not) is not going to have any impact on the prevailing market price. Another term for this is that each individual buyer or seller is a "price-taker"; neither can individually have any effect on the price that prevails in this market, which is determined by the collective decisions of numerous buyers and sellers.

We sometimes make some additional assumptions. For example, each seller sells an identical good (think salt, sugar, potatoes or broccoli) so that buyers are indifferent between which seller they buy from and will buy from the seller whose product is the cheapest. We also assume that there are no barriers to entry or exit in this market: sellers do not need a patent or a permit to sell. If you have a vegetable patch in your garden and you have grown a large quantity of zucchini, then there is nothing to prevent you from taking this zucchini to your local market and selling it there.

Clearly, as you most likely know from introductory economics courses, this is a stylized market. Economists use this for two reasons. First, for some goods (as in the examples above and others that I will discuss below), this is a good approximation. Second, this stylized perfectly competitive market acts as a benchmark. As I will discuss below (and as you may already know), prices tend to be lowest in such markets. In other words, the more competitive the market (the more buyers and sellers), the lower are the prices that prevail; the less competitive the market, the higher the prices. Prices tend to be the highest in monopolies where there is only one producer that sells the good.[4] So, a good measure of how competitive (or not) a market is would be to examine how much prices which prevail in that market deviate from the perfectly competitive benchmark.

So, we now have a bunch of buyers and sellers who have all come together in this place called the "market". How do they decide at what price to buy and sell? Different buyers are willing to pay different prices while different sellers want to charge different prices too. How do they come to an agreement? Leon Walras (1834–1910) was Professor of Political Economy at the University of Lausanne in Switzerland and provided a way that buyers and sellers can arrive at a price they can all agree on.

■ Behavioural analyses of markets

Walras was inspired by his experience with French bourses in the 19th century; essentially, markets for various goods. These markets were governed by an auctioneer. The auctioneer would call out various prices. At each of these prices, the buyers would indicate how much they intended to buy at that price. Adding these up gave a measure of total demand in the market. Similarly, the sellers would also indicate how much they were willing to sell at those prices, which, in turn, provided an estimate of how much was available for sale. The auctioneer would keep calling out prices and calculating estimates of demand and supply until, by a process called *tatonnement* (French for "trial and error") he/she arrived at a price where the total demand and total supply were exactly equal. Once this price was discovered, all sales and purchases were conducted at this price.

Figure 14.5 illustrates the *tatonnement* process. Suppose the auctioneer calls out a price of $1.50. Clearly, at this point, the total amount buyers want to buy is greater than the amount that the sellers are willing to sell. This is a situation of excess demand (or shortage). So, in the next step, the auctioneer calls out $1.60. The gap between demand and supply falls, but demand is still greater than supply and, hence, there is still a shortage. So, the auctioneer knows that the price needs to go higher, but how much? He/she goes to $2.50. Now, the total amount that the sellers want to sell exceeds the amount that the buyers want to buy, resulting in excess supply (or a surplus). The auctioneer now knows that $1.60 is too low while $2.50 is too high. He/she keeps going back and forth until he/she arrives at a price of $2.00. Here, the total quantity demanded by the buyers exactly equals the total available for sale from the sellers. This is usually referred to as the "market equilibrium". The equilibrium price is $2.00 and the equilibrium quantity is seven (measured in some relevant units).

Why is this an equilibrium? Because, once this price has been established, in the absence of an external shock to the demand and supply curves, it will tend to persist because individual buyers and sellers cannot impact this price any more. Obviously, every buyer who was willing to pay $2.00, or possibly a little more (say, all the way down to $2.05), is happy to buy at this price. Any buyer who is not willing to pay $2.00 cannot buy. Similarly, every seller who was willing to sell at $2.00 or a little less (say, those who have costs of $1.95 or less) will be able to sell. Any seller whose costs exceed $2.00 will not be able to sell in this market.

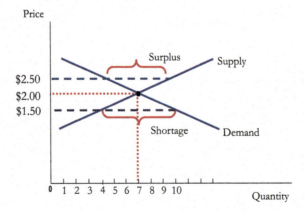

Figure 14.5
The process of achieving market equilibrium

348 □

CASE STUDY 14.1 PETROL PRICES DURING THE COVID-19 PANDEMIC

I mentioned above that, during the pandemic, petrol prices fell sharply. There were two primary factors behind this, one affecting demand and the other supply. Once the virus started spreading, more and more countries asked their citizens to stay home. People worked from home, while schools and colleges delivered lessons online. This meant people were driving a lot less than before, regardless of petrol prices. This had the effect of reducing demand for petrol.

The vast bulk of the market supply of petrol is controlled by a group of countries that collectively form the Organization of the Petroleum Exporting Countries, or OPEC. These include countries such as Algeria, Angola, Iran, Iraq, Kuwait, Libya, Nigeria, Saudi Arabia, United Arab Emirates and Venezuela, with Saudi Arabia being the *de facto* leader of the group. There are other countries, such as Russia, who have oil reserves but these reserves are small compared to the amount controlled by OPEC.

OPEC does not behave as a "price-taker". Being virtually a monopoly, OPEC can dictate the market price of oil by tightly controlling the supply. It does so by assigning a quota to each OPEC member. As long as the members abide by their quotas, the supply curve stays where OPEC wants it to be. But periodically, whether due to internal dissension or due to miscalculation, one or more countries exceed their quota and produce more oil. For OPEC members, this is a social dilemma. As long as each member country abides by the quota, everyone is better off and enjoys large profit. However, if everyone else abides by the quota but one member increases production a little, then that country is better off at the expense of the others. But if one country does so, then the other countries do not wish to be left behind and are tempted to increase their production too. This results in an increase in supply until everyone gets together and negotiates a truce and reduces production to abide by their quotas. During the pandemic, while demand decreased, at least for a while OPEC members increased production, resulting in increased supply. The result was lower price.

Figure 14.6 explains. Suppose pre-pandemic demand for petrol is shown by D1, while pre-pandemic supply is S1. Then the initial equilibrium in this market is at E, where the equilibrium price is $P1 and the equilibrium quantity is Q1. Post-pandemic, demand drops from D1 to D2, while supply from OPEC increases from S1 to S2. The new market equilibrium is now F, where the market price has fallen to $P2, and, given the relative magnitudes of the shifts in demand and supply, total quantity bought and sold, post-pandemic, has dropped to Q2. So, even with the lower price, demand has fallen so much that people are still buying less petrol than they used to.

■ Behavioural analyses of markets

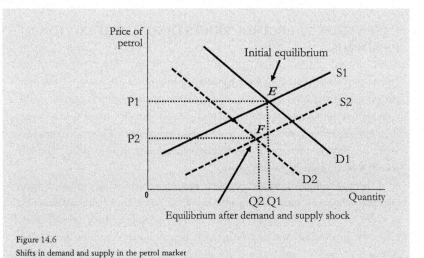

Figure 14.6
Shifts in demand and supply in the petrol market

CONSUMER AND PRODUCER SURPLUS

Once the market arrives at the equilibrium via Walras' *tatonnement* process, there is no longer any tendency for the price to change in the absence of any shocks to demand and/or supply. But this does not mean that everyone is equally happy or satisfied at this market outcome. Clearly, there are some low-valuation buyers and high-cost sellers who cannot transact in this market at all. But, leaving those aside, even among those who do end up buying and selling in this market, not everyone enjoys the same pay-off (or "surplus").

Consider the market shown in Figure 14.7, with an equilibrium price of $8. This implies that all goods will be bought and sold at this price. Look at a buyer like Avala. She was actually willing to pay much more than $8. Suppose she was willing to pay $14 to buy one unit of this good. Why? Because Avala believes that buying one unit of the good will bring her $14 worth of happiness (utility) and, therefore, at most, she was willing to pay $14 (or something a little less, say, $13.90). To keep things simple, let us say that, at the limit, Avala would pay $14. But she gets to buy this unit for $8. So, it is as if Avala has experienced a psychological "surplus" of $6 ($14 − $8). This psychological surplus, which is the difference between how much Avala was willing to pay and how much she actually pays is defined as the *consumer surplus*. Take another buyer, like Erik. Erik does not value this good as highly as Avala, and at the limit, was willing to pay $12 for it. When Erik buys this for $8, he gets a surplus of $4. This implies that if we add up the surplus from all the buyers who were willing to pay $8 or more, then we get a measure of aggregate consumer surplus in this market. This is depicted by the vertically striped triangle that lies between the demand curve and the equilibrium price. Once we know the demand intercept, the price and the equilibrium, it is easy to calculate the magnitude of this aggregate consumer surplus. It is the area of the vertically striped triangle = (1/2)×(base)×(height).

Next, let us look at the supply side and consider two sellers, Emilio and Evie. Emilio is a lower cost seller than Evie. He can produce and sell his goods for $5 apiece. When Emilio gets $8 per unit of his good, he makes a surplus (profit) of $3 per unit. Evie produces her

Figure 14.7
Consumer and producer surplus

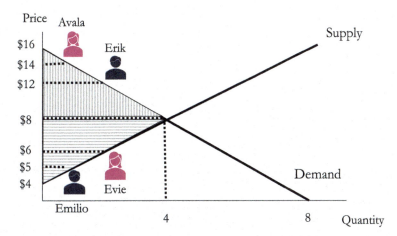

units at a higher cost of $6 per unit. So, at a price of $8, Evie makes a surplus (profit) of $2 per unit. Once again, if we add up the surplus of all the sellers who can produce the good for $8 or less, we get a measure of the aggregate *producer (seller) surplus*. The interpretation of the producer surplus is more straightforward than that of the consumer surplus. In the case of consumers, we had to appeal to their psychological utility and valuation of the good to get a measure of their welfare. For producers, surplus is simply the difference between the price the seller gets per unit of his/her good and the cost of producing that unit. So, producers' surplus is the same as profit. In the market equilibrium of Figure 14.7, the aggregate producer surplus (profit) is shown by the horizontally striped area above the supply curve and below the equilibrium price. The magnitude of this producer surplus is the same as the area of the horizontally striped triangle = $(1/2) \times (base) \times (height)$.

In fact, the concepts of producer surplus and consumer surplus feature prominently in making policy decisions. For example, if a country is considering imposing a tariff (tax) on foreign imports (such as cars), a frequent consideration is what this will do to aggregate consumer surplus and aggregate producer surplus. In the tariff example, prices will be higher following a tariff, resulting in an increase in producer surplus but a reduction in consumer surplus, and the question would be whether the gain in one makes up for a loss in the other.

To iterate: why do economists talk so much about competitive markets? As I noted earlier, because lots of markets share these features. And second, because it is an important benchmark. If you had a market set-up where the equilibrium price is arrived at via this Walrasian *tatonnement* process, then typically you are guaranteed lowest prices and the *highest efficiency*. What does efficiency mean? It can be expressed in a few different ways, which essentially imply the same thing. One way of thinking about efficiency is that every buyer who values the good at more than the equilibrium price gets to buy, and each seller who can produce the good at a cost less than the equilibrium price gets to sell. So, in the market equilibrium of this market, all possible gains from exchange have been realized. This, in turn, implies that the sum of producer and consumer surplus taken together is the maximum possible. It is important to understand that this notion of "efficiency" is purely descriptive (or "positive" as economists like to say); there is no normative component to this; there is no value judgement involved. Walras is not claiming that the market equilibrium is fair or unfair, just or unjust, equal or unequal. Walras is simply saying that if we organized markets in this manner, then each unit of the good that can be profitably sold and bought will be sold and bought. Every seller willing to sell at the equilibrium price will be able to sell and every buyer willing to pay the equilibrium price or more will be able to buy. This maximizes the sum of consumer and producer surplus, which implies maximum efficiency.

BUT ... DOES IT WORK IN REAL LIFE?

The Walrasian model of perfectly competitive markets is an elegant theory. But, a reader (or student) is justified in thinking: this does not look like the markets I know; when I go to a store I don't see an auctioneer calling out prices. In fact, the only times I have seen an auctioneer is when I bought/sold my last house or bought/sold an antique. There are actually two different issues here: First, the Walrasian auctioneer is, of course, a fictional artefact, a *deux ex machina* designed to highlight how markets may reach equilibrium. In fact, as I will show in this section, the process of market equilibration does not require the presence of an auctioneer. Buyers and sellers looking for profitable trades will be able to achieve the same outcome subject to some caveats. Then in a later section (headed "Posted offer markets"), I will take up the second issue: that this does not seem to resemble the markets where we shop. When I go to the supermarket, I don't usually haggle over the price. The prices are clearly displayed and I decide how much to buy or not. These are called *posted offer* markets and I will come to this shortly.[5]

So, if we took a bunch of buyers with different valuations of a good and another bunch of sellers with different costs of production and mixed them together in a market, will they be able to achieve equilibrium outcomes in the absence of an auctioneer? Will the market clear; meaning, will everyone willing to buy get to buy? Will everyone willing to sell get to sell and will the market reach the equilibrium price predicted by the underlying demand and supply curves? If there is no auctioneer, then who will guarantee that such an outcome will indeed come to prevail? And, what type of markets look like this anyway?

To take the second issue first, as I mentioned before, Walras was inspired by what transpired in the French bourses, but, in general, lots of markets may look like this. Any market that allows for bargaining over the price can be depicted in this manner. This can be farmers' markets, or markets for Dutch tulips and even markets for used cars. In fact, the set-up Walras had in mind is very similar to the stock exchanges, such as the New York Stock Exchange (NYSE). So, one thing to bear in mind is that the market institution is crucial. What we have here is a group of buyers with different willingness to pay and a group of sellers with different costs of production and, therefore, different prices they are willing to accept for their goods. How they get together and transact is a matter of market design. For instance, one really does not need an auctioneer. In this day and age, each buyer can enter into a computer the price he/she wants to pay (typically called a *bid*) and how much he/she wants to buy. A seller can do the same; insert the price he/she wants to charge (the *ask*) and how many units he/she wants to sell at this price. The computer can then calculate the underlying demand and supply curves, figure out the equilibrium price and let everyone know what the price is. Every buyer who wants to buy at that price gets to buy and every seller willing to sell at that price gets to sell, subject to availability of stock. This would be a feasible way to set up a market.

In 1990, Steven Wunsch set up a stock exchange in Phoenix, Arizona (called the Arizona Stock Exchange) that worked exactly like this. Buyers and sellers could input their buying prices (bids) and selling prices (asks) into a computer, which then created the underlying demand and supply function and the resulting equilibrium price. All trades then occurred at this equilibrium price, exactly like a Walrasian market. (The fancy name for a market that works like this is a *call market*, where all transactions take place at a specific time once the demand and supply curve information has been aggregated.) However, this stock exchange closed in 2001 due to a very low volume of transactions. The Walrasian markets (and the idea of the auctioneer) then corresponds to a *centralized* system, where an auctioneer (or a computer) does the calculations and tells everyone what price they should buy and sell at. But even the markets that rely on getting buyers and sellers together do not usually rely on such a centralized mechanism. Instead, they allow buyers and sellers to engage in *decentralized* trades. This means that buyers and sellers in this market are allowed to wander around (maybe in the digital world) and strike trades that they fancy. The primary concerns are: is there any reason to believe that such decentralized trading between buyers and sellers, each trying to find the best possible deal, works? Will the market clear? Will the market reach the predicted equilibrium price?

At the very outset, we said that a key component to rationality is to maximize pay-offs and those who consistently fail to do so may find themselves under selection pressure. If some sellers consistently fail to maximize their profit, then they would fall behind others who did better and may be driven out of the market. Buyers who consistently paid a higher than necessary price would soon run out of money to make other essential purchases.

In 1948, Edward Chamberlin at Harvard University decided to see if this can possibly work. He had students play the role of buyers and sellers. For the sake of simplicity, Chamberlin assumed that each seller could sell one unit and each buyer could buy one unit too. So, once a buyer and seller got together and completed their transaction, they had finished. This is a simplifying assumption that I will carry through, realizing that nothing will change even if we let buyers and sellers transact multiple units at the same time. All this does is to make the steps on the demand and supply curves longer. If we allow for few buyers and sellers each buying/selling multiple units, then the steps on the demand–supply curves become longer and the market is "thinner". This is the situation depicted in the left-hand panels of Figures 14.1 (for demand) and 14.3 (for supply). If we allow lots of buyers and sellers each buying/selling small amounts (one unit is my shorthand for a small amount) then the steps become shorter, there are lots more such steps and the market becomes "thicker". This is shown in the right-hand panels of Figures 14.1 and 14.3.

Each buyer is given a slip of paper with a number written on it. This was that buyer's valuation of the good; the maximum amount he/she is willing to pay to buy the good. Each buyer is instructed that he/she should try to maximize his/her surplus by buying at the lowest possible price. Each seller is also given a piece of paper with a number written on it. This is the seller's cost of production and, therefore, the minimum price he/she is willing to accept for his/her good. Each seller is told that he/she should try to sell at the highest price that he/

■ Behavioural analyses of markets

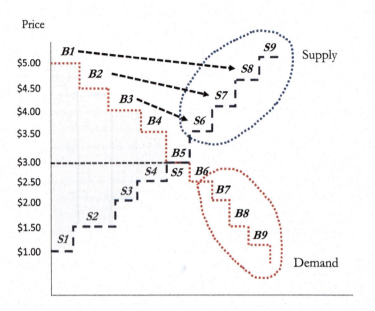

Figure 14.8
Step-like demand and supply functions with buyers and sellers (Smith 1962)

she can, in order to maximize his/her profit. Before I explain what Chamberlin and those who followed him find, let me explain the set-up a little bit more with the aid of Figure 14.8.

This figure shows the step-like demand and supply functions that we have seen before. I have arranged the buyers (B1, B2, B3 …) in decreasing order of their valuation (maximum price they are willing to pay) and the sellers (S1, S2, S3 …) in increasing order of their costs (minimum price they are willing to accept). Now, suppose we put these buyers and sellers in a room and let them engage in completely unsupervised decentralized trading. Given the underlying demand and supply curves, the equilibrium price in this market should be $3.00 and either four or five units of the good should be traded. This is because we have a buyer B5, with a valuation of $3.00, and a seller S5, with a cost of production of $3.00. They are indifferent between buying or not and selling or not since they get zero surplus. Alternatively, you can think of this as this buyer and seller may get a very small surplus if their valuation and cost are marginally higher and lower than $3.00, respectively. But we are more interested in the price that prevails in a market like this. Will this price be equal or close to $3.00?

Ideally, if you could direct matters, then you might ask B1 to get together with S1, B2 with S2, etc., and work out a price somewhere between the buyer's valuation and seller's cost. But notice, if you could conceivably do this, what you have established is a set of bilateral ultimatum games between each buyer and each seller. B1 is willing to pay $5.00 to buy one unit of the good. S1 can produce that unit at a cost of $1.00. So, they could easily agree on a price of $3.00, with each getting a surplus of $2.00. Sounds fair, right? Similarly, B2 and S2 get together. B2 is willing to pay $4.50, while S2 should be willing to accept $1.50. Strike a deal at $3.00 and each walk away with $1.50 in surplus. If every pair did so and simply split the difference, then each pair strikes a deal at $3.00 and the market price should be at least close to, if not exactly equal to, $3.00.

But there are two potential problems with this story. First, as I just noted, what you have set up here is a series of ultimatum games. What if either the buyers or the sellers are really hard-nosed? What if B1 is willing to pay $3.00 but S1 insists on getting more than $3.00? What if S2 is willing to settle for $3.00 but B2 insists on paying less? Clearly, trades are possible in the lightly shaded area to the left between the demand and supply curves. But who guarantees that they will agree on $3.00? And if they do not, then we could end up with a wide range of prices different from $3.00.

Here is the other problem. In the absence of an auctioneer or someone else directing action, what is to prevent B1 from getting together with S8? B1 is willing to pay $5.00 while S8 is willing to settle for $4.50. They could strike a deal at $4.75. This is because, in such a decentralized market, B1 does not know that there are lots of other sellers who have lower cost and that he/she may be able to get a much better deal if he/she traded with S1 or S2. Similarly, B2 could get together with S7, B3 with S6. Each of them can take part in a profitable trade albeit with very small surpluses. But normally, sellers like S6, S7 and S8 should not even be able to trade at the equilibrium price. So, how do B1, B2 or B3 learn about the lower cost sellers like S1, S2 or S3? Information about the respective values and costs become critical, which, in turn, implies that the way the market is designed is fundamental to achieving equilibrium outcomes.

This is where Chamberlin's experiments fell short to an extent. Chamberlin found that prices in his market did not track the equilibrium price well, and market efficiency, as measured by the total surplus enjoyed by the buyers and sellers, fell short of what would be expected under a Walrasian market clearing process. This led Chamberlin to conclude that, in the absence of some central clearing authority, markets such as these may fail to clear and may not reach the predicted equilibrium. Chamberlin did not adequately appreciate the fact that while he had set the market up properly, where things went wrong was in the information aggregation and dissemination. Buyers and sellers found themselves in a rather sterile environment, where *price discovery* was difficult. This meant that buyers and sellers had a hard time figuring out the potential distributions of valuations and costs and did not have an accurate estimation of what potential profits may look like. Simply put, the B1 or B2-type high valuation buyers did not understand that they should hold out until they found the S1 or S2-type low cost sellers rather than transact with S7 or S8-types.

Vernon Smith (who would go on to receive the Nobel Prize in Economics in 2002, along with Daniel Kahneman) was a student of Chamberlin at Harvard. Upon starting his academic career as an assistant professor at Purdue University, Smith realized that the Chamberlin approach was actually well suited to studying markets but needed some modifications; in particular, in the way information is conveyed to the traders in the market. Smith set up a market that does not require an auctioneer calling out prices and is very similar to the way stock exchanges such as the NYSE operate.

Figure 14.8 illustrates Smith's approach too. Each buyer starts by entering a bid, a price that this buyer is willing to pay (and, if relevant, can also enter how many units he/she wants to buy but, for the time being, let us continue to assume that each buyer and seller will transact one unit only). Each seller enters an ask, the price at which this seller is willing to sell. Remember that buyers have an incentive to try to buy at the lowest possible price while sellers want to sell at the highest possible price. Another way to think of this is to let the lowest valuation buyer go first. Alternatively, if you are not sure whether you are a high or low valuation buyer, then wait to see what happens. If no one is entering a bid, then enter a bid that makes sense given your own valuation. A similar argument applies to the seller. In terms of Figure 14.8, this means that, in all likelihood, Buyer 9 and Seller 9 will move first. S9 asks for $5.00 while B9 is willing to pay $1.00. Obviously, no trade is possible. Actually, it does not have to be B9 who makes a bid. It is entirely feasible for B1 to bid "low" at $1.00, at which point B9 may also put in a bid for $1.00. But the same argument applies. At this point, there are two buyers who are each willing to pay $1.00 but no seller is willing to sell at this price. Then B8 may jump in by raising the "bid" to $1.50 (one of the other buyers could do this too), while S8 enters the market and lowers the ask to $4.50. Any buyer is free to put in a bid at any point in time, just as a seller can put in an ask.

Smith established one constraint. Any bid must be an improvement on the previous one. So, if the current highest bid is $1.50, then the next bid must either be higher, or, if lower (say $1.00), then it will be placed in a *rank queue* behind the current highest bid of $1.50. The same thing applies to sellers' asks. Either the ask must be lower than the current "ask", or else it is placed behind the current low ask in the queue of asks. So, essentially, while we intuitively think of the demand curve as starting high on the Y-axis and sloping down negatively to the right, in Smith's implementation of the market, the demand curve "starts" low on the right with the lowest bid and then moves "up" as bids increase. Similarly, instead of the supply curve starting low on the left from the Y-axis and sloping up to the right, here, it starts "high" on the right and moves "down" as the asks decline.

Over time, as more and more high-valuation buyers and low-cost sellers enter the market, the step-like demand and supply functions are created. This still does not prevent, say, B1 trading with S7 or S8 at higher than equilibrium prices. But in this market, everyone gets to see all the standing bids and asks, which gives traders a broad idea of how these are distributed. Traders also get to see the price at which a contract is struck. Suppose B2 (willing to pay $4.50) and S7 (willing to accept $4.00) get together and conduct a transaction at $4.20, then this tells others something. If B1 (willing to pay $5.00) was contemplating getting together with S7 (willing to accept $4.00) and conducting a trade at $4.50, then B1 quickly realizes that this is more than B2 paid. Therefore, B1 now has an incentive to hold out for someone willing to sell at $4.00 or lower.

It turns out that these two innovations: the *ascending bid–descending ask* process (where each successive bid or ask must be an improvement over the previous one) and the revelation of the contract prices work like magic. Smith dubbed this market institution a *continuous double auction*. In Figure 14.9, I show the results from one of Smith's early experiments. The left-hand panel shows the same information as in Figure 14.8, but, on the right-hand panel, I have shown what happens when a group of people assigned to the role of buyers and sellers actually take part in this market. There are typically 8–10 buyers and sellers in this market. Each buyer and seller transact one unit and the contract price is made public. In the right-hand panel, I show two things: one, each dot represents a transaction price; two, the dotted line represents the time path of the average price to keep things simple, but, in each case, just about five or six trades should take place with a few buyers and a few sellers being excluded for either having too low a valuation or too high a cost. While buyer and seller roles remain the same for the entire session, the buyers are given different valuations in each period, just

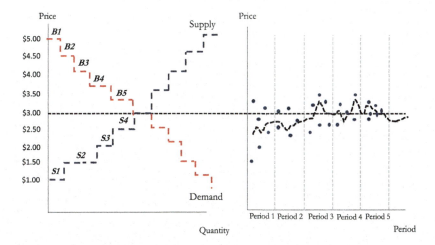

Figure 14.9 Results from a continuous double auction market. Re-created on the basis of data in Smith (1962)

as the sellers are assigned different costs. They each trade for a number of market periods lasting around 2–3 minutes each. A bell rings to indicate the trading period has either opened or closed. Each buyer has a record sheet where he/she writes down the price he/she paid if he/she bought a unit. His/her valuation minus the price paid is his/her profit for that round. Similarly, the seller notes down the price he/she received. This price minus his/her cost of production is his/her profit. At the end of the session, these profits are added up and the traders are paid in cash.

In Figure 14.9, I have shown data for five periods. As noted, the dots show the price at which each transaction occurs and the dotted line shows the *average* transaction price for all the units traded in that period. Three things are clear. First, over time, the average price tracks the equilibrium price extremely well and second, while there is considerable dispersion in the prices at the beginning, over time, even the individual transactions take place at prices that are close to the equilibrium price. Third, in each period, roughly the predicted number of trades (five or six) take place. So, even in the absence of an auctioneer, the respective incentives of the buyers and sellers to maximize their surplus leads to the predicted equilibrium outcome in terms of both price and quantity. This was clear vindication that the Walrasian model of market equilibrium was accurate and can be used to predict equilibrium price and quantity in a market. So, in this instance, individual rationality in the sense of each trader trying to maximize his/her surplus, implemented via Smith's "continuous double auction" market mechanism, leads to the market clearing and the highest possible efficiency in terms of aggregate producer and consumer surplus.[6]

ROBUSTNESS OF THE MARKET EQUILIBRATION PROCESS

Smith had clearly demonstrated that even a completely decentralized trading process based on bilateral trading between self-interested buyers and sellers, in the form of a double auction, can generate the market equilibrium that will be predicted by the Walrasian *tatonnement* process. But does this work for all kinds of demand and supply curves? These curves can be flat or steep. You could have markets where all sellers have the same cost of production

■ Behavioural analyses of markets

resulting in a horizontal supply curve along with a downward sloping demand. Or you could have an upward sloping supply but all the buyers have the same valuation for the good, resulting in a horizontal demand curve. Does the decentralized trading process guarantee that the market will arrive at the predicted equilibrium in all of these cases? This is what I mean by "robustness"; does the insight of Figure 14.9 apply widely? The answer turns out to be "yes" and "no". This is what I discuss next.

Figure 14.10 shows a situation where the demand and supply curves are relatively flat, say, compared to the case in Figure 14.9, where the two curves are relatively steeper. According to Walras, markets should equilibrate more quickly in this situation with relatively flat demand and supply. Walras' idea was that, in such a market, any price that is higher or lower than the equilibrium price will result in large surpluses or shortages, respectively. These should lead to faster trial and error learning and quicker convergence to the equilibrium price. As Figure 14.10 shows, this is clearly the case, even in Smith's decentralized trading institution. In fact, Smith found that whether the demand and supply curves were steeper or flatter did not matter much in relation to whether the average price tracked the equilibrium price and how quickly the two converged. Effectively, the trajectory of contract prices is not different between Figures 14.9 and 14.10.

But what did seem to make a significant difference (and something Walras did not anticipate) was that things did not work as well when Smith used demand and supply curves with large differences in the magnitudes of producer and consumer surplus. Figure 14.11 illustrates this. This is a situation where the surplus accruing to the sellers (the magnitude of the area above the supply curve and below the equilibrium price) is significantly larger than the consumer surplus (the magnitude of the area below the demand curve and above the equilibrium price). Prices start out well below the predicted equilibrium and, while they show some convergence to the equilibrium, it is clear that there are large peaks and troughs along the way and, by and large, average prices are below the equilibrium. This is a situation where the predicted equilibrium will probably not do a good job of capturing the actual (or average) contract prices. Why?

The intuition is not hard to understand in light of our earlier discussion on the ultimatum game. In Figure 14.11, the predicted equilibrium price is $8.00. Now, a buyer like

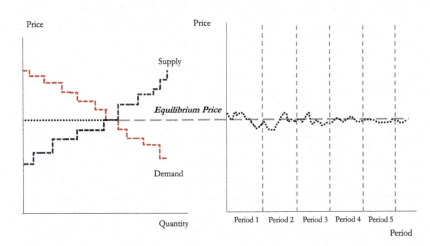

Figure 14.10 Results from a continuous double auction market with relatively flat demand and supply curves. Re-created on the basis of data in Smith (1962)

Figure 14.11
Results from a continuous double auction market with producer surplus larger than consumer surplus. Re-created on the basis of data in Smith (1962)

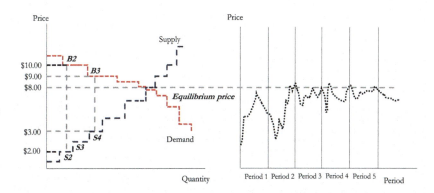

B2, who is willing to pay $10.00, meets a seller like S2, whose cost is $2.00. If they agree to trade at the equilibrium price, then the buyer gets a surplus of $2.00 while the seller gets $6.00. Similarly, if B3 (willing to pay $9) and S3 (willing to accept $3) get together and agree on $8.00, then B3 gets a surplus of $1.00 while S3 gets $5.00. It soon becomes clear to the buyers that they are on the losing end of this market. Therefore, they negotiate much harder to keep the price below $8.00. Sellers are now faced with the prospect of taking a smaller surplus or not making the sale at all. Not surprisingly, the sellers are willing to sell at a price less than $8.00 on average. The insight from this market is that, in situations where the magnitude of the producer surplus is larger than that of the consumer surplus, decentralized bilateral trading will lead to market prices that are, on average, lower than the predicted equilibrium. While I have not shown this in the diagram, this also usually implies that fewer than the predicted number of units will change hands (owing to the fact that some buyers may choose not to buy if the consumer surplus is small) and, consequently, this market will also result in lower efficiency than predicted.

Armed with this insight, Smith decided to check if a similar result holds true when the magnitude of consumer surplus is much larger than that of producer surplus. In fact, Smith decided to look at an extreme case to make his point. He decided to make the supply curve horizontal. As I mentioned before, this corresponds to a situation where all the sellers have the same cost and, therefore, are all willing to accept the same minimum price. Figure 14.12 illustrates this situation. In addition, Smith also decided to introduce a shift in demand partway through the session with demand decreasing from Demand 1 to Demand 2.

We will first look at what happens in this market with the horizontal supply curve and demand given by Demand 1. It will be clear from our discussion around Figure 14.11 that this is a situation where the consumer surplus accruing to the buyers is larger than the producer surplus accruing to the sellers. In fact, in equilibrium, the sellers do not get any surplus at all and just about break even, in the sense that the price they get just about covers their cost of production. Using an argument similar to the one we used for Figure 14.11, it is easy to see that for each bilateral trade in this market, the seller gets close to zero surplus. We expect that sellers will bargain much harder in this market (or even walk away from a sale) if they cannot get some positive surplus. Not surprisingly, this is what happens. As can be seen from the right-hand panel, prices start much above the predicted equilibrium and, while they seem to settle after a few periods, it is clear that the average price is higher than the predicted equilibrium.

■ Behavioural analyses of markets

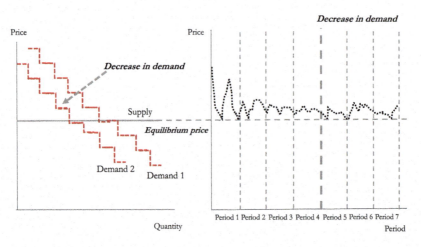

Figure 14.12
Results from a continuous double auction market with a horizontal supply curve and a shift in demand. Re-created on the basis of data in Smith (1962)

At this point, starting from Period 5, Smith implemented a reduction in demand from Demand 1 to Demand 2. Walras would say that this is not going to make any difference to this market. The equilibrium price will remain unchanged. But, as a behavioural economist, Smith knew better. He realized that with a decrease in demand, there would be some downward pressure on prices since buyers are now looking at obtaining a smaller surplus than before. They would, therefore, bargain harder than before. This is borne out by the data. Starting in Period 5, the average prices are lower and the large peaks visible in the first couple of rounds have subsided. But, nevertheless, and not surprisingly, given that producers are still looking at getting zero surplus, prices converge to a level that still remains higher than the predicted equilibrium price.

What do we learn from this? First, the Walrasian model seems to be a good approximation of how markets work in real life via a double auction involving decentralized trading between buyers and sellers submitting bids and asks, respectively. But whether these markets will converge to the predicted equilibrium or not and whether efficiency will be maximized (via all profitable trades taking place or not) depends crucially on the degree of market power, as measured by the magnitude of the consumer and producer surplus. When these magnitudes are roughly equal, markets work as predicted, prices converge to the predicted equilibrium and efficiency is high. But, if there are large discrepancies in market power, in the sense that either consumer surplus is larger than producer surplus (market power on the buyer side) or producer surplus is larger than consumer surplus (market power on the seller side), then the equilibration process is not as smooth. In the first case, prices will tend to settle above the predicted equilibrium, and in the latter case, prices will settle below. In both cases, the volume of transactions (number of units bought and sold) will be lower resulting in lower efficiency.

POSTED OFFER MARKETS

As I noted earlier, most of the markets we encounter in our day-to-day lives do not look like the ones discussed above. Yes, those markets may be reasonable for buying and selling stocks, but when you go to buy a pair of sneakers or a pair of jeans or your groceries, you typically do not haggle over the price. You look at the "posted" price on the item (essentially the sticker price) and decide whether to buy or not. Sometimes, you may decide to wait for a big sale and see if the item is sold for a cheaper price. This type of posted offer pricing is the dominant model for pretty much all of the retail sector and was brought in as an innovation by Macy's and Woolworth's in the second half of the 19th century. The new mass retailers implemented a separation between the ownership of the store and the actual sale of the goods by a large number of clerks. This resulted in the posted-offer "take-it-or-leave-it" pricing strategy which replaced the haggling that characterized the transactions at the general store prior to this. By the 1930s, this form of pricing was referred to as "administered" pricing and there was a general feeling among economists that this pricing strategy would result in a less competitive process.

Having explored the workings of the demand and supply mechanism in competitive markets, Smith, along with his collaborators Jon Ketcham of the University of Arizona (Smith had, by this time, moved to the University of Arizona also) and Arlington Williams of Indiana, now turned his attention to understanding the process of price formation and convergence in such posted offer markets. It needs to be noted that a posted offer market institution is just another variation on the rules governing a market. In a double auction, buyers and sellers simultaneously submit bids and asks, respectively. We could think of various other rules for clearing the market. For example, the Arizona stock exchange where, rather than allowing decentralized trading, all trading takes place at the equilibrium price computed by considering the underlying demand and supply curves. In a posted offer market, the sellers are, in a way, inactive. Once they have posted their prices, that's it. The buyers get to decide whether to buy or not at this price. The question that Smith and his colleagues wanted to ask is: suppose we took a market like the one shown in Figure 14.9. We know what happens if this market is operationalized as a double auction. What would happen if the market is set up as a posted offer market? Will the prices still converge to the theoretical and predicted equilibrium? Will the predicted number of trades take place? Will efficiency be high or low compared to what happens under a double auction?

Smith and his collaborators look at a number of different metrics of market performance. Are prices in a double auction market, in general, closer to the equilibrium price than those in posted offer markets? Are the efficiencies comparable? It turns out that the answers to both questions are in the negative. Market prices (and their dispersion from the predicted equilibrium price) are higher and efficiency is lower in posted offer markets. However, Smith and colleagues found that some of this difference dissipates if traders get more experience with the market, often by bringing in participants who have taken part before and are therefore familiar with the set-up.

In a follow-up, Smith and his colleagues look at what happens if the market supply is horizontal, as in the case of Figure 14.12. Surprisingly, here, the differences between a double auction mechanism and a posted offer mechanism do not seem to matter as much. Prices are higher than equilibrium in both cases, and efficiency lower. But the reason for this will be obvious from our discussion around Figure 14.12. It is not so much that posting offers reduces prices or improves efficiency in these markets. Prices in posted offer markets tend to be higher and efficiency lower. It is just that, in a situation like this, the buyers have more market power than sellers. As we discussed in the case of the market in Figure 14.12, this implies that sellers bargain harder in this market. This leads to a lower transaction volume and higher price even in the double auction set-up. So, the reason that posted offer markets perform as well as double auction in this market is due to the fact that the double auction is less successful in achieving the equilibrium price.

POSTED OFFER MARKETS AND MARKET POWER

As Smith and his colleagues point out, it is not hard to understand why posted offer markets would tend to work in favour of the sellers and against the buyers. In order to understand this, take a look at Figure 14.13. In this market, there are lots of buyers and three sellers. Seller 1 has eight units for sale, Seller 2 has ten units and Seller 3 has four units. So, a total of 22 units are available for sale. Before proceeding, I should note that the very structure of this market, with lots of buyers and three sellers, would work in the sellers' advantage. This is because there is a lot more competition among the buyers (given that there are more of them) and much less competition on the seller side (given that there are fewer of them). So, in general, it is always the case that if one side of the market is a lot thicker than the other side, then the thinner side of the market will have more market power.[7]

But, leaving that aside, let us think of what may transpire in a market like the one in Figure 14.13. Walrasian reasoning suggests a straightforward resolution. The equilibrium price is $5.00 and 11 units should be sold (with each buyer buying one unit). Seller 1 should sell all of his/her eight units at a price of $3.00 each and Seller 2 should sell three out of his/her ten units at a price close to $5.00. To keep things simple, I have drawn the graph such that Seller 2's supply coincides with the market equilibrium price. But, one can easily assume that Seller 2's costs are marginally less than $5.00. By this time, readers should not have difficulty with the basic concept at work here. So, Seller 1 makes a profit of $2.00 per unit, Seller 2 makes a very small profit per unit and Seller 3 would be out of this market since his/her costs are "too high". But is that what will happen, especially if the sellers can see what price each is posting, as Smith and colleagues quite correctly assume?

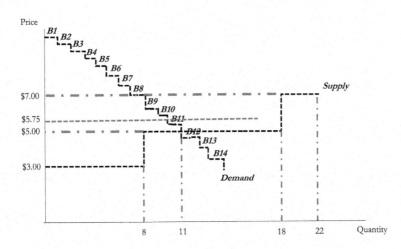

Figure 14.13
Posted offer market with lots of buyers and three sellers

Suppose Seller 3 posts a price of $7.00 (or a fraction less). There are, at least, seven or eight buyers in the market who are willing to pay more than $7.00 (depending on whether we include B8 or not, who is, effectively, indifferent between buying and not buying at this price). If S1 and S2 follow suit and also charge $7.00 (or a little less), then eight units are sold in this market, assuming that B8, who gets a small surplus, buys. Depending on who ends up doing the selling, and especially if these sales end up going to S1 and S2, then they stand to make a much higher profit than if they sold at $5. Alternatively, Sellers 1 and 2 can cut out Seller 3 and settle on a price of $5.75. If they do so, then they lose one buyer (B11) but Seller 1 potentially earns $2.75 per unit while Seller 2 earns $0.75 per unit. What this means is that there is no longer a compelling reason why the price would converge to the equilibrium price of $5.00, but may well settle somewhere between $5.00 and $7.00. Given that the buyers do not know the underlying selling costs but the sellers have a reasonable idea of these, there is little downward pressure on prices to drive them toward the equilibrium outcome.

In fact, this is exactly what Smith and his colleagues find. They find plenty of *price signalling*, where higher cost producers post higher prices, in order to entice some of the high valuation buyers and lower cost sellers to follow this lead. Smith et al. also find that posted offer markets are vulnerable to *tacit collusion*. This is a situation where Sellers 1 and 2 may tacitly agree to a price like $5.75, which guarantees both of them higher profits than in the competitive equilibrium. The incentives for Seller 2 to do so is obvious. But why does Seller 1 not undercut this price and charge less since he/she can afford to do so? This is possible, but notice that in the competitive equilibrium of this market, the best Seller 1 can hope to do is to sell eight units at a per unit profit of $2.00 for a total profit of $16.00. But if the price is at $5.75, then some quick calculations suggest that Seller 1 is better off even if he/she sells six or seven units at this higher price.[8] Therefore, Seller 1 has little incentive to undercut Seller 2 below $5.75. These are all examples, but the basic point remains. Given the potential for price signalling and tacit collusion among sellers, there is little downward pressure on prices in posted offer markets. What the posted offer institution has done is to disable part of the Walrasian trial and error process. The result is almost always higher prices than would prevail if both sides of the market were equally competitive and the price was decided by a double auction through an ascending bid and descending ask process. This is why I suggested that my aversion to haggling and tendency to gravitate toward posted offer sellers most likely implies that I miss out on bargains and end up paying more for things!

FAIRNESS IN POSTED OFFER MARKETS REVISITED

In Chapter 8, I discussed the implications of the ultimatum game results for such posted offer markets. I provided an overview of the results from work done by Kahneman and his colleagues, to show that people are willing to accept price increases resulting from cost increases but not price increases induced by demand shocks and/or increased vulnerability of buyers (snowstorms causing higher demand for shovels; unemployment in the region resulting in lower demand for labour and, therefore, lower wages, etc.); that is, price increases designed for greater profitability. I also presented findings from work done by Ruffle showing that buyers do often withhold demand (and buy less than they otherwise would) if they believe the price is higher than it should be. Such demand withholding is higher when there are fewer buyers in the market and when these buyers are made aware of the discrepancy between the magnitude of the consumer surplus and the producer surplus, especially if the latter is much higher than the former.

Along with a different set of collaborators, Smith provides a somewhat different perspective on this debate on how fairness concerns may impact markets.[9] Smith and his collaborators start with the Kahneman et al. conjecture that people are far more willing to accept price increases when this comes about due to increases in seller costs, but are much less willing to do so if they believe that this is designed to take undue advantage of customers (and possibly the latter's lack of market power). Franciosi et al. look at two different scenarios: First, where there is an increase in seller costs; this implies that the original supply curve will move back and to the left, resulting in a higher equilibrium price and lower quantity sold. The second situation is where sellers are subject to a profit tax. This does not change seller costs and therefore, leaves the supply curve unchanged. But, any seller profit is taxed, leaving sellers with less money than before. Here, there are no cost-based arguments for raising price. The only reason a seller may raise price under a tax on profits is to safeguard those profits, especially if sellers behave as if they have a reference level of profit that they wish to achieve or preserve. This second situation, then, corresponds to a situation where sellers are increasing prices primarily as a way of protecting their profits, which may well be thought of as taking advantage of the buyers (especially if the sellers were making reasonable profit to start with).

Franciosi et al. conjecture: first, prices will be higher when costs go up than under a tax on profits, and second, demand withholding will be less pronounced in the former case than in the latter. As in the case of results reported by Ruffle, Franciosi et al. also find that this is true, but with some caveats. First, prices are certainly higher when costs increase than when profits are taxed but the amount of demand withholding is not that different. Franciosi et al. calculate demand withholding by counting the number of buyers who could have bought the good profitably, that is, at a price less than their valuation, but chose not to do so. Moreover, the price differentials are present initially but tend to disappear over time.

Why do the results differ from Ruffle? For one thing, go back to Figure 14.13 with the three sellers. Remember that if costs increase, the supply curve moves back and to the left as a result. We know this will raise prices. We can see this via a thought exercise in the context of the same diagram, without drawing yet another graph. Suppose the market price used to be $3.00 but has gone to $5.00. Seller 1 is still charging $3.00. At $3.00, there are at least 14 people who are willing to buy but Seller 1 has capacity to sell only eight units. This may mean that Seller 1 has to ration how many each buyer can get or there may be long lines outside Seller 1's store since his/her price is lower. But this, in turn, means that some of the higher valuation buyers may decide that they are not interested in standing in line and these buyers gravitate towards Seller 2 or even Seller 3. Eventually, if enough buyers do so, then the higher price of (say) $5.00 or $7.00 no longer seems outrageous. Franciosi et al. argue that what is considered to be "fair" or not may well depend on buyer expectations. We saw this earlier in Chapter 7 as part of the ultimatum game results from Al Roth and his collaborators. What is considered fair in Pittsburgh or Ljubljana is quite different from the perceptions in Jerusalem or Tokyo (or, for that matter, among the Machiguenga or the Lamelara). So, it is not surprising that, over time, prices in the different treatments are not different.

There is also the issue of market (or bargaining) power. I noted above that a crucial issue behind what happens to prices is countervailing power on the two sides. If the number of buyers and sellers on both sides are similar, then, at least in a double auction, prices converge to the market equilibrium. But if there are many more buyers (sellers) than there are sellers (buyers), then prices will tend to be higher (lower). This is simply because smaller numbers make it easier to undertake coordinated actions. In the Ruffle study, demand withholding is most pronounced when there are two buyers rather than four buyers. In the Franciosi et al. study there are always six buyers and six sellers. When there are few buyers, it is a lot easier for them to coordinate their actions and withhold demand. Similarly, when there are few sellers, it is a lot easier for them to signal to each other and act in tacit collusion. As the number of sellers goes up, the incentive (and pressure) to undercut other sellers increases since this will increase sales. Larger numbers make tacit coordination of actions more difficult.

POLICY INTERVENTIONS IN MARKETS

Earlier in the chapter, I mentioned that the Walrasian view of the market is value-free. Walras has nothing to say about whether the equilibrium price is fair or unfair, whether this outcome is just or unjust. The Walrasian view simply posits that, given the valuation expressed by buyers in the form of a demand curve and the cost structure (and the minimum willingness to accept) of sellers expressed via the supply curve, one would expect to see a particular equilibrium outcome. Once this equilibrium is arrived at, in the absence of an external shock to demand and/or supply, the equilibrium price should not change.

But what if you felt that the price so arrived at is "unfair" and that something needs to be done about this? After all, prices of goods need to be considered in the context of people's incomes and the affordability of various goods, especially necessities like food or utilities. For example, in 2010, Jimmy McMillan contested the gubernatorial election in New York state with the slogan: "The rent is too damn high!" This, in fact, quickly became a meme. Similarly, in cities and countries around the world, there is a growing "living wage" movement. If you look at the website of the organization Living Wage Aotearoa, you will find the following:

> The Living Wage has emerged as a response to growing poverty and inequality that continues to hold back so many Kiwi workers, their families and our economy. Living Wage Movement Aotearoa New Zealand brings together community/secular, union and faith-based groups to campaign for a Living Wage.

These people are suggesting that the equilibrium price arrived at via the workings of demand and supply are not fair and that something needs to be done about this. McMillan is suggesting that the rent (a large component of the budget for many people, especially those less well-off) is too high and, therefore, unaffordable for many people in big cities such as New York. Living Wage Aotearoa is saying that the hourly wage dictated by the demand for, and supply of, blue-collar workers is so low that people cannot survive on it. This is not the place to adjudicate these issues. But it is certainly true that governments at various levels, city, state or country, often legislate prices that are different from what would be dictated by the market. These interventions are typically labelled a *price ceiling* or a *price floor*.

■ Behavioural analyses of markets

Price ceiling

An example of a price ceiling is rent control. Many cities, such as New York, have rent controlled apartments. What does this mean? This means that, left to the market, the rent of a (say) small studio apartment in New York City will be $2,000 per month. The City Council believes that this is too high. They legislate that landlords cannot charge more than $1,500 per month for an apartment like this. The left-hand panel of Figure 14.14 illustrates the situation. The market equilibrium price is $2,000 per month but the City Council has established a price ceiling at $1,500. This means that the price cannot go above $1,500. By now, you know that doing this will prevent the market from reaching the market equilibrium price of $2,000, at which point quantity demanded and quantity supplied are equal. At $1,500, there are many more renters (Q_D) looking to rent an apartment than there are apartments available (Q_S), resulting in a shortage of apartments. There will be many more people looking for apartments, which will require some form of rationing; people having to compete with many applications for the same apartment and the landlord getting to choose the tenant.[10]

Now, typically, economists suggest that a price ceiling will be "binding", implying that it will have an impact on the market, and result in lower prices, if, and only if, the ceiling price is less than the equilibrium price. So, the price ceiling will only matter when it is set at $1,500 or anything less than the equilibrium price of $2,000. This, in turn, suggests that if, for some reason, the City Council imposes a price ceiling that is above the equilibrium, such as $2,500, this should not have any effect on the market equilibrium price and quantity.[11] But, it turns out that even a price ceiling above an equilibrium (such as the one at $2,500) can have a significant moderating effect on the market via lowering prices.

In order to see this, Vernon Smith teamed up with long-time collaborator Arlington Williams. They implemented a market very similar to that shown in Figures 14.9 or 14.10, except that they had participants take part in two different treatments, one where there is a price ceiling and one where there is a price floor. Participants start by taking part in a market where there is no intervention followed by the introduction of a price ceiling or price floor. What happens when there is a price ceiling above the equilibrium price? According to theory, this should not have an impact at all and the market should reach the predicted equilibrium price and quantity. Figure 14.15 illustrates the impact of this price ceiling, which is set at a price a little above the predicted equilibrium price. The solid line with squares represents bids to buy, the solid line with crosses represents offers (asks) to sell, and

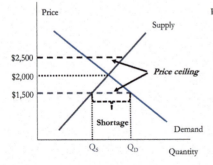
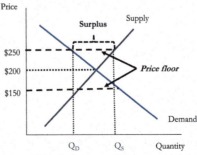

Figure 14.14 Price ceiling and price floor

366

Figure 14.15 Impact of a price ceiling. Figure re-created by author on the basis of data in Smith and Williams (2008)

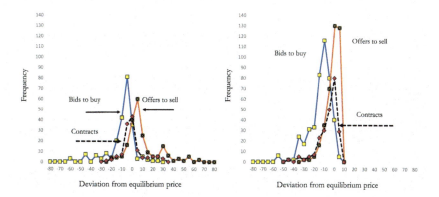

the dashed line with diamonds represents contracts struck. The left-hand panel shows the situation prior to the imposition of a price ceiling, while the right-hand panel does so for the situation following the imposition of the ceiling. Even at a first glance, it is clear that things are different in the two different situations. Remember that the case where a price ceiling is imposed below the equilibrium price (and is therefore binding) is subsumed under this case, where the price ceiling is not binding. With a binding price ceiling, the effects will just be much more pronounced.

The horizontal axis here measures deviations from the predicted equilibrium from $0.80 below the equilibrium price to $0.80 above. The price ceiling is imposed at $0.05 above the equilibrium price. The vertical axis measures how many bids and asks are being presented at each of those price points. By comparing the left and right-hand panels, we can see that the immediate impact of the price ceiling is to truncate the offers to sell to just about $0.05 above the equilibrium, that is, just around the price ceiling. As opposed to the left-hand panel, there are no longer any asks in the right tail, since asking for a higher price, such as, say, $0.40 or $0.50 above the equilibrium, is no longer possible given the ceiling price. Essentially, there are no asks at any price that is higher than approx. $0.05 above equilibrium price. Instead, now there is a sharp spike in the asks at prices just around the equilibrium price. Remember what I said when I discussed Figure 14.8. It is as if the supply curve starts high to the right and then slopes down to the left as sellers reduce their asks. But in the presence of the price ceiling, those high asks are no longer possible since the highest sellers can start at is the ceiling price. This effectively means that the distribution of the asks moves to the left (meaning towards lower prices).

The impact on bids is less pronounced because the price ceiling does not impact the bid process as much. Again, remember that you can think of the demand curve as starting low on the right-hand side of Figure 14.8 and then sloping upward as buyers increase their bids over time. The price ceiling does not impact those low bids and starts to bite only for bids that are at or above the ceiling. Further, given that both buyers and sellers have already experienced the market without a price ceiling, once the price ceiling is brought in, buyers, seeing lower asks from the sellers (under the price ceiling) find it in their self-interest to begin negotiations at a lower level and, therefore, start with bids that are lower than before. There are very few bids at higher prices now for two reasons. First, bids above the ceiling are not possible in any event. Second, realizing that the price ceiling lowers seller asks, buyers also

■ Behavioural analyses of markets

correspondingly reduce their bids. The net result is not hard to predict. Even with a price ceiling that is non-binding, there is a shift in the bids and asks to the left, implying that, on average, the bids and asks are lower with a price ceiling than without one. This results in lower prices and a transfer of surplus from the sellers to the buyers.

Price floor

The right-hand panel of Figure 14.14 depicts a price floor. This is where we have an intervention in the form of a minimum price. An example of this is agricultural support price. Suppose the equilibrium price of wheat in the US Midwest tends to hover around approx. $250 per metric ton. Let us say that, due to a bumper harvest and increase in supply, the equilibrium price has dropped to $200 per metric ton. The government decides that the equilibrium price is too low and is going to cause significant hardship to farmers. The government imposes a price floor at $250 per ton. This implies that all sale and purchase of wheat must take place at this price. Obviously, at this price, there is less demand and there will be a surplus of wheat. Typically, in such situations, the government will buy up the surplus at the floor price to make sure that the price does not drop below the floor. Does it make any sense for the government to set a price floor below the equilibrium such as $150 per metric ton? Not really, because this should not prevent the market from reaching equilibrium at $200.

But, as would be clear from our previous discussion, even a price floor like $150 will have an impact. The results are similar to the ones for the price ceiling in Figure 14.15. In this case, with a price floor, the primary impact will be on the buyer side by eliminating some of the low bids to the right of Figure 14.8. This means that the bid prices will be truncated to the left by the price floor, which rules out bids below the floor. This will also have a moderating effect on the ask prices, since the sellers will now realize that they do not need to lower their ask as much and can start their negotiations at higher prices than in the absence of a price floor. The net effect of this will be to shift the distribution of both bids and asks to the right, resulting in higher prices and a transfer of surplus from the buyers to the sellers. I have not drawn a graph to illustrate this because this graph would be very similar to Figure 14.15. In that figure, the truncation in bids and asks happens from the right due to a price ceiling, which cuts off the high bids and high asks. A price floor cuts off the bids and asks from the left, that is, gets rid of low bids and low asks. This results in an increase in the price and a transfer of surplus from the buyers to the sellers.

A similar argument would be applicable to the minimum wage. Typically, the minimum wage is set to a value that is higher than the equilibrium wage for blue-collar workers. But, if the prevailing equilibrium wage is considered low from the point of view of sustainability, then even if a city or a state imposes a minimum wage that is less than the market equilibrium, this will still have the impact of raising the effective wage and transferring some surplus from the employers to the workers.

CONCLUDING REMARKS

In this chapter, I have discussed how the interaction between buyers and sellers via a decentralized descending-ask–ascending-bid process leads to equilibrium outcomes as predicted by the Walrasian *tatonnement* process. Smith referred to this process as a continuous double auction, with buyers and sellers simultaneously submitting bids to buy and offers to sell respectively. I have shown that this decentralized process, guided by the mutual self-interest of buyers and sellers, will maximize efficiency. This is what Adam Smith meant by the "invisible hand"; that even in the absence of an auctioneer or another central authority, bilateral bargaining between buyers and sellers would lead to the predicted equilibrium.

A key lesson from this is that, contrary to the oft-expressed scepticism by non-economists, there is nothing inherently immoral or questionable about markets. In fact, as I argued earlier, all evidence suggests that markets actually serve a moderating influence and help achieve the maximization of aggregate producer and consumer surplus. But this does come with some caveats. For one thing, the efficient functioning of markets does require an approximate balance between buyer and seller market power. When the approximate sizes of the consumer and producer surplus (which can serve as good proxies for buyer and seller countervailing power, respectively) are equal, markets operate efficiently.

It is when one side or the other has excessive market power that problems emerge. One extreme of this is a single seller (a monopoly; think Google or Microsoft) or a single buyer (monopsony; think company towns with one large employer). But even without the extreme cases, we can think of situations where a market is dominated by a few big sellers. Think of the US airline market with three big "legacy" carriers: American, Delta and United, with a number of other smaller carriers like Alaska, JetBlue and Southwest. But the answer to this is typically not the abandonment of the market system, but, rather, some light-touch regulation to moderate some of the seller power in these markets. We will have to leave this discussion for a different course and a different book.

A second issue is that while the decentralized ascending-bid–descending-ask double auction explored by Smith appears to be the epitome of individual rationality at play, this rationality is not ubiquitous. In the next and final chapter of this book, I will examine the phenomenon of asset bubbles, which are, at least partly, the outcome of a degree of irrationality on the part of buyers and sellers. So, it does not seem guaranteed that, even with balanced market power on both sides, markets will achieve efficient outcomes. A certain amount of rationality and the nature of the market institution seems to be of great importance. I will address this in more detail in the next chapter.

I have also pointed out that most markets we participate in are not the decentralized double auction introduced by Smith. Rather, these are posted offer markets where sellers post a take-it-or-leave-it-price and buyers decide whether to buy or not. I have shown that prices in such posted offer markets will typically be higher than the competitive equilibrium price dictated by the underlying demand and supply curves. This tendency for the price to be higher in posted offer markets will be exacerbated if the market is characterized by a few sellers with heterogenous costs. There is a possibility that such markets will end up settling at a price close to the minimum acceptable price for the highest cost seller. This is partly due to the ability of sellers in these markets to engage in price signalling and tacit collusion.

I revisited the debate over fairness in markets to explore whether buyers actually withhold demand in markets where they realize that the bulk of the surplus is accruing to the sellers. I showed that is true but it depends crucially on the thickness of the buyer side. If there are lots of buyers, making coordinated action difficult, then demand withholding is hard to sustain. For demand withholding to be successful, one needs fewer buyers (consequently, with greater bargaining power). I also showed that the time horizon may matter. A lower cost seller may not raise the price immediately due to fairness considerations, but if and when this seller runs out of stock, the other sellers will charge higher prices, and, over time, the market price will increase as buyer expectations adjust to what a "fair" price is.

I ended by discussing some policy interventions in the form of price ceilings and price floors. Economic theory suggests that a price ceiling will have an impact on the market price if, and only if, it is imposed at a price that is below the equilibrium price. I discussed Smith's work in this area showing that while this is certainly true, even a price ceiling imposed above the equilibrium price will lead to a lowering of prices via truncating the high bids and high asks. This in turn will transfer some surplus from sellers to buyers. A similar argument applies to price floors. These will tend to cut off the low bids and low asks and result in market prices that are higher than equilibrium and thereby transfer some surplus from buyers to sellers.

So, where does that leave us? I noted earlier that I am a big fan of Leonard Cohen. In one of his songs "Everybody Knows", Cohen summarizes what a lot of people seem to think when it comes to markets[12]: Cohen sings that the "dice are loaded" and the "fight was fixed". The game is always rigged against the good guys and the rich get rich and the poor stay poor. I would disagree with Leonard Cohen. Yes, the dice may be loaded and the fight may be fixed, but this is not really a fundamental part of the operation of markets. If the playing field is level, with market power balanced on both sides, then markets are efficient. Of course, the playing field is often, even frequently, not level. This does not mean that we cannot rely on markets. It simply means that we need to level the playing field as far as practicable via regulation and policy interventions. But, to repeat: markets may have their drawbacks but we have yet to discover a better way of organizing trade and exchange. There are broad philosophical questions here that are, unfortunately, beyond our scope for now. My hope is that the discussion in this chapter and in this volume has inspired you to study these topics in more depth.

NOTES

1 Of course, concerts do have prices set at different levels. One way to think of this is that we are making a simplifying assumption that everyone will pay the same price. Another way of thinking of this is to assume that these are tickets to a particular section, say Gold Reserve or Silver Reserve. So, tickets bought for $P2 will be seated further back than tickets bought for $P1. But if the organizers charge $P2 instead of $P1 for (say) Gold Reserve, then they will have to charge everyone $P2; they cannot sell some of the Gold Reserve seats at a different price than some others.

2 We usually refer to it as a demand curve even though it should be called a demand line. Also, if and when we write price as the dependent variable (and put it on the Y-axis) and quantity as the independent variable (and put it on the X-axis), what we have created is technically the inverse demand function. Chances are that you have seen this material before. But, in any event, we are not going to worry too much about this. I will refer to this line as the demand curve.

3 For instance, if you sell Coca-Cola, then demand for your product will be strongly affected by what is happening in the market for Pepsi, a close substitute. If Pepsi lowers its prices and demand for Pepsi rises, then demand for Coca-Cola will fall. Similarly, if you produce coffee creamers, and for some reason the consumption of coffee goes down, then demand for your coffee creamers will also go down. This is because coffee and coffee creamers are complements. If demand for coffee rises/falls, demand for coffee creamers will rise/fall along with it.

4   Many life-saving drugs such as insulin are produced by large pharmaceutical companies that hold a patent on the drug and become the sole supplier of the same. Given that there are no substitutes, the prices for these drugs often tend to be much higher than they would be had the market been more competitive. Often, there are generic producers of these drugs resulting in lower prices, but often not. This is an involved debate and this is not the place to debate the pros and cons of patents (and there are pros, in the sense that, in the absence of patent protection, companies have little incentive to innovate or engage in research and development). This is only to highlight the fact that the fewer the firms there are in a market, the higher the prices will tend to be. I will have more to say on this below.

5   I find haggling painful and, as my wife likes to point out, my salary would probably have been a lot lower had I accepted the offers I received without negotiating. In the US, I dreaded the thought of haggling over car purchases and the cars I bought in New Zealand were all bought from firms that had a "no haggling" or "posted price" model. In the next section, I will discuss what this implies for such markets and buyers like me. In short, we are doomed to pay a much higher price than others.

6   In fact, the ranking of bids and asks is possibly less important to price discovery than announcing the prices at which contracts have been struck. I, along with many others, have carried out plenty of classroom experiments with the Smith set-up. Give buyers a set of valuations and sellers a set of costs (minimum acceptable price) on pieces of paper (I usually use post-it notes of different colours so that it is easy to see who is a buyer and who is a seller) and ask them to walk around the room trying to find the best possible deal. Typically, each buyer can buy one unit and a seller can sell one unit. As soon as a contract is arrived at, these buyers and sellers are out of the market and take their seats. I then write up the contract price on the board (or document camera). This is typically enough for people to figure out where the possible equilibrium is. While there is considerable variation in the prices early on, in four to five rounds, the dispersion reduces and prices tend to cluster tightly around the equilibrium price, so that the average price tracks the equilibrium price closely. However, one important caveat to those planning on trying this out: for reasons you will see shortly, it is important to make sure that the demand and supply curves you use result in consumer and producer surplus that are roughly equal in magnitude. Otherwise, the market price will not track the equilibrium price.

7   While examples of markets where buyers outnumber sellers come to mind more readily, this does not have to be the case. There are many markets where the opposite is true. Think about a situation with a large number of small suppliers selling to a large chain like Woolworths, Carrefour, or Walmart or small producers of meat and vegetables selling to a large franchise chain like McDonalds. In these cases, the buyer has a lot more bargaining power and will most likely be able to pay lower prices than if the buyer side was more competitive. Other examples include markets for labour. For instance, consider the city of Gary, Indiana, just south of Chicago, Illinois. The city was named after Elbert Henry Gary, who was the founding chairman of the United States Steel Corporation. For a very long time in Gary's history, much of the adult population had jobs in the steel industry. Needless to mention, in such cases, the wages of those workers would tend to be lower than would be true if workers could choose among multiple employers. The 1941 film *How Green Was My Valley*, based on the book of the same name by Richard Llewellyn and directed by John Ford, provides a captivating portrayal of the rise and fall of such a company town, in this case, the coal-fields of South Wales.

8   Remember that if Seller 1 sells eight units at $5.00, then he/she makes $16.00 in profit. Assuming that it costs Seller 1 $3.00 to produce and sell each unit, if he/she sells eight units at $5.75, then his/her revenue is $5.75×8 = $46.00 and his/her cost is $3.00×8 = $24.00. So, his/her profit is $22.00. For seven units, his/her revenue is $5.75×7 = $40.25 and his/her cost is $3.00×7 = $21.00, so his/her profit is $19.25. Profit if he/she sells six units is $5.75×6 - $3.00×6, which is $16.50, marginally higher than making $16.00 by selling eight units at $5.00. So, in all of these cases, Seller 1 makes a higher profit than in the competitive equilibrium.

9   This set of collaborators includes Robert Franciosi, Praveen Kujal, Roland Michelitsch and Gang Deng.

■ Behavioural analyses of markets

10 In one of the early episodes of *Seinfeld*, a rent-controlled apartment becomes free in Jerry Seinfeld's apartment building. The building manager is willing to let Elaine Benes, Jerry's ex-girlfriend have the apartment in return for a $5,000 fee, essentially a bribe. Initially, Jerry is willing to lend Elaine the money before realizing that it may not be such a good idea to have your ex-girlfriend staying in the same building as you. This footnote is probably redundant. I put this in to show that a price ceiling in the form of rent control is not an abstract idea and does apply to real life. Also, I am a big fan of *Seinfeld* and felt that this would be a good chance to put in a reference to the show for those of you who were too young (or not yet born) at the time the show ran. At the time of writing, it is available on Amazon Prime and certainly worth checking out. My "hip" teenager agrees with this assessment.

11 It could be that the City Council got this wrong or, by the time the bill was sent out for public consultation, debated in chambers and then finally voted on and (possibly) survived vetoes by the Mayor or the Governor, the market conditions have changed such that the equilibrium price has actually gone down to $2,000, which is below the proposed ceiling at $2,500.

12 "Everybody knows", written by Leonard Cohen and Sharon Robinson from the Album: *I'm Your Man*, from Columbia Records.

15 Asset bubbles in markets

In this chapter I:

- *Discuss what is meant by an asset market bubble, where prices of financial assets rise far in excess of what the asset is really worth;*
- *Explore some historical asset bubbles to set the scene;*
- *Show how we can study such asset bubbles in the lab and what we know about factors that contribute to such bubbles;*
- *Highlight the role of cognitive biases in the generation of such bubbles, which, in turn, also provides clues as to how we can avoid creating such bubbles in the first place.*

INTRODUCTION

I wrote much of this book in 2020, while the world was grappling with the COVID-19 pandemic and the fallout from it. At that point, it was pretty clear that we were looking at a global recession with shrinking gross domestic products (GDP) and rising unemployment. It was not yet clear whether this recession would equal the Great Depression of the 1930s but it was clear that this was going to be worse than the global financial crisis (GFC) of 2008–2009. For many of us, the GFC was the most serious recession that we had encountered until we came face to face with the COVID-19 pandemic.

In many ways, the GFC started as a financial crisis with a bursting of the housing bubble in the US. Figure 15.1 shows what happened to inflation adjusted average house prices during the latter part of the 1990s and the first decade of the 2000s. As can be seen from this figure, starting from around 1998, house prices increased sharply till around 2006. At that point, the recession hit. House prices fell and a large number of homeowners were saddled with negative equity. This meant that the loans they had taken out to buy the house (the mortgage) was now larger than the value of the house. So, they could no longer afford to repay their mortgages by simply selling their house. How did this come about, and how did this in turn set off a massive global recession?[1]

By the late 1990s, competition between mortgage lenders for revenue and market share led to more relaxed underwriting standards and riskier mortgages to borrowers whose creditworthiness (ability to repay these loans) was questionable. This resulted in the so-called "subprime" loans. These were loans made at interest rates much below the "prime" (i.e., market) interest rates to start with but the rates increased sharply later on. They were potentially

■ Asset bubbles in markets

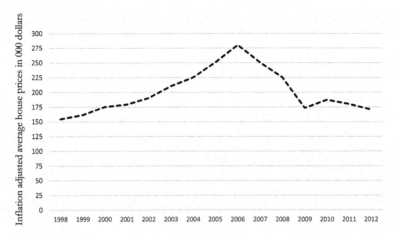

Figure 15.1
US housing market bubble

risky but Wall Street seemed to be willing to accept this higher risk. Some have suggested that the government owned Federal National Mortgage Association (FNMA, popularly known as Fannie Mae) and Federal Home Loan Mortgage Corporation (FHLMC or Freddie Mac) may have encouraged more relaxed underwriting standards by promoting automated underwriting and appraisal systems (by thousands of small mortgage brokers) as well as by often not requiring down payments.

In turn, investment banks, such as Lehman Brothers, created a set of bonds called collateralized debt obligations (CDOs) on the basis of those mortgage payments. These are essentially bonds (pieces of paper) that people hold where the payment on the bonds depends on a steady stream of people making regular mortgage payments. If and when those mortgage payments stopped or even fluctuated widely, the CDOs would have trouble meeting their financial obligations to the holders. In 2000, banks had made $130 billion in sub-prime loans and created $55 billion worth of mortgage bonds. By 2005, sub-prime loans had grown to $625 billion, of which $507 billion were turned into mortgage bonds. These sub-prime loans were highly risky to start with, since there was a high probability of default from the homeowners. This implied, in turn, that the CDOs backed by these loans were also highly risky and should have been rated as such. Yet, these bonds were rated "AAA" by ratings agencies such as Moody's and S&P. A large number of people, as well as big pension funds, who are often constrained to invest in AAA rated bonds only, invested in these CDOs. When the homeowners, who often had little ability to service the loans, defaulted, so did these mortgage assets, resulting in heavy losses.

But how did we get from this financial crisis to a deep global recession? For one thing, as banks became more cautious about lending money, credit became more difficult to obtain, thereby severely hampering business activities. This was the "supply side" effect. But another important factor is the widespread pessimism and loss of confidence among businesses and individuals. What the financial crisis did was to serve as a tipping point. When the housing market went bust, the suppliers of materials to that market took a hit. Houseowners, for many of whom their houses represented their major asset, sharply cut back on spending when faced with steep declines in the value of their houses. So, the contagion spread to the market for cars and other durables. This is the "demand side" effect.

Another fundamental problem in deep recessions is that the economy gets caught in an under-employment trap, where no firm wishes to expand production unless it can be assured that others will do so, yet not doing so leads to an outcome that is worse for everyone concerned. This is a classic coordination problem, which we discussed in Chapter 13. Such loss of faith, which often tends to be self-fulfilling, can have devastating economic consequences. But, as I mentioned, this chapter is not about the GFC, but, rather, our focus in this chapter will be the housing bubble that started it all. In this chapter, I will discuss what is meant by a bubble; how they arise, how they can be studied in the lab and what we know about factors that contribute to such bubbles or their cessation.

CASE STUDY 15.1 THE SOUTH SEA COMPANY BUBBLE

In August 1710, Robert Harley was appointed Britain's Chancellor of the Exchequer, essentially the Minister of Finance. Since 1694, the privately-owned Bank of England had acted as the monopoly broker of all borrowing and lending for the government. The government had become dissatisfied with the service it was receiving and Harley was actively seeking new ways to improve the national finances. Harley's investigations led to the conclusion that the government owed a total of £9 million, with not much in the way of income to pay it off. Harley devised a scheme to consolidate this debt in much the same way that the Bank of England had consolidated previous debts. The creditors who held this debt were required to surrender it to a new company formed for the purpose, the South Sea Company, which, in return, would issue them shares in the company of the same nominal value. The government would make an annual payment to the company, equating to 6% interest plus expenses, which would then be redistributed to the shareholders as a dividend.

In turn, the company received an "asiento" for the South Seas, implying South America and surrounding waters.[2] In reality, this meant very little because, while the company did gain the right to trade slaves to South America, this particular trade was dominated by Spain, with which country Britain was at war at the time.[3] The originators of the scheme knew that there was no realistic expectation that there would ever be a trade to exploit, but, nevertheless, the potential for great wealth was talked up at length. There was also significant insider trading, with company funds used to buy its own shares. Government officials who had oversight responsibilities for the company were gifted shares and were given cash loans backed by those same shares to spend on purchasing more shares. All of this led to a speculative frenzy. Figure 15.2 shows what happened to the share prices of the South Sea Company between 1719 and 1721.[4] During the course of 1720, share prices of the company increased dramatically before coming down to earth.

Many investors were ruined by the share-price collapse, and, as a result, the national economy reduced substantially. A parliamentary inquiry was held after the bursting of the bubble to discover its causes. A number of politicians were disgraced, and people found to have profited immorally from the company had personal assets confiscated proportionate to their gains. The South Sea Company was restructured

■ Asset bubbles in markets

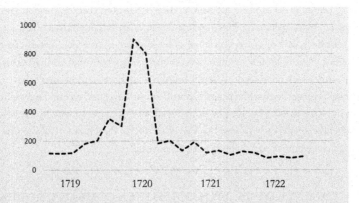

Figure 15.2
South Sea Company bubble

but continued to operate for more than a century after. The crash of the South Sea Company restored the position of the Bank of England as banker to the British government. On an interesting side note: it appears that Sir Isaac Newton also held stocks in the South Sea Company. When asked about the price bubble, he is rumoured to have said: "I can calculate the movement of the stars, but not the madness of men". It is not known how much money Newton may have lost or gained.

There are many other such historical instances of bubbles. In 1637, there was a huge speculative bubble in the price of tulip bulbs, as recorded in the book *Extraordinary Popular Delusions and the Madness of Crowds* by the British journalist, Charles Mackay. Tulips were probably introduced to Europe in the middle of the 16th century from Turkey. They were different from other European flowers and quickly became a status symbol. As the flowers grew in popularity, professional growers paid higher and higher prices for bulbs and prices rose steadily. By 1636, tulip bulbs became one of the Netherlands' leading exports. The price of tulips skyrocketed because of speculation in tulip futures among people who never saw the bulbs. Tulip mania reached its peak during the winter of 1636–1637, when some bulbs were reportedly changing hands ten times in a day. The collapse began when buyers refused to show up at a tulip bulb auction in Haarlem, which was suffering from an outbreak of bubonic plague. This outbreak might also have helped to burst the bubble.

STUDYING ASSET BUBBLES IN THE LAB

An asset or price bubble is a situation where the price of an asset far exceeds the asset's fundamental value. For instance, consider a house. The price of the house should reflect the value of the land on which the house stands as well as the total cost of the building itself. While there is certainly scope for differences in valuation and, therefore, some deviation in the price of the house from its underlying value, these deviations should not be huge, and, in any event, should not persist for long periods of time. A similar argument is true of shares in a company.

The current price of the share should reflect the risk adjusted discounted value of expected future dividends to be paid on it.[5] So, the current price should subsume all the relevant information and this price should not change unless something fundamental changes about the company, people's expectations or the market conditions. This, in turn, implies that prices should track the fundamental value closely and that it should be difficult to "beat the market" by buying and selling such shares. If all traders are perfectly rational and equally well informed about the market conditions, then they should all price the share in a similar way. This idea that prices of financial assets such as shares should track the fundamental value is the essence of the *efficient markets hypothesis*, as proposed by Eugene Fama of the University of Chicago in the 1970s.

But, as we know now, not everyone is rational, or at least not rational to the same extent. They are also not equally well informed and, more importantly, we know that people are subject to a wide range of biases. All of these suggest that, while the efficient markets hypothesis may be an elegant theory, in practice this may not quite hold. But there are problems in trying to understand bubble formation in markets with naturally occurring data on prices and quantities. For one thing, it is not always obvious when a bubble is forming due to speculative frenzy as opposed to shifts in underlying demand and supply conditions. It is also not always easy to separate the price dynamics from other potential confounds.

Vernon Smith, fresh from his success in demonstrating the rationality of traders and the ability of the decentralized ascending bid–descending ask double auction mechanism to corroborate the Walrasian *tatonnement* conjecture, now decided to turn his attention to the efficient markets hypothesis. Smith's question was: are bubbles feasible and realistic or are they merely artefacts of particular historical or social circumstances? If we took an asset whose fundamental value is known and common knowledge, should we expect to see speculative bubbles arise as a routine matter? Or are price bubbles anomalies that occur infrequently?

Smith's *ex ante* conjecture was that, just as he found in the case of double auctions that decentralized trading between rational, self-interested buyers and sellers will lead to efficient outcomes, the same would be true in related markets where people trade financial assets. What he found was that these markets (or the buyers and sellers in these markets) behaved dramatically differently. There are large and persistent asset bubbles with prices hovering far above any feasible fundamental value for long periods.

For this work, Smith teamed up with a colleague at Arizona, Gerry Suchanek, and one of Smith's long-time collaborators, Arlington Williams (of Indiana), whom we met in Chapter 14. Smith and his colleagues have done voluminous work in this area, which has become the standard paradigm for studying and understanding the formation of asset bubbles in markets. I am going to provide a broad overview of their design and use that as the benchmark for the rest of this chapter.

Suppose you own a financial asset in the form of shares in a company. If you hold on to these shares, then you can earn dividends from the company. To keep things simple, I will use the term "share" to indicate one unit of this financial asset. Further, suppose that these shares last for a finite amount of time after which point they become valueless.[6] Let us say that, because company earnings are not certain, the dividend payments are uncertain too. But you know for sure that, for each share you hold, there is a one-quarter chance that this dividend payment will take one of four values: $0, $0.08, $0.28, and $0.60. This implies that in any period, the expected dividend is (1/4)*(0 + 0.08 + 0.28 + 0.60) = $0.24. So, in any given period, on average, you would expect to earn $0.24 in dividend payment for each share held.

Smith et al. then set up a large number of experiments, where each experiment acts as a market. Typically, each market consists of somewhere between nine and 12 traders. These traders are going to interact for 15 periods. At the start of the experiment, each trader receives some cash money and some shares. The cash held earns interest but it can also be used to buy shares. Now, remember that each share earns you an expected dividend of $0.24 per period. This means that if you hold on to one share for the entire 15 periods, then your expected earnings from that share is ($0.24)*(15) = $3.60. For the sake of simplicity, we are not going to discount future pay-offs since it does not make any difference to the underlying intuition of this exercise. Typically, Smith et al. set up their markets such that in a market with nine (12) traders, there are three (four) traders of each of the following three types: one group with three shares and $2.25 in cash; a second group with two shares and $5.85 in cash and a third group with one share and $9.45 in cash. Notice that the effective endowment of each group is the same: $13.05. For example, given an expected value of $3.60 per share, the first group received $10.80 in shares and $2.25 in cash; the second $7.20 in shares plus $5.85 in cash and so on. A trader's total earnings from the entire session is given by cash endowments to start with, plus any interest earned, plus any dividends received, plus any profit from selling shares, minus any payments made for buying shares.

Trading of shares is done using a continuous double-auction mechanism. Buyers of shares can submit bids to buy, sellers can submit asking prices (asks) to sell. In any period, each bid (ask) must be higher (lower) than the previous bid (ask). Bids that are lower than the current highest bid or asks that are higher than the current lowest ask are put in a rank queue behind the current low bid or high ask. Buyers and sellers are also able to accept standing asks or bids, respectively, if they wish to buy or sell at that price. Each period lasts somewhere between 3 to 5 minutes during which time buyers and sellers can submit bids and asks, respectively, or accept standing asks or bids. They are, of course, free to not do anything and simply hang on to their cash endowment, which earns interest, and their share endowment, which earns dividends.

Three points are worth noting at the outset. First, as opposed to real-life markets, where there are many things happening at the same time and the degree of uncertainty is high and level of common knowledge low, the variables within the experiment are controlled tightly. Not only that, all the experimental parameters are common knowledge. Participants know what the expected dividends and interest rates are; they know how many periods they will interact for; they know exactly who has how much cash and/or shares. This is vastly different from real markets, where not all participants are aware of relevant opportunity costs. For example, if Grace opens a day-trading account and decides to buy some shares of Air New Zealand, she may or may not know accurately the value of other variables that might impact her choice. Would she be better off investing in gold? Or via buying NZ/US dollars or euros? The advantage to the stylized markets set up by Smith et al. is that it allows us to identify specific mechanisms at work behind the formation of bubbles. If bubbles arise in the fairly sanitized confines of the lab where all information is common knowledge, then we can plausibly expect that they are more likely to arise in situations where there are many more potential confounds.

Second, given this experimental control over the parameters and common knowledge of those parameters among participants, the fundamental value of a share should also be commonly understood. Given that each share becomes valueless at the end of the 15th period and yields an expected dividend payment of $3.60 per share, it would seem unlikely that the price at which these shares are bought and sold should deviate significantly from the underlying fundamental value. So, at the beginning of the session, the expected value of a share is $3.60, which is the sum of the expected dividends over time. With ten periods left, the expected value of the share is $2.40; with two periods left, the share is worth only $0.48 and so on.

Finally, note that the earnings of the traders include the possibility of capital gains. For instance, if a trader hangs on to a share, then his/her expected earnings for the share would be $3.60, but if he/she could sell this share to another trader for $5.60, then he/she can make a profit (or capital gain) of $2.00. If this second trader then manages to sell that share for $8.00, then he/she, in turn, makes a capital gain of $2.40. Why another trader should be willing to buy at $5.60 (or $8.00) is a question that we will discuss later and at length.

Figure 15.3 shows what happens in a typical such session. As noted, there is voluminous work done by Smith et al. and many successors. The finding is ubiquitous with some exceptions that I will discuss below. All of these markets reliably demonstrate a bubble and crash pattern just like the US housing market or the South Sea Company shares. In this figure, I have taken data from one of my own replications, which contained a larger number of traders than in the Smith markets but, nevertheless, does a good job of illustrating the typical price pattern of shares in such a market. This is a busy graph; so, let me explain. The solid black horizontal bars going down like a step from the left to the right is the fundamental value of a share. At the beginning of Period 1, this value is equal to $3.60, which is depicted as 360 in the diagram. At the beginning of Period 2, the fundamental value is ($0.24*14) = $3.36 and so on. The vertical grey dashed lines indicate the periods. The lighter shaded dots indicate the transactions that took place in each of the 15 periods. The dark dashed line tracks the average transaction price over time. It is worth noting that we will often focus on the average market price over an entire trading period but the average price may sometimes mask the price dispersions from the average within a period.

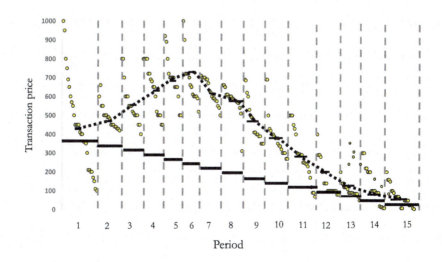

Figure 15.3
Results from an asset market experiment

As noted, this figure does a comprehensive job of presenting the main findings of Smith et al. First, prices usually tend to start low, often below the fundamental value. Smith et al. argued that, by and large, participants tend to be risk averse in the beginning such that trading starts at prices below the fundamental value. In this particular market, average price started marginally above the fundamental value of $3.60 in Period 1, where there is a large volume of transactions with a number of shares changing hands. From then onward, the average transaction price ticks upward, partly fuelled by participant expectations that prices will continue to rise, until it reaches an average value of approx. $7.40 in Period 6. It is noteworthy that this is more than twice the share's initial expected value of $3.60. It is also the case that in Period 6, with nine periods left, the expected remaining dividend stream from this share is only $2.16. So, if Grace buys that share at $7.40, she can expect to receive at most $2.16 from holding on to the asset, a loss of $5.24, unless, of course, she manages to find another buyer who is willing to pay an even higher price for the share. In this particular case though, Grace will most likely find that she was the one with the most inflated expectation of future price increases. She ends up buying the share at the peak of the bubble, with prices crashing toward the fundamental value after that. Smith et al. also find that not only does this bubble and crash pattern arise repeatedly in their markets towards the end of the session, there is also a reduction in the volume of transactions, with many fewer shares changing hands.

These results raised questions about the validity of the efficient markets hypothesis. It became clear that even in the very controlled atmosphere of the lab with common knowledge of outcomes and opportunity costs, bubbles and crashes happen reliably. Smith et al., however, note that the fact that prices do crash and return to the fundamental value provides some affirmation of efficient markets: that such bubbles will probably not be infinitely lived either and prices will eventually come back down to earth. However, it is also clear that there may be extended periods where prices are dissociated from underlying fundamental values. The same double-auction mechanism that provides strong support for individual rationality and ensures smooth convergence to equilibrium in markets for goods does not provide similar vindication for rationality in financial markets, where there is no distinction between buyers and sellers and the potential for speculative gains loom large.

Smith et al. concluded by saying that a common dividend and common knowledge thereof is insufficient to induce common expectations. They interpreted this as uncertainty among the participants about the actions of other buyers. These authors posit a lack of common knowledge regarding the rationality of other traders in generating this bubble phenomenon. Obviously, while the experimenter can control all other aspects of the experiment, he/she has less control over the home-grown beliefs of participants or their inherent preferences. However, whether the bubble-and-crash pattern can be attributed entirely to irrationality or not is a topic I will return to shortly.

I DON'T UNDERSTAND WHY THE FUNDAMENTAL VALUE IS DECLINING!

A common refrain from students is: why is the fundamental value declining? When someone owns a house, the value of the house typically does not decline; it may well increase over time and the horizon is longer lasting than the 15 periods in the lab. As I noted earlier, these bubbles and crashes are not an artefact of the finite lives of the assets. These patterns arise even when the fundamental value is flat. Charles Holt of Virginia, along with long-time collaborator Jacob Goeree and others, has done extensive work looking at situations where the fundamental value is constant, often referred to as a "flat" fundamental value. Given that we cannot really run infinitely long experiments, the flat fundamental value paradigm is a good approximation of an asset (such as a house) that is long-lasting and does not lose value over time.

Like Smith, participants in the Holt et al. studies also start out with cash, that earns interest, and shares, with the exception that these shares will be redeemed at a fixed value at the end of the session. In Figure 15.4, I show what happens in such markets. In doing this, I am presenting data from a study by David Dickinson (of Appalachian State) along with Ananish Chaudhuri and Ryan Greenaway-McGrevy (both at Auckland). (The results reported in Holt's studies are similar.) I will discuss this study in greater detail in Case Study 15.2. The basic set-up is the same as that in the Holt studies. Groups of 7–13 subjects (median group size = 11 subjects) participated in the online asset market experiment. Here, all participants have the same endowment of cash and 6 shares. Each share has a constant fundamental value of $7 in all rounds of all treatments. Cash held at the end of each round received 10% interest. In each round, each share earns a dividend of either $0.40 or $1.00 (so, the expected dividend is $0.70 per round) and shares are redeemed for $7.00 at the end of the final period of the treatment.[7]

Dickinson et al. collect data from many markets and I have presented data for only three of those. I have chosen these because they help establish my point but they are not all that different from many other markets in that study or in studies done by other researchers, for that matter. As in Smith, participants interact for 15 periods. More in keeping with Smith's arguments, in all three markets, initial prices start at less than the fundamental value. But then the prices take off. In Market 1, prices rise steadily to $45 until Period

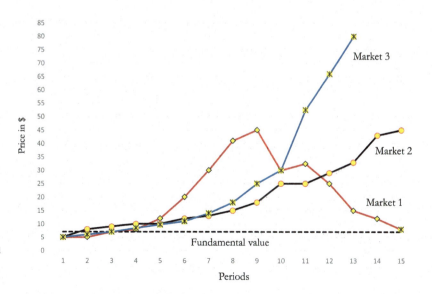

Figure 15.4
Results from asset markets with flat fundamental value. Re-created on the basis of data in Dickinson et al. (2019)

9 before declining relatively smoothly down to the fundamental value of $7 by the last round. In Market 2, however, the bubble never crashes! Prices increase slowly but inexorably till, even in Period 15, the average price is more than $40, for shares that are worth only $7. Market 3 demonstrates a huge bubble and a precipitous crash. Prices reach $80 in round 13. Then, no shares change hands in Period 14, in line with Smith's observation that trading volume reduces dramatically towards the end. Finally, in Period 15, the market crashes to the fundamental value.

Holt's findings show that the bubble-and-crash pattern arises even where the financial asset is long (or infinitely) lived and has a flat fundamental value rather than a declining value. This also shows that one does not need to have traders with different endowments of cash and shares for bubbles to arise. In Holt's work and Dickinson et al.'s, all participants have the exact same endowment of cash and shares, yet both observe significant bubbles. We know a few other things. The bubble phenomenon tends to be more pronounced in Smith-type markets with declining fundamental value as opposed to Holt-type markets with flat fundamental value. Further, even in markets with flat fundamental value, the magnitude and duration of bubbles tend to be larger with more liquidity. For the markets in Figure 15.4, if we doubled the dividend payments from $0.40 and $1.00 to $0.80 and $2.00, such that the expected dividend is now $1.40, and also doubled the interest rate from 10% to 20%, such that the fundamental value remains unchanged at $7 ($1.40/$0.20), the bubbles will be larger (in the sense of greater dispersion of prices from fundamental value) and longer lasting. So, in terms of Figure 15.4, one way to think about this is that if you took the participants from Market 2 but doubled the expected dividend and interest rates, then the bubble-and-crash pattern will be similar to Market 3.

This is not an artefact of having students take part. In their work, Smith et al. brought in business people including people familiar with stock trading from the local community. Those markets generated similar bubbles as well, a finding replicated by others subsequently. What about introducing some confederates of the experimenters who are well versed with the issue and understand the underlying problems, such as graduate students in Economics? This does not make a difference. Neither does communication among the traders. Arlington Williams ran very large markets with more than 300 students, who could take part over a number of days, during which the students are talking to one another and the instructor is also often discussing the phenomenon in class. This, too, does not minimize bubbles.[8]

What about various forms of short-selling? Since this is not a course in behavioural finance, I am going to refrain from going too much into the details of such financial manoeuvres. But, briefly, we can define short-selling in two ways. First, suppose you are in Period 9 of Market 2 of Figure 15.4. The share price has gone up to $45. You understand that a crash is coming. You strike a future deal (enter into a contract to be conducted in the future) with another trader that at the end of Period 15, you will sell a certain number of shares to him/her at $30 per share. You do this even though you actually do not possess any shares currently. The other trader may be willing to accept this offer, given that it appears that you are offering to sell shares that are currently trading at $45 per share at a discount of $15 per share. But, in Round 14, prices have fallen to $12 per share. You buy up those shares at $12 per share and then sell it to the other trader for $30 per share according to the terms of your deal, thereby earning a profit of $18 per share. Of course, if the price does not crash and ends up above $30, then you will make a loss since you will have to buy those shares at a higher price and then re-sell them at $30 to fulfil the terms of your contract.[9]

A second option is that, in Period 9, you borrow money against shares from a stockbroker. Currently, the shares are selling for $45 per share. You borrow $4,500, which is the equivalent of 100 shares at $45 per share. However, here, the deal is that you will have to repay the broker 100 shares rather than $4,500. You wait until Period 15, when the share price drops to $8. You buy 100 shares at $800, return them to the broker and make a profit of $3,700. But once again, if, for some reason, the price does not drop and remains above $45, then you are looking at making heavy losses. For example, if you followed this strategy in Market 2, you may be in trouble. Suppose you are in Period 10 of Market 2 with prices at $25 per share. You expect them to drop to $10 per share by Period 15. You borrow $2,500 from the broker as the current price of 100 shares, expecting that the price will drop to $10. If and when it does, you can buy 100 shares for $1,000, return them to the broker and make a profit of $1,500. But, when Period 15 arrives, the share price is at $45. This means that in order to return 100 shares to the broker, you now need to pay $4,500 against your earlier borrowing of $2,500. Now, you are looking at a loss of $20 per share.[10]

Why is this relevant? Because, if there are a lot of people who are doing this, then the traders or brokers whom they are striking deals with should begin to get the impression that someone or more than one out there thinks that the prices are going to crash. After all, the only way you can make money is if the market crashes. But this should signal an impending crash to others and they should, in turn, shy away from buying and/or selling at very high prices. If and when that happens, prices should converge to fundamental value more rapidly. The evidence here is mixed. Some of the early studies in the area, including that done by Smith, suggested that short-selling does not have an impact on bubbles. But some subsequent studies have suggested that short-selling may indeed lead to smaller bubbles. It is also the case that the greater the short-selling capacity (or the more the number of traders who anticipate a market crash and engage in short-selling), the more the price tracks the fundamental value, but even large amounts of short-selling does not get rid of bubbles completely or quickly. The only thing that reliably seems to get rid of the bubbles is experience with these markets. The more experience traders have, the less the tendency to bid up prices and the fewer the bubbles, with market prices tracking fundamental values with greater experience.[11]

RATIONAL SPECULATION AND THE ROLE OF EXPECTATIONS

At some level, the pattern of behaviour seems obvious, given what we know about human decision making. The possibility of speculative gains unleashes "animal spirits" among inexperienced traders. Further, cognitive limitation may play a role in this more complex market where there is no longer a clear delineation in the roles of buyers and sellers. This makes the potential for cognitive and/or decision errors larger. While all of those things are at play, it is useful to tease out some of these in greater detail.

First, speculation may not be irrational. If we assume that different traders have different expectations in the market, then it may well make sense for someone like Grace to buy shares at an inflated price as long as Grace is certain that there is another trader, Izzy, who is willing to pay an even higher price for the share. Izzy, in turn, may be able to sell her shares to a third trader Becky, who is willing to pay an even higher price. It is possible that either Izzy or Becky finds that she is the last person to buy at an inflated price and the market crashes after that. But, as long as there are Izzy and Becky type traders, Grace's initial speculative move in order to enjoy capital gains may not be irrational. Speculation may also be profitable, even with a capital loss, where the sale price is less than the purchase price, if the stream of future dividends on that share is larger than the magnitude of this capital loss. So, clearly, if nothing else, the bubble-and-crash pattern may be generated by a mixture of rational and irrational traders, the latter referring to traders who are more liable to make mistakes in terms of when to buy or sell. Equally, they may also happen even if all traders are rational but this rationality is not common knowledge; in the sense that some traders believe that there are some others in the market who are not behaving rationally or are liable to make mistakes in the process of buying and selling.

But a key question is: given that prices in most, albeit not all, markets eventually crash back down toward the fundamental value, why are traders not able to anticipate this crash? For one thing, as we saw above, not all markets crash. Second, anticipating the crash requires the traders to engage in rather sophisticated backward induction arguments, which is not easy and particularly not easy for those who do not have much experience in the institution. Instead, many of these traders engage in more naïve behaviour based on their (often myopic) forecasts of what they expect to happen to the price. Smith et al. explore this by explicitly eliciting trader forecasts of (average) prices prior to a round and the actual (average) prices that prevail in that round. If traders are mostly rational and take all or much of the relevant information into account when forming their expectations, then we would expect their forecasts prior to a particular round to be closely correlated with the prices that prevail during that round. Smith et al. find that, on average, this is not true. Forecasts are not accurate and most traders use current prices as the basis of their future forecasts. Once the price starts to deviate from the fundamental value, traders seem to believe that the fundamental value is no longer the primary concern but base their future forecasts on current prices. This is generally known as *adaptive* expectations as opposed to *rational* expectations; that is, in forming their price expectations, the traders are not taking all salient information into consideration, such as the fundamental value or the length of the time horizon, but are myopically basing their future forecasts on current prices alone.[12] But even there, most traders tend to underestimate price increases during the boom and overestimate price declines during the slump. They are also not very good at predicting large price changes or turning points. But there is one caveat to this: those who are better at forecasting prices end up earning more, thereby providing support to the thesis that, at least for some traders, but certainly not all, speculative moves in anticipation of capital gains can be entirely rational.

It is clear that traders do not do a good job of anticipating prices and expect the price that they forecast. This in turn implies that, during the boom when the price rises, there is an excess of bids to buy over offers to sell, with many of the bids going unfulfilled. This leads to an increase in those bids in order to buy and the bids rise faster than the forecasts made by the traders. During the downturn, the exact opposite happens. Offers to sell start to exceed bids to buy, signalling a downturn, and the price starts dropping quickly, far outstripping predicted prices.

Charles Noussair (currently at Arizona) and Charles Plott (of Caltech) had also been working on such violations of the efficient markets hypothesis and the formation of price bubbles in markets. Along with another colleague, Vivian Lei, they wondered about the Smith et al. explanation that the bubbles are partially due to rational speculation and partly due to myopic (or adaptive) expectations where traders simply base future forecasts on current prices and do not necessarily take account of other factors, such as the rationality of others or the time horizon. Lei, Noussair and Plott wondered whether some of this may be due to a form of bounded rationality where traders, placed in a demanding cognitive environment, make decision errors that compound these bubbles. If this is the case, then bubbles may arise not only due to a failure on the part of traders to allow for others' rationality, but also because some trader behaviour does actually deviate from rationality.

Lei et al. also wondered whether, given the complexities of the Smith et al. market, it could be the case that Smith et al. are actually overestimating the size and frequency of bubbles. In the context of such lab experiments, there is nothing else for traders to do other than take part in trades. It is conceivable that this "excess trading" on the part of traders who have nothing better to do during a lab session magnifies the bubbles. If traders end up buying and selling since they need something to do during the course of the session, then they may well be engaging in trades without much deliberation, which exacerbates the tendency to make mistakes.

In order to distinguish between rational speculative motives and mistakes, Lei et al. decided to completely turn off the speculative channel. They essentially recreated the original Smith double auction goods market experiments that we studied in Chapter 14 by assigning a single role to each trader, either as a buyer or a seller. A buyer is endowed with cash, with which he/she can buy shares, but does not have any shares to sell and is also prevented from reselling any shares bought. Similarly, sellers have shares to sell, but no cash, and are also not allowed purchase shares. The main difference is that the buyers and sellers are buying and selling the same financial asset and, realistically, this asset should have the same fundamental value for the buyers and sellers. So, as opposed to the earlier double auction markets for goods, there is no systematic variation in buyer valuations and seller costs. Therefore, this design should do away with the possibility of speculative gains and, in turn, bubbles.

Lei et al. also provided their participants with detailed information regarding the expected dividends, which corresponds to the fundamental value of the shares. This should ideally make the fundamental value common knowledge for all traders and, thereby, ensure that trading prices do not deviate much from the underlying fundamental value of the asset. Lei et al. run three sessions of their *no speculation* markets. The left panel of Figure 15.5 shows the outcomes over 12 periods of trading. The thick dashed line shows the declining fundamental value of the asset. Surprisingly, two out of three markets (Markets 1 and 2) exhibit the now familiar bubble-and-crash pattern while, in Market 3, the prices do not deviate that much from the underlying fundamental value but there is also no tendency in this market for the prices to converge to the fundamental value. In Markets 1 and 2, more than 40% of transactions take place at prices that are higher than the maximum possible gains from future dividends. In Market 3, this proportion is lower at around 28%. The presence of bubbles in these markets show that the bubble-and-crash phenomenon can arise even in the absence of speculation. It also suggests that there may be no obvious reason for all traders to

■ Asset bubbles in markets

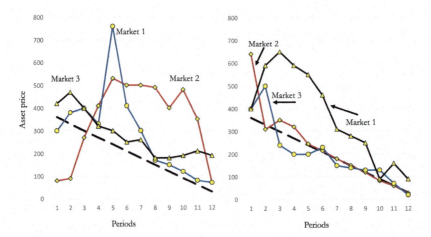

Figure 15.5
Results from no speculation asset markets. Re-created on the basis of data in Lei et al. (2001)

assume rationality on the part of all other traders, given that some do seem to make mistakes in their trades.

Lei and her colleagues go on to suggest that the large volume of trading partially explains why prices diverge from the fundamental value even when there is no possibility of speculative gains. They find that, even in the absence of speculation, the sellers sell more than 80% of the shares at their disposal to the buyers. This is counter-intuitive, since if all the traders have similar risk attitudes and given that there are an equal number of buyers and sellers and that the fundamental value is the same for everyone, one would only expect about one-half of these shares to change hands. Lei et al. conjecture that these excessive levels of trade may arise due to the fact that, within a session, buyers and sellers have nothing else to do other than to trade, and, thereby, end up trading much more than they should.

In order to test this excess trading conjecture, Lei and her colleagues allow traders to simultaneously participate in two different markets. One of these markets is set up exactly like Smith's double auction markets for goods where buyers and sellers respectively buy and sell a good as in Chapter 14. The other market is for a financial asset, but this is set up exactly like Lei et al.'s earlier work that prevents the possibility of speculative gains. Here, the goods market runs for 15 periods, while the asset market opens in Period 4 and runs simultaneously with the goods market for the remaining 12 periods. The asset market has the same structure as before, with buyers endowed with cash and the ability to buy shares but not resell them and sellers in possession of shares who can sell those shares but not buy them back. The right panel of Figure 15.5 shows the outcomes of three sessions, each of which had both of these two markets, an asset market and a goods market, operating side by side. Traders now have the choice of trading either in the goods market or in the asset market.

In the right panel of Figure 15.5, I have shown only what happens in the asset market. A few things stand out. Even here, there is still a bubble in one market, Market 1. But in the other two markets, prices track the fundamental value closely; in fact, in Market 3, we can see almost a negative bubble with prices below fundamental value in some periods. In Market 2, prices start high at 640 but drop down sharply in the very next period and then track the fundamental value closely for the rest of the duration of the market. Overall, 55% of shares change hands, which is very much in keeping with the fact that, as long as the buyers and sellers do not differ significantly in terms of their risk attitudes and given equal numbers of buyers and sellers, just about half of the shares should be sold.

The work done by Lei, Noussair and Plott leaves us with the following conclusions. First, the frequently observed bubble-and-crash pattern can arise even in markets where there are no possibilities for speculative gains. Here, bubbles and crashes are being caused by decision errors made in a relatively demanding cognitive environment. Earlier, I suggested that bubbles may arise even if all traders are rational but are just not convinced of the rationality of others. Lei and her colleagues are suggesting that this need not be the case; there are some traders who do make mistakes and, therefore, some traders may anticipate these errors and exploit these to their own advantage. As I noted earlier, traders who are better at forecasting price changes do earn more.

Second, part of the bubble-and-crash phenomenon may be due to excess trading by traders who engage in trades since they have nothing else to do during the course of the experiment. Allowing these traders an alternative activity leads to a dampening of the bubble phenomenon. This suggests that lab tests of asset market bubbles may be, at times, overestimating the frequency, amplitude and duration of bubbles. So, one way to think of this is that the lab studies provide an upper bound of the bubble phenomena in real-life markets.

So, where does this leave us? First, by and large, deviations from the efficient markets hypothesis seem well documented. Yes, prices do eventually converge to the fundamental value but it is a stretch to suggest that this is the equilibrium outcome; prices may diverge from the fundamental value for extended periods of time. Second, part of this bubble-and-crash pattern is driven by the potential for speculation and capital gains. This speculation may well be rational as long as traders are not convinced of the rationality of all other traders. Third, by and large, the traders behave in a myopic manner and base their future forecasts on current prices alone; they also underestimate prices during booms and overestimate prices during slumps. Consequently, traders are not good at forecasting turning points or large price changes. Fourth, some traders do make mistakes in their decisions and so not all traders need to be rational. Therefore, the possibility of such errors and the anticipation of the same by other traders may also lead to speculative bubbles. Those traders who are better at forecasting market movements earn more. Finally, a part of the bubble-and-crash phenomenon may be attributable to the fact that, in most such experiments, traders have no alternative activity. Therefore, they engage in much more buying and selling than is optimal. Providing traders with an alternative market activity ameliorates bubbles. In that sense, the magnitude of asset bubbles generated in a lab environment may be thought of as an upper bound of what is likely to happen in actual markets.

UNLEASHING (AND LEASHING) OUR ANIMAL SPIRITS

In his book, *The General Theory of Employment, Interest and Money*, John Maynard Keynes referred to "animal spirits" at the heart of much financial decision making. Keynes wrote:

> Even apart from the instability due to speculation, there is the instability due to the characteristic of human nature (…). Most, probably, of our decisions to do something positive (…)

can only be taken as the result of animal spirits – a spontaneous urge to action rather than inaction, and not as the outcome of a weighted average of quantitative benefits multiplied by quantitative probabilities.

Here, Keynes is clearly suggesting that many of our decisions, financial, economic and others, are born out of "animal spirits" rather than a deliberate calculation of the expected gains and losses. For those of you who have arrived at this chapter via the previous chapters, this conclusion will appear almost facile. But remember Keynes was writing at a time when almost none of the research described in this book had been undertaken. Many of you may also understand that economics as it stood at the time was essentially microeconomic in nature, with a pronounced emphasis on competitive markets. Keynes was essentially developing, *de novo*, the entire field of modern macroeconomics.

By now, we have a much better understanding of the causes and consequences of Keynesian "animal spirits"; the fact many of our decisions are subject to biases and heuristics and they are often conditional on observing the actions of others and imitating them. Trading in financial assets is a complex undertaking requiring traders to rely on concepts such as expected return, fundamental value, backward induction, and opportunity costs (of buying or selling shares for speculative gain versus holding them for dividend realizations). It is no wonder, then, that many of the biases which affect our decision making in other arenas will come into play with even greater force in this area, which is ripe with both risk and uncertainty (in terms of what other traders may believe or do).

It is also highly likely that traders may fall back on heuristics in this complex task, except the use of heuristics here may backfire for many. We have seen, and this is a point that I have made earlier, that those with greater experience in such markets fare much better than those who are inexperienced. Among other things, as I will show below, experience enables traders to make much better forecasts of market movements and we have seen already from the work of Smith et al. that those who make better forecasts earn more. So, while the role of heuristics (or other biases) may not lead to loss of earnings for everyone, it certainly depends crucially on the degree of experience that one brings to the table. We have seen before that Tom Brady's or Sully Sullenberger's split-second decision making arises primarily from their long experience at the task. In the absence of that experience and familiarity (in some sense, their "muscle memory"), relying on intuitive decision making or gut feelings may lead as astray.

Given the nature of these financial markets, many of the biases we have studied at this point will be likely to play a role in decision making. This has been the subject of many books, including Robert Shiller's *Irrational Exuberance*, Michael Lewis's *The Big Short*, Burton Malkiel's *A Random Walk Down Wall Street*, William Cohan's *House of Cards: A Tale of Hubris and Wretched Excess on Wall Street* and others. Therefore, in the interest of parsimony, I will discuss two aspects of decision making in financial trading: The role of *self-control* and the role of *over-confidence*. This is partly because we have addressed both of these at length in prior chapters and so this material will appeal to readers. Another author may well have chosen other topics and other papers.

Martin Kocher (of Vienna), Konstantin Lucks (of Munich) and David Schindler (Tilburg University) interpret Keynes' animal spirits to imply that the formation of price bubbles in financial markets may owe their existence to a lack of self-control on the part of traders. When some traders see other traders buying, even at inflated prices, the urge to buy becomes overpowering. In writing about their work on asset bubbles and classroom demonstrations, Arlington Williams relates an anecdote, where one student asked something along the lines of: "Why are so many people buying at such high prices?" Williams goes on to comment that the typical buyer who is buying at grossly inflated prices usually does not say much about his or her strategy. This also applies to the Lei, Noussair and Plott findings that the magnitude of trading is much higher when there is no other alternative available. Sometimes, this kind of behaviour is referred to as *momentum trading*; a type of "herd mentality" where traders feel the urge to trade because everyone else is doing so. While, I concede the point made by Lei, Noussair and Plott about the role of an alternative activity in reducing asset bubbles, I think that the assumption of activity concentrated in a single market may not be off the mark in many cases. In the context of real-life markets, information is often incomplete. Yes, there are many potential markets out there, but if most people I know are all buying and selling houses, then I am much more inclined to do the same with my wealth. We have already seen the role of advice in decision making in many contexts. So, if all my friends are investing their nest-egg in houses (or shares of the South Sea Company), I may be sorely tempted to do so too, instead of diversifying my portfolio. This is only to suggest that people may become excessively focused on one particular market even if other markets are available. It is not so much a question of having access to multiple markets but one of realizing the need for diversification and the pitfalls associated with chasing capital gains.

Kocher and his colleagues start by noting that there is enough correlational evidence to suggest that self-control (or lack thereof) may play a role in momentum trading and price bubbles. For example, Andrew Lo at MIT's Sloan School of Management and colleagues examine the behaviour of 80 anonymous day-traders. They find that subjects who possess worse self-control, that is., those traders who exhibit much more emotional reactions to both gains and losses, end up performing worse than those who exercise greater self-control. But what Kocher and his colleagues were interested in was establishing causality; that it is the lack of self-control that leads to bad trades, rather than bad trading outcomes resulting in stronger emotional responses or a third factor affecting both self-control as well as poor decision making.

In order to study this, Kocher et al. turn to the Stroop Task that we discussed in Chapter 3. All participants take part in the asset trading market introduced by Smith, Suchanek and Williams where the fundamental value of the asset is declining over time. Except, prior to the market interaction, participants take part in a variant of the Stroop Task.[13] Participants are assigned to two different groups, one with *depleted* and the second with *non-depleted* self-control. Both groups perform the Stroop Task for five minutes and are presented with many such words on successive screens. Those in the former group saw the conflicting messages on every screen for those five minutes, while those in the latter group saw this conflict once every 70th screen. The idea here is that the former group, which has to exercise much greater self-control than the latter, will end up depleting their reservoir of self-control and will find it much harder to desist from driving prices up in the ensuing asset trading game, especially when others are doing so. In short, we should expect to see greater amounts of momentum trading as well as larger and longer lasting asset bubbles among those traders whose self-control has been depleted. Kocher and his colleagues confirm that those in the former group made more mistakes and correctly answered fewer problems in the Stroop Task. This group also reported that they found the task much more difficult in a post-study questionnaire. Therefore, their manipulation in terms of one group going into the asset trading game with less self-control than the other was successful.

In the study by Kocher et al., there are 160 participants who are assigned to 16 markets of ten traders each. Eight markets consist of 80 traders whose self-control has been depleted while the other eight consist of traders whose self-control is intact. In addition, there are another 24 *mixed* markets of ten traders each, where half of the traders have had their self-control depleted while the other half have not. Following this, participants take part in the Smith et al. market game for ten periods. At the end, they provide demographic information and also take part in other tasks that measure their emotional states, risk attitudes and cognitive abilities, given evidence that those who are cognitively more able (say, are better at solving mathematical problems) perform better in the Smith et al. asset trading game in terms of earning more money. All of these are measured via well-validated scales.

Figure 15.6 shows the results. The thick dashed black line shows the declining fundamental value of the asset. The other three lines show the trajectory of the asset price in the three markets; depleted, non-depleted and mixed. Two things stand out clearly. First, the magnitude of the price bubble is much higher in the market consisting of depleted self-control traders compared to that consisting of non-depleted ones. Second, the trajectory of the price in the mixed markets (consisting of one-half depleted and the other half non-depleted traders) behaves similarly to that in the market with depleted traders. This suggests that, in order for price bubbles to form, it is not essential for all traders to have depleted their self-control; the presence of some depleted traders seems sufficient to generate the "animal spirits" necessary for other traders to join in on momentum trading and drive prices up during the boom.

Looking at the mixed groups, Kocher and colleagues find that the traders whose self-control is depleted tend to post their bids quickly and much earlier than their non-depleted

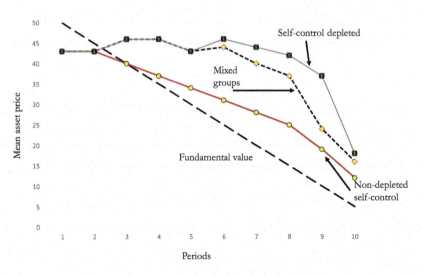

Figure 15.6 Results from asset markets with depleted self-control traders, non-depleted self-control traders, and a mix of both types of traders. Re-created on the basis of data in Kocher et al. (2019)

colleagues. But, differences disappear quickly, because the non-depleted traders, who are unaware that the market consists of both types, start to mimic the depleted traders very quickly on the assumption that these "early movers" know something about the market that they do not. The result is that the behaviour of traders in these mixed markets resembles that in the depleted self-control markets.

Kocher et al. find that the act of following the actions of depleted self-control traders has a significantly detrimental effect on the earnings of those traders who are non-depleted. In a follow-up study, they brought in a group of non-depleted traders and asked them to divide their investment between two assets, one with a known value and the second with an unknown dividend value. Except, the asset with the known value resulted in higher earnings than the one with the probabilistic dividends. Each group could choose between the deterministic value asset or the asset with probabilistic dividends, except, for the probabilistic dividend asset, half of the traders were shown the (higher) prices generated by depleted traders in the prior study while the other half saw the (lower) prices generated by the non-depleted traders. Probably not surprisingly at this point, the traders who saw the price trajectory generated by the depleted traders invested a lot more in the probabilistic dividend asset. The net result is that these traders earn less.

Next, Kocher et al. look into the channels through which self-control, or lack thereof, affects decision making. Two potential channels are risk attitudes and cognitive abilities. They find that their self-control manipulation via the Stroop Task has no impact on subsequent risk attitudes. However, in post-task questionnaires, the self-control depleted subjects report feeling stronger emotions, such as excitement, that are commonly associated with asset bubbles. Finally, Kocher et al. find that while higher cognitive abilities do play a role in moderating the magnitude of bubbles and result in higher earnings, the role of such cognitive skills is much less pronounced for self-control depleted traders. So, when depleted of self-control, even superior cognitive ability does not prevent these traders from generating price bubbles. Kocher et al. conclude that:

> Together, these findings suggest that self-control depleted traders become more reliant on heuristics, are much more emotion driven, and rely less on their cognitive skills to find optimal trading strategies.

While Kocher and his colleagues examine the role of self-control or lack thereof, Julija Michailova of Hamburg and Ulrich Schmidt of Kiel look at another likely culprit: overconfidence. In their study, participants first take part in a general knowledge quiz. Each question has three possible answers of which the participant has to choose one. For each question, each participant indicates how confident he/she is about his/her answer. These can range from 33% (complete uncertainty; since given three options, there is a 33% chance that one of them will be correct) to 100% (complete certainty). Michailova and Schmidt then compute a *bias score* for each participant. They do this by looking at each participant's mean confidence score across all questions and the mean proportion of correct answers. So, suppose a participant said that he/she was 100% sure of all his/her answers but, in reality, only 60% of his/her answers were correct, then his/her bias score is 40%. A positive bias score means overconfidence, a negative bias score means underconfidence and a bias score of zero implies a

■ Asset bubbles in markets

person who is accurately calibrated (confidence neutral). In keeping with prior findings, these authors find that participants tend to be overconfident, with mean overconfidence of approx. 12% and a fairly large standard deviation of 11.

A few weeks later, these participants are invited to come to the lab and take part in an asset market study using the same protocols as in Smith et al. Participants are endowed with cash and some shares and trade for 15 periods. In any period, the potential dividend values are $0, $0.08, $0.28 or $0.60, implying an expected dividend of $0.24. So, at the beginning of the session, the expected dividend from the asset is $3.60, declining to $0.24 by Period 15. There are ten markets, each with six participants. However, half of these markets consist of high overconfidence subjects (those who were in the highest overconfidence band; mean bias score of 21%) while the other half consist of participants who were in the lowest band (mean bias score of 1%). The participants, of course, are unaware that overconfidence is the subject of the study. The general knowledge questions they answered did not deal with economics or finance and the two groups were invited to sign up for distinct sets of sessions.

Figure 15.7 shows the outcome. Again, and possibly unsurprisingly at this point, the overconfident participants generate a much larger price bubble. Michailova and Schmidt look at other measures and conclude that markets with highly overconfident traders display greater volatility, greater turnover (many more transactions with lots of shares changing hands) and much higher dispersion of prices from fundamental value. Again, not surprisingly, highly overconfident traders also have inflated expectations and forecast much higher prices than traders low on overconfidence. In fact, the trajectory of price forecasts (not shown on the graph) by highly overconfident participants almost exactly mirrors the trajectory of actual prices as shown in Figure 15.7.

Michailova and Schmidt conclude by saying that this pre-eminent role of overconfidence is bad news for market level phenomena. Evidence suggests that professional traders tend to be much more overconfident than students. This counters the Lei et al. argument

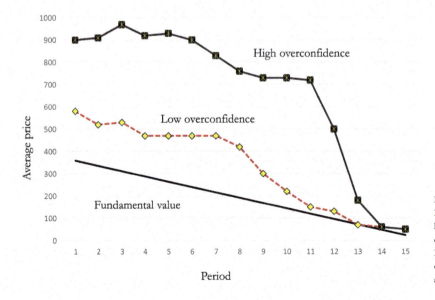

Figure 15.7 Results from asset markets with high and low overconfidence traders. Re-created on the basis of data in Michailova and Schmidt (2016)

that lab bubbles may be seen as upper bounds of actual bubbles. If traders in actual markets are highly overconfident, then they may tend to generate even larger bubbles than students. Of course, we do not know what professional traders would do if they had to choose between investing in more than one market. Brad Barber of UC-Davis and Terrance Odean of UC-Berkeley have done extensive work in this area and have shown that overconfidence motivates mutual fund managers to undertake excessive trades, even though these traders, typically, do not outperform markets. For most people, the best strategy is to invest in a highly diversified portfolio and not make frequent changes. Those who trade excessively usually earn less than the market return. There is also evidence that investment activities of firms are positively correlated with the CEO's level of overconfidence.

PASSIONS WITHIN REASON: THE ROLE OF EXPERIENCE IN CURBING BUBBLES

So, are we then doomed to succumb to such "animal spirits" in our trading activities? Not necessarily. The papers that show the existence of these also provide implicit clues as to how they may be curbed. We have seen earlier from the work done by Margaret Neale and Max Bazerman that people can learn not to fall prey to overconfidence by being made aware of its existence. Similarly, we have discussed the issue of exercising self-control on different occasions along the way and shown how this may enable people to do things such as save more for retirement. One way this can be achieved is via entering into a commitment scheme, which prevents us from succumbing to temptation. So, how do we curb unbridled passions by infusing them with a dash of clear-headed reasoning?

As Smith et al. noted, the best prescription for reducing asset bubbles is greater experience on the part of traders. Ernan Haruvy of UT-Dallas (now at McGill), Yaron Lahav (then at Emory and now at Ben Gurion University in Israel) and Charles Noussair (at Tilburg then but at Arizona at the time of writing) extend the early path-breaking work of Smith and his colleagues by delving into how it is that experience makes such a difference. This is important because, if it is indeed the case that traders rely on simple rules-of-thumb as suggested by Kocher and his colleagues, then such heuristics are more likely to be successful when traders have more experience at the task at hand.

Haruvy and colleagues invited 53 participants to take part in their study. There are nine participants in each one of five sessions and eight in the other one. In each session, the participants take part in four different markets in sequence, with each market lasting for 15 periods. So, all in all, these participants interact for 60 rounds over four markets. Each of the four markets within a session resemble the Smith et al. markets. Participants start out with an initial endowment of cash and shares. The share pays dividends, which takes one of four values in each round: $0.00, $0.04, $0.14 and $0.30, with an expected dividend of $0.12 in each round. Participants accumulate earnings during the 15 rounds in each market but they are paid their balances at the end of one market and before the beginning of the next, so that they do not carry their earnings from one market to the next. The market is implemented as a call-market, which we discussed in Chapter 14, as opposed to the double auction implemented by Smith et al. This means that, in any round, buyers submit bids to buy and how many shares they wish to buy at that price and sellers submit offers to sell and how many shares they are willing to sell at that price. Once the "bids" and "asks" have been submitted, the computer programme works out the implicit demand and supply curves and calculates the equilibrium price. All trades take place at this equilibrium price.

In a major deviation from the Smith et al. structure, Haruvy and colleagues also elicit price expectations from their traders for all future rounds in each of the four markets. This means that, rather than asking traders in one period what they think the price will be in the next period, Haruvy et al. ask them about price expectations for all future periods. This means that at the start of a market and before Period 1, traders are asked what they think the price will be for each of the 15 market periods coming up; before Period 2, they are asked about their predictions for the remaining 14 rounds; before Period 3, they are asked to predict the same for the remaining 13 periods and so on. Traders get paid for the accuracy of their predictions over and above the money they make from the trading game itself.[14] The reader will immediately realize the value of asking people to make such long-term predictions. This alters the frame of reference by asking participants to look much further ahead instead of just one period ahead and the act of doing so should also encourage backward induction. When asked to look 15 periods ahead, participants are much more inclined to anticipate that the share is valueless at the end of the 15th period. This should enable them to work their way backwards better and prices should more closely track the fundamental value of the asset.

Haruvy and colleagues make a number of interesting discoveries. First, in spite of the ability to look ahead over a much longer horizon than usual, both Markets 1 and 2 exhibit the usual bubble-and-crash pattern. The price trajectory in these two markets is similar to that of Market 1 in the left-hand panel of Figure 15.5. But, by the third and fourth markets, the prices start to track the fundamental value more closely. The evolution of the price path in Markets 3 and 4 looks more like Market 3 in the right-hand panel of Figure 15.5. So, by the third market, the bubble-and-crash phenomenon has pretty much disappeared.

In order to look more closely at this, Haruvy and colleagues focus on the "peak price". This is the highest share price attained during the operation of a market and is easy to pinpoint. The highest price in a market represents a turning point, in that the price will start to decrease from this point on. Let us think for a minute what we would expect if prices followed the fundamental value. In that case, we expect the market price to be highest in Period 1 and then decline from that point on; much like Market 3 on the right panel of Figure 15.5. However, if there are indeed bubbles in the market, then we expect the price to start low, then peak in a later period and then crash. Remember that Smith et al. found that prices often start below the fundamental value in Period 1. So, the price peaking earlier in the market is consistent with convergence to the fundamental value.

Figure 15.8 shows what happens to peak prices across the different markets and sessions. There are five sessions with four markets running consecutively and one session with three markets but not the fourth. In Market 1, the price reached its highest level in Period 13 in two out of six sessions. In the remaining four sessions, the price peaked at Periods 10, 11, 12 and 14. In Market 2, the price peaked at Period 2 in one market, at Period 4 in two markets and at Periods 7, 9 and 12 in the three remaining markets. By the third market, the change is obvious, here prices peaked by Period 6 at the latest in all six sessions. Finally, in Market 4, which was run in only five sessions, the price peaked in Period 1 for two sessions,

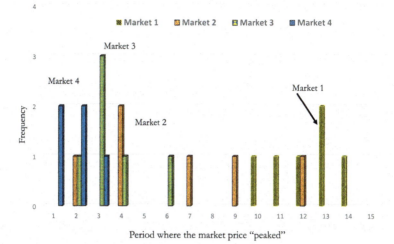

Figure 15.8
Peak price periods in asset markets. Re-created on the basis of data in Haruvy et al. (2007)

in Period 2 for two sessions and in Period 3 for one session. By the fourth market, price peaks were very much in keeping with prices tracking the fundamental value. People do learn not to "over-bid" over time but it does take a long time for people to understand this.

A closer look at participant expectations regarding market prices provides details of how this convergence occurs. In the early periods of Market 1, most participants predict that prices will remain at current levels. After a few periods, when the price starts to increase, most predict that prices will continue to increase and very few (in fact, only five out of 53 participants) anticipate the eventual market crash. At the outset of Market 2, most participants predict a price trajectory that is similar to that of Market 1, though, on average, they expect the price bubble to be smaller and they expect the price peak to occur at the same time as in the first market. But, in anticipating the price peak, the traders run the prices up in early periods and then attempt to reduce their purchases and increase their sales before they expect the price peak to occur. This process continues in Markets 3 and 4, where actual price peaks occur earlier than expected as traders put upward pressure on prices in anticipation of the peak they expect to occur. This process moves the price peak earlier and closer to Period 1, which is consistent with prices tracking the fundamental value. By Market 4, average expectations are that prices will, more or less, track fundamentals.

This finding also explains and elaborates on the original Smith et al. finding that actual prices lie above forecast prices during booms and below forecast prices during slumps. In other words, the prices forecast by traders lag behind the actual market price. Haruvy and colleagues find that this is primarily because trader forecasts of prices adjust more slowly than their actual behaviour. In forecasting prices, traders look not only at what is happening in the current market, but also look back to earlier markets. So, for Market 2, they consider prices in both Markets 1 and 2; for Market 3, they consider all three markets 1, 2 and 3 and so on. Except, they put twice as much weight on what happened in the immediately preceding market. So, for Market 4, traders put twice as much weight on Market 3 than on the other markets. This tendency to look back to the past markets (which typically exhibit larger bubbles than the current one) explains why price forecasts adjust slowly, and, therefore, lag behind actual market prices.

The Haruvy et al. results shed light on the inner workings of trader minds. Initially, inexperienced traders expect a price trajectory that is constant over the remaining life of the asset. Later, their predictions start to change but still reflect a continuation of past and current market trends, implying that these expectations lag behind actual market prices. With greater experience in more markets, trader forecasts come to correspond to the fundamental value and their prediction bias decreases. These results, in many ways, corroborate the earlier ones of Smith and his colleagues. Prediction biases appear during a bubble because traders base their forecasts on history but adjust their behaviour accordingly: they attempt to reduce purchases and increase sales when they believe the price peak is imminent and prices are going to start declining. The effect of this behaviour brings the price peaks earlier over time and attenuates the bubbles. Furthermore, while the expectation formation process is backward looking, Haruvy et al. show that the process via which they are formed and updated can provide useful guides for predicting future price peaks. They conclude by saying:

> Convergence of asset markets to fundamental values in our markets thus appears to occur because traders use trading strategies that are profitable given their expectations, which are in turn based on history. That is, adaptive expectations, coupled with profit maximization, characterize a dynamic process of convergence toward fundamental pricing.

CASE STUDY 15.2 ARE ALL THE COOL KIDS NIGHT TRADING?

We have all heard of day-trading, but, as a 2011 Forbes article pointed out, these days "all the cool kids are night-trading". Globalization has led to the creation of global financial markets (e.g., markets for foreign exchange, treasuries, commodities and crypto-currencies) and technological advances have made it easier for a trader in Auckland to participate in overseas markets in London, New York or Tokyo. But such global markets involve traders who are geographically dispersed, which raises an under-appreciated issue with implications for pricing in such markets. The fact that the traders are globally dispersed implies that some are operating during the day, when they are well-rested and alert, while others are operating late at night, where they are most likely to be less sharp. Because no matter how much coffee you drink, at 4:00 in the morning everyone feels tired and is, at least partially, cognitively impaired. Our bodies are conditioned to operate on the basis of circadian rhythms; simply put, we are more alert during the day and less so at night.

David Dickinson of Appalachian State University has spent a lot of time and energy trying to understand the effects of sleep deprivation on decision making. As Dickinson points out, evidence suggests that insufficient sleep is a condition that affects large segments of the population across the globe. In the US, insufficient sleep has been recently labelled a public health problem by the US Centers for Disease Control and Prevention. This is not surprising, given that 30% of adults are considered to be chronically sleep deprived due to habitual sleep levels of six hours per night or less. Additionally, more than 20 million adults perform shift work each year, which implies an additional challenge to being well rested physically. Not only that, such shift work is often concentrated in sectors where public health is at stake, such as emergency service workers, long-haul trucking, and air traffic control, to name a few. This problem of sleepy decision makers is not reserved for the US, however, as similar levels of insufficient sleep have been found in recent survey data from Mexico, Canada, the UK, Germany and Japan.

So, as markets become more globalized and the incidence of night trading increases, what should we expect? In order to answer this question, Dickinson teamed up with Ananish Chaudhuri and Ryan Greenaway-McGrevy (of the University of Auckland) and set up an asset trading experiment. They recruited university students in the US east coast and in New Zealand and invited them to take part in a stock-trading game for real money. Participants are recruited for different time slots during the entire day: 4:00 a.m., 8:00 a.m., 12:00 noon, 4:00 p.m., 8:00 p.m. and 12:00 midnight. They set up two types of markets: *local* markets, involving people in the same location and, therefore, playing at the same time of the day, and *global* markets involving people at both locations and, therefore, playing at different times of the day. Participants can log in to the software from home; they are put in groups of 7–13 (median group size = 11) and participate for about an hour. They are not aware where the other participants are located. For the global markets, the different time-slots and the 16-hour time difference between the two locations imply that one group is typically taking part at a "good" time of the day when they are alert and awake, while the other group is at a "bad" time, when they are more likely to be sleepy and cognitively impaired.

Instead of the Smith et al. design of declining fundamental value of the shares, Dickinson et al. adopt the Holt framework of flat fundamental value. Each participant has some cash and some shares to trade. Cash earns interest and the shares have a fundamental value of $7 (NZ$10.50), meaning that any shares held at the end of the session can be redeemed for $7 (NZ$10.50). Participants can buy or sell shares for two markets, each lasting 15 rounds, for a total of 30 rounds. The difference is that, in one of those two markets (sometimes during the first 15 rounds and at other times during the second 15 rounds), the market interest rate and the prospective share dividends are doubled, resulting in much greater liquidity in the market. The objective of the traders is to earn the most money. Average earnings in this study are around $30 (NZ$45).

Dickinson et al. find that global markets, that involved players at different times of day, are particularly susceptible to bubbles, where the assets sell at inflated values, much higher than the fundamental value of $7. This, in turn, suggests that as markets become more globalized, attracting traders from all over the world, we should expect to see much greater mispricing, that is, market prices showing greater deviation from the underlying fundamental value. But, equally importantly, these researchers find that tired traders, playing at a bad time of day, make systematic mistakes. They are much more likely to take risky positions by buying shares at inflated prices and holding on to those shares for longer periods. In other words, they are not good at anticipating that the market will crash at the end of the 15 rounds and all shares held will be redeemed at their fundamental value. This in turn allows the more alert traders to take advantage of the tired traders, who end up earning less.

Dickinson and colleagues find that our "animal spirits" are stronger when we are sleep deprived and cognitively impaired. Being sleep deprived is similar to being drunk. It makes us unable to think through future consequences and seriously underestimate the downside risk. This is why we get behind the steering wheel even when drunk. Similarly, we take out more risky positions by failing to anticipate market crashes and hanging on to the riskier shares for longer than we should. People who are sleep deprived are especially bad at anticipating the crash.

This is not to suggest that no one should be night trading, but, rather, to point out the obvious pitfalls. Night traders are much more likely to be taken advantage of by day traders. Given that overconfidence is a common human failing, it is important to consider the opportunity costs. Not only: *Am I doing well by night trading?*, the question is: *Could I do better in an alternative venture?* And be aware that you are much more prone to taking risks that you would normally avoid. What if people were playing for millions of dollars rather than the smaller sums in this study? While Dickinson et al. could not provide millions of dollars, as noted above, they could and did manipulate the amount of liquidity in these markets by doubling the dividend values and increasing the interest rate on cash. Evidence in the paper suggests that if the markets are flooded with more cash, then the bubbles would be much bigger and the losses for the tired traders much larger. So, with the advent of night trading, we should expect to see greater market volatility.[15]

CONCLUDING REMARKS

This chapter has been devoted to the issue of price bubbles in markets for financial assets. These are situations where a particular financial asset is trading at a price much higher than it really should be worth. I have discussed some notable historical bubbles, including the South Sea Bubble in the early 18th century, tulip mania in the 17th century and the US housing bubble in the early part of the 21st century. There were others, such as the so-called "dotcom" bubble, also during the late 1990s and early 2000s, where the prices of internet based "tech" companies went through the roof. This led the then Chairman of the Federal Reserve, Alan Greenspan, to talk about "irrational exuberance" of investors, and a best-seller book of the same name by Robert Shiller of Yale. The effects of some of these bubbles were more localized and when the bubbles burst, the majority of the damage was confined to the investors. But, in some cases, such as the bursting of the US housing bubble, the consequences were far more widespread and devastating, resulting in a global recession. Given this, researchers, policy makers, investors and even ordinary citizens have an obvious interest in how, why and when such bubbles form.

I have discussed the path-breaking work undertaken by Vernon Smith and his colleagues, showing that lab experiments can be set up as microcosms of such macroeconomic phenomena. The work done by Smith in this area has subsequently generated a very large literature and added to our knowledge of why and how such bubbles form. We have seen that such bubbles may form in markets for assets with declining fundamental value as well as flat fundamental values. The formation of bubbles depends not only on speculative motives, but may also come about due to decision errors by traders. Well-known behavioural biases, such as lack of self-control and overconfidence, can exacerbate such market bubbles, to an extent by fuelling speculation in the anticipation of capital gains. We have learned that trader expectations play a crucial role in the formation of asset bubbles. Those who make better forecasts benefit at the expense of those who do not.

By and large, the major factor behind attenuating asset bubbles is trader experience. With greater experience the trajectory of prices track the fundamental value closely. But, acquiring this level of insight takes time and happens via the interaction of expectations, which depend on past history and behaviour. As traders gain experience over markets, they anticipate prices to peak earlier. Accordingly, they seek to lock in potential capital gains and increase sales earlier during the life of the market. But the act of doing so implies that price forecasts tend to lag behind actual prices. They also imply that, over successive markets, the price starts to peak earlier, which is consistent with prices tracking the fundamental value over time. But, while such expectations are backward looking, nevertheless such trader expectations, coupled with market trends, can tell us what to expect in terms of price peaks in the future.

So, what does that mean for regular people? One issue is that it is not always obvious to participants when a market bubble has formed. Bubbles are often obvious only after they burst. But, in terms of day-to-day investment decisions, it is probably worth paying attention to those with much greater experience. Diversify. Be aware of the opportunity costs of various actions. If the returns on a particular asset seem too good to be true, they probably are. It is difficult to outperform the market on a continual basis. One way of acquiring experience is to seek advice from those who have experience with a particular situation. In many cases, particularly where potentially large sums of money may be involved, learning by listening/observing may be better than learning by doing. And finally, try to be aware of the behavioural biases that plague many of our decisions. Before taking the plunge, seek counter-arguments and get someone to play devil's advocate.

In the words of Dennis Miller from *Saturday Night Live*: "That is my story and I am sticking with it." For all those of you who have persevered till this point, thank you. I hope you have enjoyed the ride. As I said at the very outset, this is an exciting area of research and study. Another writer may well have chosen to write about a different set of topics. I wanted to provide you with a glimpse of the exhilarating world of behavioural economics and the various factors that affect our decision making. There is a fairly extensive References section for those who wish to pursue these topics further. There are many open questions and new avenues for research available to enterprising students. To repeat what I said in the Preface: it is said that you can get the horse near the water, but you cannot make it drink. My fervent hope is that this volume has made you thirsty!

■ Asset bubbles in markets

NOTES

1 The primary focus of this chapter is the phenomenon of price bubbles in asset markets, which is where prices increase far in excess of the fundamental value of an asset. It is not about the GFC. I am providing a very cursory overview of the financial crisis as a segue into my discussion of asset bubbles. There is a voluminous scholarly literature in this area. There is no way I am going to do justice to the various facets of this crisis in a couple of pages. Much of what appears here is based on my interpretation and understanding of things written by Michael Lewis, the best-selling author of books like *Liar's Poker*, *The Blind Side* (the film version earned a Best Actress Oscar for Sandra Bullock) and *Moneyball* (starring Brad Pitt). Lewis explored the causes and consequences of the GFC in his book *The Big Short* (made into a film starring Christian Bale, Steve Carrell, Ryan Gosling and Brad Pitt), but a lot of this material appeared earlier in the popular media, including articles in *Vanity Fair* and elsewhere. I have adapted some of his arguments here, taken mostly from these various articles. If you have nits to pick with this, then do feel free to check out https://michaellewiswrites.com and express your displeasure with him.

2 The *Asiento* was a contract granted by the Spanish crown to an individual or company, allowing the holder exclusive rights in the slave trade with Spain's American colonies; it constituted the principal legal means of supplying slaves to Spanish America.

3 This was the War of Spanish Succession (1701–1714). It was set off with the death of the childless Charles II of Spain in 1700. Philip of Anjou, grandson of Louis XIV of France, inherited an undivided Spanish Empire. Disputes over territorial and commercial rights led to war in 1701 between the Bourbons of France and Spain and the Grand Alliance, including Britain, Holland and Austria, whose candidate was Charles, younger son of Leopold I, Holy Roman Emperor.

4 The Y-axis in this figure is drawn on a logarithmic scale and this is not the same as share prices. A logarithmic (or log) scale is a way of displaying numerical data over a wide range of values in a compact way, where often the largest numbers in the data are much larger than the smaller ones. In such cases, one may take log transformations of the actual values. This allows us to interpret the changes as proportional changes rather than changes in absolute magnitude.

5 Here, the term "risk adjusted" simply means that different assets have different risks and returns. Some assets promise a higher return but come with a higher risk of losing one's money if the project or the company fails. Other assets promise lower returns but also come with lower risk. The lowest risk assets are things like term deposits where the chance of losing one's money is virtually zero. So, the key point here is that in calculating expected pay-offs from a particular financial asset, one must take into account the prospective risk in that investment; hence, "risk adjusted". We already know what discounted means. This simply means that future pay-offs need to be adequately discounted by using the concept of time discounting that we discussed all the way back in Chapter 3. But, behind all the jargon, the main contention is simple: Rational traders should have a pretty good idea of the price (or value) of an asset and, therefore, these assets should not continue to trade at values that are considerably higher (or lower) than the fundamental value of the asset, just as we, typically, should not expect to buy or sell a house or a car at a price that is much higher than the house or the car is worth.

6 The assumption of a finite length of time is a simplification. I will show shortly that even if we allow for infinitely lived assets, we still observe similar bubble phenomena. One way to think of an asset that loses value after a certain period of time is to think of holding shares of a company with investments in a depletable natural resource, such as a copper, gold or coal mine. This natural resource will generate cash flow in the form of dividends while the company is in operation but, at some point in time, the resource will be depleted, rendering those shares valueless.

7 Here is a way to think of how this flat fundamental value works. Suppose you have a share that you can hold for only two periods. Suppose the value of the asset in the second and last period is V; that is, if you keep the shares until the second period, then each share can be redeemed for $V. Everyone knows this. Suppose the expected dividend in the first period is E(D). So, anyone who holds on to this asset expects to get E(D) + V after the second period. What price should you be

willing to pay for this share at the beginning of Period 1? Suppose the prevailing interest rate is r. Ignoring issues of quasi-hyperbolic discounting and such for the time being, the two-period discounted value of the share is $P = \dfrac{E(D)+V}{1+r}$. But suppose, instead of lasting two periods, the asset lasted for infinitely longer with expected dividend of E(D) in each period. So, the discounted value of the asset in the second period can be thought of as $V = \dfrac{E(D)}{1+r} + \dfrac{E(D)}{(1+r)^2} \ldots$ all the way to infinity. (Remember, we are not discounting future pay-offs for the sake of simplicity.) This is a geometric series, sometimes called a "perpetuity" formula, where each successive term is being multiplied by $\dfrac{1}{1+r}$ and the. value can be calculated as $V = \dfrac{E(D)}{r}$. If you substitute this value of V in the equation for P and solve, then you get $P = \dfrac{E(D)}{r}$. So, effectively, the value of the asset becomes the expected dividend in any period divided by the interest rate. Notice that Holt sets the expected dividend to $0.70 and the interest rate to 10% (0.10), thereby yielding a constant price of the share at $7.

8 For these large markets, students are paid in extra credit points rather than cash. In case you are wondering about the efficacy of this approach, I can assure you that this works quite well in providing appropriate incentives, possibly even better than cash.

9 A version of this type of short-selling is depicted in the film *Trading Places*, starring Eddie Murphy and Dan Ackroyd. It is an older film but well worth watching. In the film, Murphy and Ackroyd get to learn beforehand that a bumper orange crop will lead to a crash in orange prices, a report that was going to be delivered to the nefarious Dukes brothers who were illegally bribing an official to get their hands on the report. Murphy and Ackroyd provide a false report to the Dukes that prices will go up but, in the meantime, they short-sell orange futures. When the actual news comes out and the price crashes, they buy up those stocks cheaply and get their revenge on the Dukes, who had bet on prices being much higher.

10 Versions of this show up on Wall Street-related films all the time. A selective list includes *The Big Short*, which I mentioned above, as well as *Margin Call*, *Wall Street* and others.

11 Short-selling was possible in Europe from possibly the 16th century onward and would probably have been available as a strategy to Isaac Newton during the South Sea Bubble in the early parts of the 18th century. One wonders whether, in spite of his protestations about not being able to predict the affairs of men, Newton was astute enough to engage in some short-selling to make money out of the crash. Wikipedia suggests that Newton held approx. £22,000 in South Sea Company stock after the crash. This suggests that he probably did not benefit, since otherwise he would have sold them to turn in a profit when the crash happened. But it is not clear how much South Sea stock he held prior to the crash.

12 I should point out that I am using the term *adaptive expectations* in the way the concept was defined in the past. People currently think of adaptive expectations as adjusting one's beliefs in a specific direction to correct the prediction error of the previous period. What I am calling adaptive expectations may be better called *backward looking* or *trend-following* expectations. I have chosen to stick with the adaptive expectations nomenclature since this is what the original writers used. Discerning readers should bear the distinction in mind. When I say expectations are adaptive, I really mean expectations that are backward looking. I thank Charles Noussair for highlighting this distinction.

13 In this version of the Stroop Task, participants have to name the colour of the words they see on the screen. For example, they may see the word BLUE on the screen when it is written in the colour BLUE, or they may see it written in the colour RED. Since participants have to name the colour, they need to say "BLUE" in the former instance and they need to say "RED" in the latter. But much evidence suggests that we instinctively tend to "read" what is on the screen, rather than think about the colour it is written in. And so, the tendency to say BLUE in both cases is very strong. It takes self-control to rein in the instinct to say BLUE when the word is written in RED.

14 This is a common practice to ensure that the participants are taking the forecasting task seriously. In general, experimenters make sure that the payments for such forecasting tasks, while salient, are not very large vis-à-vis the payments for the actual experimental task. Otherwise, if the forecasting payments are very large, participants may put more effort into this and then adjust their strategies during the game to match their forecasts. Usually, such payments follow a "scoring rule". Most scoring rules reward participants according to how accurate their forecasts are and penalize participants more the further away they are from the correct answer. For example, in the Haruvy et al. study, participants earn five times more if their forecasts are within 10% of the price in the period as opposed to if they are within 50% of the actual price. Other scoring rules may reward participants based on the absolute distance between the actual price and the predicted price or the squared distance between the actual price and the predicted price.

15 While this is not directly related, it may have some tangential relation. During the early part of 2020, as the world grappled with the COVID-19 pandemic and it was clear that a recession was around the corner, prices in global stock markets continued to soar for extended periods, where these prices seemed to be completely dissociated from the underlying market fundamentals. One conjecture behind this phenomenon is that with many countries in lockdown, lots of people with nothing else to do entered the markets. Given their overall lack of familiarity, the sudden influx of these traders led to an increase in prices, since we have seen that inexperienced traders are more liable to create bubbles. Some of this must have involved night trading as well, with traders undertaking trades in far-flung parts of the world at odd hours of the day. The relevance to the work done by Dickinson and his colleagues is the finding that inexperience coupled with impaired cognitive control can result in large market bubbles. At the time of writing, this is merely a conjecture (though I hope a reasonable conjecture). For an argument along these lines, see: Fitzgerald, Maggie, "Penny stock-loving Robinhood traders raised bubble concerns, but most retail investors are selling". CNBC.com. June 25, 2020. www.cnbc.com/2020/06/25/penny-stock-loving-robinhood-traders-raised-bubble-concerns-but-most-retail-investors-are-selling.html.

References

Abadie, A., & Gay, S. (2006). The impact of presumed consent legislation on cadaveric organ donation: a cross-country study. *Journal of Health Economics*, *25*(4), 599–620.

Akerlof, G. A. (1982). Labor contracts as partial gift exchange. *Quarterly Journal of Economics*, *97*(4), 543–569.

Allais, M. (1953). Le comportement de l'homme rationnel devant le risque: Critique des postulats et axiomes de l'école Américaine. *Econometrica*, *21*(4), 503–546.

Almas, I., Cappelen, A., Sorensen, E., & Tunggoden, B. (2019, November 25–26). Fairness across the world: Preferences and beliefs [Keynote presentation]. Australia New Zealand Workshop in Experimental Economics, Monash University, Clayton, Victoria, Australia.

Anderson, C. M., & Putterman, L. (2006). Do non-strategic sanctions obey the law of demand? The demand for punishment in the voluntary contribution mechanism. *Games and Economic Behavior*, *54*(1), 1–24.

Andreoni, J. (1988). Why free ride? Strategies and learning in public goods experiments. *Journal of Public Economics*, *37*(3), 291–304.

Andreoni, J. (1990). Impure altruism and donations to public goods: A theory of warm-glow giving. *Economic Journal*, *100*(401), 464–477.

Andreoni, J. (1995a). Cooperation in public-goods experiments: Kindness or confusion? *American Economic Review*, *85*(4), 891–904.

Andreoni, J. (1995b). Warm-glow versus cold-prickle: The effects of positive and negative framing on cooperation in experiments. *Quarterly Journal of Economics*, *110*(1), 1–21.

Andreoni, J., & Croson, R. (2008). Partners versus strangers: Random rematching in public goods experiments. In C. R. Plott & V. L. Smith (Eds.), *Handbook of Experimental Economics Results* (Vol. 1, pp. 776–783). North-Holland.

Andreoni, J., & Petrie, R. (2004). Public goods experiments without confidentiality: A glimpse into fund-raising. *Journal of Public Economics*, *88*(7–8), 1605–1623.

Ariely, D. (2008). *Predictably Irrational*. HarperCollins.

Asch, S. E. (1951). Effects of group pressure upon the modification and distortion of judgments. In H. Guetzkow (Ed.), *Groups, Leadership and Men: Research in Human Relations* (pp. 177–190). Carnegie Press.

Asch, S. E. (1956). Studies of independence and conformity: I. A minority of one against a unanimous majority. *Psychological Monographs: General and Applied*, *70*(9), 1–70.

Ashraf, N., Bohnet, I., & Piankov, N. (2006). Decomposing trust and trustworthiness. *Experimental Economics*, *9*(3), 193–208.

Ashraf, N., Karlan, D., & Yin, W. (2006). Tying Odysseus to the mast: Evidence from a commitment savings product in the Philippines. *Quarterly Journal of Economics*, *121*(2), 635–672.

Axelrod, R. (1980). Effective choice in the prisoner's dilemma. *Journal of Conflict Resolution*, *24*(1), 3–25.

Axelrod, R. (1984). *The Evolution of Cooperation*. Basic Books.

Axelrod, R. (1986). An evolutionary approach to norms. *American Political Science Review*, *80*(4), 1095–1111.

References

Axelrod, R. (1997). *The Complexity of Cooperation: Agent-based Models of Competition and Collaboration.* Princeton University Press.

Axelrod, R., & Hamilton, W. D. (1981). The evolution of cooperation. *Science, 211*(4489), 1390–1396.

Banerjee, A. V., & Duflo, E. (2011). *Poor Economics: A Radical Rethinking of the Way to Fight Global Poverty.* PublicAffairs.

Barber, B. M., & Odean, T. (2000). Trading is hazardous to your wealth: The common stock investment performance of individual investors. *Journal of Finance, 55*(2), 773–806.

Barber, B. M., & Odean, T. (2001). Boys will be boys: Gender, overconfidence, and common stock investment. *Quarterly Journal of Economics, 116*(1), 261–292.

Bardsley, N., & Sausgruber, R. (2005). Conformity and reciprocity in public good provision. *Journal of Economic Psychology, 26*(5), 664–681.

Baron, J. N., Hannan, M. T., & Burton, M. D. (2001). Labor pains: Change in organizational models and employee turnover in young, high-tech firms. *American Journal of Sociology, 106*(4), 960–1012.

Baumeister, R. F., Bratslavsky, E., Muraven, M., & Tice, D. M. (1998). Ego depletion: Is the active self a limited resource? *Journal of Personality and Social Psychology, 74*(5), 1252–1265.

Bayes, T. (1763). An essay towards solving a problem in the doctrine of chances. *Philosophical Transactions of the Royal Society of London, 53,* 370–418.

Bazerman, M. H., & Moore, D. A. (2012). *Judgment in Managerial Decision Making* (8th ed.). Wiley Global Education.

Ben-David, I., Graham, J. R., & Harvey. C. R. (2013). Managerial miscalibration. *Quarterly Journal of Economics, 128*(4), 1547–1584.

Bentham, J. [1789] 2009. *An Introduction to the Principles of Morals and Legislation* (Dover Philosophical Classics). Dover.

Berg, J., Dickhaut, J., & McCabe, K. (1995). Trust, reciprocity, and social history. *Games and Economic Behavior, 10*(1), 122–142.

Bernoulli, D. (1954). Exposition of a new theory on the measurement of risk (L. Sommer, Trans.). *Econometrica, 22*(1), 23–36. (Original work published 1738.)

Bertrand, M., & Mullainathan, S. (2004). Are Emily and Greg more employable than Lakisha and Jamal? A field experiment on labor market discrimination. *American Economic Review, 94*(4), 991–1013.

Bewley, T. (1999). *Why Wages Don't Fall During a Recession.* Harvard University Press.

Bewley, T. (2005). Fairness, reciprocity and wage rigidity. In H. Gintis, S. Bowles, R. Boyd, & E. Fehr (Eds.), *Moral Sentiments and Material Interests: The Foundations of Cooperation in Economic Life* (pp. 303–338). MIT Press.

Blount, S. (1995). When social outcomes aren't fair: The effect of causal attributions on preferences. *Organizational Behavior and Human Decision Processes, 63*(2), 131–144.

Blume, A., & Ortmann, A. (2007). The effects of costless pre-play communication: Experimental evidence from games with Pareto-ranked equilibria. *Journal of Economic Theory, 132*(1), 274–290.

Bochet, O., & Putterman, L. (2009). Not just babble: Opening the black box of communication in a voluntary contribution experiment. *European Economic Review, 53*(3), 309–326.

Bochet, O., Page, T., & Putterman, L. (2006). Communication and punishment in voluntary contribution experiments. *Journal of Economic Behavior & Organization, 60*(1), 11–26.

Bohnet, I. (2016). *What Works: Gender Equality by Design.* Harvard University Press.

Bohnet, I., & Zeckhauser, R. (2004a). Social comparisons in ultimatum bargaining. *Scandinavian Journal of Economics, 106*(3), 495–510.

Bohnet, I., & Zeckhauser, R. (2004b). Trust, risk and betrayal. *Journal of Economic Behavior & Organization, 55*(4), 467–484.

Bolton, G. E., & Zwick, R. (1995). Anonymity versus punishment in ultimatum bargaining. *Games and Economic Behavior, 10*(1), 95–121.

Bolton, G. E., & Ockenfels, A. (2000). ERC: A theory of equity, reciprocity, and competition. *American Economic Review, 90*(1), 166–193.

Bolton, G. E., Brandts, J., & Ockenfels, A. (2005). Fair procedures: Evidence from games involving lotteries. *Economic Journal*, 115(506), 1054–1076.

Bostian, A. J., Goeree, J., & Holt, C. A. (2005). Price bubbles in asset market experiments with a flat fundamental value. In Draft for the Experimental Finance Conference, Federal Reserve Bank of Atlanta September, 23: 2005.

Bostian, A. J., & Holt, C. A. (2009). Price bubbles with discounting: A web-based classroom experiment. *Journal of Economic Education*, 40(1), 27–37.

Bowles, S., & Gintis, H. (2002). Homo reciprocans. *Nature*, 415(6868), 125–127.

Boyd, R., & Richerson, P. J. (1985). *Culture and the Evolutionary Process*. University of Chicago Press.

Brandts, J., & Charness, G. (2000). Hot vs. cold: Sequential responses and preference stability in experimental games. *Experimental Economics*, 2(3), 227–238.

Brandts, J., & Cooper, D. J. (2006). A change would do you good ... An experimental study on how to overcome coordination failure in organizations. *American Economic Review*, 96(3), 669–693.

Brandts, J., & Cooper, D. J. (2007). It's what you say, not what you pay: An experimental study of manager–employee relationships in overcoming coordination failure. *Journal of the European Economic Association*, 5(6), 1223–1268.

Brandts, J., & MacLeod, W. B. (1995). Equilibrium selection in experimental games with recommended play. *Games and Economic Behavior*, 11(1), 36–63.

Brandts, J., Saijo, T., & Schram, A. (2004). How universal is behavior? A four country comparison of spite and cooperation in voluntary contribution mechanisms. *Public Choice*, 119(3–4), 381–424.

Breiman, L. (1996). Bagging predictors. *Machine Learning*, 24(2), 123–140.

Brosnan, S. F., & de Waal, F. B. (2003). Monkeys reject unequal pay. *Nature*, 425(6955), 297–299.

Bryan, J. H., & Test, M. A. (1967). Models and helping: Naturalistic studies in aiding behavior. *Journal of Personality and Social Psychology*, 6(4, Pt.1), 400–407.

Burlando, R., & Hey, J. D. (1997). Do Anglo-Saxons free-ride more? *Journal of Public Economics*, 64(1), 41–60.

Camerer, C. (2015). The promise and success of lab-field generalizability in experimental economics: A critical reply to Levitt and List. In A. Schotter & G. Fréchette (Eds.), *Handbook of Experimental Economic Methodology* (Chapter 14, pp. 249-295). Oxford University Press.

Camerer, C. F. (2003). *Behavioral Game Theory: Experiments in Strategic Interaction*. Princeton University Press.

Camerer, C., & Weber, R. (2008). Growing organizational culture in the laboratory. In V. Smith & C. Plott (Eds.), *Handbook of Experimental Economics Results* (pp. 903–907). Elsevier.

Camerer, C., & Weigelt, K. (1988). Experimental tests of a sequential equilibrium reputation model. *Econometrica*, 56(1), 1–36.

Cameron, L. A. (1999). Raising the stakes in the ultimatum game: Experimental evidence from Indonesia. *Economic Inquiry*, 37(1), 47–59.

Card, D., & Krueger, A. B. (1994). Minimum wages and employment: A case study of the fast food industry in New Jersey and Pennsylvania. *American Economic Review*, 84(4), 772–793.

Cardenas, J. C., Stranlund, J., & Willis, C. (2002). Economic inequality and burden-sharing in the provision of local environmental quality. *Ecological Economics*, 40(3), 379–395.

Carpenter, J. P. (2004). When in Rome: Conformity and the provision of public goods. *Journal of Socio-Economics*, 33(4), 395–408.

Carpenter, J. P. (2007a). Punishing free-riders: How group size affects mutual monitoring and the provision of public goods. *Games and Economic Behavior*, 60(1), 31–51.

Carpenter, J. P. (2007b). The demand for punishment. *Journal of Economic Behavior & Organization*, 62(4), 522–542.

Carpenter, J. P., Harrison, G. W., & List, J. A. (Eds.). (2005). *Field Experiments in Economics*. JAI Press.

Chamberlin, E. H. (1948). An experimental imperfect market. *Journal of Political Economy*, 56(2), 95–108.

Chandor, J. C. (Director). (2011). *Margin Call* [Film]. Before the Door Pictures.

Charness, G., & Rabin, M. (2002). Understanding social preferences with simple tests. *Quarterly Journal of Economics*, 117(3), 817–869.

References

Charness, G., & Yang, C. Endogenous group formation and public goods provision: Exclusion, exit, mergers, and redemption. Available at SSRN: https://ssrn.com/abstract=932251 or http://dx.doi.org/10.2139/ssrn.932251.

Chaudhuri, A. (2009). *Experiments in Economics: Playing Fair with Money*. Routledge.

Chaudhuri, A. (2011). Sustaining cooperation in laboratory public goods experiments: A selective survey of the literature. *Experimental Economics, 14*(1), 47–83.

Chaudhuri, A. (2013). "Experimental economics" in the *Encyclopaedia of Life Support Systems* (EOLSS; http://eolss.net), UNESCO, New York, NY.

Chaudhuri, A. (2018). Belief heterogeneity and the restart effect in a public goods game. *Games, 9*(4), Article 96.

Chaudhuri, A. (Ed.). (2021). *Research Agenda in Experimental Economics*. Edward Elgar.

Chaudhuri, A., & Gangadharan, L. (2007). An experimental analysis of trust and trustworthiness. *Southern Economic Journal, 73*(4), 959–985.

Chaudhuri, A., & Paichayontvijit, T. (2006). Conditional cooperation and voluntary contributions to a public good. *Economics Bulletin, 3*(8), 1–14.

Chaudhuri, A., & Paichayontvijit, T. (2010). Recommended play and performance bonuses in the minimum effort coordination game. *Experimental Economics, 13*(3), 346–363.

Chaudhuri, A., & Paichayontvijit, T. (2011). Recommended play versus costly punishments in a laboratory public goods experiment. In K. G. Dastidar, H. Mukhopadhyay, & U. B. Sinha (Eds.), *Dimensions of Economic Theory and Policy: Essays for Anjan Mukherji* (pp. 282–298). Oxford University Press.

Chaudhuri, A., & Paichayontvijit, T. (2017). On the long-run efficacy of punishments and recommendations in a laboratory public goods game. *Scientific Reports, 7*(1), 1–8.

Chaudhuri, A., Ali Khan, S., Lakshmiratan, A., Py, A. L., & Shah, L. (2003). Trust and trustworthiness in a sequential bargaining game. *Journal of Behavioral Decision Making, 16*(5), 331–340.

Chaudhuri, A., Cruickshank, A., & Sbai, E. (2015). Gender differences in personnel management: Some experimental evidence. *Journal of Behavioral and Experimental Economics, 58*, 20–32.

Chaudhuri, A., Graziano, S., & Maitra, P. (2006). Social learning and norms in a public goods experiment with inter-generational advice. *Review of Economic Studies, 73*(2), 357–380.

Chaudhuri, A., Li, Y., & Paichayontvijit, T. (2016). What's in a frame? Goal framing, trust and reciprocity. *Journal of Economic Psychology, 57*, 117–135.

Chaudhuri, A., Paichayontvijit, T., & Smith, A. (2017). Belief heterogeneity and contributions decay among conditional cooperators in public goods games. *Journal of Economic Psychology, 58*, 15–30.

Chaudhuri, A., Schotter, A., & Sopher, B. (2009). Talking ourselves to efficiency: Coordination in inter-generational minimum effort games with private, almost common and common knowledge of advice. *Economic Journal, 119*(534), 91–122.

Chaudhuri, A., Sopher, B., & Strand, P. (2002). Cooperation in social dilemmas, trust and reciprocity. *Journal of Economic Psychology, 23*(2), 231–249.

Chwe, M.-S. (2001) *Rational Ritual: Culture, Coordination, and Common Knowledge*. Princeton University Press.

Cinyabuguma, M., Page, T., & Putterman, L. (2005). Cooperation under the threat of expulsion in a public goods experiment. *Journal of Public Economics, 89*(8), 1421–1435.

Cinyabuguma, M., Page, T., & Putterman, L. (2006). Can second-order punishment deter perverse punishment? *Experimental Economics, 9*(3), 265–279.

Claessens, S., Fischer, K., Chaudhuri, A., Sibley, C. G., & Atkinson, Q. D. (2020a). The dual evolutionary foundations of political ideology. *Nature Human Behaviour, 4*, 336–345. https://doi.org/10.1038/s41562-020-0850-9.

Claessens, S., Sibley, C., Chaudhuri, A., & Atkinson, Q. (2020b). Cooperative phenotype predicts economic conservatism, policy views, and political party support. PsyArXive preprints. https://psyarxiv.com/t7rqb/

Clark, K., & Sefton, M. (2001). Repetition and signalling: Experimental evidence from games with efficient equilibria. *Economics Letters, 70*(3), 357–362.

Cohan, W. D. (2009). *House of Cards: A Tale of Hubris and Wretched Excess on Wall Street*. Doubleday.
Cohen, L. and Robinson, S. (1988). "Everybody knows". Album: *I'm Your Man*. Columbia Records.
Cookson, R. (2000). Framing effects in public goods experiments. *Experimental Economics*, 3(1), 55–79.
Cooper, D. J. (2006). Are experienced managers experts at overcoming coordination failure? *B.E. Journal of Economic Analysis & Policy*, 6(2), Article 6. www.bepress.com/bejeap/advances/vol6/iss2/art6.
Cooper, D. J., & Kagel, J. H. (2003). The impact of meaningful context on strategic play in signaling games. *Journal of Economic Behavior & Organization*, 50(3), 311–337.
Cooper, D., & Kagel, J. (2015). Other regarding preferences: A survey of experimental results. In J. H. Kagel & A. E. Roth (Eds.), *The Handbook of Experimental Economics* (Vol. 2, pp. 217–289). Princeton University Press.
Cooper, R., DeJong, D. V., Forsythe, R., & Ross, T. W. (1989). Communication in the battle of the sexes game: Some experimental results. *RAND Journal of Economics*, 20(4), 568–587.
Cooper, R., DeJong, D. V., Forsythe, R., & Ross, T. W. (1992). Communication in coordination games. *Quarterly Journal of Economics*, 107(2), 739–771.
Cooper, R. W. (1999). *Coordination Games: Complementarities and Macroeconomics*. Cambridge University Press.
Cooper, R. W., DeJong, D. V., Forsythe, R., & Ross, T. W. (1990). Selection criteria in coordination games: Some experimental results. *American Economic Review*, 80(1), 218–233.
Cox, J. C. (2004). How to identify trust and reciprocity. *Games and Economic Behavior*, 46(2), 260–281.
Cronk, L. (2007). The influence of cultural framing on play in the trust game: A Maasai example. *Evolution and Human Behavior*, 28(5), 352–358.
Croson, R. (2000). Thinking like a game theorist: Factors affecting the frequency of equilibrium play. *Journal of Economic Behavior & Organization*, 41(3), 299–314.
Croson, R. (2007). Theories of commitment, altruism and reciprocity: Evidence from linear public goods games. *Economic Inquiry*, 45(2), 199–216.
Damásio, A. (1994). *Descartes' Error: Emotion, Reason, and the Human Brain*. Putnam; Harper Perennial; Penguin.
Davis, D. D., & Holt, C. A. (1992). *Experimental Economics*. Princeton University Press.
Davis, D., & Holt, C. (2008). The exercise of market power in laboratory experiments. In C. R. Plott & V. L. Smith (Eds.), *Handbook of Experimental Economics Results* (Vol. 1, pp. 138–145). North-Holland.
Dawes, R. M. (1980). Social dilemmas. *Annual Review of Psychology*, 31(1), 169–193.
Dawes, R. M., & Thaler, R. H. (1988). Anomalies: Cooperation. *Journal of Economic Perspectives*, 2(3), 187–197.
Dawes, R. M., McTavish, J., & Shaklee, H. (1977). Behavior, communication, and assumptions about other people's behavior in a commons dilemma situation. *Journal of Personality and Social Psychology*, 35(1), 1–11.
Dawes, R. M., Orbell, J. M., Simmons, R. T., & Van De Kragt, A. J. (1986). Organizing groups for collective action. *American Political Science Review*, 80(4), 1171–1185.
Dawkins, R. (1976). *The Selfish Gene*. Oxford University Press.
Day, R. H., & Knuth, H. (1981). The contributions of F. C. Müller-Lyer. *Perception*, 10(2), 126–146.
Dell'Antonia, K. J. (2018, August 18). Happy children do chores. *New York Times*. www.nytimes.com /2018/08/18/opinion/sunday/children-chores-parenting.html
Denant-Boemont, L., Masclet, D., & Noussair, C. N. (2007). Punishment, counterpunishment and sanction enforcement in a social dilemma experiment. *Economic Theory*, 33(1), 145–167.
de Oliveira, A., Croson, R., & Eckel, C. (2015). One bad apple? Heterogeneity and information in public good provision. *Experimental Economics*, 18(1), 116–135.
De Palma, B. (Director). (1983). *Scarface* [Film]. Universal Pictures.
de Quervain, D. J. F., Fischbacher, U., Treyer, V., Schallhammer, M., Schnyder, U., Buck, A., & Fehr, E. (2004). The neural basis of altruistic punishment. *Science*, 305(5688), 1254–1258.
Diamond, D. W., & Dybvig, P. H. (1983). Bank runs, deposit insurance, and liquidity. *Journal of Political Economy*, 91(3), 401–419.

References

Diamond, J. M. (2005). *Collapse: How Societies Choose to Fail or Succeed*. Viking Press.

Dickinson, D. L., Chaudhuri, A., & Greenaway-McGrevy, R. (2019). Trading while sleepy? Circadian mismatch and mispricing in a global experimental asset market. *Experimental Economics*, 23(2), 526–553.

Donne, J., & Savage, E. (1975). *John Donne's Devotions upon emergent occasions: A critical edition with introduction & commentary*. Salzburg: Institut für Englische Sprache und Literatur, Universität Salzburg.

Dufwenberg, M., & Kirchsteiger, G. (2004). A theory of sequential reciprocity. *Games and Economic Behavior*, 47(2), 268–298.

Dufwenberg, M., Gächter, S., & Hennig-Schmidt, H. (2011). The framing of games and the psychology of play. *Games and Economic Behavior*, 73(2), 459–478.

Eckel, C. C., & Wilson, R. K. (2004). Is trust a risky decision? *Journal of Economic Behavior & Organization*, 55(4), 447–465.

Egas, M., & Riedl, A. (2008). The economics of altruistic punishment and the maintenance of cooperation. *Proceedings of the Royal Society B: Biological Sciences*, 275(1637), 871–878.

Ehrhart, K.-M., & Keser, C. (1999). Cooperation and mobility: On the run. Working Paper, CIRANO and University of Karlsruhe.

Emerson, R. W. (1911). *Essays (first, second and third series)*. Ward Lock.

Ephron, N. (Director). (1993). *Sleepless in Seattle* [Film]. TriStar Pictures.

Ertan, A., Page, T., & Putterman, L. (2009). Who to punish? Individual decisions and majority rule in mitigating the free rider problem. *European Economic Review*, 53(5), 495–511.

Falk, A., & Fischbacher, U. (2006). A theory of reciprocity. *Games and Economic Behavior*, 54(2), 293–315.

Falk, A., Fehr, E., & Fischbacher, U. (2003a). On the nature of fair behavior. *Economic Inquiry*, 41(1), 20–26.

Falk, A., Fehr, E., & Fischbacher, U. (2003b). Reasons for conflict: Lessons from bargaining experiments. *Journal of Institutional and Theoretical Economics*, 159(1), 171–187.

Falk, A., Fehr, E., & Fischbacher, U. (2005). Driving forces behind informal sanctions. *Econometrica*, 73(6), 2017–2030.

Fama, E. F. (1970). Efficient capital markets: A review of theory and empirical work. *Journal of Finance*, 25(2), 383–417.

Fathi, M., Bateson, M., & Nettle, D. (2014). Effects of watching eyes and norm cues on charitable giving in a surreptitious behavioral experiment. *Evolutionary Psychology*, 12(5), 878–887.

Fehr, E., & Fischbacher, U. (2002). Why social preferences matter: The impact of non-selfish motives on competition, cooperation and incentives. *Economic Journal*, 112(478), C1–C33.

Fehr, E., & Fischbacher, U. (2004a). Social norms and human cooperation. *Trends in Cognitive Sciences*, 8(4), 185–190.

Fehr, E., & Fischbacher, U. (2004b). Third-party punishment and social norms. *Evolution and Human Behavior*, 25(2), 63–87.

Fehr, E., & Fischbacher, U. (2005a). Altruists with green beards. *Analyse & Kritik*, 27(1), 73–84.

Fehr, E., & Fischbacher, U. (2005b). Human altruism: Proximate patterns and evolutionary origins. *Analyse & Kritik*, 27(1), 6–47.

Fehr, E., & Gächter, S. (1998). Reciprocity and economics: The economic implications of homo reciprocans. *European Economic Review*, 42(3–5), 845–859.

Fehr, E., & Gächter, S. (2000). Cooperation and punishment in public goods experiments. *American Economic Review*, 90(4), 980–994.

Fehr, E., & Gächter, S. (2002a). Altruistic punishment in humans. *Nature*, 415(6868), 137–140.

Fehr, E., & Gächter, S. (2002b). Do incentive contracts undermine voluntary cooperation? (April 2002). Zurich IEER Working Paper No. 34, Available at SSRN: https://ssrn.com/abstract=313028 or http://dx.doi.org/10.2139/ssrn.313028.

Fehr, E., & List, J. A. (2004). The hidden costs and returns of incentives – Trust and trustworthiness among CEOs. *Journal of the European Economic Association*, 2(5), 743–771.

Fehr, E., & Rockenbach, B. (2003). Detrimental effects of sanctions on human altruism. *Nature*, *422*(6928), 137–140.

Fehr, E., & Rockenbach, B. (2004). Human altruism: Economic, neural, and evolutionary perspectives. *Current Opinion in Neurobiology*, *14*(6), 784–790.

Fehr, E., & Schmidt, K. M. (1999). A theory of fairness, competition, and cooperation. *Quarterly Journal of Economics*, *114*(3), 817–868.

Fehr, E., Fischbacher, U., & Gächter, S. (2002). Strong reciprocity, human cooperation, and the enforcement of social norms. *Human Nature*, *13*(1), 1–25.

Fehr, E., Gächter, S., & Kirchsteiger, G. (1997). Reciprocity as a contract enforcement device: Experimental evidence. *Econometrica*, *65*(4), 833–860.

Fehr, E., Kirchler, E., Weichbold, A., & Gächter, S. (1998). When social norms overpower competition: Gift exchange in experimental labor markets. *Journal of Labor Economics*, *16*(2), 324–351.

Fehr, E., Kirchsteiger, G., & Riedl, A. (1993). Does fairness prevent market clearing? An experimental investigation. *Quarterly Journal of Economics*, *108*(2), 437–459.

Fehr, E., Kirchsteiger, G., & Riedl, A. (1996). Involuntary unemployment and non-compensating wage differentials in an experimental labour market. *Economic Journal*, *106*(434), 106–121.

Fehr, E., Kirchsteiger, G., & Riedl, A. (1998). Gift exchange and reciprocity in competitive experimental markets. *European Economic Review*, *42*(1), 1–34.

Fehr, E., Klein, A., & Schmidt, K. M. (2007). Fairness and contract design. *Econometrica*, *75*(1), 121–154.

Fiorina, M. P., & Plott, C. R. (1978). Committee decisions under majority rule: An experimental study. *American Political Science Review*, *72*(2), 575–598.

Fischbacher, U., & Gächter, S. (2010). Social preferences, beliefs, and the dynamics of free riding in public goods experiments. *American Economic Review*, *100*(1), 541–556.

Fischbacher, U., Gächter, S., & Fehr, E. (2001). Are people conditionally cooperative? Evidence from a public goods experiment. *Economics Letters*, *71*(3), 397–404.

Fischbacher, U., Gächter, S., & Quercia, S. (2012). The behavioral validity of the strategy method in public good experiments. *Journal of Economic Psychology*, *33*(4), 897–913.

Fischhoff, B. (1975). Hindsight is not equal to foresight: The effect of outcome knowledge on judgment under uncertainty. *Journal of Experimental Psychology: Human Perception and Performance*, *1*(3), 288–299.

Flood, M. M. (1958). Some experimental games. *Management Science*, *5*(1), 5–26.

Ford, J. (Director). (1941). *How Green Was My Valley* [Film]. 20th Century Fox.

Forsythe, R., Horowitz, J. L., Savin, N. E., & Sefton, M. (1994). Fairness in simple bargaining experiments. *Games and Economic Behavior*, *6*(3), 347–369.

Franciosi, R., Kujal, P., Michelitsch, R., Smith, V., & Deng, G. (1995). Fairness: Effect on temporary and equilibrium prices in posted-offer markets. *Economic Journal*, *105*(431), 938–950.

Frank, R. H. (1985). *Choosing the Right Pond: Human Behavior and the Quest for Status*. Oxford University Press.

Frank, R. H. (1999). *Luxury Fever: Money and Happiness in an Era of Excess*. Free Press.

Frank, R. H. (2005). Does absolute income matter? In L. Bruni & P. L. Porta (Eds.), *Economics and Happiness: Framing the Analysis* (pp. 65–90). Oxford University Press.

Frank, R. H. (2007). *The Economic Naturalist: In Search of Explanations for Everyday Enigmas*. Basic Books.

Frederick, S. (2005). Cognitive reflection and decision making. *Journal of Economic Perspectives*, *19*(4), 25–42.

Frey, B. S. (1997). *Not Just for the Money: An Economic Theory of Personal Motivation*. Edward Elgar.

Frey, B. S., & Meier, S. (2004). Social comparisons and pro-social behavior: Testing 'conditional cooperation' in a field experiment. *American Economic Review*, *94*(5), 1717–1722.

Frey, B. S., & Oberholzer-Gee, F. (1997). The cost of price incentives: An empirical analysis of motivation crowding-out. *American Economic Review*, *87*(4), 746–755.

Frey, B. S., & Torgler, B. (2007). Tax morale and conditional cooperation. *Journal of Comparative Economics*, *35*(1), 136–159.

References

Friedman, D., & Sunder, S. (1994). *Experimental Methods: A Primer for Economists*. Cambridge University Press.
Friedman, M. (1953). The methodology of positive economics. In M. Friedman (Ed.), *Essays in Positive Economics* (pp. 3–43). Chicago University Press.
Fukuyama, F. (1995). *Trust: The Social Virtues and the Creation of Prosperity*. Free Press.
Gächter, S. (2007). Conditional cooperation. Behavioral regularities from the lab and the field and their policy implications. In B. S. Frey & A. Stutzer (Eds.), CESifo seminar series. *Economics and Psychology: A Promising New Cross-disciplinary Field* (pp. 19–50). MIT Press.
Gächter, S., & Fehr, E. (1999). Collective action as a social exchange. *Journal of Economic Behavior & Organization, 39*(4), 341–369.
Gächter, S., & Herrmann, B. (2009). Reciprocity, culture and human cooperation: Previous insights and a new cross-cultural experiment. *Philosophical Transactions of the Royal Society B: Biological Sciences, 364*(1518), 791–806.
Gächter, S., & Herrmann, B. (2011). The limits of self-governance when cooperators get punished: Experimental evidence from urban and rural Russia. *European Economic Review, 55*(2), 193–210.
Gächter, S., & Thöni, C. (2005). Social learning and voluntary cooperation among like-minded people. *Journal of the European Economic Association, 3*(2–3), 303–314.
Gächter, S., & Thöni, C. (2007). Rationality and commitment in voluntary cooperation: Insights from experimental economics. In P. Fabienne & H. B. Schmidt (Eds.), *Rationality and Commitment* (pp. 175–208). Oxford University Press.
Gächter, S., Herrmann, B., & Thöni, C. (2004). Trust, voluntary cooperation, and socio-economic background: Survey and experimental evidence. *Journal of Economic Behavior & Organization, 55*(4), 505–531.
Gächter, S., Renner, E., & Sefton, M. (2008). The long-run benefits of punishment. *Science, 322*(5907), 1510.
Galton, F. (1886). Regression towards mediocrity in hereditary stature. *Journal of the Anthropological Institute of Great Britain and Ireland, 15*, 246–263.
Geisel, Theodore (Dr Seuss). (1990). *Oh, the Places You'll Go!* Random House.
Gigerenzer, G. (1996). On narrow norms and vague heuristics: A reply to Kahneman and Tversky. *Psychological Review, 103*(3), 592–596.
Gigerenzer, G. (2007). *Gut Feelings: The Intelligence of the Unconscious*. Viking Books.
Gigerenzer, G. (2013). *Risk Savvy: How to Make Good Decisions*. Penguin Books.
Gigerenzer, G., Todd, P. M., & The ABC Research Group. (1999). Fast and frugal heuristics: The adaptive toolbox. In *Simple Heuristics That Make Us Smart* (pp. 3–34). Oxford University Press.
Gilovich, T., Vallone, R., & Tversky, A. (1985). The hot hand in basketball: On the misperception of random sequences. *Cognitive Psychology, 17*(3), 295–314.
Gintis, H., Bowles, S., Boyd, R., & Fehr, E. (Eds.). (2004). *Moral Sentiments and Material Interests: The Foundations of Cooperation in Economic Life*. MIT Press.
Gladwell, M. (2005). *Blink: The Power of Thinking Without Thinking*. Little, Brown.
Glimcher, P. (2003). *Decisions, Uncertainty, and the Brain: The Science of Neuroeconomics*. MIT Press.
Glimcher, P. (2010). *Foundations of Neuroeconomic Analysis*. Oxford University Press.
Gneezy, U., & Rustichini, A. (2000a). A fine is a price. *Journal of Legal Studies, 29*(1), 1–17.
Gneezy, U., & Rustichini, A. (2000b). Pay enough or don't pay at all. *Quarterly Journal of Economics, 115*(3), 791–810.
Gneezy, U., Güth, W., & Verboven, F. (2000). Presents or investments? An experimental analysis. *Journal of Economic Psychology, 21*(5), 481–493.
Goeree, J. K., & Holt, C. A. (2001). Ten little treasures of game theory and ten intuitive contradictions. *American Economic Review, 91*(5), 1402–1422.
Goldstein, D. G., & Gigerenzer, G. (2002). Models of ecological rationality: The recognition heuristic. *Psychological Review, 109*(1), 75–90.

Guala F. (2012). Reciprocity: Weak or strong? What punishment experiments do (and do not) demonstrate. *Behavioral and Brain Sciences, 35*(1), 1–15. doi: 10.1017/S0140525X11000069. PMID: 22289303.

Gunnthorsdottir, A., Houser, D., & McCabe, K. (2007). Disposition, history and contributions in public goods experiments. *Journal of Economic Behavior & Organization, 62*(2), 304–315.

Gürerk, Ö., Irlenbusch, B., & Rockenbach, B. (2006). The competitive advantage of sanctioning institutions. *Science, 312*(5770), 108–111.

Güth, W., Schmittberger, R., & Schwarze, B. (1982). An experimental analysis of ultimatum bargaining. *Journal of Economic Behavior & Organization, 3*(4), 367–388.

Hamilton, W. D. (1964). The genetical evolution of social behaviour. *Journal of Theoretical Biology, 7*(1), 1–52.

Hannan, M. T., Burton, M. D., & Baron, J. N. (1996). Inertia and change in the early years: Employment relations in young, high technology firms. *Industrial and Corporate Change, 5*(2), 503–536.

Harding, S. (Ed.). (1975). *Can Theories be Refuted? Essays on the Duhem-Quine Thesis* (Vol. 81). Springer Science & Business Media.

Harford, T. (2005). *The Undercover Economist*. Little, Brown.

Harrison, G. W., & List, J. A. (2004). Field experiments. *Journal of Economic Literature, 42*(4), 1009–1055.

Harsanyi, J. C. (1953). Cardinal utility in welfare economics and in the theory of risk-taking. *Journal of Political Economy, 61*(5), 434–435.

Harsanyi, J. C. (1955). Cardinal welfare, individualistic ethics, and interpersonal comparisons of utility. *Journal of Political Economy, 63*(4), 309–321.

Harsanyi, J. C. (1962). Bargaining in ignorance of the opponent's utility function. *Journal of Conflict Resolution, 6*(1), 29–38.

Harsanyi, J. C. (1967). Games with incomplete information played by "Bayesian" players, I–III Part I. The basic model. *Management Science, 14*(3), 159–182.

Haruvy, E., Lahav, Y., & Noussair, C. N. (2007). Traders' expectations in asset markets: Experimental evidence. *American Economic Review, 97*(5), 1901–1920.

Heller, J. (1961). *Catch-22*. Simon & Schuster.

Henrich, J. (2000). Does culture matter in economic behavior? Ultimatum game bargaining among the Machiguenga of the Peruvian Amazon. *American Economic Review, 90*(4), 973–979.

Henrich, J., & Boyd, R. (2001). Why people punish defectors: Weak conformist transmission can stabilize costly enforcement of norms in cooperative dilemmas. *Journal of Theoretical Biology, 208*(1), 79–89.

Henrich, J., Heine, S. J., & Norenzayan, A. (2010). Most people are not WEIRD. *Nature, 466*(7302), 29.

Henrich, J. P., Boyd, R., Bowles, S., Camerer, C., Fehr, E., & Gintis, H. (Eds.). (2004). *Foundations of Human Sociality: Economic Experiments and Ethnographic Evidence from Fifteen Small-scale Societies*. Oxford University Press.

Henry, O. (1992). *The Gift of the Magi and Other Short Stories*. Dover.

Herrmann, B., Thöni, C., & Gächter, S. (2008). Antisocial punishment across societies. *Science, 319*(5868), 1362–1367.

Hoffman, E., McCabe, K., Shachat, K., & Smith, V. (1994). Preferences, property rights, and anonymity in bargaining games. *Games and Economic Behavior, 7*(3), 346–380.

Hoffman, E., McCabe, K. A., & Smith, V. L. (1996a). On expectations and the monetary stakes in ultimatum games. *International Journal of Game Theory, 25*(3), 289–301.

Hoffman, E., McCabe, K., & Smith, V. L. (1996b). Social distance and other-regarding behavior in dictator games. *American Economic Review, 86*(3), 653–660.

Holt, C. A. (1995). Industrial organization: A survey of laboratory research. In J. Kagel & A. E. Roth (Eds.), *Handbook of Experimental Economics* (pp. 349–443). Princeton University Press.

Homans, G. C. (1954). The cash posters: A study of a group of working girls. *American Sociological Review, 19*(6), 724–733.

References

Homer (1996). *The Odyssey* (R. Fagles, Trans.). Penguin Classics.

Houser, D., & Kurzban, R. (2002). Revisiting kindness and confusion in public goods experiments. *American Economic Review*, 92(4), 1062–1069.

Howard, R. (Director). (2001). *A Beautiful Mind* [Film]. Imagine Entertainment.

Hugo, V. (1987). *Les Misérables* (L. Fahnestock, & N. MacAfee, Trans.). Signet Classics. (Original work published 1862.)

Hume, D. (1739–1740). *A Treatise of Human Nature: Being an Attempt to Introduce the Experimental Method of Reasoning into Moral Subjects*. Clarendon Press.

Hume, D. (1748). *An Inquiry Concerning Human Understanding*. J. B. Bebbington.

Hunt, G. R., Corballis, M. C., & Gray, R. D. (2001). Laterality in tool manufacture by crows. *Nature*, 414(6865), 707.

Hunt, G. R., & Gray, R. D. (2004). The crafting of hook tools by wild New Caledonian crows. *Proceedings of the Royal Society B: Biological Sciences*, 271(suppl. 3), S88–S90.

Ichniowski, C., Shaw, K., & Prennushi, G. (1997). The effects of human resource management practices on productivity: A study of steel finishing lines. *American Economic Review*, 87(3), 291–313.

Isaac, R. M., & Walker, J. M. (1988a). Communication and free-riding behavior: The voluntary contribution mechanism. *Economic Inquiry*, 26(4), 585–608.

Isaac, R. M., & Walker, J. M. (1988b). Group size effects in public goods provision: The voluntary contributions mechanism. *Quarterly Journal of Economics*, 103(1), 179–199.

Isaac, R. M., McCue, K. F., & Plott, C. R. (1985). Public goods provision in an experimental environment. *Journal of Public Economics*, 26(1), 51–74.

Isaac, R. M., Walker, J. M., & Thomas, S. H. (1984). Divergent evidence on free riding: An experimental examination of possible explanations. *Public Choice*, 43(2), 113–149.

Isaac, R. M., Walker, J. M., & Williams, A. W. (1994). Group size and the voluntary provision of public goods: Experimental evidence utilizing large groups. *Journal of Public Economics*, 54(1), 1–36.

Jensen, K., Call, J., & Tomasello, M. (2007). Chimpanzees are rational maximizers in an ultimatum game. *Science*, 318(5847), 107–109.

Johnson, N. D., & Mislin, A. A. (2011). Trust games: A meta-analysis. *Journal of Economic Psychology*, 32(5), 865–889.

Kagel, J. H., & Roth, A. E. (Eds.). (1995). *The Handbook of Experimental Economics*. Princeton University Press.

Kahneman, D. (2011). *Thinking, Fast and Slow*. Farrar, Straus and Giroux.

Kahneman, D., & Tversky, A. (1973). On the psychology of prediction. *Psychological Review*, 80(4), 237–251.

Kahneman, D., & Tversky, A. (1979). Prospect theory: An analysis of decision under risk. *Econometrica*, 47(2), 263–292.

Kahneman, D., Knetsch, J. L., & Thaler, R. H. (1986a). Fairness and the assumptions of economics. *Journal of Business*, 59(4), S285–S300.

Kahneman, D., Knetsch, J. L., & Thaler, R. (1986b). Fairness as a constraint on profit seeking: Entitlements in the market. *American Economic Review*, 76(4), 728–741.

Kahneman, D., Knetsch, J. L., & Thaler, R. H. (1990). Experimental tests of the endowment effect and the Coase theorem. *Journal of Political Economy*, 98(6), 1325–1348.

Karlan, D. S. (2005). Using experimental economics to measure social capital and predict financial decisions. *American Economic Review*, 95(5), 1688–1699.

Kelley, H. H., & Stahelski, A. J. (1970). Social interaction basis of cooperators' and competitors' beliefs about others. *Journal of Personality and Social Psychology*, 16(1), 66–91.

Keser, C., & van Winden, F. (2000). Conditional cooperation and voluntary contributions to public goods. *Scandinavian Journal of Economics*, 102(1), 23–39.

Ketcham, J., Smith, V. L., & Williams, A. W. (1984). A comparison of posted-offer and double-auction pricing institutions. *Review of Economic Studies*, 51(4), 595–614.

Keynes, J. M. (1936). *The General Theory of Employment, Interest and Money*. Palgrave Macmillan.

Kim, O., & Walker, M. (1984). The free rider problem: Experimental evidence. *Public Choice*, *43*(1), 3–24.

Knack, S., & Keefer, P. (1997). Does social capital have an economic payoff? A cross-country investigation. *Quarterly Journal of Economics*, *112*(4), 1251–1288.

Knez, M., & Camerer, C. (1994). Creating expectational assets in the laboratory: Coordination in 'weakest-link' games. *Strategic Management Journal*, *15*(S1), 101–119.

Knez, M., & Simester, D. (2001). Firm-wide incentives and mutual monitoring at Continental Airlines. *Journal of Labor Economics*, *19*(4), 743–772.

Knoch, D., Gianotti, L. R., Baumgartner, T., & Fehr, E. (2010). A neural marker of costly punishment behavior. *Psychological Science*, *21*(3), 337–342.

Knutson, B., Rick, S., Wimmer, G. E., Prelec, D., & Loewenstein, G. (2007). Neural predictors of purchases. *Neuron*, *53*(1), 147–156.

Kocher, M. G., Cherry, T., Kroll, S., Netzer, R. J., & Sutter, M. (2008). Conditional cooperation on three continents. *Economics Letters*, *101*(3), 175–178.

Kocher, M. G., Lucks, K. E., & Schindler, D. (2019). Unleashing animal spirits: Self-control and overpricing in experimental asset markets. *Review of Financial Studies*, *32*(6), 2149–2178.

Kosfeld, M., Heinrichs, M., Zak, P. J., Fischbacher, U., & Fehr, E. (2005). Oxytocin increases trust in humans. *Nature*, *435*(7042), 673–676.

Kremer, M. (1993). The O-ring theory of economic development. *Quarterly Journal of Economics*, *108*(3), 551–575.

Kreps, D. M., Milgrom, P., Roberts, J., & Wilson, R. (1982). Rational cooperation in the finitely repeated prisoners' dilemma. *Journal of Economic Theory*, *27*(2), 245–252.

Kujal, P., & Smith, V. L. (2008). Fairness and short run price adjustment in posted offer markets. In C. R. Plott & V. L. Smith (Eds.), *Handbook of Experimental Economics Results* (Vol. 1, pp. 55–61). North-Holland.

Kunreuther, H., & Easterling, D. (1990). Are risk-benefit tradeoffs possible in siting hazardous facilities? *American Economic Review*, *80*(2), 252–256.

Kunreuther, H., & Easterling, D. (1992). Gaining acceptance for noxious facilities with economic incentives. In D. W. Bromley & K. Segerson (Eds.), *The Social Response to Environmental Risk* (pp. 151–186). Springer.

Kunreuther, H., & Easterling, D. (1996). The role of compensation in siting hazardous facilities. *Journal of Policy Analysis and Management*, *15*(4), 601–622.

Kunreuther, H., Easterling, D., Desvousges, W., & Slovic, P. (1990). Public attitudes toward siting a high-level nuclear waste repository in Nevada. *Risk Analysis*, *10*(4), 469–484.

Kurzban, R., & Houser, D. (2005). Experiments investigating cooperative types in humans: A complement to evolutionary theory and simulations. *Proceedings of the National Academy of Sciences*, *102*(5), 1803–1807.

Laibson, D. (1997). Golden eggs and hyperbolic discounting. *Quarterly Journal of Economics*, *112*(2), 443–477.

Lambert, E. (2011, March 17). All the cool kids are night trading. *Forbes*. www.forbes.com/sites/emilylambert/2011/03/17/all-the-cool-kids-are-night-trading/#69cb9bcf4f6a

Landis, J. (Director). (1983). *Trading Places* [Film]. Paramount Pictures.

LaPiere, R. T. (1934). Attitudes vs. actions. *Social Forces*, *13*(2), 230–237.

LaPiere, R. T., & Farnsworth, P. R. (1936). *Social Psychology*. McGraw-Hill.

Ledyard, J. O. (1995). Public goods: Some experimental results. In J. Kagel & A. Roth (Eds.), *Handbook of Experimental Economics* (pp. 111–194). Princeton University Press.

Lei, V., Noussair, C. N., & Plott, C. R. (2001). Nonspeculative bubbles in experimental asset markets: Lack of common knowledge of rationality vs. actual irrationality. *Econometrica*, *69*(4), 831–859.

Levitt, S. D., & List, J. A. (2007a). Viewpoint: On the generalizability of lab behaviour to the field. *Canadian Journal of Economics*, *40*(2), 347–370.

Levitt, S. D., & List, J. A. (2007b). What do laboratory experiments measuring social preferences reveal about the real world? *Journal of Economic Perspectives*, *21*(2), 153–174.

References

Lewis, M. (2010a, March 1). Betting on the blind side. *Vanity Fair.* www.vanityfair.com/news/2010/04/wall-street-excerpt-201004

Lewis, M. (2010b). *The Big Short: Inside the Doomsday Machine.* W. W. Norton.

Lewis, M. (2016). *The Undoing Project: A Friendship That Changed Our Minds.* W. W. Norton.

Lipsey, R. (1979). *An Introduction to Positive Economics* (5th ed.). Weidenfeld & Nicolson.

List, J. A. (2006). The behavioralist meets the market: Measuring social preferences and reputation effects in actual transactions. *Journal of Political Economy, 114*(1), 1–37.

Living Wage Aotearoa New Zealand. (n.d.). *Living Wage Aotearoa New Zealand Homepage. www.livingwage.org.nz/*

Lo, A. W., Repin, D. V., & Steenbarger, B. N. (2005). Fear and greed in financial markets: A clinical study of day-traders. *American Economic Review, 95*(2), 352–359.

Loewenstein, G., & Elster, J. (Eds.). (1992). *Choice Over Time.* Russell Sage Foundation Press.

Loewenstein, G., & Prelec, D. (1992). Anomalies in intertemporal choice: Evidence and an interpretation. *Quarterly Journal of Economics, 107*(2), 573–597.

Lopez-de-Silanes, F., La Porta, R. F., Shleifer, A., & Vishny, R. W. (1997). Trust in large organizations. *American Economic Review Papers and Proceedings, 87*(2), 333–338.

Lord, C. G., Ross, L., & Lepper, M. R. (1979). Biased assimilation and attitude polarization: The effects of prior theories on subsequently considered evidence. *Journal of Personality and Social Psychology, 37*(11), 2098–2109.

Mackay, C. (1841). *Extraordinary Popular Delusions and the Madness of Crowds.* Richard Bentley.

Malkiel, B. (1973). *A Random Walk Down Wall Street: Including a Life-cycle Guide to Personal Investing.* W. W. Norton.

Mankiw, N. G. (1997) *Principles of Economics.* South-Western.

Markowitz, H. M. (1952). Portfolio selection. *Journal of Finance, 7*(1), 77–91.

Marlowe, F. W. (2004). Dictators and ultimatums in an egalitarian society of hunter-gatherers: The Hadza of Tanzania. In J. P. Henrich, R. Boyd, S. Bowles, C. Camerer, E. Fehr, & H. Gintis (Eds.), *Foundations of Human Sociality: Economic Experiments and Ethnographic Evidence from Fifteen Small-scale Societies* (pp. 168–193). Oxford University Press.

Marwell, G., & Ames, R. E. (1979). Experiments on the provision of public goods. I. Resources, interest, group size, and the free-rider problem. *American Journal of Sociology, 84*(6), 1335–1360.

Marwell, G., & Ames, R. E. (1980). Experiments on the provision of public goods. II. Provision points, stakes, experience, and the free-rider problem. *American Journal of Sociology, 85*(4), 926–937.

Marwell, G., & Ames, R. E. (1981). Economists free ride, does anyone else? *Journal of Public Economics, 15*(3), 295–310.

Masclet, D., Noussair, C., Tucker, S., & Villeval, M. C. (2003). Monetary and nonmonetary punishment in the voluntary contributions mechanism. *American Economic Review, 93*(1), 366–380.

McCarey, L. (Director). (1957). *An Affair to Remember* [Film]. Jerry Wald.

McKay, A. (Director). (2015). *The Big Short* [Film]. Regency Enterprises; Plan B Entertainment.

Merlo, A., & Schotter, A. (1999). A surprise-quiz view of learning in economic experiments. *Games and Economic Behavior, 28*(1), 25–54.

Michailova, J., & Schmidt, U. (2016). Overconfidence and bubbles in experimental asset markets. *Journal of Behavioral Finance, 17*(3), 280–292.

Milgram, S. (1974). *Obedience to Authority: An Experimental View.* Harper & Row.

Mischel, W. (1968). *Personality and Assessment.* Wiley.

Mischel, W. (2004). Toward an integrative science of the person. *Annual Review of Psychology, 55*, 1–22.

Müller-Lyer, F. C. (1889a) "Psychophysische Untersuchungen. Über die Abhängigkeit der relativen Unterschiedsempfindlichkeit von Intensität und Extension des Reizes. *Archiv für Anatomie und Physiologie,* Physiologische Abteilung 2 (Supplement) 91–140.

Müller-Lyer, F. C. (1889b). Optische Urteilstäuschungen. *Archiv für Anatomie und Physiologie,* Physiologische Abteilung 2 (Supplement) 263–270.

Nagel, R. (1995). Unravelling in guessing games: An experimental study. *American Economic Review, 85*(5), 1313–1326.

Nasar, S. (1998). *A Beautiful Mind*. Simon & Schuster.

Nash, J. F., Jr. (1950). Equilibrium points in n-person games. *Proceedings of the National Academy of Sciences, 36*(1), 48–49.

Nash, J. F., Jr. (1951). Non-cooperative games. *Annals of Mathematics, 54*(2), 286–295.

Neale, M. A., & Bazerman, M. H. (1985). The effects of framing and negotiator overconfidence on bargaining behaviors and outcomes. *Academy of Management Journal, 28*(1), 34–49.

Nikiforakis, N. (2008). Punishment and counter-punishment in public good games: Can we really govern ourselves? *Journal of Public Economics, 92*(1–2), 91–112.

Nikiforakis, N. (2010). Feedback, punishment and cooperation in public good experiments. *Games and Economic Behavior, 68*(2), 689–702.

Nikiforakis, N., & Normann, H. T. (2008). A comparative statics analysis of punishment in public-good experiments. *Experimental Economics, 11*(4), 358–369.

Northcraft, G. B., & Neale, M. A. (1987). Experts, amateurs, and real estate: An anchoring-and-adjustment perspective on property pricing decisions. *Organizational Behavior and Human Decision Processes, 39*(1), 84–97.

Norton, M. I., & Ariely, D. (2011). Building a better America—One wealth quintile at a time. *Perspectives on Psychological Science, 6*(1), 9–12.

Noussair, C. (2011, November 16–18). *Trends in academic publishing in experimental economics* [Keynote address]. Communications with Economists: Current and Future Trends, Wiley Economics Online Conference.

Noussair, C., & Plott, C. R. (2008). Bubbles and crashes in experimental asset markets: Common knowledge failure? In C. R. Plott & V. L. Smith (Eds.), *Handbook of Experimental Economics Results* (Vol. 1, pp. 260–263). North-Holland.

Noussair, C., & Tucker, S. (2005). Combining monetary and social sanctions to promote cooperation. *Economic Inquiry, 43*(3), 649–660.

Olson, M. (1965). *The Logic of Collective Action: Public Goods and the Theory of Groups*. Harvard University Press.

Ones, U., & Putterman, L. (2007). The ecology of collective action: A public goods and sanctions experiment with controlled group formation. *Journal of Economic Behavior & Organization, 62*(4), 495–521.

Orbell, J., Dawes, R., & van de Kragt, A. (1990). The limits of multilateral promising. *Ethics, 100*(3), 616–627.

Ortmann, A., Fitzgerald, J., & Boeing, C. (2000). Trust, reciprocity, and social history: A re-examination. *Experimental Economics, 3*(1), 81–100.

Ostrom, E. (1990). *Governing the Commons: The Evolution of Institutions for Collective Action*. Cambridge University Press.

Ostrom, E., & Gardner, R. (1993). Coping with asymmetries in the commons: Self-governing irrigation systems can work. *Journal of Economic Perspectives, 7*(4), 93–112.

Ostrom, E., Gardner, R., & Walker, J. (1994). *Rules, Games, and Common-pool Resources*. University of Michigan Press.

Ostrom, E., Walker, J., & Gardner, R. (1992). Covenants with and without a sword: Self-governance is possible. *American Political Science Review, 86*(2), 404–417.

Oswald, A. (2010). Notes on economics and the future of quantitative social science. Unpublished manuscript, Department of Economics, University of Warwick. Available from: warwick.ac.uk/fac/soc/economics/staff/ajoswald/maysciencedata2010.pdf

Page, T., Putterman, L., & Unel, B. (2005). Voluntary association in public goods experiments: Reciprocity, mimicry and efficiency. *Economic Journal, 115*(506), 1032–1053.

Penn, A. (Director). (1967). *Bonnie and Clyde* [Film]. Warner Bros.-Seven Arts; Tatira-Hiller.

Pfungst, O. (2010). *Clever Hans (the horse of Mr. von Osten): A Contribution to Experimental Animal and Human Psychology* (C. L. Rahn, Trans.). Henry Holt. (Original work published 1911.)

Piketty, T. (2014). *Capital in the Twenty-first Century* (A. Goldhammer, Trans.). Harvard University Press. (Original work published 2013.)

References

Plassmann, H., O'Doherty, J., & Rangel, A. (2007). Orbitofrontal cortex encodes willingness to pay in everyday economic transactions. *Journal of Neuroscience, 27*(37), 9984–9988.

Plott, C. R. (1991). Will economics become an experimental science? *Southern Economic Journal, 57*(4), 901–919.

Plott, C. R. (2008). Properties of disequilibrium adjustment in double auction markets. In C. R. Plott & V. L. Smith (Eds.), *Handbook of Experimental Economics Results* (Vol. 1, pp. 16–21). North-Holland.

Plott, C. R., & Smith, V. L. (1978). An experimental examination of two exchange institutions. *Review of Economic Studies, 45*(1), 133–153.

Porter, D. P., & Smith, V. L. (2003). Stock market bubbles in the laboratory. *Journal of Behavioral Finance, 4*(1), 7–20.

Porter, D., & Smith, V. L. (2008). Price bubbles. In C. R. Plott & V. L. Smith (Eds.), *Handbook of Experimental Economics Results* (Vol. 1, pp. 247–255). North-Holland.

Putnam, R. D. (2000). *Bowling Alone: The Collapse and Revival of American Community*. Simon & Schuster.

Rabin, M. (1993). Incorporating fairness into game theory and economics. *American Economic Review, 83*(5), 1281–1302.

Reiner, R. (Director). (1987). *The Princess Bride* [Film]. Act III Communications; Buttercup Films; The Princess Bride.

Richerson, P. J., & Boyd, R. (2004). *Not by Genes Alone: How Culture Transformed Human Evolution*. University of Chicago Press.

Rigdon, M., Ishii, K., Watabe, M., & Kitayama, S. (2009). Minimal social cues in the dictator game. *Journal of Economic Psychology, 30*(3), 358–367.

Rosling, H., Rosling, O., & Rönnlund, A. R. (2018). *Factfulness: Ten Reasons We're Wrong About the World – And Why Things Are Better Than You Think*. Flatiron Books.

Roth, A. (2015). *Who Gets What — and Why: The New Economics of Matchmaking and Market Design*. Houghton Mifflin Harcourt.

Roth, A. E. (Ed.). (1987). *Laboratory Experimentation in Economics: Six Points of View*. Cambridge University Press.

Roth, A. (1995a). Introduction to experimental economics. In J. Kagel & A. Roth (Eds.), *Handbook of Experimental Economics* (pp. 3–109). Princeton University Press.

Roth, A. (1995b). Bargaining experiments. In J. Kagel & A. Roth (Eds.), *Handbook of Experimental Economics* (pp. 253–348). Princeton University Press.

Roth, A. E. (1993). On the early history of experimental economics. *Journal of the History of Economic Thought, 15*(2), 184–209.

Roth, A. E., Prasnikar, V., Okuno-Fujiwara, M., & Zamir, S. (1991). Bargaining and market behavior in Jerusalem, Ljubljana, Pittsburgh, and Tokyo: An experimental study. *American Economic Review, 81*(5), 1068–1095.

Roth, A. E., Sönmez, T., & Ünver, M. U. (2004). Kidney exchange. *Quarterly Journal of Economics, 119*(2), 457–488.

Roth, A. E., Sönmez, T., & Ünver, M. U. (2005). Pairwise kidney exchange. *Journal of Economic Theory, 125*(2), 151–188.

Rousseau, J.-J. (1994). *Discourse on the Origin of Inequality* (F. Philip, Trans.). Oxford University Press. (Original work published 1755.)

Ruffle, B. J. (2000). Some factors affecting demand withholding in posted-offer markets. *Economic Theory, 16*(3), 529–544.

Samuelson, P. A. (1938). A note on the pure theory of consumer's behaviour. *Economica, 5*(17), 61–71.

Samuelson, P. A. (1948). Consumption theory in terms of revealed preference. *Economica, 15*(60), 243–253.

Samuelson, P., & Nordhaus, W. (1948). *Economics*. McGraw-Hill.

Sanfey, A. G., Rilling, J. K., Aronson, J. A., Nystrom, L. E., & Cohen, J. D. (2003). The neural basis of economic decision-making in the ultimatum game. *Science, 300*(5626), 1755–1758.

Schelling, T. C. (1960). *The Strategy of Conflict*. Harvard University Press.

Schelling, T. C. (1978). *Micromotives and Macrobehavior*. W. W. Norton

Schotter, A. (2003). Decision making with naive advice. *American Economic Review*, 93(2), 196–201.

Schotter, A., & Sopher, B. (2003). Social learning and coordination conventions in intergenerational games: An experimental study. *Journal of Political Economy*, 111(3), 498–529.

Schotter, A., & Sopher, B. (2006). Trust and trustworthiness in games: An experimental study of intergenerational advice. *Experimental Economics*, 9(2), 123–145.

Schotter, A., & Sopher, B. (2007). Advice and behavior in intergenerational ultimatum games: An experimental approach. *Games and Economic Behavior*, 58(2), 365–393.

Seabright, P. (2004). *The Company of Strangers: A Natural History of Economic Life*. Princeton University Press.

Shakespeare, W. 1564–1616. (1994). *The Merchant of Venice*. Longman.

Shiller, R. J. (2000). *Irrational Exuberance*. Princeton University Press.

Shubik, M. (1992). Game theory at Princeton, 1949–1955: A personal reminiscence. *History of Political Economy*, 24(5), 151–163.

Simon, H. A. (1955). A behavioral model of rational choice. *Quarterly Journal of Economics*, 69(1), 99–118.

Simon, H. A. (1990). Bounded rationality. In J. Eatwell, M. Milgate, & P. Newman (Eds.), *Utility and Probability* (pp. 15–18). Palgrave Macmillan.

Smith, A. (1759). *The Theory of Moral Sentiments*. Printed for A. Millar; A. Kincaid and J. Bell: Edinburgh.

Smith, A. (1776). *An Inquiry into the Nature and Causes of the Wealth of Nations*. W. Strahan and T. Cadell.

Smith, V. L. (1962). An experimental study of competitive market behavior. *Journal of Political Economy*, 70(2), 111–137.

Smith, V. L. (1964). Effect of market organization on competitive equilibrium. *Quarterly Journal of Economics*, 78(2), 181–201.

Smith, V. L. (1965). Experimental auction markets and the Walrasian hypothesis. *Journal of Political Economy*, 73(4), 387–393.

Smith, V. L. (1976). Experimental economics: Induced value theory. *American Economic Review*, 66(2), 274–279.

Smith, V. L. (1982). Microeconomic systems as an experimental science. *The American Economic Review*, 72(5), 923–955.

Smith, V. L. (1989). Theory, experiment and economics. *Journal of Economic Perspectives*, 3(1), 151–169.

Smith, V. L. (2007). *Rationality in Economics: Constructivist and Ecological Forms*. Cambridge University Press.

Smith, V. L., & Williams, A. W. (1981). On nonbinding price controls in a competitive market. *American Economic Review*, 71(3), 467–474.

Smith, V. L., & Williams, A. W. (2008). The effect of non-binding price controls in double auction trading. In C. R. Plott & V. L. Smith (Eds.), *Handbook of Experimental Economics Results* (Vol. 1, pp. 46–54). North-Holland.

Smith, V. L., Suchanek, G. L., & Williams, A. W. (1988). Bubbles, crashes, and endogenous expectations in experimental spot asset markets. *Econometrica*, 56(5), 1119–1151.

Snijders, C., & Keren, G. (1998). Determinants of trust. In D. V. Budescu, I. Erev, & R. Zwick (Eds.), *Games and Human Behavior: Essays in Honor of Amnon Rapoport* (pp. 355–385). Lawrence Erlbaum.

Sober, E., & Wilson, D. S. (1998). *Unto Others: The Evolution and Psychology of Unselfish Behavior*. Harvard University Press.

Spitzer, M., Fischbacher, U., Herrnberger, B., Grön, G., & Fehr, E. (2007). The neural signature of social norm compliance. *Neuron*, 56(1), 185–196.

Starmans, C., Sheskin, M., & Bloom, P. (2017). Why people prefer unequal societies. *Nature Human Behaviour*, 1(4), Article 0082.

Steele, C. M., & Aronson, J. (1995). Stereotype threat and the intellectual test performance of African Americans. *Journal of Personality and Social Psychology*, 69(5), 797–811.

Steele, C. M., & Aronson, J. (1998). Stereotype threat and the test performance of academically successful African Americans. In C. Jencks & M. Phillips (Eds.), *The Black–White Test Score Gap* (pp. 401–427). Brookings Institution Press.

References

Steele, J. R., & Ambady, N. (2006). "Math is hard!" The effect of gender priming on women's attitudes. *Journal of Experimental Social Psychology*, 42(4), 428–436.

Stiglitz, J. (2002). *Globalization and Its Discontents*. W.W. Norton.

Stone, O. (Director). (1987). *Wall Street* [Film]. American Entertainment Partners; Amercent Films.

Sugden, R. (1984). Reciprocity: The supply of public goods through voluntary contributions. *Economic Journal*, 94(376), 772–787.

Tagell, K. (2013, September 29). Auto-enrolment pensions: Key questions on saving for your retirement. *Guardian*. www.theguardian.com/money/2013/sep/29/auto-enrolment-pensions-saving-retirement

Thaler, R. (1987). The psychology of choice and the assumptions of economics. In A. E. Roth (Ed.), *Laboratory Experimentation in Economics: Six Points of View* (pp. 99–130). Cambridge University Press.

Thaler, R. H., & Benartzi, S. (2004). Save more tomorrow™: Using behavioral economics to increase employee saving. *Journal of Political Economy*, 112(S1), S164–S187.

Thaler, R. H., & Sunstein, C. R. (2008). *Nudge: Improving Decisions About Health, Wealth, and Happiness*. Yale University Press.

Thurstone, L. L. (1931). The indifference function. *Journal of Social Psychology*, 2(2), 139–167.

Titmuss, R. M. (1970). *The Gift Relationship*. Allen & Unwin.

Toll, B. A., Salovey, P., O'Malley, S. S., Mazure, C. M., Latimer, A., & McKee, S. A. (2008). Message framing for smoking cessation: The interaction of risk perceptions and gender. *Nicotine & Tobacco Research*, 10(1), 195–200.

Trivers, R. L. (1971). The evolution of reciprocal altruism. *Quarterly Review of Biology*, 46(1), 35–57.

Tucker, A. W., & Straffin, P. D., Jr. (1983). The mathematics of Tucker: A sampler. *Two-Year College Mathematics Journal*, 14(3), 228–232.

Tversky, A., & Kahneman, D. (1983). Extensional versus intuitive reasoning: The conjunction fallacy in probability judgment. *Psychological Review*, 90(4), 293–315.

Van Huyck, J. B., Battalio, R. C., & Beil, R. O. (1990). Tacit coordination games, strategic uncertainty, and coordination failure. *American Economic Review*, 80(1), 234–248.

Van Huyck, J. B., Gillette, A. B., & Battalio, R. C. (1992). Credible assignments in coordination games. *Games and Economic Behavior*, 4(4), 606–626.

von Neumann, J., & Morgenstern, O. (1944). *The Theory of Games and Economic Behavior*. Princeton University Press.

Walras, L. (2014). *Elements of Theoretical Economics or the Theory of Social Wealth* (D. A. Walker, & J. van Daal, Trans.). Cambridge University Press. (Original work published 1874.)

Wason, P. C. (1968). Reasoning about a rule. *Quarterly Journal of Experimental Psychology*, 20(3), 273–281.

Weber, R. A. (2006). Managing growth to achieve efficient coordination in large groups. *American Economic Review*, 96(1), 114–126.

Wilkinson, R., & Pickett, K. (2009). *The Spirit Level: Why Greater Equality Makes Societies Stronger*. Bloomsbury Press.

Williams, A. W. (2008). Price bubbles in large financial asset markets. In C. R. Plott & V. L. Smith (Eds.), *Handbook of Experimental Economics Results* (Vol. 1, pp. 242–246). North-Holland.

Yamagishi, T. (1986). The provision of a sanctioning system as a public good. *Journal of Personality and Social Psychology*, 51(1), 110–116.

Yamagishi, T. (1988). The provision of a sanctioning system in the United States and Japan. *Social Psychology Quarterly*, 51(3), 265–271.

Yunus, M., & Jolis, A. (1998). *Banker to the Poor: Micro-lending and the Battle Against World Poverty*. PublicAffairs.

Zahavi, A., & A. Zahavi. (1997). *The Handicap Principle: A Missing Piece of Darwin's Puzzle*. Oxford University Press.

Zak, P. J., & Knack, S. (2001). Trust and growth. *Economic Journal*, 111(470), 295–321.

Zizzo, D. J. (2010). Experimenter demand effects in economic experiments. *Experimental Economics*, 13(1), 75–98.

Index

Page numbers in *italics* refer to figures, those in **bold** indicate tables.

adaptive expectations 384, 385
agency relationships 242–52
Akerlof, G. G. 243–4
Allais paradox 101–6, 110
Almäs, I. et al. 214–15
altruism: evolution of cooperative behaviour 283–4, 307; and fairness 183–4; and reciprocity 223–5
altruistic punishers 287–8, 290–1
anchoring and anchoring index 70–1
Andreoni, J. 270–3; and Petrie, R. 63
animal spirits and asset bubbles 387–93
animals: prisoner's dilemma 155–6; ultimatum game 181–2
anterior cingulate cortex (ACC) 194
anti-social and pro-social punishments 297
arbitration and negotiations 112–13
Ariely, D. 4, 70; Norton, M. and 212–13
Arizona Stock Exchange 353
ascending bid–descending ask process *see* continuous double auction market mechanism
Asch, S. E. 41, 65, 66, 277
Ashraf, N. et al. 84, 225, 233
asset bubbles in markets 373–6, 398–9; and animal spirits 387–93; decline of fundamental value 380–3; laboratory studies 42, 376–80; night-trading (case study) 396–8; rational speculation and role of expectations 383–7; role of experience in curbing 393–6
assurance game *see* stag hunt game
Atkinson, Q. D. et al. 307
attitudes and behaviour dichotomy 30–3
Auckland's City Rail Link (case study) 75–6
auction markets *see* continuous double auction market mechanism; Walras, L./Walrasian model (*tatonnement* process)

autocracy model 251–2
Axelrod, R. 156, 297, 306

backward induction 166, 167–8, 170–1, 175, 219
Barber, B. M. and Odean, T. 114
bargaining 12, 37–8, 112–13; *see also* ultimatum game
Baron, J. N. et al. 250–2
base rates 132, 142
baseball players 54, 138; "hot hands" fallacy (case study) 139–42; Major League (vignette) 1–2
battle of the sexes game 160–2, 165–8, *312*, **313**, **314**
Baumeister, R. F. 7–8
Bayes' Rule 125–6, 128, 130, 142
Bazerman, M. H. 132, 133; Neale, M. and 113
Bentham, J. 5
Berg, J. et al. 218–23, 225, 226, 228–9, 233, 234, 237, 254, 260
Bernoulli, D. 36–7, 92
Bertrand, M. and Mullainathan, S. 86–7
best responses 161–2
betrayal cost 230
between-subjects and within-subjects designs 35
Bewley, T. 244
bias 388–9; confirmation 72–3; hindsight 73–4; present 78–83, 157; representativeness 122; self-serving 275
Bloomberg, Michael 128–9
Blount, S. 179–80, 194, 213
Blue Cab–Green Cab problem 117, *118*, 123, 127, 128
Blume, A. and Ortmann, A. 324–5
Bochet, O. et al. 300
Bohnet, I. 71; Ashraf, N. et al. 225, 233; and Zeckhauser, R. 229–30

419

Index

Bolton, G. E.et al. 213; and Zwick, R. 189–93
bounded rationality 4, 39, 40
Brady, Tom 56
brain: frontal lobe damage 5–6, 26; limbic system 54; reward centres 25, 26, 238; *see also* neuroeconomics
Brandts, J.: Bolton, G. et al. 213; and Cooper, D. 325–9; et al. 273; and McLeod, B. 324
Brosnan, S. and de Waal, F. 181
bubble-and-crash patterns *see* asset bubbles in markets
bureaucracy model 251–2
Burlando, R. and Hey, J. D. 273
Bush, George W. 50

Camerer, C. 11, 46–7, 173, 198, 233; Knez, M. and 319; and Weigelt, K. 220
Cameron, L. A. 43, 186–8
capital gains 379
Cardenas, J. C. et al. 256–7, 263
Carpenter, J. P. 292–3
cash posters experiment 243
Catch-22 (Yossarian and Nately characters) 147–8, 152–5, 158–9, 312–13
caudate nucleus 238
causal inferences 41, 44–5
causality: poverty and birth rates (case study) 119–20; vs correlation 120–1
centralized markets: vs decentralized markets 353; *see also* Walras, L./Walrasian model (*tatonnement* process)
certainty equivalent 96
ceteris paribus and demand 344
Challenger space shuttle disaster 135, 340–1
Chamberlin, E. H. 37–8, 353–4, 355
changing the default option 68, 77
Charness, G. and Yang, C. 304
Chaudhuri, A.: Dickinson, D. et al. 381–2, 397–8; and Gangadharan, L. 227–8, 232; Li, S. and Pichayontvijit, T. 234–7; Maitra, P. and Graziano, S. 305–6; and Pichayontvijit, T. 276–7, 301–2, 304, 339; Pichayontvijit, T. and Smith, A. 281, 282; Schotter, A. and Sopher, B. 332–5
choice: "choice architecture" 63; "choice overload" 26; constrained 4, 13–23; equitable and inequitable 190–1; over time 76–85
Chwe, M. S. 323
Cinyabuguma, M. et al. 294
civic cooperation norms 261
Claessens, S. et al. 307
Clark, K. and Sefton, M. 338

Clever Hans experiment 43
climate change, intrinsic motivations, sustainability and 256–8
cognitive bias *see* bias
cognitive hierarchy models 11
Colbert, Stephen 50
collateralized debt obligations (CDOs) 374
collective action problems *see* cooperation in social dilemmas
commitment model 251, 252
common consequence effect 101, 102, 103–4
common knowledge treatment 234
common ratio effect 103, 110
communication 321–5; and incentive bonuses 328–30, 336–7, 339–40; intergenerational approach 305–6, 333–5; in non-sorted groups 298–300
competitive equilibrium *see* market system
computerised econometric analysis 34
concave utility function 94, 95, 96
conditional co-operators/co-operation 148, 297–8, 303–4; as altruistic punishers 287–8; and free-riders 274–5, 276–8, 280–1, 285
conditional probabilities 124
confirmation bias 72–3
conjunction fallacy 123; case study 134–5; and disjunctive fallacies 131–7, 142
constrained choices 4, 13–23
consumer surplus and producer surplus 208, 350–2
consumption of goods, budget constraint and price change 13–23
Continental Airlines 309–10, 335–7
continuous double auction market mechanism 356–60, 378, 380; vs posted offer markets 361–2
control conditions 35
Cookson, R. 233, 234, 273
Cooper, D. J. 329–30; Brandts, J. and 325–9
Cooper, R. et al. 314–16, 319, 321–2, 323–4
cooperation, benefits of 155,
cooperation in social dilemmas: example of social dilemma 264–8; explanations for decaying contributions 270–7; and herd mentality 277–8; prisoner's dilemma and stag hunt games 278–82; small vs large groups 268–70
cooperation in social dilemmas, sustaining 287–90, 306–7; cost effectiveness of punishment 290–3; effectiveness of punishment 295–6; intergenerational approach 305–6, 332–5; means other than punishment 297–8; neuroeconomics of trust

and reciprocity (case study) 237–9; non-sorted groups 298–302; "perverse" punishment 293–5; sorted groups 302–5; verdict 296–7
coordination failures in organizations: communication 321–5; creating culture in laboratory 330–5; examples of coordination failure 309–13; experimental evidence 313–16; laboratory and real world interventions 335–40; minimum effort coordination game 316–20; role of incentives 325–30
coordination games 170
coordination problems 39
correlation vs causation 120–1
cost effectiveness of punishments 290–3
counter-punishments 293–4, 297
COVID-19 pandemic 69, 74–5, 262–3, 342, 373; identified vs statistical lives (case study) 61–2; loss aversion (case study) 107–8; petrol prices (case study) 349, 350
Cox, J. C. 223–5
Cronk, L. 234
Croson, R.: and Andreoni, J. 273; de Oliveira, A. et al. 303–4
cross-country studies: fairness and ultimatum game 195–201; inequality 209–12, 214–15; public goods game 273; trust 261
crowding out effect 254–6, 258–60

Damasio, A. 5–6, 26
"dark side" of priming (case study) 65–6
Davis, D. and Holt, C. 35
Dawes, R. M.: et al. 299; and Thaler, R. 240
day-care centre study, Israel 258–9
de Oliveira, A. et al. 303–4
de Quervain, D. J. F. et al. 237–9
de Waal, F. and Brosnan, S. 181
decaying contributions: explanations for 270–7; public goods game 267, 268, 280, 281, 282
decentralized markets: vs centralized markets 353; see also continuous double auction market mechanism
deception, use in experiments 41
decision making 2–3, 26–7; economics and psychology 6–12; neuroeconomics perspective 23–6; problem of choice 13–23; types of 12–13; vignettes 1–2
Deewan, Afzaal and Natalie 242
demand 343–5; and supply see market system; withholding by buyers 209, 363–4, 365
dependent and independent events 131–7, 142
Descartes's error 5–6

descriptive psychology 8
Dickinson, D. L. 396–7; et al. 381–2, 397–8
dictator game 183–4, 223–4; modified 223, 224–5; risky 230; triple 225
diminishing marginal utility 20, 95
discounting future pay-offs 79, 157
discrimination see price discrimination; racial stereotypes and discrimination
dominant strategy 151, 154; free-riding as 279–80; modified 158–9; stag hunt game 315–16
Donne, John 283
dopamine 25, 26
dorsolateral prefrontal cortext (DLPFC) 194
double-blind designs 188–9; and single-blind designs 35, 188, 189–92; trust experiments 221, 231
Down's Syndrome case 129–31
Duchenne and forced smiles 52, 53
Dufwenberg, M. et al. 234
Duhem–Quine problem 32, 45

Eckel, C. C.: de Oliveira, A. et al. 303–4; and Wilson, R. 230
ecological rationality 53–4
economic growth 260–2
efficiency of markets 351–2
efficient market hypothesis 377, 380, 387
ego depletion theory 7–8
emotions: frontal lobe damage 5–6, 26; see also neuroeconomics; psychology and economics
employee attachment 251
employment: job offers (case study) 98–9; racial discrimination (case study) 86–7; relationships 242–52
endowment effect 111–12
equitable and inequitable choices 190–1
evolution of cooperative behaviour 283–4, 305–6, 307, 332–5
excess trading and asset bubbles 385–7
expectations: in decision to trust 225–8; and rational speculation 383–7
expected utility theory and prospect theory 37, 89–91, 114–15; Allais paradox 101–6, 110; elements of prospect theory 103, 106–9 (see also loss aversion); risk attitudes and paradoxical behaviour 110–11; risk neutrality and risk aversion 91–101
expected value, concept and calculation of 89–97
experience, role in trading behaviour 393–6
experimental economics: criticism of 41–7; development of 32–5; elements of design

421

35–6; future of 47–8; history of 36–40; and non-experimental approaches 30–2; and psychology: similarities and differences 40–1
experimenter demand effects 34, 41, 43–4, 183
external validity of laboratory experiments 41–2, 45–6
extrinsic incentives and intrinsic motivations 254–6, 258–60

fairness: posted offer markets 207–9, 363–5; and trust 252–4; *see also* ultimatum game
Falk, A. et al. 180–1, 193
false positive situation 127, 129–31
Fathi, M. et al. 63–4
Fehr, E.: et al. 244–5, 284–5; Fischbacher, U. et al. 273–5, 278, 282; and Gächter, S. 246–7, 248, 287–9; Gächter, S. and Kirchsteiger, G. 249–50; Kirchsteiger, G. and Riedl, A. 245–6; and Kosfeld, M. et al. 231; and List, J. 42; and Rockenbach, B. 260; and Schmidt, K. 282
field data 31–2, 33, 34
field settings vs laboratory experiment design 42, 45–7
FINCA (Foundation for International Community Assistance), Peru 254
finitely repeated prisoner's dilemma 170–1
Fiorina, M. P. and Plott, C. R. 39–40
Fischbacher, U. et al. 273–5, 278, 282; Kosfield, M. et al. 231
Fischhoff, B. 74
fitness trade-offs 156, 307
flat-screen TV (case study) 97–8
Flood, M. M. and Drescher, M. 38
Forsythe, R.: Cooper, R. et al. 314–16, 319, 321–2, 323–4; et al. 183
framing 68–70, 234–7; gain frame and loss frame 104–6, 112–13; "osotua" 234
Franciosi, R. et al. 364
Frank, R. H. 24, 215
free-riding 147–8, 152–5, 158–9, 265; and conditional co-operators 274–5, 276–8, 280–1, 285; and coordination problem 312–13; as dominant strategy 279–80; *see also* cooperation in social dilemmas, sustaining; decaying contributions
Frey, B. S. 262; and Oberholzer-Gee, F. 254–5
Friedman, M. 32
frontal lobe damage 5–6, 26
functional magnetic resonance imaging (fMRI) 24, 25, 193
fundamental value: decline of 380–3; flat 381, 382, 397; peak price 394–6

Gächter, S.: Fehr, E. and 246–7, 248, 287–9; Fehr, E. et al. 249–50; Fischbacher, U. et al. 273–5, 278, 282; Herrmann, B. and Thöni, C. 294–5; Renner, E. and Sefton, M. 296; and Thöni, C. 303
Gage, Phineas 5, 26
gain frame and loss frame 104–6, 112–13
Galton, F. 138–9
gambling *see* lotteries
game theory 32–3, 34, 37, 38–40, 145–6
game trees 165–7
Geisel, Theodore (Dr Seuss) 3
gender stereotypes 67
"gift-exchange", employment relationship as 243–6, 250–2
gift-giving relationships, Kenya 234
Gigerenzer, G. 53–4, 55–7, 61, 134
Gilovich, T. et al. 139–42
Gini coefficient 210, 211, 214–15
Gintis, H. 198
Gladwell, M. 54
Glimcher, P. 24
global financial crisis (GFC) 2008-9 373–4
Gneezy, U.: et al. 226; and Rustichini, A. 258–9
Golden Balls show (vignette) 2
Grameen Bank, Bangladesh 253–4
Greenspan, Alan 398
grim trigger strategy (GTS) 157–8
group size *see* small vs large groups
guessing game 8–12
Gunnthorsdottir, A. et al. 275–6, 302
Gürerk, O. et al. 289–90
gut feelings and effortful thinking *see* System 1 and System 2 thinking
Güth, W. et al. 174–8, 182–3, 184, 195; Gneezy, U. et al. 226

Hamilton, W. D. 284, 307
Harford, T. 69–70
Harley, Robert 375
Haruvy, E. et al. 393–6
Hazledine, T. 75–6
Heinrich, John 42
Heller, Joseph 147
Henrich, J.: and Boyd, R. 295–6; et al. 198–201
Henry, O. 160, 313
herd mentality: cooperation in social dilemmas 277–8; momentum trading 389
heuristics/rule of thumb 54, 55–6, 388, 393
high-tech start ups, Silicon Valley 251–2
hindsight bias 73–4
Hodson, N. 135–7

Hoffman, E. et al. 182, 184–5, 188–9
Holly, Buddy (vignette) 1
Holt, C. A.: Davis, D. and 35; et al. 381, 382
Holzhauer, James (vignette) 1
Homans, G. C. 243
"hot hands" fallacy (case study) 139–40
Hugo, Victor: *Les Misérables* 217
Hume, D. 5, 26

Ichigo Asset Management 172–3
identified vs statistical lives (COVID-19 pandemic case study) 61–2
impunity game 189–92
imputed value 3
incentives: communication and 328–30, 336–7, 339–40; extrinsic, and intrinsic motivations 254–6, 258–60; role of 325–30; ultimatum game 184–8; *see also* payment of participants
income effect 23
income inequality 209–15
independence of irrelevant alternatives 316
indifference curves (consumption bundles) 18–22, 37
insula 25, 194
intergenerational approach 305–6, 332–5
intrinsic motivations: extrinsic incentives and 254–6, 258–60; sustainability and climate change 256–8
investment game *see* trust game/investment game; trust and trustworthiness
invisible hand 215
Isaac, R. M. 267; and Walker, J. 268–70, 298–9
Itzhak, B-D. et al. 113–14

Jensen, K. et al. 182
Johnson, N. D. and Mislin, A. A. 234
jury decision-making problem 117–18, 123–8

Kahneman, D. 57, 59–60, 62–3, 68, 118, 121–3, 134, 137; Knetsch, J. and Thaler, R. 111–12, 204, 207, 363, 364; and Tversky, A. 102–6, 107, 122
Karlan, D. S. 254
Kelley, H. H. and Stahelski, A. J. 277
Keser, C. and van Winden, F. 276
Key, John 172
Keynes, J. M. 12, 387–9
kidney cancer, incidence of 59, 121–2, 139
kin selection theory 284, 307
Knack, S. et al. 261
Knez, M. and Camerer, C. 319; and Simester, D. 335–7

Knutson, B. et al. 25–6
Kocher, M. G. et al. 388–91
Kosfeld, M. et al. 231
Kremer, M. 340–1
Kreps, D. M. et al. 271
Kunreuther, H. and Easterling, D. 255
Kurzban, R. and Houser, D. 277–8

labour contracts *see* trust and trustworthiness in markets; wages
Laibson, D. 84
LaPiere, R. T. 31
learning hypothesis 271, 272, 273
less developed countries: climate change issues 256–8; Grameen Bank, Bangladesh 253–4; monetary stakes in ultimatum game 185–8; tolerance for income inequality 214–15
Let's Make a Deal game show 124
Level-k thinking models 11
Levitt, S. D. and List, J. A. 42, 45, 46
life expectancy and inequality 210
Lipsey, R. 31
living wage movement 365
Lo, A. W. et al. 389
Lord, C. G. et al. 73
loss aversion 108; COVID-19 pandemic (case study) 107–8; mental accounting and endowment effect 111–12; and overconfidence 112–14
lotteries 90–7; Allais paradox 101–6, 110; symmetric and asymmetric 213; trusting and risky decisions 228–31
luck vs skill in income inequality 214–15
Lynch, Patrick 129

MacArthur Foundation Norms and Preferences Network 198
Mackay, C. 376
McMillan, Jimmy 365
Major League baseball players (vignette) 1–2
Mankiw, N. G. 242
marginal per capita return (MPCR) 268–70, 293, 302, 303
marginal utility 16–17, 20–1, 24; diminishing 20, 95
market power 360; exploitation of increased 204–5; posted offer markets 362–3, 365
market share competition (case study) 168–9
market system 342–3, 368–70; competitive equilibrium in reality 352–7; competitive equilibrium theory 347–50; demand 343–5; policy interventions 365–8; robustness of

equilibrium process 357–60; supply 345–6, 347; *see also* asset bubbles in markets; posted offer markets
marketing and framing (case study) 69–70
Markowitz, H. M. 56
Marlowe, F. W. 164
Marschak, J. 39
marshmallow test 76–7
Masclet, D. et al. 300–1
medial orbitofrontal cortex (mOFC) 25–6
medial prefrontal cortex (mPFC) 25
mental accounting and endowment effect 111–12
Michailova, J. and Schmidt, U. 391–2
micro-credit 253–4
Milgram, S. 41
mind–body dualism 5
minimum effort coordination game 316–20, 331–5, 338–9
minimum wage 368
Mischel, W. 76
"model" and economic theory 6–7
modern portfolio theory 56
modified dictator game 223, 224–5
momentum trading 389
money *see* incentives; payment of participants
monitoring: and group size 270, 292–3; mutual 336–7; peer 253
monkeys and chimpanzees: ultimatum game and fairness 181–2
motivations *see* incentives; intrinsic motivations; payment of participants
Müller–Lyer Illusion 60, *61*
multiple equilibria 160–5, 170, 315; *see also* coordination failures in organizations
mutual monitoring 336–7

Nagel, R. 9–11
Nash, J. F., Jr. 38, 147
Nash equilibrium 147–8, 151–2, 154, 155, 159, 235, 279, 288; backward induction 167–8, 175; *see also* multiple equilibria
Neale, M. A.: and Bazerman, M. 113; Northcraft, G. B. and 71
negotiating *see* bargaining; ultimatum game
neuroeconomics: decision making 23–6; trust and reciprocity (case study) 237–9; ultimatum game (case study) 193–4
night-trading (case study) 396–8
Nikiforakis, N. 293–4; and Normann, H. T. 290–2
NIMBY (Not in My Backyard) problem 254–5
no history experiment 222–3, 226

non-monetary punishments 300–1
Northcraft, G. B. and Neale, M. A. 71
Norton, M. I. and Ariely, D. 212–13
Noussair, C.: Haruvy, E. et al. 393–6; Lei, V. et al. 385–7, 389, 392–3; and Tucker, S. 300–1
nucleus accumbens (NAcc) 25, 26

Obama, Barak 56
The Odyssey (Homer) 83–4, 268
omitted variable 120–1
OPEC *see* petrol prices (COVID-19 pandemic case study)
opportunity costs 2–3
optimistic beliefs regarding peers 319, 338
optimists, pessimists and realists 281–2
Ortmann, A.: Blume, A. and 324–5; et al. 226–7, 228
Osaka Steel Company, Tokyo Kohtetsu company takeover bid 172–3
Ostrom, E. 257–8; et al. 299–300
Oswald, A. 47, 48
other-regarding/social preferences 46, 223–4, 225
over-confidence 388, 391–3
oxytocin 231

Page, T.: Bochet, O. et al. 300; Cinyabuguma, M. et al. 294; et al. 304
partners vs strangers: cooperation/coordination 271–3, 288–9, 337–40
pay-offs: battle of the sexes game 161, *312*, 313; discounting future 79, 157; minimum effort coordination game **317**, 318–19, 318–20; prisoner's dilemma 149–55, 158–9, 279–80; stag hunt game 162–5, *312*, 313, 315–16
payment of participants 33, 34–5, 40, 41; countering wealth effect 35–6; less developed countries 43
peak price 394–6
perspective taking in negotiations 113
PET scans 237–9
petrol prices (COVID-19 pandemic case study) 349, *350*
Pfungst, O. 43
Pickett, K. and Wilkinson, R. 209–12
Picketty, T. 212
Plassmann, H. et al. 25–6
Plott, C. R. 33, 39–40, 47; et al. 267; Lei, V. et al. 385–7, 389, 392–3
posted offer markets 360–2; and fairness 207–9, 363–5; and market power 362–3, 365; prices 37–8, 39, 352

poverty and birth rates (case study) 119–20
prediction biases 396
preference reversals 106
preferences 24, 26; other-regarding/social 46, 223–4, 225; self-regarding 223; "transitive" 17–18
prefrontal cortex 25, 26, 194
present bias 78–83, 157
price ceiling 366–8
price discrimination 204–5
price floor 368
price increases 204–6; and budget constraints 15, 16, 22–3
price signalling 363
price–quantity relationship: and demand 344–5; and supply 345–6
"price-taker" 347
priming 63–7, 277; plus reference point (anchoring) 70
"principal–agent" problem 242
The Princess Bride (case study) 148–9
prior probability and posterior probability 124, 125, 130, 142
prisoner's dilemma 149–55; in animal world 155–6; case study 157–8; as public goods game 278–82; tit-for-tat strategies 156–8
private knowledge treatment 234
probabilistic thinking 117–21, 142; conjunctive and disjunctive fallacies 131–7; difficulties with 121–3; Down's Syndrome case 129–31; jury decision-making 117–18, 123–8; regression to the mean 137–42; stop-and-frisk policy 128–9
probability weight function 106–8, 110
producer surplus and consumer surplus 208, 350–2
proposers and responders *see* ultimatum game
prospect theory 103, 106–9; *see also* loss aversion
protests, PCs, buying groceries and green lights (case study) 310–11
psychology and economics: decision making 6–12; experiments: similarities and differences 40–1; renumeration of participants 34–5; ultimatum game and fairness 177–8
public goods game *see* cooperation in social dilemmas
public playground: "Little Rangitoto Reserve" 146, 264–8
punishment: fear of 188–94; *see also* cooperation in social dilemmas, sustaining
Putnam, R. D. 232–3

Rabin, M. 278–80, 281
racial stereotypes and discrimination 65–7, 86–7, 128–9
Radner, R. 39
RAND Corporation 38–9
rational speculation and role of expectations 383–7
rationality: bounded 4, 39, 40; ecological 53–4; economists' definition and understanding of 3–4; and emotion 5–6
reasoning 5, 12
reciprocal altruism theory 280, 284, 307
reciprocity *see* trust and trustworthiness
regression to the mean 137–42
rent offered in contract 247–8
representativeness bias 122
restart in public goods game 272–3
restaurants: tipping rule 206; trust 241–2
Revealed Preference Theory 24
revenue flow: high-tech start-ups 252
Rigdon, M. et al. 64–5
risk attitudes and paradoxical behaviour 110–11
risk neutrality and risk aversion 91–101
risk premium 96, 97
risk seeker (case study) 99–101
risk and trade-offs (COVID-19 pandemic case study) 61–2
risky dictator game 230
risky and trusting decisions 228–31
Rösling, H. et al. 119
Roth, A. E. 36–7; et al. 195–8, 200, 364
Rousseau, J.-J. 162–3, 164
Ruffle, B. J. 207–9, 363–4, 365
rule of thumb/heuristics 54, 55–6, 388, 393

St John, S. 69
St Petersburg Paradox 36–7, 91–2
Samuelson, P. A. 24, 31
sanctioning and sanction-free institutions 289–90
Sanfey, A. G. et al. 193–4
Schelling, T. C. 39
Schotter, A.: and Merlo, A. 36; and Sopher, B. 332
Seabright, P. 53, 239
self-control 7–8, 388–91, 393; long-term (Odysseus case study) 83–4
self-interest 146, 170–1, 203; and other factors in decision making 4–5; trust game 219; ultimatum game 183, 185, 191, 199, 201; *see also* free-riding
self-regarding preferences 223

self-serving bias 275
Selten, R. 39, 40
sender and receiver *see* trust game/investment game
sequential move games 165–9, 175
shares trading *see* asset bubbles in markets
Shiller, R. J. 398
short-selling 382–3
Silicon Valley: high-tech start ups 251–2
Simon, H. A. 39
single-blind designs 35, 188; *see also* double-blind designs
sleep deprivation effects (night-trading case study) 396–8
small vs large groups: cooperation in social dilemmas 268–70; minimum effort coordination game 319, 331–2; monitoring 270, 292–3
Smith, A. 16–17, 203, 215, 369
Smith, V. L. 32, 33, 38, 39, 40, 45, 355–60; et al. 364, 384, 385; Hoffman, E. et al. 182, 184–5, 188–9; Ketcham, J. and Williams, A. 361–3; Suchanek, G. and Williams, A. 377–80, 389; and Williams, A. 366–7, 382
Snijders, C. and Keren, G. 228–9
social capital 260–1
social and health outcomes of inequality 211
social history experiment 222–3, 226, 233, 237
social mobility 216
social norms 13, 26–7; civic cooperation 261; *see also* fairness
social/other-regarding preferences 46, 223–4, 225
South Sea Company Bubble (case study) 375–6
"Split or Steal" game 51–3
sports 55–6, 172, 323; *see also* baseball players
stag hunt game 314–15; coordination interventions 320, 322–5, 338; pay-offs 162–5, *312*, 313, 315–16; prisoner's dilemma and 278–82; role of incentives 325–30
Starmans, C. et al. 212, 213
Steele, C. M. and Aronson, J. 66–7
Steele, J. R. and Ambady, N. 67
Stiglitz, J. 252
stock exchanges/bourses 348, 352–3
stop-and-frisk policy 128–9
strangers vs partners: cooperation/coordination 271–3, 288–9, 337–40
strategic thinking 145–9, 170–1; battle of the sexes game 160–2, 165, *312*, 313; *Catch-22* (Yossarian and Nately characters) 147–8, 152–5, 158–9; sequential move games 165–9,

175; stag hunt game and pay-off-ranked equilibria 162–5; *see also* prisoner's dilemma
strategies hypothesis 271, 272–3
strong reciprocity theory 284–5, 307
strong reciprocity treatment (SRT) 250
Stroop Task 60, 389–90
students as subjects 41, 42, 45–6
sub-prime mortgages 373–4
substitution effect 23
Sullenberger, Chesley 56–7
sunk cost fallacy 74–5
supply 345–6, *347*; and demand *see* market system
survey questionnaires 30, 31, 33, 34
System 1 thinking: limits of 57–62; power of 53–7
System 1 and System 2 thinking 54, 62–76; conflicts between 76–85; *Twelve Angry Men* (film) 117–18

take-it-or-leave-it *see* ultimatum game
tatonnement process *see* Walras, L./Walrasian model (*tatonnement* process)
teenage pregnancies and inequality 211–12
"10/0 game" 181
Thaler, R. H. 78, 111; Dawes, R. and 240; Kahneman, D. et al. 111–12, 204, 207; and Sunstein, C. 63, 68
third party treatment 179
Thurstone, L. L. 37
time, choice over 76–85
tipping rule in restaurants 206
tit-for-tat strategies 156–8
Toll, B. A. et al. 68–9
"total utility" and "marginal utility", distinctions 16–17
trade-offs: fitness 156, 307; over time 76–85; and risk (COVID-19 pandemic case study) 61–2
"transitive" preferences 17–18
triple dictator game 225
Trivers, R. L. 284, 307
trust game/investment game 51–3; *see also* trust and trustworthiness
trust and trustworthiness 217–23, 239–40; altruism and reciprocity 223–5; does trust pay? 233–9; neuroeconomics of trust and reciprocity (case study) 237–9; and risk 228–31; role of expectations in decision to trust 225–8; similarities 231–3
trust and trustworthiness in markets 241–2, 262–3; agency relationships 242–52; extrinsic incentives and intrinsic motivations 254–6, 258–60; further economic implications of

252; growth 260–2; intrinsic motivations, sustainability and climate change 256–8
Tucker, A. W. 149
tulip bulb bubble 376
Twelve Angry Men (film) 117–18
$20 auction and sunk cost fallacy 74–5
Tyrannosaurus Rex model 6–7

ultimatum game 173–8, 201; brain activity (case study) 193–4; competitive equilibrium market 354–5, 358–9; criticism of findings 182–3; fair or altruistic behaviour: dictator game 183–4; fairness controversies 172–3; fairness norms and cross-cultural studies 195–201; fear of punishment vs embarrassment 188–94; intentions and outcomes 179–82; posted offer markets 363–5; raising monetary stakes in 184–8
ultimatum game, market implications of 203, 215–16; economic consequences of fairness norms 207–9; fairness as constraint on profit-making 204–7; fairness and income inequality 209–15
Utilitarianism 5
utility 3; normative model of decision making 16–23; and preferences 24, 26; as subjective value 92–3; *see also* expected utility theory and prospect theory

value, paradox of 16–17
value function 108–9, 110; and loss aversion (case study) 109

van Huyck, J. B. et al. 316–20, 322–3, 329
ventral tegmental area (VTA) 25
voluntary contributions mechanism *see* cooperation in social dilemmas
von Neumann, J. and Morgenstern, O. 37, 38, 146
von Osten, W. 43

wages 246–50; cash posters experiment 243–4; fairness in labour markets 206–7; and "gift-exchange" in employment relationships 243–6; and pricing decisions 205
Walker, J.: et al. 267; Isaac, M. and 268–70, 298–9; Ostrom, E. et al. 299–300
Walras, L./Walrasian model (*tatonnement* process) 347–8, 350, 351–2, 357–8, 360, 362, 365
"watching eyes" experiment 63–5
weak reciprocity treatment (WRT) 250
wealth effect 35–6
Weber, R. A. 330–1, 332
Wilkinson, R. and Pickett, K. 209–12
Williams, A. W. 389
willing to pay (WTO) 25, 26
within-subjects and between-subjects designs 35
Wunsch, S. 353
WYSIATI paradigm 57, 118, 127

Yunus, M. 253, 254

Zizzo, D. J. 43–4
Zuckerman Sensation Seeking Scale 230

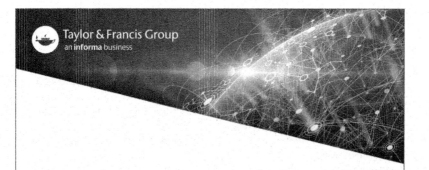